Handbook of Positive Psychology Assessment

About the Editors

Willibald Ruch, PhD, is Professor for Personality and Assessment in the Department of Psychology at the University of Zurich, Switzerland. He is a fellow of the International Positive Psychology Association, a senior scientist at the VIA Institute of Character in Cincinnati, OH, USA, and past president of the Swiss Association for Positive Psychology and the International Society for Humor Studies. His research interests concern issues of defining and measuring personality and character, in particular character strengths, virtues, humor, cheerfulness, and positive emotions.

Arnold B. Bakker, PhD, is Professor of Work and Organizational Psychology at Erasmus University Rotterdam, The Netherlands, as well as a (distinguished) visiting professor at the University of Johannesburg and North-West University, South Africa, the University of Zagreb, Croatia, and the University of Bergen, Norway. He is a fellow of the Association for Psychological Science, the International Association of Applied Psychology, and the European Academy of Occupational Health Psychology as well as former president of the European Association of Work and Organizational Psychology. His research interests cover positive organizational phenomena such as job demands-resources theory, work engagement, flow, playful work design, and job crafting.

Louis Tay, PhD, is William C. Byham Associate Professor of Industrial-Organizational Psychology at Purdue University, West Lafayette, IN, USA. He obtained his PhD in industrial-organizational psychology at the University of Illinois at Urbana-Champaign. His research interests cover methodology (i.e., measurement, continuum specification, latent class modeling, Big Data / data science) and well-being (i.e., societal well-being, wellness programs, work–leisure [e.g., arts/humanities activities] interface).

Fabian Gander, PhD, is a postdoc in the Department of Psychology at the University of Basel, Switzerland. He received his PhD from the University of Zurich and he serves as co-editor of the *Journal of Happiness Studies*. His research interests are personality traits and well-being, with a special focus on changes in personality and well-being and their assessment.

Psychological Assessment – Science and Practice

Each volume in the series *Psychological Assessment – Science and Practice* presents the state-of-the-art of assessment in a particular domain of psychology, with regard to theory, research, and practical applications. Editors and contributors are leading authorities in their respective fields. Each volume discusses, in a reader-friendly manner, critical issues and developments in assessment, as well as well-known and novel assessment tools. The series is an ideal educational resource for researchers, teachers, and students of assessment, as well as practitioners.

Psychological Assessment – Science and Practice is edited with the support of the European Association of Psychological Assessment (EAPA).

Psychological Assessment – Science and Practice, Vol. 5

Handbook of Positive Psychology Assessment

Edited by
Willibald Ruch, Arnold B. Bakker, Louis Tay, and Fabian Gander

hogrefe

Library of Congress Cataloging in Publication information for the print version of this book is available via the Library of Congress Marc Database under the LC Control Number 2022942205

Library and Archives Canada Cataloguing in Publication
Title: Handbook of positive psychology assessment / edited by Willibald Ruch, Arnold B. Bakker, Louis Tay, and Fabian Gander.
Names: Ruch, W. (Willibald), editor. | Bakker, Arnold B., editor. | Tay, Louis (Psychologist), editor. | Gander, Fabian, editor.
Series: Psychological assessment--science and practice ; v. 5.
Description: Series statement: Psychological assessment--science and practice ; v. 5 | Includes bibliographical references.
Identifiers: Canadiana (print) 20220398461 | Canadiana (ebook) 20220398577 | ISBN 9780889376199 (softcover) | ISBN 9781616766191 (PDF) | ISBN 9781613346198 (EPUB)
Subjects: LCSH: Positive psychology. | LCSH: Psychological tests—Handbooks, manuals, etc.
Classification: LCC BF204.6 .H36 2022 | DDC 150.19/88—dc23

http://www.hogrefe.com

PUBLISHING OFFICES
USA: Hogrefe Publishing Corporation, 44 Merrimac St., Suite 207, Newburyport, MA 01950
Phone (978) 255 3700; E-mail customersupport@hogrefe.com
EUROPE: Hogrefe Publishing GmbH, Merkelstr. 3, 37085 Göttingen, Germany
Phone +49 551 99950-0, Fax +49 551 99950-111; E-mail publishing@hogrefe.com
SALES & DISTRIBUTION
USA: Hogrefe Publishing, Customer Services Department,
30 Amberwood Parkway, Ashland, OH 44805
Phone (800) 228-3749, Fax (419) 281-6883; E-mail customersupport@hogrefe.com
UK: Hogrefe Publishing, c/o Marston Book Services Ltd., 160 Eastern Ave., Milton Park, Abingdon, OX14 4SB
Phone +44 1235 465577, Fax +44 1235 465556; E-mail direct.orders@marston.co.uk
EUROPE: Hogrefe Publishing, Merkelstr. 3, 37085 Göttingen, Germany
Phone +49 551 99950-0, Fax +49 551 99950-111; E-mail publishing@hogrefe.com
OTHER OFFICES
CANADA: Hogrefe Publishing, 82 Laird Drive, East York, Ontario, M4G 3V1
SWITZERLAND: Hogrefe Publishing, Länggass-Strasse 76, 3012 Bern

Printed and bound in Germany

ISBN 978-0-88937-619-9 (print) • ISBN 978-1-61676-619-1 (PDF) • ISBN 978-1-61334-619-8 (EPUB)
https://doi.org/10.1027/00619-000

Contents

Part I

Introduction

Chapter 1
Introduction

Willibald Ruch[1], Arnold B. Bakker[2], Louis Tay[3], and Fabian Gander[4]

[1]Department of Psychology, University of Zurich, Switzerland
[2]Center of Excellence for Positive Organizational Psychology, Erasmus University Rotterdam, The Netherlands
[3]Department of Psychological Sciences, Purdue University, West Lafayette, IN, USA
[4]Department of Psychology, University of Basel, Switzerland

Since the advent of positive psychology around the turn of the millennium, research and practice in this area have flourished. Not only has research into existing positive concepts increased but numerous new concepts have also been introduced and new assessment instruments and methods have been developed. For many topics, this has led to a plethora of – often competing – approaches to measurement. Today, researchers and practitioners alike are often faced with the challenging task of finding their way through a maze of alternative approaches when aiming to assess a particular concept. In addition, relatively little research explicitly addresses diagnostic issues, compares instruments, or even offers specific guidelines and recommendations about which measure is particularly suitable for which situation.

This handbook aims to relieve that predicament by providing a state-of-the-art overview of current theories, approaches, issues, and assessment instruments in the field of positive psychology. It is aimed at researchers, instructors, students, and practitioners and serves to guide both researchers and practitioners in selecting appropriate instruments by providing specific recommendations. Thus, the book's overarching goal is to contribute to both theory *and* practice of positive psychological assessment and stimulate further advances in the field by illuminating current gaps in the literature and discussing general issues in the assessment of positive psychological concepts.

Of course, given the breadth of the field and the numerous existing concepts and measurement approaches, this handbook cannot provide an exhaustive overview of the field but rather must be selective. In our selection of topics, we aimed to both cover rather traditional positive psychological concepts and include comparatively new and emerging ones as well. We believe this approach provides readers with the foundational positive psychological concepts while also introducing more novel perspectives.

The chapters are authored by renowned experts in their field. The authors were asked to describe their own work as well as other important contributions to the respective topic. Also, they were invited to not just give a purely neutral and descriptive view of their field but to include their expert evaluations and opinions on the topic to provide some guidance for the interested reader.

Each chapter begins with an introduction to the theoretical background, which elaborates on the relevance of the topic at hand, followed by an overview of the most relevant assessment instruments in the field, including a discussion of their psychometric properties and a selection of key research findings. Finally, each chapter discusses specific assessment-related challenges regarding the respective topic and provides recommendations for selecting assessment instruments.

The book is divided into four main sections. The first section focuses on well-being. Given the large number of competing theories, models, and assessment instruments on well-being and related concepts (e.g., happiness, flourishing, thriving, positive affect, quality of life), we deemed a current overview of existing approaches to be urgently needed.

The second section of the book covers traits, states, and behaviors. In this section, we had to be the most selective and decided to focus on certain specific topics and cover them in considerable detail: character, humor, playfulness, meaning and purpose, flow, self-efficacy, appreciation of beauty, posttraumatic growth, passion, and work engagement.

The third section of the book focuses on assessment in specific contexts, namely, in school settings, romantic relationships, health and clinical settings, leisure, and positive psychology interventions.

The fourth and final section covers topics that have recently been introduced or have yet to be considered from a positive psychology perspective: primal world beliefs, imagination, self-transcendent experiences, and nostalgia.

Acknowledgments

We thank everyone who contributed to the creation of this book. Foremost, of course, we acknowledge the invaluable contributions of the authors of the individual chapters, who invested their effort and expertise in creating comprehensive overviews of the role of psychological assessment in their respective field. Furthermore, we are very grateful for the contributions of numerous anonymous reviewers who provided critical feedback on the manuscripts and thereby helped to improve the quality of the individual chapters.

Part II

Well-Being

Chapter 2

Assessing Psychological Flourishing

A Review of Theory and Instruments

Fanyi Zhang and Louis Tay

Department of Psychological Sciences, Purdue University, West Lafayette, IN, USA

In psychology, the concept of flourishing is often mentioned in the same breath as positive psychology (Seligman & Csikszentmihalyi, 2000). The hallmarks of flourishing – positive experiences, positive individual traits, and positive institutions – are aspirational goals and key topics of study in positive psychology. As individuals and societies seek to flourish, they recognize that economic metrics, while important, need to be supplemented by other metrics that directly index human flourishing (Diener & Seligman, 2004). Many of these indices and assessments are directed toward the dimension of positive experiences – which we term psychological flourishing (e.g., Diener, 2000; Su et al., 2014). In this review, we examine the concept of psychological flourishing and the more established major instruments used to assess it.

Human Flourishing and Psychological Flourishing

The concept of human flourishing can be traced back to the Greek concept of *eudaimonia*, which has been translated as happiness, human welfare, and – pertinent to this chapter – human flourishing. Human flourishing points to the highest human good and an objectively desirable life. Indeed, Aristotle noted that human flourishing is "something complete and self-sufficient, since it is the end of the things achievable in action" (Aristotle & Irwin, 1999, p. 8). Yet, what exactly comprises human flourishing? Based on positive psychology (Seligman & Csikszentmihalyi, 2000) and positive health (Seligman, 2008), the term denotes multiple senses: positive individual traits, positive physical health, positive institutions, and positive experiences.

In terms of *positive individual traits*, the Aristotelian conception of human flourishing emphasizes living in accordance with the highest virtue (*arête*; Aristotle & Irwin, 1999). Historically, moral psychology sought to examine this through the efforts of cognitive approaches. For example, in Kohlberg's theory of moral development (Kohlberg, 1958), moral reasoning and judgment are the means for evaluating moral growth. More recently, affective approaches have increased in popularity. Discrete emotions such as disgust undergird violations of moral offenses (Rozin et al., 2009) and awe can inspire virtuous action (Keltner & Haidt, 2003; Yaden et al., 2018). Work on character strengths and virtues (Peterson & Seligman, 2004) has resulted in assessments of positive individual attributes and actions (McGrath, 2014; Ng et al., 2018).

The concept of *positive physical health* was recognized by the World Health Organization in 1948 as denoting not merely the absence of illness or infirmity but a complete state of physical wellness, an idea that has since been extended into the field of positive health, which proposes the assessments of healthy functioning (Seligman, 2008). *Positive institutions* include the positive functioning of communities, businesses, and organizations, which means seeking structures and policies that promote fairness and inclusion and enabling collective well-being, for example, in the form of organizational policies that build interpersonal trust (Six & Sorge, 2008).

Our chapter focuses on psychological flourishing, which is the dimension of *positive experiences* in positive psychology. Broadly understood, this comprises both positive subjective experiences (e.g., happiness, flow) and positive interpersonal relationships (e.g., friendships) (see also Park et al., 2016). Psychological flourishing has its roots in the humanistic movement within psychology. The humanists emphasized self-actualization, which refers to the optimal functioning of a person (Maslow, 1956; Rogers, 1961). Indeed, self-actualization, according to the hierarchy of needs, emphasizes the fulfillment of psychological needs (i.e., esteem needs and belongingness needs) beyond physical needs to achieve one's full potential (Maslow, 1943, 1956). Often, psychology has instantiated dimensions of psychological flourishing as both subjective well-being (i.e., positive emotions, low negative emotions, and life satisfaction) (Diener, 1984) and psychological well-being (i.e., self-acceptance, environmental mastery, positive relations, purpose in life, personal growth, and autonomy) (Ryff & Keyes, 1995). Others consider this both hedonic and eudaimonic well-being (Waterman, 1993). Therefore, the concept of psychological flourishing goes beyond positive emotions alone (e.g., Tay et al., 2019), although these are important in their own right. Within positive psychology, psychological flourishing has its incarnation in the PERMA notion of well-being, an acronym for **p**ositive emotions, **e**ngagement, positive **r**elationships, **m**eaning, and **a**ccomplishment (Seligman, 2011).

We distinguish the concept of human flourishing from psychological flourishing: The former comprises positive actions, attributes, and experiences for entities at different levels of analysis (e.g., individual, group, community, organization, nation) (e.g., Tay et al., 2018), whereas the latter is a subset of human flourishing. The focus lies on the individual experience of positivity, which goes beyond the mere experience of pleasure to encompass positive psychological fulfillment.

Assessing Psychological Flourishing

There are many different means of assessments within and outside of psychology to evaluate specific aspects of psychological flourishing. For example, researchers have developed assessments for meaning in life (Steger et al., 2006), positive affect (Watson et al., 1988), and social support (Zimet et al., 1988). In the assessment of psychological flourishing, we want to review measures that capture multiple constructs rather than single-ones or that encompass multiple aspects in terms of their content. There are several reasons for this. It is increasingly being recognized that the assessment of human flourishing must be approached in an integrative rather than a piecemeal fashion (VanderWeele, 2017; VanderWeele et al., 2020) to enable communities and societies to better understand the different aspects of human flourishing simultaneously. Methodologically, the use of measures with the same wording style and response scale enables a level of stylistic and rating equivalence (Tay et al., 2021). This is important for researchers when they compare different constructs. For example, past work has shown that measurement of the same constructs on different scale lengths can lead to nonequivalence – even when using linear-stretch methods to place them on a common scale (Batz et al., 2016).

Below, we review psychological flourishing scales that have been validated and well-received in the field, including broad scales that assess multiple dimensions: the Mental Health Continuum (MHC), the Flourishing Scale (FS), the PERMA-Profiler, and the Comprehensive Inventory of Thriving (CIT). Further, we review both Ryff's Psychological Well-Being Scale (PWBS) and the Personal Well-Being Index (PWI), widely used measures that assess different dimensions of psychological wellness and life domains. At the time of this review, the original works of each scale had been cited over 300 times. We provide a general description of the scales, the key dimensions they assess, and their psychometric properties, including reliability, (factorial) validity, and translation/equivalence across cultures. This chapter draws on studies that focus on examining the psychometric properties of the scales (i.e., reliability, validity, measurement equivalence). We conducted a literature search in ERIC, Google Scholar, PsycARTICLES, PsycINFO, and Social Sciences Full-Text databases using the applicable scale name in combination with the terms "psychometrics" or "validation" as keywords. We also checked the reference lists from the retrieved studies. This initial search yielded 235 articles as well as data presented at professional conferences. We examined and included contributions if they (1) were empirical, (2) aimed at developing or validating the target scale, and (3) provided information on at least one of the psychometric properties mentioned above. The final list of articles utilized in the current review numbered 190 studies; a list of the studies can be found in a supplement at www.wam-lab.com.

Review of Psychological Flourishing Scales

Mental Health Continuum-Short Form (MHC-SF)

Keyes (2005) outlined the two-continua model, where mental health and mental illness were hypothesized to be two related but distinct continua. More specifically, the paper pointed out that the absence of mental illness is not necessarily evidence of high levels of mental health. Based on a review of the previous well-being literature, the state of mental health was operationalized as "a syndrome of a set of symptoms of an individual's subjective well-being," with "subjective well-being" referring to the composite of affective states, psychological well-being, and social functioning. The conceptualization and measurement of affective states followed the hedonic approach (e.g., Diener et al., 1999) to capture individuals' positive feelings and emotions. The latter two followed the eudaimonic approach and focused on two important aspects of optimal functioning. Psychological well-being targeted one's own evaluation of functioning in life, based on Ryff's (1989) characterization of a positive psychological functioning that covered self-acceptance, personal growth, positive relationships with others, environmental mastery, purpose in life, and autonomy. Finally, social functioning focused on how people evaluated their functioning in life in terms of the social standard, based on the rationale in Keyes (1998), which included social contribution, social acceptance, social actualization, social integration, and social coherence.

Originally, researchers used the Mental Health Continuum-Long Form (MHC-LF) to measure these individual aspects, but it was a slightly lengthy scale that consisted of 40 items in total (Keyes, 2002). The Mental Health Continuum-Short Form (MHC-SF) was thus developed to serve as a brief questionnaire to cover the hypothesized three aspects of mental health: emotional (EWB, 3 items), social (SWB, 5 items), and psychological well-being (PWB, 6 items). Respondents are asked to rate the frequency of their feelings on a scale from 1 (*never*) to 6 (*every day*). As a diagnostic tool, the results are categorized into three levels of well-being: flourishing (those who rate 5 or 6 on at least 1 EWB item and at least 6 SWB and PWB items), languishing (those who rate 1 or 2 on at least 1 EWB item and at least 6 SWB and PWB items), and moderate (those who are neither flourishing nor languishing). We found 59 articles in our initial literature search. After excluding those primarily elaborating on theoretical backgrounds, we included 47 in our final review.

Reliability

The initial studies with U.S. adolescents reported acceptable Cronbach's alphas for the subscales (.67 to .84 range; Keyes, 2006). Further studies on Western populations (Canadian and U.S. adults) reported similar data (.77 to .87 range; Gilmour, 2014; Keyes et al., 2012; Orpana et al., 2017).

Hides et al. (2016) reported McDonald's omega coefficients to further validate the subscales. The MHC-SF overall score showed high reliability, with omega coefficients reaching .96 and .90 for classical and hierarchical tests, respectively. The classical omega tests for the subscales ranged from .89 to .91, which appeared to be acceptable. However, the specific omega hierarchical scores for subscales ranged from .03 to .23, none of which met the cutoff of .50 suggested by Reise (2012). These statistics indicated that the variance attributed to the subscales was on the lower end, which was also supported in further studies on more diverse samples. We did not find any temporal reliability information using Western adult samples.

Validity

The MHC-SF was originally validated on a U.S. adolescent sample (Keyes, 2006). PWB correlated positively with self-concept ($r=.54$) and self-determination ($r=.46$); SWB correlated with school integration ($r=.42$), and perceived closeness ($r=.31$); EWB correlated negatively with depression ($r=-.30$). All subscales correlated negligibly with perceived math and reading skills ($r=.13$ to $.22$), showing discriminant validity evidence. Moreover, 90 % of the studies agreed upon a correlated two-factor structure (compared with one- or orthogonal two-factor structure) between mental health and mental illness (r=-.34 to -.84 between latent factors), supporting Keyes' overarching two-continua model of human flourishing.

Regarding MHC-SF factorial validity evidence, early researchers tested the proposed three-factor CFA model (Keyes, 2002, 2006; Keyes et al., 2008). In a comparison of one-, two-, and three-factor CFA results, 22 of the 22 factorial validation studies showed that the correlated three-factor CFA yielded the best model fit. The observed interfactor correlations ranged from .53 to .94, 60 % of which were above .70. This raises concerns over the distinctiveness of the three subscales. Because MHC-SF may be viewed as capturing a broad psychological flourishing factor, researchers then hypothesized a bifactor structure (i.e., a broad psychological flourishing factor and three subfactors). 80 % of the studies demonstrated a better model fit of bifactor (with one general factor and three group factors) over three-factor models, while the remaining two studies on the Spanish version showed comparable model fit indices between the two (Echeverria et al., 2017; Peña Contretras et al., 2017). The item-level analysis also supports a broad psychological flourishing factor (e.g., Lamborn et al., 2018; Longo et al., 2020; Rogoza et al., 2018; Schutte & Wissing, 2017; Silverman et al., 2018). The overall item loadings suggest that items loaded more strongly on the general factor rather than their target factor. These results again indicate the presence of a strong general flourishing factor.

Applications in Diverse Samples

The MHC-SF has been tested in 52 countries in over 30 languages. Two studies reported the temporal stability of the MHC-SF. One study with Dutch adults (Lamers et al., 2011) reported stable reliability of the total scale over 9 months, reaching a .65 test-retest correlation. The temporal stability of the subscales ranged from .46 to .53, which also suggested good temporal stability. Further, the test-retest correlations over 3 months ranged from .65 to .70 for the total scale and .45 to .56 across all three subscales. Another study with Italian adults (Petrillo et al., 2015) suggested only moderate temporal reliability over a 1-month interval, with correlations ranging from .27 to .32.

Reliability information for the MHC-SF was reported in 42 studies that examined diverse samples. Cronbach's alpha ranged from .72 to .96 for the overall score, with 94.1 % of the statistics above .80. The subscales exhibited slightly lower but good alphas: EWB had a range from .70 to .92, PWB a range from .66 to .93. The lowest among the three, SWB, ranged from .49 to .88, with 92.5 % of the statistics above .70, which can be considered acceptable (Nunnally & Bernstein, 1994).

Six articles further tested McDonald's omega. The MHC-SF overall score again showed high reliability, with omega coefficients (both classical and hierarchical tests) ranging from .74 to .95. When the results were replicated in Western cultures, while the classical omega tests for the subscales appeared to be acceptable (.55 to .94, with only one exception below .50 cutoff with Setswana-speaking African adults; Schutte & Wissing, 2017), the specific omega hierarchical scores for subscales ranged from .00 to .38, none meeting the cutoff. These statistics again suggested that, while the MHC-SF total score might be treated as a highly reliable measure of positive mental health, subscale score reliability should be considered carefully, as most of the variance was attributable to the general factor; the ability of the subscales to reliably measure the specific domains of psychological flourishing beyond the general dimension is relatively low.

The overall MHC-SF positively correlated with mental health (r=.40 to .82) and subjective happiness (r=.57 to .78). MHC-SF negatively correlated with psychological distress (r=-.50 to -.70), depression (r=-.67 to -.38), anxiety (r=-.49 to -.36) and stress (r=-.60 to -.41). The MHC-SF subscales of EWB were positively correlated with life satisfaction (.49 to .65); PWB was positively correlated with self-esteem (r=.33 to .69), and SWB was positively correlated with sense of belonging (r=.40 to .50). The only exception was a study with Indian adolescents, which showed only nonsignificant or weak correlations (r=-.34 to -.10) with other constructs (Singh et al., 2015).

A total of 19 studies reported measurement invariance over sex, age, countries, ethnicity, education, and geographic location. All 14 studies reached scalar invariance across both sexes, meaning that scores can be compared between males and females. 80 % of the studies reached scalar invariance across age, with one study on Portuguese children reaching only metric invariance (Carvalho et al., 2016). Three studies reported partial scalar invariance across countries. Joshanloo et al. (2013) identified four noninvariant items being items 1 ("How often did you feel happy?"), 4 ("How often did you feel that you had something important to contribute to society?"), 8 ("How often did you feel that the way our society works made sense to you?"), and 12 ("How often did you feel that you had experiences that challenged you to grow and become a better person?"). Another large international study reported 10 out of 36 countries reaching full scalar invariance (Żemojtel-Piotrowska et al., 2018). These results provide some initial basis to make meaningful comparisons across age and sex. However, researchers should be careful when making crosscultural conclusions.

As noted above, MHC-SF can serve as a diagnostic tool. The results can be categorized into three levels of well-being: flourishing (those who rate 5 or 6 on at least 1 EWB item and at least 6 SWB and PWB items), languishing (those who rate 1 or 2 on at least 1 EWB item and at least six SWB and PWB items), and moderate (those who are neither flourishing nor languishing). Among the 19 samples that reported the categorical diagnosis, 15 roughly demonstrated a similar pattern, with 32.9 % flourishing, 57.0 % moderate, and 8.9 % languishing on average. These results suggest that the MHC-SF may be useful as a diagnostic tool, given that they reveal similar norms across samples. However, two Korean samples (one on adults and the other on high-school students) demonstrated much lower flourishing (8.0 % and 11.7 %, respectively) compared to other samples (Lim et al., 2013; Lim, 2014), whereas a U.S. university student sample and a Canadian adult sample demonstrated much higher percentages of flourishing (51.8 % and 76.9 %, respectively; Gilmour, 2014; Keyes et al., 2012). These differences may suggest that the MHC-SF is useful at revealing potential differences in flourishing, or that there are significant differences in how different cultures use the MHC-SF.

Summary

Overall, the MHC-SF demonstrates good reliability (internal consistency and temporal reliability) and validity evidence for both the overall scale and individual subdimensions. It serves as a useful diagnostic tool to identify individual levels of flourishing. The findings well support a three-factor structure, although more recent studies reported a better fit of a bifactor model, suggesting an overarching psychological flourishing dimension informed by the content of the specific dimension. Once this general dimension is accounted for, the specific factors from the subscales do not account for substantial reliable variance beyond that. Future researchers should seek to better understand the role of the MHC-SF total score, as the findings suggested higher reliability compared with the individual subscales. In addition, the subjective well-being dimension consistently shows lower levels of reliability and validity coefficients, especially when adopted to non-Western cultures. Moreover, while the MHC-SF generally shows measurement equivalence on age and sex, there is less evidence of measurement equivalence across countries. Care needs to be taken when using the MHC-SF to compare psychological flourishing across cultures.

PERMA-Profiler

To provide insight into identifying the building blocks of flourishing, Seligman (2011) identified five pillars and proposed the PERMA model in Seligman's Well-Being Theory: Positive emotions (subjective experience of happiness for the past, present, and future), Engagement (the use of the force of character and an individual's talents and capacity), Relationships (creativity and altruism in social relations), Meaning (achieving purpose in life), and Accomplishment (striving for success and victory in the pursuit of self-realization). Empirical research has shown evidence of each component contributing to a variety of life domains, including resilience (Tugade & Fredrickson, 2004), life satisfaction (Kashdan et al., 2009), and reduced risk of depression (Manderscheid et al., 2010).

Following this model, the PERMA-Profiler was developed to measure these five elements, along with negative emotions and health (Butler & Kern, 2016). The measure consists of 23 items in total: 15 items were designed to cover the five core dimensions (3 items each), with 8 filler items on health (3 items), negative emotions (3 items), loneliness (1 item), and overall happiness (1 item). Sample items include "In general, how often do you feel joyful?" and "To what extent do you feel loved?" rated on an 11-point scale ranging from 0 to 10. Overall psychological flourishing is calculated by averaging all the responses, which range from below 5 (*languishing*) to 9 and above (*very high functioning*). Our initial search rendered 14 articles, all of which were included in the current review.

Reliability

The main psychometric properties of the scale came from the development studies by Butler and Kern (2016), who recruited eight English-speaking samples internationally to validate the scale. The mean Cronbach's alpha was .94, with all samples except for one reporting the alpha above .90. All dimensions showed acceptable internal consistencies. The mean Cronbach's alpha was .88 (.84 to .89 range) for Positive emotions, .72 (.60 to .80 range) for Engagement, .82 (.75 to .85 range) for Relationships, .90 (.85 to .91 range) for Meaning, and .79 (.70 to .84 range) for Achievement. Additionally, the mean Cronbach's alpha was .71 (.71 to .77 range) for Negative emotions and .92 (.92 to .94 range) for Health. We also examined three other articles that provided reliability information with the PERMA English version. All studies reported a Cronbach's alpha higher than

.90. All individual PERMA dimensions exhibited good internal consistency, with Cronbach's alphas ranging from .66 to .88.

The test-retest correlations reported in the development studies ranged from .69 (over 1 year) to .88 (over 2 weeks) for the overall PERMA score (Butler & Kern, 2016). The individual dimensions reported acceptable temporal reliability as well. Test-retest correlations ranged from .51 (Engagement over 1 year) to .90 (Relationships over 2 weeks), with 93.3 % over .60. In general, these results support that the PERMA-Profiler appears to show a high level of internal consistency and stability over time.

Validity

The development studies confirmed the five-factor proposed structure across all online adult samples from the US, the UK, Australia, Hong Kong, and Malaysia. This provided initial support for the factorial structure of the scale. However, there occurred to be some issues when applying to other cultural contexts, which is covered in the following section.

Regarding the criterion-validity evidence of the measure, the overall PERMA factor correlates positively with flourishing (r=.84), health (r=.50), and life satisfaction (r=.78) in the development studies. These correlations are expected and consistent, which reflect the concept of psychological flourishing that emphasizes positive experiences. The measure was also negatively correlated to psychological symptoms including anxiety (r=–.50), perceived stress (r=–.55), and depression (r=–.61). Ryan et al. (2019) reported that, while the construct correlated moderately to strongly with subjective measures (r=.63 with mental health, r=–.65 with depression, r=–.37 with anxiety, and r=–.46 with stress), it correlates only negligibly (r=–.03 with objective activity and r=–.05 with sleep) or not at all significantly with objective ones (r=.15 with physical health).

Individual dimensions also demonstrated acceptable convergent validity evidence (Butler & Kern, 2016; Ryan et al., 2019). Positive emotions were found to be positively correlated with self-acceptance (r=–.75 to –.73) and negatively correlated with depression (r=–.75 to –.49), anxiety (r=–.53 to –.27), perceived stress (r=–.58 to –.28), and negative emotions (r=–.61 to –.29). Engagement reported weak but statistically significant correlations with compassion (r=.25), activist identification (r=.18), and work performance (r=.25). Relationships were found to be positively correlated with social support (r=.50 to .68) and negatively correlated with loneliness (r=–.63 to –.50). Meaning was positively correlated with purpose in life (r=.30) and self-acceptance (r=.45), and Achievement with self-efficacy (r=.65) and less burn-out (r=.57).

Application in Diverse Samples

The original English version has been validated in different cultural contexts, including in Australia, the United States, the United Kingdom, Hong Kong, Canada, etc. It has been translated into more than 10 languages, including German, Turkish, Italian, and Korean (see https://www.peggykern.org/questionnaires.html for many of these scales). Five articles provided reliability information from international samples, including Indonesia, Italy, Greece, etc. (e.g., Hidayat et al., 2018; Giangrasso, 2018; Pezirkianidis et al., 2021), all of which reported a Cronbach's alpha of .80 and above. In these articles, we note that Engagement (.56 to .84) showed slightly lower reliabilities than the other dimensions (.77 to .90 for Positive Emotions, .70 to .96 for Relationships, .78 to .91 for Meaning, and .70 to .93 for Achievement). Test-retest reliabilities reported were .81 over 2 weeks (Ayse, 2018) and .88 over 1 month (Watanabe et al., 2018).

We examined the convergent and discriminant validity evidence, which was supported in three international samples covering German-speaking adults (Wammerl et al., 2019), Italian university students (Giangrasso, 2018), and Greek adults (Pezirkianidis et al., 2021). The overall score was found to correlate positively with subjective happiness in an Italian university student sample (r=.81) and psychological well-being in the Greek adult sample (r=.77). It negatively correlated with depression in the German-speaking adult sample (r=–.76). External validity evidence as the correlation coefficients reached –.59 between Positive Emotions and negative affect and .61 between Achievement and environmental mastery (Wammerl et al., 2019). Giangrasso (2018) also reported positive correlations between Relationships and positive relationships (r=.68) and between Meaning and purpose in life (r=.82). Nonetheless, Pezirkianidis et al. (2021) used confirmatory factor analysis to examine the discriminant validity evidence of the different PERMA dimensions and found that the Engagement factor was not well distinguished from other dimensions. This appears to be aligned with the findings that Engagement also has lower reliability than the other dimensions in international samples.

Applied to a diverse cultural context including India, Greece, Germany, Austria, Italy, and Turkey, most of the eight factorial validation articles supported the intercorrelated five-factor structure of the originally proposed model (e.g., Ayse, 2018; Giangrasso, 2018; Pezirkianidis et al., 2021). Nevertheless, there were instances where the results failed to extract the proposed five factors. Two articles, with physically inactive Australian adults and U.S. student veterans respectively, suggested a two-factor solution in further exploratory factor analyses (Ryan et al., 2019; Umucu, Grenawalt et al., 2019). One article, with English-speaking Malaysian adults, revealed a three-factor solution according to the Kaiser-Guttman criterion (Khaw & Kern, 2015). We note that researchers also hypothesized and explored other factor structures (such as higher-order structure and bifactor structure) (e.g., Hidayat et al., 2018; Wammerl et al., 2019). In general, there appears to be support for the structure of the PERMA-Profiler in a variety of cultural contexts, though specific studies may not show the five-factor structure.

We found two articles that tested measurement invariance of the scale, both supporting full scalar invariance of sex (Pezirkianidis et al., 2021; Wammerl et al., 2019). The former article also reported full scalar invariance across age groups. The latter tested the German version across three countries. A strict invariance model was reached between Austria and Germany (the Swiss data were excluded from analysis because of the small sample size). These results provided preliminary evidence that the PERMA-Profiler might be interpreted similarly across sexes and age groups. However, more research is necessary to comprehensively understand the measurement equivalence across cultures, as the factor model only converges for some samples.

Summary

Across multiple studies, there is evidence of the reliability and validity of the PERMA-Profiler. However, some researchers also pointed out the potential issues (e.g., lower reliabilities, low discriminant validity evidence with other dimensions) with the Engagement dimension when applied to diverse cultural contexts. Future researchers are encouraged to test the measurement equivalence of the measure and to validate its factor structure in international contexts as there is competing evidence that failed to replicate the five-factor model. In terms of its usage, Wammerl et al. (2019) noted that the PERMA theory is insightful for addressing at least some of the building blocks of subjective well-being, which might be useful for developing interventions in the context of psychotherapy, coaching, or counseling.

Comprehensive Inventory of Thriving and Brief Inventory of Thriving

The Comprehensive Inventory of Thriving (CIT) was developed rather recently to "measure a broad range of psychological well-being constructs and represent a holistic view of positive functioning" (Su et al., 2014). The concept of "thriving" was used to connote a comprehensive image of well-being beyond the traditional split between the hedonic and eudaimonic framework. The CIT integrated key hedonic and eudaimonic models, including subjective well-being (Diener, 1994), psychological well-being (Ryff & Keyes, 1995), self-determination theory (Ryan & Deci, 2000), and the PERMA theory of well-being (Seligman, 2011). Based on these previous well-being frameworks, researchers identified 18 subscales under seven dimensions as the overarching theoretical framework: Relationships (Support, Community, Trust, Respect, Loneliness, and Belongingness subscales), Engagement (Engagement subscale), Mastery (Skills, Learning, Self-Efficacy, Self-Worth, and Accomplishment subscales), Autonomy (Lack of Control subscale), Optimism (Optimism subscale), Subjective well-being (Life Satisfaction, Positive Emotions, and Negative Emotions subscales), and Meaning (Meaning subscale). The CIT was built upon this structure with 3 items under each subscale, for a total of 54 items. Respondents rate their agreement on a 5-point scale from 1 (*strongly disagree*) to 5 (*strongly agree*). Su et al. (2014) presented scale norms in a large adult sample within the U.S. We identified nine recent studies validating the scale (and/or its variant) and presented the key psychometric properties below.

Reliability

In the development studies, the Cronbach's alphas ranged from .71 to .96 across samples (one college student sample, one elder adult sample, one lower-income adult sample, and two adult samples) and dimensions (Su et al., 2014). Test-retest reliabilities were around .60 and above over 4 months for all subscales. In general, the CIT scale showed good internal consistency and test-retest reliability.

Validity

The 18-factor correlated model had an excellent model fit and was thus supported in the original studies (Su et al., 2014). This indicated the correlated, yet distinct, dimensions assessed by the subscales. As for convergent validity evidence, CIT was found to correlate moderately to strongly with extant measures: flourishing (r=.30 to .73 range), self-mastery (r=.26 to .69 range, the highest with the Self-Efficacy subscale), Optimism (r=.26 to .82 to range, the highest with the Optimism subscale), satisfaction with life (r=.20 to .90, the highest with the Life Satisfaction subscale), and core self-evaluations (r=.26 to .78 range). In line with theory, it negatively correlated with scales that measure psychological symptoms, including PHQ-9 (r=–.59 to –.18 range) and GAD-7 (r=–.51 to –.12 range). Su et al. (2014) also examined the incremental validity of the CIT compared with Satisfaction with Life Scale (SWLS; Diener, Emmons, Larsen, & Griffin, 1985), Flourishing Scale (Diener et al., 2010), Life Orientation Test-Revised (Scheier, Carver, & Bridges, 1994), Self-Mastery Scale (Pearlin & Schooler, 1978), and Core Self-Evaluations Scale (Judge, Erez, Bono, & Thoresen, 2003). Results showed an average of 59.63 % in the additional variance accounted for across health-related outcomes (existence of medical conditions, level of physical functioning, etc.), suggesting its utility beyond the existing measures.

Application in Diverse Samples

Eight translations of the scale can be found on Dr. Ed Diener's personal website (http://labs.psychology.illinois.edu/~ediener/CIT_BIT.html). Research has validated the scale in a diverse cultural background, including German, Italian, Chinese, Turkish, and Spanish contexts covering 14 countries. Regarding reliability, in an international study across several countries, including the United States, Argentina, Australia, China, Germany, India, Spain, Singapore, Turkey, Mexico, and Russia, Cronbach's alphas were above .70 for all dimensions except for Engagement (.37 in Argentina, .37 in Mexico and .54 in Spain; Wiese et al., 2018). In another Brazilian sample, the Cronbach's alphas ranged from .70 to .95 (Martins & Ferreira, 2018). We did not find any article reporting the test-retest reliability of the CIT in other cultures.

Convergent validity evidence of both the general scale and the subscales was established in the Chinese and Brazilian samples. For example, Duan et al. (2020) reported positive correlations between the CIT overall score with life satisfaction (r=.57) and flourishing (r=.68); negative correlations were found with depression (r=–.46), anxiety (r=–.34), and stress (r=–.35). As for the subscales, strong correlations were reported in expected directions, Life Satisfaction with life satisfaction (r=.78), Optimism with optimism (r=.57), Positive feelings with flourishing (r=.73), etc. CIT was also positively correlated to students' life satisfaction in a sample of Italian elementary-school students (r=.16 to .56 across subscales; Andolfi et al., 2017).

The correlated 18-factor model showed satisfactory model fit indices (compared with single-factor, bifactor, seven-factor, or 18 first-order factors with seven second-order factors models) in a Chinese community sample (Duan et al., 2020), a Brazilian adult sample (Martins & Ferreira, 2018), and international samples in five out of eight countries (Wiese et al., 2018). The three countries that failed to replicate the factor structure were

Argentina, China, and Mexico, with no acceptable alternative solution. Strict measurement invariance was reported across eight out of 11 countries, further suggesting the measurement equivalence across cultures (Wiese et al., 2018). However, higher-order structure models attained the best fit in a study with German-speaking adults (Hausler et al., 2017) and a study with Italian children (Andolfi et al., 2017). In sum, though some minor disparities in factor models do occur, the multidimensionality of the scale is supported across studies. Further, the CIT measure appears to show measurement equivalence across nations.

BIT: Variant of CIT

Ten core items were selected from the CIT to develop the Brief Inventory of Thriving (BIT), to serve as a comparatively shorter screening tool for mental health status and as an index of general psychological flourishing. We examined five articles that tested its psychometric properties. Cronbach's alphas ranged from .75 to .93 across samples, suggesting good internal consistency of the scale. The one-factor structure was confirmed in all studies, while results suggested error correlations for Turkish and Russian samples (Wiese et al., 2018).

Two articles tested measurement equivalence across countries of the BIT. Sorgente et al. (2018) reported full configural, full metric, partial scalar, and partial unique invariance across Italian, Portuguese, and Chinese young adults. Further, Wiese et al. (2018) reported full configural, full metric, and partial scalar invariance across 11 countries, including Argentina, Australia, China, Germany, India, Mexico, Russia, Singapore, Spain, Turkey, and the United States. These results again support the hypothetical monodimensional structure of the BIT and expand its applicability over diverse cultural backgrounds.

For convergent validity evidence, BIT was found to positively correlate with flourishing, life satisfaction, optimism, self-mastery, meaning in life, and core self-evaluations. Negative correlations were found between BIT and negative emotions, depression, anxiety, and stress. These results provided discriminant and convergent validity evidence of the scale. In terms of incremental validity, it explained an average of 29.48 % additional variance over other established scales in most health outcomes. More importantly, it improved upon FS in predicting the health outcomes by 20.08 %, suggesting its unique predictive ability is different from FS (Su et al., 2014). In a Chinese community sample, BIT was found to be the only significant contributing factor (together with FS and SWLS) in explaining the variance of ill-being (depression, stress, and anxiety) in the risk group. These results suggest BIT's strong predictability of various behavior and health outcomes, enlarging its breadth of application.

Summary

There appears to be good reliability and validity evidence for the CIT and especially for its shorter variant, the BIT. There is also evidence of its incremental validity beyond extant measures for predicting outcomes such as health. However, the Engagement dimension showed lower reliabilities when applied to other cultures (Wiese et al., 2018). Interestingly, we observed similarly lower reliabilities of the Engagement subscale in the

PERMA-Profiler. Future efforts are encouraged to delve deeper into this aspect. Further, there have been relatively large-scale studies to examine the use of the CIT and BIT across multiple different countries, generally showing measurement invariance (except for Argentina, China, and Mexico).

Flourishing Scale (FS)

The Flourishing Scale (Diener et al., 2010) is a brief measure designed to capture optimal human flourishing across reasonably comprehensive domains. Rather than separating into individual facets, the FS consists of eight items providing an overall score of social-psychological functioning, including meaning and purpose in life, relationships, engagement, competence, and optimism. Although the FS was developed to be unidimensional in terms of its factor structure, it encompassed content from multiple sources and conceptualized psychological flourishing as a construct contributed by various psychosocial dimensions. This seems analogous to the MHC-SF bifactor models that seek to extract a general factor from the different subscales. Considering its integrative nature and economy of time in its application, we decided to include the scale in the current review to provide future researchers and practitioners with a useful measurement tool to consider when seeking to broadly assess psychological flourishing.

Sample items of the FS include "People respect me" and "I am a good person and live a good life," rated on a 7-point scale ranging from 1 (*strongly disagree*) to 7 (*strongly agree*). An overall flourishing score is calculated by summing up all the responses, with higher scores implying higher levels of psychological flourishing. We found 30 articles and included 26 of them in our final review.

Reliability

The alpha reliability was .87, and the test-retest correlation over 1 month was .71 in the original paper on U.S. college students (Diener et al., 2010). Howell and Buro (2015) reported a similar alpha of .89 in Canadian college students. The following studies covering diverse samples reported similar results, which are described in the following section. In sum, the statistics provided initial support for the satisfactory internal consistency and temporal stability over 1 month of the FS.

Validity

The FS generally displayed good validity evidence in Western cultures. It showed positive correlations with Cantril's Ladder (r=.57; Diener et al., 2010) and subjective happiness (r=.67; Hone et al., 2013). Positive correlations with life satisfaction were also reported (r=.62 and .64, respectively). The FS was negatively correlated with loneliness (r=–.28; Diener et al., 2010), anxiety (r=–.65), depression (r=–.65), and stress (r=–.60; Umucu, Grenawalt et al., 2019). In terms of factorial validity evidence, results showed a consistent one-factor structure across the five articles on Western populations, which agreed upon its overarching theoretical framework. However, some minor issues occurred, which are described in more detail below. In all, the results showed satisfactory psychometric properties as a measure of flourishing.

Application in Diverse Samples

The FS has been translated into 25 languages to date (https://eddiener.com/scales/9). The original English version was developed and validated in the United States and Singapore (Diener et al., 2010). Following studies validated this scale in countries over the globe targeting different populations, including Japanese college students (Sumi, 2014), Indian adolescents (Singh et al., 2016), and patients with chronic back pain (Perera et al., 2018). All 30 studies demonstrated satisfactory reliability, reporting a Cronbach's alpha equal to or greater than .80 (range .80 to .95), except for one study of Spanish parents with children of cancer reporting an alpha of .74 (Pozo Muñoz & Bretones Nieto, 2019) and another with Portuguese university students of .78 (Silva & Caetano, 2013). These results together supported the reliability of the FS across international contexts.

The FS scores correlated with measures of well-being in diverse samples among Italian (Giuntoli et al., 2017), Russian (Didino et al., 2019), Egyptian (Salama-Younes, 2017), and Portuguese adults (Silva & Caetano, 2013). Among college students and adults in Brazil, FS correlated positively with positivity at r=.65 level (Fonseca et al., 2015). Further, among Greek adults (Kyriazos et al., 2018) FS was positively correlated with gratitude (r=.47) and resilience (r=.35). In a sample of Chinese adults, the FS showed positive correlations with virtues (r=.55), including relationship (r=.44), vitality (r=.38), and conscientiousness (r=.49; Tang et al., 2016). Therefore, there is good validity evidence for the FS scale across different countries.

Across demographic groups, configural invariance was supported across ages (adolescents vs. adults), majors, employment status (employed vs. unemployed), and administration methods (online vs. paper; Giuntoli et al., 2017; Singh et al., 2016; Villieux et al., 2016). Scalar equivalence was also reported in a Spanish sample between two universities (De la Fuente et al., 2017) and in a Greek adult sample across sexes (Kyriazos et al., 2018).

Although the FS has been applied in many countries, we did not find studies conducted to examine the measurement equivalence of FS across nations or cultures. Some initial evidence of measurement equivalence comes from the FS factor structure across diverse samples. There seems to be strong support for the one-factor solution across samples, suggesting at least configural equivalence. However, numerous studies required the specification of error covariances between items to reach satisfactory model fit, suggesting that there may not be scalar or metric invariance (e.g., Didino et al., 2019; Hone et al., 2013; Kyriazos et al., 2018; Perera et al., 2018; Tong & Wang, 2017; Umucu, Grenawalt et al., 2019). We suggest that more research on cultural equivalence is necessary before making a conclusion.

Summary

In general, the FS showed good reliability and validity evidence. It has been translated and used in many countries and shows a robust one-factor solution to capture psychological flourishing. From the evidence presented so far, it appears that the FS is a useful tool to integratively measure psychological flourishing, especially considering its length and breadth. Future researchers should seek to examine whether the FS is measurement invariant across nations to determine whether FS scores are comparable across cultures and languages.

Psychological Well-Being Scale

At a time when most researchers understood well-being from a hedonic perspective, Ryff argued for the importance of psychological well-being, which should include positive human functioning beyond just experiencing positive feelings (Ryff, 1989). A scale was developed to measure psychological well-being from six aspects, including Autonomy (AU), Environmental Mastery (EM), Personal Growth (PG), Positive Relations with others (PR), Purpose in Life (PL), and Self-Acceptance (SA; Ryff, 1989). The initial inventory had 120 items in total. The scale established various shorter versions afterward with modifications and development. The most used versions have a length of 84 items (14 items per subscale), 54 items (9 items per subscale), or 18 items (3 items per subscale). To adapt it to diverse cultural and linguistic contexts, researchers also developed various other forms of different item selection based on the original inventory. Generally, the scale is rated on a 6-point Likert-type scale from 1 (*strongly disagree*) to 6 (*strongly agree*). In our current review, we summarized results from a total of 45 studies that validated the scale.

Reliability

The original PWBS inventory (120 items) was tested on 321 adults and showed good internal consistency across subscales (Ryff, 1989). Cronbach's alphas ranged from .86 to .93 across subscales. The test-retest correlations ranged from .81 to .88 over a 6-week interval, establishing acceptable temporal consistency. A shortened form (84 items) was then developed and tested on midlife and aging adults. Cronbach's alphas reported similar results, ranging from .82 to .91 across subscales (Ryff & Essex, 1992; Ryff et al., 1994; Schmutte & Ryff, 1997). However, the subscales showed a trend of decreasing reliability with a smaller number of items. While the 18-item version showed acceptable reliability in the overall score, reporting an alpha of .81 (Keyes et al., 2002), the subscales only reported low alphas ranging from .33 to .59 (Keyes et al., 2002; Ryff & Keyes, 1995). While the longer forms of PWBS reported acceptable internal consistency, the results raised concern over the ability of items to reliably measure the subscales in the 18-item version.

Validity

Four studies reported validity evidence for the PWBS (Keyes et al., 2002; Ryff, 1989; Ryff et al., 1994; Ryff & Keyes, 1995). Most subscales showed moderate to strong correlations with life satisfaction (r=.35 to .73), except for PG (r=.18 to .38) and AU (r=.12 to .30). In general, the subscales displayed lower correlations with hedonic well-being measures, including positive affect (r=.19 to .50) and subjective happiness (r=.08 to .54), which aligned with the hypothesis. Individual subscales also showed acceptable convergent validity evidence with relevant external measures. For example, SA positively correlated with self-esteem at r=.62, EM with internal control at r=.52, and PL with morale at r=.55 (Ryff, 1989). PR, AU, and PG again showed relatively lower correlations with other indexes. Ryff (1989) pointed out that these three dimensions were not well represented at the time of research. Indeed, the following research provided more convergent validity evidence, which is covered in the following section.

Regarding factorial validity evidence, the proposed factor structure by Ryff (1989) was a correlated six-factor model. As mentioned earlier, Ryff and Keyes (1995) also introduced a hierarchical second-order factor as all the subscales theoretically contribute to general psychological well-being. Only one study tested the factor structure on the 120-item version of PWBS and failed to replicate the a priori 6-factor model (Kafka & Kozma, 2002). Further research also revealed competing results in 42- and 54-item versions. For example, Boers (2014) reported an acceptable 6-factor structure, while other studies reported the opposite (Abbott et al., 2006; Burns & Machin, 2009). On the contrary, the 18-item version best supported the proposed factor models, with all five articles confirming the existence of six first-order factors corresponding to the a priori dimensions. These results raised questions over the factorial structure of the scales, especially the longer forms. We compare more results from diverse samples in the following section as well.

Application in Diverse Samples

Ryff's PWBS has been translated into multiple languages and applied in more than 20 countries over the globe. The trend persisted so that the subscales showed lower reliability with smaller numbers of items. Specifically, the 18-item version reported Cronbach's alphas ranging from .17 to .68 (90.0% under .60) in four studies. An exception was with a sample of Swedish white-collar workers (median=.65), where the only subscales with low reliability were PL (.24) and AU (.53; Lindfors et al., 2006). Among all, PL showed the lowest reliability (.17 to .33) compared to other dimensions.

Nevertheless, the longer forms of the PWBS showed comparatively higher reliabilities. Of the nine articles that provided reliability information for the 54-item version, most reported moderate to high Cronbach's alpha (.39 to .84, 86.3% were over .60), except for Hong Kong adults (.39 to .51; Cheng & Chan, 2005) and Iranian university students (.53 to .68; Shokri et al., 2008).

The 84-item version also demonstrated moderate to acceptable reliability across 16 studies (.37 to .96), with 83.3% of alpha statistics over .60. More specifically, the results showed relatively lower reliability in Japanese university students (.45 to .83; Kitamura et al., 2004), Hong Kong university students (.55 to .70; Cheng & Chan, 2005), Iranian university students (.57 to .76; Bayani et al., 2008), and Portuguese adolescents (.36 to

.50; Fernandes et al., 2010). Test-retest reliability across a 1-month interval was established with Turkish university students (.78 to .97; Akin, 2008) and Italian university students (.78 to .82, except for .21 for Autonomy and .31 for Environmental Mastery; Ruini et al., 2003); 2-month temporal reliability (.70 to .82) was established with a sample of Iranian undergraduates (Bayani et al., 2008).

Across different samples around the world, the overall score and the individual dimensions of the scales were found to correlate moderately to strongly with life satisfaction, positive affect, and happiness (e.g., Chan et al., 2019; Akin, 2008). A negative relationship was found with negative affect and depression (Machado et al., 2013). More specifically, in a Hong Kong adolescent sample, SA was found to correlate strongly with self-esteem (.61), EM with self-efficacy (.56), PG with personal growth initiative (.54), PL with the presence of meaning in life (.65), AU with adolescent autonomy (.57), and PR with social self-efficacy (.51; Chan et al., 2019). These findings provide convergent validity evidence of both the general scale and the individual dimensions.

The issues with the factor structure of the longer-form PWBS (i.e., 84-, 54-, and 42-item versions) persisted in non-Western cultures. The six-factor structure was supported in nine articles (e.g., Costea-Bărluțiu et al., 2018; Freire et al., 2019; Shokri et al., 2008), while another 12 articles failed to report acceptable model fit indices (e.g., Burns & Machin, 2009; Van Dierendonck, 2004; Villarosa & Ganotice, 2018). The 18-item version again showed better results. Eight out of 10 studies found acceptable model fit indices for the proposed six-factor structure.

A potential issue that researchers commonly identified is the overlap among PG, PL, EM, and SA in the longer forms (van Dierendonck, 2004; Springer & Hauser, 2006). These four dimensions typically showed moderate to high intercorrelations, with approximately 66.7% over .60 out of 22 studies. These results suggest that items from these four dimensions might contribute to an underlying construct. Moreover, factor analyses indicated that items from these dimensions had significant crossloadings on other factors (Abbott et al., 2006; Burns & Machin, 2009; Sirigatti et al., 2009; Tomás et al., 2008; van Dierendonck et al., 2008).

Three studies tested measurement invariance on gender groups. Two supported configural, metric, and scalar invariance across sexes, with the other one on UK adults suggesting that metric invariance did not hold, as men and women exhibited different factor loadings (Guidon et al., 2005). One study reported full metric invariance between Italy and Belarus (Sirigatti et al., 2013). Another study suggested a similar factor structure between Australian and international teacher samples, but the Norweigian sample differed from the previous two (Burns & Machin, 2009). Because research testing the relevant field is relatively scarce, future research should devote more to establishing the equivalence across samples.

Summary

The Ryff's PWBS generally showed satisfactory psychometric properties. From the research examined, there seems to be a trade-off with the length of the scale. The 18-item version showed better factorial validity evidence than the longer forms. However, with fewer items, there appear to be more challenges with reliability, particularly on the PL subscale. A common means researchers have used to alleviate this issue is to shorten the scale with different item construction (e.g., Gao & McLellan, 2018; Kállay & Rus, 2014; Machado et al., 2013). For instance, van Dierendonck (2004) selected 39 items based on the original 84-item version. The new scale yielded a satisfactory six-factor structure in CFA and showed acceptable reliability. Similar results were replicated in a Spanish version (van Dierendonck et al., 2008). Based on these results, we suggest that, in an application of the PWBS, it may be helpful to consider these variations or to pilot test and examine the reliability and factor structure of the PWBS in the target population.

Personal Well-Being Index (PWI)

The PWI (Cummins et al., 2003; International Wellbeing Group, 2013) was developed as a multiitem indicator of subjective quality of life to supplement the traditional single-item measurement of life satisfaction. It consists of 7 items, each of which represents one specific domain of global life satisfaction: standard of living, achieving in life, relationships, personal safety, community-connectedness, and future security. In theory, these areas should collectively indicate people's satisfaction with their life as a whole. It has been thus recommended that the scale be administered with a global question: "How satisfied are you with your life as a whole?" to confirm that all individual domains contribute unique variance to the global life satisfaction (GLS) score. There is also an eighth item representing the spiritual/religious domain which is optional and not included in the core set of PWI domains. This item should be included when spirituality/religion contributes unique variance to GLS in the target population.

The PWI is administered as a part of the Australian Unity Wellbeing Index (UWI), a regular quarterly survey that has targeted the general Australian population since 2001. It provides a large amount of data from the general population which are useful for norm-referencing findings obtained from various subpopulations of interest.

The scale is rated on an 11-point scale (0 = *no satisfaction at all*, 10 = *completely satisfied*) and has been validated on large samples internationally. Detailed instructions on administration can be found on the Australian Centre on Quality of Life (ACQOL) website (http://www.acqol.com.au/instruments). We identified 49 articles that reported psychometric information.

Reliability

The International Wellbeing Group (2013) provided the normative range of Cronbach's alpha for the adult 7-item version (PWI7-A) between .70 and .85. Our review of 10 articles on nationally representative Australian, Canadian, and U.S. adults revealed a range between .77 and .89. The test-retest correlation across 1- to 2-week intervals was .84, according to the report by the International Wellbeing Group (2013). Further, data from the Australian Unity Wellbeing Index suggested that the group means varied 3.2 points (on a 0–100 standardized scale) across 29 national surveys over 12 years, suggesting the temporal stability of the scale (Cummins et al., 2013). Altogether, these results provide good reliability evidence of the PWI.

Validity

The UWI comprises the National Wellbeing Index and Personal Wellbeing Index. The two-factor structure of UWI was supported according to Cummins et al. (2013), with PWI explaining 38.3% of the total variance. Six following studies replicated the one-factor structure in Western contexts of the PWI itself, supporting the unidimensionality of the measure (e.g., Tomyn et al., 2013; Weinberg et al., 2016; Richardson et al., 2016). Nonetheless, the order of the items seemed to have an impact in one study. Weinberg and colleagues (2018) noted that although a one-factor structure emerged when the order of items was fixed, it yielded poor model fit indices when the order was randomized.

The PWI total score correlated positively with GLS across three studies (r=.67 to .78; Cummins et al., 2003; Lau, 2005; International Wellbeing Group, 2013). In the regression analyses, the seven domains together explained 56.0% and 71.0% total in two Australian adult samples as expected. Researchers also reported a negative correlation with belief in the likelihood of terrorist attacks (r=–.77; Cummins et al., 2008). Altogether, these results support the ability of the PWI to measure psychological flourishing and suggest the presence of such an underlying factor. This evidence supports the validity of the scale.

Applications in Diverse Samples

The PWI has been translated into around 30 languages and used across over 40 countries. Most translated versions can be found on the ACQOL website mentioned above. Our review of 29 articles reported Cronbach's alphas between .72 to .92 across diverse samples, better than the normative range (.70 to .85) proposed by the International Wellbeing Group (2013). Five articles used the 8-item version, with Cronbach's alpha ranging from .82 to .90, supporting the internal consistency of the scale for both versions. Temporal reliability was supported in both an Iranian mother sample and a Chinese adult sample over a 2-week interval, reaching .81 and .84 test-retest correlation, respectively (Agha Yousefi et al., 2011; Lau, 2014).

Six studies examined the factor structure of the UWI, and all replicated the two-factor structure, with PWI explaining 28.2% to 41.8% of the total variance. The items loaded at .51 to .79 on the target factor with no significant loadings on NWI. A total of 26 studies investigated the factor structure of PWI alone, most supporting the hypothesis with few exceptions. A study with Australian, Bosnian, Croatian, and Serbian adults found a one-factor structure with Australian and Serbian females. They suggested that it improved model fit indices in all four countries and reached the cutoff criteria by deleting 2 items ("community" and "future") and allowing for error covariance between "standard" and "relationships." Only on two occasions did the items not meet the .40 cutoff of factor loadings. "Safety" loaded at .31 in a Chilean sample with lower-income adults (Oyanedel et al., 2015), and "health" loaded at .37 in a sample of Chinese taxi drivers (Nielsen, Paritski & Smyth, 2010). Further, the one-factor model of PWI explained 34.0% to 65.3% variance, with the majority falling in the 35% to 50% normative range suggested by the International Wellbeing Group (2013).

As for the 8-item version, seven out of nine studies confirmed its one-factor structure. One study on international samples reported an acceptable one-factor CFA model fit for

19 out of 26 countries (Żemojtel-Piotrowska et al., 2017). After allowing for error covariances, however, all samples met the cutoff criteria ("relationships"-"safety" in Hispanic countries, including Spain, Panama, and Puerto Rico, "safety"-"future" in Brazil and Poland, etc.). Moreover, Sarriera et al. (2014)reported that "spirituality" was distinguished from "religion," and that "spirituality" improved PWI model fit indices rather than "religion."

PWI showed an acceptable validity evidence across diverse samples, showing strong correlations with GLS (.50 to .88 range across 17 studies). However, three studies with Chinese samples showed weaker correlations (.15 to .66 range, mostly on .30 and .40 level; Nielsen, Paritski, & Smyth, 2010; Nielsen, Smyth, & Zhai, 2010; Smyth, Nielsen, & Zhai, 2010). In the regression analyses, the seven domains explained 32.1 % to 77.1 % of the total variance in GLS across 15 studies. The unique explained variance ranged from 8.0 % to 21.0 % and ranged from 26.6 % to 50.0 %. These results support the validity of the PWI to be used across diverse samples.

Full metric invariance was established across three Spanish-speaking countries (Chile, Spain, Brazil; Casas et al., 2012). However, only partial metric and partial scalar invariance were supported across larger international samples, which included countries and regions of different cultural backgrounds and economic statuses (Żemojtel-Piotrowska et al., 2017; Jovanović et al., 2019). Further, Jovanovic et al. (2019) reported full scalar invariance across sex; and Richardson et al. (2016) reported noninvariance across mental health status. These results rendered initial support that PWI measures the same underlying construct across sexes. At the same time, it is more appropriate to compare correlates of life satisfaction rather than raw scores across different cultural backgrounds. Further, it is also suggested that PWI is perceived differently by those who are positively functioning vs. those who are homeostatically defeated.

According to Cummins et al. (2003), the normative range of PWI means lies between 70 % to 80 % of the maximum scale score among Western populations, and they hypothesized the normative score to lie at around 75 %SM. Combined results of 33 national surveys from Australia across 16 years fall well in this normative range (M=75.37 %SM, SD=.77). Countries that fall in this range include Spain, Slovakia, the United Kingdom, Estonia, the United States, Brazil, Israel, Chile, Canada, Austria, Panama, Colombia, and Norway. However, only 20 % of the samples reported a mean score above 75 %SM. Lau (2014) also suggested that Asian countries report a lower PWI (60 % to 70 %SM) because of cultural differences. Results from Korea, China (including Hong Kong and Macau), Russia, Nepal, Indonesia, Vietnam, and Thailand support this hypothesis. If we combine all of these results, the PWI well represents life satisfaction as hypothesized. Although some minor issues occurred, we believe that it demonstrates excellent factorial and criterion validity evidence in general and can be used as a valid tool to measure subjective dimensions of quality of life across cultures.

Variants

There are two variants of the PWI. PWI-SC is adapted for school-age children and adolescents, using simplified wording in both item stems and response options (Cummins & Lau, 2005a). For example, "satisfied" is replaced by "happy," and the 11-point scale is rated with *very sad* to *very happy*. Specific domains such as "standard of living" and "achievement in life" are paraphrased using "things you have" and "things you want to be good at." All nine studies reported Cronbach's alphas above .70, with most (over 70 %) above .80. The PWI-SC score positively correlated with GLS (.53 to .70 range), and its one-factor structure was confirmed in all studies. Tomyn et al. (2017) suggested that while 12-year-olds did not differ from adults, the 10- and 11-year-olds did yield significantly different results in terms of McDonald's coefficients, the explained variance of the model, and factor loadings. In sum, the PWI-SC produced very similar results to the original adult version, suggesting that the two versions are much more likely to measure the same constructs. However, researchers need to use the scale with caution as there is concern over the reliability and validity of PWI-SC with decreasing age.

The PWI-ID is adapted for people with an intellectual disability or any form of cognitive impairment, using a series of screening and administrating procedures (Cummins & Lau, 2005b). Reduced-choice response scales were provided to match the cognitive ability of the respondents. Two articles with multiple Chinese samples provided psychometric properties of the PWI-ID (Lau, 2014; McGillivray et al., 2009). Cronbach's alpha ranged from .67 to .76. Test-retest reliability reached .58 across 1- to 2-week intervals (though the sample size was fairly small, $n = 31$; McGillivray et al., 2009). Two studies provided convergent validity evidence with GLS (.27 to .44) and factorial validity evidence of the one-factor structure.

Summary

In general, the PWI showed high reliability and good validity across multiple populations. The results from UWI also revealed high reliability over time. The insertion of the eighth item did not significantly improve or worsen the psychometric properties of the PWI-A. It proved to be measurement equivalent across cultures in general, and the decision of whether to include it depends on the cultural context (i.e., whether religion/spirituality plays a role in the evaluation of the quality of life in the target population). The PWI-SC demonstrated similar psychometric properties, although validity evidence is weaker with younger children. Moreover, the PWI-ID showed slightly weaker reliability and validity evidence. This might suggest that cognitive ability is necessary for the PWI as these populations might not be able to distinguish different aspects of their lives as well as the general population. In sum, the PWI is a reliable and valid measure that can be administered across diverse samples. Researchers and practitioners are encouraged to compare their statistics with the normative data which can be found on the ACQOL website, and make important decisions based on that.

Conclusion

We recognize that other validated scales might serve as appropriate tools in various situations. Researchers and practitioners should consider the contexts, target population, and research questions to select the best scale. For example, the EPOCH Measure of Adolescent Well-Being adapts the PERMA model to be developmentally appropriate for a younger population (Kern et al., 2016), which might make it appropriate for developmental researchers and school counselors for a multidimensional understanding of adolescent flourishing. This measure is also reviewed in Chapter 16 in this book. Other useful scales that researchers and practitioners could also consider include the Warwick-Edinburgh Mental Well-Being Scale (Tennant et al., 2007), the Orientations to Happiness Questionnaire (Peterson, 2002), the Authentic Happiness Inventory (Proyer et al., 2017), the Well-Being Profile (Marsh et al., 2020), and the Scales of General Well-Being (Longo et al., 2017). These measures also seek to assess psychological flourishing but were not identified in our literature search.

The current review provides an overview of some of the most frequently used and acknowledged well-being models and measures that follow an integrative approach. While we have striven to be as integrative and systematic in reviewing the psychological flourishing scales as possible, we recognize that our review may not be comprehensive, and it leaves out newer scales that may not be as well-established. Moreover, validation work of these psychological flourishing scales we reviewed is still ongoing. Nevertheless, we hope that this provides a useful start for researchers to identify the different psychological flourishing scales and recognize their respective strengths and weaknesses. We also hope that, by identifying specific gaps in the validation of psychological flourishing scales, this review can spur future research.

References

Abbott, R., Ploubidis, G., Huppert, F., Kuh, D., Wadsworth, M., & Croudace, T. (2006). Psychometric evaluation and predictive validity of Ryff's psychological well-being items in a UK birth cohort sample of women. *Health and Quality of Life Outcomes, 4*, Article 76. https://doi.org/10.1186/1477-7525-4-76

Agha Yousefi, A., Alipour, A., & Sharif, N. (2011). Reliability and validity of the Personal Well-Being Index-Adult in mothers of mentally retarded students in North of Tehran-Iran. *Iranian Journal of Psychiatry and Behavioral Sciences, 5*(2), 106–113.

Akin, A. (2008). The Scales of Psychological Well-Being: A study of validity and reliability. *Educational Sciences: Theory & Practice, 8*(3), 741–750.

Andolfi, V., Tay, L., Confalonieri, E., & Traficante, D. (2017). Assessing well-being in children: Italian adaptation of the comprehensive inventory of thriving for children (CIT-Child). *Testing, Psychometrics, Methodology in Applied Psychology, 24*, 127–145. https://doi.org/10.4473/TPM24.1.8

Aristotle, A., & Irwin, T. (1999). *Nicomachean ethics* (2nd ed.). Hackett.

Ayse, E. (2018). Adaptation of the PERMA Well-Being Scale into Turkish: Validity and reliability studies. *Educational Research and Reviews, 13*(4), 129–135. https://doi.org/10.5897/ERR2017.3435

Batz, C., Parrigon, S., & Tay, L. (2016). The impact of scale transformations on national subjective well-being scores. *Social Indicators Research, 129*, 13–27. https://doi.org/10.1007/s11205-015-1088-1

Bayani, A. A., Koocheky, A. M., & Bayani, A. (2008). Reliability and validity of Ryff's psychological well-being scales. *Iranian Journal of Psychiatry and Clinical Psychology, 14*, 146–151.

Boers, M. (2014). *Empirical evaluation of the Steyn-Boers structural model of psychological well-being at work.* Unpublished master's dissertation, Stellenbosch University, South Africa.

Burns, R., & Machin, A. (2009). Investigating the Structural Validity of Ryff's Psychological Well-Being Scales Across Two Samples. *Social Indicators Research, 93*(2), 359–375. https://doi.org/10.1007/s11205-008-9329-1

Butler, J., & Kern, M. L. (2016). The PERMA-Profiler: A brief multidimensional measure of flourishing. *International Journal of Wellbeing, 6*(3), 1–48.

Carvalho, J., Pereira, S., Pinto, N., & Marôco, S. (2016). Psychometric properties of the Mental Health Continuum-Short Form: A study of Portuguese speaking children/youths. *Journal of Child and Family Studies, 25*(7), 2141–2154. https://doi.org/10.1007/s10826-016-0396-7

Casas, F., Sarriera, J. C., Alfaro, J., González, J., Malo, M., Bertran, S., Figuer, C., da Cruz, D. A., Bedin, L., Paradiso, A., Weinreich, K., & Valdenegro, B. (2012). Testing the Personal Wellbeing Index on 12–16-year-old adolescents in 3 different countries with 2 new items. *Social Indicators Research, 105*(3), 461–482. https://doi.org/10.1007/s11205-011-9781-1

Chan, D. W., Chan, L., & Sun, X. (2019). Developing a brief version of Ryff's Scale to assess the psychological well-being of adolescents in Hong Kong. *European Journal of Psychological Assessment, 35*(3), 414–422. https://doi.org/10.1027/1015-5759/a000403

Cheng, S., & Chan, A. (2005). Measuring psychological well-being in the Chinese. *Personality and Individual Differences, 38*(6), 1307–1316. https://doi.org/10.1016/j.paid.2004.08.013

Costea-Bărluțiu, C., Bălaș-Baconschi, C., & Hathazi, A. (2018). Romanian adaptation of the Ryff's Psychological Well-Being Scale: Brief report of the factor structure and psychometric properties. *Journal of Evidence-Based Psychotherapies, 18*, 21–33. https://doi.org/10.24193/jebp.2018.1.2

Cummins, R. A., Eckersley, A., Pallant, R., Van Vugt, J., & Misajon, J. (2003). Developing a National Index of Subjective Wellbeing: The Australian Unity Wellbeing Index. *Social Indicators Research, 64*(2), 159–190. https://doi.org/10.1023/A:1024704320683

Cummins, R. A., & Lau, A. L. D. (2005a). *Personal Wellbeing Index - Intellectual Disability* (3rd ed.). Deakin University.

Cummins, R. A., & Lau, A. L. D. (2005b). *Personal Wellbeing Index - School Children* (3rd ed.). Deakin University.

Cummins, R. A., Mellør, D., Stokes, M. A., Lau, A. A. (2008). Quality of life down-under: The Australian Unity Wellbeing Index. In V. Møller, D. Huschka, & A. C. Michalos (Eds.), *Barometers of quality of life around the globe.* (Social Indicators Research Series, Vol. 33). Springer.

Cummins, R. A., Woerner, J., Weinberg, M., Collard, J., Hartley-Clark, L., Horfiniak, K., & Perera, C. (2013). *Australian Unity Wellbeing Index, Report 29.0: The wellbeing of Australians - 2 extra hours, mothers and mothers-in-law.* Australian Centre on Quality of Life, School of Psychology, Deakin University.

De La Fuente, R., Parra, A., & Sánchez-Queija, I. (2017). Psychometric properties of the Flourishing Scale and measurement invariance between two samples of Spanish university students. *Evaluation & the Health Professions, 40*(4), 409–424. https://doi.org/10.1177/0163278717703446

Didino, D., Taran, E. A., Barysheva, G. A., & Casati, F. (2019). Psychometric evaluation of the Russian version of the flourishing scale in a sample of older adults living in Siberia. *Health and Quality of Life Outcomes, 17*(1), 1–12. https://doi.org/10.1186/s12955-019-1100-6

Diener, E. (1984). Subjective well-being. *Psychological Bulletin, 95*, 542–575. https://doi.org/10.1037/0033-2909.95.3.542

Diener, E. (1994). Assessing subjective well-being: Progress and opportunities. *Social Indicators Research, 31*(2), 103–157. https://doi.org/10.1007/BF01207052

Diener, E. (2000). Subjective well-being: The science of happiness and a proposal for a national index. *American Psychologist, 55*(1), 34–43. https://doi.org/10.1037//0003-066x.55.1.34

Diener, E., Emmons, R. A., Larsen, R. J., & Griffin, S. (1985). The Satisfaction with Life Scale. *Journal of Personality Assessment, 49*, 71–75. https://doi.org/10.1207/s15327752jpa4901_13

Diener, E., & Seligman, M. E. P. (2004). Beyond money: Toward an economy of well-being. *Psychological Science in the Public Interest, 5*, 1–31. https://doi.org/10.1111/j.0963-7214.2004.00501001.x

Diener, E., Suh, E. M., Lucas, R. E., & Smith, H. L. (1999). Subjective well-being: Three decades of progress. *Psychological Bulletin, 125*(2), 276–302. https://doi.org/10.1037/0033-2909.125.2.276

Diener, E., Wirtz, D., Tov, W., Kim-Prieto, C., Choi, D., Oishi, S., & Biswas-Diener, R. (2010). New well-being measures: Short scales to assess flourishing and positive and negative feelings. *Social Indicators Research, 97*(2), 143–156. https://doi.org/10.1007/s11205-009-9493-y

Duan, W., Fei, Y., Zhao, J., & Guo, X. (2020). Incremental validity of the comprehensive inventory of thriving in predicting self-reporting mental and physical health among community populations. *Journal of Health Psychology, 25*(10–11), 1366–1373. https://doi.org/10.1177/1359105318755265

Echeverria, G., Torres, M., Pedrals, N., Padilla, O., Rigotti, A., & Bitran, M. (2017). Validacion de la version en espanol del Cuestionario del Continuo de Salud Mental-Version Corta [Validation of a Spanish version of the Mental Health Continuum-Short Form questionnaire]. *Psicothema, 29*(1), 96–102. https://doi.org/10.7334/psicothema2016.3

Fernandes, H., Vasconcelos-Raposo, J., & Teixeira, C. (2010). Preliminary analysis of the psychometric properties of Ryff's Scales of Psychological Well-Being in Portuguese adolescents. *The Spanish Journal of Psychology, 13*(2), 1032–1043. https://doi.org/10.1017/S1138741600002675

Fonseca, P.N., Nascimento, B.S., Barbosa, L.H. G.M., Vione, K.C., & Gouveia, V.V. (2015). Flourishing Scale: Evidence of its suitability to the Brazilian context. *Social Inquiry into Well-Being, 1*(2), 33–40.

Freire, R.M., Sousa, M.R., Pereira, F., & Martins, T. (2019). Estudo das propriedades psicométricas da Escala de Bem-Estar Psicológico de 42 itens [Psychometric properties of the 42-item Psychological Well-Being Scale]. *Revista Portuguesa de Enfermagem de Saúde Mental, 21*, 31–39. https://doi.org/10.19131/rpesm.0235

Gao, J., & McLellan, R. (2018). Using Ryff's scales of psychological well-being in adolescents in mainland China. *BMC Psychology, 6*, Article 17. https://doi.org/10.1186/s40359-018-0231-6

Giangrasso, B. (2018). Psychometric properties of the PERMA-Profiler as hedonic and eudaimonic well-being measure in an Italian context. *Current Psychology, 40*, 1175–1184.https://doi.org/10.1007/s12144-018-0040-3

Gilmour, H. (2014). Positive mental health and mental illness. *Health Reports, 25*(9), 3–9.

Giuntoli, L., Ceccarini, F., Sica, C., & Caudek, C. (2017). Validation of the Italian versions of the Flourishing Scale and of the Scale of Positive and Negative Experience. *SAGE Open, 7*(1). https://doi.org/10.1177/2158244016682293

Guidon, S., & Norm, O., & Philippe, C. (2005). Factor structure and invariance of responses by older men and women to an abridged version of the Ryff Scale of Psychological Well-Being. *Journal of Mental Health and Aging, 10*, 301–310.

Hausler, M., Huber, A., Strecker, C., Brenner, M., Höge, T., & Höfer, S. (2017). Validierung eines Fragebogens zur umfassenden Operationalisierung von Wohlbefinden: Die deutsche Version des Comprehensive Inventory of Thriving (CIT) und die Kurzversion Brief Inventory of Thriving (BIT) [Validation of a questionnaire for the comprehensive operationalization of well-being: The German version of the Comprehensive Inventory of Thriving (CIT) and the short version Brief Inventory of Thriving (BIT)]. *Diagnostica, 63*(3), 219–228. https://doi.org/10.1026/0012-1924/a000174

Hidayat, R., Habibi, A., Saad, M.R. M., Mukminin, A., & bin Wan Idris, W.I. (2018). Exploratory and confirmatory factor analysis of PERMA for Indonesian students in mathematics education programmes. *Pedagogika, 132*(4), 147–165. https://doi.org/10.15823/p.2018.132.9

Hides, L., Quinn, C., Stoyanov, S., Cockshaw, W., Mitchell, T., & Kavanagh, D.J. (2016). Is the mental wellbeing of young Australians best represented by a single, multidimensional or bifactor model? *Psychiatry Research, 241*, 1–7. https://doi.org/10.1016/j.psychres.2016.04.077

Hone, L., Jarden, A., & Schofield, G. (2013). Psychometric properties of the Flourishing Scale in a New Zealand sample. *Social Indicators Research, 1*, 1–15. https://doi.org/10.1007/s11205-013-0501-x

Howell, A., & Buro, K. (2015). Measuring and predicting student well-being: Further evidence in support of the Flourishing Scale and the Scale of Positive and Negative Experiences. *Social Indicators Research, 121*, 903–915. https://doi.org/10.1007/s11205-014-0663-1

International Wellbeing Group. (2013). *Personal wellbeing index* (5th ed.). Melbourne: Australian Centre on Quality of Life, Deakin University. https://www.acqol.com.au/instruments#measures

Joshanloo, M., Wissing, M., Khumalo, I., & Lamers, S. (2013). Measurement invariance of the Mental Health Continuum-Short Form (MHC-SF) across three cultural groups. *Personality and Individual Differences, 55*(7), 755–759. https://doi.org/10.1016/j.paid.2013.06.002

Jovanović, V., Cummins, R., Weinberg, A., Kaliterna, M., & Prizmic-Larsen, L. (2019). Personal Wellbeing Index: A cross-cultural measurement invariance study across four countries. *Journal of Happiness Studies, 20*(3), 759–775. https://doi.org/10.1007/s10902-018-9966-2

Judge, T.A., Erez, A., Bono, J.E., & Thoresen, C.J. (2003). The core self-evaluations scale: Development of a measure. *Personnel Psychology, 56*(2), 303–331. https://doi.org/10.1111/j.1744-6570.2003.tb00152

Kafka, G.J., Kozma, A. (2002). The construct validity of Ryff's Scales of Psychological Well-Being (SPWB) and their relationship to measures of subjective well-being. *Social Indicators Research, 57*, 171–190. https://doi.org/10.1023/A:1014451725204

Kállay, E., & Rus, C. (2014). Psychometric properties of the 44-item version of Ryff's Psychological Well-Being Scale. *European Journal of Psychological Assessment, 30*(1), 15–21. https://doi.org/10.1027/1015-5759/a000163

Kashdan, T.B., Mishra, A., Breen, W.E., & Froh, J.J. (2009). Gender differences in gratitude: Examining appraisals, narratives, the willingness to express emotions, and changes in psychological needs. *Journal of Personality, 77*(3), 691–730. https://doi.org/10.1111/j.1467-6494.2009.00562.x

Keltner, D., & Haidt, J. (2003). Approaching awe, a moral, spiritual, and esthetic emotion. *Cognition & Emotion, 17*, 297–314. https://doi.org/10.1080/02699930302297

Kern, M.L., Benson, L., Steinberg, E.A., & Steinberg, L. (2016). The EPOCH Measure of Adolescent Well-Being. *Psychological Assessment, 28*(5), 586–597. https://doi.org/10.1037/pas0000201

Keyes, C.L.M. (1998). Social well-being. *Social Psychology Quarterly, 61*(2), 121–140. https://doi.org/10.2307/2787065

Keyes, C.L.M. (2002). The Mental Health Continuum: From languishing to flourishing in life. *Journal of Health and Social Behavior, 43*(2), 207–222. https://doi.org/10.2307/3090197

Keyes, C.L. M. (2005). Mental illness and/or mental health? Investigating axioms of the complete state model of health. *Journal of Consulting and Clinical Psychology, 73*(3), 539–548. https://doi.org/10.1037/0022-006X.73.3.539

Keyes, C.L.M. (2006). Mental health in adolescence: Is America's youth flourishing? *The American Journal of Orthopsychiatry, 76*(3), 395–402. https://doi.org/10.1037/0002-9432.76.3.395

Keyes, C.L.M., Eisenberg, D., Perry, G., Dube, S., Kroenke, K., & Dhingra, S. (2012). The relationship of level of positive mental health with current mental disorders in predicting suicidal behavior and academic impairment in college students. *Journal of American College Health, 60*(2), 126–133. https://doi.org/10.1080/07448481.2011.608393

Keyes, C.L.M., Shmotkin, D., & Ryff, C. (2002). Optimizing well-being: The empirical encounter of two traditions. *Journal of Personality and Social Psychology, 82*(6), 1007–1022. https://doi.org/10.1037/0022-3514.82.6.1007

Keyes, C.L.M., Wissing, M., Potgieter, J., Temane, M., Kruger, A., Van Rooy, S., & Schmidt, S. (2008). Evaluation of the Mental Health Continuum–Short Form (MHC–SF) in Setswana-speaking South Africans. *Clinical Psychology & Psychotherapy, 15*(3), 181–192. https://doi.org/10.1002/cpp.572

Khaw, M., & Kern, D. (2015). A Cross-cultural comparison of the PERMA model of well-being. *Undergraduate Journal of Psychology at Berkeley, University of California, 8*, 10–23.

Kitamura, T., Kishida, Y., Gatayama, R., Matsuoka, T., Miura, S., & Yamabe, K. (2004). Ryff's Psychological Well-Being Inventory: Factorial structure and life history correlates among Japanese university students. *Psychological Reports, 94*(1), 83–103. https://doi.org/10.2466/pr0.94.1.83-103

Kohlberg, L. (1958). *The development of modes of moral thinking and choice in the years 10 to 16.* PhD thesis, University of Chicago.

Kyriazos, T., Stalikas, A., Prassa, K., Yotsidi, V., Galanakis, M., & Pezirkianidis, C. (2018). Validation of the Flourishing Scale (FS), Greek Version and evaluation of two well-being models. *Psychology, 9*, 1789–1813. https://doi.org/10.4236/psych.2018.97105

Lamborn, P., Cramer, K., & Riberdy, M. (2018). The structural validity and measurement invariance of the Mental Health Continuum–Short Form (MHC-SF) in a large Canadian sample. *Journal of Well-Being Assessment, 2*(1), 1–19. https://doi.org/10.1007/s41543-018-0007-z

Lamers, S., Westerhof, G., Bohlmeijer, E., Ten Klooster, P., & Keyes, C. (2011). Evaluating the psychometric properties of the Mental Health Continuum-Short Form (MHC-SF). *Journal of Clinical Psychology, 67*(1), 99–110. https://doi.org/10.1002/jclp.20741

Lau, A. (2014). China, personal well-being index. In A.C. Michalos (Ed.), *Encyclopedia of quality of life and well-being research* (pp. 813–822). Springer. https://doi.org/10.1007/978-94-007-0753-5_3992

Lau, A. L. D., Cummins, R. A., & Mcpherson, W. (2005). An investigation into the cross-cultural equivalence of the Personal Wellbeing Index. *Social Indicators Research, 72*(3), 403–430. https://doi.org/10.1007/s11205-004-0561-z

Lim, Y. (2014). Psychometric characteristics of the Korean Mental Health Continuum-Short Form in an adolescent sample. *Journal of Psychoeducational Assessment, 32*(4), 356–364. https://doi.org/10.1177/0734282913511431

Lim, Y., Go, Y., Shin, H., & Cho, Y. (2013). Prevalence and correlates of complete mental health in the South Korean adult population. In C. Keyes (Ed.), *Mental well-being: International contributions to the study of positive mental health* (pp. 91–110). Springer. https://doi.org/10.1007/978-94-007-5195-8_5

Lindfors, P., Berntsson, L., & Lundberg, U. (2006). Factor structure of Ryff's psychological well-being scales in Swedish female and male white-collar workers. *Personality and Individual Differences, 40*(6), 1213–1222. https://doi.org/10.1016/j.paid.2005.10.016

Longo, Y., Coyne, I., & Joseph, S. (2017). The Scales of General Well-Being (SGWB). *Personality and Individual Differences, 109,* 148–159. https://doi.org/10.1016/j.paid.2017.01.005

Longo, Y., Jovanović, V., Sampaio de Carvalho, J., & Karaś, D. (2020). The general factor of well-being: Multinational evidence using bifactor ESEM on the Mental Health Continuum-Short Form. *Assessment, 27*(3), 596–606. https://doi.org/10.1177/1073191117748394

Machado, W. de L., Bandeira, D. R., & Pawlowski, J. (2013). Validação da Psychological Well-being Scale em uma amostra de estudantes universitários [Validation of the Psychological Well-being Scale in an undergraduate student sample]. *Avaliaçao Psicológica, 12*(2), 263–272.

Manderscheid, R. W., Ryff, C. D., Freeman, E. J., McKnight-Eily, L. R., Dhingra, S., & Strine, T. W. (2010). Evolving definitions of mental illness and wellness. *Preventing Chronic Disease, 7*(1), Article 19.

Marsh, H. W., Huppert, F. A., Donald, J. N., Horwood, M. S., & Sahdra, B. K. (2020). The Well-Being Profile (WB-Pro): Creating a theoretically based multidimensional measure of well-being to advance theory, research, policy, and practice. *Psychological Assessment, 32*(3), 294–313. https://doi.org/10.1037/pas0000787

Martins, L., & Ferreira, M. (2018). Psychometric properties of the inventory of thriving: Brief and comprehensive versions. *Trends in Psychology, 26*(3), 1557–1571. https://doi.org/10.9788/TP2018.3-15En

Maslow, A. H. (1943). A theory of human motivation. *Psychological Review, 50,* 370–396. https://doi.org/10.1037/h0054346

Maslow, A. H. (1956). Self-actualizing people: A study of psychological health. In C. E. Moustakas (Ed.), *The self: Explorations in personal growth* (pp. 161–162). Harper & Row.

McGillivray, J., Lau, A., Cummins, R., & Davey, G. (2009). The utility of the Personal Wellbeing Index Intellectual Disability Scale in an Australian Sample. *Journal of Applied Research in Intellectual Disabilities, 22*(3), 276–286. https://doi.org/10.1111/j.1468-3148.2008.00460.x

McGrath, R. E. (2014). Scale- and item-level factor analyses of the VIA inventory of strengths. *Assessment, 21,* 4–14. https://doi.org/10.1177/1073191112450612

Ng, V., Tay, L., & Kuykendall, L. (2018). The development and validation of a measure of character: The CIVIC. *Journal of Positive Psychology, 13,* 346–372. https://doi.org/10.1080/17439760.2017.1291850

Nielsen, I., Paritski, O., & Smyth, R. (2010). Subjective well-being of Beijing taxi drivers. *Journal of Happiness Studies, 11*(6), 721–733. https://doi.org/10.1007/s10902-009-9170-5

Nielsen, I., Smyth, R., & Zhai, Q. (2010). Subjective well-being of China's off-farm migrants. *Journal of Happiness Studies, 11*(3), 315–333. https://doi.org/10.1007/s10902-009-9142-9

Nunnally, J. C., & Bernstein, I. H. (1994). *Psychometric theory* (3rd ed.). McGraw-Hill.

Orpana, H., Vachon, J., Dykxhoorn, J., & Jayaraman, G. (2017). Measuring positive mental health in Canada: Construct validation of the Mental Health Continuum-Short Form. *Health Promotion and Chronic Disease Prevention in Canada, 37*(4), 123–130. https://doi.org/10.24095/hpcdp.37.4.03

Oyanedel, J., Vargas, S., Mella, C., & Páez, D. (2015). Validación del índice de bienestar personal (PWI) en usuarios vulnerables de servicios de salud en Santiago, Chile [Validation of the Personal Wellbeing Index (PWI) in vulnerable users of health care services in Santiago, Chile]. *Revista Médica de Chile, 143,* 1144–1151. https://doi.org/10.4067/S0034-98872015000900007

Park, N., Peterson, C., Szvarca, D., Vander Molen, R. J., Kim, E. S., & Collon, K. (2016). Positive psychology and physical health: Research and applications. *American Journal of Lifestyle Medicine, 10*(3), 200–206. https://doi.org/10.1177/1559827614550277

Pearlin, L. I., & Schooler, C. (1978). The structure of coping. *Journal of Health and Social Behavior, 19*, 2–21. https://doi.org/10.2307/2136319

Peña Contreras, E. K., Lima Castro, S. E., Bueno Pacheco, G. A., Aguilar Sizer, M. E., Keyes Lee, C., & Arias Medina, W. P. (2017). Fiabilidad y validez de la Escala del Contínuum de Salud Mental (MHC-SF) en el contexto ecuatoriano [Reliability and validity of the Mental Health Continuum (MHC-SF) in the Ecuadorian context]. *Ciencias Psicológicas, 11*(2), 223–232. https://doi.org/10.22235/cp.v11i2.1499

Perera, M., Meade, M., & DiPonio, L. (2018). Use and psychometric properties of the Flourishing Scale among adults with spinal cord injury. *Rehabilitation Psychology, 63*(2), 250–257. https://doi.org/10.1037/rep0000184

Peterson, C., & Seligman, M. E. P. (2004). *Character strengths and virtues*. Oxford University Press.

Peterson, D. K. (2002). Deviant workplace behavior and the organization's ethical climate. *Journal of Business and Psychology, 17*(1), 47–61. https://doi.org/10.1023/A:1016296116093

Petrillo, G., Capone, V., Caso, D., & Keyes, C. (2015). The Mental Health Continuum-Short Form (MHC-SF) as a measure of well-being in the Italian context. *Social Indicators Research, 121*(1), 291–312. https://doi.org/10.1007/s11205-014-0629-3

Pezirkianidis, C., Stalikas, A., Lakioti, A., & Yotsidi, V. (2021). Validating a multidimensional measure of wellbeing in Greece: Translation, factor structure, and measurement invariance of the PERMA Profiler. *Current Psychology, 40*, 3030–3047.https://doi.org/10.1007/s12144-019-00236-7

Pozo Muñoz, C., & Bretones Nieto, B. (2019). Spanish version of the Flourishing Scale (FS) on the Parents of Children with Cancer: A validation through Rasch analysis. *Frontiers in Psychology, 10*, Article 35. https://doi.org/10.3389/fpsyg.2019.00035

Proyer, R. T., Gander, F., Wellenzohn, S., & Ruch, W. (2017). The Authentic Happiness Inventory revisited: Addressing its psychometric properties, validity, and role in intervention studies. *Journal of Well-Being Assessment, 1*(1), 77–96. https://doi.org/10.1007/s41543-018-0006-0

Reise, S. P. (2012). The rediscovery of bifactor measurement models. *Multivariate Behavioral Research, 47*, 667–696. https://doi.org/10.1080/00273171.2012.715555

Richardson, B., Fuller Tyszkiewicz, M., Tomyn, D., & Cummins, A. (2016). The psychometric equivalence of the Personal Wellbeing Index for normally functioning and homeostatically defeated Australian adults. *Journal of Happiness Studies, 17*(2), 627–641. https://doi.org/10.1007/s10902-015-9613-0

Rogers, C. (1961). *On becoming a person*. Houghton Mifflin.

Rogoza, R., Truong Thi, K. H., Różycka-Tran, J., Piotrowski, J., & Żemojtel-Piotrowska, M. (2018). Psychometric properties of the MHC-SF: An integration of the existing measurement approaches. *Journal of Clinical Psychology, 74*(10), 1742–1758. https://doi.org/10.1002/jclp.22626

Rozin, P., Haidt, J., & Fincher, K. (2009). From oral to moral. *Science, 323*, 1179–1180. https://doi.org/10.1126/science.1170492

Ruini, C., Ottolini, F., Rafanelli, C., Ryff, C., & Fava, G. A. (2003). La validazione italiana delle Psychological Well-being Scales (PWB) [Italian validation of Psychological Well-being Scales (PWB)]. *Rivista di Psichiatria, 38*(3), 117–130.

Ryan, J., Curtis, R., Olds, T., Edney, S., Vandelanotte, C., Plotnikoff, R., & Maher, C. (2019). Psychometric properties of the PERMA Profiler for measuring well-being in Australian adults. *PLoS ONE, 14*(12), E0225932. https://doi.org/10.1371/journal.pone.0225932

Ryan, R. M., & Deci, E. L. (2000). Self-determination theory and the facilitation of intrinsic motivation, social development, and well-being. *American Psychologist, 55*(1), 68–78. https://doi.org/10.1037/0003-066X.55.1.68

Ryff, C. D. (1989). Happiness is everything, or is it? Explorations on the meaning of psychological well-being. *Journal of Personality and Social Psychology, 57*(6), 1069–1081. https://doi.org/10.1037/0022-3514.57.6.1069

Ryff, C.D., & Essex, M.J. (1992). The interpretation of life experience and well-being: The sample case of relocation. *Psychology and Aging, 7*(4), 507–517. https://doi.org/10.1037/0882-7974.7.4.507

Ryff, C.D., & Keyes, C.L.M. (1995). The structure of psychological well-being revisited. *Journal of Personality and Social Psychology, 69*, 719–727. https://doi.org/10.1037/0022-3514.69.4.719

Ryff, C.D., Lee, Y., Essex, M., & Schmutte, P. (1994). My children and me: Midlife evaluations of grown children and of self. *Psychology and Aging, 9*(2), 195–205. https://doi.org/10.1037/0882-7974.9.2.195

Salama-Younes, M. (2017). Psychometric properties of the Psychological Flourishing Scale in an Egyptian setting. *Journal of Psychology in Africa, 27*(4), 310–315. https://doi.org/10.1080/14330237.2017.1347749

Sarriera, J.C., Casas, F., Alfaro, J., Bedin, L., Strelhow, M.R.W., Abs, D., Valdenegro, B., García, C., & Oyarzún, D. (2014). Psychometric properties of the personal wellbeing index in Brazilian and Chilean adolescents including spirituality and religion. *Psicologia: Reflexão e Crítica, 27*, 710–719. https://doi.org/10.1590/1678-7153.201427411

Scheier, M.E., Carver, C.S., & Bridges, M.W. (1994). Distinguishing optimism from neuroticism (and trait anxiety, self-mastery, and self-esteem): A re-evaluation of the Life Orientation Test. *Journal of Personality and Social Psychology, 67*, 1063–1078. https://doi.org/10.1037/0022-3514.67.6.1063

Schmutte, P., & Ryff, C. (1997). Personality and well-being: Reexamining methods and meanings. *Journal of Personality and Social Psychology, 73*(3), 549–559. https://doi.org/10.1037/0022-3514.73.3.549

Schutte, L., & Wissing, M.P. (2017). Clarifying the factor structure of the Mental Health Continuum–Short Form in three languages: A bifactor exploratory structural equation modeling approach. *Society and Mental Health, 7*(3), 142–158. https://doi.org/10.1177/2156869317707793

Seligman, M.E.P. (2008). Positive health. *Applied Psychology, 57*(s1), 3–18. https://doi.org/10.1111/j.1464-0597.2008.00351.x

Seligman, M.E.P. (2011). *Flourish: A visionary new understanding of happiness and well-being.* Free Press.

Seligman, M.E.P., & Csikszentmihalyi, M. (2000). Positive psychology: An introduction. *American Psychologist, 55*, 5–14. https://doi.org/10.1037/0003-066X.55.1.5

Shokri, O., Kadivar, P., Farzad, V., Daneshvarpour, Z., Dastjerdi, R., Paeezi, M. (2008). A study of factor structure of 3, 9 and 14-item Persian versions of Ryff's Scales Psychological Well-Being in university students. *Iranian Journal of Psychiatry and Clinical Psychology, 14*(2), 152–161. Retrieved from http://ijpcp.iums.ac.ir/article-1-465-en.html

Silva, A.J., & Caetano, A. (2013). Validation of the flourishing scale and scale of positive and negative experience in Portugal. *Social Indicators Research, 110*, 469–478. https://doi.org/10.1007/s11205-011-9938-y

Silverman, A., Forgeard, L., Beard, M., & Björgvinsson, C. (2018). Psychometric properties of the Mental Health Continuum–Short Form in a psychiatric sample. *Journal of Well-Being Assessment, 2*(1), 57–73. https://doi.org/10.1007/s41543-018-0011-3

Singh, K., Bassi, M., Junnarkar, M., & Negri, L. (2015). Mental health and psychosocial functioning in adolescence: An investigation among Indian students from Delhi. *Journal of Adolescence, 39*(5), 59–69. https://doi.org/10.1016/j.adolescence.2014.12.008

Singh, K., Junnarkar, M., & Jaswal, S. (2016). Validating the Flourishing Scale and the Scale of Positive and Negative Experience in India. *Mental Health, Religion & Culture: Assessment of Mental Health, Religion and Culture: The Development and Examination of Psychometric Measures (Part II), 19*(8), 943–954. https://doi.org/10.1080/13674676.2016.1229289

Sirigatti, S., Penzo, I., Iani, L., Mazzeschi, A., Hatalskaja, H., Giannetti, E., & Stefanile, C. (2013). Measurement Invariance of Ryff's Psychological Well-Being Scales across Italian and Belarusian students. *Social Indicators Research, 113*, 67–80. https://doi.org/10.1007/s11205-012-0082-0

Sirigatti, S., Stefanile, C., Giannetti, E., Iani, L., Penzo, I., & Mazzeschi, A. (2009). Assessment of factor structure of Ryff's Psychological Well-Being Scales in Italian adolescents. *Bollettino di Psicologia Applicata, 259*, 30–50.

Six, F., & Sorge, A. (2008). Creating a high-trust organization: An exploration into organizational policies that stimulate interpersonal trust building. *Journal of Management Studies, 45*(5), 857–884. https://doi.org/10.1111/j.1467-6486.2007.00763.x

Smyth, R., Nielsen, I., & Zhai, Q. (2010). Personal well-being in urban China. *Social Indicators Research, 95*, 231–251. https://doi.org/10.1007/s11205-009-9457-2.

Sorgente, A., Tagliabue, S., Andrade, C., Oliveira, J., Duan, W., & Lanz, M. (2018, July 3–6). *Brief Inventory of Thriving: The development of the Italian version and the cross-cultural invariance between Italian, Portuguese, and Chinese versions.* Presented at the Joint Conference of Sepex – Sepneca – AIPexperimental, Madrid, Spain.

Springer, K.W., & Hauser, R.M. (2006). An assessment of the construct validity of Ryff's Scales of Psychological Well-Being: Method, mode, and measurement effects. *Social Science Research, 35*(4), 1080–1102. https://doi.org/10.1016/j.ssresearch.2005.07.004

Steger, M.F., Frazier, P., Oishi, S., & Kaler, M. (2006). The meaning in life questionnaire: Assessing the presence of and search for meaning in life. *Journal of Counseling Psychology, 53*(1), 80-93. https://doi.org/10.1037/0022-0167.53.1.80

Su, R., Tay, L., & Diener, E. (2014). The development and validation of the Comprehensive Inventory of Thriving (CIT) and the Brief Inventory of Thriving (BIT). *Applied Psychology: Health and Well-Being, 6*, 251–279.

Sumi, K. (2014). Reliability and validity of Japanese versions of the Flourishing Scale and the Scale of Positive and Negative Experience. *Social Indicators Research, 118*(2), 601–615. https://doi.org/10.1007/s11205-013-0432-6

Tang, X., Duan, W., Wang, Z., Liu, T. (2016). Psychometric evaluation of the simplified Chinese version of flourishing scale. *Research on Social Work Practice, 26*(5), 591–599. https://doi.org/10.1177/1049731514557832

Tay, L., Diener, E., Lucas, R.E., & Larsen, R.J. (2019). Measuring positive emotions. In S. Lopez., & M. Gallagher. (Eds.), *Positive psychological assessment handbook* (2nd ed., pp. 179–202). American Psychological Association. https://doi.org/10.1037/0000138-012

Tay, L., Jebb, A.T., & Scotney, V.S. (2021). Assessments of societal subjective well-being: Ten methodological issues for consideration. In M.T. Lee, L.D. Kubzansky, & T.J. VanderWeele (Eds.), *Measuring well-being: Interdisciplinary perspectives from the social sciences and the humanities* (pp. 70–91). Oxford University Press. https://doi.org/10.1093/oso/9780197512531.003.0004

Tay, L., Pawelski, J.O., & Keith, M.G. (2018). The role of the arts and humanities in human flourishing: A conceptual model. *Journal of Positive Psychology, 13*(3), 215–225. https://doi.org/10.1080/17439760.2017.1279207

Tennant, R., Hiller, L., Fishwick, R., Platt, S., Joseph, S., Weich, S., Parkinson, J., Secker, J., & Stewart-Brown, S. (2007). The Warwick-Edinburgh Mental Well-Being Scale (WEMWBS): Development and UK validation. *Health and Quality of Life Outcomes, 5*(1), Article 63. https://doi.org/10.1186/1477-7525-5-63

Tomás, J.M., Meléndez, J.C., & Navarro, E. (2008). Modelos factoriales confirmatorios de las escalas de Ryff en una muestra de personas mayores [Factorial confirmatory models of Ryff's scales in a sample of elderly people]. *Psicothema, 20*, 304–310.

Tomyn, A., Fuller-Tyszkiewicz, J., & Cummins, R.A. (2013). The Personal Wellbeing Index: Psychometric equivalence for adults and school children. *Social Indicators Research, 110*(3), 913–924. https://doi.org/10.1007/s11205-011-9964-9

Tomyn, A., Fuller-Tyszkiewicz, J., Cummins, R.A., & Norrish, D. (2017). The validity of subjective well-being measurement for children: Evidence using the Personal Wellbeing Index–School Children. *Journal of Happiness Studies, 18*(6), 1859–1875. https://doi.org/10.1007/s10902-016-9804-3

Tong, K.K., & Wang, Y.Y. (2017). Validation of the flourishing scale and scale of positive and negative experience in a Chinese community sample. *PLoS ONE, 12*(8), E0181616. https://doi.org/10.1371/journal.pone.0181616

Tugade, M.M., & Fredrickson, B.L. (2004). Resilient individuals use positive emotions to bounce back from negative emotional experiences. *Journal of Personality and Social Psychology, 86*(2), 320–333. https://doi.org/10.1037/0022-3514.86.2.320

Umucu, E., Grenawalt, T., Reyes, A., Tansey, T., Brooks, J., Lee, B., Gleason, C., & Chan, F. (2019). Flourishing in student veterans with and without service-connected disability: Psychometric validation of the Flourishing Scale and exploration of its relationships with personality and disability. *Rehabilitation Counseling Bulletin, 63*(1), 3–12. https://doi.org/10.1177/0034355218808061

VanderWeele, T.J. (2017). On the promotion of human flourishing. *Procedures of the National Academy of Sciences USA, 114*(31), 8148–8156. https://doi.org/10.1073/pnas.1702996114

VanderWeele, T.J., Trudel-Fitzgerald, C., Allin, P., Farrelly, C., Fletcher, G., Frederick, D.E., Hall, J., Helliwell, J.F., Kim, E.S., Lauinger, W.A., Lee, M.T., Lyubomirsky, S., Margolis, S., NcNeely, E., Messer, N., Tay, L., Visvanath, V., Węziak-Białowolska, D., & Kubzansky, L.D. (2020). Current recommendations on the selection of measures for well-being. *Preventive Medicine, 133*, 106004. https://doi.org/10.1016/j.ypmed.2020.106004

Van Dierendonck, D. (2004). The construct validity of Ryff's Scales of Psychological Well-being and its extension with spiritual well-being. *Personality and Individual Differences, 36*(3), 629–643. https://doi.org/10.1016/S0191-8869(03)00122-3

Van Dierendonck, D., Díaz, D., Rodríguez-Carvajal, R., Blanco, A., & Moreno-Jiménez, B. (2008). Ryff's six-factor model of psychological well-being: A Spanish exploration. *Social Indicators Research, 87*(3), 473–479. https://doi.org/10.1007/s11205-007-9174-7

Villarosa, J., & Ganotice, F. (2018). Construct validation of Ryff's Psychological Well-Being Scale: Evidence from Filipino teachers in the Philippines. *Philippine Journal of Psychology, 51*(1), 1–20. https://doi.org/10.31710/pjp/0051.01.01

Villieux, A., Sovet, L., Jung, S.-C., & Guilbert, L. (2016). Psychological flourishing: Validation of the French version of the Flourishing Scale and exploration of its relationships with personality traits. *Personality and Individual Differences, 88*, 1–5. https://doi.org/10.1016/j.paid.2015.08.027

Wammerl, M., Jaunig, J., Mairunteregger, T., & Streit, P. (2019). The German version of the PERMA-Profiler: Evidence for construct and convergent validity of the PERMA theory of well-being in German-speaking countries. *Journal of Well-Being Assessment, 3*, 75–96. https://doi.org/10.1007/s41543-019-00021-0

Watanabe, K., Kawakami, N., Shiotani, T., Adachi, H., Matsumoto, K., Imamura, K., Matsumoto, K., Yamagami, F., Fusejima, A., Muraoka, T., Kagami, T., Shimazu, A., & Kern, M.L. (2018). The Japanese Workplace PERMA-Profiler: A validation study among Japanese workers. *Journal of Occupational Health, 60*(5), 383–393. https://doi.org/10.1539/joh.2018-0050-OA

Waterman, A.S. (1993). Two conceptions of happiness: Contrasts of personal expressiveness (eudaimonia) and hedonic enjoyment. *Journal of Personality and Social Psychology, 64*(4), 678–691. https://doi.org/10.1037/0022-3514.64.4.678

Watson, D., Clark, L.A., & Tellegen, A. (1988). Development and validation of brief measures of Positive and Negative Affect: The PANAS scales. *Journal of Personality and Social Psychology, 54*, 1063–1070. https://doi.org/10.1037/0022-3514.54.6.1063

Weinberg, M., Bennett, K., & Cummins, P. (2016). Validation of the Personal Wellbeing Index for people with end stage kidney disease. *Applied Research in Quality of Life, 11*(4), 1227–1240. https://doi.org/10.1007/s11482-015-9431-x

Weinberg, M.K., Seton, C., & Cameron, N. (2018). The measurement of subjective wellbeing: Item-order effects in the Personal Wellbeing Index—Adult. *Journal of Happiness Studies, 19*(1), 315–332. https://doi.org/10.1007/s10902-016-9822-1

Wiese, C., Tay, L., Su, R., & Diener, E. (2018). Measuring thriving across nations: Examining the measurement equivalence of the Comprehensive Inventory of Thriving (CIT) and the Brief Inventory of Thriving (BIT). *Applied Psychology: Health and Well-Being, 10*(1), 127–148. https://doi.org/10.1111/aphw.12119

World Health Organization. (1948). *Preamble to the Constitution of the World Health Organization.* Adopted by the International Health Conference, New York, 19–22 June 1946, signed on 22 July 1946 by the representatives of 61 States (Official Records of the World Health Organization, no. 2, p. 100) and entered into force on 7 April 1948. Retrieved from http://www.who.int/governance/eb/who_constitution_en.pdf

Yaden, D.B., Kaufman, S.B., Hyde, E., Chirico, A., Gaggioli, A., Zhang, J.W., & Keltner, D. (2018). The development of the Awe Experience Scale (AWE-S): A multifactorial measure for a complex emotion. *The Journal of Positive Psychology, 14*(4), 474–488. https://doi.org/10.1080/17439760.2018.1484940

Żemojtel-Piotrowska, M., Piotrowski, J.P., Cieciuch, J., Adams, B.G., Osin, E.N., Ardi, R., Bălțătescu, S., Lal Bhomi, A., Clinton, A., de Clunie, G.T., Esteves, C., Gouveia, V., Hosseini, A., Seyedhosseini Ghaheh, H., Khachatryan, N., Vasant Kamble, S., Kawula, A., Liik, K., Letovancova, E., ... Maltby, J. (2017). Measurement invariance of Personal Well-Being Index (PWI-8) across 26 countries. *Journal of Happiness Studies, 18*(6), 1697–1711. https://doi.org/10.1007/s10902-016-9795-0

Żemojtel-Piotrowska, M., Piotrowski, J.P., Osin, E.N., Cieciuch, J., Adams, B.G., Ardi, R., Bălțătescu, S.,Bogomaz, S., Lal Bhomi, A., Clinton, A., de Clunie, G.T., Czarna, A.Z., Esteves, C., Gouveia, V., Halik, M.H.J., Hosseini, A., Khachatryan, N., Vasant Kamble, S., ... Maltby, J. (2018). The Mental Health Continuum-Short Form: The structure and application for cross-cultural studies: A 38-nation study. *Journal of Clinical Psychology, 74*(6), 1034–1052. https://doi.org/10.1002/jclp.22570

Zimet, G.D., Dahlem, N.W., Zimet, S.G., & Farley, G.K. (1988). The Multidimensional Scale of Perceived Social Support. *Journal of Personality Assessment, 52,* 30–41. https://doi.org/10.1207/s15327752jpa5201_2

Chapter 3

Assessing Subjective Well-Being

A Review of Common Measures

William Tov, Jun Sheng Keh, Yan Qiang Tan, Qin Ying Tan, and Indra Alam Syah Bin Aziz

School of Social Sciences, Singapore Management University, Republic of Singapore

Subjective well-being (SWB) refers to the various ways we experience and evaluate our lives positively (Diener, 1984; Diener et al., 1999). It includes frequent feelings of pleasant or positive affect (PA) as well as infrequent feelings of unpleasant or negative affect (NA). Together, PA and NA constitute the *affective* components of SWB. Also relevant are our evaluations of life (e.g., life satisfaction), which are distinct from affective experiences in that they often require us to reflect broadly upon our circumstances and whether they meet our standards. Judgments of life satisfaction or life evaluation constitute the *cognitive* component of SWB. Although the affective and cognitive components are often correlated with each other, they are associated with different outcomes (Tay & Diener, 2011). Thus, the assessment of SWB ideally involves the separate measurement of each component (Pavot, 2008).

SWB is sometimes referred to as *hedonic* well-being because of its emphasis on a pleasant and satisfying quality of life (Tov, 2018). This contrasts with *eudaimonic* well-being, which includes a variety of constructs like meaning, personal growth, and authenticity (Huta & Waterman, 2014; Vittersø, 2016). Theories of eudaimonic well-being focus less on the pleasantness of experience and more on the needs that people must fulfill to reach their full potential. In contrast, the SWB approach does not specify the "ingredients" required for well-being. The assessment of SWB is subjective in that people report their own happiness and satisfaction without reference to any particular template of life conditions or experiences; rather, they assess their well-being using whichever standards are personally relevant and important to them.

Although eudaimonic aspects of well-being are important topics of study, our chapter focuses on measures of SWB. It is worth noting that eudaimonic well-being measures are strongly correlated with SWB measures (Kashdan et al., 2008; Tov & Lee, 2016). Thus, although SWB is considered hedonic, many experiences that make us happy and satisfied are also those in which we experience meaning, growth, and authenticity. This is not to say that SWB measures can substitute for measures of eudaimonic well-being, only that the experiences captured by the former should not be dismissed as trivial and unimportant.

SWB measures are associated with important outcomes. For example, higher levels of life satisfaction and PA predict lower susceptibility to health problems and increased longevity, whereas higher levels of NA tend to predict poorer health outcomes (Diener et al., 2017). Employees who experience more PA and satisfaction at work are more likely to help their colleagues and have lower levels of absenteeism and intentions to quit (Borman et al., 2001). Subjective reports of well-being provide valuable information beyond objective economic indicators in the evaluation of social and economic policies (Diener & Seligman, 2004; Diener & Tov, 2012; Dolan & White, 2007).

This chapter expands on previous reviews of SWB measures (Boyle et al., 2015; Diener, 1994; Weber et al., 2015). Because of space constraints, this review is not comprehensive; instead, we focus primarily on measures that have been validated for use on adult samples and are free to use for research purposes. Consequently, the scales we selected are highly accessible and have been widely used, thus establishing a deep empirical base. We review four of the most used measures in depth: Two scales assess the cognitive component of SWB (the Satisfaction with Life Scale, SWLS, and Cantril's Ladder); two scales assess the affective components of SWB (the Positive and Negative Affect Schedule, PANAS, and the Scale of Positive and Negative Experiences, SPANE).

We supplement our review with meta-analyses of the reliabilities of these scales and their correlation with each other. Thus, we report meta-analytic average reliabilities (Cronbach's alpha;) and correlations ($\bar{r}$). To provide a clear reference for researchers, we included studies in our meta-analyses only if they used the standard format of the scale (i.e., the original number of items and rating scale) and excluded studies that used a subset of items or a different number of scale points or rating labels. We caution readers that our selection of studies was limited to studies published from 1999 to 2019, with special attention to those that (1) employed non-Western samples or (2) examined change and stability in SWB. We intended to highlight the diverse contexts in which these measures have been employed. Thus, although we provide meta-analytic estimates, we also report heterogeneity across studies. Detailed listings of the studies we reviewed and included in our meta-analysis as well as supplementary information on our meta-analytic approach and codes used to perform the analyses are available as online supplements at https://osf.io/q2vtx. Where appropriate, we highlight other measures of SWB that may also be useful to researchers depending on their goals and objectives.

Measuring Cognitive Well-Being

Researchers often ask respondents to evaluate how they think and feel in general. Such evaluations are referred to as *global* judgments. In the case of cognitive well-being, global measures ask people to evaluate their life "as a whole." Other measures elicit satisfaction with more specific life domains (e.g., health or relationships); we introduce some of them later on. The two measures of cognitive well-being we review, however, are strictly global measures. Both scales draw on discrepancy theories of well-being (e.g., Campbell, 1976; Michalos, 1985), which assume a comparison process whereby people evaluate their current life conditions with how they would like things to be (i.e., their standards).

The smaller the discrepancy between their current circumstances and what they desire, the more positively they should evaluate their lives as a whole. Other processes may also be involved. Bottom-up theories propose that people summarize their momentary experiences over time with the final balance of pleasant (versus unpleasant) experiences influencing how they feel about their lives overall. In contrast, top-down theories suggest that certain people are predisposed to experience and interpret their lives positively or negatively. Support for both theories exists (Heller et al., 2004; Tov, 2012), and the measures we discuss do not preclude the influence of other factors and mechanisms. For a review of theoretical accounts of well-being, see Diener (1984).

Cantril's Ladder (Self-Anchoring Striving Scale)

The Self-Anchoring Striving Scale invites respondents to evaluate their life according to their own goals, values, and standards (Cantril, 1965; Kilpatrick & Cantril, 1960); it is commonly referred to as Cantril's Ladder. In its original form, an interviewer asked respondents to describe the *best possible* life for themselves by reporting their wishes and hopes for the future. They were then asked to describe the *worst possible* life for themselves by reporting their fears and worries for the future. The interviewer wrote down verbatim these descriptions, which were then content coded. The entire exercise served to establish a "self-defined continuum" (Kilpatrick & Cantril, 1960, p. 158), along which respondents placed their current life. To facilitate this placement, a picture of a ladder with 10 rungs was shown to the respondent – with 10 (at the top of the ladder) representing the best possible life and 0 (the bottom of the ladder) representing the worst possible life. Respondents indicated where they "stand at the present time." They would then be asked to evaluate where they stood 5 years ago and where they think they will stand 5 years into the future.

In its more common use, respondents are instructed to imagine a ladder with steps numbered from 0 to 10, with 0 representing the "worst possible life for you" and 10 representing the "best possible life for you." The respondents' hopes and fears are not often collected. Although some surveys assess life evaluations of the past and future (e.g., Gallup Organization, n.d.), many researchers use the single-item evaluation of current or present life. We examined 26 studies that used the ladder and summarize its psychometric properties.

Reliability

Responses to the ladder appear to be substantially stable over the short term. Over intervals ranging from 2 to 4 weeks, retest intervals ranged from .58 to .70 in Scottish adolescents (ages 11–15; Levin & Currie, 2014) and .71 in a sample of U.S. adults (Kapteyn et al., 2015).

Validity

Cantril's Ladder correlates strongly with the SWLS. Across five studies (N=762), the average r was .68 (95% CI [.56; .76]). Ladder scores are also positively associated with measures of PA and negatively with NA (see Table 3.1 as well as Joshanloo, 2019). Cantril's Ladder is also associated with higher levels of eudaimonic well-being (Keyes et al., 2002), greater income (Diener et al., 2010), better self-reported health, being employed, and having a partner (Kapteyn et al., 2015). In large samples representative of 95% of the world population, ladder scores were positively associated with meeting basic needs and income (Tay & Diener, 2011). The online materials summarize additional studies using the ladder.

Table 3.1. Meta-analytic correlations among measures of subjective well-being

Measure	1	2	3	4	5	6	7
1. LADDER	–	5 (762)	3 (358)	3 (358)	4 (539)	4 (539)	4 (539)
2. SWLS	.68	–	7 (1316)	7 (1316)	15 (28508)	15 (28508)	12 (26731)
3. PANAS-PA	.53	.46	–	9 (1840)	9 (2159)	9 (2159)	7 (1351)
4. PANAS-NA	−.42	−.39	−.35	–	9 (2159)	9 (2159)	7 (1351)
5. SPANE-P	.63	.59	.61	−.48	–	22 (31519)	18 (29595)
6. SPANE-N	−.50	−.43	−.45	.71	−.57	–	18 (29595)
7. SPANE-B	.63	.58	.57	−.65	.87	−.89	–

Note. LADDER = Cantril's Ladder (Self-Anchoring Striving Scale); SWLS = Satisfaction with Life Scale; PANAS = Positive Affect and Negative Affect Schedule; PA = Positive Affect; NA = Negative Affect; SPANE = Scale of Positive and Negative Experiences; P = Positive Feelings; N = Negative Feelings; B = Affect Balance. These analyses consist only of studies that specified a timeframe of the *past month* or *past 4 weeks* for PANAS and SPANE. Meta-analytic correlations appear below the diagonal, whereas the number of studies (total number of individuals) contributing to each correlation appears above the diagonal. All correlations were statistically significant at $p < .05$.

Use in Interventions

Shapira et al. (2007) conducted a 15-week computer skills course for older adults. After controlling for pretest scores, they found the posttest ladder scores were higher for those in the treatment group. However, the effect could be attributed to the control group decreasing (rather than the treatment increasing) their ladder evaluation. Few other studies have used Cantril's Ladder to evaluate intervention effectiveness, although it is commonly used to assess the quality of life in clinical and medical research.

Satisfaction with Life Scale (SWLS)

The SWLS (Diener et al., 1985) is a widely used measure of global cognitive well-being. There are over 30 translations of the scale, many of which can be downloaded from Ed Diener's website (https://eddiener.com/scales/7). The SWLS consists of 5 items including "In most ways, my life is close to my ideal" and "I am satisfied with my life," rated on a scale from 1 (*strongly disagree*) to 7 (*strongly agree*). When responses are summed across the 5 items, the scores range from 5 (*low satisfaction*) to 35 (*high satisfaction*). This is the standard format of the SWLS, and our review and meta-analysis only include studies that used this format.

Reliability

Across 103 samples (N=106,599 individuals), the SWLS generally exhibited high levels of internal consistency ($\overline{\alpha}$=.86, 95% CI [.85; .87]). However, there was significant heterogeneity across samples, $Q(102)=3348.22$, $p<.001$. Table 3.2 presents the reliabilities by different subgroups. Although the alphas were over .80 in most translations of the scale, they were lower among Bulgarian, Arabic, and Cantonese versions. The reliabilities did not vary with gender composition (i.e., percentage of female respondents) but were somewhat higher in older age samples. Recent studies reported test-retest correlations from .80 over 1 month (Steger et al., 2006) to .73 over 1 year (Ilies et al., 2019). Life satisfaction as measured by the SWLS appears to be highly stable over the short-term (1-month period) but may also change in the long term as suggested by lower test-retest correlations over time.

Validity

The one-factor structure of the SWLS was supported in 41 countries (Vittersø et al., 2002). SWLS scores are associated with higher scores on measures of PA ($\bar{r}$'s$\geq$.46) and lower scores on measures of NA ($\bar{r}$'s$\leq$-.39; Table 3.1). These correlations are not extremely high, suggesting that the SWLS captures aspects of well-being that are distinct from affective experience. By comparison, the SWLS correlates more strongly with Cantril's Ladder and other single-item measures of life satisfaction (.62 to .64; Cheung & Lucas, 2014). This pattern is consistent with the notion that SWB consists of distinct cognitive and affective components. The SWLS also shows convergent validity with other relevant constructs, such as optimism (Chang et al., 2020) and meaning in life (Steger et al., 2006). Although the SWLS does not specify the standards people use to judge their life satisfaction, it correlates with major aspects of life such as income, satisfaction with health, and satisfaction with work (Ilies et al., 2019; Kapteyn et al., 2015).

Use in Interventions

There is some evidence that positive psychology interventions (PPI) aimed at improving well-being can enhance life satisfaction as measured by SWLS (Boehm et al., 2011; Lam & Kahler, 2018; Lambert et al., 2019). However, an 8-week intervention teaching older adults how to cultivate meaningful positive experiences found no change in SWLS (Friedman et al., 2019). Thus, although SWLS scores can change meaningfully in response to psychological interventions, other factors such as sample characteristics and type of intervention may affect the extent to which changes are observed.

Table 3.2. Reliabilities for SWLS by different subgroups

Group	*N*	*k*	α	95% CI
Language				
Arabic	193	1	.74	–
Bulgarian	286	1	.60	–
Cantonese[a]	931	1	.79	–
Chinese	2566	12	.85	[.82; .88]
Dutch	7295	4	.84	[.81; .87]
English	72463	50	.87	[.86; .89]
Estonian	249	1	.86	–
Finnish	259	1	.88	–
French	638	1	.91	–
German	684	2	.85	[.82; .88]
Greek	4318	3	.87	[.84; .90]
Japanese	841	2	.86	[.82; .90]
Korean	625	3	.87	[.82; .91]
Polish	261	1	.86	–
Romanian	271	1	.88	–
Serbian	1777	3	.85	[.80; .90]
Slovene	306	1	.89	–
Spanish	2057	7	.87	[.84; .89]
Turkish	1134	3	.84	[.80; .88]
Ukrainian	228	1	.88	–
Age				
Under 18	676	4	.85	[.82; .89]
18 to 25	9725	37	.85	[.83; .86]
26 to 65	80588	48	.87	[.86; .88]
Over 65	257	2	.93	[.84; .98]

Note. *N* = number of individuals; *k* = number of studies; α = Cronbach's α; CI = confidence interval. [a] Refers to spoken language because items were administered by telephone survey.

Considerations for Selecting Cognitive Well-Being Measures

The appeal of the single-item Cantril's Ladder lies in its brevity. The layout of the ladder scale may also provide a helpful visual metaphor for evaluating one's life. Even over the telephone, Cantril's ladder may be a simpler way to elicit evaluations of life as a whole. However, as a paper-based or internet-based survey item, it is unclear whether Cantril's Ladder provides any distinct advantages over the SWLS. The time saved by using a single item is offset by longer written instructions encouraging respondents to think about the best and worst possible life they could live. Although Cheung and Lucas (2014) provided evidence that single-item life satisfaction scales were as valid as the SWLS, their analyses were based on large survey samples often exceeding 1,000 people. It is unclear whether similar results apply to smaller sample sizes, especially so when evaluating the effect of an intervention, since the change from pretest to posttest of a single-item measure may contain more measurement error than that of a multiitem measure (Schneider & Schimmack, 2009). Thus, if sample sizes are smaller than those commonly found in large surveys, a multiitem instrument like the SWLS might be preferable.

Another consideration is whether the researcher wants to know *how* satisfied a person is with specific areas of life. The SWLS and Cantril's Ladder assess only global life satisfaction. In contrast, measures that assess *domain satisfaction* include the Personal Wellbeing Index (PWI; International Wellbeing Group, 2013) and the Extended Life Satisfaction Scale (ESWLS; Alfonso et al., 1996). The PWI assesses satisfaction with standard of living, health, achievement, relationships, safety, community, future security, and spirituality. The ESWLS measures satisfaction with social life, sex life, physical appearance, family life, education, job, and relationship/marriage. In theory, one could average satisfaction across the domains to derive a measure of overall satisfaction. However, such an index may not be the same as global satisfaction measured by the SWLS or Cantril's Ladder. Although domain satisfaction measures tap major aspects of life, they cannot capture standards idiosyncratic to each person. In recognition of this possibility, both the PWI and ESWLS include items to assess global satisfaction.

Finally, most measures focus on how people feel about their current life. Researchers interested in how people evaluate their past or future might consider the Temporal Satisfaction with Life Scale (Pavot et al., 1998), which contains 15 items divided equally among assessments of past life, current life, and future life satisfaction. Cantril's Ladder has also been used in a similar manner (Cantril, 1965; Kilpatrick & Cantril, 1960). One assumption of such measures is that how a person evaluates their life currently may not fully reflect their experiences or motivation. Busseri et al. (2009) showed that a temporally expanded assessment of well-being may yield insights beyond current levels of well-being.

Measuring Affective Well-Being

Affective measures of SWB emphasize the valence (pleasantness or unpleasantness) of our moods and emotion. According to some theories (Ellsworth & Scherer, 2009; Weiner, 1985), the valence of an event is one of the first features we appraise ("Did something good or bad happen?"), often followed by subjective feelings of PA or NA. Affective well-being and cognitive well-being often correlate with each other. Our standards for what we desire in life are likely to influence how we evaluate the current conditions of our life (cognitive well-being) as well as whether we experience certain events as positive or negative (affective well-being). A key difference may be that cognitive well-being tends to reflect more stable aspects of life (Schimmack & Oishi, 2005), whereas affective well-being tends to reflect our reactions to ongoing events or experiences (Luhmann et al., 2012).

Self-reported affect can be measured at different levels (Kim-Prieto et al., 2005; Tov, 2012, 2018). *Global* measures ask respondents to report how they feel in general; *retrospective* measures ask respondents to report how they felt during a specific timeframe (e.g., over the past month); *online* measures ask respondents to report how they feel in the current moment. The two measures of affective well-being that we review could be used to assess affect at any level by modifying the instructions accordingly.

The Positive and Negative Affect Schedule (PANAS)

The PANAS (Watson et al., 1988) consists of two 10-item scales, focusing on positive and negative states that are somewhat independent. The Positive Affect scale (PANAS-PA) measures the extent to which a person feels pleasantly alert (e.g., *excited, attentive, inspired*); the Negative Affect (PANAS-NA) scale measures the extent of distress and unpleasurable engagement (e.g., *nervous, hostile, upset*). Each item is rated on a 5-point scale (1=*very slightly or not at all*, 5=*extremely*). In its original development, the PANAS was administered using seven different timeframe instructions: (1) *right now* (at the present moment), (2) *today*, (3) during the *past few days*, (4) during the *past week*, (5) during the *past few weeks*, (6) during the *past year*, and (7) *in general* (on average). Below we summarize our observations of the PANAS across 54 published articles.

Reliability

Across 64 samples (N_{PA}=22,920 and N_{NA}=25,887), the average reliabilities were acceptable for both PANAS-PA ($\bar{\alpha}$=.86, 95% CI [.85; .87]) and PANAS-NA ($\bar{\alpha}$=.85, 95% CI [.84; .86]). However, significant heterogeneity remained for PANAS-PA (Q[63]=924.00) and PANAS-NA (Q[63]=1143.91), ps<.001. Table 3.3 presents the reliabilities across different subgroups and timeframe instructions. Alphas were generally acceptable, ranging from .80 to .92, across different translations and timeframe instructions. However, the reliabilities of PANAS-PA and PANAS-NA were positively related to the mean age of the sample ($\bar{r}$'s>.37, p-values≤.006). Lower alphas were observed among respondents younger than 18. For younger respondents, researchers may consider using the child version of the PANAS (Laurent et al., 1999).

Test-retest correlations of the PANAS may depend on the timeframe specified, with higher correlations for *in general* instructions, and smaller correlations for *present moment* instructions (Watson et al., 1988). For instance, Terraciano et al. (2003) reported 3-month retest correlations for PANAS-PA and PANAS-NA of .65 and .52 (*present moment*) and .76 and .73 (*general*), respectively. This pattern is expected given that global affect should be more stable than retrospective and online affect.

Table 3.3. Reliabilities for PANAS-PA and and PANAS-NA PANAS across different subgroups and time-frame instructions

	PANAS-PA				PANAS-NA			
Group	***N***	***k***	**α**	**95% CI**	***N***	***k***	**α**	**95% CI**
Language								
Arabic	193	1	.80	–	193	1	.81	–
Chinese	694	3	.81	[.80; .82]	1097	4	.85	[.81; .89]
Dutch	4074	4	.86	[.85; .88]	4074	4	.87	[.82; .91]
English	9175	38	.86	[.85; .88]	8665	38	.85	[.83; .87]
German	684	2	.85	[.82; .88]	684	2	.82	[.79; .85]
Hindi	179	1	.80	–	179	1	.78	–
Italian	945	2	.87	[.78; .94]	945	2	.88	[.82; .92]
Korean	587	3	.83	[.78; .88]	587	3	.87	[.81; .91]
Persian	300	1	.88	–	300	1	.86	–
Portuguese	1291	1	.92	–	5019	2	.88	[.86; .89]
Serbian	808	2	.82	[.76; .88]	808	2	.82	[.74; .88]
Spanish	3336	4	.86	[.82; .90]	3336	4	.82	[.68; .92]
Timeframe								
General	10670	20	.84	[.82; .86]	13834	18	.84	[.82; .86]
Past month	5248	21	.84	[.82; .86]	5248	21	.82	[.80; .84]
Past few weeks	498	1	.86	–	498	1	.83	–
Past week	3544	9	.88	[.86; .89]	3544	9	.87	[.86; .89]
Past few days	138	1	.90	–	138	1	.89	–
Past day	276	1	.92	–	276	1	.91	–
Present moment	1480	7	.88	[.84; .91]	1480	7	.86	[.78; .91]
Recalled event	190	1	.87	–	–	–	–	–
Unknown[a]	876	3	.91	[.90; .91]	869	6	.90	[.85; .93]
Age								
Under 18	3137	7	.80	[.77; .83]	3137	7	.80	[.78; .82]
18 to 25	6020	28	.86	[.84; .87]	5176	25	.84	[.81; .86]
26 to 65	6839	16	.88	[.86; .90]	10650	19	.88	[.86; .90]
Over 65	1923	3	.89	[.84; .92]	1923	3	.86	[.82; .89]

Note. PANAS = Positive and Negative Affect Schedule; PA = positive affect; NA = negative affect. *N* = number of individuals; *k* = number of studies; α = Cronbach's α; CI = confidence interval. [a] Timeframe was not reported in the article.

Validity

Recent studies support the two-factor structure of the PANAS, with PA items and NA items loading more strongly on their respective factors. However, correlated errors are also present among subsets of items (Crawford & Henry, 2004; Lim et al., 2010; Merz & Roesch, 2011). For example, *guilty* and *ashamed* are correlated with other NA items (e.g., *angry* and *hostile*) but also reflect experiences that the latter do not – such as reactions to one's own wrongdoing. Table 3.1 presents correlations with past-month PANAS (to facilitate comparisons with the SPANE). Although PANAS-PA and PANAS-NA are conceptualized as independent factors, they tend to be inversely related (e.g.,$\bar{r}$=-.35; Table 3.1). Past-month PANAS-PA was associated with higher levels of cognitive well-being ($\bar{r}$'s≥.46), whereas past-month PANAS-NA was associated with lower levels ($\bar{r}$'s≤-.39). The online materials report PANAS correlations at other timeframes and the results of additional studies using the PANAS.

Use in Interventions

A 1-month mindfulness-based intervention led to increased PANAS-PA and decreased PANAS-NA (past-week; Bailey et al., 2018). An 8-week PPI led to significant increases in PANAS-PA but did not affect PANAS-NA within a chronic pain population (present moment; Boselie et al., 2018). However, other PPIs had no overall effect on PANAS scores (Lam & Kahler, 2018; Woodworth et al., 2016). We discuss possible reasons for these inconsistencies later (see "Considerations for Selecting Affective Well-Being Measures").

The Scale of Positive and Negative Experience (SPANE)

The SPANE (Diener, Wirtz et al., 2010) consists of 12 items with 6 items each measuring PA (SPANE-P scale) and NA (SPANE-N scale). Although two separate scores are produced, a difference score is sometimes computed (SPANE-B) by subtracting SPANE-N from SPANE-P. The SPANE was developed to address the limitations of the PANAS as a measure of SWB. As a hedonic well-being construct, SWB emphasizes the pleasantness and unpleasantness of affective experience. Although the PANAS measures valence, the items refer primarily to high arousal affective states (e.g., *excited* and *jittery*). Common emotions like happiness and sadness are not directly assessed by the PANAS.

The SPANE includes both general affective terms (e.g., *good, bad, pleasant, unpleasant*) along with more specific but commonly experienced states (e.g., *happy, sad, contented, angry*). By including more general terms, a range of affective experiences may be captured by the SPANE – whether they are high or low arousal states. The SPANE also uses a frequency-based rating scale (1 = *very rarely or never*, 5 = *very often or always*) in line with research showing that well-being judgments (e.g., life satisfaction) correlate more strongly with the frequency than intensity of affective experiences (Diener et al., 1991). In the original SPANE, participants rate how often they experienced each feeling during the *past 4 weeks,* and most of the studies we reviewed used this timeframe (67%). Busseri (2018) conducted a meta-analysis of the SPANE based on studies published through 2015. We supplemented his analysis with more recent studies. However, given our focus on the instrument itself, we excluded studies that used only a subset of the

SPANE items. We also restricted our review to studies that used a 5-point frequency-based rating scale.

Reliability

Across 46 samples (N=38,823), the average reliabilities were acceptable for the SPANE-P ($\bar{\alpha}$=.87, 95% CI [.85; 89]) and SPANE-N ($\bar{\alpha}$=.82, 95% CI [.80; .85]). Across 33 samples (N=33,913), the reliability of SPANE-B ($\bar{\alpha}$=.87, 95% CI [.85; 89]) was comparable to SPANE-P. Nevertheless, significant heterogeneity was observed for SPANE-P (Q[45]=1750.61), SPANE-N (Q[45]=2331.11), and SPANE-B (Q[32]=1157.24), ps<.001. The reliabilities for different translations, timeframe instructions, and age groups are presented in Table 3.4. The alphas were extremely poor (≤ .59) for a Persian and Swedish version of the SPANE (Kormi-Nouri et al., 2013). Kormi-Nouri et al. (2013) attributed these low reliabilities to four items (*joyful, contented, angry, afraid*) that had low item-total correlations on their respective scales; it is unclear how the items were translated. Otherwise, the alphas were above .82 for SPANE-P and above .78 for SPANE-N across most translations, timeframe instructions, and age groups. The reliability of SPANE scores did not vary significantly as a function of age or sex composition of the sample, although more research is needed on both adolescent and older adult samples. One-month retest correlations for the SPANE scales were above .57 (Diener, Wirtz et al., 2010; Rahm et al., 2017; Sumi, 2014b). Despite referencing the past 4 weeks, SPANE scores appear to reflect fairly stable levels of affective well-being.

Validity

Several studies suggest that the items constituting SPANE-P and SPANE-N represent distinct but correlated factors (e.g., Jovanović, 2015; Rahm et al., 2017; Sumi, 2014a). However, correlated errors were present in some studies (Kyriazos et al., 2018; Li et al., 2013). Thus, although the items broadly measure positive and negative feelings, subsets of items may share other characteristics (e.g., *good*, *pleasant*, and *positive* are more general in nature). On average, SPANE-P and SPANE-N scores are inversely correlated ($\bar{r}$=–.57; Table 3.1). Moreover, SPANE-P is associated with higher levels of cognitive well-being ($\bar{r}$'s≥.59), whereas SPANE-N is associated with lower levels ($\bar{r}$'s<–.43). The online materials include a detailed list of 41 studies and additional correlates of the SPANE scales.

Use in Interventions

Participants who used a mindfulness-based smartphone app over 10 sessions experienced a significant increase in affect balance (SPANE-B) compared to an active control group (Economides et al., 2018). Rahm et al. (2017) observed significant increases (decreases) in SPANE-P (SPANE-N) after a 4-week PPI. Killen and Macaskill (2015) observed significant increases in SPANE-B after a 14-day PPI.

Table 3.4. Reliabilities for SPANE across different translations, timeframe instructions, and age groups

			SPANE-P		SPANE-N				SPANE-B	
Group	***N***	***k***	**α**	**95% CI**	**α**	**95% CI**	***N***	***k***	**α**	**95% CI**
Language										
Cantonese[a]	931	1	.82	–	.81	–	931	1	.85	–
Chinese	22092	3	.88	[.81; .93]	.86	[.77; .93]	21322	1	.92	–
Dutch	–	–	–	–	–	–	226	1	.81	–
English	4835	16	.88	[.85; .90]	.81	[.78; .84]	4505	13	.84	[.78; .88]
German	719	3	.88	[.87; .88]	.83	[.79; .86]	719	3	.90	[.89; .91]
Greek	2272	1	.90	–	.85	–	2272	1	.91	–
Hebrew	211	2	.82	[.74; .89]	.79	[.75; .82]	–	–	–	–
Italian	1737	6	.90	[.89; .92]	.86	[.82; .90]	1737	6	.92	[.91; .92]
Japanese	856	2	.91	[.90; .91]	.89	[.85; .91]	856	2	.88	[.87; .88]
Persian	296	1	.42	–	.07	–	–	–	–	–
Portuguese[b]	911	2	.90	[.89; .91]	.84	–	911	2	.88	[.88; .88]
Serbian	1777	3	.90	[.88; .92]	.84	[.79; .88]	–	–	–	–
Spanish	489	1	.92	–	.83	–	170	1	.89	–
Swedish	310	1	.34	–	.59	–	–	–	–	–
Turkish	1273	3	.87	[.82; .91]	.81	[.72; .88]	–	–	–	–
Timeframe										
Past 4 weeks	34041	31	.89	[.87; .90]	.84	[.82; .85]	31851	26	.89	[.87; .90]
Past 3 weeks	191	1	.93	–	.91	–	–	–	–	–
Past 2 weeks	147	1	.80	–	.78	–	–	–	–	–
Unknown[c]	4444	13	.83	[.75; .90]	.78	[.69; .84]	2062	7	.78	[.65; .88]
Age										
Under 18	1392	3	.87	[.79; .93]	.79	[.75; .84]	837	3	.84	[.77; .89]
18 to 25	7128	21	.85	[.80; .89]	.81	[.75; .85]	4603	13	.88	[.86; .89]
26 to 65	29624	18	.89	[.86; .90]	.85	[.82; .87]	27907	13	.88	[.83; .92]
Over 65	88	1	.96	–	.81	–	–	–	–	–

Note. SPANE = Scale of Positive and Negative Experience; SPANE-P = positive feelings; SPANE-N = negative feelings; SPANE-B = affect balance (full scale with negative experience items reverse scored). *N* = number of individuals; *k* = number of studies; α = Cronbach's α; CI = confidence interval. For SPANE-PA and SPANE-N, *N*s and *k*s were identical. [a] Refers to spoken language because items were administered by telephone survey; [b] 95% CIs could not be computed for SPANE-N because of a lack of variation in alphas in the meta-analysis; [c] timeframe was not reported in the article.

Considerations for Selecting Affective Well-Being Measures

The PANAS has been the dominant measure of affect over the past 20 years, with strong psychometric properties across global, retrospective, and online instructions. The SPANE, as typically used, measures affect over the past 4 weeks and is thus a retrospective measure. It can be adapted to measure global and online affect by modifying the instructions like the PANAS. However, the SPANES' frequency-based response scale can be awkward when assessing current mood (e.g., "How much are you experiencing each of the following feelings *right now*?"). We suggest that the response scale be modified if the SPANE is used to measure online affect; an intensity format like the one used by the PANAS may suffice.

Although one strength of the PANAS is its versatility across different timeframes, a limitation lies in its emphasis on high arousal affective states. Conceptually, SWB encompasses the full range of pleasant and unpleasant affects – including *both* high and low arousal states. In contrast to the PANAS, the SPANE aims to measure a wide variety of pleasant and unpleasant states regardless of how arousing they are. Moreover, the SPANE rating scale emphasizes the frequency of affective experiences, which is more predictive of SWB judgments than the intensity of such experiences (Diener et al., 1991). These differences may have important implications for researchers.

In selecting an intervention outcome measure, researchers should consider whether high arousal states (e.g., alertness or hostility) are necessarily targeted by the intervention. For example, many PPIs (e.g., writing three good things that happened today) are intended to increase positive feelings but not necessarily arousal. This may partly explain why mixed results were obtained when affective well-being was assessed using the PANAS (Boselie et al., 2018; Lam & Kahler, 2018; Woodworth et al., 2016), whereas studies using the SPANE yielded positive results (Killen & Macaskill, 2015; Rahm et al., 2017).

Another consideration is the cultural context in which participants are sampled. East Asian cultures tend to deemphasize high arousal positive emotions in favor of low arousal emotions such as feeling *calm* and *relaxed* (Tsai et al., 2006). These low arousal states can influence a person's sense of well-being but are not directly measured by PANAS. If the goal is to broadly assess SWB, the SPANE may be preferred given its generality and emphasis on affective frequency (Busseri, 2018; Diener, Wirtz et al., 2010). This is further supported by our meta-analytic results (Table 1). For instance, the SWLS correlated more strongly with past-month SPANE-P ($\bar{r}$=.59, 95% CI [.54; .63]) than past-month PANAS-PA ($\bar{r}$=.46, 95% CI [.40; .52]). Moreover, past-month SPANE-P and SPANE-N are more strongly correlated with each other (95% CI [-.62; -.52]) than are past-month PANAS-PA and PANAS-NA (95% CI [-.42; -.27]). Stronger intercorrelations among the SWLS and SPANE may be desirable for researchers seeking reliable indicators of overall SWB.

A limitation of the PANAS and SPANE is that they primarily measure the valence of affective experiences. However, there are important differences among both positive and negative emotions. For example, feelings of gratitude predict helping behavior in ways that general happiness may not (Bartlett & DeSteno, 2006). Scales designed to measure more specific emotions include the PANAS-X (Watson & Clark, 1994) and the Differential Emotions Scale (DES-IV; Izard et al., 1993). In addition, researchers interested in the full range of valence and arousal might consider the UWIST Mood Adjective Checklist (UMACL; Matthews et al., 1990) and the Brief Mood Introspection Scale (BMIS; Mayer & Gaschke, 1988).

In the interest of reducing recall biases, methods for assessing online affect are becoming increasingly popular. For example, the experience-sampling method makes use of handheld devices (e.g., smartphones) to survey people on how they are feeling at randomly selected moments during the day (for reviews, see Augustine & Larsen, 2012; Scollon et al., 2003). Another popular approach is the day-reconstruction method (DRM; Kahneman et al., 2004), in which respondents recall the events they experienced the previous day and rate how they felt during these events. For a useful comparison of these two approaches, see Lucas et al. (2020).

Remaining Issues and Future Directions

Many researchers have translated SWB scales and evaluated their factor structure, reliability, and validity in new samples of respondents. However, there is a need for researchers to assess the crosscultural equivalence of SWB measures. This is critical insofar as there is much interest in comparing well-being across cultures by researchers (Tov & Au, 2013; Tov & Nai, 2018), policymakers (Helliwell et al., 2018), and the general public (e.g., Hetter, 2019). Jang et al. (2017) examined the equivalence of SWLS items across 26 countries and observed possible bias in some items. Their analyses suggested that items 1 and 3 (reported in the "Satisfaction with Life Scale" section) were interpreted most consistently across nations.

Fewer studies have evaluated the measurement equivalence of the PANAS and SPANE. Some researchers have employed the original English version of the PANAS to culturally diverse samples and examined the factor structure of the items. In one study, several items including *proud* and *jittery* did not load onto their hypothesized factors (Thompson, 2007). The item *alert* loaded on both the PA and NA factors in a Chinese sample that completed the PANAS in Chinese (Zhang et al., 2009). These discrepancies could be because of nonequivalent translations. However, when Singaporean and U.S. respondents both completed the PANAS in English, the extent to which certain items loaded onto their hypothesized factors differed (Lee et al., 2019). The item *proud* (*guilty*) did not load as strongly on the PA (NA) factor in the Singaporean sample as it did in the U.S. sample. Thus, other factors may be important such as cultural norms that influence emotional experiences (Eid & Diener, 2001). For additional discussion of cultural measurement issues, refer to Oishi (2018).

Another concern with SWB measures is the potential for biases in memory and judgment to distort ratings of self-reported global well-being. These include possible effects of mood, question framing, and item order on participants' responses (Schwarz & Strack, 1999). For example, a low rating on life satisfaction might simply reflect a person's bad mood when reporting. To minimize these effects, some scholars promoted online measures or detailed assessments such as the DRM (Kahneman et al., 2004). However, recent studies suggest that mood and order effects have a minimal impact on self-reported global SWB (Jayawickreme et al., 2017; Schimmack & Oishi, 2005; Yap et al., 2017). In addition, Tov (2012) showed that global SWB was predicted by the *cumulative effects* of events experienced over the past few weeks. Importantly, biases in the specific events that were recalled or how they were remembered did not affect global judgments above and beyond these cumulative effects.

Instead of viewing online reports of well-being as "accurate" and global or retrospective reports as "inaccurate," we suggest that each type of measure captures information that is relevant to understanding a person's well-being. Global and retrospective measures are not simply aggregates of momentary well-being; they are related to our online experiences, although they are also influenced by our personality, our values, and the cultural norms, which in turn influence our behavior and standards (Scollon et al., 2009; Suh et al., 1998; Tov, 2012). An important direction for future research is to better understand the interrelationships among online, retrospective, and global measures (Kim-Prieto et al., 2005), how these may differ for affective and cognitive well-being, and whether they are associated with different outcomes.

The past decades have seen many advances in our understanding of well-being and the broader notion of happiness. These would not have been possible without some way to measure SWB. Much work remains to improve these scales and better understand their properties. Nevertheless, existing measures have provided a good foundation for future measures to build upon.

Acknowledgments

We thank Xinyao Yu for her help compiling relevant articles.

Supplementary Material

Supplemental material and R analysis codes are available at https://osf.io/q2vtx

References

Alfonso, V.C., Allison, D.B., & Rader, D.E. (1996). The Extended Satisfaction with Life Scale: Development and psychometric properties. *Social Indicators Research, 38*, 275–301. https://doi.org/10.1007/BF00292049

Augustine, A.A., & Larsen, R.J. (2012). Emotion research. In M.R. Mehl & T.S. Conner (Eds.), *Handbook of research methods for studying daily life*. (pp. 497–510). Guilford.

Bailey, N.W., Nguyen, J., Bialylew, E., Corin, S.E., Gilbertson, T., Chambers, R., & Fitzgerald, P.B. (2018). Effect on well-being from an online mindfulness intervention: "Mindful in May". *Mindfulness, 9*(5), 1637–1647. https://doi.org/10.1007/s12671-018-0910-7

Bartlett, M.Y., & DeSteno, D. (2006). Gratitude and prosocial behavior: Helping when it costs you. *Psychological Science, 17*, 319–325. https://doi.org/10.1111/j.1467-9280.2006.01705.x

Boehm, J.K., Lyubomirsky, S., & Sheldon, K.M. (2011). A longitudinal experimental study comparing the effectiveness of happiness-enhancing strategies in Anglo Americans and Asian Americans. *Cognition and Emotion, 25*, 1263–1272. https://doi.org/10.1080/02699931.2010.541227

Borman, W.C., Penner, L.A., Allen, T.D., & Motowidlo, S.J. (2001). Personality predictors of citizenship performance. *International Journal of Selection and Assessment, 9*, 52–69. https://doi.org/10.1111/1468-2389.00163

Boselie, J. J. L. M., Vancleef, L. M. G., & Peters, M. L. (2018). Filling the glass: Effects of a positive psychology intervention on executive task performance in chronic pain patients. *European Journal of Pain, 22*, 1268–1280. https://doi.org/10.1002/ejp.1214

Boyle, G. J., Helmes, E., Matthews, G., & Izard, C. E. (2015). Measures of affect dimensions. In G. J. Boyle, D. H. Saklofske, & G. Matthews (Eds.), *Measures of personality and social psychological constructs* (pp. 190–224). Academic Press. https://doi.org/10.1016/B978-0-12-386915-9.00008-5

Busseri, M. A. (2018). Examining the structure of subjective well-being through meta-analysis of the associations among positive affect, negative affect, and life satisfaction. *Personality and Individual Differences, 122*, 68–71. https://doi.org/10.1016/j.paid.2017.10.003

Busseri, M. A., Choma, B. L., & Sadava, S. W. (2009). Functional or fantasy? Examining the implications of subjective temporal perspective "trajectories" for life satisfaction. *Personality and Social Psychology Bulletin, 35*, 295–308. https://doi.org/10.1177/0146167208327215

Campbell, A. (1976). Subjective measures of well-being. *American Psychologist, 31*, 117–124. https://doi.org/10.1037/0003-066X.31.2.117

Cantril, H. (1965). *The pattern of human concerns*. Rutgers University Press.

Chang, E. C., Yi, S., Liu, J., Kamble, S. V., Zhang, Y., Shi, B. Ye, Y., Fang, Y., Cheng, K., Xu, J., Shen, J., Li, M., & Chang, O. D. (2020). Coping behaviors as predictors of hedonic well-being in Asian Indians: Does being optimistic still make a difference? *Journal of Happiness Studies, 21*, 289–304. https://doi.org/10.1007/s10902-019-00087-w

Cheung, F., & Lucas, R. E. (2014). Assessing the validity of single-item life satisfaction measures: Results from three large samples. *Quality of Life Research, 23*, 2809–2818. https://doi.org/10.1007/s11136-014-0726-4

Crawford, J. R., & Henry, J. D. (2004). The Positive and Negative Affect Schedule (PANAS): Construct validity, measurement properties and normative data in a large non-clinical sample. *British Journal of Clinical Psychology, 43*, 245–265. https://doi.org/10.1348/0144665031752934

Diener, E. (1984). Subjective well-being. *Psychological Bulletin, 95*, 542–575. https://doi.org/10.1037/0033-2909.95.3.542

Diener, E. (1994). Assessing subjective well-being: Progress and opportunities. *Social Indicators Research, 31*, 103–157. https://doi.org/10.1007/BF01207052

Diener, E., Emmons, R. A., Larsen, R. J., & Griffin, S. (1985). The Satisfaction with Life Scale. *Journal of Personality Assessment, 49*, 71–75. https://doi.org/10.1207/s15327752jpa4901_13

Diener, E., Ng, W., Harter, J., & Arora, R. (2010). Wealth and happiness across the world: Material prosperity predicts life evaluation, whereas psychosocial prosperity predicts positive feeling. *Journal of Personality and Social Psychology, 99*, 52–61. https://doi.org/10.1037/a0018066

Diener, E., Pressman, S. D., Hunter, J., & Delgadillo-Chase, D. (2017). If, why, and when subjective well-being influences health, and future needed research. *Applied Psychology: Health and Well-Being, 9*, 133–167. https://doi.org/10.1111/aphw.12090

Diener, E., Sandvik, E., & Pavot, W. (1991). Happiness is the frequency, not the intensity, of positive vs. negative affect. In F. Strack, M. Argyle, & N. Schwarz (Eds.), *Subjective well-being: An interdisciplinary perspective* (pp. 119–139). Pergamon Press.

Diener, E., & Seligman, M. E. P. (2004). Beyond money: Toward an economy of well-being. *Psychological Science in the Public Interest, 5*, 1–31. https://doi.org/10.1111/j.0963-7214.2004.00501001.x

Diener, E., Suh, E. M., Lucas, R. E., & Smith, H. L. (1999). Subjective well-being: Three decades of progress. *Psychological Bulletin, 125*, 276–302. https://doi.org/10.1037/0033-2909.125.2.276

Diener, E., & Tov, W. (2012). National accounts of well-being. In K. C. Land, A. C. Michalos, & M. J. Sirgy (Eds.), *Handbook of social indicators and quality of life research* (pp. 137–156). Springer. https://doi.org/10.1007/978-94-007-2421-1_7

Diener, E., Wirtz, D., Tov, W., Kim-Prieto, C., Choi, D., Oishi, S., & Biswas-Diener, R. (2010). New well-being measures: Short scales to assess flourishing and positive and negative feelings. *Social Indicators Research, 97*, 143–156. https://doi.org/10.1007/s11205-009-9493-y

Dolan, P., & White, M.P. (2007). How can measures of subjective well-being be used to inform public policy? *Perspectives on Psychological Science, 2*, 71–85. https://doi.org/10.1111/j.1745-6916.2007.00030.x

Economides, M., Martman, J., Bell, M., & Sanderson, B. (2018). Improvements in stress, affect, and irritability following brief use of a mindfulness-based smartphone app: A randomized controlled trial. *Mindfulness, 9*, 1584–1593. https://doi.org/10.1007/s12671-018-0905-4

Eid, M., & Diener, E. (2001). Norms for experiencing emotions in different cultures: Inter- and intranational differences. *Journal of Personality and Social Psychology, 81*, 869–885. https://doi.org/10.1037//0022-3514.81.5.869

Ellsworth, P.C., & Scherer, K.R. (2009). Appraisal processes in emotion. In R.J. Davidson, K.R. Scherer, & H.H. Goldsmith (Eds.), *Handbook of affective sciences* (pp. 572–595). Oxford University Press.

Friedman, E.M., Ruini, C., Foy, C.R., Jaros, L., Love, G., & Ryff, C.D. (2019). Lighten up! A community-based group intervention to promote eudaimonic well-being in older adults: A multi-site replication with 6-month follow-up. *Clinical Gerontologist, 42*(4), 387–397. https://doi.org/10.1080/07317115.2019.1574944

Gallup Organization. (n.d.). *Understanding how Gallup uses the Cantril scale.* Retrieved from https://news.gallup.com/poll/122453/Understanding-Gallup-Uses-Cantril-Scale.aspx

Heller, D., Watson, D., & Ilies, R. (2004). The role of person vs. situation in life satisfaction: A critical examination. *Psychological Bulletin, 130*, 574–600. https://doi.org/10.1037/0033-2909.130.4.574

Helliwell, J.F., Layard, R., & Sachs, J. (Eds.). (2018). *World happiness report 2018.* Sustainable Development Solutions Network.

Hetter, K. (2019, March 20). *World's happiest country for 2019 revealed.* Retrieved from https://www.cnn.com/travel/article/worlds-happiest-countries-united-nations-2019/index.html

Huta, V., & Waterman, A.S. (2014). Eudaimonia and its distinction from hedonia: Developing a classification and terminology for understanding conceptual and operational definitions. *Journal of Happiness Studies, 15*, 1425–1456. https://doi.org/10.1007/s10902-013-9485-0

Ilies, R., Yao, J., Curseu, P.L., & Liang, A.X. (2019). Educated and happy: A four-year study explaining the links between education, job fit, and life satisfaction. *Applied Psychology, 68*, 150–176. https://doi.org/10.1111/apps.12158

International Wellbeing Group. (2013). *Personal well-being index* (5th ed.). Retrieved from http://www.acqol.com.au/instruments#measures

Izard, C.E., Libero, D.Z., Putnam, P., & Haynes, O.M. (1993). Stability of emotion experiences and their relations to traits of personality. *Journal of Personality and Social Psychology, 64*, 847–860. https://doi.org/10.1037/0022-3514.64.5.847

Jang, S., Kim, E.S., Cao, C., Allen, T.D., Cooper, C.L., Lapierre, L.M., O'Driscoll, M.P., Sanchez, J.I., Spector, P.E., Poelmans, S.A. Y., Abarca, N., Alexandrova, M., Antoniou, A.-S., Beham, B., Brough, P., Carikci, I., Ferreiro, P., Fraile, G., Geurts, S., ... Woo, J.-M. (2017). Measurement invariance of The Satisfaction with Life Scale across 26 countries. *Journal of Cross-Cultural Psychology, 48*(4), 560–576. https://doi.org/10.1177/0022022117697844

Jayawickreme, E., Tsukayama, E., & Kashdan, T.B. (2017). Examining the effect of affect on life satisfaction judgments: A within-person perspective. *Journal of Research in Personality, 68*, 32–37. https://doi.org/10.1016/j.jrp.2017.04.005

Joshanloo, M. (2019). Cultural religiosity as the moderator of the relationship between affective experience and life satisfaction: A study in 147 countries. *Emotion, 19*, 629–636. https://doi.org/10.1037/emo0000469

Jovanović, V. (2015). Beyond the PANAS: Incremental validity of the Scale of Positive and Negative Experience (SPANE) in relation to well-being. *Personality and Individual Differences, 86*, 487–491. https://doi.org/10.1016/j.paid.2015.07.015

Kahneman, D., Krueger, A.B., Schkade, D.A., Schwarz, N., & Stone, A.A. (2004). A survey method for characterizing daily life experience: The day reconstruction method. *Science, 306*, 1776–1780. https://doi.org/10.1126/science.1103572

Kapteyn, A., Lee, J., Tassot, C., Vonkova, H., & Zamarro, G. (2015). Dimensions of subjective well-being. *Social Indicators Research, 123*, 625–660. https://doi.org/10.1007/s11205-014-0753-0

Kashdan, T.B., Biswas-Diener, R., & King, L. (2008). Reconsidering happiness: The costs of distinguishing between hedonics and eudaimonia. *Journal of Positive Psychology, 3*, 219–233. https://doi.org/10.1080/17439760802303044

Keyes, C.L. M., Shmotkin, D., & Ryff, C.D. (2002). Optimizing well-being: The empirical encounter of two traditions. *Journal of Personality and Social Psychology, 82*, 1007–1022. https://doi.org/10.1037/0022-3514.82.6.1007

Killen, A., & Macaskill, A. (2015). Using a gratitude intervention to enhance well-being in older adults. *Journal of Happiness Studies, 16*, 947–964. https://doi.org/10.1007/s10902-014-9542-3

Kilpatrick, F.P., & Cantril, H. (1960). Self-anchoring scaling: A measure of individuals' unique reality worlds. *Journal of Individual Psychology, 16*, 158–173.

Kim-Prieto, C., Diener, E., Tamir, M., Scollon, C.N., & Diener, M. (2005). Integrating the diverse definitions of happiness: A time-sequential framework of subjective well-being. *Journal of Happiness Studies, 6*, 261–300. https://doi.org/10.1007/s10902-005-7226-8

Kormi-Nouri, R., Farahani, M.-N., & Trost, K. (2013). The role of positive and negative affect on well-being amongst Swedish and Iranian university students. *Journal of Positive Psychology, 8*, 435–443. https://doi.org/10.1080/17439760.2013.823511

Kyriazos, T.A., Stalikas, A., Prassa, K., & Yotsidi, V. (2018). A 3-faced construct validation and a bifactor subjective well-being model using the Scale of Positive and Negative Experience, Greek Version. *Psychology, 09*, 1143–1175. https://doi.org/10.4236/psych.2018.95071

Lam, J.A., & Kahler, C.W. (2018). A randomized crossover trial to test the effects of positive psychology intervention delivered by text messaging. *Journal of Positive Psychology, 13*, 393–405. https://doi.org/10.1080/17439760.2017.1315649

Lambert, L., Passmore, H.-A., & Joshanloo, M. (2019). A positive psychology intervention program in a culturally-diverse university: Boosting happiness and reducing fear. *Journal of Happiness Studies, 20*, 1141–1162. https://doi.org/10.1007/s10902-018-9993-z

Laurent, J., Catanzaro, S.J., Joiner, T.E. Jr., Rudolph, K.D., Potter, K.I., Lambert, S. Osborne, L., & Gathright, T. (1999). A measure of positive and negative affect for children: Scale development and preliminary validation. *Psychological Assessment, 11*, 326–338. https://doi.org/10.1037/1040-3590.11.3.326

Lee, S.T.H., Hartanto, A., Yong, J.C., Koh, B., & Leung, A.K.-y. (2019). Examining the cross-cultural validity of the Positive Affect and Negative Affect Schedule between an Asian (Singaporean) sample and a Western (American) sample. *Asian Journal of Social Psychology, 23*(1), 109–116. https://doi.org/10.1111/ajsp.12390

Levin, K.A., & Currie, C. (2014). Reliability and validity of an adapted version of the Cantril Ladder for use with adolescent samples. *Social Indicators Research, 119*, 1047–1063. https://doi.org/10.1007/s11205-013-0507-4

Li, F., Bai, X., & Wang, Y. (2013). The Scale of Positive and Negative Experience (SPANE): Psychometric properties and normative data in a large Chinese sample. *PloS ONE, 8*, 1–9. https://doi.org/10.1371/journal.pone.0061137

Lim, Y.-J., Yu, B.-H., Kim, D.-K., & Kim, J.-H. (2010). The Positive and Negative Affect Schedule: Psychometric properties of the Korean version. *Psychiatry Investigation, 7*(3), 163–169. https://doi.org/10.4306/pi.2010.7.3.163

Lucas, R.E., Wallsworth, C., Anusic, I., & Donnellan, M.B. (2020). A direct comparison of the day reconstruction method (DRM) and the experience sampling method (ESM). *Journal of Personality and Social Psychology, 120*(3), 816–835. https://doi.org/10.1037/pspp0000289

Luhmann, M., Hawkley, L.C., Eid, M., & Cacioppo, J.T. (2012). Time frames and the distinction between affective and cognitive well-being. *Journal of Research in Personality, 46*, 431–441. https://doi.org/10.1016/j.jrp.2012.04.004

Matthews, G., Jones, D.M., & Chamberlain, A.G. (1990). Refining the measurement of mood: The UWIST Mood Adjective Checklist. *British Journal of Psychology, 81*, 17–42. https://doi.org/10.1111/j.2044-8295.1990.tb02343.x

Mayer, J. D., & Gaschke, Y. N. (1988). The experience and meta-experience of mood. *Journal of Personality and Social Psychology, 55*, 102–111. https://doi.org/10.1037/0022-3514.55.1.102

Merz, E. L., & Roesch, S. C. (2011). Modeling trait and state variation using multilevel factor analysis with PANAS daily diary data. *Journal of Research in Personality, 45*, 2–9. https://doi.org/10.1016/j.jrp.2010.11.003

Michalos, A. C. (1985). Multiple discrepancies theory (MDT). *Social Indicators Research, 16*, 347–413. https://doi.org/10.1007/BF00333288

Oishi, S. (2018). Culture and subjective well-being: Conceptual and measurement issues. In E. Diener, S. Oishi, & L. Tay (Eds.), *Handbook of well-being.* DEF. https://www.nobascholar.com/chapters/46

Pavot, W. (2008). The assessment of subjective well-being: Successes and shortfalls. In M. Eid & R. J. Larsen (Eds.), *The science of subjective well-being.* (pp. 124–140). Guilford.

Pavot, W., Diener, E., & Suh, E. M. (1998). The Temporal Satisfaction with Life Scale. *Journal of Personality Assessment, 70*, 340–354. https://doi.org/10.1207/s15327752jpa7002_11

Rahm, T., Heise, E., & Schuldt, M. (2017). Measuring the frequency of emotions: Validation of the Scale of Positive and Negative Experience (SPANE) in Germany. *PloS ONE, 12*(2), e0171288. https://doi.org/10.1371/journal.pone.0171288

Schimmack, U., & Oishi, S. (2005). The influence of chronically and temporarily accessible information on life satisfaction judgments. *Journal of Personality and Social Psychology, 89*, 395–406. https://doi.org/10.1037/0022-3514.89.3.395

Schneider, L., & Schimmack, U. (2009). Self-informant agreement in well-being ratings: A meta-analysis. *Social Indicators Research, 94*, 363–376. https://doi.org/10.1007/s11205-009-9440-y

Schwarz, N., & Strack, F. (1999). Reports of subjective well-being: Judgmental processes and their methodological implications. In D. Kahneman, E. Diener, & N. Schwarz (Eds.), *Well-being: The foundations of hedonic psychology* (pp. 61–84). Russell Sage Foundation.

Scollon, C. N., Howard, A. H., Caldwell, A. E., & Ito, S. (2009). The role of ideal affect in the experience and memory of emotions. *Journal of Happiness Studies, 10*, 257–269. https://doi.org/10.1007/s10902-007-9079-9

Scollon, C. N., Kim-Prieto, C., & Diener, E. (2003). Experience sampling: Promises and pitfalls, strengths and weaknesses. *Journal of Happiness Studies, 4*, 5–34. https://doi.org/10.1023/A:1023605205115

Shapira, N., Barak, A., & Gal, I. (2007). Promoting older adults' well-being through internet training and use. *Aging & Mental Health, 11*, 477–484. https://doi.org/10.1080/13607860601086546

Steger, M. F., Frazier, P., Oishi, S., & Kaler, M. (2006). The Meaning in Life Questionnaire: Assessing the presence of and search for meaning in life. *Journal of Counseling Psychology, 53*, 80–93. https://doi.org/10.1037/0022-0167.53.1.80

Suh, E. M., Diener, E., Oishi, S., & Triandis, H. C. (1998). The shifting basis of life satisfaction judgments across cultures: Emotions versus norms. *Journal of Personality and Social Psychology, 74*, 482–493. https://doi.org/10.1037/0022-3514.74.2.482

Sumi, K. (2014a). Reliability and validity of Japanese versions of the Flourishing Scale and the Scale of Positive and Negative Experience. *Social Indicators Research, 118*, 601–615. https://doi.org/10.1007/s11205-013-0432-6

Sumi, K. (2014b). Temporal stability of the Japanese versions of the Flourishing Scale and the Scale of Positive and Negative Experience. *Journal of Psychology & Psychotherapy, 4*(2), Article 1000140. https://doi.org/10.4172/2161-0487.1000140

Tay, L., & Diener, E. (2011). Needs and subjective well-being around the world. *Journal of Personality and Social Psychology, 101*, 354–365. https://doi.org/10.1037/a0023779

Terraciano, A., McCrae, R. R., & Costa, P. T. Jr. (2003). Factorial and construct validity of the Italian Positive and Negative Affect Schedule (PANAS). *European Journal of Psychological Assessment, 19*, 131–141. https://doi.org/10.1027//1015-5759.19.2.131

Thompson, E. R. (2007). Development and validation of an internationally reliable short-form of the Positive and Negative Affect Schedule (PANAS). *Journal of Cross-Cultural Psychology, 38*, 227–242. https://doi.org/10.1177/0022022106297301

Tov, W. (2012). Daily experiences and well-being: Do memories of events matter? *Cognition & Emotion, 26*, 1371–1389. https://doi.org/10.1080/02699931.2012.660135

Tov, W. (2018). Well-being concepts and components. In E. Diener, S. Oishi, & L. Tay (Eds.), *Handbook of subjective well-being* (pp. 1–15). DEF.

Tov, W., & Au, E.W.M. (2013). Comparing well-being across nations: Conceptual and empirical issues. In S.A. David, I. Boniwell, & A. Conley Ayers (Eds.), *The Oxford handbook of happiness.* (pp. 449–464). Oxford University Press. https://doi.org/10.1093/oxfordhb/9780199557257.013.0035

Tov, W., & Lee, H.W. (2016). A closer look at the hedonics of everyday meaning and satisfaction. *Journal of Personality and Social Psychology, 111*, 585–609. https://doi.org/10.1037/pspp0000081

Tov, W., & Nai, Z.L.S. (2018). Cultural differences in subjective well-being: How and why. In J.E. Maddux (Ed.), *Subjective well-being and life satisfaction* (pp. 50–73). Routledge.

Tsai, J.L., Knutson, B., & Fung, H.H. (2006). Cultural variation in affect valuation. *Journal of Personality and Social Psychology, 90*, 288–307. https://doi.org/10.1037/0022-3514.90.2.288

Vittersø, J. (Ed.). (2016). *Handbook of eudaimonic well-being.* Springer. https://doi.org/10.1007/978-3-319-42445-3

Vittersø, J., Røysamb, E., & Diener, E. (2002). The concept of life satisfaction across cultures: Exploring its diverse meaning and relation to economic wealth. In E. Gullone & R.A. Cummins (Eds.), *The universality of subjective wellbeing indicators: A multi-disciplinary and multi-national perspective* (pp. 81–103). Kluwer Academic. https://doi.org/10.1007/978-94-010-0271-4_6

Watson, D., & Clark, L.A. (1994). *The PANAS-X: Manual for the Positive and Negative Affect Schedule-Expanded Form.* University of Iowa. https://doi.org/10.17077/48vt-m4t2

Watson, D., Clark, L.A., & Tellegen, A. (1988). Development and validation of brief measures of positive and negative affect: The PANAS scales. *Journal of Personality and Social Psychology, 54*, 1063–1070. https://doi.org/10.1037/0022-3514.54.6.1063

Weber, M., Harzer, C., Huebner, E.S., & Hills, K.J. (2015). Measures of life satisfaction across the lifespan. In G.J. Boyle, D.H. Saklofske, & G. Matthews (Eds.), *Measures of personality and social psychological constructs* (pp. 101–130). https://doi.org/10.1016/B978-0-12-386915-9.00005-X

Weiner, B. (1985). An attributional theory of achievement motivation and emotion. *Psychological Review, 92*, 548–573. https://doi.org/10.1037/0033-295X.92.4.548

Woodworth, R.J., O'Brien-Malone, A., Diamond, M.R., & Schüz, B. (2016). Happy Days: Positive Psychology interventions effects on affect in an N-of-1 trial. *International Journal of Clinical and Health Psychology, 16*, 21–29. https://doi.org/10.1016/j.ijchp.2015.07.006

Yap, S.C.Y., Wortman, J., Anusic, I., Baker, S.G., Scherer, L.D., Donnellan, M.B., & Lucas, R.E. (2017). The effect of mood on judgments of subjective well-being: Nine tests of the judgment model. *Journal of Personality and Social Psychology, 113*, 939–961. https://doi.org/10.1037/pspp0000115

Zhang, J., Yang, Y., & Wang, H. (2009). Measuring subjective well-being: A comparison of China and the USA. *Asian Journal of Social Psychology, 12*, 221–225. https://doi.org/10.1111/j.1467-839X.2009.01287.x

Chapter 4

Measuring Positive Affect, Positive Emotions, and Positivity Resonance

Jieni Zhou and Barbara L. Fredrickson

Department of Psychology and Neuroscience, University of North Carolina, Chapel Hill, NC, USA

Positive emotions – and positive affective phenomena more generally – are key drivers of positive psychology. By definition, emotions are subtle and fleeting experiences. Even so, in aggregate, everyday pleasant affective states become potent drivers of positive human processes. Past studies have shown, for instance, that when sufficiently frequent, even mild positive affective states can (a) enhance individuals' mental health and life satisfaction by raising mindfulness and resilience (Catalino & Fredrickson, 2011; Cohn et al., 2009), (b) energize dyadic interactions to build trust, comradery, and physical health (Fredrickson, 2016; Kok et al., 2013), and (c) fuel positive organizing, teamwork, and improve group performance (Meneghel et al., 2016). This chapter serves to aid researchers who endeavor to deepen the scientific knowledge base regarding the value of pleasant affective phenomena within positive psychology.

The rise of affective science over the past 30 years began with a near-exclusive focus on negative emotions, such as fear, anger, and despair. A robust scientific literature on positive emotions has emerged only over the past 15 years or so. Early theoretical accounts cast the function of pleasant affect as to reward adaptive actions and motivate subsequent approach behaviors to regain natural rewards (Cabanac, 1971; Cacioppo et al., 1999; Clore 1994). Extending this view, Fredrickson's broaden-and-build theory of positive emotions (1998, 2001; for a review, see 2013) identified an additional function of positive emotions as to build an individual's enduring resources for survival, resources such as resilience, social bonds, intelligence, and physical health. This adaptive "build" function is supported by the "broaden" effect of positive emotions – the observation that many positive emotional states temporarily expand cognitive awareness in ways that enable individuals to take in "the bigger picture" and to creatively integrate disparate ideas. Such openness is theorized to fuel trajectories of growth marked by the accrual of beneficial resources. A subset of these resources (termed "vantage resources") also increase the odds that individuals experience subsequent positive emotions, with their further broaden-and-build benefits, thus establishing the conditions for reciprocal "upward spiral" dynamics. These are the processes that allow positive affective phenomena to energize human well-being and thus form a foundation within the field of positive psychology.

The structure of this chapter reflects the fact that pleasant affective phenomena can be conceptualized and assessed at multiple levels of analysis. At the most biologically primitive level, researchers have identified "core affect" as the combination of two underlying dimensions in body and brain states, one as affective valence (i.e., degrees of pleasantness or unpleasantness) and another as arousal (i.e., degrees of activation or calm; Barrett, 2005). Stepping up one level of analysis, a more differentiated emotion, such as anger or gratitude, can result when core affect is combined with situational specifics plus an individual's unique history. Up yet another level of analysis, to the interpersonal level, Fredrickson (2016) has argued for the unique value of "positivity resonance" defined as the coexperience – between and among individuals – of (a) shared positive affect, (b) mutual care and concern, and (c) synchrony evident in both behavior and biology. The measurement approaches we feature in this chapter follow these three levels of analyses, targeting positive affect, positive emotions, and positivity resonance in turn.

Consider Theoretical Stance

Dimensional Perspectives

Multiple dimensional perspectives have been advanced to describe variations in human affective experiences. Whether or not positive and negative affect are best represented as independent vs. opposing (bipolar) dimensions forms the crux of differing perspectives. The concept of "core affect" takes pleasant and unpleasant affect to oppose one another on a single, bipolar dimension of affective valance. This view stems from Russell's (1980) circumplex model of affect, which holds that each affective state can be decomposed into a linear combination of valence and arousal. Contentment, for instance, is defined as a pleasant affective state associated with low activation/arousal. An important finding relevant to assessment is that people tend to weigh the valence dimension more than the arousal dimension when making self-ratings of their affective states (Feldman, 1995).

A contrasting approach – one that has shaped considerable research on positive affect – is Watson and Tellegen's (1985) two-factor model, which posits two independent dimensions of positive and negative affect. Positive affect, in this view, is defined as the extent to which people experience pleasant activation, whereas negative affect is the extent to which they feel unpleasant activation. Accordingly, interest and enjoyment comprise high positive affect, whereas sadness is an example of low positive affect, and anger and fear are considered high negative affect. Following this model, Watson et al. developed the Positive and Negative Affect Schedule (PANAS), described in a later section (Watson et al., 1988). Although rarely recognized, in the late 1990s the authors of the PANAS renamed their scale to emphasize activation over affect: "To avoid terminological ambiguity, we have renamed the two factors Positive Activation and Negative Activation, respectively, and use the abbreviations PA and NA in reference to these new labels only" (Tellegen et al., 1999, p. 298).

Discrete Emotions Perspectives

Another way to conceptualize emotions is to emphasize their categorical differences from one another. For instance, although gratitude and pride (like anger and fear) may be described similarly from a dimensional perspective, they also differ in consequential ways. Discrete-emotion theorists emphasize these categorical differences when they frame emotion as a package of coordinated changes across different response systems (e.g., physiological, experiential, behavioral) that have evolved to provide distinct adaptive functions that address distinct, survival-relevant threats and opportunities (Levenson, 2014; Shiota, 2014). Because events of profound evolutionary significance are categorically distinct from one another (e.g., a threat to one's own physical safety is categorically distinct from losing a loved one), so too are emotions, which are conceptualized as evolved adaptations to such events that have been shaped over millennia by the discerning chisel of natural selection. This logic does not imply that all (or even most) present-day emotions are adaptive (i.e., advantageous), but rather that, on average, the emotions of our ancestors prompted behavioral responses that increased their odds of survival, either by overcoming a dire threat or by best capitalizing on an opportunity. These two event structures – threats vs. opportunities – map onto negative vs. positive emotions, respectively. Working from this perspective, affective scientists have identified emotion-specific prototypical facial movements (Ekman 1994; Keltner 1995, 1996; Keltner et al., 2003) and appraisal themes (Smith & Ellsworth, 1985; aka, core relational themes, Lazarus, 1991), and thought-action tendencies (Fredrickson, 2013). Table 4.1 identifies the appraisal themes, thought-action tendencies, and functions of 12 distinct positive emotions. (We exclude facial actions from Table 4.1 because facial actions have a better empirical track record of distinguishing among discrete negative emotions than discrete positive emotion.)

An alternate theoretical account for the existence of discrete emotions is offered by the theory of constructed emotions (Barrett, 2006, 2012, formerly called the conceptual act theory). This theory posits that discrete emotions represent individuals' situated conceptualizations that interpret changes in core affect and guide their responses to align with their behavioral and regulation goals. Situated conceptualization, in this view, refers to the process of accessing stored conceptual knowledge (based on experience) within a given situation to disambiguate core affect. For instance, the experience of high-activation pleasant core affect in the situation of receiving an unexpected gift vs. the situation of accomplishing a valued goal would activate categorically distinct memories and in turn activate the categorically distinct emotions of gratitude vs. pride. Distinct emotions "constructed" in this way serve to guide people's emotion-specific behavioral responses and communication patterns. The theory of constructed emotion also explains variations in prototypical categorizations of emotions. For example, compassion is often defined as a positive emotion, yet it can be experienced as subjectively pleasant or unpleasant depending on a person's situational context, goals, and/or coping resources (Condon & Barrett, 2013). When exposed to another person's suffering, one can experience heightened negative affect alongside feelings of compassion. In this chapter, we refer to compassion as a positive emotion to the extent that people feel pleasant affect alongside feelings of compassion, perhaps by being able to reduce another's suffering.

Table 4.1. Appraisal themes, thought–action tendencies, and functions of 12 distinct positive emotions

Emotion label	Appraisal theme	Thought-action tendency	Function
Joy (aka happiness)	Safe, familiar, unexpectedly good	Play, get involved	Activates engagement and playfulness
Serenity (aka contentment)	Safe, familiar, low effort	Savor and integrate	Allows people to savor the present moments and thus redefine their understanding of self-identity and life priorities
Interest	Safe, novel	Explore, learn	Promotes self-expansion to gather cognitive resources to understand the phenomenon
Amusement	Nonserious social incongruity	Share joviality, laugh	Promotes cognitive shifts and enhances social boding
Hope	Fearing the worst yet yearning for better	Plan for a better future	Builds optimism and resilience to adversity
Pride	Socially valued achievement	Dream big	Activates achievement motivation
Awe	Perception of vastness and needs for accommodation	Absorb and accommodate	Enhances prosocial behaviors, humility, and group cohesion
Elevation	Witness virtuous behaviors and acts of kindness	Identify exemplary cooperators and good trade partners	promotes voluntary helping behaviors, perceived meaning in life, and life satisfaction
Inspiration	Witness human excellence	Strive toward own higher ground	Cultivates creativity and productivity
Love	Tendency of affiliation	Concern for another person's welfare	Enhances social boding and self-expansion
Gratitude	Receive a gift or benefit	Creative urge to be prosocial and reciprocate	Strengthens high-quality relationship
Compassion*	Feeling sorrow and concern for another person's suffering	Making efforts to ameliorate the other person's suffering	Enhances approach motivation, and motivates helping and comforting behaviors

Note. *Broader personal and social contexts contribute to whether compassion is a positive or negative emotion.

Interpersonal Perspectives

Whether dimensional or discrete, scientists (and lay people in many cultures, see Mesquita, 2001) typically conceptualize affect and emotions as individual-level experiences, such as "my" pride or "your" gratitude. Stepping up one level of analysis, to the dyadic (or group) level, we have theorized that positive affect and emotions may also be "coexperienced"; we refer to such moments as "positivity resonance" and have argued that these interpersonally coexperienced states powerfully impact people's health, well-being, and social belonging (Fredrickson, 2016). Building on the logic of Izard (1977), we conceptualize "positivity resonance" as a description of the positive emotion of love, experienced at the episodic level (vs. at the level of a bond or relationship). Two additional episodic features of positivity resonance, beyond the feature of shared positive affect, are mutual care and concern, and synchrony in both behavior and biology.

Conceptualized in this way, love is not unconditional. That is, two situation-specific preconditions determine whether and to what degree positivity resonance can emerge. The first precondition is perceived safety. When people feel unsafe (e.g., vigilant about an uncertain environment), their hyperalert state will thwart interpersonal trust and the emergence of coexperienced positive affect. The second precondition is a sensory connection that unfolds in real-time. Eye contact is one major form of sensory connection. Previous research has demonstrated that eye contact functions as a gateway to facial mimicry (Schrammel et al., 2009), which in turn activates a neurally mediated embodied simulation that can generate both behavioral and biological synchrony across individuals (Niedenthal et al., 2010). With real-time sensory connection, then, positive emotions can "jump the gap" between people to become shared experiences of positivity resonance. Recent research has demonstrated that positivity resonance, both perceived and enacted, predicts individual and relational well-being (e.g., lower depressive symptoms, higher marital satisfaction) better than individual-level positive affect (Major et al., 2018; Otero et al., 2019). For completeness, then, we also include measures of positivity resonance in this chapter.

Consider Assessment Approach

Survey-Based Measures

For ease and economy, many researchers rely on survey-based measures to capture positive affective phenomena. Fortunately, many such measures are readily available (see Table 4.2). Because we suspect that ease and economy may be chief considerations for many readers of this chapter, we emphasize survey-based measures before moving on to alternatives. In the selection of any assessment approach within affective science, however, the choice can be made easier if researchers consider whether or not their planned research espouses a particular theoretical stance (i.e., does it favor affect dimensions, discrete emotions, or an interpersonal level of analysis?). We provide a simplified flowchart at the end of this chapter to demonstrate the measurement selection processes (see Figure 4.1). Most survey-based measures rely on respondents to self-reflect and self-report their subjective experiences. We review these self-report assessments before turning to implicit survey measures, which do not rely on introspection.

Table 4.2. Measures of positive affect, positive emotions, and positivity resonance

Measures title	Response scale	Example items	Time instructions	Reliability	Citation
PANAS (Positive and Negative Activation/Affect Schedule)	20 items 1 = *very slightly/not at all*, 5 = *extremely*	Enthusiastic, nervous	Indicate the extent you have felt this way at the moment/today/during the past few days/the past week/the past few weeks/the past year/general).	Ranges reflect different time instructions Positive affect: Cronbach's $\alpha = [.86, .90]$ Negative affect: Cronbach's $\alpha = [.84, .87]$ Internal consistency	Watson et al. (1988)
Affect Grid	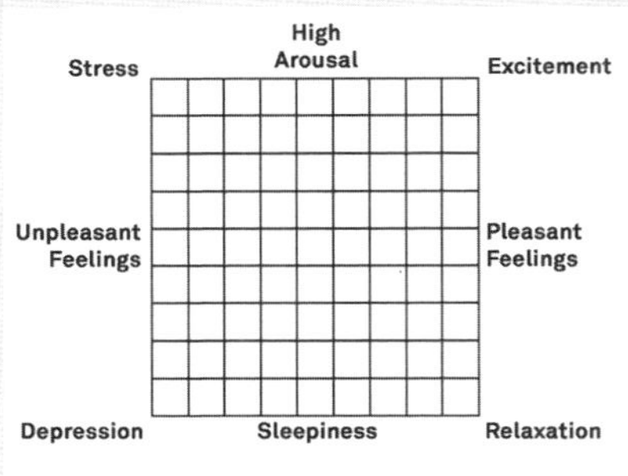 (© 1989 by American Psychological Association. Reproduced with permission from J. A. Russell, A. Weiss, & G. A. Mendelsohn, Affect grid: a single-item scale of pleasure and arousal. *Journal of Personality and Social Psychology, 57*(3), p. 494)		Please rate how you are feeling RIGHT NOW.	Correlations between Affect Grid and other measures on pleasure and arousal (e.g., PANAS) Pleasure: $r = [.77, .97]$ Arousal: $r = [.80, .95]$	Russell et al. (1989)

Table 4.2. continued

Measures title	Response scale	Example items	Time instructions	Reliability	Citation
SAM (Self-Assessment Manikin)	Pictorial assessment, 3 scales: Valence, Arousal, Dominance (different scale versions in use may differ in the number of response options and the direction of the response scale; sample scale reproduced with permission from Bradley & Lang, 1994, p. 51) 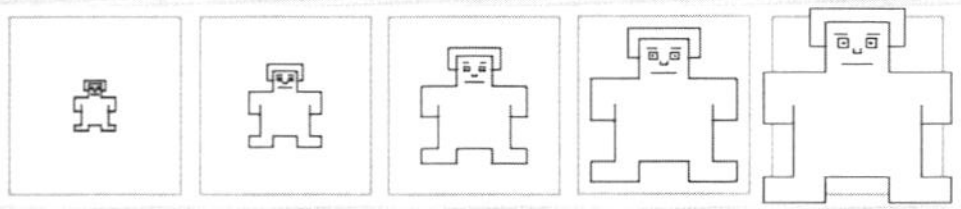	The first picture shows an individual who feels a lack of control and agency – relevant states could include subordination, intimidation, subjugation, withdrawal, submission, or resignation. The last picture shows a dominant person in control of the situation – relevant states could include control, influence, being important, dominant, recognized, or decisive.	Rate the extent to which your emotion makes you feel that you are in control of the situation, ranging from not in control at all to being 100 % in control.	Correlations between SAM and Mehrabian and Russell's semantical differential procedure (PP = Pencil and Paper version; CS = Computerized version) Valence: r (PP) = .96 r (CS) = .97 Arousal: r (PP) = .95 r (CS) = .94 Dominance: r (PP) = .23 r (CS) = .18	Bradley & Lang (1994)
UMACL (UWIST Mood Adjective Checklist)	29 items 1 = *definitely*, 4 = *definitely not* Four subscales: Energetic Arousal (8 items), Tense Arousal (8 items), Hedonic Tone (8 items), General Arousal (5 items)	Happy, jittery, vigorous	Here is a list of words that describe people's moods or feelings. Please indicate how well each word describes how you feel AT THE MOMENT.	Internal consistency Energetic Arousal: Cronbach's α = .88 Tense Arousal: Cronbach's α = .86 Hedonic Tone: Cronbach's α = .88 General Arousal: Cronbach's α = .75	Matthews et al. (1990)

Table 4.2. continued

Measures title	Response scale	Example items	Time instructions	Reliability	Citation
MAACL-R (Multiple Affect Adjective Check List)	Five dimensions: Anxiety, Depression, Hostility, Positive Affect, and Sensation Seeking Long form: 132 adjectives Short form: 66 adjectives	Nervous, lonely, good-natured, adventurous	The State Form asks subjects to describe how they feel "now-today," the Trait Form asks them to check adjectives describing how they "generally feel."	Internal consistency Long Form Cronbach's αs of the subscales [.70, .92] Short Form Cronbach's αs of the subscales [.68, .91] Sensation Seeking subscale has the lowest internal consistency among others in both short and long forms	Zuckerman & Lubin (1985) Lubin & Zuckerman (1999)
DES (Differential Emotional Scale)	36 items 1 = *never/rarely*, 5 = *very often* 12 subscales: Interest, Joy, Surprise, Sadness, Anger, Disgust, Contempt, Self-Hostility, Fear, Shame, Shyness, and Guilt	1. Feel regret, sorry about something you did 2. Feel like something stinks, puts a bad taste in your mouth	Rate how often you experienced each emotion item during the experience you described	Trait version: Test–retest reliability Cronbach's α = .77	Izard (1977, 1993) Boyle (1984) McHugo et al. (1982) Philippot (1993)
			Rate the extent to which you felt each state as you were watching the film clip.	State version: Internal consistency Cronbach's α = .81 (Average; subscales ranges [.56, .88])	

Table 4.2. continued

Measures title	Response scale	Example items	Time instructions	Reliability	Citation
DPES (Dispositional Positive Emotion Scales)	38-item self-report instrument with seven 5- or 6-item scales 1 = *strongly disagree*, 7 = *strongly agree*	Joy: I often feel bursts of joy. Awe: I see beauty all around me.	Participants report their level of agreement with each statement	Internal consistency Cronbach's α for the seven subscales [.75, .92]	Shiota et al. (2006)
mDES (modified Differential Emotional Scale)	Three-adjective groups for 10 positive emotions and 10 negative emotions 0 = *not at all*, 4 = *extremely*	What is the most amused, fun-loving, or silly you felt? (peak/end of day)	Please think back to how you felt during THE PAST TWENTY-FOUR HOURS. Using the 0–4 scale below, indicate the greatest amount that you've experienced each of the following feelings.	Internal consistency Positive emotions: Cronbach's α = .87 Negative emotions: Cronbach's α = .79 Test-retest reliability: Cronbach's α = .96 (both positive emotions and negative emotions)	Fredrickson et al. (2003) Fredrickson (2013) Fredrickson et al. (2017)
	0 = *never*, 4 = *most of the time*	I felt amused, fun-loving, or silly	Please think back to how you felt during the past 2 WEEKS. Using the 0–4 scale below, indicate how often you experienced each of the following feelings	Internal consistency Positive emotions: Cronbach's α = .79 Negative emotions: Cronbach's α = .69	

Table 4.2. continued

Measures title	Response scale	Example items	Time instructions	Reliability	Citation
PPRS (Perceived Positivity Resonance Scale)	7 items 0–100 %	... were you able to attune to and connect with the other(s)' experiences?	Episodic level: For what proportion of time during this episode ...	Within-persons: Cronbach's $\alpha = .96$ $\omega = .961$ Between-persons: Cronbach's $\alpha = .977$ $\omega = .977$	Major et al. (2018)
		... you can attune to other peoples' words and experiences?	Trait level: Of all your experiences and encounters with other people – the people you interact with regularly daily, including family, friends, neighbors, work colleagues, customers, etc. (do not just focus on one person individually but how you feel collectively with other people, in general)" and to estimate how much of the time that ...	Within-persons: Cronbach's $\alpha = .925$ $\omega = 0.924$ Between-persons: Cronbach's $\alpha = .984$ $\omega = 0.986$	

Table 4.2. continued

Measures title	Response scale	Example items	Time instructions	Reliability	Citation
IPANAT (Implicit Positive and Negative Affect Task)	1 = *doesn't fit at all*, 4 = *fits very well*	SAFEME VIKES	To what extent does the sound of this artificial word convey each of the following moods? Happy, Helpless, Energetic, Tense, Cheerful, Inhibited	Internal consistency PA and NA: Cronbach's α = .81 Test-retest reliability PA: Cronbach's α = .72 NA: Cronbach's α = .76	Quirin et al. (2009) van der Ploeg et al. (2016)
WFCT (Word Fragment Completion Task)	16 stems of positive emotion words; 16 stems of negative emotion words	ANG__ HA___	Please complete these items to form a word in English (no proper names). Write the first word that comes to mind that fits.	Not available	Rusting & Larsen (1998)
Facial Coding	FACS (Facial Action Coding System) , FACES (Facial Expression Coding System) i-MOTIONS (https://imotions.com/psychology/) FaceReader (https://www.noldus.com/facereader/facereader-online?gclid = Cj0KCQjwivbsBRDsARIsADyISJ-1E_nAYHLs8dUYmexxZXmjncuKWUoCIMTlqKvDtzT2CxGuiou9Cl0aAmexEALw_wcB)	1. Happiness = AU6 (Cheek raiser) + AU12 (Lip corner puller) 2. Code valence and intensity; report dominant emotion and overall expressiveness 3. Computer-based facial expression analysis			Ekman & Friesen (1978) Kring & Sloan (1991, 2007)

Table 4.2. continued

Measures title	Response scale	Example items	Time instructions	Reliability	Citation
BIPR (Behavioral Indicators of Positivity Resonance)	Each 30-second bin of video coded as 0, 1, or 2.		"Did positivity resonate between the two partners? That is, did they show actions, words, or voice intonation that conveyed mutual warmth, mutual concern, mutual affection, and/or a shared tempo (i.e., shared smiles and laughter)?"		Otero et al. (2019)
Psychophysiology	fEMG (Facial electromyography) captures the underlying electrical activity that's generated when muscles contract	Joy (eye-closured smile) = Orbicularis occuli + Zygomaticus major			

One of the most commonly used self-report scales in positive psychology is the Positive and Negative Activation Schedule (PANAS; Watson et al., 1999; formerly known as the Positive and Negative Affect Schedule; Watson et al., 1988). The positive activation subscale consists of 10 items: interested, alert, excited, inspired, strong, determined, attentive, enthusiastic, active, and proud. Although many users present the PANAS as a measure of positive affect, as noted previously, one limitation is that it centers exclusively on high-activation pleasant states. For instance, several subtle pleasant affective states known to be important for well-being, such as serenity (aka, contentment) and love (aka positivity resonance) go unmeasured with the PANAS. In addition, several items on the PANAS (e.g., alert, attentive) would not be regarded as emotion terms by most affective scientists (Shiota et al., 2006).

In place of providing a list of adjective labels describing emotional states, researchers have also developed a single-item scale to visually depict affective states in terms of the underlying dimensions of valence and intensity. The Affect Grid (shown in Table 4.2) is one such measure (Russell et al., 1989). Participants are instructed to place a mark within the cell of the grid that best indicates how they are/were feeling along the pleasantness and arousal dimensions. As a single-item scale, the Affect Grid is less time-consuming, and potentially less likely to cause participant fatigue with repeated assessments (Russell et al., 1989), it can also be useful as a quick manipulation check in laboratory experiments that seek to induce nonspecific positive affective states.

Like the graphic display of the Affect Grid, the Self-Assessment Manikin (SAM; shown in Table 4.2) uses a simple cartoon figure to depict emotions in terms of valence, arousal, and dominance (Hodes et al., 1985; Lang, 1980). Across response options, this cartoon figure changes from smiling to frowning to represent the underlying dimension of valence; to represent the underlying dimension of arousal, the cartoon figure changes from excited and wide-eyed to relaxed and asleep. Since SAM is a nonverbal picture-based scale, it overcomes the prerequisite for linguistic understanding for participants. The SAM is useful for non-English speakers, young children, individuals with language disorders, or clinical syndromes (Bradley & Lang, 1994; Lang, 1980; Lang et al., 1993, Morris, 1995).

Another scale that conceptualizes affect in terms of underlying dimensions, the UWIST Mood Adjective Checklist (UMACL; Matthews et al., 1990) represents a refinement of the Activation and Deactivation Affect Checklist (AD-ACL; Thayer, 1986). The UMACL consists of four subscales, three of which include 8 items and one that includes 5 items. The original AD-ACL categorizes affective states into two facets: energetic arousal (e.g., vigorous, sluggish) and tense arousal (e.g., nervous, composed). By contrast, the UMACL adds two more facets, including hedonic tone (e.g., cheerful, depressed) and anger-frustration (e.g., irritated, frustrated). The greater specificity of the UMACL has enabled its wider use in clinical research (Boyle et al., 2015; Matthews et al., 1990).

The final self-report scale to assess affect in terms of underlying dimensions we would like to point to is the Multiple Affect Adjective Check List – Revised (MAACL-R; Zuckerman & Lubin, 1985), which is widely used in clinical settings. This scale divides affective states into five dimensions: anxiety (e.g., nervous), depression (e.g., lonely), hostility (e.g., angry), positive affect (e.g., good-natured), and sensation seeking (e.g., adventurous). The MAACL-R is available in both long-form and short-form, each of which has been shown to be equally reliable (Lubin et al., 2001). One caution – that likely applies to all self-report assessment approaches – is that social desirability can distort participant responses, even more so for the negative affect dimension (Lubin & Zuckerman, 1999).

We now turn to self-report assessments of discrete emotion. Differential emotion theory (Izard, 1977, 1991) identifies 12 basic emotions including interest, joy, surprise, sadness, anger, disgust, contempt, self-hostility, fear, shame, shyness, and guilt. These 12 emotions were considered universally discernible from human facial movements and in the Differential Emotional Scale (DES; Izard, 1977) are each measured using three brief descriptions, e.g., feel sad and gloomy, almost like crying; feel amazed, like you can't believe what's happened, it was so unusual). Typical of the scientific era from which this scale emerged, the DES emphasizes negative more than positive emotions. Not assessed were specific, discernable positive emotions, which are increasingly known to carry psychological and social benefits.

More recently, to investigate links between personality and positive emotional experiences, Shiota et al. (2006) devised the Dispositional Positive Emotion Scale (DPES), which assesses dispositional proneness to experience distinct positive emotions. This scale comprises 38 items with seven 5-item or 6-item subscales for each positive emotion, including joy, contentment, pride, love, compassion, amusement, and awe. The DPES thus contains more positive emotions than previous self-report scales. According to the broaden-and-build theory (Fredrickson, 1998), each of these positive emotions builds and strengthens personal and social resources that ancestrally aided survival. Unlike other self-report surveys that impose a time constraint on affective experience (e.g., this past week or right now), the DPES assesses respondents' general tendencies to experience specific discrete positive emotions in pervasive, dispositional ways. However, if a given research program centers on transient emotional states, the DPES would not be appropriate.

Inspired equally by Izard's (1977) DES and Shiota et al.'s (2006) DPES, Fredrickson's team developed the modified Differential Emotional Scale (mDES; Fredrickson, 2013), which incorporates the distinct positive emotions identified in preliminary work by Shiota et al. (2006) to expand on the small set of positive emotions assessed in the original DES. The resulting mDES is a 20-item scale that asks respondents to rate their experience of positive and negative emotions in terms of either the intensity of those feelings or their frequency over a specified time interval (depending on the research purpose). Each of the 10 positive and the 10 negative emotions are represented by a trio of emotional adjectives (e.g., I felt awe, wonder, or amazement). To the six positive emotions targeted in the DPES (all but compassion), the mDES adds interest (from the DES) as well as gratitude, hope, and inspiration. An early version of the mDES (Tugade & Fredrickson, 2004) measured compassion, but this item was removed in the later versions because of the ambiguous valence. The item can and should be added back for research projects that target compassion.

The positive emotions on the mDES are not intended to be exhaustive; rather, researchers are encouraged to add items such as elevation or compassion as demanded by their own research questions. One advantage of the mDES is its flexibility in targeting specific, discrete emotions (e.g., gratitude or pride) at the item level or aggregating the 10 positive emotion and 10 negative emotion items separately to create independent positive and negative emotion subscale scores, respectively. These subscales yield high internal reliability, ranging from 0.82 to 0.94 (Cohn et al., 2009; Fredrickson et al., 2008). Specifically, between-person reliability is 0.87 for positive emotions and 0.79 for negative emotions, whereas within-person reliability across consecutive daily reports is 0.96 for both positive emotion and negative emotions (Fredrickson et al., 2017).

To assess the shared experience of positive emotions in interpersonal contexts, our team has developed the Perceived Positivity Resonance Scale (PPRS; Major et al., 2018). The PPRS is a 7-item scale that uses sliding response options (ranging from 0 % to 100 %) to assess the proportion of time respondents report positive affective experiences with others which are consistent with the concept of positivity resonance (Major et al., 2018). For example, items target "a mutual sense of warmth and concern," "being energized and uplifted," and feeling "in sync" with others. The items of the PPRS may be used either to target specific social episodes, specific social contacts (e.g., strangers and acquaintances), or a respondent's typical ways of connecting with other people in general. (Again, in a later section, we present various methods for capturing different temporal framings.)

Although self-reports of subjective experience may be the easiest and most economical way to measure positive affect and positive emotions, all self-reported surveys risk producing a hodgepodge of information: experiential knowledge, episodic memory, situation-specific belief, and identity-related belief, each of which may potentially bias responses (Robinson & Clore, 2002). In addition to these cognitive processes, which may override elementary emotional experiences, individuals often fall prey to social desirability and may be motivated to exaggerate their pleasant and desirable emotions, deny their unpleasant and undesirable emotions – or both (Larsen & Fredrickson, 1999). To circumvent biases that arise from both cognitive and motivational processes, researchers have introduced implicit measures of emotional experiences, several of which are also survey-based and therefore are just as easy and economical to use as are direct self-reports.

One such measure is the Implicit Positive and Negative Affect Task (IPANAT; Quirin et al., 2009; van der Ploeg et al., 2016), which asks participants to rate the extent to which each of the six artificial words (SAFME, VIKES, TUNBA, TALEP, BELNI, SUKOV) expresses certain affective states (three positive: happy, cheerful, energetic; three negative: helpless, tense, inhibited) using a 6-point Likert scale. The six artificial words were selected to be comparably neutral and equated in terms of a low level of familiarity and presumed meaning. Respondents are informed that the rationale for this task is rooted in the concept of onomatopoeia, which holds that the way a word sounds may help to express its meaning. The IPANAT has demonstrated reliability as well as validity compared to explicit self-report measures, such as the PANAS (Quirin et al., 2009). Interestingly, some studies find that implicit affect measures relate to physiological aspects of emotion, whereas explicit self-reports do not (van der Ploeg et al., 2016). Such findings imply that implicit and explicit measures may potentially tap into two different processes that may have different associations with psychological and physical well-being. Furthermore, although implicit measures of affect may guard against potential biases associated with conscious reflection or social desirability, research has shown that the IPANAT reflects variance in both trait and state affectivity, which may be a shortcoming in some contexts (Quirin et al., 2009; Schmukle & Egloff, 2004).

Another survey-based implicit affect measure is the word fragment completion task (DeWall & Baumeister, 2007; Rusting & Larsen, 1998). Respondents are asked to fill in the missing letters to complete a word fragment that can be completed either as a neutral word or as a positively or negatively valenced word. For example, "AN_ _ _" can be completed as "anger" or "angel." One potential drawback is that the word fragment completion task can be susceptible to individual personalities, as extraverts can be more attuned to cues for positive emotional information, whereas more neurotic people can be more sensitive to cues for negative emotional information (Rusting & Larsen, 1998). Also, including a measure of personality traits such as the NEO Five-Factor Inventory (Costa & McCrae, 1992; German version: Borkenau & Ostendorf, 1993) or the Ten Item Personality Inventory (TIPI; Gosling et al., 2003) can be a useful way to control for any influence of personalities on affective states measures by survey-based implicit measures of affect.

Beyond Survey-Based Measures

The assessments identified above, whether implicit or explicit, emphasize the subjective aspects of affect and emotion. Here, we briefly touch on assessments of affect and emotion that target other, more objective features, such as facial movements or physiological responses. (A full review is beyond the scope of this chapter.) One strength of such observational approaches is that they allow for emotional processes to continue to unfold without interruption. If researchers are interested in evaluating emotional experiences in real time rather than retrospectively, observational assessments may be less intrusive than self-reports. One such microlevel measure is the Facial Action Coding System (FACS; Ekman & Friesen 1978), a behavioral coding system that consists of 46 anatomically based "action units" (Aus), each of which indicates a specific form of muscle movement in the face, selected for its association with emotion experiences and expressions. The combination of AU6 (cheek raiser) and AU12 (lip corner puller), for instance, is widely used as an indicator of the genuine smiles associated with positive emotions. It can take around 100 hours or even months to self-teach the coding system using the manual for FACS. To rise to the level of a certified FACS coder, trained individuals need to take the final FACS test, which consists of 34 video segments. Coders need to agree with gold standard criterion codes at a level of .7 or higher for certification.

Using FACS with human coders not only requires extensive training but also considerable time to code. To overcome these limitations, automated computer programs such as Facial Expression Analysis (FEA; developed by i-Motions) and FaceReader (developed by Noldus) build on the FACS system to identify Aus and thereby infer emotions. Researchers have demonstrated the reliability of FEA by comparing its emotion recognition performance to facial electromyography (EMG), which picks up the electrical signals responsible for facial muscle movements. Likewise, FaceReader has been validated using the Warsaw Set of Emotional Facial Expression Pictures (WSEFEP) and the Amsterdam Dynamic Facial Expression Set (ADFES; Lewinski et al., 2014). FaceReader has been found to recognize the expressed target emotions at high rates (88% accuracy), comparable to human FACS coders (Lewinski et al., 2014).

A coding system (for use by human coders) has also been developed to assess macrolevel behavioral indicators of positivity resonance (BIPR) at the dyadic level (Otero et al., 2019) and has been validated using video-recordings of married couples who had a 15-minute conversation about an area of ongoing conflict. Coders divided each video into 30-second bins and coded the level of positivity resonance evident in behaviors (e.g., in actions, words, voice intonation, or a shared nonverbal tempo) using a scale of 0 (*not present*) ,1 (*low intensity*), and 2 (*high intensity*) based on the overall frequency, duration and clarity of the behaviors. One advantage of the BIPR coding system is that coders can be trained to reliability in 1 or 2 weeks, and coding videotapes of dyadic interaction using these macrolevel codes is far faster than using microlevel codes, such as those used for FACS.

As implied above, emotion-related facial movements may also be assessed using facial electromyography (EMG), a system of physiological recordings that measure even unobservable muscle contractions through the placement of small sensors over targeted muscle sites known to be engaged during emotions (e.g., the activation of the *orbicularis oculi* and *zygomatic major* muscle sites can signal the presence of positive emotions much like Aus 6 and 12 of FACS which are taken to represent smile-related movements near the eyes and lip corners, respectively. Importantly, consistency of electrode placement is essential for comparing and replicating findings across studies. Guidelines developed by Fridlund and Cacioppo (1986) provide detailed specifications to researchers looking to adopt the facial EMG approach. Besides tracking facial muscle movements associated with positive affect, recent research also identifies muscles elsewhere such as the postauricular reflex – the muscular response behind the ear – as linked to positive affect (Benning, 2011; Benning & Molina, 2018).

Either facial movement or behavioral coding can be a useful tool for assessing dynamic shifts in affective experience. However, such measurements can be limited by cultural variations in emotional display and expressivity (App et al., 2011; Matsumoto et al., 2008; Safdar et al., 2009). In addition, physiological measures do not necessarily correspond to self-reports of emotional states (Mauss & Robinson, 2009). Therefore, researchers should select measurement tools that best target the processes of interest.

Consider the Timeframes of Assessments

Depending on the form of any given research questions, the choice of timeframes attached to the self-reports of subjective experience presents crucial decision points. Based on evidence that people are better at recalling peak emotional experiences than they are at aggregating across multiple affective episodes (Fredrickson & Kahneman,1993; Kahneman et al., 1993), in our daily diary studies we most often ask participants to indicate, on the mDES, the greatest amount they have experienced of each of the feeling states included in the scale. By contrast, for longer periods, such "the past week," the mDES inquires respondents to report on the frequency of their experience of each identified feeling state. We advise researchers to limit the timeframe of self-reported affect to the past week. This is because research has indicated that self-reports of emotions over short vs. long periods prompt individuals to access different forms of introspection (Robinson & Clore, 2002). As the periods grow longer (e.g., the past month), individuals become less able to retrieve specific episodic information and thus tend to use more general semantic knowledge, which reflects their beliefs about their emotional experiences more than their emotion experiences per se (Robinson & Clore, 2002). For instance, gender stereotypes exist about the specific emotions that men and women experience more frequently. Men are believed to experience more anger and hostility than women, whereas women are believed to experience more sympathy and guilt. Previous research demonstrated that these gender stereotypes are evident when male and female respondents are asked to recall long periods (e.g., the past month) or hypothetical conditions, yet do not emerge when male and female respondents provide self-reports of their current affective state (Robinson et al., 1998).

Because global, retrospective self-reports based on long timespans (greater than "the past week") can inadvertently generate bias responses toward generic beliefs and away from actual affective experiences, aggregates of momentary self-reports are often best suited to capture affective responses with fidelity. Ecological Momentary Assessment (EMA, Stone & Shiffman, 1994; aka, the Experience Sampling Method, or ESM, Larson & Csikszentmihalyi, 2014) is one such assessment approach. EMA is implemented by pinging participants through text messages or specific mobile phone applications several times during the day and asking them to complete brief self-reports on their current or very recent (e.g., past 10 min) experiences. EMA is very flexible, in that any form of self-reported affect (e.g., dimensional, discrete, or interpersonal) can be deployed within it, albeit with an emphasis on brevity to avoid respondent fatigue. EMA can also be used to collect event-contingent experiences such as before and after every bout of physical activity or every social interaction lasting longer than 10 min. Immediately after such events, participants are instructed to complete brief self-reports of their experiences.

Another assessment approach that aggregates momentary self-reports to reduce response biases is the day reconstruction method (DRM; Kahneman et al., 2004). The DRM involves first asking respondents to list all the episodes from the beginning to the end of their day, by providing a short name for each episode, noting its duration, and adding some private notes to remind them about how they felt during that episode. Afterward, for each recalled episode in succession, respondents complete a brief self-report scale. Depending on the research aims, our team has embedded within the DRM either the mDES (to assess positive and negative emotions) or the PPRS (to assess positivity resonance). Akin to the DRM, the Event Reconstruction Method (ERM; Schwarz et al., 2009) asks participants to reflect on one specific recent event (e.g., the last time they interacted with a stranger, or engaged in a bout of physical activity) and to complete a brief self-report of their affective experiences during this specific episode. One benefit of the ERM relative to the DRM is that it takes much less time to complete.

Decision Flowchart for Selecting Suitable Assessment

As we hope is now evident to readers that how and when to best assess positive affect (or positive emotions, or positivity resonance) depends both on the theoretical stance of researchers toward affective phenomena and on the particulars of the research question they aim to address. To aid new researchers in their selection of measures, we have distilled the advice we have offered in this chapter into a decision-making flowchart (see Figure 4.1).

Positive psychology is a vibrant area of empirical research that provides vital evidence-based insights on how to raise individual, relational, and societal well-being. We urge

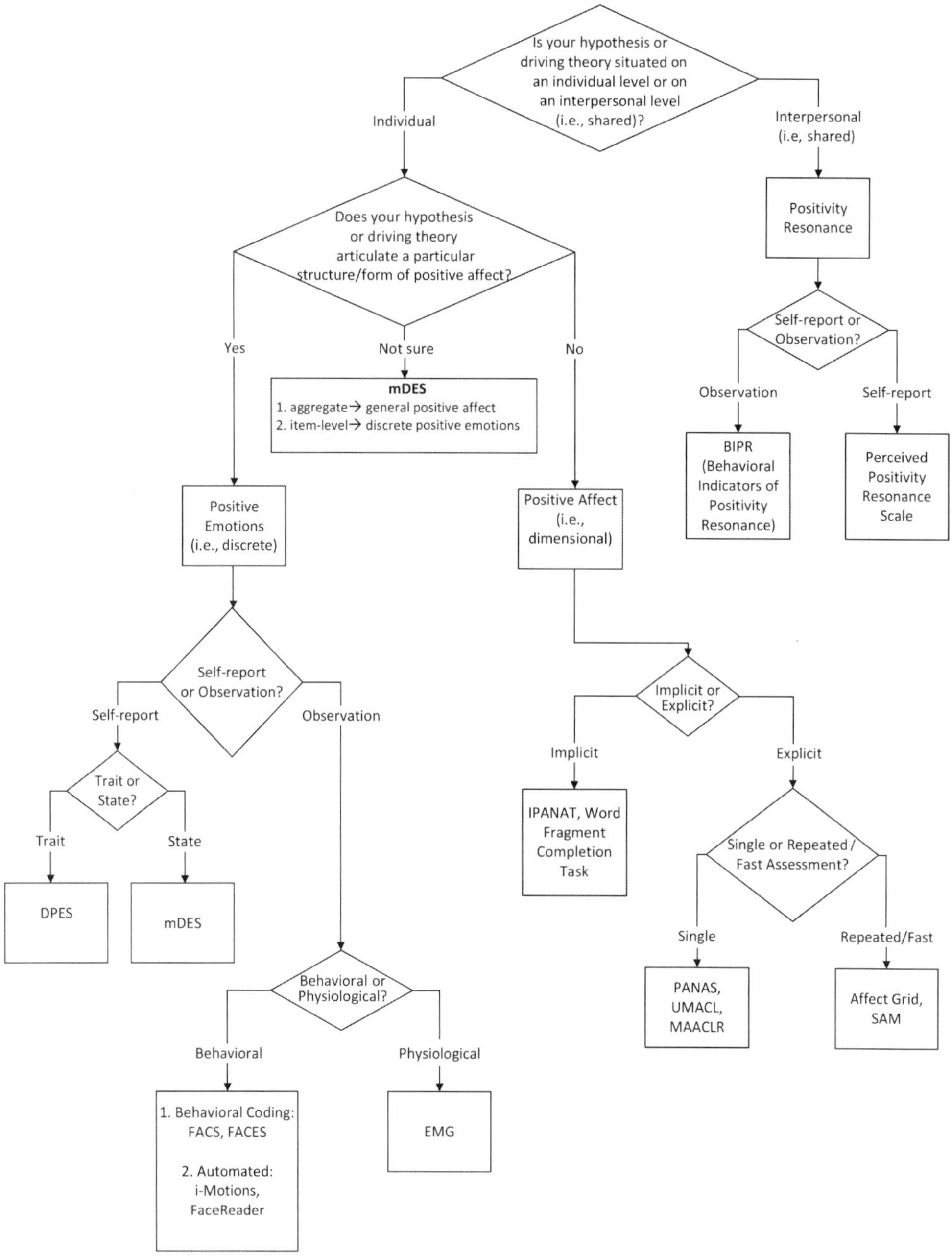

Figure 4.1. Flowchart of the decision process in measure selection.

readers to join us in adding to this research literature by training their eyes and their measures to best capture the tiny engines that drive a multitude of positive psychological processes – positive affect, positive emotions, and positivity resonance.

References

App, B., McIntosh, D.N., Reed, C.L., & Hertenstein, M.J. (2011). Nonverbal channel use in communication of emotion: How may depend on why. *Emotion, 11*(3), 603–617. https://doi.org/10.1037/a0023164

Barrett, L.F. (2005). Feeling is perceiving: Core affect and conceptualization in the experience of emotion. In L.F. Barrett, P.M. Niedenthal, & P. Winkielman (Eds.), *Emotion and consciousness* (pp. 255–284). Guilford.

Barrett, L.F. (2006). Are emotions natural kinds? *Perspectives on Psychological Science, 1*(1), 28–58. https://doi.org/10.1111/j.1745-6916.2006.00003.x

Barrett, L.F. (2012). Emotions are real. *Emotion, 12*(3), 413–429.. https://doi.org/10.1037/a0027555

Benning, S.D. (2011). Postauricular and superior auricular reflex modulation during emotional pictures and sounds. *Psychophysiology, 48*(3), 410–414. https://doi.org/10.1111/j.1469-8986.2010.01071.x

Benning, S., & Molina, S. (2018). The postauricular reflex measures positive emotion, not (angry) approach. *Psychophysiology, 55*(S1), S54.

Borkenau, P., & Ostendorf, F. (1993). *NEO-Fünf-Faktoren-Inventar (NEO-FFI) nach Costa und McCrae: Handanweisung* [NEO Five-Factor Inventory (NEO FFI) after Costa and McCrae: Manual]. Hogrefe.

Boyle, G.J. (1984). Reliability and validity of Izard's differential emotions scale. *Personality and Individual Differences, 5*(6), 747–750. https://doi.org/10.1016/0191-8869(84)90124-7

Boyle, G.J., Helmes, E., Matthews, G., & Izard, C.E. (2015). Measures of affect dimensions. In G. Boyle, D.H. Saklofske, & G. Matthews (Eds.), *Measures of personality and social psychological constructs* (pp. 190–224). Academic Press. https://doi.org/10.1016/B978-0-12-386915-9.00008-5

Bradley, M.M., & Lang, P.J. (1994). Measuring emotion: The self-assessment manikin and the semantic differential. *Journal of Behavior Therapy and Experimental Psychiatry, 25*(1), 49–59. https://doi.org/10.1016/0005-7916(94)90063-9

Cabanac, M. (1971). Physiological role of pleasure. *Science, 173*(4002), 1103–1107.

Cacioppo, J.T., Gardner, W.L., & Berntson, G.G. (1999). The affect system has parallel and integrative processing components: Form follows function. *Journal of Personality and Social Psychology, 76*(5), 839–855. https://doi.org/10.1037/0022-3514.76.5.839

Catalino, L.I., & Fredrickson, B.L. (2011). A Tuesday in the life of a flourisher: The role of positive emotional reactivity in optimal mental health. *Emotion, 11*(4), 938–950. https://doi.org/10.1037/a0024889

Clore, G.L. (1994). Why emotions are felt. In P. Ekman & R.J. Davidson (Eds.), *The nature of emotion: Fundamental questions* (pp. 103–111). Oxford University Press.

Cohn, M.A., Fredrickson, B.L., Brown, S.L., Mikels, J.A., & Conway, A.M. (2009). Happiness unpacked: Positive emotions increase life satisfaction by building resilience. *Emotion, 9*(3), 361–368. https://doi.org/10.1037/a0015952

Condon, P., & Barrett, L.F. (2013). Conceptualizing and experiencing compassion. *Emotion (Washington, D.C.), 13*(5), 817–821. https://doi.org/10.1037/a0033747

Costa, P.T., & McCrae, R.R. (1992). Normal personality assessment in clinical practice: The NEO Personality Inventory. *Psychological Assessment, 4*(1), 5–13. https://doi.org/10.1037/1040-3590.4.1.5

DeWall, C.N., & Baumeister, R.F. (2007). From terror to joy: Automatic tuning to positive affective information following mortality salience. *Psychological Science, 18*(11), 984–990. https://doi.org/10.1111/j.1467-9280.2007.02013.x

Ekman, P. (1994). All emotions are basic. In P. Ekman & R.J. Davidson (Eds.), *The nature of emotion: Fundamental questions* (pp. 15–19). Oxford University Press.

Ekman, P., & Friesen, W.V. (1978). *Facial action coding system: Investigator's guide*. Consulting Psychologists Press.

Feldman, L.A. (1995). Variations in the circumplex structure of mood. *Personality and Social Psychology Bulletin, 21*(8), 806–817. https://doi.org/10.1177/0146167295218003

Fredrickson, B.L. (1998). What good are positive emotions? *Review of General Psychology, 2*(3), 300–319. https://doi.org/10.1037/1089-2680.2.3.300

Fredrickson, B.L. (2001). The role of positive emotions in positive psychology: The broaden-and-build theory of positive emotions. *American Psychologist, 56*(3), 218–226. https://doi.org/10.1037/0003-066X.56.3.218

Fredrickson, B.L. (2013). Positive emotions broaden and build. In P. Devine & A. Plant, *Advances in Experimental Social Psychology* (Vol. 47, pp. 1–53). Academic Press. https://doi.org/10.1016/B978-0-12-407236-7.00001-2

Fredrickson, B.L. (2016). Love: Positivity resonance as a fresh, evidence-based perspective on an age-old topic. In F. Barrett, M. Lewis, & J.M. Haviland-Jones (Eds.), *Handbook of emotions* (pp. 847–858). Guilford Press.

Fredrickson, B.L., Boulton, A.J., Firestine, A.M., Van Cappellen, P., Algoe, S.B., Brantley, M.M., Loundon Kim, S., Brantley, J., & Salzberg, S. (2017). Positive emotion correlates of meditation practice: A comparison of mindfulness meditation and loving-kindness meditation. *Mindfulness, 8*(6), 1623–1633. https://doi.org/10.1007/s12671-017-0735-9

Fredrickson, B.L., Cohn, M.A., Coffey, K.A., Pek, J., & Finkel, S.M. (2008). Open hearts build lives: Positive emotions, induced through loving-kindness meditation, build consequential personal resources. *Journal of Personality and Social Psychology, 95*(5), 1045–1062. https://doi.org/10.1037/a0013262

Fredrickson, B.L., & Kahneman, D. (1993). Duration neglect in retrospective evaluations of affective episodes. *Journal of Personality and Social Psychology, 65*(1), 45–55. https://doi.org/10.1037/0022-3514.65.1.45

Fredrickson, B.L., Tugade, M.M., Waugh, C.E., & Larkin, G.R. (2003). What good are positive emotions in crisis? A prospective study of resilience and emotions following the terrorist attacks on the United States on September 11th, 2001. *Journal of Personality and Social Psychology, 84*(2), 365–376. https://doi.org/10.1037//0022-3514.84.2.365

Fridlund, A.J., & Cacioppo, J.T. (1986). Guidelines for human electromyographic research. *Psychophysiology, 23*(5), 567–589. https://doi.org/10.1111/j.1469-8986.1986.tb00676.x

Gosling, S.D., Rentfrow, P.J., & Swann Jr, W.B. (2003). A very brief measure of the Big-Five personality domains. *Journal of Research in Personality, 37*(6), 504–528. https://doi.org/10.1016/S0092-6566(03)00046-1

Hodes, R.L., Cook III, E.W., & Lang, P.J. (1985). Individual differences in autonomic response: Conditioned association or conditioned fear? *Psychophysiology, 22*(5), 545–560. https://doi.org/10.1111/j.1469-8986.1985.tb01649.x

Izard, C.E. (1977). *Human emotions.* Plenum. https://doi.org/10.1007/978-1-4899-2209-0

Izard, C.E. (1991). *The psychology of emotions.* Springer Science & Business Media. https://doi.org/10.1007/978-1-4899-0615-1

Izard, C.E. (1993). Four systems for emotion activation: Cognitive and noncognitive processes. *Psychological Review, 100*(1), 68–90. https://doi.org/10.1037/0033-295X.100.1.68

Kahneman, D., Fredrickson, B.L., Schreiber, C.A., & Redelmeier, D.A. (1993). When more pain is preferred to less: Adding a better end. *Psychological Science, 4*(6), 401–405. https://doi.org/10.1111/j.1467-9280.1993.tb00589.x

Kahneman, D., Krueger, A.B., Schkade, D.A., Schwarz, N., & Stone, A.A. (2004). A survey method for characterizing daily life experience: The day reconstruction method. *Science, 306*(5702), 1776–1780.

Keltner, D. (1995). Signs of appeasement: Evidence for the distinct displays of embarrassment, amusement, and shame. *Journal of Personality and Social Psychology, 68*(3), 441–454. https://doi.org/10.1037/0022-3514.68.3.441

Keltner, D. (1996). Evidence for the distinctness of embarrassment, shame, and guilt: A study of recalled antecedents and facial expressions of emotion. *Cognition & Emotion, 10*(2), 155–172. https://doi.org/10.1080/026999396380312

Keltner, D., Ekman, P., Gonzaga, G.C., & Beer, J. (2003). Facial expression of emotion. In R.J. Davidson, K.R. Scherer, & H.H. Goldsmith (Eds.), *Handbook of affective sciences* (pp. 415–432). Oxford University Press.

Kok, B.E., Coffey, K.A., Cohn, M.A., Catalino, L.I., Vacharkulksemsuk, T., Algoe, S.B., Brantley, M., &Fredrickson, B.L. (2013). How positive emotions build physical health: Perceived positive social connections account for the upward spiral between positive emotions and vagal tone. *Psychological Science, 24*(7), 1123–1132. https://doi.org/10.1177/0956797612470827

Kring, A.M., & Sloan, D. (1991). *The Facial Expression Coding System (FACES): A user's guide.* Unpublished manuscript.

Kring, A.M., & Sloan, D.M. (2007). The Facial Expression Coding System (FACES): Development, validation, and utility. *Psychological Assessment, 19*(2), 210–224. https://doi.org/10.1037/1040-3590.19.2.210

Lang, P.J. (1980). Behavioral treatment and bio-behavioral assessment: Computer applications. In J.B. Sidowski, J.H. Johnson, & T.A. Williams (Eds.), *Technology in mental health care delivery systems* (pp. 119–137). Ablex.

Lang, P.J., Greenwald, M.K., Bradley, M.M., & Hamm, A.O. (1993). Looking at pictures: Affective, facial, visceral, and behavioral reactions. *Psychophysiology, 30*(3), 261–273. https://doi.org/10.1111/j.1469-8986.1993.tb03352.x

Larsen, R.J., & Fredrickson, B.L. (1999). Measurement issues in emotion research. In D. Kahneman, E. Diener, & N. Schwarz (Eds.), *Well-being: The foundations of hedonic psychology* (pp. 40–60). Russell Sage Foundation.

Larson, R., & Csikszentmihalyi, M. (2014). The experience sampling method. In M. Csikszentmihalyi, *Flow and the foundations of positive psychology: The Collected Works of Mihaly Csikszentmihalyi* (pp. 21–34). Springer.

Lazarus, R.S. (1991). Progress on a cognitive-motivational-relational theory of emotion. *American Psychologist, 46,* 819–834. https://doi.org/10.1037/0003-066X.46.8.819

Levenson, R.W. (2014). The autonomic nervous system and emotion. *Emotion Review, 6*(2), 100–112. https://doi.org/10.1177/1754073913512003

Lewinski, P., den Uyl, T.M., & Butler, C. (2014). Automated facial coding: Validation of basic emotions and FACS Aus in FaceReader. *Journal of Neuroscience, Psychology, and Economics, 7*(4), 227–236. https://doi.org/10.1037/npe0000028

Lubin, B., Van Whitlock, R., Reddy, D., & Petren, S. (2001). A comparison of the short and long forms of the Multiple Affect Adjective Check List–Revised (MAACL-R). *Journal of Clinical Psychology, 57*(3), 411–416. https://doi.org/10.1002/jclp.1023

Lubin, B., & Zuckerman, M. (1999). *Manual for the MAACL-R: Multiple affect adjective check list – revised.* EdITS/Educational and Industrial Testing Service.

Major, B.C., Le Nguyen, K.D., Lundberg, K.B., & Fredrickson, B.L. (2018). Well-being correlates of perceived positivity resonance: Evidence from trait and episode-level assessments. *Personality and Social Psychology Bulletin, 44*(12), 1631–1647. https://doi.org/10.1177/0146167218771324

Matsumoto, D., Yoo, S.H., & Fontaine, J. (2008). Mapping expressive differences around the world: The relationship between emotional display rules and individualismversus collectivism. *Journal of Cross-Cultural Psychology, 39*(1), 55–74. https://doi.org/10.1177/0022022107311854

Matthews, G., Jones, D.M., & Chamberlain, A.G. (1990). Refining the measurement of mood: The UWIST mood adjective checklist. *British Journal of Psychology, 81*(1), 17–42. https://doi.org/10.1111/j.2044-8295.1990.tb02343.x

Mauss, I.B., & Robinson, M.D. (2009). Measures of emotion: A review. *Cognition & Emotion, 23*(2), 209–237. https://doi.org/10.1080/02699930802204677

McHugo, G.J., Smith, C.A. & Lanzetta, J.T. (1982). The structure of self-reports of emotional responses to film segments. *Motiv Emot, 6,* 365–385. https://doi.org/10.1007/BF00998191

Meneghel, I., Salanova, M., & Martínez, I.M. (2016). Feeling good makes us stronger: How team resilience mediates the effect of positive emotions on team performance. *Journal of Happiness Studies, 17*(1), 239–255. https://doi.org/10.1007/s10902-014-9592-6

Mesquita, B. (2001). Emotions in collectivist and individualist contexts. *Journal of Personality and Social Psychology, 80,* 68–74. https://doi.org/10.1037/0022-3514.80.1.68

Morris, J. D. (1995). Observations: SAM, the Self-Assessment Manikin, an efficient cross-cultural measurement of emotional response. *Journal of Advertising Research, 35*(6), 63–68.

Niedenthal, P. M., Mermillod, M., Maringer, M., & Hess, U. (2010). The Simulation of Smiles (SIMS) model: Embodied simulation and the meaning of facial expression. *Behavioral and Brain Sciences, 33*(6), 417–433. https://doi.org/10.1017/S0140525X10000865

Otero, M. C., Wells, J. L., Chen, K. H., Brown, C. L., Connelly, D. E., Levenson, R. W., & Fredrickson, B. L. (2019). Behavioral indices of positivity resonance associated with long-term marital satisfaction. *Emotion, 20*(7), 1225–1233. https://doi.org/10.1037/emo0000634

Philippot, P. (1993). Inducing and assessing differentiated emotion-feeling states in the laboratory. *Cognition and Emotion*, *7*(2), 171–193. https://doi.org/10.1080/02699939308409183

Quirin, M., Kazén, M., & Kuhl, J. (2009). When nonsense sounds happy or helpless: the implicit positive and negative affect test (IPANAT). *Journal of Personality and Social Psychology, 97*(3), 500–516. https://doi.org/10.1037/a0016063

Robinson, M., & Clore, G. (2002). Belief and Feeling: Evidence for an accessibility model of emotional self-report. *Psychological Bulletin, 128*, 934–960. https://doi.org/10.1037//0033-2909.128.6.934

Robinson, M. D., Johnson, J. T., & Shields, S. A. (1998). The gender heuristic and the database: Factors affecting the perception of gender-related differences in the experience and display of emotions. *Basic and Applied Social Psychology, 20*(3), 206–219. https://doi.org/10.1207/s15324834basp2003_3

Russell, J. A. (1980). A circumplex model of affect. *Journal of Personality and Social Psychology, 39*(6), 1161–1178. https://doi.org/10.1037/h0077714

Russell, J. A., Weiss, A., & Mendelsohn, G. A. (1989). Affect grid: a single-item scale of pleasure and arousal. *Journal of Personality and Social Psychology, 57*(3), 493–502. https://doi.org/10.1037/0022-3514.57.3.493

Rusting, C. L., & Larsen, R. J. (1998). Personality and cognitive processing of affective information. *Personality and Social Psychology Bulletin, 24*(2), 200–213. https://doi.org/10.1177/0146167298242008

Safdar, S., Friedlmeier, W., Matsumoto, D., Yoo, S. H., Kwantes, C. T., Kakai, H., & Shigemasu, E. (2009). Variations of emotional display rules within and across cultures: A comparison between Canada, USA, and Japan. *Canadian Journal of Behavioural Science/Revue Canadienne des Sciences du Comportement, 41*(1), 1–10. https://doi.org/10.1037/a0014387

Schmukle, S. C., & Egloff, B. (2004). Does the Implicit Association Test for assessing anxiety measure trait and state variance? *European Journal of Personality*, *18*(6), 483–494. https://doi.org/10.1002/per.525

Schrammel, F., Pannasch, S., Graupner, S. T., Mojzisch, A., & Velichkovsky, B. M. (2009). Virtual friend or threat? The effects of facial expression and gaze interaction on psychophysiological responses and emotional experience. *Psychophysiology, 46*(5), 922–931. https://doi.org/10.1111/j.1469-8986.2009.00831.x

Schwarz, N., Kahneman, D., & Xu, J. (2009). Global and episodic reports of hedonic experience. In R. F. Belli, F. P. Stafford, & D. F. Alwin (Eds.), *Calendar and time diary* (pp. 156–174). Sage. https://doi.org/10.4135/9781412990295

Shiota, M. N. (2014). The evolutionary perspective in positive emotion research. In M. M. Tugade, M. N. Shiota, & L. D. Kirby, *Handbook of positive emotions* (pp. 44–59). Guilford.

Shiota, M. N., Keltner, D., & John, O. P. (2006). Positive emotion dispositions differentially associated with Big Five personality and attachment style. *Journal of Positive Psychology, 1*(2), 61–71. https://doi.org/10.1080/17439760500510833

Smith, C. A., & Ellsworth, P. C. (1985). Patterns of cognitive appraisal in emotion. *Journal of Personality and Social Psychology, 48*(4), 813–838. https://doi.org/10.1037/0022-3514.48.4.813

Stone, A. A., & Shiffman, S. (1994). Ecological momentary assessment (EMA) in behavioral medicine. *Annals of Behavioral Medicine, 16*(3), 199–202. https://doi.org/10.1093/abm/16.3.199

Tellegen, A., Watson, D., & Clark, L. A. (1999). On the dimensional and hierarchical structure of affect. *Psychological Science, 10*(4), 297–303. https://doi.org/10.1111/1467-9280.00157

Thayer, R. E. (1986). Activation-deactivation adjective check list: Current overview and structural analysis. *Psychological Reports, 58*(2), 607–614. https://doi.org/10.2466/pr0.1986.58.2.607

van der Ploeg, M. M., Brosschot, J. F., Thayer, J. F., & Verkuil, B. (2016). The implicit positive and negative affect test: Validity and relationship with cardiovascular stress-responses. *Frontiers in Psychology, 7*, Article 425. https://doi.org/10.3389/fpsyg.2016.00425

Watson, D., Clark, L. A., & Tellegen, A. (1988). Development and validation of brief measures of positive and negative affect: the PANAS scales. *Journal of Personality and Social Psychology, 54*(6), 1063–1070. https://doi.org/10.1037/0022-3514.54.6.1063

Watson, D., & Tellegen, A. (1985). Toward a consensual structure of mood. *Psychological Bulletin, 98*(2), 219–235. https://doi.org/10.1037/0033-2909.98.2.219

Watson, D., Wiese, D., Vaidya, J., & Tellegen, A. (1999). The two general activation systems of affect: Structural findings, evolutionary considerations, and psychobiological evidence. *Journal of Personality and Social Psychology, 76*(5), 820–838. https://doi.org/10.1037/0022-3514.76.5.820

Zuckerman, M., & Lubin, B. (1985). *Manual for the MAACL-R: The Multiple Affect Adjective Check List Revised*. Educational and Industrial Testing Service.

Chapter 5

Health-Related Quality of Life

Stefan Höfer

Department of Medical Psychology, Medical University Innsbruck, Innsbruck, Austria

Quality of life (QoL) has been the focus of various scientific disciplines across the history of humankind. Early philosophers, social scientists, psychologists, and medical professionals all embraced the concept and entered the field of QoL research with a certain focus and purpose. Some researchers argue that QoL is the overall umbrella term for combining research on psychological and subjective well-being (Ring et al., 2006). The term QoL is used for various purposes sometimes lacking a specific definition behind it. Different academic and nonacademic disciplines captured the term and supplemented it by adding specific words to it such as health (e.g., health-related QoL). It has become a popular phrase in research, policy, and public discourse, although a unanimous understanding of the terminology is still lacking in scientific literature and public discussions (Skevington & Bohnke, 2018).

More recently, the mainstream of QoL research and development has taken place in the field of social indicators research and medicine. Both disciplines are confronted with the conflict between objective measures for social progress (such as gross domestic product [GDP] in social indicators research) or health (survival rates [mortality, morbidity] in medicine) and the subjective perceptions of these objective conditions. To date, GDP has become a measure for everything except what makes life worthwhile living; and mortality rates were everything medicine was looking into for a long time as the main indicator for progress. The United Nations took an active interest in the 1950s in measuring "levels of living," which added to the increasing interest of social indicators research or QoL measurement. Michalos (2017) stressed that QoL assessment may take a two-variable theory into account: the actual condition of one's life and what individuals (communities or society at large) make of these conditions. Based on that assumption, one can construct four scenarios: (1) People's living conditions are good, and people accurately perceive them and act accordingly. (2) People's living conditions are poor, and people accurately judge them so. (3) People's living conditions are poor, although people inaccurately judge them as good. (4) People's living conditions are good, although people inaccurately judge them as poor. Michalos (2017) labeled these four scenarios as (1) Real Paradise, (2) Real Hell, (3) Fool's Paradise, and (4) Fool's Hell. These scenarios contrast with the perspectives of other QoL researchers (e.g., Diener et al., 2010), in which the individual assessment is the ultimate indicator regardless of the objective situation. One of the goals of social indicators research, however, is not only to strive for the good life based on an individual's subjective assessment of feeling good – no matter how terrible their real- life conditions are – but one in which they feel good for the best of reasons (Michalos, 2017). Another perspective on QoL was introduced by Veenhoven (2000), who proposed four qualities of life based on chances and outcomes, external and internal qualities. The combination of these allows for the following classifications: (1) livability of the environment, (2) life-ability of the person, (3) utility of life for the environment, and (4) appreciation of life by the person. The first refers to good living conditions based on the environment one lives in; the second mainly focuses on how well an individual can cope with situations in life. The third presumes some higher values, with the notion that a good life must be good for something more than itself. The last and fourth aspect refers to the appreciation of life by the person themselves; mostly this refers to happiness research.

The other main scientific discipline adopting QoL measurement was medicine. In healthcare, it became relevant once the traditional outcomes of medicine such as laboratory or clinical indicators of mortality and morbidity were considered too narrow in scope. When it comes to decisions about duration of life and QoL, subjective indicators become important. The trend toward QoL assessments was fueled by the availability of more and more aggressive cancer treatments. One of the first measures of QoL – the Karnofsky Performance Status Scale (Karnofsky & Burchenal, 1949) – was introduced in the area of cancer treatment. These days, QoL measures in medicine are known under the umbrella term "patient-reported outcome measures," as QoL proved to be difficult to define and operationalize. The conflict between subjective assessment and objective health status is as relevant here as within the social indicators research area. The definition of health by the World Health Organizationin its constitution that came into force in 1948 further triggered the rapid uptake of QoL assessments in medicine, as it stipulated that health is "a state of complete physical, mental and social well-being and not merely the absence of disease or infirmity" (WHO, 2020, p. 1). The term QoL is considered to encompass all aspects of patients' well-being (including aspects such as spiritual or economic health). To increase its relevance in clinical trials, the term "health-related QoL" (HRQOL) has been introduced, sometimes used interchangeably with the term "health status." It largely refers to the patients' appraisal of their current level of functioning and satisfaction compared with what they perceive to be ideal. The term QoL has been used in different ways in medicine (e.g., Farquhar, 1995). The popularity of the terms QoL or "health-related QoL" is also reflected in the "branding" or "labeling" of results measured by various instruments. For example, the 36-Item Short Form Health Survey explicitly developed as a health survey, has been widely used for "(health-related) QoL" claims. The most widely accepted definition of the term QoL has been provided by the WHO (1997), which defined QoL as being as broad and inclusive as the definition of health. According to the WHO, QoL is defined as an individual's perception of their position in life in the context of the culture and value systems in which they live and in relation to their goals, expectations, standards, and concerns. Health economics also boarded the rapidly moving train of QoL assessment and research. With the introduction of patient-preference approaches, an attempt was made to weigh the dimension of health and to provide a single unitary expression of health status (Kaplan & Bush, 1982). Quality-adjusted life years (QALYs) represent the attempt to combine QoL assessment with the number of life years lived. QALYs are being used to evaluate medical treatment regimes, health programs as well as informed decision-making processes. QUALYs introduced disability-adjusted life years (DALYs), a measure of the number of years of life that are lost by a disability resulting from an illness.

Despite the notion that QoL assessment and research in general focus on the individual, particularly in medicine, theory and practice do not fully live up to this idea. The individual QoL approach is just one of many in QoL research (Bowling, 2001; Joyce et al., 1999). Despite the widespread agreement about the importance of QoL assessment in healthcare, few researchers define the concept or state the theoretical model of QoL they want to assess or use (Patrick & Chiang, 2000). Most researchers opt for an operational definition based on what an instrument measures, with only a small proportion of research investigating theoretical models and underlying pathways of QoL assessments (e.g., Höfer et al., 2005, Ring et al., 2006). Many of the QoL instruments focus on symptoms and functioning and would be better described as measures of health status. Hardly any of these instruments assess individual values or preferences. Using a set of predefined questions, the measurement already defines the range of outcomes and does not necessarily represent the choice or preference of an individual. The general implication is that QoL means the same thing to everyone and can be defined and measured in general terms, based on a set of items. Also, scoring presents problems as the answer to each question is given an equal weight based on the assumption that the importance for different life areas is the same for all individuals. Some instruments do use weights based on normative samples, though the meaningfulness for the individual remains unclear. Even if the development of instruments is based on focus groups, allowing patient groups, careers, and healthcare professionals alike to highlight relevant domains considered critical and important to be measured during the instrument development phase, data may still be gathered on the level of functional limitations, symptoms, distress, or global well-being, without fully understanding the meaning these terms carry for each patient (Rapkin et al., 1994).

This highlights the complexity of QoL assessment from a truly individual perspective. The challenge is to allow the individual to specify the content of their concept of QoL (domains), to rate the importance of these domains (weighing schema), and to assess the level of functioning or satisfaction with these (O'Boyle et al., 2005). Even with the wide acceptance of the importance of patient perception and values, there are ongoing developments to estimate patients' perceptions through physicians or algorithms undermining the principal concept of QoL assessment in medicine (e.g., Pakhomov et al., 2008).

Relevance

The necessity to assess the impact medical interventions have on the patient and not only on the body, in particular in patients with chronic diseases such as heart disease or cancer, or for terminally ill patients, became one of the driving forces for the exponential uptake of QoL research in healthcare. Rapid development of medical knowledge led to an increase in diagnostic and therapeutic options, which implicitly also created more medical decision-making situations. Medical paternalism was for a long time (and in part still is) standard when it comes to these decision-making processes. However, decision-making may not be always straightforward, and respect for patient autonomy or preferences is increasing. Ultimately, the goal is to achieve shared decision-making by taking patients' preferences and choices into account (Drolet & White, 2012). The shift toward patient-centered healthcare and the paradigm shift in medicine based on a bio-psycho-social model fueled this movement as well (Engel, 1977). Efforts of the Food and Drug Administration to support product claims by the pharmaceutical and medical device industry based on improvements in patient-reported outcomes (QoL) got the healthcare industry on board and enhanced the momentum of QoL assessment even further. From a broader perspective, the relevance of measuring QoL is currently not only purely altruistic with a patient-centered focus; there are also economic aspects at stake.

Practical relevance has been demonstrated in how QoL assessment can change the doctor–patient interaction with cancer patients (Velikova et al., 2002; Velikova et al., 2004). In particular, the assessment of QoL before counseling sessions with immediate feedback of the patients' QoL enables the physician to perform better, more focused consultations, with both physicians and patients being more satisfied with the interaction. Another prime example of the clinical relevance of using QoL measures is the ability to predict disease trajectory, including rehospitalization, relapse, or mortality for heart disease patients (Benzer et al., 2016; Hansen et al., 2015). Benzer et al. (2016) studied 791 patients after coronary artery revascularization and showed that patients with a low or moderate health-related QoL score were at an 80 % higher risk for unplanned hospital readmission compared to patients reporting high health-related QoL scores over 3 years. Hansen et al. (2015) reported similar results, demonstrating a linear relationship of lower global health-related QoL over 5 years in ischemic heart disease patients and all-cause mortality and cardiac readmission. Both studies controlled for confounding variables such as age, sex, disease severity, comorbidities, etc., and reported the predictive validity of health-related QoL scores over time for heart disease patients. Extending these observations in heart disease patients, Höfer et al. (2014), who followed 385 patients from preintervention baseline to 1 month and 3 months postintervention, found that changes in scores in health-related QoL over time following clinical interventions also predict 4-year survival rates.

Despite the great momentum in QoL research in healthcare, some challenges require further research. One very basic challenge that is still not fully resolved relates to the meaning and interpretation of QoL scores, in particular change scores. This is a high-priority issue as these measures are more and more in place when it comes to patient-centered care and policy. QoL change can be meaningful from different perspectives such as the societalone, taking population levels into account with small differences, or the institutional angle, which focuses on the degree of change required to influence healthcare policies. These contrast with the individual perspective, which focuses on the meaningful change of QoL for an individual. The minimal important difference (MID) is a relevant patient-centered concept that captures both the magnitude of improvement and the value patients place on such change. Minimal important differences and minimal clinically important differences (MICD) are often used synonymously in the literature. A recent literature review revealed that the methodology to develop MIDs/MICDs is not consistently applied and varies between anchor-based and distribution-based methods. Further, most MIDs are reported as single numbers, lacking information about confidence intervals around the MIDs (Jayadevappa et al., 2017).

Besides the challenge of interpreting change scores in HRQOL, there are the response-shift phenomena (Sprangers & Schwartz, 1999). Individuals actively construct meaning from their environment and display a range of cognitive mechanisms to continually adapt to changing circumstances. Response shift refers to a change in the meaning of one's evaluation of a construct (such as QoL) resulting from a change in one's internal standards of measurement, a change in one's values, or a change in one's definition of the construct. These changes may spring from external factors such as a treatment, a change in health status, or other circumstances as well as from within a person. Three different types of response shift have been described so far (Sprangers & Schwartz, 1999): (1) Reconceptualization: a change in one's definition of the target construct; (2) Recalibration: a change in one's internal standards of measurement; (3) Reprioritization: a change in one's values. Repeated measurements as a standard methodology in clinical trials may seriously be affected by response-shift phenomena. This variety of potential changes has important implications for reliably assessing the true effects of treatments. Change in QoL scores may reflect a response shift, a true treatment effect, or a complex combination thereof; reversely, no identified change over time may be masked by a response shift. Ring et al. (2005) demonstrated in 117 dental patients that the true improvement in QoL of denture treatment for edentulous patients would have been missed if only common pre/post measurement had been carried out. By using the so-called thentest (Sprangers et al., 1999) and an individualized measure of QoL assessment (SEIQOL; O'Boyle et al., 1992), the authors showed that the treatment effect was hidden by response shift phenomena.

Other challenges relate to crosscultural issues. It is common practice that QoL life instruments are developed in one language from one cultural background and then translated into other languages. However, translation is not enough: Cultural values and aspects need to be integrated, which is rarely done.

A very practical challenge when developing new QoL instruments is cost. The development of QoL instruments is time consuming and cost intensive as these instruments have to meet well-established scientific criteria (Scientific Advisory Committee of the Medical Outcomes Trust, 2002). Even if some instruments are funded through public grants, exploitation strategies and licensing considerations are rarely part of the initial development to ensure the long-term impact and integrity of these instruments. Changes to existing instruments are usually prohibited without written formal agreement of the original authors. Hence, it is strongly recommended that, when embarking on the journey of developing a QoL instrument, exploitation strategies be considered from an early stage, including resolving issues of intellectual property rights.

Assessment Instruments

To date, assessment of QoL has proceeded largely via paper-pencil instruments. Over the last decade, however, more and more studies have started to present surveys on touchscreens, computers, tablets, mobile phones, etc., using offline standalone programs or online platforms to collect data. With the advancement of technology, such experience-sampling methods are becoming a viable option for collecting multiple self-reports of an individual's (near) real-time feelings or thoughts regarding their QoL. Experience-sampling methods let participants assess their QoL at random time intervals through questionnaires and allow its tracking over time.

The following section gives examples of well-established QoL measures, considered state of the art in their respective field (see Table 5.1 for an overview of the measures). It is not comprehensive. Because of the plethora of instruments available, we recommend a thorough literature research before selecting a suitable instrument for an individual research project.

Table 5.1. Overview of QoL measures

Instrument name	Authors	Focus	Number of items	Reliability	Validity	Further information
SF-36 (V1, V2)		Generic (adults)	36	α: .57–.93	CV, DV, PV	https://www.optum.com/ https://rand.org
WHOQOL		Generic (adults)	100	α: .59–91	CV, DV, PV	https://who.int
EQ-5D	EuroQoL Group (1990)	Generic (adults)	5	ICC: 0.43–82	CV, DV, PV	https://www.euroqol.org
SEIQoL	O'Boyle et al. (1992)	Generic (adults)	30	R^2 > .70	CV, DV, PV	e-publications@RCSI
PedsQL	Varni et al. (1999)	Generic (children)	23	α: .88–.90	CV, DV, PV	https://www.pedsql.org/
KINDL	Bullinger et al. (1994)	Generic (children)	24	α: .85	CV, DV, PV	http://kindl.org
QLQ-C30	Aaronson et al. (1993)	Disease-specific (cancer, adults)	30	α: .62–.92 r_{tt}: .63–.91	CV, DV, PV	https://qol.eortc.org
MacNew	Oldridge et al. (1991)	Disease-specific (heart disease, adults)	27	α: .91–.96 r_{tt}: .75–.86	CV, DV, PV	http://www.macnew.org
QOLIBRI	v. Steinbüchel et al. (2010)	Disease-specific (traumatic brain injury, adults)	37	α: .75–89 r_{tt}: .78–85	CV, DV, PV	http://www.qolibrinet.com

Note. SF-36 = 36-Item Short Form Survey (V1 = version 1, V2 = version 2); SEIQoL = Schedule for the Evaluation of Individual Quality of Life; PedsQL = Pediatric Quality of Life Inventory; QLQ-C30 = Quality of Life of Cancer Patients Questionnaire; MacNew = MacNew Heart Disease Health-Related Quality of Life Instrument; QOLIBRI = Quality of Life After Brain Injury. α = Cronbach's α. CV = content validity, DV = discriminant validity, PV = predictive validity.

Brief Description of the Main Instruments

The WHOQOL

The WHOQOL is based on the WHO definition of QoL (see above) and is also considered a generic QoL instrument. Its development took particular cultural aspects into account, making it a truly global QoL measure for various reasons. In contrast to other QoL measures it also takes the environment and religion/spirituality into account. 100 items are grouped into six domains: physical health, psychological, level of independence, social relations, environment, and religion/spirituality. The WHOQOL has been extensively validated worldwide, and national language versions can be obtained through the local developers. The average duration to complete the instrument is 30–45 min.

A short version, the WHOQOL BREF, based on 26 questions, was developed as the long version might not be useful in every context. The WHOQOL BREF consists of four domains: physical health, psychological, social relationships, and environment, which correlate well with the original domains based on the WHOQOL 100 (r=. 89 to .95). The WHOQOL BREF is completed within 5–10 min.

The 36-Item Short Form Survey (SF-36)

The SF-36 version 1 is probably the most used generic QoL measure worldwide. It was developed within the Medical Outcome Study in the U.S. and is freely available from the RAND cooperation at https://www.rand.org/. It comprises eight scales based on 36 items: Four scales focus on physical health (physical functioning, role-physical, bodily pain, and general heath) and four assess mental health (vitality, social functioning, role-emotional, and mental health). Each of the four scales is summarized into two summary component scales measuring physical health and mental health. It is available in almost all languages worldwide, and detailed documentation of its psychometric properties is available for different languages and different diseases. Besides a self-rating version, a proxy-rating version is also available. The SF-36 has been further refined, and a commercial version 2 is available at https://www.optum.com/. One of the differences between the two versions is the norm-based scoring system of the SF-36 v2, where all eight scale scores are converted to an average of 50 ± 10 *SD*, allowing for easier interpretation. This needs to be carefully reflected on by researchers and clinicians as it may lead to confusion with previous SF-36 reports based on the traditional scoring range of 0–100. A short form, the SF-12, is also available. Additionally, there have been efforts within the scientific community to develop health utility values for the SF by generating a SF-6D (Brazier et al., 2002). The SF-6D allows for the assessment of up to 18,000 different health states that can be derived from data collected through either the SF-36 or the SF-12.

In contrast to the WHOQoL, the SF-36 has been translated from English into other languages, and cultural aspects reflecting particular patient values may have been disregarded in the development of the national versions of the SF-36. However, this critique may very well extend to other more or less established QoL measures (also discussed here); to date, this has been a common process and developing an instrument in one language based on one cultural value system and then translating it into other languages or adapting it for other cultures is the gold standard. Therefore, generally speaking, exporting implicit social values and norms reflected in the items chosen in a particular QoL measure may well become an issue when QoL is compared across cultures using the value set of a specific nation.

The EQ-5D

Another widespread generic QoL measure is the EuroQoL-5D (EQ-5D; EuroQol Group, 1990), which is based on five health dimensions (mobility, self-care, usual activities, pain and discomfort, and anxiety and depression). These dimensions are rated on a 3-point scale allowing for 243 different health states. These states can be related with a global scale (ranging from 0–100) also called the "health thermometer." It further has been extensively used to develop health utility sets, allowing the calculation for QUALYs. Hence, the most widespread use of the EQ-5D is typically in health economics, including patient outcomes. The length of the instrument is a true benefit, though with five dimensions and three answer options the scope is limited, so its use should be accompanied by disease-specific instruments. Later, the EQ-5D-5L was introduced to improve the instrument's sensitivity and to reduce ceiling effects. The main difference is that the 3-point answering scale was transformed to five answering options (no problems, slight problems, moderate problems, severe problems, and extreme problems). Also, the wording of one item was modified from "confined to bed" to "unable to walk about." A child- and adolescent-friendly version was also introduced for the age group 8–15 years, with a proxy-version also available.

The Schedule for the Evaluation of Individual Quality of Life (SEIQoL)

The SEIQoL is a rather unique QoL instrument, as it assumes that QoL is defined as "what the individual determines it to be" (O'Boyle et al., 1993). Hence, it presents no specific items but rather open questions. First, subjects are asked to nominate and describe those five areas of their lives (cues) they consider to be most central to their perceived QoL. In a second step, subjects are then asked to assess the current status or level of satisfaction/functioning on each cue using a visual analog scale. In a third step, they rate their current overall QoL on a visual analog scale. After that, they assess the relevant weight of each cue, which is done by a weighting procedure designed to examine the importance attached by the individual to each cue based on judgment analysis (Hammond et al., 1975). Judgment analysis, a method derived from social judgment theory, makes use of multiple regression analysis to model the structure of an individual's "judgment policy" by quantifying the weight they give to each cue in judging the QoL associated with 30 hypothetical cases. These 30 hypothetical cases are predefined variations in the level of functioning for the cues used by the individual. By examining its importance, this step quantifies the relative contribution of each cue to the individual's judgment of their overall QoL. Since the individual is not explicitly asked to rank the importance of each cue, the derived values incorporate implicit ("unconscious") elements into the weighting procedure. A single score (the SEIQoL Index Score) is calculated by multiplying each cue weight by its corresponding level and summing the products across the five cues. Because this is quite a complex method of determining cue weights, Hickey et al. (1996) developed a direct weighing (SEIQoL-DW) procedure that replaces the 30 hypothetical cases weighting procedure by allocating 100 points to each cue using a pie chart. The pie chart contains five overlapping discs, each of which represents one QoL cue nominated and rated by the respondent. The subject is asked to optically arrange the five overlapping discs such that each visible part of the disc reflects the importance of each cue (e.g., the more weight the person gives to a cue, the larger the visible part of the section). The SEIQoL-DW appears to be a feasible and valid instrument (Wettergren et al., 2009), and the direct weighting method is becoming increasingly popular, though it cannot provide the depth of information collected through the full SEIQoL. Both the SEIQoL-DW and the SEIQoL are more or less semistructured interviews and hence time consuming (Becker et al., 2014).

The SEIQoL and the SEIQoL-DW have been employed in a range of interventions such as in hip-replacement surgery (O'Boyle et al., 1992), in terminally ill patients (Waldron et al., 1999), in patients with ALS (Felgoise et al., 2009), in edentulous patients (Lena Ring et al., 2005), and many more. Medical staff have noticed that it provides potentially valuable information for doctor–patient consultations, although it is probably too time consuming for standard medical clerking (Mountain et al., 2004).

The Pediatric Quality of Life Inventory (PedsQL)

The PedsQL takes a modular approach to measuring health-related QoL in healthy children and adolescents and in those with acute and chronic health conditions. The PedsQL measurement model seamlessly integrates both generic core scales and disease-specific modules into a single measurement system. The core PedsQL consists of 23 items assigned to four scales (Physical functioning, Emotional functioning, Social functioning, and School functioning). Different versions adjusted for the developmental phases of children and adolescents are available (5–7, 8–12, 13–18 years). Additionally, there are proxy versions for parents or caretakers. In addition to the above age brackets, a proxy version for 2–4 years is available. The instrument is available in over 60 languages. A short version with 15 items has also been developed. Disease-specific modules include arthritis, asthma, brain tumor, cancer, cardiac, diabetes, epilepsy, pain, and many more (Varni et al., 1999).

The KINDL

Another child-specific QoL instrument is the so-called KINDL, which is a generic instrument for assessing health-related QoL in children and adolescents aged 3 years and older. The KINDL has now been translated into over 25 languages with norm values available. It consists of 24 items, and three versions based on the developmental stage of the children are provided (4–6, 7–13, 14–17 years). A proxy version to be completed by the parents or caretaker is also available. The 24 items are combined in 6 scales (Physical well-being, Emotional well-being, Self-esteem, Family, Friends, and Everyday functioning). Because it is a generic QoL insert, additional modules for certain diseases/conditions have been developed (e.g., cancer, obesity, asthma bronchial, diabetes, epilepsy) (Bullinger et al., 2008; Ravens-Sieberer & Bullinger, 1998).

The Quality of Life of Cancer Patients Questionnaire (QLQ-C30)

The QLQ was developed by the European Organization for Research and Treatment of Cancer (EORTC), an independent, nonprofit cancer research organization with the mission to coordinate and conduct international translational and clinical research to improve the standard of cancer treatment for patients. The original version of the QLQ was published by Aaronson et al. (1993) as a 36-item version capturing QoL, symptoms, and health status of adult cancer patients. Since then, the questionnaire has undergone several changes. The current version, the QLQ-C30, is designed to assess generic aspects of QOL in cancerwith 30 items split into scales: functional scales (e.g., physical, emotional, cognitive, etc.) and symptom scales (e.g., fatigue, pain, etc.). Additionally, 6 single-item questions are presented (e.g., constipation, sleep, etc.) and 2 items comprise a global QoL scale. Most of these scales consist of only 2 items (Hjermstad et al., 1995; Kaasa et al., 1995; Osoba et al., 1994). Additionally, to address aspects specific to particular tumor sites, treatment modalities, or symptoms, a modular approach has been adopted with further cancer-specific items included alongside the 30 core items. A highly standardized approach has been adopted for the development of these modules to ensure uniformly high quality.

The QLQ-C30 is currently available in over 40 languages, has extensively been shown to be valid, reliable, and responsive to change, and has been used in over 600 studies with cancer patients. On a critical note, despite focusing and being called a QoL questionnaire, it mainly concerns health status and symptoms, with only 2 items focusing on QoL.

The MacNew Heart Disease Health-Related Quality of Life Instrument (MacNew)

An example for a disease-specific, health-related QoL instrument in the field of cardiology is the MacNew, which was originally developed as the Quality of Life After Myocardial Infarction Questionnaire (Oldridge et al., 1991) but has since been further developed into the MacNew (Höfer et al., 2004). The MacNew comprises 27 items in 3 scales (physical, emotional, and social HRQOL); a total score is also available. The instrument has been translated and culturally adopted for over 40 languages. The MacNew is based on the WHO definition of health and measures the perception of physical, emotional, and social aspects related to heart disease. It is the only health-related QoL instrument for heart-disease patients with items formulated to address physical, emotional, or social health-related QoL from a subjective perspective. This differs from other instruments that generally address the functional status. Also, rarely do patient-reported outcome measures in heart disease use the full definition of health when measuring QoL. Although originally developed as a myocardial infarction-specific questionnaire, today the MacNew is considered a core heart disease health-related QoL measure, valid and reliable for myocardial infarction (e.g., Alphin et al., 2015), angina (e.g., Alphin et al., 2015), and heart failure (e.g., Mozenska et al., 2019). It has been extensively used in evaluating cardiac rehabilitation programs (e.g., Salavati et al., 2015) but also has been successfully applied in clinical trials with patients undergoing bypass surgery (e.g., Wauthy et al., 2019), percutaneous coronary interventions (e.g., Al Abdi et al., 2019), pacemaker implantations (e.g., Höfer, Anelli-Monti et al., 2005), or defibrillators (e.g., Undavia et al., 2008). There are also established reference values for minimal important differences.

The Quality of Life After Brain Injury (QOLIBRI)

The QOLIBRI is the first instrument specifically developed to assess disease-specific health-related QoL of adults (>18) years after traumatic brain injury (TBI) It was developed by an international task force in two multilanguage studies involving over 2,000 individuals after TBI (von Steinbüchel et al., 2010, von Steinbuechel et al., 2012). The questionnaire is based on 37 items, combined in six dimensions. The first four dimensions "Cognition," "Self," "Daily Life and Autonomy," and "Social Relationships" assess satisfaction with them, while the remaining two scales "Emotions" and "Physical Problems" assess how bothersome they are. A total score can be calculated. It is easy to fill in and can be completed in 7–10 min. It is suitable for use in clinical settings, research studies, and population surveys. A short version of the QOLIBRI, the QOLIBRI Overall Scale (QOLIBRI OS) is also available, with 6 items asking for the overall satisfaction or feeling bothered of the six dimensions. The reliability of the QOLIBRI-OS is good (Cronbach's α=.86, test-retest reliability=.81) and strongly correlates with the total QOLIBRI scores (r=.87). It performs equally well in participants with higher and lower cognitive performance. Factor analysis indicated that the scale is unidimensional (von Steinbuechel et al., 2012).

Recommendations for Instrument Selection

One of the most important questions to be answered when selecting an existing instrument is its fit for purpose. Most instruments these days provide solid background information on their conceptual models, scales, and items as well as their psychometric performance in the past. Despite the label of instruments or their respective scales indicating what they intend to measure, it is most important to read through each question of an instrument under consideration to ensure the content is actually what you intend to measure in the planned study or project. Hence, the first recommendation for instrument selection is to closely read the instrument and the respective response options. The second recommendation concerns past psychometric performance indicators, which can be an excellent aid in helping to narrow down the selection process. However, past excellent performance may not always guarantee that the instrument will perform well in the population selected for research purposes. Therefore, basic psychometric checking of the investigated sample is mandatory before analyzing and reporting the actual results of the study. Among the psychometric properties to guide one through the selection process, indicators for reliability have a higher priority than indicators for validity. If the performance of an instrument is not reliable, the validity may be of concern as well. Finally, if the intention is to measure change over time, responsiveness indicators and availability of interpretation guidance, for example, on minimal important differences, should be taken into account.

A good resource for selecting outcome measures is the COSMIN project (www.cosmin.nl), which aims to improve the selection of outcome measurement instruments both in research and in clinical practice by developing methodology and practical tools for selecting the most suitable outcome measurement instrument. The project authors have developed guidelines on how to conduct systematic reviews on patient-reported outcome measures and recommend 10 steps to do so (Prinsen et al., 2018).

When it comes to product claim aspects, which quite often is the case in medical research, the US Food and Drug Administration (FDA) and its European counterpart, the European Medicine Agency (EMA), provide guidance papers that can help select appropriate outcome measures (Revicki et al., 2007). Finally, before selecting an instrument, one can apply the criteria for instrument development provided by the Scientific Advisory Board of the Medical Outcomes Trust (2002) as a reference to check the candidate instruments.

Conclusion, Comments, and Future Directions

QoL assessment, particularly within healthcare, triggered the start of a change in how medicine captures and integrates patients' views. For the first time, the introduction of QoL assessments allowed the systematic registration of the so-called patient's voice within the medical discipline. Of course, there are still conceptual and measurement problems, such as validly capturing individual QoL or dealing with response shift phenomena over time. An unresolved question concerns how to integrate QoL assessment into clinical routine care. The emerging trend toward computer adaptive testing and the utilization of mobile devices may prove to help overcome this obstacle. Overall, there is ample evidence that it is worthwhile to measure QoL in all medical disciplines, and that it has implications for treatment decisions and may also improve the quality of doctor-patient interaction in the long term.

References

Aaronson, N. K., Ahmedzai, S., Bergman, B., Bullinger, M., Cull, A., Duez, N. J., Filiberti, A., Flechtner, H., Fleishman, S. B., de Haes, J. C. J. M., Kaasa, S., Klee, M., Osoba, D., Razavi, D., Rofe, P. B., Schraub, S., Sneeuw, K., Sullivan, M., & Takeda, F. (1993). The European Organization for Research and Treatment of Cancer QLQ-C30: A quality-of-life instrument for use in international clinical trials in oncology. *Journal of the National Cancer Institute, 85*(5), 365–376. https://doi.org/10.1093/jnci/85.5.365

Al Abdi, R. M., Alshraideh, H., Hijazi, H. H., Jarrah, M., & Alyahya, M. S. (2019). The use of echocardiographic and clinical data recorded on admission to simplify decision making for elective percutaneous coronary intervention: A prospective cohort study. *BMC Medical Informatics and Decision-making, 19*(1), Article 46. https://doi.org/10.1186/s12911-019-0797-9

Alphin, S., Höfer, S., Perk, J., Slørdahl, S., Zwisler, A. D. O., & Oldridge, N. (2015). The MacNew Heart Disease Health-Related Quality of Life Questionnaire: A Scandinavian validation study. *Social Indicators Research, 122*(2), 519–537. https://doi.org/10.1007/s11205-014-0694-7

Becker, G., Merk, C. S., Meffert, C., & Momm, F. (2014). Measuring individual quality of life in patients receiving radiation therapy: The SEIQoL-Questionnaire. *Quality of Life Research, 23*(7), 2025–2030. https://doi.org/10.1007/s11136-014-0661-4

Benzer, W., Philippi, A., Höfer, S., Friedrich, O., & Oldridge, N. (2016). Health-related quality of life predicts unplanned rehospitalization following coronary revascularization. *Herz, 41*(2), 138–143. https://doi.org/10.1007/s00059-015-4351-y

Bowling, A. (2001). *Measuring disease*. Open University Press.

Brazier, J., Roberts, J., & Deverill, M. (2002). The estimation of a preference-based measure of health from the SF-36. *Journal of Health Economics, 21*(2), 271–292. https://doi.org/10.1016/S0167-6296(01)00130-8

Bullinger, M., Brütt, A.L., Erhart, M., & Ravens-Sieberer, U. (2008). Psychometric properties of the KINDL-R questionnaire: Results of the BELLA study. *European Child and Adolescent Psychiatry, 17*(Suppl. 1), 125–132. https://doi.org/10.1007/s00787-008-1014-z

Bullinger, M., von Mackensen, S., & Kirchberger, I. (1994). KINDL – Ein Fragebogen zur Erfassung der gesundheitsbezogenen Lebensqualität von Kindern [KINDL – questionnaire for the assessment of health-related quality of life in children]. *Zeitschrift für Gesundheitspsychologie, 2*, 64–77.

Diener, E., Lucas, R., Schimmack, U., & Helliwell, J. (2010). *Well-being for public policy*. Oxford University Press. https://doi.org/10.1093/acprof:oso/9780195334074.001.0001

Drolet, B.C., & White, C.L. (2012). Selective paternalism. *The Virtual Mentor, 14*(7), 582–588. https://doi.org/10.1001/virtualmentor.2012.14.7.oped2-1207

Engel, G.L. (1977). The need for a new medical model: A challenge for biomedicine. *Science, 196*(4286), 129–136. https://doi.org/10.1126/science.847460

EuroQol Group. (1990). EuroQol: A new facility for the measurement of health-related quality of life. *Health Policy, 16*(3), 199–208. https://doi.org/10.1016/0168-8510(90)90421-9

Farquhar, M. (1995). Definitions of quality of life: A taxonomy. *Journal of Advanced Nursing, 22*(3), 502–508. https://doi.org/10.1046/j.1365-2648.1995.22030502.x

Felgoise, S.H., Stewart, J.L., Bremer, B.A., Walsh, S.M., Bromberg, M.B., & Simmons, Z. (2009). The SEIQoL-DW for assessing quality of life in ALS: Strengths and limitations. *Amyotrophic Lateral Sclerosis, 10*(5–6), 456–462. https://doi.org/10.3109/17482960802444840

Hammond, K., Stewart, T., Brehmer, B., & D, S. (1975). Social judgment theory. In M. Kaplan & S. Schwarz (Eds.), *Human judgment and decision making* (pp. 272–312). Academic Press. https://doi.org/10.1016/B978-0-12-397250-7.50016-7

Hansen, T.B., Thygesen, L.C., Zwisler, A.D., Helmark, L., Hoogwegt, M., Versteeg, H., Höfer, S., & Oldridge, N. (2015). Self-reported health-related quality of life predicts 5-year mortality and hospital readmissions in patients with ischaemic heart disease. *European Journal of Preventive Cardiology, 22*(7), 882–889. https://doi.org/10.1177/2047487314535682

Hickey, A.M., Bury, G., O'Boyle, C.A., Bradley, F., O'Kelly, F.D., & Shannon, W. (1996). A new short form individual quality of life measure (SEIQoL-DW): Application in a cohort of individuals with HIV/AIDS. *BMJ (Clinical Research Ed.), 313*(7048), 29–33. https://doi.org/10.1136/bmj.313.7048.29

Hjermstad, M.J., Fossa, S.D., Bjordal, K., & Kaasa, S. (1995). Test/retest study of the European Organization for Research and Treatment of Cancer Core Quality-of-Life Questionnaire. *Journal of Clinical Oncology, 13*(5), 1249–1254. https://doi.org/10.1200/JCO.1995.13.5.1249

Höfer, S., Anelli-Monti, M., Berger, T., Hintringer, F., Oldridge, N., & Benzer, W. (2005). Psychometric properties of an established heart disease specific health-related quality of life questionnaire for pacemaker patients. *Quality of Life Research, 14*(8), 1937–1942. https://doi.org/10.1007/s11136-005-4347-9

Höfer, S., Benzer, W., Alber, H., Ruttmann, E., Kopp, M., Schüssler, G., & Doering, S. (2005). Determinants of health-related quality of life in coronary artery disease patients: A prospective study generating a structural equation model. *Psychosomatics, 46*(3), 212–223. https://doi.org/10.1176/appi.psy.46.3.212

Höfer, S., Benzer, W., & Oldridge, N. (2014). Change in health-related quality of life in patients with coronary artery disease predicts 4-year mortality. *International Journal of Cardiology, 174*(1), 7–12. https://doi.org/10.1016/j.ijcard.2014.03.144

Höfer, S., Lim, L., Guyatt, G., & Oldridge, N. (2004). The MacNew Heart Disease health-related quality of life instrument: A summary. *Health and Quality of Life Outcomes, 2*, Article 3. https://doi.org/10.1186/1477-7525-2-3

Jayadevappa, R., Cook, R., & Chhatre, S. (2017). Minimal important difference to infer changes in health-related quality of life: A systematic review. *Journal of Clinical Epidemiology, 89*, 188–198. https://doi.org/10.1016/j.jclinepi.2017.06.009

Joyce, C., McGee, H., & O'Boyle, C. (Eds.). (1999). *Individual quality of life: Approaches to conceptualisation and assessment*. Harwood.

Kaasa, S., Bjordal, K., Aaronson, N., Moum, T., Wist, E., Hagen, S., & Kvikstad, A. (1995). The EORTC Core Quality of Life Questionnaire (QLQ-C30): Validity and reliability when analysed with patients treated with palliative radiotherapy. *European Journal of Cancer, 31*(13–14), 2260–2263. https://doi.org/10.1016/0959-8049(95)00296-0

Kaplan, R., & Bush, J. (1982). Health-related quality of life measurement for evaluation research and policy analysis. *Health Psychology, 1*(1), 61–80. https://doi.org/10.1037/0278-6133.1.1.61

Karnofsky, D., & Burchenal, J. (1949). The clinical evaluation of chemotherapeutic agents in cancer. In C. MacLeod (Ed.), *Evaluation of chemotherapeutic agents* (pp. 191–205). Columbia University Press.

Michalos, A.C. (2017). Quality of life, two-variable theory. In *Development of quality of life theory and its instruments: The selected works of Alex. C. Michalos* (pp. 1–4). Springer. https://doi.org/10.1007/978-3-319-51149-8_1

Mountain, L.A., Campbell, S.E., Seymour, D.G., Primrose, W.R., & Whyte, M.I. (2004). Assessment of individual quality of life using the SEIQoL-DW in older medical patients. *QJM : Monthly Journal of the Association of Physicians, 97*(8), 519–524. https://doi.org/10.1093/qjmed/hch081

Mozenska, O., Bil, J., Segiet, A., & Kosior, D.A. (2019). The influence of calcium-phosphate metabolism abnormalities on the quality of life in patients with hemodynamically significant mitral regurgitation. *BMC Cardiovascular Disorders, 19*, Article 116. https://doi.org/10.1186/s12872-019-1094-3

O'Boyle, C., Höfer, S., & Ring, L. (2005). Individualized quality of life. In P. Fayers & R. Hays (Eds.), *Assessing quality of life in clincal trials. Methods and practice* (2nd ed., pp. 225–242). Oxford University Press.

O'Boyle, C., McGee, H., Hickey, A., Joyce, C., Browne, J., O'Malley, K., & Hiltbrunner, B. (1993). *The Schedule for the Evaluation of Individual Quality of Life (SEIQoL). Administration manual.* Royal College of Surgeons in Ireland.

O'Boyle, C., McGee, H., Hickey, A., & O'Malley, K. (1992). Individual quality of life in patients undergoing hip replacement. *Lancet, 339*(10), 1088–1091. https://doi.org/10.1016/0140-6736(92)90673-Q

Oldridge, N., Guyatt, G., Jones, N., Crowe, J., Singer, J., Feeny, D., McKelvie, R., Runions, J., Streiner, D., & Torrance, G. (1991). Effects on quality of life with comprehensive rehabilitation after acute myocardial infarction. *The American Journal of Cardiology, 67*(13), 1084–1089. https://doi.org/10.1016/0002-9149(91)90870-Q

Osoba, D., Zee, B., Pater, J., Warr, D., Kaizer, L., & Latreille, J. (1994). Psychometric properties and responsiveness of the EORTC Quality of Life Questionnaire (QLQ-C30) in patients with breast, ovarian and lung cancer. *Quality of Life Research, 3*, 353–364. https://doi.org/10.1007/BF00451727

Pakhomov, S. V., Jacobsen, S.J., Chute, C.G., & Roger, V.L. (2008). Agreement between patient-reported symptoms and their documentation in the medical record. *The American Journal of Managed Care, 14*(8), 530–539.

Patrick, D.L., & Chiang, Y.P. (2000). Measurement of health outcomes in treatment effectiveness evaluations: Conceptual and methodological challenges. *Medical Care, 38*(9 Suppl), II14–25. https://doi.org/10.1097/00005650-200009002-00005

Prinsen, C.A.C., Mokkink, L.B., Bouter, L.M., Alonso, J., Patrick, D.L., de Vet, H.C.W., & Terwee, C.B. (2018). COSMIN guideline for systematic reviews of patient-reported outcome measures. *Quality of Life Research, 27*(5), 1147–1157. https://doi.org/10.1007/s11136-018-1798-3

Rapkin, B.D., Smith, M.Y., Dumont, K., Correa, A.M.P.A., Palmer, S., & Cohen, S. (1994). Development of the Idiographic functional status assessment: A measure of the personal goals and goal attainment activities of people with AIDS. *Psychology and Health, 98*, 111–129. https://doi.org/10.1080/08870449408407463

Ravens-Sieberer, U., & Bullinger, M. (1998). Assessing health-related quality of life in chronically ill children with the German KINDL: First psychometric and content analytical results. *Quality of Life Research, 7*, 399–407. https://doi.org/10.1023/A:1008853819715

Revicki, D.A., Gnanasakthy, A., & Weinfurt, K. (2007). Documenting the rationale and psychometric characteristics of patient reported outcomes for labeling and promotional claims: The PRO Evidence Dossier. *Quality of Life Research, 16*, Article 717. https://doi.org/10.1007/s11136-006-9153-5

Ring, L., Höfer, S., Heuston, F., Harris, D., & O'Boyle, C.A. (2005). Response shift masks the treatment impact on patient reported outcomes (PROs): The example of individual quality of life in edentulous patients. *Health and Quality of Life Outcomes, 3*, Article 55. https://doi.org/10.1186/1477-7525-3-55

Ring, L., Höfer, S., McGee, H., Hickey, A., & O'Boyle, C.A. (2006). Individual quality of life: Can it be accounted for by psychological or subjective well-being? *Social Indicators Research, 82*(3), 443–461. https://doi.org/10.1007/s11205-006-9041-y

Salavati, M., Fallahinia, G., Vardanjani, A.E., Rafiei, H., Mousavi, S., & Torkamani, M. (2015). Comparison between effects of home based cardiac rehabilitation programs versus usual care on the patients' health related quality of life after coronary artery bypass graft. *Global Journal of Health Science, 8*(4), 196–202. https://doi.org/10.5539/gjhs.v8n4p196

Scientific Advisory Committee of the Medical Outcomes Trust. (2002). Assessing health status and quality-of-life instruments: Attributes and review criteria. *Quality of Life Research, 11*(3), 193–205. https://doi.org/10.1023/A:1015291021312

Skevington, S.M., & Bohnke, J.R. (2018). How is subjective well-being related to quality of life? Do we need two concepts and both measures? *Social Science & Medicine (1982), 206*, 22–30. https://doi.org/10.1016/j.socscimed.2018.04.005

Sprangers, M.A.G., & Schwartz, C.E. (1999). Integrating response shift into health-related quality of life research: A theoretical model. *Social Science and Medicine, 48*(11), 1507–1515. https://doi.org/10.1016/S0277-9536(99)00045-3

Sprangers, M.A.G., Van Dam, F.S.A.M., Broersen, J., Lodder, L., Wever, L.,Visser, M.R.M., Oosterveld, P., & Smets, E.M.A. (1999). Revealing response shift in longitudinal research on fatigue: The use of the thentest approach. *Acta Oncologica, 38*(6), 709–718. https://doi.org/10.1080/028418699432860

Undavia, M., Goldstein, N.E., Cohen, P., Sinthawanarong, K., Singson, M., Bhutani, D., Munson, T., Gomes, J.A., Fischer, A., & Mehta, D. (2008). Impact of implantable cardioverter-defibrillator recalls on patients' anxiety, depression, and quality of life. *Pacing and Clinical Electrophysiology, 31*(11), 1411–1418. https://doi.org/10.1111/j.1540-8159.2008.01204.x

Varni, J., Seid, M., & Rode, C. (1999). The PedsQL: Measurement model for the pediatric quality of life inventory. *Medical Care, 37*(2), 126–139. https://doi.org/10.1097/00005650-199902000-00003

Veenhoven, R. (2000). The four qualities of life. *Journal of Happiness Studies, 1*, 1–39. https://doi.org/10.1023/A:1010072010360

Velikova, G., Booth, L., Smith, A.B., Brown, P.M., Lynch, P., Brown, J.M., & Selby, P.J. (2004). Measuring quality of life in routine oncology practice improves communication and patient well-being: A randomized controlled trial. *Journal of Clinical Oncology, 22*(4), 714–724. https://doi.org/10.1200/JCO.2004.06.078

Velikova, G., Brown, J.M., Smith, A.B., & Selby, P.J. (2002). Computer-based quality of life questionnaires may contribute to doctor-patient interactions in oncology. *British Journal of Cancer, 86*, 51–59. https://doi.org/10.1038/sj.bjc.6600001

von Steinbüchel, N., Wilson, L., Gibbons, H., Hawthorne, G., Höfer, S., Schmidt, S., Bullinger, M., Maas, A., Neugebauer, E., Powell, J., von Wild, K., Zitnay, G., Bakx, W., Christensen, A.-L., Koskinen, S., Formisano, R., Saarajuri, J., Sasse, N., & Truelle, J.-L. (2010). Quality of Life after Brain Injury (QOLIBRI): Scale validity and correlates of quality of life. *Journal of Neurotrauma, 27*(7), 1157–1165. https://doi.org/10.1089/neu.2009.1077

von Steinbuechel, N., Wilson, L., Gibbons, H., Muehlan, H., Schmidt, H., Schmidt, S., Sasse, N., Koskinen, S.,Sarajuuri, J., Höfer, S., Bullinger, M., Maas, A., Neugebauer, E., Powell, J., von Wild, K., Zitnay, G., Bakx, W., Christensen, A.-L.,Formisano, R., Hawthorne, G., & Truelle, J.-L. (2012). QOLIBRI overall scale: A brief index of health-related quality of life after traumatic brain injury. *Journal of Neurology, Neurosurgery, and Psychiatry, 83*(11), 1041–1047. https://doi.org/10.1136/jnnp-2012-302361

Waldron, D., O'Boyle, C.A., Kearney, M., Moriarty, M., & Carney, D. (1999). Quality-of-life measurement in advanced cancer: Assessing the individual. *Journal of Clinical Oncology, 17*(11), 3603–3611. https://doi.org/10.1200/JCO.1999.17.11.3603

Wauthy, P., Pierrakos, C., Chebli, L., & Tortora, R. (2019). Long-term survival and quality of life in Jehovah's witnesses after cardiac surgery: A case control study. *BMC Cardiovascular Disorders, 19*(1), Article 73. https://doi.org/10.1186/s12872-019-1061-z

Wettergren, L., Kettis-Lindblad, A., Sprangers, M., & Ring, L. (2009). The use, feasibility and psychometric properties of an individualised quality-of-life instrument: a systematic review of the SEIQoL-DW. *Quality of Life Research, 18*(6), 737–746. https://doi.org/10.1007/s11136-009-9490-2

World Health Organization. (2020). Basic documents (49th ed., including amendments adopted up to 31 May 2019). https://apps.who.int/gb/bd/pdf_files/BD_49th-en.pdf#page=1

World Health Organization. Division of Mental Health and Prevention of Substance Abuse. (1997). *WHOQOL: Measuring quality of life*. https://apps.who.int/iris/handle/10665/63482

Part III

Positive Traits, States, and Behaviors

Chapter 6
Assessing Character Strengths

Lisa Wagner and Willibald Ruch

Department of Psychology, University of Zurich, Zurich, Switzerland

Character strengths are among the most frequently studied research topics in positive psychology (Donaldson et al., 2015). This chapter briefly introduces the VIA classification of character strengths and virtues (Peterson & Seligman, 2004) and discusses some general considerations when assessing character strengths. We then focus on reviewing different instruments that have been used to assess character strengths across different age groups and contexts. We provide an overview of the instruments available and the challenges that accompany assessing character strengths.

In 2004, as a result of a multiyear collaborative project, Christopher Peterson and Martin Seligman published *Character Strengths and Virtues: A Handbook and Classification*, which presents the VIA classification of character strengths and virtues. The VIA classification provides a framework for describing positively valued traits believed to contribute to a "good life." In creating this framework, Peterson and Seligman considered a wide range of sources, such as virtue lists from various world religions and philosophical traditions, developmental theories, youth programs, and organizations as well as other sources ranging from literature to popular culture.

To select character strengths, they used a set of criteria, most of which had to be met. These criteria included the following: A strength should (1) contribute to fulfillments that constitute the "good life," both for the individual and for other people, (2) be morally valuable in its own right (see Stahlmann & Ruch, 2020), (3) not demean others when displayed, (4) not have an opposite term that could also be seen as a strength (see Seligman, 2015), (5) be manifested in thoughts, feelings, and actions and consequently be measurable, and (6) be sufficiently distinct from all other strengths in the classification. Moreover, each character strength should have (7) universally recognized paragons, (8) prodigies (see Park & Peterson, 2006a), and (9) "imbeciles" who do not display the strength at all. Lastly, (10) societies should have institutions and rituals that are aimed at promoting the character strength. Later publications listed 12 criteria (see the discussion in Ruch & Stahlmann, 2019). Box 6.1 displays the VIA classification (Peterson & Seligman, 2004).

Relevant Definitions

The VIA classification assigned the 24 character strengths to six core virtues (see Box 6.1), which resulted from reviewing various philosophical and religious traditions across time and space (Dahlsgaard et al., 2005). On a hierarchically lower level lie situational themes. In their handbook, Peterson and Seligman (2004) define character strengths as "the psychological ingredients – processes or mechanisms – that define the virtues. Said another way, they are distinguishable routes to displaying one or another of the virtues" (p. 13). They also describe that character strengths "make the good life possible" (p. 4). For assessment purposes, a more operational definition would be helpful, therefore we define the relevant constructs of the VIA classification (Peterson & Seligman, 2004) as follows in this chapter:

- *Character strengths* are positively valued traits that contribute to "the good life" for an individual and others.
- *Virtues* are core characteristics that have been described and valued by both moral philosophers and religious thinkers across time and cultures.
- *Situational themes* are habits that allow individuals to display a certain character strength in a specific situation.

Peterson and Seligman (2004) argue that virtues are too abstract to be assessed in individuals. While ad-hoc measures based on the descriptions of the virtues (e.g., Ruch, Heintz et al., 2020) or on items assessing character strengths (e.g., McGrath, 2019) do exist for research purposes, their use for other purposes it is not recommended. We are not aware of instruments designed specifically for assessing situational themes. For this reason, we focus only on the assessment of character strengths in the following.

Box 6.1. VIA classification of character strengths and virtues

Wisdom and knowledge – Cognitive strengths that entail the acquisition and use of knowledge

- **Creativity** [originality, ingenuity]: Thinking of novel and productive ways to conceptualize and do things; includes artistic achievement but is not limited to it
- **Curiosity** [interest, novelty-seeking, openness to experience]: Taking an interest in ongoing experience for its own sake; finding subjects and topics fascinating; exploring and discovering
- **Judgment** [critical thinking]: Thinking things through and examining them from all sides; not jumping to conclusions; being able to change one's mind in light of evidence; weighing all evidence fairly
- **Love of Learning:** Mastering new skills, topics, and bodies of knowledge, whether on one's own or formally; obviously related to the strength of curiosity but goes beyond it to describe the tendency to add systematically to what one knows
- **Perspective** [wisdom]: Being able to provide wise counsel to others; having ways of looking at the world that make sense to oneself and to other people

Courage – Emotional strengths that involve the exercise of will to accomplish goals in the face of opposition, external or internal

- **Bravery** [valor]: Not shrinking from threat, challenge, difficulty, or pain; speaking up for what is right even if there is opposition; acting on convictions even if unpopular; includes physical bravery but is not limited to it
- **Perseverance** [persistence, industriousness]: Finishing what one starts; persisting in a course of action in spite of obstacles; "getting it out the door"; taking pleasure in completing tasks
- **Honesty** [authenticity, integrity]: Speaking the truth but more broadly presenting oneself in a genuine way and acting in a sincere way; being without pretense; taking responsibility for one's feelings and actions
- **Zest** [vitality, enthusiasm, vigor, energy]: Approaching life with excitement and energy; not doing things halfway or halfheartedly; living life as an adventure; feeling alive and activated

Humanity – Interpersonal strengths that involve tending and befriending others

- **Love:** Valuing close relations with others, in particular those in which sharing and caring are reciprocated; being close to people
- **Kindness** [generosity, nurturance, care, compassion, altruistic love, "niceness"]: Doing favors and good deeds for others; helping them; taking care of them
- **Social intelligence** [emotional intelligence, personal intelligence]: Being aware of the motives and feelings of other people and oneself; knowing what to do to fit into different social situations; knowing what makes other people tick

Justice – Civic strengths that underlie healthy community life

- **Teamwork** [citizenship, social responsibility, loyalty]: Working well as a member of a group or team; being loyal to the group; doing one's share
- **Fairness:** Treating all people the same according to notions of fairness and justice; not letting personal feelings bias decisions about others; giving everyone a fair chance
- **Leadership:** Encouraging a group of which one is a member to get things done and at the time maintain good relations within the group; organizing group activities and seeing that they happen

Temperance – Strengths that protect against excess

- **Forgiveness:** Forgiving those who have done wrong; accepting the shortcomings of others; giving people a second chance; not being vengeful
- **Humility:** Letting one's accomplishments speak for themselves; not regarding oneself as more special than one is
- **Prudence:** Being careful about one's choices; not taking undue risks; not saying or doing things that might later be regretted
- **Self-regulation** [self-control]: regulating what one feels and does; being disciplined; controlling one's appetites and emotions

Transcendence – Strengths that forge connections to the larger universe and provide meaning

- **Appreciation of beauty and excellence** [awe, wonder, elevation]: Noticing and appreciating beauty, excellence, and/or skilled performance in various domains of life, from nature to art to mathematics to science to everyday experience
- **Gratitude:** Being aware of and thankful for the good things that happen; taking time to express thanks
- **Hope** [optimism, future-mindedness, future orientation]: Expecting the best in the future and working to achieve it; believing that a good future is something that can be brought about
- **Humor** [playfulness]: Liking to laugh and tease; bringing smiles to other people; seeing the light side; making (not necessarily telling) jokes
- **Spirituality** [faith, purpose]: Having coherent beliefs about the higher purpose and meaning of the universe; knowing where one fits within the larger scheme; having beliefs about the meaning of life that shape conduct and provide comfort

Relevance: Why Assess Character Strengths?

From a research perspective, we need sound measures of character strengths to empirically study their relationship with indicators of the "good life" (the first criterion described by Peterson & Seligman, 2004). In addition, of course, it is also relevant to study their relationships with related constructs, such as the Five-Factor Model of personality (e.g., McGrath et al., 2020). However, besides their relevance for advancing research in positive psychology (Donaldson et al., 2015), the assessment of character strengths is important in many practical contexts, including, but not limited to, psychotherapy (e.g., Chaves et al., 2019; Flückiger & Beesdo-Baum, 2020), vocational counseling (e.g., Littman-Ovadia et al., 2014), coaching (e.g., Burke & Passmore, 2019), education (e.g., Norrish et al., 2013), and character strengths-based positive psychological interventions (e.g., Niemiec, 2017; Ruch, Niemiec et al., 2020). The specific relevance might vary across different fields, but in many cases, the main function of assessing character strengths in practice can be described as *resource activation* (see Flückiger & Beesdo-Baum, 2020). Character strengths are typically assessed to enable individuals to recognize their strengths and then work with these strengths in a coaching or therapy process.

General Considerations in the Assessment of Character Strengths

Before we review the different instruments for assessing character strengths, we need to mention some general questions in the assessment of character strengths. These questions include: Is social desirability relevant to the assessment of character strengths? Should measures of character strengths be scored normatively or ipsatively? Which aspects of character strengths are assessed besides their trait levels?

Role of Social Desirability

Given the positive and morally valued nature of character strengths (Stahlmann & Ruch, 2020), researchers and practitioners might be concerned about the potential influence of a self-enhancement bias created by the social desirability of character strengths toward the results obtained. In the past, researchers relied on scales that assessed social desirability to determine the extent to which self-enhancement tendencies influence the scores obtained on personality questionnaires. When using such a scale together with the standard assessment of character strengths, the VIA-Inventory of Strengths (VIA-IS), between two (Peterson & Seligman, 2004: prudence and spirituality) and five (Macdonald et al., 2008: curiosity, honesty, fairness, kindness, forgiveness) character strengths showed correlations of at least $r=.30$ to a social desirability scale. Overall, the size of the correlations did not differ from a measure of the Five-Factor Model of personality traits also used by Macdonald et al. (2008). Ruch, Proyer, Harzer et al. (2010) concluded that social desirability is not a strong threat to the validity of the scores obtained by the VIA-IS. This conclusion was based on small correlations between the Lie Scale of the Eysenck Personality Questionnaire-Revised (Eysenck & Eysenck, 1991) and the VIA-IS scales (using self-ratings, median $r=.06$, and informant ratings, median $r=.06$) as well as on a low correlation between a derived desirability index (difference between self and informant rating) and the Lie scale (median $r=.05$). Still, the correlations for prudence and teamwork were noteworthy and need to be considered. Because "lie" items often contain virtuous behaviors, substance is more likely responsible for these correlations and not just response style. Work on impression management or social desirability scales supports this idea (see, e.g., Zettler et al., 2015).

Another frequently used operationalization of self-enhancement is the discrepancy between self-reports and informant ratings (e.g., Müller & Moshagen, 2019). One might assume that the discrepancy between these two should be larger for ratings strongly affected by social desirability. For both the VIA-IS and the VIA-Youth (i.e., the standard instrument to assess character strengths in youth), median self-informant correlations around .40 have been reported (Ruch, Proyer, Harzer et al., 2010; Ruch, Weber et al., 2014). These values are highly comparable to coefficients obtained for other, not explicitly positively valued, personality traits (for a meta-analysis, see, e.g., Connelly & Ones, 2010). Of note, if any differences were observed, informants typically gave (at least descriptively) higher ratings than self-raters (e.g., Ruch, Proyer, Harzer et al., 2010). This observation suggests that the desirable nature of character strengths does not lead self-reports to be disproportionally inflated by self-enhancement.

Ipsative vs. Normative Scoring and Assessing Signature Strengths

While most research studies apply a normative approach to scoring measures of character strengths, ipsative scoring is relevant to many practical contexts. In many settings, knowing which character strengths are ranked highest within an individual is more important than knowing how a person's scores compare to others. Also, many strengths-based interventions build on so-called *signature strengths*, which are those character strengths that are highly typical of an individual and whose display is rewarding (Peterson & Seligman, 2004), not unlike Allport's (1961) notion of personal traits. Peterson and Seligman (2004) claimed that individuals have three to seven such strengths. However, empirical studies show that, while the mean is typically between five and six, the actual number of signature strengths individuals identify with varies widely (Blanchard et al., 2020; McGrath, 2019).

In some character strengths-based interventions, individuals complete the VIA-IS or the VIA-Youth to identify their most pronounced strengths. Then, they are asked to display one (e.g., Seligman et al., 2005), three (e.g., Toback et al., 2016), four (e.g., Harzer & Ruch, 2016), or five (e.g., Proyer et al., 2015) of these highest-ranking character strengths in new ways. Overall, though, there is very little evidence that it makes a difference whether the strengths used in an intervention are at the top or the bottom in an individuals' rank order of strengths (see Proyer et al., 2015). In addition, instruments intending to assess the individual's level of each of the character strengths and instruments intending to assess signature strengths directly converge only modestly with each other (Blanchard et al., 2020: McGrath, 2019). This finding suggests that what individuals consider their signature strengths is not directly aligned with what character strengths measures assess. Consequently, it seems useful to always include an individual's perception when determining signature strengths.

Given that the items across all scales of the VIA-IS were not constructed to be of the same psychometric difficulty, it would also seem useful to determine norms for any data before providing an individual's rank order of character strengths. Such a procedure is done by some platforms that allow individuals to complete the VIA-IS online and to receive personal feedback (e.g., the German-speaking site www.charakterstaerken.org), but by far not in all cases.

Relatedly, some research articles make statements such as "the highest strengths in this group of people (for instance, a certain profession) are X, Y, and Z" when comparing the means across all 24 character strengths within this group. Such statements are not particularly meaningful considering varying psychometric difficulty across the scales. Of course, it is possible to compare the rank order or the means of strengths between different groups, but making claims about the rank order within one group without comparisons seems problematic. Thus, comparisons among character strengths should be based on normed data. Normative data for the US have recently been published (McGrath et al., 2022).

Assessing the Application of Character Strengths in Different Life Domains

Even if two individuals can be characterized by the same level of a given character strength, such as creativity, we would not expect both individuals to show the same level of creative behavior in their workplaces. The idea of differentiating between the "possession" or "endorsement,“ on the one hand, and the "use,“ "application,“ "display," or "deployment" of character strengths, on the other hand, led to the development of several scales that capture this aspect. Generic measures of strengths use, such as the Strengths Knowledge Scale and the Strengths Use Scale (Govindji & Linley, 2007), are independent of a specific understanding of strengths. Such scales assess strengths without restricting respondents' understanding of what strengths to consider (the items refer to "my strengths" and "things I am good at"). Consequently, individuals will vary greatly in the traits they include in this very broad definition. It is thus not surprising that strengths use correlates highly with self-esteem and self-efficacy (e.g., Govindji & Linley, 2007): It describes whether a person perceives opportunities to do what they think they are good at and whether they believe they show these behaviors. Recent research has revealed that two dimensions underlying the scores in the Strengths Use Scale can be distinguished: (1) perceiving many opportunities to display one's strengths and (2) displaying strengths-related behavior (van Zyl et al., 2021).

These two aspects have also been considered when explicitly using the VIA classification (Peterson & Seligman, 2004) as a framework for assessing character strengths. It is of interest to assess both the extent to which individuals (1) perceive their environment as conducive to displaying behavior in accordance with one's character strengths and (2) show character strengths-related behaviors. Harzer and Ruch (2013) define the *applicability* of a character strength as "the degree to which situational circumstances allow an individual to display strengths-relevant behavior" (p. 967). The applicability of strengths has been assessed to complement an individual's level of a given character strength. Individuals within the same workplace showed a relatively strong interrater agreement regarding the aspects that relate to perceived characteristics of a workplace (i.e., the degree to which a given character strength is demanded and helpful; Harzer & Ruch, 2013). Thus, it is reasonable to assume that these ratings indeed relate to characteristics of the (work) environment.

The life domains assessed were also extended beyond work and studies (Kachel et al., 2020) to include domains such as leisure, romantic relationships, or close personal relationships (Wagner et al., 2021), and it has been suggested to separate the items relating to the relevance of strengths in a given environment (i.e., "it is demanded," "it is helpful," and "it is important to me") from the item relating to behavior (i.e., "I do it"). The ACS-RS was also adapted for use with adolescents in the context of school (Wagner & Ruch, 2022). In this version, only one external or environmental ("it is desired") and one internal or behavioral aspect ("I behave this way") is rated for each character strength.

Assessing the "Underuse" and "Overuse" of Character Strengths

By offering a systematic description of positive individual traits, Peterson and Seligman (2004) view the VIA classification as a positive counterpart to classifications that describe mental illness, such as the Diagnostic and Statistical Manual of Mental Disorders (DSM; American Psychiatric Association, 2013). There are also attempts to characterize mental illnesses by the opposite, namely, the absence or the excess of the 24 character strengths (Seligman, 2015). One attempt to assess the underuse and overuse (roughly corresponding to absence and excess) of character strengths is the Overuse/Underuse/Optimal Use inventory of strengths (OUOU; Freidlin et al., 2017), which asks participants to consider three so-called facets (underuse, optimal use, and overuse) of each of the 24 character strengths and allocate 100 % among the three facets for each respective strength. For example, the overuse of love of learning is described as "I seek knowledge so much that this negatively impacts my relationships or my work/school."

This approach has certain drawbacks: The three answers for each character strength are not independent (in fact, the answers to one facet depend on the answers to the other two facets), so that no comparisons between individuals regarding their level of character strengths can be made. Also, the validity of the OUOU can be questioned. In particular, no documentation exists on how the conceptualizations of underuse and overuse were constructed or validated. Is there only one type of overuse and underuse or many different ones that also may relate to different pathologies? There is also no evidence that the level of a character strength is related to underuse, optimal use, and, especially, overuse. Such evidence would be important to support the claim that the same construct (namely, the same character strength) underlies all three facets. Previous studies on single character strengths have also failed to identify the suggested "too much of a good thing" (e.g., Ruch, Proyer, & Weber, 2010; Wiese et al., 2018; see Ng & Tay, 2020, for a discussion) and have instead found a linear relationship between character strengths and well-being. In addition, Freidlin et al. (2017) report a relatively high internal consistency ($\alpha=.75$) for the 24 items assessing the overuse of all character strengths. This finding is somewhat surprising as one would expect that individuals show overuse of specific character strengths and not of all character strengths at the same time.

One might draw a parallel to other debates on the assessment of positively valued constructs, such as the question of whether one can value happiness too much (Mauss et al., 2011). As Luhmann et al. (2016) demonstrated for the case of the Valuing Happiness Scale (Mauss et al., 2011), correlations with negative outcomes can be artifacts of the negative wording of a few items. Considering the example item mentioned above, it is not surprising that the perception that one's behavior negatively impacts life domains is related to negative outcomes.

In light of these considerations and open questions, theoretical interpretations seem unwarranted before the scale has been systematically validated. One could also argue that the criteria put forward to describe character strengths do not apply to the overuse of strengths, which thus cannot be an expression of character strengths. Overall, it seems that "strengths overuse" cannot be described as an expression of a character strength at a high level but rather as a construct separate from character strengths, which is related to a generally negative self-evaluation.

Overview of Instruments Assessing Character Strengths

Table 6.1 gives an overview of commonly used instruments for the assessment of character strengths. This overview is structured by the target group (adults vs. children/adolescents). It first describes the standard instruments, then several shorter forms, and, finally, instruments assessing specific aspects of character strengths (i.e., signature strengths, application of character strengths in different life domains, and overuse/underuse of character strengths). This overview is by no means comprehensive. In particular, it does not include measures that used the VIA Classification as a starting point for their construction but assess traits beyond the 24 character strengths (e.g., CIVIC; Ng et al., 2018) nor instruments that were presented by Peterson and Seligman (2004) in their handbook, but never published or otherwise validated (e.g., the VIA Structured Interview for the assessment of signature strengths or the VIA Rising to the Occasion Inventory, which asks participants to reflect on their behavior in specific strengths-relevant situations). Thus, Table 6.1 does not represent a complete overview of all existing measures of character strengths.

Key Research Findings on the Described Measures

Only very scare validity evidence has been presented for several of the measures reviewed in Table 6.1. For instance, for some of the measures, it is even unclear to which extent they converge with other established methods for assessing character strengths (convergent validity). Overall, we also know relatively little about the test-retest stability of the measures, in particular over longer time intervals. Except for the VIA-IS, the VIA-IS-R, the VIA-Youth, and the CSRF, we are not aware of data on the stability. This gap in the literature should be addressed in future studies because knowledge on the test-retest stability is of high relevance for evaluating the effects of interventions on character strengths. The same is true for divergent validity: For many of the measures, there is little to no evidence on their associations with conceptually overlapping or distinct constructs, such as the Big Five or HEXACO personality traits (McGrath et al., 2020) or intelligence (Kretzschmar et al., 2022).

Research using the measures presented in Table 6.1 has mainly focusedon criterion validity. For instance, there are studies on the relationships with well-being (e.g., Buschor et al., 2013; Hausler et al., 2017; Wagner, Gander et al., 2020), achievement (e.g., Datu & Bernardo, 2020; Harzer & Ruch, 2014; Wagner, Holenstein et al., 2020), and interpersonal relationships (e.g., Boiman-Meshita, & Littman-Ovadia, 2022; Wagner, 2019), whereas to date, very little research has considered joint and interactive effects of character strengths (for an exception, see Ruch, Platt et al., 2014), which might be a valuable avenue for future research.

Studying Factor Structure vs. Assessing Virtues

The VIA Classification was developed with a focus on the outcomes that character strengths predict. In assessment terms, this means that the focus has been on criterion validity. Even though the hierarchical structure of the classification reminds readers of factor models, it was not conceptualized as nor intended to be a factor model. That is, the classification – and the instruments used to assess the character strengths in the classification – were *not* developed with ideas about the structure of these strengths. In other words, the VIA Classification was not constructed with the goal of developing a factorial model in mind. Instead, Peterson and Seligman (2004) describe character strengths as "distinguishable routes to displaying one or another of the virtues" (p. 13), which implies that an individual does not necessarily (or perhaps even rather unlikely) pursue all of those routes simultaneously, as a factorial model would imply (see the discussion in Ruch & Proyer, 2015, pp. 10–11). In addition, Miller (2019) argued that character strengths and virtues could be related in several ways because Peterson and Seligman's (2004) descriptions were not sufficiently clear in describing these relationships.

Table 6.1. Psychometric properties of prevalent instruments assessing character strengths (sorted chronologically by category)

Instrument	Informant and number of items	Reliability	(Convergent) validity	Languages available	Notes
Adults					
VIA Inventory of Strengths (Peterson & Seligman, 2004)	Self-ratings (240 items; 10 items per strength)	α = >.70 r_{tt} = >.70 (4 months) (Peterson et al., 2004) α = .71–.90 (median α = .76) r_{tt} = .69–.87 (over 3 months) r_{tt} = .65–.85 (over 6 months) r_{tt} = .62–.85 (over 9 months) (Ruch, Proyer, Harzer et al., 2010)	With informant-rating r = .26–.69 (mean r = .42) (Ruch, Proyer, Harzer et al., 2010)	Afrikaans, Arabic, Chinese (Simplified), Chinese (Traditional), Croatian, Danish, Dutch, French, German, Greek, Hebrew, Hindi, Italian, Japanese, Korean, Portuguese (Brazil), Portuguese (Portugal), Russian, Spanish, Swedish, Turkish, Urdu, see supplementary Table S2 for an overview of published adaptations (https://osf.io/2rzj3/)	
VIA-IS-R (McGrath, 2019)[a]	Self-ratings (192 items; 8 items per strength)	αs = .77–.91 (median α = .85), (McGrath, 2019) α = .75–.91 (median α = .85), r_{tt} = .76–.89 (mean r = .82, over 3 months) (McGrath & Wallace, 2021)	With VIA-IS-120 r = .59–.94 (mean r = .83) With SSS r = .30–.64 (mean r = .45) (McGrath, 2019) With VIA-IS-120 r = .58–.88 (mean r = .77), (McGrath & Wallace, 2021)	English	Data from a sample demographically representative of the US population available (McGrath et al., 2022)
IPIP-VIA (Goldberg et al., 2006)	Self-ratings (213/217 items; 7–10 per scale)	α = .70–.91 (McGrath, 2015)	Convergent validity not tested	English, German, Polish	Short form containing 96 items used in Partsch et al. (2021) Version derived using Rasch modeling (du Plessis & de Bruin, 2015)

Table 6.1. continued

Instrument	Informant and number of items	Reliability	(Convergent) validity	Languages available	Notes
Children and adolescents					
VIA-Youth (Park & Peterson, 2006b)	Self-ratings (adolescents aged 10–17) of 24 character strengths (198 items; 7–9 per character strength)	$\alpha = .72–.91$ (median $\alpha = .81$) $r_{tt} = .46–.71$ (over 6 months; mean $r = .58$, 50 % overlapping items) (Park & Peterson, 2006b) $\alpha = .65–.91$ (median $\alpha = .77$) $r_{tt} = .61–.85$ (over 4 months; mean $r = .73$) (Ruch, Weber et al., 2014)	With abstract judgments (summary self-ratings) $r = .18–.55$ (mean $r = .36$) With teacher ratings $r = .14–.33$ (mean $r = .23$) (Park & Peterson, 2006b) With parent-rating $r = .22–.70$ (mean $r = .40$) (Ruch, Weber et al., 2014)	English, German, Spanish	
Character Strengths Inventory for Children (CSI-C; Shoshani & Shwartz, 2018)	Self-ratings (children aged 7–12) of 24 character strengths (96 items; 4 per character strength)	$\alpha = .73–.91$ (median $\alpha = .82$) r_{tt} n/a	Convergent validity not tested	English, Hebrew	
Character Strengths Inventory for Early Childhood (CSI-EC; Shoshani, 2019)	Parent ratings (children aged 3–6) of 24 character strengths (96 items; 4 per character strength)	$\alpha = .71–.92$ (median $\alpha = .83$) r_{tt} n/a	Convergent validity not tested	English, Hebrew	

Table 6.1. continued

Instrument	Informant and number of items	Reliability	(Convergent) validity	Languages available	Notes
Short forms					
VIA-120 (Littman-Ovadia, 2015)	Self-ratings (120 items; 5 per scale)	α = .64–.90 (median α = .78) (Littman-Ovadia, 2015, Study 5) α = .58–.89 (median α = .77) (Höfer et al., 2019, Study 1) r_{tt} n/a	With VIA-IS rs = .88–.96 (mean r = .93) (Littman-Ovadia, 2015, Study 1) rs = .52–.87 (mean r = .75) (Höfer et al., 2019, Study 1) No evidence from independent administrations of both measures	Arabic, Chinese (Simplified), English, German, Hebrew, Greek, Spanish	5 VIA-IS items for each character strength with the highest corrected item-total correlations
VIA-72	Self-ratings (72 items; 3 per scale)	α = .61–.81 (Moreira et al., 2021) r_{tt} n/a	Convergent validity not tested	English, Portuguese, Urdu	3 VIA-IS items for each character strength with the highest corrected item-total correlations
Self-rated measure of character strengths (Furnham & Lester, 2012)	Self-ratings (24 items)	r_{tt} n/a	Convergent validity not tested	English	
Character strengths rating form (CSRF; Ruch, Martínez-Martí et al., 2014)	Self-ratings (24 items)	r_{tt} = .37–.69 (over 2 years; median r_{tt} = .46, Gander et al., 2020)	Convergence with VIA-IS ranging from r = .41 to r = .77 (mean r = .58) (Ruch, Martínez-Martí et al., 2014)	German	Adapted for use in daily diary studies (Gander et al., 2021) and for informant ratings (Ruch, Heintz et al., 2020)
Abbreviated Character Strengths Test (ACST: Vanhove et al., 2016)	Self-ratings (24 items, only 21 items/character strengths retained after analysis)	Six virtue dimensions: α = .70–.84 r_{tt} n/a	Correlations of virtue dimensions with Big Five personality traits ranging from r = −.27 to r = .54	English	

Table 6.1. continued

Instrument	Informant and number of items	Reliability	(Convergent) validity	Languages available	Notes
Measures of specific aspects					
Applicability of Character Strengths – Rating Scale (ACS-RS; Harzer & Ruch, 2013)	Self-ratings of applicability (96 items in total; 4 per character strength)	Work life: $\alpha = .71–.90$ (median $\alpha = .80$) Private life: $\alpha = .76–.94$ (median $\alpha = .84$) (Harzer & Ruch, 2013) r_{tt} n/a	Median of correlations with VIA-IS: $r = .66$ for work life and $r = .70$ for private life (Harzer & Ruch, 2013)	German	Has been adapted for use with adolescents (Wagner & Ruch, 2021) and several life domains (Wagner et al., 2021)
Optimal/Over/Under Used Strengths (OUOU; Freidlin et al., 2017)	Self-ratings of underuse, optimal use, and overuse of the 24 character strengths	$\alpha = .84$ underuse, $\alpha = .89$ optimal use, $\alpha = .75$ overuse r_{tt} n/a	Convergent validity not tested	English	Answer format: Respondents are asked to distribute 100 % across three facets
Signature Strengths Survey (SSS; McGrath, 2019)	Overview of the 24 character strengths, participants select essential strengths in two rounds	α n/a r_{tt} n/a	With VIA-IS-R $r = .30–.34$ (mean $r = .45$) (McGrath, 2019) With VIA-120 $r = .24–.59$ (mean $r = .35$) (Blanchard et al., 2020)	English	
Short forms assessing only some aspects of character strengths					
Chinese Virtues Questionnaire (CVQ-96; Duan et al., 2012)	Self-ratings of three virtues (Interpersonal, vitality, cautiousness) (96 items; 32 items for interpersonal, 40 items for vitality, and 24 items for cautiousness)	$\alpha = .83–.90$ (Duan et al., 2012) $\alpha = .88–.92$ $r_{tt} = .70–.76$ (10 weeks) (Duan et al., 2013)	With Gratitude Questionnaire-6 $r = .27–.47$ With Hope Scale $r = .42–.52$ (Duan et al., 2013)	Chinese	

Table 6.1. continued

Instrument	Informant and number of items	Reliability	(Convergent) validity	Languages available	Notes
Brief Strengths Scale-12 (BSS-12; Ho et al., 2016)	Self-ratings (12 items in total; 4 items each for temperance strength, interpersonal strength, and intellectual strength)	α = .72–.89 r_{tt} n/a	Convergent validity not tested	Chinese, English	
Three-dimensional Inventory of Character Strengths (TICS; Duan & Bu, 2017)	Self-ratings (15 items in total; 1 item each for curiosity, humor, creativity, social intelligence, zest, fairness, leadership, teamwork, authenticity, kindness, regulation, prudence, judgment, perseverance, and love of learning)	α = .79–.86 r_{tt} n/a	Convergent validity not tested	Chinese	

Note. α = Cronbach's alpha, ω = McDonald's omega, r_{tt} = test-retest reliability. [a]The VIA Assessment Suite (McGrath, 2019) also contains several additional versions: VIA Inventory of Strengths-M (VIA-IS-M; containing the 96 items of the VIA-IS-R with the highest item-total correlations); VIA Inventory of Strengths-P (VIA-IS-P; 96 items, exclusively positive-keyed items), Global Assessment of Character Strengths-72 (GACS-72; three items per strength to assess its similarity to a signature strength), and Global Assessment of Character Strengths – 24 (GACS-24; version of the GAS-24 with one item per strength).

With these considerations in mind, it becomes evident that averaging those character strengths theoretically assigned to a virtue to form a virtue score is not meaningful. The items assessing character strengths were never constructed to assess virtues, and their contents do not reflect the descriptions of the virtues. This also means that any success or failure to show a six-factorial structure does not provide direct information on the appropriateness or validity of the VIA Classification. Recently, more direct approaches to testing the assignment of character strengths to virtues (Gander et al., 2021; Giuliani et al., 2020; Ruch & Proyer, 2015; Ruch, Heintz et al., 2020; Ruch et al., 2021) have been suggested. The results provided relatively consistent evidence for most assignments, although these studies also suggested that character strengths may be assigned to more than one virtue, and that the character strength of humor may be better assigned to the virtue of humanity (instead of transcendence).

Nonetheless, the higher-order structure of the instruments assessing the character strengths of the VIA classification has been addressed repeatedly. However, in many cases, items or scales had to be excluded to arrive at acceptable factor solutions; thus, many factor solutions do not represent all 24 character strengths. We also hasten to emphasize that, while such higher-order factors describing which character strengths typically occur together might be useful for certain purposes, they hardly can be expected to represent the virtues described in the VIA Classification. Many solutions regarding higher-order factors have been identified (see Supplementary Table S1 available on the Open Science Framework: https://osf.io/2rzj3/). These factor solutions range from one to six factors, suggesting that there is no stable factor structure across the instruments and, in most cases, not even within one instrument. This makes comparing any two results based on factor scores very difficult. Recently, McGrath (2015) and Partsch et al. (2021) argued in favor of three-factor structures, which showed some degree of robustness across different samples. However, the content and composition of the three factors suggested differed between the instruments (e.g., the three factors extracted from the IPIP-VIA-R by Partsch et al. are not comparable to those extracted from the VIA-IS or VIA-IS-R by McGrath), which makes a coherent account of how to interpret the higher-order factors very difficult.

Using higher-order factors of character strengths also seems of limited usefulness for many applications in research and practice. Studies often conclude that those strengths with the highest relationships to relevant criteria load onto different factors (e.g., Wagner & Ruch, 2022). Therefore, reporting results on the level of factors may obscure the results and would not allow conclusions on the specific contributions of the single character strengths. In practice, most strengths-based interventions operate at the level of character strengths (e.g., Niemiec, 2017), as these are more concrete and arguably easier to implement than interventions based on more abstract, higher-order concepts.

Equivalence Between Different Measures

Given the availability of different measures of character strengths based on the VIA Classification, the question arises whether the scores assessed using different instruments can be interpreted similarly. Several studies that address the equivalence between different measures of character strengths were recently undertaken to answer this question. First, the convergence of the revised (VIA-IS-R) with the original (VIA-IS-R) questionnaire is of interest to determine whether the results that were obtained using one or the other questionnaire are sufficiently comparable. Using the German version of both instruments, Vylobkova et al. (2022) showed that, overall, the VIA-IS and the VIA-IS-R could be considered equivalent regarding internal consistency, correlations between the scales as well as criterion-related validity (relationships with well-being, moral behaviors, and core virtues). Neither of the measures is clearly superior to the other in any of these criteria, and, with a few exceptions, the overlap between the homologous scales was high. McGrath and Wallace (2021) also report a high level of convergence between the different instruments within the VIA Assessment Suite (VIA-IS-R, VIA-IS-P, VIA-IS-M, GACS). We tentatively conclude from these results that the results achieved with the VIA-IS and the VIA Assessment Suite, in particular with the VIA-IS-R, can be readily compared.

Second, despite some differences in the structure of the instruments, it is also of interest to investigate the convergence of instruments designed for different age groups. To this end, Kretzschmar et al. (2022) used a sample of 18-year-old students who completed both the VIA-Youth and the VIA-IS, in addition to several well-being measures. The results highlighted that the two instruments assessing character strengths converged well for many strengths but less well for others (e.g., curiosity and leadership). In sum, Kretzschmar et al. considered these differences to be too large to allow comparing scores between the two instruments. Also, a meta-analysis on cross-sectional age differences in the 24 character strengths (Heintz & Ruch, 2022) using 47 samples yielded a more substantial gap between ages 17 and 18 (i.e., the oldest group that completed the VIA-Youth and the youngest that completed in the VIA-IS) than between other age groups. Together, these findings suggest that making statements about which character strengths are more or less pronounced in adolescents compared to adults is not valid if such statements are based on different questionnaires in both samples.

As mentioned previously, only a moderate amount of agreement (mean $r=.45$) between the VIA-IS-R and the SSS has been reported (McGrath et al., 2019). To our knowledge, no studies have directly compared versions of the IPIP-VIA to the original version(s). Therefore, we can make no conclusions regarding their equivalence.

Recommendations for Instrument Selection

Assessment contexts vary in their requirements, but some general recommendations for instrument selection can be put forward. First, (very) short measures assessing character strengths with only 1–3 items each, such as the CSRF and the VIA-72, should only be used in large-scale studies in which considerations of participant burden exclude the use of longer measures and in which only group-level comparisons are of interest. However, researchers should be aware that using these short forms comes at the cost of reliability and validity. Second, for assessments in individual contexts (e.g., in counseling), we recommend the use of neither shortened versions nor any instruments that primarily rely on factor-level scales. Most applied work (e.g., Niemiec, 2017) focuses on the level of character strengths or is interested in identifying signature strengths. Hence, it is most informative for practitioners to use measures that allow assessing individual character strengths with sufficient reliability and validity, that is, VIA-IS, VIA-IS-R, IPIP-VIA, and VIA-Youth.

Author Note

Disclosure statement: The second author is a senior scientist at the VIA Institute on Character, which holds the copyright to the VIA Inventory of Strengths.

References

Allport, G.W. (1961). *Pattern and growth in personality*. Holt, Reinhart & Winston.

American Psychiatric Association. (2013). *Diagnostic and statistical manual of mental disorders (DSM-5)* (5th ed.). American Psychiatric Association.

Blanchard, T., Kerbeykian, T., & McGrath, R.E. (2020). Why are signature strengths and well-being related? Tests of multiple hypotheses. *Journal of Happiness Studies, 21*(6), 2095–2114. https://doi.org/10.1007/s10902-019-00170-2

Boiman-Meshita, M., & Littman-Ovadia, H. (2022). Is it me or you? An actor-partner examination of the relationship between partners' character strengths and marital quality. *Journal of Happiness Studies, 23*(1), 195–210. https://doi.org/10.1007/s10902-021-00394-1

Burke, J., & Passmore, J. (2019). Strengths based coaching: A positive psychology intervention. In L.E. Van Zyl & S. Rothmann Sr. (Eds.), *Theoretical approaches to multi-cultural positive psychological interventions* (pp. 463–475). Springer International Publishing. https://doi.org/10.1007/978-3-030-20583-6_21

Buschor, C., Proyer, R.T., & Ruch, W. (2013). Self- and peer-rated character strengths: How do they relate to satisfaction with life and orientations to happiness? *The Journal of Positive Psychology, 8*(2), 116–127. https://doi.org/10.1080/17439760.2012.758305

Chaves, C., Lopez-Gomez, I., Hervas, G., & Vazquez, C. (2019). The Integrative Positive Psychological Intervention for Depression (IPPI-D). *Journal of Contemporary Psychotherapy, 49*(3), 177–185. https://doi.org/10.1007/s10879-018-9412-0

Connelly, B.S., & Ones, D.S. (2010). An other perspective on personality: Meta-analytic integration of observers' accuracy and predictive validity. *Psychological Bulletin, 136*(6), 1092–1122. https://doi.org/10.1037/a0021212

Dahlsgaard, K., Peterson, C., & Seligman, M.E. P. (2005). Shared virtue: The convergence of valued human strengths across culture and history. *Review of General Psychology, 9*(3), 203–213. https://doi.org/10.1037/1089-2680.9.3.203

Datu, J.A. D., & Bernardo, A.B. I. (2020). The blessings of social-oriented virtues: Interpersonal character strengths are linked to increased life satisfaction and academic success among Filipino high-school students. *Social Psychological and Personality Science, 11*(7), 983–990. https://doi.org/10.1177/1948550620906294

Donaldson, S.I., Dollwet, M., & Rao, M.A. (2015). Happiness, excellence, and optimal human functioning revisited: Examining the peer-reviewed literature linked to positive psychology. *The Journal of Positive Psychology, 10*(3), 185–195. https://doi.org/10.1080/17439760.2014.943801

Duan, W., & Bu, H. (2017). Development and initial validation of a short three-dimensional inventory of character strengths. *Quality of Life Research, 26*(9), 2519–2531. https://doi.org/10.1007/s11136-017-1579-4

Duan, W., Ho, S.M.Y., Yu, B., Tang, X., Zhang, Y., Li, T., & Yuen, T. (2012). Factor structure of the Chinese Virtues Questionnaire. *Research on Social Work Practice, 22*(6), 680–688. https://doi.org/10.1177/1049731512450074

Duan, W., Ho, S.M.Y., Bai, Y., & Tang, X. (2013). Psychometric evaluation of the Chinese Virtues Questionnaire. *Research on Social Work Practice, 23*(3), 336–345. http://doi.org/10.1177/1049731513477214 https://doi.org/10.1177/1049731513477214

du Plessis, G.A., & de Bruin, G.P. (2015). Using Rasch modelling to examine the international personality item pool (IPIP) values in action (VIA) measure of character strengths. *Journal of Psychology in Africa, 25*(6), 512–521. https://doi.org/10.1080/14330237.2015.1124603

Eysenck, H.J., & Eysenck, S.B.G. (1991). *Manual of the Eysenck Personality Scales (EPQ adults)*. Hodder and Stoughton.

Flückiger, C., & Beesdo-Baum, K. (2020). Ressourcenaktivierung [Resource activation]. In J. Hoyer & S. Knappe (Eds.), *Klinische Psychologie & Psychotherapie* (pp. 575–588). Springer. https://doi.org/10.1007/978-3-662-61814-1_23

Freidlin, P., Littman-Ovadia, H., & Niemiec, R.M. (2017). Positive psychopathology: Social anxiety via character strengths underuse and overuse. *Personality and Individual Differences, 108*, 50–54. https://doi.org/10.1016/j.paid.2016.12.003

Furnham, A., & Lester, D. (2012). The development of a short measure of character strength. *European Journal of Psychological Assessment, 28*(2), 95–101. https://doi.org/10.1027/1015-5759/a000096

Gander, F., Hofmann, J., Proyer, R.T., & Ruch, W. (2020). Character strengths: Stability, change, and relationships with well-being changes. *Applied Research in Quality of Life, 15*(2), 349–367. https://doi.org/10.1007/s11482-018-9690-4

Gander, F., Wagner, L., Amann, L., & Ruch, W. (2021). What are character strengths good for? A daily diary study on character strengths enactment. *The Journal of Positive Psychology*. Advance online publication. https://doi.org/10.1080/17439760.2021.1926532

Giuliani, F., Ruch, W., & Gander, F. (2020). Does the excellent enactment of highest strengths reveal virtues? *Frontiers in Psychology, 11*, Article 1545. https://doi.org/10.3389/fpsyg.2020.01545

Goldberg, L.R., Johnson, J.A., Eber, H.W., Hogan, R., Ashton, M.C., Cloninger, C.R., & Gough, H.G. (2006). The international personality item pool and the future of public-domain personality measures. *Journal of Research in Personality, 40*(1), 84–96. https://doi.org/10.1016/j.jrp.2005.08.007

Govindji, R., & Linley, P.A. (2007). Strengths use, self-concordance and well-being: Implications for strengths coaching and coaching psychologists. *International Coaching Psychology Review, 2*(2), 143–153.

Harzer, C., & Ruch, W. (2013). The application of signature character strengths and positive experiences at work. *Journal of Happiness Studies, 14*(3), 965–983. https://doi.org/10.1007/s10902-012-9364-0

Harzer, C., & Ruch, W. (2014). The role of character strengths for task performance, job dedication, interpersonal facilitation, and organizational support. *Human Performance, 27*(3), 183–205. https://doi.org/10.1080/08959285.2014.913592

Harzer, C., & Ruch, W. (2016). Your strengths are calling: Preliminary results of a web-based strengths intervention to increase calling. *Journal of Happiness Studies, 17*(6), 2237–2256. https://doi.org/10.1007/s10902-015-9692-y

Hausler, M., Strecker, C., Huber, A., Brenner, M., Höge, T., & Höfer, S. (2017). Distinguishing relational aspects of character strengths with subjective and psychological well-being. *Frontiers in Psychology, 8*, Article 1159. https://doi.org/10.3389/fpsyg.2017.01159

Heintz, S., & Ruch, W. (2022). Cross-sectional age differences in 24 character strengths: Five meta-analyses from early adolescence to late adulthood. *The Journal of Positive Psychology, 17*(3), 356–374. https://doi.org/10.1080/17439760.2021.1871938

Ho, S.M.Y., Li, W.L., Duan, W., Siu, B.P.Y., Yau, S., Yeung, G., & Wong, K. (2016). A Brief Strengths Scale for individuals with mental health issues. *Psychological Assessment, 28*(2), 147–157. https://doi.org/10.1037/pas0000164

Höfer, S., Hausler, M., Huber, A., Strecker, C., Renn, D., & Höge, T. (2019). Psychometric characteristics of the German Values in Action Inventory of Strengths 120-Item Short Form. *Applied Research in Quality of Life, 15*(2), 597–611. https://doi.org/10.1007/s11482-018-9696-y

Kachel, T., Huber, A., Strecker, C., Höge, T., & Höfer, S. (2020). Development of cynicism in medical students: Exploring the role of signature character strengths and well-being. *Frontiers in Psychology, 11*, Article 328. https://doi.org/10.3389/fpsyg.2020.00328

Kretzschmar, A., Harzer, C., & Ruch, W. (2022). Character strengths in adults and adolescents: Their measurement and association with well-being. *Journal of Personality Assessment*. Advance online publication. https://doi.org/10.1080/00223891.2022.2043879

Kretzschmar, A., Wagner, L., Gander, F., Hofmann, J., Proyer, R.T., & Ruch, W. (2022). Character strengths and fluid intelligence. *Journal of Personality*. Advance online publication. https://doi.org/10.1111/jopy.12715

Littman-Ovadia, H. (2015). Short form of the VIA Inventory of Strengths: Construction and initial tests of reliability and validity. *International Journal of Humanities Social Sciences and Education, 2*(4), 229–237.

Littman-Ovadia, H., Lazar-Butbul, V., & Benjamin, B.A. (2014). Strengths-based career counseling: Overview and initial evaluation. *Journal of Career Assessment, 22*(3), 403–419. https://doi.org/10.1177/1069072713498483

Luhmann, M., Necka, E.A., Schönbrodt, F.D., & Hawkley, L.C. (2016). Is valuing happiness associated with lower well-being? A factor-level analysis using the Valuing Happiness Scale. *Journal of Research in Personality, 60*, 46–50. https://doi.org/10.1016/j.jrp.2015.11.003

Macdonald, C., Bore, M., & Munro, D. (2008). Values in action scale and the Big 5: An empirical indication of structure. *Journal of Research in Personality, 42*(4), 787–799. https://doi.org/10.1016/j.jrp.2007.10.003

Mauss, I.B., Tamir, M., Anderson, C.L., & Savino, N.S. (2011). Can seeking happiness make people unhappy? Paradoxical effects of valuing happiness. *Emotion, 11*(4), 807–815. https://doi.org/10.1037/a0022010

McGrath, R.E. (2015). Integrating psychological and cultural perspectives on virtue: The hierarchical structure of character strengths. *The Journal of Positive Psychology, 10*(5), 407–424. https://doi.org/10.1080/17439760.2014.994222

McGrath, R.E. (2019). *The VIA Assessment Suite for Adults: Development and initial evaluation* (rev. ed.) [Technical report]. VIA Institute on Character.

McGrath, R.E., Brown, M., Westrich, B., & Han, H. (2022). Representative sampling of the VIA Assessment Suite for Adults. *Journal of Personality Assessment, 104*(3), 380–394. https://doi.org/10.1080/00223891.2021.1955692

McGrath, R.E., Hall-Simmonds, A., & Goldberg, L.R. (2020). Are measures of character and personality distinct? Evidence from observed-score and true-score analyses. *Assessment, 27*(1), 117–135. https://doi.org/10.1177/1073191117738047

McGrath, R.E., & Wallace, N. (2021). Cross-validation of the VIA Inventory of Strengths-Revised and its short forms. *Journal of Personality Assessment, 103*(1), 120–131. https://doi.org/10.1080/00223891.2019.1705465

Miller, C.B. (2019). Some philosophical concerns about how the VIA classifies character traits and the VIA-IS measures them. *The Journal of Positive Psychology, 14*(1), 6–19. https://doi.org/10.1080/17439760.2018.1528377

Moreira, P.A.S., Inman, R.A., & Cloninger, C.R. (2021). Virtues in action are related to the integration of both temperament and character: Comparing the VIA classification of virtues and Cloninger's biopsychosocial model of personality. *The Journal of Positive Psychology*. Advance online publication. https://doi.org/10.1080/17439760.2021.1975158

Müller, S., & Moshagen, M. (2019). Controlling for response bias in self-ratings of personality: A comparison of impression management scales and the overclaiming technique. *Journal of Personality Assessment, 101*(3), 229–236. https://doi.org/10.1080/00223891.2018.1451870

Niemiec, R.M. (2017). *Character strengths interventions: A field guide for practitioners*. Hogrefe Publishing. https://doi.org/10.1027/00492-000

Ng, V., & Tay, L. (2020). Lost in translation: The construct representation of character virtues. *Perspectives on Psychological Science, 15*(2), 309–326. https://doi.org/10.1177/1745691619886014

Ng, V., Tay, L., & Kuykendall, L. (2018). The development and validation of a measure of character: The CIVIC. *The Journal of Positive Psychology, 13*(4), 346–372. https://doi.org/10.1080/17439760.2017.1291850

Norrish, J.M., Williams, P., O'Connor, M., & Robinson, J. (2013). An applied framework for positive education. *International Journal of Wellbeing, 3*(2), 147–161. Retrieved from https://internationaljournalofwell-being.org/index.php/ijow/article/view/250

Park, N., & Peterson, C. (2006a). Character strengths and happiness among young children: Content analysis of parental descriptions. *Journal of Happiness Studies, 7*, 323–341. https://doi.org/10.1007/s10902-005-3648-6

Park, N., & Peterson, C. (2006b). Moral competence and character strengths among adolescents: The development and validation of the Values in Action Inventory of Strengths for Youth. *Journal of Adolescence, 29*, 891–909. https://doi.org/10.1016/j.adolescence.2006.04.011

Partsch, M.V., Bluemke, M., & Lechner, C.M. (2021). Revisiting the hierarchical structure of the 24 VIA character strengths: Three global dimensions may suffice to capture their essence. *European Journal of Personality*. Advance online publication. https://doi.org/10.1177/08902070211017760

Peterson, C., & Seligman, M. (2004). *Character strengths and virtues: A handbook and classification*. Oxford University Press.

Proyer, R.T., Gander, F., Wellenzohn, S., & Ruch, W. (2015). Strengths-based positive psychology interventions: A randomized placebo-controlled online trial on long-term effects for a signature strengths- vs. a lesser strengths-intervention. *Frontiers in Psychology, 6*, Article 456. https://doi.org/10.3389/fpsyg.2015.00456

Ruch, W., Gander, F., Wagner, L., & Giuliani, F. (2021). The structure of character: On the relationships between character strengths and virtues. *The Journal of Positive Psychology, 16*(1), 116–128. https://doi.org/10.1080/17439760.2019.1689418

Ruch, W., Heintz, S., & Wagner, L. (2020). Co-occurrence patterns of character strengths and measured core virtues in German-speaking adults. *Frontiers in Psychology, 11*, 599094. https://doi.org/10.3389/fpsyg.2020.599094

Ruch, W., Martínez-Martí, M.L., Proyer, R.T., & Harzer, C. (2014). The Character Strengths Rating Form (CSRF): Development and initial assessment of a 24-item rating scale to assess character strengths. *Personality and Individual Differences, 68*, 53–58. https://doi.org/10.1016/j.paid.2014.03.042

Ruch, W., Niemiec, R.M., McGrath, R.E., Gander, F., & Proyer, R.T. (2020). Character strengths-based interventions: Open questions and ideas for future research. *The Journal of Positive Psychology, 15*(5), 680–684. https://doi.org/10.1080/17439760.2020.1789700

Ruch, W., Platt, T., & Hofmann, J. (2014). The character strengths of class clowns. *Frontiers in Psychology, 5*, Article 1075. https://doi.org/10.3389/fpsyg.2014.01075

Ruch, W., & Proyer, R.T. (2015). Mapping strengths into virtues: The relation of the 24 VIA-strengths to six ubiquitous virtues. *Frontiers in Psychology, 6*, Article 460. https://doi.org/10.3389/fpsyg.2015.00460

Ruch, W., Proyer, R.T., Harzer, C., Park, N., Peterson, C., & Seligman, M.E.P. (2010). Values in Action Inventory of Strengths (VIA-IS): Adaptation and validation of the German version and the development of a peer-rating form. *Journal of Individual Differences, 31*, 138–149. https://doi.org/10.1027/1614-0001/a000022

Ruch, W., Proyer, R.T., & Weber, M. (2010). Humor as a character strength among the elderly: Empirical findings on age-related changes and its contribution to satisfaction with life. *Zeitschrift für Gerontologie und Geriatrie, 43*(1), 13–18. https://doi.org/10.1007/s00391-009-0090-0

Ruch, W., & Stahlmann, A.G. (2019). 15 years after Peterson and Seligman (2004): A brief narrative review of the research on the 12 criteria for character strengths – The forgotten treasure of the VIA classification. In M. Brohm-Badry, C. Peifer, J.M. Greve, & B. Berend (Eds.), *Zusammen wachsen – Förderung der positiv-psychologischen Entwicklung von Individuen, Organisationen und Gesellschaft* (pp. 142–172). Pabst Science Publishers.

Ruch, W., Weber, M., Park, N., & Peterson, C. (2014). Character strengths in children and adolescents: Reliability and initial validity of the German Values in Action Inventory of Strengths for Youth (German VIA-Youth). *European Journal of Psychological Assessment, 30*, 57–64. https://doi.org/10.1027/1015-5759/a000169

Seligman, M.E.P. (2015). Chris Peterson's unfinished masterwork: The real mental illnesses. *The Journal of Positive Psychology, 10*(1), 3–6. https://doi.org/10.1080/17439760.2014.888582

Seligman, M.E.P., Steen, T.A., Park, N., & Peterson, C. (2005). Positive psychology progress: Empirical validation of interventions. *American Psychologist, 60*(5), 410–421. https://doi.org/10.1037/0003-066X.60.5.410

Shoshani, A. (2019). Young children's character strengths and emotional well-being: Development of the Character Strengths Inventory for Early Childhood (CSI-EC). *The Journal of Positive Psychology, 14*, 86–102. https://doi.org/10.1080/17439760.2018.1424925

Shoshani, A., & Shwartz, L. (2018). From character strengths to children's well-being: Development and validation of the Character Strengths Inventory for Elementary School Children. *Frontiers in Psychology, 9*, Article 2123. https://doi.org/10.3389/fpsyg.2018.02123

Stahlmann, A.G., & Ruch, W. (2020). Scrutinizing the criteria for character strengths: Laypersons assert that every strength is positively morally valued, even in the absence of tangible outcomes. *Frontiers in Psychology, 11*, 591028. https://doi.org/10.3389/fpsyg.2020.591028

Toback, R.L., Graham-Bermann, S.A., & Patel, P.D. (2016). Outcomes of a character strengths-based intervention on self-esteem and self-efficacy of psychiatrically hospitalized youths. *Psychiatric Services, 67*(5), 574–577. https://doi.org/10.1176/appi.ps.201500021

Vanhove, A.J., Harms, P.D., & DeSimone, J.A. (2016). The Abbreviated Character Strengths Test (ACST): A preliminary assessment of test validity. *Journal of Personality Assessment, 98*(5), 536–544. https://doi.org/10.1080/00223891.2016.1148044

van Zyl, L.E., Arijs, D., Cole, M.L., Gliíska-Newes, A., Roll, L.C., Rothmann, S., Shankland, R., Stavros, J.M., & Verger, N.B. (2021). The Strengths Use Scale: Psychometric properties, longitudinal invariance and criterion validity. *Frontiers in Psychology, 12*, Article 2135. https://doi.org/10.3389/fpsyg.2021.676153

Vylobkova, V., Heintz, S., Gander, F., Wagner, L., & Ruch, W. (2022). Convergence and psychometric properties of character strengths measures: The VIA-IS and the VIA-IS-R. *Journal of Personality Assessment*. Advance online publication. https://doi.org/10.1080/00223891.2022.2044342

Wagner, L. (2019). Good character is what we look for in a friend: Character strengths are positively related to peer acceptance and friendship quality in early adolescents. *The Journal of Early Adolescence, 39*(6), 864–903. https://doi.org/10.1177/0272431618791286

Wagner, L., Gander, F., Proyer, R.T., & Ruch, W. (2020). Character strengths and PERMA: Investigating the relationships of character strengths with a multidimensional framework of well-Being. *Applied Research in Quality of Life, 15*(2), 307–328. https://doi.org/10.1007/s11482-018-9695-z

Wagner, L., Holenstein, M., Wepf, H., & Ruch, W. (2020). Character strengths are related to students' achievement, flow experiences and enjoyment in teacher-centered learning, individual, and group work above the influence of cognitive ability. *Frontiers in Psychology, 11*, Article 1324. https://doi.org/10.3389/fpsyg.2020.01324

Wagner, L., Pindeus, L., & Ruch, W. (2021). Character strengths in the life domains of work, education, leisure, and relationships, and their associations with flourishing. *Frontiers in Psychology, 12*, Article 597534. https://doi.org/10.3389/fpsyg.2021.597534

Wagner, L., & Ruch, W. (2022). Displaying character strengths in behavior is related to well-being and achievement at school: Evidence from between- and within-person analyses. *Journal of Positive Psychology*. Advance online publication. https://doi.org/10.1080/17439760.2022.2109196

Wiese, C.W., Tay, L., Duckworth, A.L., D'Mello, S., Kuykendall, L., Hofmann, W., Baumeister, R.F., & Vohs, K.D. (2018). Too much of a good thing? Exploring the inverted-U relationship between self-control and happiness. *Journal of Personality, 86*(3), 380–396. https://doi.org/10.1111/jopy.12322

Zettler, I., Hilbig, B.E., Moshagen, M., & de Vries, R.E. (2015). Dishonest responding or true virtue? A behavioral test of impression management. *Personality and Individual Differences, 81*, 107–111. https://doi.org/10.1016/j.paid.2014.10.007

Chapter 7

Assessing Humor and Its Kin

Sonja Heintz[1] and Jennifer Hofmann[2]

[1]School of Psychology, Faculty of Health, University of Plymouth, UK
[2]Department of Psychology, University of Zurich, Switzerland

This chapter first defines humor and introduces unidimensional and multidimensional approaches. It then outlines the relevance of humor for positive psychology (well-being, virtuousness, and humor interventions). The main focus of this chapter lies on different assessment instruments, such as questionnaires, behavior tests, and behavior observations. Next, we discuss the challenges in assessing humor and suggest steps for overcoming these challenges as well as make recommendations when selecting measures for research and applications. Finally, we present important steps for future research and applications in the assessment of humor.

Humor is a term that has had different connotations throughout history and that is still used with different meanings nowadays (Martin & Ford, 2018; Ruch, 2008; Ruch, Heintz et al., 2018). The most prevalent interpretation of the term "humor" in current psychological research is as an umbrella term that entails all funny or comic phenomena. In this sense, humor by itself is a rather broad and neutral term (see Roeckelein, 2002; cf. Ruch, Heintz et al., 2018) that only receives its valence or "flavor" when we specify the type or style of humor under investigation, such as aggressive, benevolent, or verbal humor. Additionally, the term "sense of humor" is often used to denote stable individual differences in humor in general (e.g., Craik et al., 1996; Martin & Lefcourt, 1984; McGhee, 2010; Ruch & Heintz, 2019; Thorson & Powell, 1993). We also need to disentangle the terms "humor" and "laughter." While the experience of amusement is often accompanied by laughter, amusement also occurs without laughter (and sometimes even without any nonverbal signal at all; see Ruch, 1995); vice versa, laughter may occur without humor.

In the context of positive psychology, positively and morally valued forms of humor are the most relevant because of their apparent connection to well-being and other positive outcomes (Hofmann & Ruch, 2019; Lefcourt, 2001; McGhee, 2010; Peterson & Seligman, 2004; Ruch & Heintz, 2016). Yet, a look at darker styles of humor (such as mockery) and humorlessness may help to identify humor-related situations or traits that may be related to negative outcomes, or that should be avoided in positive psychology interventions (see also Edwards & Martin, 2014; Kuiper, 2012). Considering both the positive and negative sides of humor thus enables a holistic perspective when assessing humor in positive psychology.

From General Sense of Humor to Narrow Traits, Styles, and Ability

Earlier conceptions of the sense of humor viewed this construct as unidimensional, ranging from no sense of humor to a great sense of humor (e.g., McGhee, 2010; Svebak, 1996). Yet, one major shortcoming of this view is that it covers neither the lack of humor (humorlessness) nor the complexity of humorous conduct. At best, a model describing the sense of humor should be multidimensional, detailing cognitive and affective factors of humor as well as humorlessness (Ruch et al., 1996). These ideas led to the development of the state-trait model of cheerfulness, which aims at explaining the temperamental basis of the sense of humor, consisting of the traits (and respective states) of cheerfulness, seriousness, and bad mood. They comprise affective and cognitive aspects of humor and account for interindividual as well as intraindividual differences (for an overview, see Hofmann et al., 2018).

Additionally, psychological humor research attempted to conceptualize humor from a multidimensional perspective. Craik et al. (1996) derived specific aspects of everyday humorous conduct from the literature, everyday observations, and acts depicted by humorous people. They collected a total of 100 statements, and principal component analyses revealed five bipolar factors underlying those items: socially warm vs. cold, reflective vs. boorish, earthy vs. repressed, benign vs. mean-spirited, and competent vs. inept styles of humorous conduct. This approach covers cognitive and affective dimensions as well as aspects of humorlessness (inept style).

In 2003, Martin et al. presented a different conceptualization of humor styles that focused on well-being functions of humor. Their four styles fall along two dimensions of enhancing oneself vs. relationships with others and doing this adaptively vs. maladaptively: affiliative (enhance relationships adaptively), self-enhancing (enhance oneself adaptively), aggressive (enhance oneself maladaptively), and self-defeating (enhance relationships maladaptively) humor styles. This model focuses mostly on affective aspects of humor. The most recent multidimensional approach to humor is a model of comic styles which adapted eight styles from literary studies to denote individual differences in humor (Ruch, Heintz et al., 2018). These styles cover lighter and darker affective aspects and more or less sophisticated cognitive aspects of humor: fun, benevolent humor, nonsense, wit, irony, satire, sarcasm, and cynicism. Humorlessness is not represented in this model.

Focusing on responses to laughter rather than on humor, another multidimensional model (Ruch et al., 2014; Ruch & Proyer, 2008, 2009) distinguishes different dispositions toward laughter, ridicule, and being laughed at. This model entails *gelotophobia*, the fear of being laughed at, which constitutes a form of humorlessness, where laughter is associated with ridicule, shame, and anxiety rather than positive emotions. The second dimension, *gelotophilia*, in turn, describes liking to be laughed at (i.e., entertaining others by making fun of oneself). The third dimension is *katagelasticism*, which entails liking to laugh at and mock others.

Moreover, interindividual differences are also apparent in aspects relating to the ability to comprehend and produce humor as well as differences in preferences for certain types of humor. Humor production targets generating something funny, ranging from spontaneous utterances in daily conversations to professional performances (i.e., comedians). Humor comprehension targets the capability of understanding humor (i.e., a punchline, a cartoon caption) and its mechanisms. Humor appreciation denotes a person's preference for certain kinds of humor. While humor appreciation is linked to prior comprehension, the two are still separate processes (see Chan et al., 2012, 2013; Ruch & Hehl, 2007). Based on comprehension and appreciation, we also experience emotional responses to humor: amusement or exhilaration, which is related to the nonverbal behavioral markers of smiling and laughter (Ruch, 1995) or sometimes other emotions, such as disgust or contempt.

General Thoughts on Assessing Humor and Its Kin

Humor has remained elusive, both in terms of its definition as well as in its measurement. Many instruments have been developed to assess humor and its kin, but only very few have been used by multiple groups of researchers – and even fewer have been thoroughly validated. Additionally, instruments sharing the same name might not necessarily measure the same construct, and instruments measuring the same construct might be labeled differently (also called "jingle-jangle-fallacies"; e.g., Marsh, 1994). This makes it hard to compare findings across studies and measures, which is eventually needed to establish a cumulative knowledge base of humor. We compiled Table 7.1 to better negotiate the maze of humor-related instruments.

An additional aspect to consider is the match between the assessment method and the construct under investigation as well as biases inherent to specific methods. Typical humor-related behavior (e.g., sense of humor, humor appreciation) can best be assessed using self-reports, other-reports, behavior tests, and behavior observations, while maximal humor-related behavior (e.g., humor comprehension and production) can best be assessed using performance measures. Laughter and smiling as behavioral markers of amusement can best be assessed using behavior observations. Historically, behavior tests have been most frequently employed in psychological humor research, yet since the 1980s self-report questionnaires have become the main method to assess humor-related constructs (see Ruch, 2007).

Although self-reports are economical to administer and score, they are prone to response biases (e.g., self-enhancement, social desirability) and memory biases (e.g., systematically underestimating or overestimating certain behaviors). Because humor is generally seen as a socially desirable construct (or undesirable in the case of mockery and forms of humorlessness; Cann & Matson, 2014; Craik et al., 1996), it is important to separate construct variance from method variance, especially in the context of positive psychology. In other words, positive correlations between humor and positive outcomes should not be driven by a common positive response bias but they should be related because the underlying constructs are genuinely and uniquely connected (see also Ruch & Heintz, 2013, 2017). Multimethod assessment can overcome biases inherent to self-reports and provide a more valid picture of humor and its kin.

The Relevance of Humor in Positive Psychology

Different criteria have been proposed in the literature to decide whether humor can be considered a positive-psychological trait. It is often seen as sufficient that humor correlates positively with positive outcomes (e.g., Lefcourt, 2001). Some authors extended this notion by also considering aspects of humor related to negative outcomes (e.g., Edwards & Martin, 2014; Kuiper, 2012). The strictest definition of humor as a positive-psychological trait is the definition of humor as a character strength by Peterson and Seligman (2004), where humor must fulfill several predefined criteria (e.g., being positive and morally valued, not having negative effects on oneself and others, contributing to individual and societal flourishing). Although we adopted the broadest definition of humor for the present chapter, it should be kept in mind that some approaches are more central to positive psychology (i.e., humor constructs that cause positive outcomes and/or are morally valued), while others are more peripheral (i.e., humor constructs that relate to negative outcomes).

Humor and Well-Being

In early theories (e.g., Freud, 1928; Hobbes, 1651/1996), humor was implied as relevant to health and well-being, and psychological humor research continued to focus on this perspective. Beneficial effects for psychological well-being were attributed both to mockery (i.e., laughing at others to feel better about oneself; Ferguson & Ford, 2008; Hobbes, 1651/1996; Martin et al., 2003) and to coping humor (i.e., humor as a mature defense mechanism; Freud, 1928; Martin & Lefcourt, 1983). Research has consistently shown that lighter forms of humor or comic styles, trait cheerfulness, laughing at oneself, and humor as a character strength correlate positively with well-being, positive affect, and work satisfaction, and negatively with negative affect, perceived stress, and depression (e.g., Hofmann et al., 2018; Martin et al., 2003; Mesmer-Magnus et al., 2012; Ruch, Wagner et al., 2018).

Correlations of mocking forms of humor (such as aggressive humor style, sarcasm, and cynicism) with negative psychological outcomes have been more mixed, and they are likely to be more relevant for negative social outcomes (e.g., Martin et al., 2003; Martin et al., 2012; Ruch, Wagner et al., 2018). Finally, forms of humorlessness, such as gelotophobia and the self-defeating humor style, typically correlate positively with depressive symptoms, anxiety, and negative affect (e.g., Martin et al., 2003; Ruch et al., 2014; Ruch, Wagner et al., 2018; cf. Heintz & Ruch, 2018; Ruch & Heintz, 2013, 2017). Overall, most humor research has focused on relationships with subjective (hedonic) well-being and less on relationships with psychological (eudaimonic) well-being – and little research has investigated social and physical well-being.

Humor and Virtue

The link between humor and virtue has been studied less often, although a benevolent and corrective function of humor was already noted in historic writings (for an overview, see Ruch & Heintz, 2016). Furthermore, humor was included as one of 24 character strengths in the VIA classification of character strengths and virtues (Peterson & Seligman, 2004). In line with the definition of character strengths as positively valued and moral traits, humor was more narrowly defined to only capture light and benevolent aspects (i.e., having a humorous worldview and entertaining others, but not mocking them). Ruch and Heintz (2016) extended this approach by defining not only benevolent humor, which captures a humorous worldview and a generally accepting attitude, but also corrective humor (or satire), which makes fun of wrongdoings to improve future behaviors and situations. Research supported the relationships of these humor constructs with virtuousness, especially the virtues of humanity, wisdom, and justice (Beermann & Ruch, 2009a, 2009b; Ruch et al., 2021; Ruch & Heintz, 2016; Ruch & Proyer, 2015; Yam et al., 2019).

Humor Interventions

In general, humor trainings are heterogeneous and focus on various goals; they have a long tradition and started before the formal foundation of positive psychology (Seligman & Csikszentmihalyi, 2000). To categorize existing interventions, Ruch and Hofmann (2017) proposed to distinguish three dimensions in which they differ: target group (individuals/individual use or focus on groups), presentation mode (offline/online), and procedure (standardized/ad hoc). According to these dimensions, huge differences exist among the best-evaluated training programs: Some trainings last 8 weeks and follow a standardized manual (e.g., McGhee's 7 Humor Habits Program, 2010; for an overview,

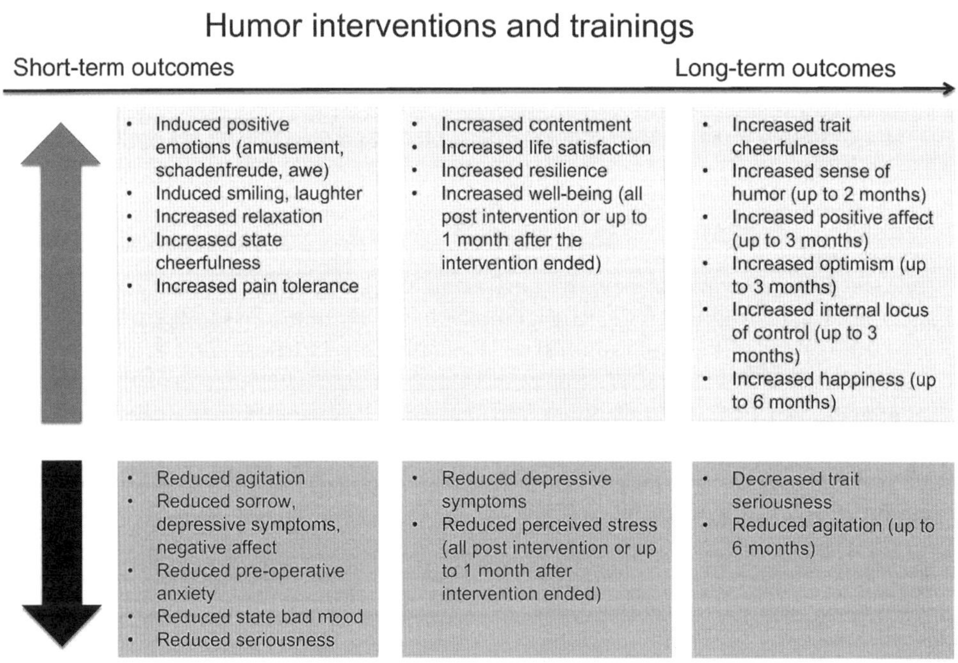

Figure 7.1. The short- and long-term effects of humor interventions on positive (top part) and negative (bottom part) psychological outcomes (adapted from Hofmann & Giuliani, 2019; all individual studies and references can be found in their chapter).

see Ruch & McGhee, 2014), while other online positive-psychology interventions last as short as 1 week with a minimal time investment of 5 min a day (e.g., Wellenzohn et al., 2018). Figure 7.1 shows the short- and long-term effects found for humor interventions. Even short interventions can enhance happiness and decrease depressive symptoms, while longer interventions have been found to also be effective in enhancing sense of humor, cheerfulness, self-efficacy, and optimism. Recent developments target specific domains (e.g., workplace; Hofmann et al., 2020) and morally valued forms of humor (Hofmann & Ruch, 2019).

Humor Assessment Instruments

General Approaches

The instruments are divided into three categories: (1) questionnaires, which comprise self-reports and other-reports of humor, the sense of humor, dispositions toward laughter and being laughed at, and cheerfulness in traits and states; (2) behavior tests, which capture habitual responses to different kinds of humorous stimuli (humor appreciation) or the ability to comprehend and to actively produce humor using performance measures; and (3) behavior observations, which assess affective responses to humor, namely, smiling and laughter, but also possible negative emotional reactions to humor (e.g., contempt, disgust, and shame).

Overview of Humor Assessment Instruments and Key Findings

Table 7.1. presents an overview of prevalent humor instruments employed in current research that have satisfying psychometric properties. All instruments listed were developed rationally (i.e., based on a model/theory, a conceptual definition, and/or existing literature) and empirically (i.e., principal components, factor, and/or reliability analyses; see Table 7.1). Table 7.2 lists other noteworthy instruments that have partially untested or insufficient psychometric properties. Ruch (2007) provides a comprehensive list of humor instruments, and further discussions can be found in Casu and Gremigni (2012), Ruch and Heintz (2014, 2019), and Martin and Ford (2018).

Table 7.1. The psychometric properties of prevalent humor instruments (in chronological order)

Instrument	Scale(s) and items	Reliability	Validity	Key findings	Norms	Notes
Questionnaires						
State-Trait Cheerfulness Inventory (Ruch et al., 1996, 1997)	Temperamental basis of the sense of humor: cheerfulness, seriousness, and bad mood as traits and states (forms with 30–106 items for traits, 18–30 items for states)	α > .90 (long/standard form; Hofmann et al., 2018); r_{tt} (traits) = 83–.84 (8 weeks; Carretero-Dios et al., 2014)	Factorial, convergent and discriminant validity supported (Carretero-Dios et al., 2011)	State forms sensitive to mood inductions; trait forms moderate effects of humor interventions (Hofmann & Ruch, 2017; Wellenzohn et al., 2018)	Adults from many countries (Hofmann et al., 2018)	Trait long-form (104/106 items) distinguishes 14 facets; state long-form (30 items) distinguishes 6 facets; several translations (see Hofmann et al., 2018)
Sense of Humor Scale (SHS; McGhee, 1999, 2010)	Six humor habits/skills: Enjoyment of humor, verbal humor, laughter, humor in everyday life laughing at yourself, and humor under stress (24 items)	α = .74–.90 (Proyer et al., 2010); parallel-test reliability *M* = .77 (Ruch & Heintz, 2018)	Factorial, convergent and discriminant validity supported (Heintz et al., 2021; Ruch & Heintz, 2018)	Seven humor habits training increases scores in the scale and well-being (Ruch & McGhee, 2014)	Adults from German-speaking countries (Proyer et al., 2010)	Often includes the two preconditions for sense of humor, playfulness/seriousness & positive/negative mood (8 items each); parallel version (Ruch & Heintz, 2018) and short version developed (Heintz et al., 2021)
Humor Styles Questionnaire (Martin et al., 2003)	Well-being functions of humor: Affiliative, self-enhancing, aggressive, and self-defeating humor styles (32 items)	α = .82–.88; r_{tt} = .80–.85 (1–2 weeks)	Factorial, convergent and discriminant validity supported except for self-defeating (Heintz, 2017, 2019b)	Relations to well-being and outcomes in romantic relationships (Caird & Martin, 2014) and workplace (Mesmer-Magnus et al., 2012); self-enhancing led to lowered state anxiety (Ford et al., 2017)	Adults from many countries (Martin, 2015); children from the UK	Adapted for children (Fox et al., 2013; James & Fox, 2016) and workplace (e.g., Cann et al., 2014); several translations; limited incremental validity beyond personality (Ruch & Heintz, 2013)

Table 7.1. continued

Instrument	Scale(s) and items	Reliability	Validity	Key findings	Norms	Notes
Humor scale of VIA Inventory of Strengths (Peterson et al., 2005) and VIA-Youth (Park & Peterson, 2006)	Humor as a character strength (10 items); 1 of 24 character strengths in the VIA-Inventory	$\alpha = .85$; $r_{tt} = .80, .81, .85$ (3, 6, 9 months, respectively; Ruch et al., 2010)	Convergent, discriminant, and factorial validity supported (McGrath, 2014; Ruch et al., 2010)	Relations to psychological well-being (Peterson et al., 2007) and positive workplace outcomes (Hofmann et al., 2020); training increased well-being (Wellenzohn et al., 2018)	Adults from 75 nations (McGrath, 2015); adolescents from several countries	Adaptations to many languages; explicitly excludes all forms of humor that are not morally valued
GELOPH, PhoPhiKat (Ruch & Proyer, 2008, 2009)	Dispositions toward laughter and being laughed at: gelotophobia, gelotophilia, and katagelasticism (15–45 items)	$\alpha > .90$; $r_{tt} = .80–.86$ and .75–.80 (3, 6 months, respectively; Ruch & Proyer, 2009)	Factorial, convergent and discriminant validity supported (see Ruch et al., 2014)	Related to responses to teasing and ridicule, physiological responses to laughter, life satisfaction, and character strengths (Ruch et al., 2014)	German-speaking adults	Adapted for children (Proyer et al., 2012) and workplace (9 items; Hofmann et al., 2017); 42 language versions (Proyer et al., 2009)
BenCor (Ruch & Heintz, 2016) and Comic Style Markers (CSM; Ruch et al., 2018)	Comic styles: Fun, (benevolent) humor, nonsense, wit, irony, satire/corrective humor, sarcasm, and cynicism (48 items); BenCor: Benevolent humor and satire (12 items)	CSM: $\alpha = .66–.89$, $r_{tt} = .74–.89$ (1–2 weeks); BenCor: $\alpha s > .60$ in 21 of 25 samples (Heintz et al., 2018)	Factorial, convergent and discriminant validity supported	Relations to well-being, character strengths, mindfulness, and behavior tests of humor (Heintz, 2019a; Hofmann et al., 2020; Ruch, Wagner et al., 2018)	Adults from German-speaking, US/UK, and Chilean samples	Entail verbally sophisticated items (more suitable for samples with higher education); revised BenCor-R for international samples (Heintz et al., 2020)

Table 7.1. continued

Instrument	Scale(s) and items	Reliability	Validity	Key findings	Norms	Notes
Behavior tests						
3 Witz-Dimensionen Test (Ruch, 1992), Forms K, A, and B	Humor appreciation (funniness, aversiveness): Incongruity-resolution, nonsense, and sexual humor (30 + 5 warm-up items)	α = .65–.95; parallel-test reliability = .54–.90; no r_{tt} because of nature of the material	Factorial and convergent validity supported (Hofmann & Ruch, 2018)	Can be used to induce positive affect (Ruch, 1992); relation to comic styles (Heintz, 2019a)	Adults & patients from German-speaking countries	A and B are parallel versions (30 items each); a structural preference index can be computed (liking incongruity-resolution rather than nonsense)
Cartoon Punchline Production Test (CPPT[-K]; Köhler & Ruch, 1993; Ruch & Heintz, 2019)	Humor creation (writing cartoon captions): Quantity and quality (wittiness and originality) (15 items, short version with 6 items)	α = .94 for quantity, .52–.75 for quality	Convergent, discriminant, and factorial validity supported (Heintz, 2019a; Köhler & Ruch, 1996)	Relations to creativity and humor self-reports (Heintz, 2019a)	Adults from German-speaking countries (Ruch & Heintz, 2019)	Free ratings usually require 6–12 raters, with standardized rating schemes 2–4 raters sufficient; optional ratings for wit and imagination of the person
Escala de Apreciación del Humor (EAHU; Carretero-Dios et al., 2010)	Humor appreciation (funniness, aversiveness): incongruity-resolution, nonsense, sexual, black, men-/women-disparagement humor (32 items)	αs>.70	Content & factorial validity supported (Carretero-Dios et al., 2009)	Relations to Schwartz' and Rokeach's values (Carretero-Dios, 2005) and comic styles (Mendiburo-Seguel & Heintz, 2020)	Adults from Spain	Three of the six scales derived from the 3 WD; added value of separating disparaging contents supported in recent research (Heintz, 2021)

Table 7.1. continued

Instrument	Scale(s) and items	Reliability	Validity	Key findings	Norms	Notes
Behavior observations						
Facial Action Coding System (FACS; Ekman, Friesen, & Hager, 2002)	Objective assessment of 44 visually discernible action units (AUs) in the human face, including gross movements (eye, head, and shoulder movements); not specific to the study of humor	Good to excellent reliabilities (κ) for 90 % of AUs; good reliability for intensity scoring (κ; Sayette et al., 2001)	Construct validity supported (Ekman & Rosenberg, 2005); standardized manual and exam for coders to ensure validity and reliability	Relations of smiling and laughter to self-reports of humor and emotions (Ekman & Rosenberg, 2005); absence of positive reactions to humorous stimuli related to gelotophobia (Platt et al., 2013)	–	Distinguishes different kinds of smiles and laughs (Ekman & Rosenberg, 2005; Ruch, 2007) and emotional responses to humor; abbreviated EMFACS allows coding emotion expression configurations (holistic ratings of full expressions)

Note. α = Cronbach's α, r_{tt} = test-retest reliability, κ = Cohen's kappa (interrater reliability).

Table 7.2. Overview of other noteworthy humor assessment instruments (in chronological order)

Instrument	Scale(s) and number of items	Notes on psychometric properties
Sense of Humor Scale and revisions (Svebak, 1974, 1996, 2010)	Sense of humor total score, subscales meta-message sensitivity (M-scale), personal liking of humor (L-scale), emotional expressiveness (E-scale; 21–27 items; short form for total score with 6 or 3 items)	Criterion validity and r_{tt} across 1 month supported; construct validity supported for M-scale and partially for L-scale; Factorial validity only supported for short scales with total score, not for longer scale (Thorson & Powell, 1991); M-scale partially with low internal consistency (Köhler & Ruch, 1996); SOC untested
Coping Humor Scale (Martin & Lefcourt, 1983)	Use of humor to cope with stressful experiences (7items)	Convergent and criterion validity supported; SOC untested; factorial validity with mixed results (Thorson & Powell, 1991); item 4 insufficient (Martin, 1996)
Situational Humor Response Questionnaire (Martin & Lefcourt, 1984)	Displaying sense of humor through conversational behavior (18 situational items and 3 general self-report items)	Internal consistency, r_{tt} (1 month), and convergent validity (SOC, laughter) supported (Martin, 1996); content validity debated (propensity to laughter vs. sense of humor; Ruch & Deckers, 1993); factorial validity not supported (Thorson & Powell, 1991)
Humor Orientation Scale (Booth-Butterfield & Booth-Butterfield, 1991)	Communicative use of humor in interpersonal situations, total score or frequency and effectiveness (17 items)	Reliability and criterion validity supported; factorial validity supports 1–2 factors; SOC untested
Multidimensional Sense of Humor Scale (Thorson & Powell, 1993)	Recognition of oneself as a humorous person, recognition of others' humor, appreciation of humor, laughing, perspective, coping humor (29 items)	Criterion validity supported; SOC and r_{tt} untested; factorial validity debated (1–4 factors with different interpretations and item compositions; Thorson et al., 1997); total score reliable, subscale humor appreciation often less reliable
Humorous Behavior Q-Sort Deck (Craik et al., 1996)	Socially warm/cold, reflective/boorish, earthy/repressed, benign/mean-spirited, and competent/inept styles of humorous conduct (100 items); ipsatively scored	Content and criterion validity supported; SOC not supported for all scales (Ruch, Proyer et al., 1996); factor structure not replicated (4–7 unidimensional factors with normative instead of ipsative scoring; Kirsh & Kuiper, 2003; Ruch & Heintz, 2019)
Relational Humor Inventory (De Koning & Weiss, 2002)	Functional humor in relationships: Negative, positive, instrumental; self, partner, and couple humor (34 items)	Criterion, construct, and factorial validity supported; internal consistencies supported; SOC and r_{tt} untested

Note. All instruments are self-report questionnaires. r_{tt} = test-retest reliability, SOC = self-other convergence (i.e., correlations between self- and other-reports).

Challenges in Assessing Humor

The selection in Table 7.1 should help to provide a list of recommended instruments among the vast variety of humor measures. Still, several challenges persist in assessing humor which should be addressed in future research to eventually provide a solid basis for developing and evaluating humor-based interventions (see also Ruch, 2007). In general, adopting a consistent terminology and using psychometrically sound instruments whenever possible would help to unify humor-related constructs and measures and to provide a common framework for researchers and practitioners.

Theory-Based Approaches

Most humor instruments have been derived rationally, based on more or less well-defined constructs. By contrast, deriving constructs from detailed models and theories (a deductive approach) would be preferable, as it would allow a better interpretation of measures and constructs as well as an empirical means of testing their validity (especially content validity) and underlying models and theories. At the very least, authors should provide a detailed definition of the construct(s) they intend to assess, a description of the high scorer on a scale, and similarities and differences to existing constructs. Eventually, theoretical and empirical approaches need to be aligned to advance and refine each other to paint a comprehensive picture of humor.

Convergent/Criterion Validity

Only a few multitrait-multimethod studies across several assessment instruments have been conducted in humor research (Babad, 1974; Köhler & Ruch, 1996; Koppel & Sechrest, 1970), and they yielded surprisingly low convergent validities; for example, self-reports and behavior tests of humor production showed only small overlaps (Köhler & Ruch, 1996). This poses the question: Which method is valid? Behavior tests possess face validity (i.e., evaluating jokes or writing punchlines), yet they might not capture humor appreciation and production in everyday life (e.g., Lampert & Ervin-Tipp, 2007). Self-reports often capture social desirability (i.e., very few people would admit that they are not humorous) to some extent (e.g., Cann & Matson, 2014; Köhler & Ruch, 1996; Martin et al., 2003; Ruch & Deckers, 1993). As mentioned above, however, a joint positivity bias seems an unlikely sole explanation of the relationships between humor and positive outcomes. Employing further methods (e.g., other-reports, behavioral observations, intensive longitudinal assessments of everyday humor experiences or behaviors) could help to solve which instruments or scales are valid. For example, humor measures should correlate higher with other humor instruments than with measures of personality or well-being (see Ruch & Heintz, 2017, for an experimental method of distinguishing humor and nonhumor variance in items). Another option is that the different methods capture valid aspects of humor, but that these aspects are different from one another (e.g., maximal humor creation performance in behavior tests vs. humor communication in social situations in self-reports; see Ruch & Heintz, 2019). Additionally, the content and structure of the items in behaviors tests and questionnaires might be different; this interpretation is strengthened by recent findings of the convergence between self-reports and behavior tests with matched contents (i.e., wit and nonsense; Heintz, 2019a; Mendiburo-Seguel & Heintz, 2020).

Incremental Validity

When investigating the relationships between humor and well-being, it is important to take other relevant variables, such as broad personality traits, into account. Humor should present an added value beyond already established traits; in other words, we need to establish the incremental validity of humor measures in predicting relevant outcomes. For example, the relationship between telling jokes and positive emotions should not only be driven by extraversion, but there should be a unique contribution of joke-telling to explaining variance in positive emotions. Recent studies supported small incremental relationships of humor in explaining psychological well-being beyond personality traits (e.g., Dyck & Holtzman, 2013; Jovanovic, 2011; Ruch & Heintz, 2013; Ruch, Wagner et al., 2018). This shows that humor might be a unique piece of the complex puzzle that fosters our well-being.

Interplay of States and Traits

The question of whether different states influence responses to trait humor measures has mainly been investigated with behavior tests of humor appreciation and production (for an overview, see Deckers, 2007). In general, inducing positive moods increased humor appreciation and production, while negative moods reduced them with small effects. Recently, Yoon (2018) also found that low-arousal moods (independent of valence) increased the perceived humor of television ads. Further research is required to determine the effects of genuine mood fluctuations, different mood induction procedures, and interactions between valence and arousal on behavior measures and self-reports of humor. In general, mood and state effects should be controlled, especially in experiments and single-case studies, by standardizing the procedure and conditions, by assessing humor-related or general mood, by minimizing the influence of other people on the test results (e.g., testing participants individually, experimenter absent or preoccupied), and by using warm-up items (see also Ruch, 1992).

Scoring of Qualitative Data

When employing behavior tests of humor comprehension and humor production, participants are usually required to produce open responses, such as explaining a joke or writing punchlines. To score this data, several independent raters code the material according to prespecified criteria (e.g., funniness, degree of comprehension). Interrater reliability then describes how well the different judgments converge, which often requires six or more raters for each punchline to balance out different humor preferences. Standardized coding schemes can be employed to make this scoring more objective and economical. For instance, Ruch and Heintz (2019) presented a coding scheme for cartoon-caption tasks, which allows a reliable coding of the wittiness and originality of punchlines with only two raters. Developing such standardized schemes for other humor comprehension and production tasks would be an important endeavor for future research to increase both the practicability of open responses and comparisons between studies.

Recommendations: Selecting a Suitable Instrument

The various aspects of humor that may be assessed require different assessment methods. Figure 7.2 presents an overview of humor-related constructs and general recommendations of assessment methods.

Figure 7.2 shows that, in general, most aspects (such as humor-related traits) are predominantly assessed with self-reports or other-reports, while other aspects, such as humor detection, production, comprehension, and appreciation, call for tests. Also, nonverbal responses may be assessed with behavior-coding methods. To find a suitable instrument for planning new research and applied projects on humor, the decision tree in Figure 7.2 and the guiding questions in Figure 7.3 can be followed to choose the appropriate method and design.

A few notes should be made on specific applications and research designs that call for distinct instruments. First, the State-Trait Cheerfulness Inventory (STCI; Ruch et al., 1996, 1997) is currently the only validated measure that includes humor-related states. Thus, if temporal changes are of interest, or if differential mood states are to be con-

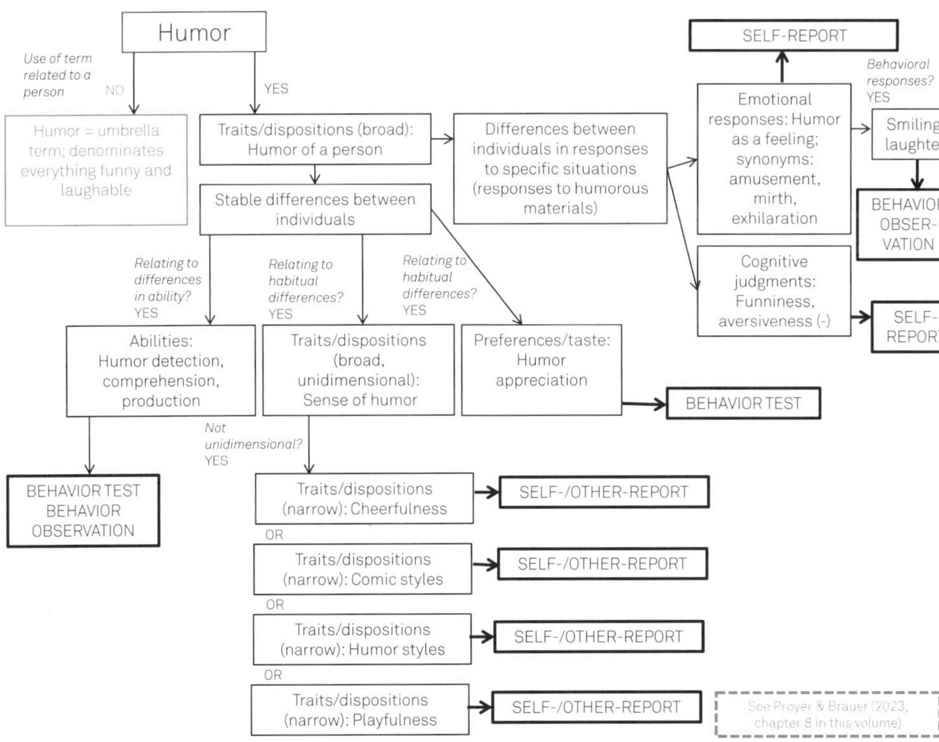

Figure 7.2. Decision tree for the assessment of aspects of humor and available methods.

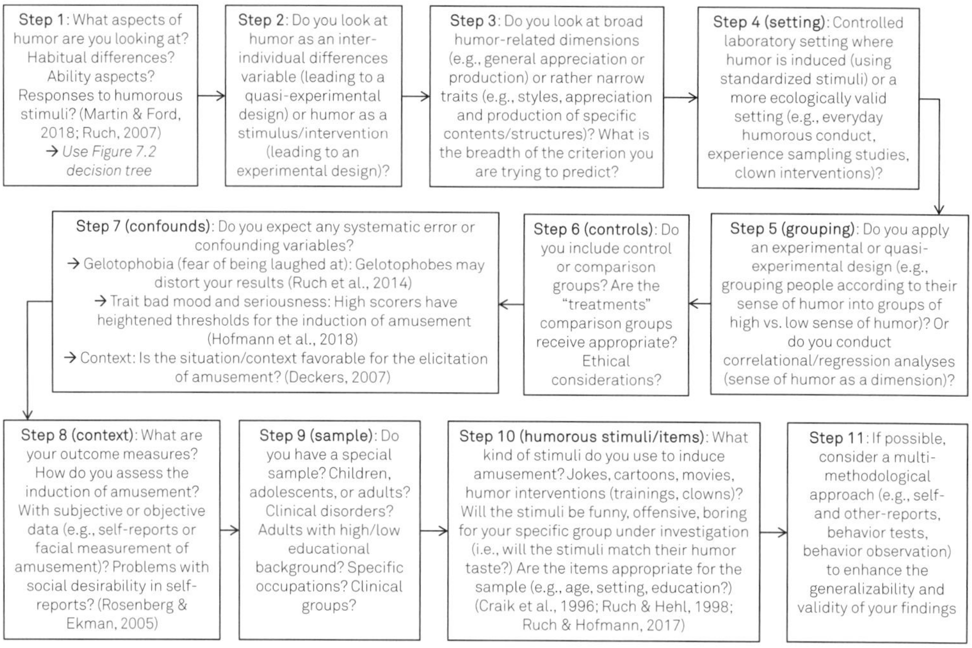

Figure 7.3. Specific decision steps to consider when planning a humor study.

trolled in experiments and interventions, the STCI is the method of choice. Second, the Sense of Humor Scale (SHS; Heintz et al., 2021; McGhee, 2010; Ruch & Heintz, 2018) is the preferred instrument to assess the effectiveness of the 7 Humor Habits Training or a humor training derived from it.

Third, behavior tests that contain humor stimuli need to be piloted before being applied in another culture, age group, context, and/or language. The stimuli might require previous knowledge (e.g., event, person, or tradition), rely on a specific format (e.g., joke setup or meme), or contain puns or word plays that cannot be easily translated (see Chiaro, 2007). If novel stimuli are to be used, extensive piloting is required to ensure that the stimuli differ only in their intended features (e.g., content, structure, funniness, offensiveness, or boringness) but are comparable in other aspects to avoid biased and potentially misleading conclusions (see also Heintz, 2021). In addition, it should be tested whether participants know the stimuli, as repeated exposure might change the evaluation of the stimuli (e.g., waxing or waning; Hollingworth, 1911).

Fourth, the context in which the study is conducted could also influence the preference for a specific method. As outlined in the Introduction, self-reports are prone to response and memory biases. To our knowledge, no studies have been conducted that compared humor self-reports in high-stakes vs. low-stakes conditions or in faking good vs. bad instructions (see Furnham, 1986). Until there is evidence that assessments of humor are comparable in these conditions, one should choose a behavior test or even better a multimethod approach in high-stakes contexts. Additionally, to best capture the humor constructs relevant for the specific population, instruments that were either developed within or adapted to a specific context (e.g., the workplace) or age group (e.g., adolescence, childhood, older age) should be preferred over general instruments. This ensures that items are well understood, and that participants can adequately respond to the items, enhancing data quality and reducing attrition. Thus far, most instruments were developed for adults (mostly university students) in general, and their applicability to other contexts or populations might be limited.

Fifth, the breadth of the constructs assessed by humor instruments ranges from specific responses to specific humor stimuli (in behavior tests) or specific humorous conduct (comic styles) to broader statements about one's humorous temperament (STCI) or well-being-related functions (humor styles). Therefore, one has to decide how broad or narrow humor should be assessed for the research or application in question. Furthermore, tests should be chosen that assess constructs relevant for the criterion, such as specific aspects of well-being (e.g., positive affect, relationships), morality, or virtue.

Sixth, although employing behavioral measures and observations of humor is advantageous and also necessary for validating a measure, it should be kept in mind that scoring humor production tests (in which participants produce punchlines or other humorous responses), humor comprehensions tests (in which participants explain why a stimulus is funny), and behavioral observations (using the FACS) requires more time and effort than utilizing and evaluating a self-report questionnaire. As outlined previously, developing standardized schemes can help to make these scoring procedures more efficient. For behavioral observations, coding time could be reduced by focusing on specific action units (e.g., those relevant for positive emotions) or by employing the EMFACS, which focuses on emotion-specific displays rather than single action units and may be used after successfully passing the FACS final test for coders.

Finally, if conducting single-case studies or assessing individuals, humor tests should be more reliable than for group-based comparisons (.90 recommended rather than .70 for groups). Furthermore, norms should be available against which the individual can be compared. Ideally, the norm group should have a comparable demographic background as the person under investigation, based on factors that could influence the resulting humor scores (e.g., sex, age, education, or nationality).

Recommendations for Future Research and Application

Several recommendations can be made for the research on humor instruments. Ideally, one should develop a comprehensive model or theory of humor from which appropriate items and scales can be derived (see Heintz & Ruch, 2019). These new instruments need to undergo thorough validation: content validity by expert ratings, convergent and discriminant validity with other measures and methods, factorial validity with exploratory and confirmatory factor analyses, and criterion and incremental validity beyond established measures to ensure that the new instruments provide an added value in predicting relevant outcomes. These measures should then be adapted into other languages and cultures to determine the degree of measurement invariance of the scale and single items (i.e., to what extent they measure the same constructs or are unique to specific contexts). Further, the nomological network (i.e., pattern of correlations) of humor instruments in different contexts should be explored. This would eventually allow building a cumulative and crosscultural line of humor research.

Establishing comprehensive theories and models and valid assessments would then allow meaningful *applications* of humor instruments. This could include adapting and assessing humor in different applied contexts, such as the workplace and clinical settings. Also, adapting humor instruments to different age groups, to allow assessments in settings such as schools or retirement homes, would be valuable future directions. Further, one might investigate short-term and long-term changes in humor because of life events, developmental changes, or changes because of trainings, which can be captured with instruments that assess both traits and states and through (intensive) longitudinal designs.

Overall, the assessment of humor has improved in the past two decades, and an increasing number of validation efforts have been carried out to ensure that the instruments actually measure what they intend to measure. While model-building and assessment are two often separate endeavors, it is to be hoped that the increasing interest in the construct of humor in psychology will lead to more global collaborations that advance humor from a theoretical and empirical perspective. These joint efforts should ideally lead to the development of theory-based, standardized, and validated instruments that help to advance research and applications of humor to explore its potential for psychosocial well-being and beyond.

References

Babad, E. Y. (1974). A multi-method approach to the assessment of humor: A critical look at humor tests. *Journal of Personality, 42*(4), 618–631. https://doi.org/10.1111/j.1467-6494.1974.tb00697.x

Beermann, U., & Ruch, W. (2009a). How virtuous is humor? Evidence from everyday behavior. *Humor: International Journal of Humor Research, 22*(4), 395–417. https://doi.org/10.1515/HUMR.2009.023

Beermann, U., & Ruch, W. (2009b). How virtuous is humor? What we can learn from current instruments. *The Journal of Positive Psychology, 4*(6), 528–539. https://doi.org/10.1080/17439760903262859

Booth-Butterfield, S., & Booth-Butterfield, M. (1991). Individual differences in the communication of humorous messages. *Southern Journal of Communication, 56*, 205–218. https://doi.org/10.1080/10417949109372831

Caird, S., & Martin, R. A. (2014). Relationship-focused humor styles and relationship satisfaction in dating couples: A repeated-measures design. *Humor: International Journal of Humor Research, 27*, 227–247. https://doi.org/10.1515/humor-2014-0015

Cann, A., & Matson, C. (2014). Sense of humor and social desirability: Understanding how humor styles are perceived. *Personality and Individual Differences, 66*, 176–180. https://doi.org/10.1016/j.paid.2014.03.029

Cann, A., Watson, A. J., & Bridgewater, E. A. (2014). Assessing humor at work: The humor climate questionnaire. *Humor: International Journal of Humor Research, 27*, 307–323. https://doi.org/10.1515/humor-2014-0019

Carretero-Dios, H. (2005). *Sentido del humor: Construcción de la escala de apreciación del humor (EAHU)* [Sense of humor: Construction of the humor appreciation scale (EAHU)]. Doctoral thesis, University of Granada, Spain. Retrieved from http://digibug.ugr.es/bitstream/handle/10481/656/15472310.pdf

Carretero-Dios, H., Benítez, I., Delgado-Rico, E., Ruch, W., & López-Benítez, R. (2014). Temperamental basis of sense of humor: The Spanish long form of the trait version of the State Trait Cheerfulness Inventory. *Personality and Individual Differences, 68*, 77–82. https://doi.org/10.1016/j.paid.2014.03.045

Carretero-Dios, H., Eid, M., & Ruch, W. (2011). Analyzing multitrait-mulitmethod data with multilevel confirmatory factor analysis: An application to the validation of the State-Trait Cheerfulness Inventory. *Journal of Research in Personality, 45*, 153–164. https://doi.org/10.1016/j.jrp.2010.12.007

Carretero-Dios, H., Pérez, C., & Buela-Casal, G. (2009). Content validity and metric properties of a pool of items developed to assess humor appreciation. *The Spanish Journal of Psychology, 12*, 773–787. https://doi.org/10.1017/S1138741600002146

Carretero-Dios, H., Pérez, C., & Buela-Casal, G. (2010). Assessing the appreciation of the content and structure of humor: Construction of a new scale. *Humor: International Journal of Humor Research, 23*, 307–325. https://doi.org/10.1515/humr.2010.014

Casu, G., & Gremigni, P. (2012). Humor measurement. In P. Gremigni (Ed.), *Humor and health promotion* (pp. 253–274). Nova Science Publishers.

Chan, Y.C., Chou, T.L., Chen, H.C., & Liang, K.C. (2012). Segregating the comprehension and elaboration processing of verbal jokes: An fMRI study. *NeuroImage, 61*, 899e906. https://doi.org/10.1016/j.neuroimage.2012.03.052

Chan, Y.C., Chou, T.L., Chen, H.-C., Yeh, Y.C., Lavallee, J.P., Liang, K.C., & Chang, K.E. (2013). Towards a neural circuit model of verbal humor processing: An fMRI study of the neural substrates of incongruity detection and resolution. *Neuroimage, 66*, 169–176. https://doi.org/10.1016/j.neuroimage.2012.10.019

Chiaro, D. (2007). The effect of translation on humour response. In Y. Gambier, M. Shlesinger, & R. Stolze (Eds.), *Doubts and directions in translation studies* (pp. 137–152). John Benjamins. https://doi.org/10.1075/btl.72.16chi

Craik, K.H., Lampert, M.D., & Nelson, A.J. (1996). Sense of humor and styles of everyday humorous conduct. *Humor: International Journal of Humor Research, 9*, 273–302. https://doi.org/10.1515/humr.1996.9.3-4.273

Deckers, L. (2007). Influence of mood on humor. In W. Ruch (Ed.), *The sense of humor: Explorations of a personality characteristic* (pp. 309–328). Mouton de Gruyter.

De Koning, E., & Weiss, R.L. (2002). The relational humor inventory: Functions of humor in close relationships. *American Journal of Family Therapy, 30*, 1–18. https://doi.org/10.1080/019261802753455615

Dyck, K.T., & Holtzman, S. (2013). Understanding humor styles and well-being: The importance of social relationships and gender. *Personality and Individual Differences, 55*, 53–58. https://doi.org/10.1016/j.paid.2013.01.023

Edwards, K.R., & Martin, R.A. (2014). The conceptualization, measurement, and role of humor as a character strength in positive psychology. *Europe's Journal of Psychology, 10*, 505–519. https://doi.org/10.5964/ejop.v10i3.759

Ekman, P., Friesen, W.V., & Hager, J.C. (2002). *Facial Action Coding System: A technique for the measurement of facial movement*. Consulting Psychologists Press.

Ekman, P., & Rosenberg, E.L. (Eds.) (2005). *What the face reveals. Basic and applied studies of spontaneous expression using the Facial Action Coding System (FACS)*. Oxford University Press. https://doi.org/10.1093/acprof:oso/9780195179644.001.0001

Ferguson, M.A., & Ford, T.E. (2008). Disparagement humor: A theoretical and empirical review of psychoanalytic, superiority, and social identity theories. *Humor: International Journal of Humor Research, 21*, 283–312. https://doi.org/10.1515/HUMOR.2008.014

Ford, T.E., Lappi, S.K., O'Connor, E.C., & Banos, N.C. (2017). Manipulating humor styles: Engaging in self-enhancing humor reduces state anxiety. *Humor, 30*(2), 169–191. https://doi.org/10.1515/humor-2016-0113

Fox, C.L., Dean, S., & Lyford, K. (2013). Development of a humor styles questionnaire for children. *Humor: International Journal of Humor Research, 26*, 295–319. https://doi.org/10.1515/humor-2013-0018

Freud, S. (1928). Humour. *International Journal of Psychoanalysis, 9*(1), 1–6. Retrieved from https://www.pep-web.org/document.php?id=SE.021.0159A

Furnham, A. (1986). Response bias, social desirability and dissimulation. *Personality and Individual Differences, 7*(3), 385–400. https://doi.org/10.1016/0191-8869(86)90014-0

Heintz, S. (2017). Putting a spotlight on daily humor behaviors: Dimensionality and relationships with personality, subjective well-being, and humor styles. *Personality and Individual Differences, 104*, 407–412. https://doi.org/10.1016/j.paid.2016.08.042

Heintz, S. (2019a). Locating eight comic styles in basic and broad concepts of humor: Findings from self-reports and behavior tests. *Current Psychology*. Advance online publication. https://doi.org/10.1007/s12144-019-00179-z

Heintz, S. (2019b). Do others judge my humor style as I do? Self-other agreement and construct validity of the Humor Styles Questionnaire. *European Journal of Psychological Assessment, 35*(5), 625–632. https://doi.org/10.1027/1015-5759/a000440

Heintz, S. (2021). Separating content and structure in humor appreciation: A bimodal structural equation modeling approach. *Journal of Individual Differences, 41*(1), 37–44. https://doi.org/10.1027/1614-0001/a000301

Heintz, S., & Ruch, W. (2018). Can self-defeating humor make you happy? Cognitive interviews reveal the adaptive side of the self-defeating humor style. *Humor: International Journal of Humor Research, 31*, 451–472. https://doi.org/10.1515/humor-2017-0089

Heintz, S., & Ruch, W. (2019). From four to nine styles: An update on individual differences in humor. *Personality and Individual Differences, 141*, 7–12. https://doi.org/10.1016/j.paid.2018.12.008

Heintz, S., Ruch, W., Aykan, S., Brdar, I., Brzozowska, D., Carretero-Dios, H. Chen, H.-C., Chłopicki, W., Choi, I., Dionigi, A., Ďurka, R., Ford, T. E., Güsewell, A., Isler, R. B., Ivanova, A., Laineste, L., Lajčiaková, P., Lau, C., Lee, M., ... Wong, P. S. O. (2020). Benevolent and corrective humor, life satisfaction, and broad humor dimensions: Extending the nomological network of the BenCor across 25 countries. *Journal of Happiness Studies, 21*(7), 2473–2492. https://doi.org/10.1007/s10902-019-00185-9

Heintz, S., Ruch, W., Lau, C., Saklofske, D. H., & McGhee, P. E. (2021). Development and validation of the Short Version of the Sense of Humor Scale (SHS-S): Paving the way for assessment of humor skills training. *European Journal of Psychological Assessment*. Advance onlinepublication. https://doi.org/10.1027/1015-5759/a000670

Heintz, S., Ruch, W., Platt, T., Pang, D., Carretero-Dios, H., Dionigi, A., Argüello Gutiérrez, C., Brdar, I., Brzozowska, D., Chen, H.-C., Chłopicki, W., Collins, M., Ďurka, R., El Yahfoufi, N. Y., Quiroga-Garza, A., Isler, R. B., Mendiburo-Seguel, A., Selvan Ramis, T., Saglam, B., ... Torres-Marín, J. (2018). Psychometric comparisons of benevolent and corrective humor across 22 countries: The virtue gap in humor goes international. *Frontiers in Psychology, 9*, Article 92. https://doi.org/10.3389/fpsyg.2018.00092

Hobbes, T. (1651/1996). *Leviathan*. Oxford University Press.

Hofmann, J., Carretero-Dios, H., & Carrell, A. (2018). Assessing the temperamental basis of the sense of humor: Adaptation of the English language version of the State-Trait Cheerfulness Inventory long and standard form. *Frontiers in Psychology, 9*, Article 2255. https://doi.org/10.3389/fpsyg.2018.02255

Hofmann, J., & Giuliani, F. (2019). Forschung: Humor ist trainierbar. [Research: Humour can be practiced]. In C. Müller (Ed.), *HumorCare – Das Heiterkeitsbuch für Pflege- und Gesundheitsberufe* (pp. 207–224). Hogrefe.

Hofmann, J., Heintz, S., Pang, D., & Ruch, W. (2020). Differential relationships of light and darker forms of humor with mindfulness. *Applied Research in Quality of Life, 15*(2), 369–393. https://doi.org/10.1007/s11482-018-9698-9

Hofmann, J., & Ruch, W. (2018). Humorous TV ads and the 3WD: Evidence for generalizability of humour appreciation across media? *European Journal of Humor Research, 5*, 194–215. https://doi.org/10.7592/EJHR2017.5.4.hofmann

Hofmann, J., & Ruch, W. (2019). Moving forward in fostering humor: Towards training lighter forms of humor in multicultural contexts. In L. E. van Zyl & S. Rothmann (Eds.), *Theoretical approaches to multicultural positive psychological interventions* (Vol. 1, pp. 1–20). Springer. https://doi.org/10.1007/978-3-030-20583-6_1

Hofmann, J., Ruch, W., Proyer, R.T., Platt, T., & Gander, F. (2017). Assessing dispositions toward ridicule and laughter in the workplace: Adapting and validating the PhoPhiKat-9 questionnaire. *Frontiers in Psychology, 8*, Article 714. https://doi.org/10.3389/fpsyg.2017.00714

Hollingworth, H.L. (1911). Experimental studies in judgment: Judgments of the comic. *Psychological Review, 18*, 132–156. https://doi.org/10.1037/h0071649

James, L., & Fox, C. (2016). The development of a humor styles questionnaire for younger children. *Humor: International Journal of Humor Research, 29*, 555–582. https://doi.org/10.1515/humor-2016-0042

Jovanovic, V. (2011). Do humor styles matter in the relationship between personality and subjective well-being? *Scandinavian Journal of Psychology, 52*, 502–507. https://doi.org/10.1111/j.1467-9450.2011.00898.x

Kirsh, G.A., & Kuiper, N.A. (2003). Positive and negative aspects of sense of humor: Associations with the constructs of individualism and relatedness. *Humor: International Journal of Humor Research, 16*(1), 33–62. https://doi.org/10.1515/humr.2003.004

Köhler, G., & Ruch, W. (1993). *The Cartoon Punchline Production Test — CPPT*. Unpublished manuscript. Department of Psychology, University of Düsseldorf, Germany.

Köhler, G., & Ruch, W. (1996). Sources of variance in current sense of humor inventories: How much substance, how much method variance? *Humor: International Journal of Humor Research, 9*, 363–398. https://doi.org/10.1515/humr.1996.9.3-4.363

Koppel, M.A., & Sechrest, L. (1970). A multitrait-multimethod matrix analysis of sense of humor. *Educational and Psychological Measurement, 30*(1), 77–85. https://doi.org/10.1177/001316447003000107

Kuiper, N.A. (2012). Humor and resiliency: Towards a process model of coping and growth. *Europe's Journal of Psychology, 8*(3), 475–491. https://doi.org/10.5964/ejop.v8i3.464

Lampert, M., & Ervin-Tipp, S. (2007). Exploring paradigms: The study of gender and sense of humor near the end of the 20th century. In W. Ruch (Ed.), *The sense of humor: Explorations of a personality characteristic* (2nd ed., pp. 231–270). Mouton de Gruyter. https://doi.org/10.1515/9783110804607-012

Lefcourt, H.M. (2001). *Humor: The psychology of living buoyantly.* Springer.

Marsh, H.W. (1994). Sport motivation orientations: Beware of jingle-jangle fallacies. *Journal of Sport and Exercise Psychology, 16*(4), 365–380. https://doi.org/10.1123/jsep.16.4.365

Martin, R.A. (1996). The situational humor response questionnaire (SHRQ) and coping humor scale (CHS): A decade of research findings. *Humor: International Journal of Humor Research, 9*, 251–272. https://doi.org/10.1515/humr.1996.9.3-4.251

Martin, R. A. (2015). On the challenges of measuring humor styles: Response to Heintz and Ruch. *Humor: International Journal of Humor Research, 28*, 635–639. https://doi.org/10.1515/humor-2015-0096

Martin, R.A., & Ford, T.E. (2018). *The psychology of humor: An integrative approach* (2nd ed.). Academic Press.

Martin, R.A., Lastuk, J.M., Jeffery, J., Vernon, P.A., & Veselka, L. (2012). Relationships between the Dark Triad and humor styles: A replication and extension. *Personality and Individual Differences, 52*(2), 178–182. https://doi.org/10.1016/j.paid.2011.10.010

Martin, R.A., & Lefcourt, H.M. (1983). Sense of humor as a moderator of the relation between stressors and moods. *Journal of Personality and Social Psychology, 45*, 1313–1324. https://doi.org/10.1037/0022-3514.45.6.1313

Martin, R.A., & Lefcourt, H.M. (1984). Situational Humor Response Questionnaire: Quantitative measure of sense of humor. *Journal of Personality and Social Psychology, 47*, 145–155. https://doi.org/10.1037/0022-3514.47.1.145

Martin, R.A., Puhlik-Doris, P., Larsen, G., Gray, J., & Weir, K. (2003). Individual differences in uses of humor and their relation to psychological well-being: Development of the Humor Styles Questionnaire. *Journal of Research in Personality, 37*, 48–75. https://doi.org/10.1016/S0092-6566(02)00534-2

McGhee, P.E. (1999). *Health, healing and the amuse system: Humor as survival training* (3rd ed.). Kendall/Hunt.

McGhee, P.E. (2010). *Humor as survival training for a stressed-out world: The 7 humor habits program*. Author House.

McGrath, R.E. (2014). Scale-and item-level factor analyses of the VIA Inventory of Strengths. *Assessment, 21*(1), 4–14. https://doi.org/10.1177/1073191112450612

McGrath, R.E. (2015). Character strengths in 75 nations: An update. *The Journal of Positive Psychology, 10*, 41–52. https://doi.org/10.1080/17439760.2014.888580

Mendiburo-Seguel, A., & Heintz, S. (2020). Comic styles and their relation to the sense of humor, humor appreciation, acceptability of prejudice, humorous self-image and happiness. *Humor, 33*(3), 381–403. https://doi.org/10.1515/humor-2018-0151

Mesmer-Magnus, J., Glew, D.J., & Viswesvaran, C. (2012). A meta-analysis of positive humour in the workplace. *Journal of Managerial Psychology, 27*, 155–190. https://doi.org/10.1108/02683941211199554

Park, N., & Peterson, C. (2006). Moral competence and character strengths among adolescents: The development and validation of the Values in Action Inventory of Strengths for Youth. *Journal of Adolescence, 29*, 891–909. https://doi.org/10.1016/j.adolescence.2006.04.011

Peterson, C., Park, N., & Seligman, M.E.P. (2005). Assessment of character strengths. In G.P. Koocher, J.C. Norcross, & S.S. Hill (Eds.), *Psychologists' desk reference* (pp. 93–98). Oxford University Press.

Peterson, C., Ruch, W., Beermann, U., Park, N., & Seligman, M.E.P. (2007). Strengths of character, orientations to happiness, and life satisfaction. *The Journal of Positive Psychology, 2*, 149–156. https://doi.org/10.1080/17439760701228938

Peterson, C., & Seligman, M.E.P. (2004). *Character strengths and virtues: A handbook and classification*. Oxford University Press.

Platt, T., Hofmann, J., Ruch, W., & Proyer, R.T. (2013). Duchenne Display responses towards sixteen enjoyable emotions: Individual differences between no and fear of being laughed at. *Motivation and Emotion, 37*, 776–786. https://doi.org/10.1007/s11031-013-9342-9

Proyer, R.T., & Brauer, K. (2023). Assessing playfulness: Current challenges and overview. In W. Ruch, A.B. Bakker, L. Tay, & F. Gander, *Handbook of positive psychology assessment* (pp. 145–161). Hogrefe Publishing.

Proyer, R.T., Neukom, M., Platt, T., & Ruch, W. (2012). Assessing gelotophobia, gelotophilia, and katagelasticism in children: An initial study on how six to nine-year-olds deal with laughter and ridicule and how this relates to bullying and victimization. *Child Indicators Research, 5*, 297–316. https://doi.org/10.1007/s12187-011-9127-1

Proyer, R.T., Ruch, W., Ali, N.S., Al-Olimat, H.S., Amemiya, T., Adal, T.A., Aziz Ansari, S., Arhar, Š., Asem, G., Baudin, N., Bawab, S., Bergen, D., Brdar, I., Brites, R., Brunner-Sciarra, M., Carrell, A., Carretero Dios, H., Celik, M., Ceschi, G., ... Yeun, E.J. (2009). Breaking ground in cross-cultural research on the fear of being laughed at (gelotophobia): A multi-national study involving 73 countries. *Humor, 22*(1–2), 253–279. https://doi.org/10.1515/humr.2009.012

Proyer, R.T., Ruch, W., & Müller, L. (2010). Sense of humor among the elderly. *Zeitschrift für Gerontologie und Geriatrie, 43*, 19–24. https://doi.org/10.1007/s00391-009-0082-0

Roeckelein, J.E. (2002). *The psychology of humor: A reference guide and annotated bibliography*. Greenwood Press.

Ruch, W. (1992). Assessment of appreciation of humor: Studies with the 3 WD humor test. In C.D. Spielberger, & J.N. Butcher (Eds.), *Advances in personality assessment* (Vol. 9, pp. 27–75). Erlbaum.

Ruch, W. (1995). Will the real relationship between facial expression and affective experience please stand up: The case of exhilaration. *Cognition and Emotion, 9*(1), 33–58. https://doi.org/10.1080/02699939508408964

Ruch, W. (2007). Humor measurement tools. In W. Ruch (Ed.), *The sense of humor: Explorations of a personality characteristic* (2nd ed., pp. 405–412). Mouton de Gruyter. https://doi.org/10.1515/9783110804607.405

Ruch, W. (2008). The psychology of humor. In V. Raskin (Ed.), *The primer of humor research* (pp. 17–100). Mouton de Gruyter. https://doi.org/10.1515/9783110198492.17

Ruch, W., & Deckers, L. (1993). Do extraverts "like to laugh"? An analysis of the Situational Humor Response Questionnaire (SHRQ). *European Journal of Personality, 7*(4), 211–220. https://doi.org/10.1002/per.2410070402

Ruch, W., Gander, F., Wagner, L., & Giuliani, F. (2021). The structure of character: On the relationships between character strengths and virtues. *The Journal of Positive Psychology, 16*(1), 116–128. https://doi.org/10.1080/17439760.2019.1689418

Ruch, W., & Hehl, F.-J. (2007). A two-mode model of humor appreciation: Its relation to esthetic appreciation and simplicity-complexity of personality. In W. Ruch (Ed.), *The sense of humor: Explorations of a personality characteristic* (2nd ed., pp. 109–142). Mouton de Gruyter. https://doi.org/10.1515/9783110804607.109

Ruch, W., & Heintz, S. (2013). Humour styles, personality, and psychological well-being: What's humour got to do with it? *European Journal of Humour Research, 1*(4), 1–24. https://doi.org/10.7592/ejhr2013.1.4.ruch

Ruch, W., & Heintz, S. (2014). Test measurements of humor. In S. Attardo (Ed.), *Encyclopedia of humor studies* (vol. 2, pp. 759–761). Sage.

Ruch, W., & Heintz, S. (2016). The virtue gap in humor: Exploring benevolent and corrective humor. *Translational Issues in Psychological Science, 2*, 35–45. https://doi.org/10.1037/tps0000063

Ruch, W., & Heintz, S. (2017). Experimentally manipulating items informs on the (limited) construct and criterion validity of the Humor Styles Questionnaire. *Frontiers in Psychology, 8*, Article 616. https://doi.org/10.3389/fpsyg.2017.00616

Ruch, W., & Heintz, S. (2018). Psychometric evaluation of the revised Sense of Humor Scale and the construction of a parallel form. *Humor: International Journal of Humor Research, 31*, 235–257. https://doi.org/10.1515/humor-2016-0085

Ruch, W., & Heintz, S. (2019). Humor production and creativity: Overview and recommendations. In S. R. Luria, J. Baer, & J. C. Kaufman (Eds.), *Creativity and humor* (pp. 1–42). Academic Press. https://doi.org/10.1016/b978-0-12-813802-1.00001-6

Ruch, W., Heintz, S., Platt, T., Wagner, L., & Proyer, R. T. (2018). Broadening humor: Comic styles differentially tap into temperament, character, and ability. *Frontiers in Psychology, 9*:6. https://doi.org/10.3389/fpsyg.2018.00006

Ruch, W., & Hofmann, J. (2017). Fostering humor. In C. Proctor (Ed.), *Positive psychology interventions in practice* (pp. 65–80). Springer.

Ruch, W., Hofmann, J., Platt, T., & Proyer, R. T. (2014). The state-of-the-art in gelotophobia research: A review and some theoretical extensions. *Humor: International Journal of Humor Research, 27*, 23–45. https://doi.org/10.1515/humor-2013-0046

Ruch, W., Köhler, G., & van Thriel, C. (1996). Assessing the "humorous temperament": Construction of the facet and standard trait forms of the State Trait Cheerfulness Inventory – STCI. *Humor: International Journal of Humor Research, 9*, 303–340. https://doi.org/10.1515/humr.1996.9.3-4.303

Ruch, W., Köhler, G., & van Thriel, C. (1997). To be in good or bad humor: Construction of the state form of the State Trait Cheerfulness Inventory – STCI. *Personality and Individual Differences, 22*, 477–491. https://doi.org/10.1016/s0191-8869(96)00231-0

Ruch, W., & McGhee, P. E. (2014). Humor intervention programs. In A. C. Parks & S. M. Schueller (Eds.), *Handbook of positive psychological interventions* (pp. 179–193). Wiley-Blackwell.

Ruch, W., & Proyer, R. T. (2008). The fear of being laughed at: Individual and group differences in gelotophobia. *Humor: International Journal of Humor Research, 21*(1), 47–67. https://doi.org/10.1515/HUMOR.2008.002

Ruch, W., & Proyer, R. T. (2009). Extending the study of gelotophobia: On gelotophiles and katagelasticists. *Humor: International Journal of Humor Research, 22*, 183–212. https://doi.org/10.1515/HUMR.2009.009

Ruch, W., & Proyer, R. T. (2015). Mapping strengths into virtues: The relation of the 24 VIA strengths to six ubiquitous virtues. *Frontiers in Psychology, 6*, Article 460. https://doi.org/10.3389/fpsyg.2015.00460

Ruch, W., Proyer, R.T., Harzer, C., Park, N., Peterson, C., & Seligman, M.E.P. (2010). Values in Action Inventory of Strengths (VIA-IS). *Journal of Individual Differences, 31*, 138–149. https://doi.org/10.1027/1614-0001/a000022

Ruch, W., Wagner, L., & Heintz, S. (2018). Humor, the PEN model of personality, and subjective well-being: Support for differential relationships with eight comic styles. *Rivista Italiana di Studi sull'Umorismo, 1*, 31–44. Retrieved from https://www.risu.biz/wp-content/uploads/2018/01/Ruch_et_al.-RISU-11-2018-31-44-1.pdf

Sayette, M.A., Cohn, J.F., Wertz, J.M., Perrott, M.A., & Parrott, D.J. (2001). A psychometric evaluation of the facial action coding system for assessing spontaneous expression. *Journal of Nonverbal Behavior, 25*, 167–185. https://doi.org/10.1023/a:1010671109788

Seligman, M.E P., & Csikszentmihalyi, M. (2000). Positive psychology: An introduction. *American Psychologist, 55*, 1–14. https://doi.org/10.1037//0003-066x.55.1.5

Svebak, S. (1974). Revised questionnaire on the sense of humor. *Scandinavian Journal of Psychology, 15*(1), 328–331. https://doi.org/10.1111/j.1467-9450.1974.tb00597.x

Svebak, S. (1996). The development of the Sense of Humor Questionnaire: From SHQ to SHQ-6. *Humor: International Journal of Humor Research, 9*, 341–362. https://doi.org/10.1515/humr.1996.9.3-4.341

Svebak, S. (2010). The Sense of Humor Questionnaire: Conceptualization and review of 40 years of findings in empirical research. *Europe's Journal of Psychology, 6*(3), 288–310. https://doi.org/10.5964/ejop.v6i3.218

Thorson, J.A., & Powell, F.C. (1991). Measurement of sense of humor. *Psychological Reports, 69*(2), 691–702. https://doi.org/10.2466/pr0.1991.69.2.691

Thorson, J.A., & Powell, F.C. (1993). Development and validation of a multidimensional sense of humor scale. *Journal of Clinical Psychology, 49*, 13–23. https://doi.org/10.1002/1097-4679(01)49:1<13::AID-JCLP2270490103>3.0.CO;2-S

Thorson, J.A., Powell, F.C., Sarmany-Schuller, I., & Hampes, W.P. (1997). Psychological health and sense of humor. *Journal of Clinical Psychology, 53*(6), 605–619. https://doi.org/10.1002/(SICI)1097-4679(199710)53:6<605::AID-JCLP9>3.0.CO;2-I

Wellenzohn, S., Proyer, R.T., & Ruch, W. (2018). Who benefits from humor-based positive psychology interventions? The moderating effects of personality traits and sense of humor. *Frontiers in Psychology, 9*: 821. https://doi.org/10.3389/fpsyg.2018.00821

Yam, K.C., Barnes, C.M., Leavitt, K., Wei, W., Lau, J., & Uhlmann, E.L. (2019). Why so serious? A laboratory and field investigation of the link between morality and humor. *Journal of Personality and Social Psychology, 117*(4), 758–772. https://doi.org/10.1037/pspi0000171

Yoon, H. (2018). Creating the mood for humor: Arousal level priming in humor advertising. *Journal of Consumer Marketing, 35*(5), 491–501. https://doi.org/10.1108/JCM-01-2017-2074

Chapter 8

Assessing Playfulness

Current Challenges and Overview

René T. Proyer and Kay Brauer

Department of Psychology, Martin Luther University Halle-Wittenberg, Halle, Germany

„[...] der Mensch spielt nur, wo er in voller Bedeutung des Worts Mensch ist, und er ist nur da ganz Mensch, wo er spielt.“

“[...] man only plays when he is in the fullest sense of the word a human being, and he is only fully a human being when he plays”

(Friedrich Schiller, 1795/1968)

Playfulness is an understudied personality trait – most certainly in adults. Several conceptualizations have been put forward and there is no agreement on a definition. One recent suggestion is “[...] an individual differences variable that allows people to frame or reframe everyday situations in a way such that they experience them as entertaining, and/or intellectually stimulating, and/or personally interesting” (Proyer, 2017, p. 114). Although state approaches do exist, playfulness has mainly been studied as a trait (i.e., relatively stable across time and situations). Moreover, there has been a debate regarding the dimensionality of adult playfulness. There are exceptions, but most models propose a multifaceted structure.

Most of the research generated in the wider field has been done on *play* (the actual *behavior*); foremost, in animals and children. In this chapter, we focus on *playfulness* (the individual differences variable associated with the disposition to *play*) across different age groups. Only recently has greater attention been attributed to the study of playfulness in adults, while earlier efforts focused on younger age groups. In as early as 1977, Lieberman suggested that playfulness permeates into adulthood and is of relevance there as well. Speaking of adult playfulness, she notes: “By this I mean the lightheartedness that we find as a quality of play in the young child’s activities and, later on, as the combinatorial play essential to imagination and creativity. I, therefore, see playfulness as behavior that goes beyond the childhood years; and, through its component parts of sense of humor, manifest joy, and spontaneity, it has major implications for childrearing practices, educational planning, career choices, and leisure pursuits” (Lieberman, 1977, p. xi) and “[...] playfulness as a quality of play would developmentally transform itself into a personality trait of the player in adolescence and adulthood" (p. 23). Even if her structural assumptions can be debated from a current perspective, the idea that playfulness is a personality trait and that there is a developmental process that extends into adulthood is important for measurement approaches.

Playfulness in Older Taxonomies of Personality

An influential early contribution to the field is Murray's (1938) *Personology* theory of personality, which comprises basic psychogenic human needs. Having a background in psychoanalytic theory, he suggested that the needs exist mainly at a subconscious level and defines them as "[...] a construct [...], which stands for a force [...] in the brain region, a force which organizes perception, apperception, intellection, conation and action in such a way as to transform in a certain direction an existing, unsatisfying situation" (p. 123). He lists *play* as one of these needs, namely, "play (playful attitude). To relax, amuse oneself, seek diversion and entertainment. To 'have fun,' to play game. To laugh, joke and be merry. To avoid serious tension" (p. 83). A further element of this need is the tendency to perform activities for joy alone and without further reasoning, or to escape reality. As in other conceptualizations, this view focuses strongly on the amusement aspect of play; there is also the notion that those with the need for play may laugh and joke more while being at work (Murray, 1938). While Murray defines the need for *play*, its measurement in the Personality Research Form (PRF; Jackson, 1984) seems to describe playfulness – in the sense of a person that likes to attend parties, enjoys telling and hearing jokes, spends lots of time relaxing, enjoys pranks and practical jokes, enjoys not being serious or reserved, prefers playing to reading, and is, overall, rather hedonistically oriented. Of course, this reflects Murray's conceptualization, though one might argue that it focuses only on one particular aspect of being playful, while others (e.g., intellectual components) are comparatively less well covered (see also Proyer, 2012a, 2014a; Proyer & Jehle, 2013). Nevertheless, the broad research generated using the PRF provides a good orientation for correlates of a particular facet of playfulness in a wide range of fields.

Playfulness has also been part of other conceptualizations. For example, Cattell (1945) aimed at analyzing principal trait clusters for describing personality. There he identified different "regions" and among these one that differentiates between "self-assertion, venturesomeness, clamorousness" vs. "general inhibition, modesty, timidity" (Region C). These regions are then grouped into so-called sectors; Sector G is "liveliness, instability, verbal expressiveness" vs. "reserve, quiescence, naturalness." Finally, the sectors are grouped into nuclear clusters, one of which is Nuclear Cluster G1 – "austerity, thoughtfulness, stability" vs. "playfulness, changeability, foolishness." Playfulness is also found in Sector L of Cattell's taxonomy; i.e., "amorousness, playfulness" vs. "propriety" (this is also Nuclear Cluster L1, which is assigned to Region C). Again, playfulness lies in an area that resembles a rather hedonistic outlook and probably more of an impulsive nature (cf. Proyer, 2017).

Goldberg and Rosolack (1994; see also Goldberg, 1990) identified a playfulness cluster that is associated with extraversion; it consists of the terms adventurous, mischievous, playful, and rambunctious. They locate this cluster in Eysenck's (1967/2017) Extraversion super factor and in Cattell's (1950) H+ (social boldness), F+ (liveliness) primary, and

E+ (extraversion) second-order factor. Playfulness is also an example of spontaneity as a category (Extraversion) in the Norman taxonomy (e.g., Norman, 1963) of trait descriptive adjectives (along with impulsive, carefree, and zany). An example of a taxonomy developed in the German-speaking countries is the approach by Wellek (1966), who differentiates among various layers of the character and postulates the components of intensity, extensity, extraversion, introversion, id-orientation ("Eshaftigkeit"), and ego-orientation ("Ichhaftigkeit"). There, he assigns playfulness as part of the broader category of esthetics to introversion. This conceptualization is of special interest because most of the later approaches seem to be biased toward extraversion (Proyer & Jehle, 2013).

A final taxonomy that includes playfulness is Peterson and Seligman's (2004) Values-in-Action (VIA) classification of character strengths (i.e., morally positively valued traits) and virtues. There, they use playfulness as a synonym of humor, which is a strength they assign to the virtue of transcendence (together with the strengths of appreciation of beauty and excellence, gratitude, hope, and religiousness). Taking the short description of the strength into account (i.e., "humor [playfulness]: liking to laugh and joke; bringing smiles to other people"), it seems as if this, again, focuses on the entertainment and social functions of playfulness (humor). Proyer and Ruch (2011) have shown that there is overlap between humor and playfulness in this approach, but that they are distinct (for a more in-depth discussion of the overlap between humor and playfulness, see Proyer, 2018). Given that the most frequently used measure for the VIA classification (the VIA-IS; Peterson et al., 2005) does not cover playful contents well (cf. Proyer & Ruch, 2011), reservation is warranted when interpreting findings of the VIA-IS humor scale in the direction of playfulness.

Relevance for the Assessment of Playfulness

Playfulness serves important functions in developmental processes and beyond. Lieberman (1977) posits that playfulness has an impact on a child's creativity, imagination, humor, and well-being. There is only a little research in adolescents, but preliminary evidence (e.g., Staempfli, 2007) suggests a robust association with well-being and coping with stress. Recently, there has been an increase in interest in the study of adult playfulness (Bittermann et al., 2021). Findings point to a contribution of playfulness to, for example, academic performance, physical activity, well-being, or relationship satisfaction (for an overview, see Proyer, 2020). There is robust evidence for assortative mating preferences in playfulness, and that playfulness may have an important signal function in selecting partners for long-term heterosexual relationships (i.e., low aggression in men and vitality and fecundity in women; Chick, 2001; see also Brauer, Proyer et al., 2021).

One recent development in the field was the introduction of the OLIW model of playfulness. This structural model was developed for adults and covers four basic facets: **O**ther-directed (enjoying playful interactions with others); **L**ighthearted (preferring improvisation to planning); **I**ntellectual (liking of problem-solving and preference for complexity than simplicity); and **W**himsical playfulness (preference for unusual things and/or persons; Proyer, 2017). The facets were derived multimethodologically covering a thorough literature search, psycholinguistic studies, and factor-analytic approaches. Recently, the model was expanded to include adolescents, with encouraging results (Proyer & Tandler, 2020).

Table 8.1. Proposed facets of playfulness (selection)

Author(s)	Year	Name of components
Barnett	2007	Gregarious; uninhibited; comedic; dynamic
Bishop & Chace	1971	Exploration; joy; liberty; spontaneity
Bundy	1993	Freedom to suspend reality; internal control; framing; intrinsic motivation
Ferland	1997	Curiosity; sense of humor; pleasure; spontaneity; initiative; challenge and in other versions: Curiosity; sense of humor; pleasure; spontaneity
Glynn & Webster	1992	Spontaneous; expressive; fun; creative; silly
Guitard et al.	2005	Pleasure; creativity; spontaneity; sense of humor; curiosity
Henriot	1969	Uncertainty; illusion; particular mimic; unpredictability
Knox	1996	Curiosity; imagination, creativity; physical activity; joy; social and verbal flexibility
Lieberman	1977	Cognitive spontaneity; physical spontaneity; sense of humor; joy; social spontaneity
Lyons	1987	Effectance; arousal; social interaction; release
Meakins et al.	2005	Intrinsic motivation; internal control; freedom to suspend reality; framing
Peterson & Seligman	2004	Playfulness is used synonymously with humor (i.e., liking to laugh and joke; bringing smiles to other people)
Proyer	2012a	Cheerful-engaged; whimsical; impulsive; intellectual-charming; imaginative; lighthearted; kind-loving
Proyer	2014a	Cheerful-engaged; whimsical; creative-loving; intellectual; impulsive
Proyer	2017	Other-directed; lighthearted; intellectual; whimsical
Proyer & Jehle	2013	Humorous; cheerful-uninhibited; expressive; other-directed; intellectual-creative
Schaefer & Greenberg	1997	Fun-loving; sense of humor; enjoys silliness; informal; whimsical
Shen et al.	2014	Fun-seeking motivation; uninhibitedness; spontaneity
Staempfli	2007	Physical animation; social engagement; mental spontaneity; emotional fluidity; humorous perspective
Yarnal & Qian	2011	Upbeat; impish; spontaneous; humorous
Yu et al.	2007	Pleasantry; initiative and concentrating; creativity

Of course, different conceptualizations and other facets of playfulness have been identified in the literature. For example, seeing adult playfulness as "[...] an internal predisposition characterized by creativity, curiosity, pleasure, sense of humor, and spontaneity" (Guitard et al., 2005, p. 9). Table 8.1 gives an overview of selected proposals for components of playfulness.

The table illustrates the diversity of the conceptualizations and the heterogeneity of the proposed facets. The components of playfulness listed in the table were derived using a broad range of methods. For example, Barnett (2007) and Yarnal and Qian (2011) used focus groups of people in the intended age range (younger and older adults), Guitard et al. (2005) used a qualitative approach, Proyer (2012a, 2014a) used a psycholinguistic approach, and Proyer and Jehle (2013) used a psychometric approach by subjecting 17 existing scales on playfulness to one joint factor analysis. However, there are concerns since some of the conceptualizations lack a theoretical foundation, have been used comparatively rarely, or were developed for usage in specialized groups (e.g., play therapists; Schaefer & Greenberg, 1997). In any case, the table shows that the approaches share similarities, but that there are also differences in the frameworks. Interestingly, none of the proposed models has a hierarchical structure, and future research will show whether such a conceptualization is feasible. Finally, an important point of concern is that several models (and their associated assessment instruments) share substantial overlap between what constitutes playfulness (i.e., its core characteristics) and its *consequences* as well as with parts of the nomological net (for an overview, see Proyer, 2018, 2020). We discuss this point with sample items when giving an overview of available instruments to assess playfulness.

Assessment Instruments

Although playfulness is not a mainstream research topic, a large number of instruments are available for its assessment(see Table 8.2). After reviewing the existing literature, we identified three major concerns; namely, many instruments are only ad-hoc developments for single studies, rely on the usage of a single item, and/or are outdated. Proyer and Jehle (2013) identified 17 subjective measures for playfulness in adults. Of these, only a few were used regularly in research. There does not seem to be a consensus about what instruments should be used and for what purposes. Table 8.2 gives an overview of measures that are more regularly being used (with one important omission).

Playfulness in Older Adults

Overall, only little research on playfulness in this age group exists. Given that research conducted with samples of younger age groups has shown positive associations with desired outcomes, there may be an undiscovered potential for research and practice in the field of positive aging (see Yarnal & Qian, 2011). Using focus groups, Yarnal and Qian (2011) developed a four-factor measure (i.e., the Older Adult Playfulness Scale). As a definition of playfulness in older adults they suggest: "Playful older adults are happy, optimistic, cheerful, amusing, positive, enthusiastic, and relaxed. In everyday exchanges, they tend toward mischief, naughtiness, clowning, joking, and teasing; they embody fun and humor in ways that translate into laughter and amusement in others. Although imp-

Table 8.2. An overview of playfulness measures

Measure	Author(s)	Number of items	Response scale	Reliability	Validity	Notes
Adult Playfulness Trait Scale (APTS)	Shen et al. (2014)	19	1 (*strongly disagree*) to 7 (*strongly agree*)	α = .87 (global); .68–.87 (subscales)	CFA; convergent and discriminant validity (e.g., social desirability); group comparison (low vs high playful participants)	Further validation: playfulness and adaptability (Shen et al., 2017)
Adolescent Playfulness Scale (APF20)	Staempfli (2007)	20	1 (*almost never true for me*) to 5 (*almost always true for me*)	α = .90 (global; subscales not reported)	PCA; correlations with coping strategies, perceived stress, and well-being	
Children's Playfulness Scale (CPS)	Barnett (1990)	23 (rated by teachers or parents)	1 (*doesn't sound at all like the child*) to 5 (*sounds exactly like the child*)	α = .79–.89 Retest-stability = .84–91 (≤ 3 months)	PCA	CFA and measurement invariance (Trevlas et al., 2003) Rasch model analysis (Bundy & Clifton, 1998) Convergence with ToP (Muys et al., 2006) Good interrater reliability (≥ .87; Boyer, 1997; Zachopoulou et al., 2004)
Older Adult Playfulness Scale	Yarnal & Qian (2011)	15	1 (*not at all*) to 10 (*very much*)	α = .63–93	PCA/CFA, convergent validity with APTS, discriminant with BIS/BAS, PANAS	
OLIW	Proyer (2017)	28	1 (*strongly disagree*) to 7 (*strongly agree*)	α = .66–.79 Test-retest = .67–.87 (≤ 3 months)	PCA & CFA; convergent with other playfulness measures; discriminant with big five personality traits; convergent with daily ratings of play behavior; self-other-ratings in the expected range	Replication of 4-factorial structure in CFA/measurement model (Brauer & Proyer, 2017); Evidence for robust self-other agreement and interrater consensus in a zero-acquaintance study (Proyer, & Brauer, 2018)
OLIW-S (Short version of the OLIW)	Proyer et al. (2020)	12	1 (*strongly disagree*) to 7 (*strongly agree*)	α/ω = .52–.74/.53–.75 (self-ratings) and .63–.77/.64–.78 (peer ratings) Test-retest: .73–.85 (for intervals of 1 and 2 weeks and 1 and 3 months)	CFA (also in peer ratings); self–other agreement in acquainted dyads Convergent (SMAP)/discriminant correlations with Big Five and maladaptive traits (PID-5)	

Table 8.2. continued

Measure	Author(s)	Number of items	Response scale	Reliability	Validity	Notes
OLIW-Youth	Proyer & Tandler (2020)	12	1 (*strongly disagree*) to 7 (*strongly agree*)	α = .60–.79	CFA Convergent (SMAP)/discriminant correlations with Big Five	Correlations with behaviors and roles in bullying-type situations, school grades, and academic goal orientations
Playfulness Scale for Young Adults (PSYA)	Barnett (2007)	15	1 (*not at all*) to 10 (*very much*)	α = .78–96	PCA and discrimination of low- vs high-scorers in self-rated playfulness (single item)	
Short Measure of Adult Playfulness (SMAP)	Proyer (2012b)	5	1 (*strongly disagree*) to 7 (*strongly agree*)	α = .80–.89 Test-retest: .74 (12–16 weeks)	PCA & CFA; convergent with other playfulness measures; discriminant with big five personality traits and temperamental basis of the sense of humor; preferences for structure/art	Evidence for robust self-other agreement and interrater consensus in a zero-acquaintance study (Proyer, & Brauer, 2018)
Test of Playfulness (ToP)	Bundy (1997)	29	0 (*rarely or never/not/unskilled*) to 3 (*almost always/highly/highly skilled*) for extent/intensity/skillfulness	Interrater reliability ≥ .96 (computed as overlap between observer ratings and prediction by Rasch-model; Bundy et al., 2001)	PCA	Rasch model analyses; convergent correlations with CPS (Bundy et al., 2001)

Note. BIS/BAS = Behavioral Inhibition Scale/Behavioral Activation Scale; CFA = confirmatory factor analysis; PANAS = Positive Affect Negative Affect Schedule; PCA = principal component analysis; PID-5 = Personality Inventory for DSM-5.

ish, they are circumspect about their behavior in ways that teenagers have not yet mastered. Nevertheless, again, they continue to approach the world with a measure of creativity and whimsy" (p. 71). One might argue that these descriptors (e.g., happy, optimistic, mischievous, naughty, creative, whimsical, funny, or humorous) describe the consequences of *being playful* rather than its core characteristic. Also, (again) questions of the distinctiveness of playfulness in this sense emerge: One of the factors is composed of the terms "funny" and "humorous." Setting the discussion of the number of variables that should be assigned to a factor to label it meaningfully aside, it will be almost impossible to find different associations with measures of "humor" (in its broadest sense). There, being funny and humorous will be used as indicators for being humorous/having a good sense of humor – and their convergence with other measures (e.g., for humor production) will be very high. Nevertheless, this research allows for an in-depth understanding of how playfulness is expressed and what shapes the perception of playfulness in higher age – and its potential to contribute to positive psychological functioning in this age group. A final question is whether there is a need for measures specifically developed for higher age groups, or whether standard measures suffice (see, e.g., Brauer, Sendatzki et al., 2021; Proyer, 2014b), for example, by testing measurement invariance across age groups.

Playfulness in Adults

It should be noted that, according to the citation frequency, the most frequently used instrument, the Adult Playfulness Scale (Glynn & Webster, 1992), is missing from Table 8.2. The scale has poor psychometric qualities, and while comparatively much research was generated with this instrument, it would require substantial revisions before it could be recommended for further use. Glynn and Webster (1992) were interested in developing a questionnaire that could be used for the assessment of playfulness in a work context. The rationale for the development of the items and their relationship with playfulness is rather unclear. Glynn and Webster used pairs of adjectives from Osgood's (1962) semantic differential and proposed a five-factor structure of their scale, which cannot be fully understood given the information provided in their paper. Other solutions have been proposed as well. Overall, the presented data are not convincing, and there also seem to be some psychometric problems in the test development. Despite being probably the most frequently quoted instrument, its further usage *cannot be recommended*.

Of the more recently developed multidimensional scales for adults, two should be highlighted in more detail. The Adult Playfulness Trait Scale (APTS; Shen et al., 2014) contains 19 items that cover three facets: fun-seeking motivation (9 items; e.g., "I try to have fun no matter what I am doing"), uninhibitedness (5 items; e.g., "I don't always follow rules"), and spontaneity (5 items; e.g., "I often do unplanned things"). The facets fit well into the literature generated in the field (e.g., Barnett, 2007; Schaefer & Greenberg, 1997); confirmatory factor analyses supported the expected multifaceted structure while a unidimensional model did not fit the data well. This was supported by the differential associations of the scales with outcomes, for example, experiencing boredom is related to fun-seeking while being independent of uninhibitedness and spontaneity. Further, Shen et al. (2014) found the expected associations with a self-as-entertainment scale, convergent validity with global measures of playfulness, and that the scales predict playful behavior well. Also, the APTS is potent in differentiating among groups with different levels of playfulness. Additionally, the scale was successfully used in a study on playfulness and adaptability among young adults and their parents (Shen et al., 2017).

The standard OLIW (Proyer, 2017) assesses four facets of playfulness with 28 items in a 7-point answer format. OLIW is an acronym for the facets covered: **o**ther-directed, **l**ight-hearted, **i**ntellectual, **w**himsical. These were derived from a multimethod approach including psycholinguistic studies and psychometric analyses of existing measures in a joint hierarchical factor analysis (Proyer & Jehle, 2013). The 4-factorial structure was tested and confirmed through principal component and confirmatory factor analyses (also replicated with the short-form across four samples; see Proyer et al., 2020). A unidimensional structure showed a substantially worse fit. There is robust evidence for its validity, for example, good convergence with daily ratings of play behaviors (averaged across 14 days) and no redundancy with broad personality traits (Big Five). Further, the convergence of self-ratings and other-ratings across the facets supports the validity (see also Proyer & Brauer, 2018; Proyer et al., 2020). The OLIW was employed to study the differential associations of the facets across different life domains, which we discuss in the "Key Research Findings" section in more detail.

Playfulness in Children and Adolescents

Lieberman (1977) conducted large-scale observational studies among children in kindergartens and schools and developed an observation scale that allows for the assessment of interindividual differences in the disposition to play. Barnett (1990) compiled a questionnaire (Children's Playfulness Scale; CPS) based on Lieberman's observation scale to allow for the measurement of playfulness in children. A major difference to the assessment of playfulness in adults is that playfulness in children is typically rated by parents or teachers (Barnett, 1990; Lieberman, 1977). For example, in Barnett's (1990) CPS ratings are given on items using the scale anchors 1 (*doesn't sound at all like the child*) and 5 (*sounds exactly like the child*). However, Barnett provides evidence for good psychometric properties including high test-retest reliabilities for timespans of up to 3 months (r_{tt} = .92 for the total score). Similarly, Bundy (1997) provided a measure of children's playfulness (Test of Playfulness; ToP), which also relies on teachers' ratings or parental ratings and shows comparatively good psychometric properties and good interrater reliability (see also Bundy et al., 2001). This stimulated research on playfulness as a personality trait and the relevance of play in children (see, e.g., Barnett, 1990; Bundy, 1997; Knox, 1996; Lautamo & Heikkilä, 2011; Lieberman, 1977; Trevlas et al., 2003, 2013).

As discussed previously, there is an overlap between the core characteristics and the consequences of playfulness in the available measures for children and adolescents. For example, Lieberman (1977) proposes that "spontaneity," "manifest joy," and "sense of humor" are basic components of playfulness in children, but it is unclear whether "manifest joy" is a component or, perhaps, a consequence of being playful. There is robust evidence that playing and being playful elicit positive emotions (e.g., Fredrickson, 2001), and that it can also be associated with flow experiences (Csikszentmihalyi, 1975). Thus, the question arises as to whether it should be considered a core component of playfulness. Moreover, such a conceptualization causes problems for studies that aim to examine the predictive power of playfulness and its components since there is overlap between the predictor (a measure of playfulness) and the criterion (e.g., humor).

Barnett (2007) focused on the study of playfulness in young adults using focus groups and collected nominations from students on what traits they commonly associate with playful adults. She reduced this list to a nonredundant selection of 42 descriptors and collected data on self-ratings and ratings of highly playful people. After comparing the data, she arrived at a selection of 16 adjectives, and a principal axis analysis of these yielded a 4-factor solution (after dropping "creative" from the initial list of adjectives that entered her study, i.e., the final solution comprised of 15 adjectives). Later, Barnett and others used this list of 15 adjectives as a questionnaire by reformulating the adjectives into items (Playfulness Scale for Young Adults, PSYA; e.g., Barnett, 2011; Magnuson & Barnett, 2013; Qian & Yarnal, 2011). However, no paper describes the construction of this questionnaire (e.g., provides basic psychometric information).

There is an important caveat that needs to be considered: The study from 2007 is an excellent approximation of how young adults perceive playfulness and what traits they commonly associate with playfulness. Hence, it is a compilation of these perceptions, but it seems difficult to derive a measure solely based on these ratings. The question emerges as to whether this assesses playfulness in its narrow sense. From the perspective of the authors, this study (Barnett, 2007) should be seen as an important contribution toward basic research in playfulness, but not for the measurement of playfulness. As discussed above, the criterion and predictor seem to be mixed for the PSYA as well. For example, the factor of "gregarious" types of playfulness contains adjectives such as "happy" or "cheerful." Considering that these items would be regressed on or correlated with a measure of, say, life satisfaction, the participant must differentiate between "happy" as an indicator of playfulness and being satisfied as an indicator of life satisfaction. Hence, the two measures are not independent of each other, and this would lead to an overestimation of the true relationship.

The assessment of adolescent playfulness is mainly related to Staempfli's study from 2007 and assessment by observations (Hess & Bundy, 2003). First studies examining whether the structure of the OLIW model is also suitable to describe the structure of playfulness in adolescents are underway. Proyer and Tandler (2020) recently introduced the OLIW-Youth, a 12-item measure that comprises the four OLIW components in 13- to 18-year-olds well. While some items of the original OLIW-Youth were retained from the standard version (e.g., lighthearted: "I am a lighthearted person"), others were rephrased to the context of adolescents (e.g., other-directed: "Among my clique/circle of friends I have a reputation for joining for every fun."). Initial evidence on the psychometric properties and validity is promising, as the OLIW-Youth shows convergent validity with the SMAP (Proyer, 2012a), the expected correlations with external criteria such as the big five, school grades, life satisfaction, or roles in bullying-type situations, and factorial validity for the 4-facet structure. The following section summarizes the research done on children with the CPS (Barnett, 1990).

Key Research Findings

Because of the large number of instruments, we restrict ourselves to research generated with the OLIW for adults (Proyer, 2017) and Barnett's (1990) CPS for children. Research using the OLIW shows good convergence of self-ratings and other ratings across different levels of acquaintanceship from zero-acquaintance settings to friends and romantic partners (Proyer, 2017; Proyer & Brauer, 2018; Proyer, Brauer et al., 2018). Further, the OLIW was used to study romantic relationships, and findings showed that there is assortative mating for the facets of playfulness, and that, primarily, other-directed playfulness is a robust predictor of relationship satisfaction – in both the individual themselves (actor effect), but also depending on the partners' level of playfulness (partner effect in APIM-designs; Brauer, Sendatzki et al., 2021; Proyer, Brauer et al., 2019). Self-ratings and peer-ratings of the four dimensions also contributed to the prediction of mental health, physical activity, and better physical functioning (Proyer, Gander et al., 2018). Also, the four OLIW facets could be well located in broad and narrow personality traits such as the Big Five personality traits, the PID-5 system of personality pathology, subjective and objective indicators of creativity, the impostor phenomenon, and quantitative text analyses showed that expressions in the facets showed were linked to language use when describing oneself (Brauer & Proyer, 2017; Proyer & Brauer, 2018; Proyer et al., 2020; Proyer, Brauer et al., 2019; Proyer, Tandler et al., 2019).

In children, the playfulness dimensions could be well localized in trait descriptors (e.g., aggressive, cheerful) and demographic variables such as age, sex, and birth order (Barnett, 1991; Zachopoulou et al., 2004). Further, motoric abilities in preschool children could be associated with playfulness (Trevlas et al., 2003) as well as inclinations toward play behaviors (e.g., social vs. nonsocial; Rentzou, 2013). Barnett (2018) studied the consequences of playfulness in the classroom and found that playful boys were perceived by their teachers as "class clowns," being disruptive and rebellious. Also, they described them as being of low social competence, while students and their peers experience them as engaging. Using a longitudinal design, Barnett showed that those associations increased in their magnitude over the course from grade 1 to 3, showing that (mis)perceptions of playful children have consequences in school settings, as it can be assumed that such perceptions would influence how teachers approach and evaluate the achievements of their students. There is initial evidence for its crosscultural validity, as the CPS showed comparable findings for the psychometric properties and expressions in samples from China and Taiwan (Holmes, 2001; Li et al., 1995). Boyer (1997) used the CPS to study whether a 10-lesson sensory stimulation training (imaginative exercises aiming to activate the senses of smell, taste, touch, and hearing) increases playfulness in 3- to 5-year-olds and found promising evidence that such trainings enhance the children's playfulness in the experimental group.

Recommendations for Instrument Selection

The number of instruments with an in-depth analysis of reliability and validity is rather limited. This field is a good example of the notion that a frequently used instrument is not necessarily the best possible choice. As discussed, a major problem is a potential overlap between how playfulness is measured and what outcomes should be predicted. Overall, those interested in the study of playfulness should check for the distinctiveness of the measures used and for their overlap with related, yet distinct variables.

Another important consideration is whether to use a global measure or a multifaceted instrument. Short scales can more easily be used in large-scale assessments when only limited testing time is available. Measures such as the 5-item Short Measure of Adult Playfulness (SMAP; Proyer, 2012a) or scales of larger test batteries such as the playfulness scale of the Sense of Humor Scale (SHS; McGhee, 1999; Ruch & Heintz, 2018) allow for an economic assessment of playfulness, as they aim at assessing playfulness in the sense of a frequent display, easy onset, and high intensity of playful behaviors but do not allow for differentiating among facets. The consideration of facets may be particularly helpful in predicting specific outcomes. For example, it was shown for the OLIW that facets such as other-directed playfulness relate positively to relationship satisfaction, while whimsical playfulness may even cause problems in relationships (Proyer, Brauer et al., 2019). Accordingly, older notions of a ludic love style (e.g., low commitment, short-term perspectives) go along with lighthearted playfulness, while, for example, other-directed playfulness relates to behavior that could be characterized as a playful love style (i.e., engaging, directed at involvement, and with a long-term perspective; Proyer, Brauer et al., 2018). Evidently, the latter is characterized by different types of behavior in the relationship, and the outlook for, for example, long-term relationships is different. Hence, taking facets into account provides a more differentiated picture of the role of playfulness in different areas of life.

Conclusion, Comments, and Future Directions

Currently, there is a lack of fully tested instruments. While older assessment instruments for playfulness in children seem comparatively well-established, more work needs to be spent on testing measures for different age groups. The assessment of playfulness across the lifespan allows researchers to conduct longitudinal studies on the trajectories of playfulness throughout life (cf. Proyer, 2014b) as well as testing their longitudinal effects on important outcomes linked to playfulness at the cross-sectional level (e.g., relationship satisfaction; physical fitness, etc.). Further, recent years have seen initial approaches to assess playfulness beyond subjective self-reports, for example, by using indicators of playful behaviors in narrow settings (e.g., with the romantic partner), but also from a broader perspective (e.g., collecting playful behaviors throughout the day). The extension and combination of self-reports, peer-ratings, and ambulatory assessment methods contribute to improving the assessment and understanding of playfulness in different age groups and stages of life.

Our literature review shows that there is much room for improvement in the assessment of playfulness across all age groups. We, therefore, encourage extensions and multimethodological approaches. The latter contribute to our understanding of open measurement issues in the field, for example, studies using multitrait-multimethod analyses (Campbell & Fiske, 1959) to examine convergent and discriminant validity seem missing. Further, the use of confirmatory factor analyses (e.g., Proyer, 2017) and/or item response theory (e.g., Bundy et al., 2001; Davis & Boone, 2021) to examine structural assumptions, testing reliability beyond internal consistency (e.g., test-retest reliability or McDonald's omega; see Dunn et al., 2014; Proyer et al., 2020) is particularly encouraged. Finally, it would be desirable to provide more evidence for the criterion validity of the measures (e.g., testing the convergence with observational data).

A further challenge is the understanding of the cross-cultural validity of the measures. Typically, models developed across the world differ. For example, Yu et al.'s (2007) Adult Playfulness Scale, developed in Taiwan, contains a pleasantry facet of playfulness (they define playfulness as "[...] a personal characteristic of pleasantry temperament, combining physical, cognitive and social spontaneity, which shows the power to begin energetically or to concentrate on events or activities, and the ability to utilize resources in solving problems or in rising to the challenge of own competence," p. 416), which is not part of models developed in Western countries. Hence, a better cross-cultural understanding of playfulness would contribute to further advancement in the field. Finally, it is not well understood whether interventions can be developed for fostering playfulness – and what outcomes such programs might produce (cf. Proyer et al., 2021). An exception is McGhee's (2010) 7 Humor Habits Program, which contains playful activities, and its accompanying measure, the SHS (McGhee, 1999; Ruch & Heintz, 2018), which contains a playfulness scale. This is probably the only measure available in the field that has been developed with an intervention perspective in mind. More research is needed to develop measures that are sensitive to upward changes in playfulness because of deliberate activities. Similarly, most of the current research focuses on a trait perspective, while playfulness may also be studied from a state perspective (cf. Apter, 1991; Bateson & Martin, 2013; Shen, 2020).

In conclusion, there is robust evidence for the contribution of playfulness to a broad number of positive outcomes. A larger number of self-report instruments exist for the assessment of playfulness across all age groups. Nevertheless, more research on playfulness is needed in areas such as the theoretical foundations, its development over the lifespan, distinctiveness from related variables, its assessment in intervention type of settings, or its basic structure. Existing research is encouraging and supports the call for a stronger consideration of playfulness and its facets in future research endeavors.

References

Apter, M. J. (1991). A structural-phenomenology of play. In J. H. Kerr & M. J. Apter, *Adult play: A reversal theory approach* (pp. 13–29). Swets & Zeitlinger.

Barnett, L. A. (1990). Playfulness: Definition, design, and measurement. *Play & Culture, 3*, 319–336.

Barnett, L. A. (1991). Characterizing playfulness: Correlates with individual attributes and personality traits. *Play & Culture, 4*, 371–393.

Barnett, L. A. (2007). The nature of playfulness in young adults. *Personality and Individual Differences, 43*, 949–958. https://doi.org/10.1016/j.paid.2007.02.018

Barnett, L. A. (2011). How do playful people play? Gendered and racial leisure perspectives, motives, and preferences of college students. *Leisure Sciences, 33*, 382–401. https://doi.org/10.1080/01490400.2011.606777

Barnett, L. A. (2018). The education of playful boys: Clowns in the classroom. *Frontiers in Psychology, 9*, Article 232. https://doi.org/10.3389/fpsyg.2018.00232

Bateson, P., & Martin, P. (2013). *Play, playfulness, creativity and innovation.* Cambridge University Press. https://doi.org/10.1017/CBO9781139057691

Bishop, D. W., & Chace, C. A. (1971). Parental conceptual systems, home play environment, and potential creativity in children. *Journal of Experimental Child Psychology, 12*, 318–338. https://doi.org/10.1016/0022-0965(71)90028-2

Bittermann, A., Batzdorfer, V., Müller, S. M., & Steinmetz, H. (2021). Mining Twitter to detect hotspots in psychology. *Zeitschrift für Psychologie, 229*(1), 3–14. https://doi.org/10.1027/2151-2604/a000437

Boyer, W. A. R. (1997). Enhancing playfulness with sensorial stimulation. *Journal of Research in Childhood Education, 12*, 78–87. https://doi.org/10.1080/02568549709594718

Brauer, K., & Proyer, R. T. (2017). Are impostors playful? Testing the association of adult playfulness with the impostor phenomenon. *Personality and Individual Differences, 116*, 57–62. https://doi.org/10.1016/j.paid.2017.04.029

Brauer, K., Proyer, R.T., & Chick, G. (2021). Adult playfulness: An update on an understudied individual differences variable and its role in romantic life. *Social and Personality Psychology Compass, 15*(4), e12589. https://doi.org/10.1111/spc3.12589

Brauer, K., Sendatzki, R., Scherrer, T., Chick, G., & Proyer, R.T. (2021). Revisiting adult playfulness and relationship satisfaction: APIM analyses of middle-aged and older couples. *International Journal of Applied Positive Psychology*. Advance online publication. https://doi.org/10.1007/s41042-021-00058-8

Bundy, A.C. (1993). Assessment of play and leisure: Delineation of the problem. *The American Journal of Occupational Therapy, 47*(3), 217–222. https://doi.org/10.5014/ajot.47.3.217

Bundy, A.C. (1997). Play and playfulness: What to look for. In L.D. Parham & L.S. Fazio (Eds.), *Play in occupational therapy for children* (pp. 56–62). Mosby.

Bundy, A.C., & Clifton, J.L. (1998). Construct validity of the Children's Playfulness Scale. In M.C. Duncan, G. Chick, & A. Aycock (Eds.), *Play and culture studies: Diversions and divergences in fields of play* (pp. 137–148). Greenford.

Bundy, A.C., Nelson, L., Metzger, M., & Bingaman, K. (2001). Reliability and validity of a Test of Playfulness. *The Occupational Journal of Therapy Research, 21*, 276–292. https://doi.org/10.1177/153944920102100405

Campbell, D.T., & Fiske, D.W. (1959). Convergent and discriminant validation by the multitrait-multimethod matrix. *Psychological Bulletin, 56*, 81–105. https://doi.org/10.1037/h0046016

Cattell, R.B. (1945). The principal trait clusters for describing personality. *Psychological Bulletin, 42*(3), 129–161. https://doi.org/10.1037/h0060679

Cattell, R.B. (1950). *Personality*. McGraw Hill.

Chick, G. (2001). What is play for? Sexual selection and the evolution of play. *Play and Culture Studies, 3*, 3–25.

Csikszentmihalyi, M. (1975). Play and intrinsic rewards. *Journal of Humanistic Psychology, 15*, 41–63. https://doi.org/10.1177/002216787501500306

Davis, D.R., & Boone, W. (2021). Using Rasch analysis to evaluate the psychometric functioning of the other-directed, lighthearted, intellectual, and whimsical (OLIW) adult playfulness scale. *International Journal of Educational Research Open, 2*, 100054. https://doi.org/10.1016/j.ijedro.2021.100054

Dunn, T.J., Baguley, T., & Brunsden, V. (2014). From alpha to omega: A practical solution to the pervasive problem of internal consistency estimation. *British Journal of Psychology, 105*, 399–412. https://doi.org/10.1111/bjop.12046

Eysenck, H.J. (1967/2017). *The biological basis of personality*. Routledge.

Ferland, F. (1997). *Play, children with physical disabilities and occupational therapy: The ludic model*. University of Ottawa Press.

Fredrickson, B.L. (2001). The role of positive emotions in positive psychology: The broaden-and-build theory of positive emotions. *American Psychologist, 56*, 218–226. https://doi.org/10.1037//0003-066X.56.3.218

Glynn, M.A., & Webster, J. (1992). The adult playfulness scale: An initial assessment. *Psychological Reports, 7*, 83–103. https://doi.org/10.2466/pr0.1992.71.1.83

Goldberg, L.R. (1990). An alternative "description of personality": The Big Five factor structure. *Journal of Personality and Social Psychology, 59*, 1216–1229. https://doi.org/10.1037//0022-3514.59.6.1216

Goldberg, L.R., & Rosolack, T.K. (1994). The Big Five factor structure as an integrative framework: An empirical comparison with Eysenck's P-E-N model. In C.F. Halverson Jr., G.A. Kohnstamm, & R.P. Martin (Eds.), *The developing structure of temperament and personality from infancy to adulthood* (pp. 7–36). Erlbaum.

Guitard, P., Ferland, F., & Dutil, É. (2005). Toward a better understanding of playfulness in adults. *Occupational Journal of Therapy Research, 25*, 9–22. https://doi.org/10.1177/153944920502500103

Henriot, J. (1969). *Le jeu* [The game]. Presses Universitaires de France.

Hess, L.M., & Bundy, A.C. (2003). The association between playfulness and coping in adolescents. *Physical and Occupational Therapy in Pediatrics, 23*, 5–17. https://doi.org/10.1080/J006v23n02_02

Holmes, R.M. (2001). Parental notions about their children's playfulness and children's notions of play in the United States and Hong Kong. *Play and Culture Studies, 3*, 291–314.

Jackson, D.N. (1984). *Personality Research Form*. Research Psychologists Press.
Knox, S. (1996). Play and playfulness in preschool children. In R. Zemke & F. Clark (Eds.), *Occupational science: The evolving discipline* (pp. 80–88). F.A. Davis.
Lautamo, T., & Heikkilä, M. (2011). Inter-rater reliability for the play assessment in group settings. *Scandinavian Journal of Occupational Therapy, 18*, 3–10. https://doi.org/10.3109/11038120903480048
Li, W., Bundy, A.C., & Beer, D. (1995). Taiwanese parental values toward an American Evaluation of Playfulness. *Occupational Therapy Journal of Research, 15*(4), 237–258. https://doi.org/10.1177/153944929501500402
Lieberman, J.N. (1977). *Playfulness: Its relationship to imagination and creativity*. Academic Press.
Lyons, M. (1987). A taxonomy of playfulness for use in occupational therapy. *Australian Journal of Occupational Therapy, 34*, 152–156. https://doi.org/10.1111/j.1440-1630.1987.tb01589.x
Magnuson, C.D., & Barnett, L.A. (2013). The playful advantage: How playfulness enhances coping with stress. *Leisure Sciences, 35*, 129–144. https://doi.org/10.1080/01490400.2013.761905
McGhee, P.E. (1999). *Health, healing and the amuse system: Humor as survival training*. Kendall/Hunt.
McGhee, P.E. (2010). *Humor as a survival training for a stressed-out world: The 7 humor habits program*. AuthorHouse.
Meakins, C.R.H., Bundy, A.C., & Gliner, J. (2005). Validity and reliability of the experience of leisure scale (TELS). In F.F. McMahon, D.E. Lytle, & B. Sutton-Smith (Eds.), *Play: An interdisciplinary synthesis* (pp. 255–267). University Press of America.
Murray, H.A. (1938). *Explorations in personality*. Oxford University Press.
Muys, V., Rodger, S., & Bundy, A.C. (2006). Assessment of playfulness in children with autistic disorder: A comparison of the Children's Playfulness Scale and the Test of Playfulness. *The Occupational Journal of Therapy Research, 26*, 159–170. https://doi.org/10.1177/153944920602600406
Norman, W.T. (1963). Toward an adequate taxonomy of personality attributes: Replicated factor structure in peer nomination personality ratings. *Journal of Abnormal and Social Psychology, 66*, 574–583. https://doi.org/10.1037/h0040291
Osgood, C.E. (1962). Studies of the generality of affective meaning systems. *American Psychologist, 17*, 10–28. https://doi.org/10.1037/h0045146
Peterson, C., Park, N., & Seligman, M.E.P. (2005). Assessment of character strengths. In G.P. Koocher, J.C. Norcross, & S.S. Hill III (Eds.), *Psychologists' desk reference* (2nd ed., pp. 93–98). Oxford University Press.
Peterson, C., & Seligman, M.E.P. (2004). *Character strengths and virtues: A handbook and classification*. Oxford University Press.
Proyer, R.T. (2012a). A psycho-linguistic study on adult playfulness: Its hierarchical structure and theoretical considerations. *Journal of Adult Development, 19*, 141–149. https://doi.org/10.1007/s10804-012-9141-7
Proyer, R.T. (2012b). Development and initial assessment of a short measure for adult playfulness: The SMAP. *Personality and Individual Differences, 53*, 989–994. https://doi.org/10.1016/j.paid.2012.07.018
Proyer, R.T. (2014a). A psycho-linguistic approach for studying adult playfulness: A replication and extension toward relations with humor. *Journal of Psychology, 148*, 717–735. https://doi.org/10.1080/00223980.2013.826165
Proyer, R.T. (2014b). Playfulness over the lifespan and its relation to happiness Results from an online survey. *Zeitschrift für Gerontologie und Geriatrie, 47*, 508–512. https://doi.org/10.1007/s00391-013-0539-z
Proyer, R.T. (2017). A new structural model for the study of adult playfulness: Assessment and exploration of an understudied individual differences variable. *Personality and Individual Differences, 108*, 113–122. https://doi.org/10.1016/j.paid.2016.12.011
Proyer, R.T. (2018). Playfulness and humor in psychology: An overview and update. *HUMOR: International Journal of Humor Research, 31*, 259–271. https://doi.org/10.1515/humor-2016-0080
Proyer, R.T. (2020). Playfulness. In V. Zeigler-Hill & T.K. Shackelford (Eds.), *Encyclopedia of personality and individual differences* (pp. 3948–3951). Springer. https://doi.org/10.1007/978-3-319-28099-8_1885-1

Proyer, R.T., & Brauer, K. (2018). Exploring adult playfulness: Examining the accuracy of personality judgments at zero-acquaintance and an LIWC analysis of textual information. *Journal of Research in Personality, 73*, 12–20. https://doi.org/10.1016/j.jrp.2017.10.002

Proyer, R.T., Brauer, K., & Wolf, A. (2020). Assessing other-directed, lighthearted, intellectual, and whimsical playfulness in adults: Development and initial validation of a short form of the OLIW using self- and peer-ratings. *European Journal of Psychological Assessment, 36*(4), 624–634. https://doi.org/10.1027/1015-5759/a000531

Proyer, R.T., Brauer, K., Wolf, A., & Chick, G. (2018). Beyond the ludic lover: Individual differences in playfulness and love styles in heterosexual relationships. *American Journal of Play, 10*, 265–289.

Proyer, R.T., Brauer, K., Wolf, A., & Chick, G. (2019). Adult playfulness and relationship satisfaction: An APIM analysis of romantic couples. *Journal of Research in Personality, 79*, 40–48. https://doi.org/10.1016/j.jrp.2019.02.001

Proyer, R.T., Gander, F., Bertenshaw, E., & Brauer, K. (2018). The positive relationships of playfulness with indicators of health, activity, and physical fitness. *Frontiers in Psychology, 9*, Article 1440. https://doi.org/10.3389/fpsyg.2018.01440

Proyer, R.T., Gander, F., Brauer, K., & Chick, G. (2021). Can playfulness be stimulated? A randomised placebo-controlled online playfulness intervention study on effects on trait playfulness, well-being, and depression. *Applied Psychology: Health and Well-Being, 13*(1), 129–151. https://doi.org/10.1111/aphw.12220

Proyer, R.T., & Jehle, N. (2013). The basic components of adult playfulness and their relation with personality: The hierarchical factor structure of seventeen instruments. *Personality and Individual Differences, 55*, 811–816. https://doi.org/10.1016/j.paid.2013.07.010

Proyer, R.T., & Ruch, W. (2011). The virtuousness of adult playfulness: The relation of playfulness with strengths of character. *Psychology of Well-Being, 1*, Article 4. https://doi.org/10.1186/2211-1522-1-4

Proyer, R.T., & Tandler, N. (2020). An update on the study of playfulness in adolescents: Its relationship with academic performance, well-being, anxiety, and roles in bullying-type situations. *Social Psychology of Education, 23*(1), 73–99. https://doi.org/10.1007/s11218-019-09526-1

Proyer, R.T., Tandler, N., & Brauer, K. (2019). Playfulness and creativity: A selective review. In S.R. Luria, J. Baer, & J.C. Kaufman (Eds.), *Creativity and humor* (pp. 43–56). Academic Press. https://doi.org/10.1016/B978-0-12-813802-1.00002-8

Qian, X.-L., & Yarnal, C. (2011). The role of leisure stress-coping process among emerging adults: An SEM analysis. *Leisure, 35*, 191–209. https://doi.org/10.1080/14927713.2011.578398

Rentzou, K. (2013). Preschool children's social and nonsocial play behaviours. Measurement and correlations with children's playfulness, behaviour problems and demographic characteristics. *Early Child Development and Care, 184*, 633–647. https://doi.org/10.1080/03004430.2013.806496

Ruch, W., & Heintz, S. (2018). Psychometric evaluation of the revised Sense of Humor Scale and the construction of a parallel form. *Humor: International Journal of Humor Research, 31*, 235–257. https://doi.org/10.1515/humor-2016-0085

Schaefer, C., & Greenberg, R. (1997). Measurement of playfulness: A neglected therapist variable. *International Journal of Play Therapy, 6*, 21–31. https://doi.org/10.1037/h0089406

Schiller, F. (1968). *On the aesthetic education of man in a series of letters* (E.M. Wilkinson & L.A. Willoughby, Trans.). Clarendon Press. (Original work published 1795)

Shen, X. (2020). Constructing an interactionist framework for playfulness research: Adding psychological situations and playful states. *Journal of Leisure Research, 51*(5), 536–558. https://doi.org/10.1080/00222216.2020.1748551

Shen, X.S., Chick, G., & Pitas, N.A. (2017). From playful parents to adaptable children: A structural equation model of the relationships between playfulness and adaptability among young adults and their parents. *International Journal of Play, 6*, 244–254. https://doi.org/10.1080/21594937.2017.1382983

Shen, X.S., Chick, G., & Zinn, H. (2014). Validatig the Adult Playfulness Trait Scale (APTS): An examination of personality, behavior, attitude, and perception in the nomological network of playfulness. *American Journal of Play, 6*, 345–369.

Staempfli, M. B. (2007). Adolescent playfulness, stress perception, coping and well-being. *Journal of Leisure Research, 39*, 393–412. https://doi.org/10.1080/00222216.2007.11950114

Trevlas, E., Grammatikopoulous, V., Tsigilis, N., & Zachopoulou, E. (2003). Evaluating playfulness: Construct validity of the Children's Playfulness Scale. *Early Childhood Education, 31*, 33–39. https://doi.org/10.1023/A:1025132701759

Trevlas, E., Matsouka, O., & Zachopoulou, E. (2013). Relationship between playfulness and motor creativity in preschool children. *Early Child Development and Care, 173*, 535–543. https://doi.org/10.1080/0300443032000070482

Wellek, A. (1966). *Die Polarität im Aufbau des Charakters. System der konkreten Charakterkunde.* [The polarity in the structure of character. System of definite characterology]. Francke.

Yarnal, C., & Qian, X. (2011). Older-adult playfulness: An innovative construct and measurement for healthy aging research. *American Journal of Play, 4*, 52–79.

Yu, P., Wu, J. J., Chen, I. H., & Lin, Y. T. (2007). Is playfulness a benefit to work? Empirical evidence of professionals in Taiwan. *International Journal of Technology Management, 39*, 412–429. https://doi.org/10.1504/IJTM.2007.013503

Zachopoulou, E., Trevlas, E., & Tsikriki, G. (2004). Perceptions of gender differences in playful behaviour among kindergarten children. *European Early Childhood Education Research Journal, 12*, 43–53. https://doi.org/10.1080/13502930485209301

Chapter 9

Measuring Meaning and Purpose in Life

A Review and Recommendations

Michael F. Steger[1,2] **and Frank Martela**[3]

[1]Center for Meaning and Purpose, Colorado State University, Fort Collins, CO, USA
[2]North-West University, Optentia Research Programme, Vanderbijlpark, South Africa
[3]Department of Industrial Engineering and Management, Aalto University, Finland

Meaning in life has progressed from its beginnings as a niche topic within therapeutic and clinical contexts for most of the 20th century to its current status as one of the most well-researched variables in positive psychology and a cornerstone of well-being, quality of life, and health. One reason for such rapid development has been the creation of psychometrically sound measurement tools, enabling greater numbers of researchers to feel confident in including meaning in life in a wider range of studies. In this chapter, we review the primary measurement tools used in meaning-in-life research, discuss the differences between them, present recommendations for the most appropriate tools to use, and identify emerging topics within meaning-in-life measurement. Before this, we briefly consider the theoretical background of meaning in life, including explaining the rationale for referring in common parlance to this area of research using the phrase "meaning and purpose in life."

Theoretical Background and Relevance

Having meaning in life is a fundamental part of human flourishing and having a fulfilling life (Baumeister & Vohs, 2002; Frankl, 1963) and has been linked to mental health, well-being (Debats et al., 1995; Steger et al., 2009; Zika & Chamberlain, 1992), and health-promoting behaviors (Brassai et al., 2015). Several studies have even demonstrated that having a purpose in life predicts longevity (Cohen et al., 2016). Lack of meaning, in contrast, is associated with mortality, depression, and even suicide ideation (Harlow et al., 1986; Steger et al., 2006; Tanno et al., 2009).

Meaning in life is a topic that has stimulated thinkers and philosophers since the 19th century, with the early existentialists such as Søren Kierkegaard, Arthur Schopenhauer, and Friedrich Nietzsche as well as authors such as Thomas Carlyle and Leo Tolstoy helping to raise the question of meaning into public awareness (Martela, 2020). In the 20th century, the Second World War with its atrocities provided a key impetus for thinkers such as the French existentialist Jean-Paul Sartre (e.g., 2007) and the Austrian psychoanalyst Victor Frankl to see the quest for meaning as central to human existence. The former was a prisoner-of-war while the latter survived the concentration camps with a vision that those among us who know the why of our existence can survive almost any how we are forced to encounter (Frankl, 1963). Along with existential psychotherapy (Yalom, 1980), Frankl's logotherapy, often seen as the "third school" of Viennese psychotherapy, brought the question of meaning into the domain of therapy. Despite these historical developments, it took a long time before empirical psychology started to show interest in measuring meaning. Key early contributions included Roy Baumeister's (1991) book *Meanings of Life,* which gathered together what the fields of psychology and sociology knew about meaning at that time. Since the start of the 21st century, however, empirical interest in the question of meaning has increased considerably, assisted by the advent of well-validated measures (Steger et al., 2006) and more clarity surrounding how to understand and define the main construct, meaning in life. Both the empirical topic and the scales used to measure meaning have proliferated. Brandstätter et al. (2012) observed that more new scales to measure meaning were developed between 2000 and 2009 than in all previous decades combined.

Psychological concepts of meaning were massively influenced by Frankl's (1963) thinking that humans are innate seekers of meaning, that we desire a purpose or something to keep living for, and that, when all else is lost, we may work to discover meaning through engaging in creative acts, nurturing bonds and relationships with others, and choosing to inhabit our own noble attitudes toward unavoidable suffering. Early theories of meaning sought to specify these ideas in ways that could support an empirical investigation. For example, Maddi (1970) emphasized the human motivational imperative to seek a purpose outside of themselves, which Klinger (1977, 1998) argued originated within our biological and evolutionary heritage as creatures who needed the motivation to accept risk and seek out nutrients and other elements necessary for our survival. To these explications of purpose, Battista and Almond (1973) added a cognitive dimension: We cannot understand who we are, what kinds of goals we ought to adopt, or how to pursue them without having a cognitive framework that holds what we know about life in an integrated model. Battista and Almond also proposed an emotional dimension: the feeling of fulfillment in life. Rather than lay out definitional dimensions of meaning, Baumeister (1991) proposed that perceptions of meaning would arise when people meet core needs for purpose, self-worth, efficacy, and value. The first 50 years of meaning in life theory extended ideas about searching for meaning, developing a sense of purpose, gaining an understanding of how the world around us is composed, and finding meaning through our ability to achieve aims in the world around us.

Currently, the field tends to draw a few key distinctions, many of which have been carried forward from early thinking. First, the presence of meaning is separate from the search for meaning (Steger et al., 2006). The former is a feeling of an abundance of meaning within one's life, the latter is about being motivated and wanting to find *more* meaning in one's life. Furthermore, it has become commonplace to distinguish between three facets of meaning: coherence, purpose, and significance (Heintzelman & King, 2014; Martela & Steger, 2016), with some researchers suggesting mattering as the third facet instead of significance (George & Park, 2016a). Coherence refers to one's life making sense and being comprehensible; purpose is about having direction and goals in one's life; significance is about a general sense of one's life having value and being worth living; mattering is about one's life being valuable in the grand scheme of things and from the point of view of the universe. While many measures tended to include elements of all these facets, there is currently more effort to develop measures that would differentiate these three facets (Costin & Vignoles, 2020; George & Park, 2016b).

Assessment Instruments – Main Instruments

The number of instruments aiming to measure meaning has proliferated in recent years; in their systematic review, Brandstätter et al. (2012) identified altogether 59 different instruments to measure meaning in life. This means that in this review we can cover the most influential and relevant ones (for previous reviews, see Brandstätter et al., 2012; Park & George, 2013), which we present mainly in chronological order (Table 9.1 provides a summary of all the measures).

Table 9.1. Summary of meaning in life measures covered in this review

Measure	Number of items	Subscales	Source
Purpose in Life Test (PIL)	22	Unidimensional, measures purpose	Crumbaugh & Maholick (1964)
Life Regard Index (LRI)	28	• Valued life framework • Fulfillment of life framework	Battista & Almond (1973)
Seeking of Noetic Goals (SONG)	20	Unidimensional, measures will to meaning, which is akin to search for meaning	Crumbaugh (1977)
Life Attitude Profile (LAP)	56	• Life purpose • Existential vacuum • Life control • Death acceptance • Will to meaning • Goal seeking • Future meaning to fulfill	Reker & Peacock (1981)
Life Attitude Profile–Revised (LAP-R)	48	• Life purpose • Existential vacuum • Coherence • Death acceptance • Choice/responsibleness • Goal-seeking	Reker (1992)
Sense of Coherence Scale (SOC)	29 original + various	• Meaningfulness • Comprehensibility • Manageability	Antonovsky (1987)

Table 9.1. continued

Measure	Number of items	Subscales	Source
Purpose in Life subscale of the Ryff Psychological Well-Being Scales (PWB)	9 original + various	Unidimensional, measures purpose	Ryff (1989)
Sources of Meaning Profile (SOMP)	17	One item each for 17 sources of meaning	Reker (1996)
Meaning in Life Questionnaire (MLQ)	10 original + 6-item	• Presence of meaning • Search for meaning	Steger et al. (2006)
Daily Meaning Scale (DMS)	2	Unidimensional, measures state meaning and purpose	Steger et al. (2008)
Subjective Meaningfulness of the Day Scale	2	Unidimensional, measures state meaning and purpose	King & Hicks (2009)
Meaningful Life Measure (MLM)	23	• Exciting life • Purposeful life • Principled life • Accomplished life • Valued life	Morgan & Farsides (2009a)
Sources of Meaning and Meaning in Life Questionnaire (SoMe)	151	• Meaningfulness • Crisis of meaning • Multi-item subscales for 26 sources of meaning – Explicit religiosity – Spirituality – Social commitment – Unison with nature – Self-knowledge – Health – Generativity – Challenge – Individualism – Power – Development – Achievement – Freedom – Knowledge – Creativity – Tradition – Practicality – Morality – Reason – Community – Fun – Love – Comfort – Care – Attentiveness – Harmony	Schnell (2009)
Multidimensional Existential Meaning Scale (MEMS)	15	• Comprehensibility • Purpose • Mattering	George & Park (2016b)

Table 9.1. continued

Measure	Number of items	Subscales	Source
Scale of Four Dimensions of Meaning in Life	49	• Need for meaning • Meaning confusion • Meaning avoidance • Meaning anxiety	Zhang et al. (2018)
Tripartite Meaning Scale	4	• General meaning • Purpose • Coherence • Significance	Costin & Vignoles (2020)

Scales to Measure Presence of Meaning

One of the earliest attempts to assess meaning was the Purpose in Life Test (PIL) by Crumbaugh and Maholick (1964), which was devised to assess Frankl's noogenic neurosis – "a breakdown because of 'existential frustration' or a lack of perceived meaning or 'purpose' in life" (p. 206). The scale included 22 items and was used in the early stages of empirical meaningfulness research, though it later received much criticism (e.g., Dyck, 1987; Schnell, 2009; Steger et al., 2006) for having a factor structure that varies from study to study (compare, e.g., Chamberlain & Zika, 1988; McGregor & Little, 1998) and for including items asking about excitement, pleasure, and suicidality, which run the danger of confounding meaning in life with its potential correlates and outcomes.

Battista and Almond (1973) conceptualized meaning in life as positive regard felt toward one's life which arises from having a valued life framework or goal and being able to fulfill it. Accordingly, their Life Regard Index (LRI) included two subscales: Framework and Fulfillment. However, despite being widely used in the past, the measurement has been criticized for inconsistent results regarding the factor structure and other psychometric problems as well as containing items that overlap with other constructs such as depression and general satisfaction with life (see, e.g., Schnell, 2009; Steger et al., 2006).

The Life Purpose subscale of the Life Attitude Profile (LAP; Reker & Peacock, 1981) is part of a seven-dimension scale aiming to assess the full scope of existential concerns people face. Its items assess having a sense of purpose, a zest for life, fulfillment, and contentment and satisfaction with the life one is living, and thus it is somewhat of a conceptual blend of the two LRI fulfillment subscales. Reker revised the Life LAP over several publications (e.g., 1992) and offered evidence of internal consistency that was generally in the acceptable range above .70, with large correlations indicating test-retest stability. Although the Life Purpose subscale has been the most psychometrically sound of these subscales, many of the others have performed poorly, which might have suppressed use of the Life Purpose subscale, along with concerns over the risk of confounding with other content, particularly life satisfaction and positive emotions such as zest and excitement.

The Sense of Coherence Scale (SOC; Antonovsky, 1987) has sometimes been used to measure meaning in life. The scale includes three dimensions: comprehensibility, manageability, and meaning. However, it is unclear whether it should be used to measure meaning as it is better seen as a coping disposition measure (Sammallahti et al., 1996) that aims primarily to capture "a way of seeing the world which facilitates successful coping with the innumerable, complex stressors confronting us in the course of living" (Antonovsky, 1993, p. 725). For example, half of the items of the meaningfulness subscale center on boredom and indifference to life.

The Purpose in Life subscale of the Psychological Well-Being Scales (PWB; Ryff, 1989) was designed by Ryff to measure what she saw as one key aspect of psychological well-being, that of having "goals, intentions, and a sense of direction" (p. 1071). There are several versions of the scale of various lengths, and it has since grown into one of the most often used scales of meaningfulness. However, it must be noted that it aims to measure one of the subfacets of meaning in life – purpose – rather than meaning more generally.

The Presence of Meaning subscale of the Meaning in Life Questionnaire (MLQ; Steger et al., 2006), which was validated in three studies, provided a significant improvement over earlier scales in terms of its psychometric validity and how rigorously that was assessed in the designing phase. In Brandstätter et al.'s (2012) evaluation of 59 scales for measuring meaning, it was the only one to receive full points for its reliability, interpretability, and validity. Yet it is still worth noting that a Rasch analysis conducted among a sample from South Africa, Australia, and New Zealand suggested that this subscale might lack sensitivity at high levels of presence of meaning, which was attributed in part to its inclusion of a reverse-scored item (Schutte et al., 2016). Because of its brief format (5 items), stable factor structure, and good psychometric properties, however, it has become clearly the most often used scale to assess the presence of meaning.

The Meaningful Life Measure (MLM; Morgan & Farsides, 2009a) explored the factor structure of items derived from several popular meaning-in-life scales to identify five latent constructs: exciting life, purposeful life, principled life, accomplished life, and valued life. They then constructed and psychometrically validated (see also Morgan & Farsides, 2009b) scales to assess each of these five constructs and show their separateness. However, given that the constructs were empirically derived, more information about what theoretically relevant constructs each of them aims to measure would be preferred, as well as whether all of them – e.g., exciting life – should be seen as facets of meaning in life.

The Meaningfulness subscale of the Sources of Meaning and Meaning in Life Questionnaire (SoMe; Schnell, 2009) aims to measure the subjective appraisal of meaningfulness using five questions. Schnell reported the internal consistency of this scale (α=.74) along with correlations with positive mood (r=.36) and life satisfaction (r=.44). An earlier 4-item version of this scale correlated with r=.46 with Antonovsky's scale (Schnell & Becker, 2006).

The Multidimensional Existential Meaning Scale (MEMS; George & Park, 2016b) included three subscales designed to assess three separate facets of the presence of meaning: comprehensibility, purpose, and mattering. Comprehensibility comprises a sense of coherence in life; purpose is about one's life being directed and motivated by valued goals; mattering concerns whether individuals feel that their existence has value in the world (George & Park, 2016a). The psychometric properties were tested in three studies and found to be satisfactory, although the intercorrelations between the facets were quite high. Thus, if one's interest is in the three facets of meaning it assesses, this scale is a good way of measuring those.

The Tripartite Meaning Scale (Costin & Vignoles, 2020) included three separate scales for coherence, purpose, and existential mattering which aimed to be acquiescence-free through including a balanced number of positively and negatively phrased items. Interestingly, the authors demonstrated in two longitudinal studies that, while mattering predicted a subsequent general sense of meaning, purpose and coherence did not.

Scales to Measure Search for Meaning

The Seeking of Noetic Goals Scale (SONG; Crumbaugh, 1977) was designed to assess the "will to meaning," but the scale has been subject to severe criticism (e.g., Dyck, 1987) to the degree of having gone almost completely unused.

The Will to Meaning subscale of the LAP and its revisions (Reker, 1996) were also developed to assess people's search for meaning as a complement to other existential scales in the LAP. Its psychometric properties were poor but improved with revision, and its items asked about people's tendencies to think about the ultimate meaning of life, their own meaning or purpose, whether they have an urge to find themselves, understanding meaning through hardship and suffering, and feeling that everyone is accountable for their life.

The Search for Meaning subscale of the MLQ (Steger et al., 2006) is a 5-item scale designed to measure search for meaning that was validated in three studies and had satisfactory psychometric properties. It has become the standard scale to assess how much people search for meaning in their lives.

Scales to Measure Episodic Meaning

The Daily Meaning Scale (DMS; Steger et al., 2008) uses two items to measure the daily experience of meaning in life. Instead of looking at life in general, it aims to examine one's current, daily level of meaning. Changes in scores on this scale correlate to changes in other psychological variables, daily events, and behavioral events, thus showing that, in addition to a general sense of meaning in life, people can make more episodic evaluations of the meaningfulness of shorter periods.

The Subjective Meaningfulness of the Day Scale (King & Hicks, 2009) uses two items to measure how meaningful 'this day' has been to the participants; it has been used in, for example, daily diary studies (e.g., Martela, Ryan, & Steger, 2018).

Scales to Measure Other Aspects and Dimensions of Meaning

The Sources of Meaning Profile (SOMP) and later revisions by Reker (1996) represent the first efforts to provide a quantitative scale for assessing sources of meaning, understood as the parts of life people find most meaningful. By the revision in 1996, the scale eventually assessed 17 sources of meaning, such as relationships, financial security, nature, service to others, everyday needs, leisure, personal growth, human rights, political causes, religious activities, or leaving a legacy. Although sources of meaning offer great potential for learning more about how people bring meaning into everyday life, only a very tiny minority of published works use these measures, including Reker's groundbreaking effort. More often, it seems as if researchers prefer to use open-ended, qualitative approaches, perhaps to avoid persistent cultural limitations inherent to lists of "what matters" (e.g., Delle Fave et al., 2011).

The Crisis of Meaning subscale of the SoMe (Schnell, 2009) measures the evaluation that one's life is frustratingly empty and lacking meaning. Schnell (2009) argues that a crisis of meaning is not a mere lack of meaningfulness but should be examined separately. Her empirical analysis finds support for this notion: For example, the two constructs have rather low correlations (-.38 and -.35), demonstrating the importance of examining them as two separate constructs rather than opposite ends of a unipolar scale.

In addition to having scales for meaningfulness and crisis of meaning discussed elsewhere, the SoMe (Schnell, 2009) includes subscales for 26 different orientations or sources of meaning such as self-knowledge, unison with nature, and generativity, which were derived through structured in-depth interviews to represent ultimate sources of meaning in the sense of being independent sources of intrinsic value.

The Scales for Four Dimensions of Meaning in Life (Zhang et al., 2018) represent scales developed to examine four meaning-related dimensions: need for meaning was about how much participants felt they need meaning in their life, meaning confusion was about being confused about meaning or how to attain it, meaning avoidance was about actively avoiding thinking about meaningfulness, and meaning anxiety was about worries about not finding meaning to one's life. Their results showed the separateness of these four dimensions thus allowing future studies to examine these aspects to meaning more deeply.

Observations on the Similarities and Differences Between the Scales

Overall, the scales that have been developed to measure meaning reflect the breadth and complexity of the construct itself. Measures of the presence of meaning yield fairly similar results in the literature, while these results diverge decidedly from those obtained for measures of the search for meaning. Research using measures of sources of meaning scales indicate that people emphasize somewhat different sources, though having a larger number and diversity of sources of meaning correlates overall with a greater sense of meaning in life (e.g., Schnell, 2009). Further, meaning measures, particularly the older ones, tend to interchange the terms meaning, purpose, mission, and significance, and also frequently include an item or two from earlier measures. In fact, one measure, the MLM (Morgan & Farsides, 2009a), is a collection of items from other measures.

Perhaps psychometric suitability provides the clearest differences among measures, with several being deemed to include extraneous themes, conflating content, or being unreliable or structurally unstable. If we take matters of measurement suitability seriously, it is problematic that many major findings have only been reported for historical and flawed measures (e.g., need for and response to therapy). However, subtler differences are present as well. For example, the presence subscale of Steger et al.'s MLQ (2009) and Ryff's Purpose Scale (1989) show divergent trends of increase vs. decrease across the lifespan (cf. Pinquart, 2002); daily search for meaning seems positive, whereas trait search for meaning often appears negative. Clearly, instrumentation is key to these differences and may indicate important nuances in the construct itself. If instrumentation is a key, the tendency for certain disciplines to use specific measures suggests areas where expanding the array of measures used may yield new insights. For example, gerontological and health research are partial to Ryff's and Antonovsky's scales, so the vast majority of research reporting longevity benefits among those with greater meaning were conducted with only those two scales or "good enough" scales from within those disciplines. Finally, there are cases where the choice of instrument shapes what can be learned. Research on the SoMe indicates that some sources are better than others but that generally having more sources is better than having few (Schnell, 2009). It is unclear whether a similar result could be gained using the 17-item Reker measure instead of the SoMe, which uses more than 145 items to assess 26 sources.

A clear trend in the literature is the movement from the unidimensional presence of meaning scales into scales that separate meaning into several facets aiming to examine them separately (e.g., Costin & Vignoles, 2020; George & Park, 2016b; Morgan & Farsides, 2009a). Theoretically, key distinctions have been drawn between coherence, purpose, significance (Heintzelman & King, 2014; Martela & Steger, 2016), and mattering (George & Park, 2016a) as key facets of meaning in life. However, it is worth noting that it is still a somewhat open question whether all the theoretical distinctions that have been proposed are practically distinct. For example, the Comprehension subscale of the MEMS correlated .79 with Steger's presence of meaning (George & Park, 2016b), and Costin and Vignole's (2020) coherence and purpose scales correlated at .72, casting doubt on how well they can be separated empirically. This is an area where further empirical work is needed.

Recommendations for Instrument Selection

As the above section strongly indicates, the essential first step of the instrument selection process is to make it clear what facet or aspect of meaning one is primarily interested in examining. Is one interested in studying the search for, the need for, or the presence of meaning? Is one interested in the general presence of meaning in life? Or does one want to examine one of its subfacets such as coherence, purpose, or significance? Is one interested in an overall sense of meaning in life or experiences of meaningfulness in particular situations, tasks, or days – or the sources from which people draw meaning? These are separate research topics, and thus it is crucial to be clear about what aspect of meaning one is interested in: the presence of meaning or the search or need for it; meaning in general or some specific facet of it; meaning in life or meaningfulness of a specific situation. Only after this has been clarified is it time to examine what specific measure would be appropriate given one's exact research interest.

Having settled the research interest, one should then examine the available scales to see how well validated they are. If one is interested in general meaning in life or search for meaning, for example, Steger et al.'s (2006) Presence of Meaning and Search for Meaning scales appear to be leading choices, enabling researchers to use popular, psychometrically robust instruments, which has the benefit of making it possible to directly compare one's results to the wide range of previous studies using that measure for examining meaning in life. For the purpose in life, on the other hand, the options include the subscales developed for purpose in life by Ryff (1989), Morgan and Farsides (2009a), George and Park (2016b), and Costin and Vignoles (2020). Like Steger et al.'s scales, Ryff's Purpose scale offers the benefit of being widely used across a vast range of studies, particularly in health and aging fields. For assessing meaning as a multidimensional construct, in turn, several new measures have been proposed for that task (Costin & Vignoles, 2020; George & Park, 2016b; Morgan & Farsides, 2009a), but research is probably too preliminary to support specific recommendations. For daily and episodic meaning assessment, research is also probably too preliminary for a specific recommendation. For measures of sources of meaning, the choices are difficult, and we cannot provide a strong recommendation because of a relative lack of research. Schnell's SoMe is comprehensive and is distinguished by using multiple items per source of meaning but is extremely long, while Reker's scale is easy to use but might fail to assess key sources that the more comprehensive SoMe covers.

Conclusion

The overall conclusion of this review is that there are many, many options to consider for measuring meaning and purpose in life, along with a massive research base of thousands of studies to back up the importance of meaning to human functioning. The number of different measures of meaning, with partially overlapping definitions of the key constructs, can, however, make the choice of a good measure hard. Systematic examinations of the distinctiveness and overlap between the various measures would be much welcomed. The good news is that a few instruments are psychometrically robust, and several are widely used for the basic dimensions of general meaning, purpose, and perhaps search for meaning, too. Researchers can feel confident in the leading recommendations of this chapter, such as using MLQ (Steger et al., 2006) to measure presence or search of meaning and Ryff's (1989) Purpose in Life subscale to assess purpose.

As much progress has been made already, significant innovation and exploration are still ongoing and lie in the future for meaning-in-life assessment and research. For example, quite interesting results are being reported from the use of single-item and short-form meaning measures to survey populations (e.g., Oishi & Diener, 2014; Steger & Samman, 2012). We anticipate that there will continue to be progress made on offering psychometrically sound versions of existing measures as well as further efforts to quantify the dimensions of meaning through measurement. Outside of progress on operational definitions of meaning, we anticipate greater attention to the overall theoretical definition and conceptualization of meaning in life, leading to greater consensus on a shared understanding of the construct of meaning. Until then, researchers will continue to add to the wealth of knowledge about meaning in life as a central human concern.

References

Antonovsky, A. (1987). *Unraveling the mystery of health: How people manage stress and stay well.* Jossey-Bass.

Antonovsky, A. (1993). The structure and properties of the sense of coherence scale. *Social Science & Medicine, 36*(6), 725–733. https://doi.org/10.1016/0277-9536(93)90033-Z

Battista, J., & Almond, R. (1973). The development of meaning in life. *Psychiatry, 36*(4), 409–427. https://doi.org/10.1080/00332747.1973.11023774

Baumeister, R.F. (1991). *Meanings of life*. Guilford.

Baumeister, R.F., & Vohs, K.D. (2002). The pursuit of meaningfulness in life. In C.R. Snyder & S.J. Lopez (Eds.), *Handbook of positive psychology* (pp. 608–618). Oxford University Press.

Brandstätter, M., Baumann, U., Borasio, G.D., & Fegg, M.J. (2012). Systematic review of meaning in life assessment instruments. *Psycho-Oncology, 21*(10), 1034–1052. https://doi.org/10.1002/pon.2113

Brassai, L., Piko, B.F., & Steger, M.F. (2015). A reason to stay healthy: The role of meaning in life in relation to physical activity and healthy eating among adolescents. *Journal of Health Psychology, 20*(5), 473–482. https://doi.org/10.1177/1359105315576604

Chamberlain, K., & Zika, S. (1988). Measuring meaning in life: An examination of three scales. *Personality and Individual Differences, 9*(3), 589–596. https://doi.org/10.1016/0191-8869(88)90157-2

Cohen, R., Bavishi, C., & Rozanski, A. (2016). Purpose in life and its relationship to all-cause mortality and cardiovascular events: A meta-analysis. *Psychosomatic Medicine, 78*(2), 122–133. https://doi.org/10.1097/PSY.0000000000000274

Costin, V., & Vignoles, V.L. (2020). Meaning is about mattering: Evaluating coherence, purpose, and existential mattering as precursors of meaning in life judgments. *Journal of Personality and Social Psychology, 118*(4), 864–884. https://doi.org/10.1037/pspp0000225

Crumbaugh, J.C. (1977). The Seeking of Noetic Goals Test (SONG): A complementary scale to the Purpose in Life Test (PIL). *Journal of Clinical Psychology, 33*, 900–907. https://doi.org/10.1002/1097-4679(197707)33:3<900::AID-JCLP2270330362>3.0.CO;2-8

Crumbaugh, J.C., & Maholick, L.T. (1964). An experimental study in existentialism: The psychometric approach to Frankl's concept of noogenic neurosis. *Journal of Clinical Psychology, 20*(2), 200–207. https://doi.org/10.1002/1097-4679(196404)20:2<200::AID-JCLP2270200203>3.0.CO;2-U

Debats, D.L., Drost, J., & Hansen, P. (1995). Experiences of meaning in life: A combined qualitative and quantitative approach. *British Journal of Psychology, 86*, 359–375. https://doi.org/10.1111/j.2044-8295.1995.tb02758.x

Delle Fave, A., Brdar, I., Freire, T., Vella-Brodrick, D., & Wissing, M.P. (2011). The eudaimonic and hedonic components of happiness: Qualitative and quantitative findings. *Social Indicators Research, 100*(2), 185–207. https://doi.org/10.1007/s11205-010-9632-5

Dyck, M.J. (1987). Assessing logotherapeutic constructs: Conceptual and psychometric status of the Purpose in Life and Seeking of Noetic Goals tests. *Clinical Psychology Review, 7*(4), 439–447. https://doi.org/10.1016/0272-7358(87)90021-3

Frankl, V.E. (1963). *Man's search for meaning: An introduction to logotherapy* (I. Lasch, trans.). Washington Square Press.

George, L.S., & Park, C.L. (2016a). Meaning in life as comprehension, purpose, and mattering: Toward integration and new research questions. *Review of General Psychology, 20*(3), 205–220. https://doi.org/10.1037/gpr0000077

George, L.S., & Park, C.L. (2016b). The Multidimensional Existential Meaning Scale: A tripartite approach to measuring meaning in life. *The Journal of Positive Psychology, 12*(6), 613–627. https://doi.org/10.1080/17439760.2016.1209546

Harlow, L.L., Newcomb, M.D., & Bentler, P.M. (1986). Depression, self-derogation, substance use, and suicide ideation: Lack of purpose in life as a mediational factor. *Journal of Clinical Psychology, 42*(1), 5–21. https://doi.org/10.1002/1097-4679(198601)42:1<5::AID-JCLP2270420102>3.0.CO;2-9

Heintzelman, S.J., & King, L.A. (2014). Life is pretty meaningful. *American Psychologist, 69*(6), 561–574. https://doi.org/10.1037/a0035049

King, L.A., & Hicks, J.A. (2009). Detecting and constructing meaning in life events. *The Journal of Positive Psychology, 4*(5), 317–330. https://doi.org/10.1080/17439760902992316

Klinger, E. (1977). *Meaning and void.* University of Minnesota Press.

Klinger, E. (1998). The search for meaning in evolutionary perspective and its clinical implications. In P.T.P. Wong & P.S. Fry (Eds.), *The human quest for meaning* (pp. 27–50). Erlbaum.

Maddi, S.R. (1970). The search for meaning. In M. Page (Ed.), *Nebraska symposium on motivation* (pp. 137–186). University of Nebraska Press.

Martela, F. (2020). *A wonderful life: Insights on finding a meaningful existence.* Harper Design.

Martela, F., Ryan, R.M., & Steger, M.F. (2018). Meaningfulness as satisfaction of autonomy, competence, relatedness, and beneficence: Comparing the four satisfactions and positive affect as predictors of meaning in life. *Journal of Happiness Studies, 19*(5), 1261–1282. https://doi.org/10.1007/s10902-017-9869-7

Martela, F., & Steger, M.F. (2016). The meaning of meaning in life: Coherence, purpose and significance as the three facets of meaning. *Journal of Positive Psychology, 11*(5), 531–545. https://doi.org/10.1080/17439760.2015.1137623

McGregor, I., & Little, B.R. (1998). Personal projects, happiness, and meaning: On doing well and being yourself. *Journal of Personality and Social Psychology, 74*, 494–512. https://doi.org/10.1037/0022-3514.74.2.494

Morgan, J., & Farsides, T. (2009a). Measuring meaning in life. *Journal of Happiness Studies, 10*(2), 197–214. https://doi.org/10.1007/s10902-007-9075-0

Morgan, J., & Farsides, T. (2009b). Psychometric evaluation of the meaningful life measure. *Journal of Happiness Studies, 10*(3), 351–366. https://doi.org/10.1007/s10902-008-9093-6

Oishi, S., & Diener, E. (2014). Residents of poor nations have a greater sense of meaning in life than residents of wealthy nations. *Psychological Science, 25*(2), 422–430. https://doi.org/10.1177/0956797613507286

Park, C.L., & George, L.S. (2013). Assessing meaning and meaning making in the context of stressful life events: Measurement tools and approaches. *The Journal of Positive Psychology, 8*(6), 483–504. https://doi.org/10.1080/17439760.2013.830762

Pinquart, M. (2002). Creating and maintaining purpose in life in old age: A meta-analysis. *Ageing International, 27*(2), 90–114. https://doi.org/10.1007/s12126-002-1004-2

Reker, G.T. (1992). *Manual: Life Attitude Profile-Revised.* Student Psychologists Press.

Reker, G.T. (1996). *Manual of the Sources of Meaning Profile-Revised (SOMP-R).* Student Psychology Press. https://doi.org/10.1037/t45961-000

Reker, G.T., & Peacock, E.J. (1981). The Life Attitude Profile (LAP): A multidimensional instrument for assessing attitudes toward life. *Canadian Journal of Behavioural Science/Revue Canadienne Des Sciences Du Comportement, 13*(3), 264–273. https://doi.org/10.1037/h0081178

Ryff, C.D. (1989). Happiness is everything, or is it? Explorations on the meaning of psychological well-being. *Journal of Personality and Social Psychology, 57*(6), 1069–1081. https://doi.org/10.1037/0022-3514.57.6.1069

Sammallahti, P.R., Holi, M.J., Komulainen, E.J., & Aalberg, V.A. (1996). Comparing two self-report measures of coping: The Sense of Coherence Scale and the Defense Styles Questionnaire. *Journal of Clinical Psychology, 52*, 517–524. https://doi.org/10.1002/(SICI)1097-4679(199609)52:5<517::AID-JCLP4>3.0.CO;2-K

Sartre, J.-P. (2007). Existentialism is a humanism. In C. Macomber (Ed., & Trans.), *Existentialism is a humanism* (pp. 17–72). Yale University Press. https://doi.org/10.2307/j.ctv15vwkgx.5

Schnell, T. (2009). The Sources of Meaning and Meaning in Life Questionnaire (SoMe): Relations to demographics and well-being. *The Journal of Positive Psychology, 4*(6), 483–499. https://doi.org/10.1080/17439760903271074

Schnell, T., & Becker, P. (2006). Personality and meaning in life. *Personality and Individual Differences, 41*(1), 117–129. https://doi.org/10.1016/j.paid.2005.11.030

Schutte, L., Wissing, M.P., Ellis, S.M., Jose, P.E., & Vella-Brodrick, D.A. (2016). Rasch analysis of the meaning in life questionnaire among adults from South Africa, Australia, and New Zealand. *Health and Quality of Life Outcomes, 14*(1), Article 12. https://doi.org/10.1186/s12955-016-0414-x

Steger, M. F., Frazier, P., Oishi, S., & Kaler, M. (2006). The Meaning in Life Questionnaire: Assessing the presence of and search for meaning in life. *Journal of Counseling Psychology, 53*(1), 80–93. https://doi.org/10.1037/0022-0167.53.1.80

Steger, M. F., Kashdan, T. B., & Oishi, S. (2008). Being good by doing good: Daily eudaimonic activity and well-being. *Journal of Research in Personality, 42*(1), 22–42. https://doi.org/10.1016/j.jrp.2007.03.004

Steger, M. F., Oishi, S., & Kashdan, T. B. (2009). Meaning in life across the life span: Levels and correlates of meaning in life from emerging adulthood to older adulthood. *The Journal of Positive Psychology, 4*(1), 43–52. https://doi.org/10.1080/17439760802303127

Steger, M. F., & Samman, E. (2012). Assessing meaning in life on an international scale: Psychometric evidence for the Meaning in Life Questionnaire-Short Form among Chilean households. *International Journal of Wellbeing, 2*, 182–195. https://doi.org/10.5502/ijw.v2i.i3.2

Tanno, K., Sakata, K., Ohsawa, M., Onoda, T., Itai, K., Yaegashi, Y., & Tamakoshi, A. (2009). Associations of ikigai as a positive psychological factor with all-cause mortality and cause-specific mortality among middle-aged and elderly Japanese people: Findings from the Japan Collaborative Cohort Study. *Journal of Psychosomatic Research, 67*(1), 67–75. https://doi.org/10.1016/j.jpsychores.2008.10.018

Yalom, I. D. (1980). *Existential Psychotherapy* (1st ed.). Basic Books.

Zhang, H., Sang, Z., Chen, C., Zhu, J., & Deng, W. (2018). Need for meaning, meaning confusion, meaning anxiety, and meaning avoidance: Additional dimensions of meaning in life. *Journal of Happiness Studies, 19*, 191–212. https://doi.org/10.1007/s10902-016-9815-0

Zika, S., & Chamberlain, K. (1992). On the relation between meaning in life and psychological well-being. *British Journal of Psychology, 83*, 133–145. https://doi.org/10.1111/j.2044-8295.1992.tb02429.x

Chapter 10

Assessing Flow

State of the Art and Challenges for the Future

Antonella Delle Fave[1] and Marta Bassi[2]

[1]Department of Pathophysiology and Transplantation, University of Milan, Italy
[2]Department of Biomedical and Clinical Sciences, University of Milan, Italy

We gratefully dedicate this chapter to the memory of Mihaly Csikszentmihalyi (1934–2021)

The availability of appropriate instruments to evaluate flow, also labeled as optimal experience, is relevant for researchers and professionals working in a variety of domains. The investigation of flow as a complex phenomenon allows researchers interested in basic processes to delve deeper into the overall structure of human experience, an area of study still relatively underexplored.

The models of analysis developed to investigate flow may be effectively adopted to identify and operationalize other different experiential states occurring in daily life. For practitioners in the domains of education, clinical psychology, business and organizations, medical and social services, the assessment of flow may be a useful way to ascertain the quality of daily experience of their students, employees, patients, and clients, and to explore pathways toward improving it.

Such a wide range of potential applications of flow has produced a variety of assessment instruments, including qualitative interviews, questionnaires, and experience-sampling procedures. Some of them sought to investigate the psychological features of flow as an optimal experience in human life; other instruments aimed at measuring flow in a specific context, such as work or sport; other ones served to identify personality characteristics that can facilitate flow. Physiological correlates of flow were investigated through an analysis of biomarkers such as cortisol. And, finally, the use of imaging techniques provided information on the neural correlates of this experience.

Based on these premises, the first section of this chapter presents a brief overview of flow as an experiential state including emotional, cognitive, and motivational components. It also discusses the antecedents and consequences of flow as well as personality traits facilitating its onset. The second section describes the main instruments developed to assess flow, by providing information on their structure, psychometric properties, and related findings. It makes a distinction between general measures and domain-related ones. The third section is devoted to the most recent frontier of flow research, namely, the assessment of the neural and physiological correlates of flow, with a description of related studies, measures, and findings. The last section focuses on the costs and benefits of each measure (or measure category) as well as on the aspects of flow that are still unexplored or need to be investigated through more adequate procedures.

Flow: The Optimal Experience

In 1975, a book entitled *Beyond Boredom and Anxiety* opened new horizons to researchers, professionals, and the general public. The book's author, Mihaly Csikszentmihalyi, brought to their attention a peculiar state of mind, well-known by lay people though neglected by scientists, which he labeled "flow." This term synthetically expressed the perception of fluidity and continuity in concentration as well as the harmonious merging between mental and physical functions people described when referring to their involvement in engaging and challenging activities, such as painting, climbing mountains, playing chess, or practicing surgery.

Based on interviews with a variety of people referring to different activities - and nevertheless providing strikingly similar descriptions of the associated experience - Csikszentmihalyi (1975) identified nine recurrent dimensions of flow: the perception of high challenges in the activity matched with high personal skills; clear goals guiding the activity; unambiguous feedback about the moment by moment quality of task performance; the merging of action and awareness, and a feeling of oneness with the activity; a deep concentration on the task at hand; loss of self-consciousness and preoccupation with oneself; a perceived control and mastery of the situation; an altered sense of time; and performing the activity as an autotelic and intrinsically rewarding experience, without concern for performance outcomes. The pervasive complexity and positivity of the flow state led Csikszentmihalyi to define it also as optimal experience; the two terms have often been used interchangeably (Csikszentmihalyi & Csikszentmihalyi, 1988).

Studies involving participants widely differing in culture, age, health conditions, educational level, and occupation have supported the universality of flow experience, which can be associated with a variety of activities, provided they are perceived as sources of concentration and engagement, and are challenging enough to foster the mobilization of personal skills (Csikszentmihalyi & Csikszentmihalyi, 1988; Delle Fave et al., 2011; Engeser, 2012; Harmat et al., 2016; Jackson & Csikszentmihalyi, 1999). Contextual dimensions promoting or hindering flow were also investigated, especially in the domains of the family (Hektner, 2001; Rathunde, 2001), school (Shernoff & Csikszentmihalyi, 2009), and work (Fullagar & Delle Fave, 2017).

Another important element emerged from these findings: By virtue of the intrinsic reward derived from experiencing flow, individuals are more likely to preferentially cultivate the associated activities, within a lifelong developmental process defined as psychological selection (Csikszentmihalyi & Massimini, 1985), shaping personal interests and competences as well as long-term goals and values (Csikszentmihalyi & Beattie, 1979). Optimal experience contributes to orienting the life trajectory and socialization pattern of each individual, by promoting the investment of attentional and motivational resources toward selected action domains. A growing amount of evidence is also available concerning the positive outcomes of flow in specific life domains: Experiencing flow promotes creativity and innovation (Csikszentmihalyi, 1996); in the context of work it fosters performance (Demerouti, 2006), well-being (Fullagar & Kelloway, 2009), and collective efficacy beliefs (Salanova et al., 2006, 2014). From a broader social perspective, the potential of specific activities to facilitate the onset of flow may involve whole human groups or communities (Paéz et al., 2015; Zumeta et al., 2016), thus promoting a sense of belonging and unity, and orienting cultural trends (Massimini & Delle Fave, 2000). At the same time, there is evidence concerning some problematic aspects of flow. Despite its experientially rewarding nature, not all the associated activities have positive consequences on individual and group development, for example, combat flow (Harari, 2008) or antisocial activities such as stealing (Delle Fave & Massimini, 2005a).

Studies have also shed light on task-related variations in the psychological structure of flow. The cognitive core of the experience, including high concentration and control of the situation, does not show remarkable differences across samples and activities (Delle Fave & Massimini, 2005b). On the contrary, affective and motivational variables widely vary across activities in relation to a core task feature: being compulsory vs. freely chosen (such as work or study vs. leisure; Bassi & Delle Fave, 2012; Csikszentmihalyi & LeFevre, 1989; Rodríguez-Sánchez et al., 2011). More specifically, in compulsory activities such as work, flow is characterized by a neutral affective tone and the perception of extrinsic rewards as well as by highly relevant short- and long-term goals. Leisure, in contrast, is associated with significantly positive affect levels, intrinsic rewards as well as low relevance of activity-related goals. Another peculiarity was detected when evaluating flow during activities involving interactions with other people (Paéz et al., 2015; van den Hout et al., 2018; Walker, 2010); in these situations, flow is often characterized by significantly high values of all psychological variables, including affective and motivational ones (Delle Fave et al., 2011).

Finally, the use of different procedures led researchers to consider some of the nine dimensions of flow, all originally considered core components of this experience, as more adequately representing antecedents and consequences of flow. A great amount of evidence has been collected throughout decades of research around the central role of challenges and skills (and more specifically their balance) in facilitating the onset of flow (Guo & Poole, 2009; Keller & Bless, 2008; Keller & Blomann, 2008; Massimini et al., 1987; Moneta & Csikszentmihalyi, 1996; Pearce et al., 2005). Clear goals and unambiguous feedback can also be more effectively understood as flow prerequisites rather than components (Hektner et al., 2007; Kawabata & Mallett, 2011), though more studies are needed to clarify this issue. The intrinsic reward and enjoyment derived from performing a flow-inducing activity can be instead described as outcomes of the experience, as they are more often perceived upon task completion than during the unfolding of the activity (Csikszentmihalyi, 1997; Nakamura & Csikszentmihalyi, 2009).

At the individual level, personality and trait-like dimensions can facilitate the flow onset as well: Researchers have explored the relationship between flow and dispositional variables, such as internal locus of control (Keller & Blomann, 2008); intrinsic motivation orientation (Moneta, 2012); the Big Five (Bassi et al., 2014; Mesurado & Richaud de Minzi, 2013; Ullén et al., 2012). Researchers have also related the frequency of flow occurrence in daily life to a dispositional trait, assessing it through various instruments (Asakawa, 2010; Jackson & Eklund, 2002; Ullén et al., 2012). Based on the conceptualization formulated by Csikzentmihalyi (1997), a specific measure of autotelic personality was recently developed and validated (Tse et al., 2020).

To better disentangle the role of specific dimensions in contributing to the phenomenology of flow, experimental studies have also been conducted, although their potential in capturing a dynamic experiential state is limited. Additional research is needed to tackle this issue.

After this brief description of flow as a theoretical construct and an object of empirical exploration, the remaining sections of this chapter offer more detailed information on the instruments developed through over 40 years of research to capture and measure this peculiar experience.

The Evolution of Flow Measurement

Seminal and Evergreen: The Original Tools to Assess Flow

Flow Questionnaire

The first research instrument specifically designed to investigate flow is the Flow Questionnaire (FQ; Csikszentmihalyi, 1975; Csikszentmihalyi & Csikszentmihalyi, 1988). It can be described as a mixed-method tool, including both open-ended questions and scales that provide researchers with a multifaceted description of flow and associated activities. In the original version, the first page included three quotations derived from free descriptions of flow collected by Csikszentmihalyi during interviews with people devoted to the most diverse flow-inducing activities. Participants were asked to read the three quotations and to report whether they had ever had similar experiences in their life. If they did, they were invited to specify the associated activities or situations (they could indicate more than one activity) and to report their frequency (from *a rare event* to *every day*). Participants were then asked to rate, through 14 items on 0–8 Likert-type scales, the levels of the nine components of flow during the associated activities (some components were investigated through more than one item, for example, challenge/skill balance was evaluated through the separate ratings of perceived challenges and perceived skills). Four open-ended questions followed, exploring the personal and environmental conditions facilitating the onset and persistence of flow during the performance of the associated activities (Massimini et al., 1988; Wilson & Moneta, 2012).

The original version of the Flow Questionnaire was subsequently revised, expanded (Delle Fave & Massimini, 1988, 1991), and used to collect data from a variety of participants across countries, giving rise to the largest international databank currently available on the measurement of flow with a single instrument (Delle Fave et al., 2011). The expansion of FQ was guided by three aims: to verify the universality of flow characteristics across activities and cultures; to contextualize flow and related activities within participants' daily routine as well as within the lifelong process of psychological selection (Csikszentmihalyi & Massimini, 1985; Massimini & Delle Fave, 2000); to relate individuals' flow experiences and associated activities to cultural, social, educational, and health-related dimensions.

To pursue these aims, open-ended questions about participants' long-term psychological investment were included in FQ, and two instruments consisting of open-ended questions were added to the international data collection: the Life Theme Questionnaire (LT;

Csikszentmihalyi & Beattie, 1979) and the Order/Disorder Questionnaire (OD; Massimini et al., 1988). Together, these three instruments contribute to a thorough investigation of participants' psychological selection throughout their lifespan. Global findings and results obtained from specific populations are reported in Delle Fave et al. (2003a), Delle Fave & Massimini (2000, 2003, 2004a, 2004b, 2005a), Delle Fave and Bassi (2009), and Delle Fave et al. (2011).

International studies allowed researchers to detect some critical issues in FQ. The three original quotations included the description of a rather "extreme" condition of absorption:

> "I am really quite oblivious to my surroundings after I really get doing in this activity. *I think that the phone could ring, and the doorbell could ring or the house burn down or something like that* ... Once I stop, I can let it back again."

Several participants, especially individuals responsible for monitoring other people's behavior or environmental conditions, whether by profession or social role (e.g., parents of young children, caregivers, nurses, teachers, policemen), denied that total isolation from external solicitations - especially the emergency described in the quotation - could take place in their lives, thus casting doubts on the possibility to experience flow as a whole. The sentence was therefore removed from the three main quotations and submitted to participants separately; this was an interesting opportunity to verify its "extremeness," as only a low percentage of participants reported having experienced it during their lives, in very rare conditions of absorption during the performance of very specific tasks, often taking place in an isolated setting (Delle Fave et al., 2011; Moneta, 2010). Except for this change, the quotations describing flow in the modified version of FQ are coincident with Csikszentmihalyi's original ones:

> "My mind isn't wandering. I am totally involved in what I am doing and I am not thinking of anything else. My body feels good ... the world seems to be cut off from me ... I am less aware of myself and my problems."
>
> "My concentration is like breathing ... I never think of it ... When I start, I really do shut out the world."
>
> "I am so involved in what I am doing ... I don't see myself as separate from what I am doing."

A further change concerned the activities to be described through the 14 scaled items. As participants are given no limitations in the number of flow-related activities they can list after reading the quotations, to limit their burden they are invited to select from the list the activity associated with the most pervasive and intense flow experience and to only refer to it when answering the rating scales (the same strategy was adopted by Wilson & Moneta, 2012).

A final, interesting, culture-related issue emerged concerning the meaning and translation of the key term "challenge." As highlighted by participants involved in early Italian pilot studies (Massimini & Inghilleri, 1986), the literal translation of the item (*sfida*) was not pertinent to many flow activities associated with the quotations. While it could be easily related to competitive games and sports as well as to work and study tasks entailing external evaluation and social expectations, it was not suited to activities perceived as intrinsically rewarding, pressure-free, enjoyable opportunities to engage in a self-chosen task. Based on this issue, the final Italian version of "challenge" included reference to both engagement and opportunity for action and self-expression. Subsequent studies involving English-speaking participants from non-Western countries further confirmed the need to adequately address this issue in international studies. In particular, Indian adults living in India as well as Indian immigrants settled in Europe pointed to the inadequacy of referring to *challenges* concerning flow activities such as meditation, creative writing, playing music, playing with children, cooking, or getting involved in social interaction, rather describing these activities as "opportunities for action and self-expression." Therefore, a new item referring to this feature was added to the rating scales in the English version of FQ. The differences observed in most participants' ratings of the perceived "challenges" and "opportunity for action and self-expression" across flow activities confirmed the usefulness of this solution (Delle Fave & Massimini, 2004b; Delle Fave et al., 2011).

Besides English and Italian, the Flow Questionnaire is also available in French (Bassi et al., 2008), Spanish (Mesurado, 2008), and Portuguese (Freire, 2006).

The Experience Sampling Method

Flow can be fruitfully investigated through experience-sampling procedures. The development and use of this typology of measurement has to be again ascribed to Csikszentmihalyi and his collaborators, who in the late 1970s launched the experience sampling method (ESM), aimed at investigating individual behaviors and the associated experiences in real-time, during the unfolding of daily life events and activities (Csikszentmihalyi et al., 1977).

ESM sessions usually last for 1 week, during which participants receive acoustic signals 6–8 times a day and are expected to fill out a form upon each signal reception. The forms include different questions, that may partially vary according to the research target. Generally, open-ended questions or checklists are used to collect data on the ongoing activity, location, social context, short- and long-term relevance of the main activity (e.g., "As you were beeped, what was the main thing you were doing?", "Where were you?", "Who were you with?"). Scaled questions are instead used to investigate the affective, cognitive, and motivational dimensions of the experience. Two scaled questions explicitly rate the levels of challenges and skills perceived in the ongoing activity. Form completion requires 2 min on average. The reliability and validity of this procedure were tested in both cross-sectional and longitudinal studies (Csikszentmihalyi & Larson, 1987; Csikszentmihalyi & Schneider, 2000; Larson & Delespaul, 1992; Van Der Poel & Delespaul, 1992). In light of the increasing popularity of ESM, a handbook was published to provide researchers with conceptual, methodological, and analytical guidelines for the appropriate use of the procedure (Hektner et al., 2007).

Compared to single-administration procedures, ESM combines the ecological validity of naturalistic observation with the descriptive nature of diaries and the precision of scaled questionnaires, avoiding memory distortions (Schimmack, 2003) and providing researchers with repeated momentary representations of the interplay between the daily environmental settings (activities, places, social contexts) and individuals' behavior and experience (Hektner et al., 2007; Napa Scollon et al., 2003). The instrument was used across cultures, with clinical and nonclinical samples, in cross-sectional and longitudinal investigations (Bassi et al., 2012; Conner et al., 2009; Delle Fave & Massimini, 1992, 2004c, 2005b; Mill et al., 2018; Moneta, 2004; Trull & Ebner-Priemer, 2009).

The risk for retrospective recall is specifically addressed by discarding from analysis forms completed over 20 min after signal receipt. A short time lag between signal and response ensures that ESM ratings validly reflect internal experiences and not an individual's response style or social desirability. Overall, a response rate of 30 % (referring to the percentage of forms completed upon signal receipt) is considered adequate for inclusion in analyses (Hektner et al., 2007). Response rate variations were detected across samples, ranging from 92 % among US managers (Csikszentmihalyi & Larson, 1987) to 68.8 % among Italian teenagers (Bassi & Delle Fave, 2012). On average, participants with mental or physical impairments correctly answered to 50–60 % of the signals (Cortinovis Intini et al., 2011; Sartori et al., 2014; Sartori et al., 2019; Sznitman et al., 2018).

Some methodological disadvantages can be also identified in ESM (Napa Scollon et al., 2003). Regarding participants, self-selection bias and attrition (a potential problem for any psychological study) may be more relevant because of the long sampling sessions and the repeated completion of forms during daily activities. Situational issues may include individuals' reluctance or impossibility to fill in forms during specific activities, such as religious rituals, job tasks that cannot be interrupted, or sports competitions. Nevertheless, the majority of ESM participants usually do not complain about activity disruptions, while acknowledging that signal distribution comprehensively captures their weekly routine (Csikszentmihalyi & Larson, 1987).

ESM is relevant to the study of flow as it allows for identifying this experience in real-time and for comparing it with the other experiences arising during the unfolding of daily tasks and events. In particular, through ESM data it was possible to empirically test the Flow Channel Model described by Csikszentmihalyi (1975), a bidimensional area with skills on the x-axis and challenges on the y-axis, in which flow was conceptually located in a "channel" extended along the bisector of the angle defined by the two axes, and corresponding to challenge and skill values balanced at different levels of intensity. Based on the view of flow as a state "beyond boredom and anxiety," boredom corresponded to the area of the model in which skills are higher than challenges, while anxiety corresponded to the opposite area, in which challenges exceed skills.

ESM studies allowed researchers to better clarify the role of challenges and skills as antecedents of flow. Using real-time sampling and the availability of repeated measures for all the experiential variables identified as flow components, the original "channel model" was implemented through different strategies of data organization and analysis, which provided empirical evidence of the multicomponential structure of flow, the predictive role of challenges and skills, and the structure of other experiential states, including boredom and anxiety (Clarke & Haworth, 1994; Delle Fave & Bassi, 2000; Delle Fave & Massimini, 2004c, 2005b; deVries, 1992). In particular, the use of ESM led to the development of the Experience Fluctuation Model (EFM; Massimini et al., 1987), an evolution of the original flow channel relying on the transformation of the raw scores of the experiential variables into standardized values (z-scores), with the individual participant's mean as a baseline.

Based on the arctangent function of standardized challenges and skills, the circumference is partitioned into eight sectors (defined channels), each identifying a specific range of challenges/skills ratios. Flow experience is expected to correspond to the sector located in the upper right quadrant between 22.5° and 67.5°, and labeled as "channel 2," where both z-challenges and z-skills show high values. Other sectors identify conditions of imbalance in favor of challenges (Channels 1, 7, 8) or skills (Channels 3, 4, 5). An additional condition of challenge/skill balance was identified in the lower left quadrant sector (Channel 6), where both variables score below average. The values of the experiential variables in the eight different channels were consistent with the theoretical expectations across studies involving participants differing in culture, age, profession, and health conditions (Bassi & Delle Fave, 2012; Delle Fave et al., 2003b; Delle Fave & Massimini, 2005b; Haworth & Evans, 1995; Inkinen et al., 2014; Sartori & Delle Fave, 2014). In channel 2, most psychological variables score significantly above average, as expected in flow. In channel 6, the challenge/skill balance below average corresponds to a state of disengagement, lack of concentration, and negative affect, defined as apathy. Channel 4 (challenges lower and skills higher than average) is associated with an experiential profile of relaxation, with positive values of affect and control, but low concentration and involvement. In channel 8, the imbalance between high challenges and low skills is associated with high alertness and concentration, negative affect, and distress, consistent with an experience of anxiety. The remaining channels correspond to states of arousal (channel 1), control (channel 3), boredom (channel 5), and worry (channel 7, average challenges/low skills).

Other studies have adopted regression models, highlighting the distinctive predictive role of challenges and skills separately on the potential onset of flow (Moneta & Csikszentmihalyi, 1996). Further clarifications were obtained through multilevel (ML) analysis, exploiting the hierarchical structure of ESM data, consisting of repeated measures nested within individuals (Raudenbush & Bryk, 2002). ML models allow for simultaneously analyzing variables from different levels, taking into account the dependence of observations (Hox, 2002) and providing more solid evidence of the predictive role of specific variables. These studies further confirmed the appropriateness of considering perceived challenges and skills as predictors of the experiential profile emerging from the performance of an activity (Bassi & Delle Fave, 2012; Bassi, Ferrario et al., 2012; Sartori et al., 2014, 2019). Another possibility provided by ESM is to study flow at the intraindividual level, as it may be described as a nonergodic process (Ceja & Navarro, 2009), whose onset and maintenance in the course of an activity depends on individual and contextual features. To this end, techniques based on nonlinear dynamic systems have been implemented to analyze the dynamics of flow occurrence at work (Ceja & Navarro, 2011).

The Flow Scales: Combining Brevity and Versatility

The empirical evidence collected through the first studies relying on the Flow Questionnaire and ESM on the experiential features of flow led researchers to develop shorter instruments structured as rating scales, to reliably detect flow in different contexts, without imposing too high a burden on participants. These instruments are described below.

The Flow State Scales (FSS) and Dispositional Flow Scales (DFS)

The first purely quantitative instruments, assessing flow through scaled items only, were designed by Susan Jackson and her colleagues (Jackson et al., 1998; Jackson & Marsh,

1996), who aimed at developing self-report tools that could be easily used in the sports context to evaluate flow in physical activity. The outcomes of this work were the Flow State Scale (FSS) and the Dispositional Flow Scale (DFS), both designed to measure all nine dimensions of flow through 36 items (4 items for each dimension) on 5-point scales. The two instruments differed in item formulation according to their assessment goal. In particular, FSS was designed to measure flow after completion of physical activity, training, or sports match; to this end, participants are invited to refer the items to their experience during the activity, rating each item from 1 (*strongly disagree*) to 5 (*strongly agree*). The DFS was, in turn, designed to evaluate the average frequency of flow occurrence during the practice of physical activity; participants are asked to rate it from 1 (*never*) to 5 (*always*).

Despite the acceptable psychometric properties of the two original instruments (Marsh & Jackson, 1999; Tenenbaum et al., 1999), some of the items were considered conceptually problematic, while other ones did not satisfy statistical requirements, especially concerning the two subscales time transformation and loss of self-consciousness (Vlachopoulos et al., 2000. Therefore, both instruments were revised in item content (Jackson & Eklund, 2002), giving rise to new versions: Flow State Scale-2 (FSS-2) and Dispositional Flow Scale-2 (DFS-2), both containing 36 items on 5-point rating scales.

The FSS-2 and DFS-2 currently represent the most conceptually exhaustive and psychometrically solid multidimensional tools to assess flow. Confirmatory factor analyses showed a satisfactory fit for a 9-first-order factor model (distinguishing each of the flow dimensions) as well as for a higher-order model representing a global flow factor (Jackson & Eklund, 2002). Since the item content is not bound to a specific activity, researchers can use both scales to assess state and dispositional flow in a variety of activity domains, simply by orienting participants' focus on the activity of interest through the formulation of the introductory instructions (Wang et al., 2009). Both scales were validated in Japanese (Kawabata et al., 2008). The FSS-2 was validated in French (Fournier et al., 2007) and Spanish (Calvo et al., 2008). Validated versions of the DFS-2 are available in Italian (Riva et al., 2017), Portuguese (Gouveia et al., 2012), and Spanish (González-Cutre et al., 2009).

To address the concerns of researchers looking for brief evaluation tools to be included in batteries of multiple instruments, or to be administered in situations incompatible with a prolonged data collection, Jackson et al. (2008) subsequently developed short versions of the two scales, the Short Flow State Scale-2 and the Short Dispositional Flow Scale-2. Both contain 9 items, each selected from the original long scales to represent one of the nine flow dimensions and loading on a single, global flow factor. The short DFS-2 showed remarkable psychometric robustness in studies involving sports professionals as well as participants from a variety of occupations, whereas FSS-2 shows overall weaker properties, and better performance in studies involving sports professionals (Jackson & Martin, 2008). Details on the structure and psychometric properties of both long and short versions of these scales are reported in a users' manual (Jackson, Eklund & Martin, 2010).

The Core Flow Scale

A conceptually different short scale was further added to the set of instruments developed by Jackson and colleagues: the Core Flow Scale, a measure including 10 items on 5-point rating scales, assessing the phenomenological features of flow experience (Martin & Jackson, 2008). The items are derived from the qualitative descriptions of flow provided by élite athletes who reported with their own words, sometimes using idiomatic expressions or colloquial terms, how they felt while experiencing flow during their practice (Jackson, 1996). Sample items are "being in the zone" or "being into the groove."

The Flow Kurz Skala (FKS)

The FKS (Engeser & Rheinberg, 2008; Rheinberg et al., 2003) is a 10-item instrument designed to assess on 7-point scales (from *not at all* to *very much*) the typical components of flow: perception of an adequate level of challenges; the smoothness of action/thoughts; neglect of time passing; ease of concentration; clear ideas; immersion in the ongoing task; effortless action/thought fluency; clear goals; feeling of control; loss of self-consciousness. Three additional items can be added to the scale to specifically assess perceived task demands, personal skills, and the fit between the two. The high internal consistency of FKS allows for calculating a global flow score. At the same time, factor analysis highlighted the presence of two distinct components (Rheinberg et al., 2003): absorption in the activity (including 4 items referring to the perception of adequate challenges, time distortion, immersion in the task, and loss of self-consciousness) and fluency of performance (including the other 6 items, referring to action smoothness and appropriateness, effortless concentration, control, and clear goal pursuit). Although high scores in both subscales lead to a high global score corresponding to a full-fledged flow experience (Schiepe-Tiska & Engeser, 2017), the two dimensions are not equivalent in terms of construct representativeness. While absorption is more closely related to flow, as it implies the perception of adequate challenges and deep immersion in the ongoing task, fluency may also arise in low-demanding situations that nevertheless allow the individual to perceive action smoothness and high control (Rheinberg et al., 2003).

Thanks to its brevity and good psychometric properties, the FKS has been used in a variety of contexts (e.g., Baumann & Scheffer, 2011; Engeser & Baumann, 2015; Schüler et al., 2013), as well as in repeated sampling studies (Peifer & Zipp, 2019; Rheinberg et al., 2007). The scale, predominantly used in German-speaking countries, was recently validated in Greek (Kyriazos et al., 2018).

The Flow Metacognition Questionnaire (FMQ)

This instrument was developed by Wilson and Moneta (2016) to quantitatively assess individuals' beliefs in the constructive role of flow for cognitive functioning and behavioral outcomes, and in their own ability to enter and maintain the state of flow, globally defined as flow metacognitions (Wilson & Moneta, 2012). This instrument is conceptually in continuity with the four open-ended questions included in the FQ and it is aimed at qualitatively investigating the personal and environmental dimensions that can facilitate or hinder the onset and maintenance of flow (Massimini et al., 1988). The FMQ consists of 12 items on 4-point Likert-like scales (from 1 = *do not agree* to 4 = *agree very much*). Factor analysis yielded a two-component solution, leading to the identification of two subscales: beliefs that flow fosters achievement (including items such as "My thinking becomes clearer when I am in flow") and confidence in the ability to self-regulate flow (sample item "I am able to sustain flow for long periods"). Initial results obtained from student and workers samples suggest a positive correlation between flow metacognitions levels and intensity of both state and dispositional flow, as well as the percentage of working time spent in flow.

The Swedish Flow Proneness Questionnaire (SFPQ)

The SFPQ (Ullén et al., 2012) was designed to evaluate flow as a trait, asking participants to report the average frequency of flow occurrence through seven items on a 5-point scale (from *never* to *every day or almost every day*). The items are formulated in three different versions, to explore flow frequency within three major daily domains: work, leisure, and maintenance activities. The item contents cover some, though not all, of the core components of flow: boredom (reverse scored), demand/skill balance, clear goals, clear feedback, deep concentration, complete control, and enjoyment. The SFPQ showed good internal consistency and reliability based on Cronbach's alpha and Spearman-Brown split-half coefficient, as well as correlations with personality traits, but not with intelligence (Ullén et al., 2012). A study conducted with twin pairs suggests moderate heritability for the three domain-related subscales (Mosing et al., 2012).

Flow in Context: Individual and Task-Related Facets

The WOrkreLated Flow Inventory (WOLF)

The scale was designed by Bakker (2005) to measure flow in the specific context of work. It was built to capture three global dimensions, deemed as core components of flow: absorption in the activity, enjoyment and positive emotions, and intrinsic motivation. The first dimension, absorption, includes 4 items representing focused attention, total immersion, forgetfulness of other environmental stimuli or thoughts, and feeling of being "transported" by the activity. The second dimension, work enjoyment, is identified through 4 emotion-related items, referring to positive feelings, enjoyment, happiness, and cheerfulness. The third dimension, intrinsic motivation, includes 5 items referring to the willingness to work during free time, regardless of the amount of salary, because of the enjoyment and reward derived from the activity per se, and based on the feeling of working for oneself. Participants are invited to report the frequency of the flow experience at work, by rating each item on a 7-point scale ranging from 0 (*never*) to 6 (*every day*). The WOLF shows good factorial validity, satisfactory internal consistencies, and good test-retest reliability within a time lag of 6 weeks (Bakker, 2008). Good content and construct validity were also detected in the Chinese version of the WOLF (Chen et al., 2016) and in the Italian one (I-WOLF; Zito et al., 2015). The I-WOLF was recently adapted for use with sports professionals (I-WOLFS, Zito et al., 2018), confirming the satisfactory psychometric properties of the instrument.

A modified version of the WOLF was also developed to evaluate flow daily through repeated samplings (Demerouti et al., 2012). Item formulation was revised to collect information on the work experience characterizing the current day. Only 3 items were selected for each dimension of flow. The item ratings were measured on a 5-point scale ranging from *not at all true* to *totally true*.

The Team Flow Monitor (TFM)

This is probably the most recent scale developed in the flow domain (van den Hout et al., 2018, 2019). It is grounded into a conceptualization of team flow as a shared flow experience arising in and among individuals performing interdependent tasks to achieve a collective outcome. The authors' core aim is to expand the understanding and assessment of collective flow, usually interpreted through constructs and measures that refer to individual experiences and behaviors. To this end, they conceptualize team flow as a phenomenon unfolding from the interactions among the team members and characterized by collective dimensions rather than simply reflecting the sum of individual contributions (Walker, 2010).

More specifically, the experience of team flow derives from a set of seven prerequisites: a collective ambition, common goals, the alignment of personal goals with shared ones, high integration of skills, open communication, safety, and mutual commitment. The joint presence of all these prerequisites allows for the onset of team flow experience, characterized by four features: a sense of unity, a sense of joint progress, mutual trust, and shared focus. Based on this conceptualization, the TFM comprises 14 items, grouped into two subscales: Team Flow Prerequisites (7 items) and Team Flow Characteristics (4 items). Factor analysis confirmed the distinct contribution of these two factors to the total Team Flow score.

The Flow State Scale for Occupational Tasks

The instrument was designed by Yoshida et al. (2013) to evaluate the occurrence of flow during occupational therapy tasks as a potential measure of rehabilitation effectiveness. The final version consists of 14 items on a 7-point rating scale. Factor analysis led to the identification of three factors corresponding to the subscales Sense of control of the task (6 items), Experience of positive emotion (4 items), and Experience of absorption by concentrating on a task (4 items). The instrument was tested on college students performing the computer game Tetris under three difficulty conditions: boredom, demand/skill balance, and overload. Discussions with occupational therapies highlighted that the computer game used for the validation study could be reasonably related to games, crafts, and other tasks typically proposed to patients during occupational therapy sessions. The scale was originally developed in Japanese, and no validation studies in other languages, including English, are currently available.

The Autotelic Personality Questionnaire (APQ)

This instrument (Tse et al., 2020) represents the first attempt to assess the autotelic personality based on Csikszentmihalyi's original multidimensional conceptualization (Csikszentmihalyi & Csikszentmihalyi, 1988; Nakamura & Csikszentmihalyi, 2009). After repeated testing and item reduction, the final questionnaire includes 26 items measured on 7-point rating scales. The items assess seven dimensions assumed to characterize autotelic individuals: persistence, low self-centeredness, intrinsic motivation, curiosity, and enjoyment and transformation of boredom (4 items each); attentional control, and enjoyment and transformation of challenges (3 items each). Significant and theoretically sound correlations were detected between APQ scores and four of the Big Five dimensions, except for agreeableness. Individuals showing higher APQ scores also reported higher flow proneness and satisfaction with life, as well as more flow during the performance of an experimental task.

Current Advancements: The Biological Correlates of Flow

Procedures

Neurological and Physiological Measurement Techniques

During the last decade, an increasing number of studies have been devoted to the identification of the brain areas associated with flow experiences. This is a daunting goal, as for flow to occur individuals have to engage in an activity sufficiently complex and demanding to attract their attention, favor their focused concentration, and mobilize specific cognitive and motor skills, globally increasing the level of arousal. Neurophysiological and neuroimaging techniques, however, set strict boundaries to the variety of tasks that can be used in experiments aimed at detecting the cerebral correlates of flow, especially concerning the need for avoiding body movements, or reducing them to the minimum. Studies in this area rely on electrophysiological tools such as EEG as well as imaging techniques such as magnetic resonance imaging (MRI) and near-infrared spectroscopy (NIRS).

MRI exploits the magnetic properties of body tissues and is based on the generation of magnetic fields that force the alignment of protons, which in its turn produces the release of energy, varying in amount across tissues (Essig et al., 2013). MRI also allows obtaining perfusion-related parameters through noninvasive endogenous contrast methods, which is especially interesting for flow researchers, considering that tissue perfusion represents an important physiological indicator of tissue activity. Near-infrared spectroscopy (NIRS) exploits a different feature of the tissues, namely, their relative transparency to light in the near-infrared range, providing information on optical absorption coefficients (Sakatani et al., 2006). In their functional versions (fMRI and fNIRS), these techniques allow researchers to evaluate the level of activity characterizing a specific brain region by measuring the associated changes in local blood volume. Activity-dependent changes in oxygenated hemoglobin concentration can be identified in real-time through both techniques, based on the principle of neurovascular coupling: Because of the relationship between neuronal activity and local blood flow, the activation of a specific brain region can be quantified in terms of the hemodynamic response in that region, defined as blood-oxygen-level-dependent (BOLD) response (Weiskopf et al., 2005).

Both fNIRS and fMRI are sensitive to similar physiological changes, and their results are highly correlated, especially in the domain of brain research. At the same time, the two techniques differ in some key features. Compared to fMRI, fNIRS is less vulnerable to head and body motion artifacts, leading to the development of wireless instrumentation that can be employed during tasks performed in daily contexts (Jones & Cooper, 2018; Leff et al., 2011). The measurement of cortical activity through fNIRS, however, is circumscribed in spatial resolution to 4 cm in depth, whereas fMRI can be used to measure activation throughout the brain, including subcortical areas.

Physiological markers of flow are – apparently – easier, and certainly less expensive to measure than brain correlates. Several studies on flow rely on the assessment of heart rate and respiratory depth, usually considered as indicators of autonomous nervous system (ANS) activation. A more sophisticated measure, heart rate variability (HRV), was more recently included (for a review, see Shaffer & Ginsberg, 2017). HRV represents the outcome of several processes, including the interplay between the sympathetic and parasympathetic branches of the ANS, regulatory control mechanisms via the vagus nerve (respiratory sinus arrhythmia, RSA), the baroreceptor reflex controlling blood pressure, and rhythmic changes in vascular tone. Electrocardiography-based spectral analysis allows identification of the different frequency bands characterizing HRV. The high-frequency band (HF) reflects central parasympathetic activity and variations related to the respiratory cycle; the low-frequency band (LF) may be produced by both branches of the ANS and by baroreceptors activity. The LF/HF ratio has been often used as an indicator of the relative prevalence of one of the ANS branches. More specifically, a low LF/HF ratio reflects parasympathetic dominance, whereas a high LF/HF ratio indicates sympathetic dominance, occurring in high arousal or stressful situations. This model, however, was currently challenged, and related findings are controversial (Shaffer et al., 2013).

Another useful marker of flow is cortisol, an indicator of the hypothalamic pituitary adrenal (HPA) axis activation characterizing high arousal and stress conditions. Because of its role in enhancing energy resources, cortisol facilitates sustained attention, a crucial component of flow. In related studies, cortisol is usually collected through repeated saliva sampling before, during, and after task performance.

Other physiological measures have been used in flow studies as indicators of ANS activation. They include transdermal vagus nerve stimulation (tVNS; Ventureyra, 2000), electrodermal activity (EDA; Critchley, 2002), and electromyography (EMG; Waterink & van Boxtel,1994).

Finally, a mobile eye tracker was recently used to investigate the quality of visual fixation of a target immediately preceding movement execution during netball and basketball shooting tasks (Harris et al., 2017). The study was aimed at verifying the relationship between flow and the phenomenon of the quiet eye (QE; Vickers, 1996), an optimal attentional condition of prolonged visual fixation that facilitates top-down control of movement, in its turn associated with high sports performance (Mann et al., 2007).

Subjective Flow Measures

Most studies aimed at investigating the biological correlates of flow also include a self-reported measure of optimal experience, usually administered after task completion. This kind of assessment is important from two different perspectives: It allows for verifying the consistency between individuals' perception of task challenges and the objective task difficulty based on experimental manipulation, and it allows for detecting convergences and divergences between self-reported dimensions of the experience and their neural correlates, not only concerning cognitive processes but also emotional and motivational/reward ones.

The instruments most frequently used in these studies are the Flow Kurz Skala (Rheinberg et al., 2003), the Flow Short Scale (Jackson et al., 2008), and the Swedish Flow Proneness Questionnaire (SFPQ; Ullén et al., 2012). The Flow Scale for Occupational Tasks was included in a single fNIRS study (Yoshida et al., 2014). In some studies, flow scales were further integrated with self-reported measures of specific psychological dimensions, such as concentration and attentional effort, and valence/arousal affect (Harmat et al., 2015).

Indirect or partial flow measures were used in other studies. For example, Keller et al. (2011) administered to participants a scale assessing involvement, as well as a single-item measure of perceived fit between task demands and personal skills. Measures of secondary-task reaction time, sustained attention, cognitive flexibility, and the intrinsic reward subscale of the Flow State Scale (Jackson & Marsh, 1996) were used by Huskey et al. (2018). Only one study did not include any subjective measure of flow, solely relying on the experimental manipulation of task difficulty to assume the onset of flow, boredom, or anxiety, and to interpret related neurophysiological patterns (Klasen et al., 2012).

Study Designs

Most studies were designed as experiments in which participants performed computer tasks across multiple sessions, varying in level of task difficulty to facilitate the onset of boredom (demands lower than personal skills), flow (demands balanced with a person's skills), and anxiety/overload (demands higher than personal skills).

The tasks used in studies based on ECG, fMRI, or fNIRS included mental solution of arithmetic tasks (Katahira et al., 2018; Ulrich et al., 2014, 2016a, 2016b) or computer games (Harmat et al., 2015; Huskey et al., 2018; Klasen et al., 2012; Yoshida et al., 2014). The assessment of physiological indicators of flow was performed through a wider range of experimental tasks, ranging from computer games (Colzato et al., 2018; Harmat et al., 2015; Keller et al., 2011; Peifer et al., 2014, 2015; Tian et al., 2017; Tozman et al., 2015) to real-life activities such as playing the piano (De Manzano et al., 2010), playing chess (Tozman et al., 2017), solving a mathematical problem, and writing a research report (Knierim et al., 2019).

Findings

Neurophysiological Correlates of Flow

Overall, data collected through EEG, fMRI, and fNIRS revealed specific patterns of brain activation during flow. Broadly speaking, flow-related activation occurred in areas included in the "multiple-demand (MD) system" (Duncan, 2010), a heterogeneous set of frontoparietal brain regions implicated in the processing of demanding cognitive tasks (Niendam et al., 2012; Woolgar et al., 2018). More specifically, cortical regions showing increased activation during flow were those involved in language, attention, and motor processes, such as the lateral prefrontal cortex, the sensorimotor network, and the pre-supplementary motor area (Jueptner et al., 1997). Regarding subcortical structures, findings highlighted the activation of basal ganglia, thalamus, and cerebellum.

The specific recurrence of basal ganglia activation in flow studies may be related to their involvement in the regulation of motor and premotor cortical areas, contributing to action selection and voluntary movement fluency. Because of their multiple connections with cortical areas, basal ganglia are also involved in cognition, emotion, and motivation/reward processes. The key structure for size and interconnections within this set of nuclei is the corpus striatum, which includes a dorsal area (caudate nucleus and putamen) and a ventral one (nucleus accumbens and olfactory tubercle, the former representing as a center of the reward network). The *substantia nigra* instead plays a key role in the production of dopamine, a neurotransmitter fostering positive affect and adaptive emotion regulation (Volkow et al., 2006).

Decreased activation during flow was instead recurrently detected in medial cortical regions, such as the medial prefrontal cortex, the posterior cingulate cortex, the inferior parietal region, and the medial temporal lobe, including the amygdala. These areas are constituents of the default mode network (DMN), activated during rest or highly automatic tasks and characterized by high levels of global connectivity, thus serving as a sort of brain hub (van den Heuvel & Sporns, 2011). The anterior, prefrontal areas are specifically activated during self-reflection tasks and deactivated during goal-directed tasks (Shulman, Fiez, Corbetta et al., 1997), such as those typically used in experiments to elicit flow states; the posterior areas are predominantly active during rest conditions. Major roles attributed to the DMN include the integration of spatial and internal body representations, and the facilitation of brain shifts across different networks, corresponding to different cognitive states, that promotes flexibility and quick adaptation to environmental changes (Gu, Satterthwaite, Medaglia et al., 2015; Davey & Harrison, 2018).

Some specific findings obtained through neuroimaging techniques during flow conditions were related to the typology of experimental task employed in the studies. For example, in the videogame used by Keller et al. (2011), the player was expected to fight against a rival group together with simulated comrades, in different scenarios such as a castle or a desert town. Findings showed a remarkable activation of the sensorimotor network during the condition of demands/skill balance, reflecting the simulation of physical activity elicited by the game (Mathiak & Weber, 2006). Experiments involving the solution of mental arithmetic tasks in conditions of low demands, demand/skill balance, and overload (Ulrich et al., 2014, 2016a, b) highlighted an inverted U-shaped activation pattern in regions corresponding to the DM, in particular the lateral prefrontal cortex, as well as in the basal ganglia. These areas were characterized by a significantly higher cerebral blood flow (rCBF) during optimal experience than during boredom and overload, suggesting a more efficient and smooth information processing. The opposite, U-shaped activation pattern was instead detected in the regions corresponding to the DMN, showing significant rCBF decreases in the demand/skill balance condition compared with the other two conditions, suggesting absorption in the ongoing task without the interference of self-conscious observation. In another study adopting the same experimental task, but using EEG for data collection (Katahira et al., 2018), increased theta activity was detected in the frontal area during flow and overload conditions compared to boredom, and moderate alpha activity in the frontal and central areas during flow, suggesting high levels of cognitive control and absorption matched with a moderate load on the working memory.

In an fNIRS-based study (Yoshida et al., 2014) administering a Tetris game task in conditions of demand/skill balance and low demand, a significant increase in oxygenated hemoglobin concentration was detected in the ventrolateral prefrontal cortex during the former, and a decrease during the latter condition; interestingly, significant increases in oxygenated hemoglobin concentrations in the same areas were observed after game performance, while participants were completing the subjective flow scale.

Finally, in an fMRI-based study using computer games as experimental tasks, Huskey et al. (2018) interpreted imaging results related to flow in terms of synchronization among neural networks, relying on the assumption that flow results in a synchronization process between cognitive control and reward networks, corresponding to an energetically-optimized brain state and an enjoyable experience. Using the degree of connectivity within and among brain networks as an outcome measure, the authors hypothesized to observe a higher synchronization between reward and cognitive control networks in the demand/skill balance condition, compared to the low demand and overload ones. In line with the other studies, an inverted U-shaped pattern was detected in the degree of network connectivity, with the balanced-difficulty condition being associated with the highest connectivity in the ventral frontoparietal control, memory, and sensory/motor networks, compared with the other two conditions. This finding suggests an effective integration of visual cues and action control during flow, with lower demands on the dorsal attention network; in addition, during the boredom condition, much more dense connections were observed within the DMN.

Contrary to expectations, and differently from previous studies (Klasen et al., 2012; de Manzano et al., 2013), no flow-related increase in the degree of connections between cognitive control and subcortical reward networks was observed in this study; however, the nucleus accumbens, that plays a key role in the reward network, was not part of the brain regions selected for analysis.

Physiological Correlates

Findings derived from physiological markers, in association with the assessment of flow state scales, were consistent with theoretical expectations and neuroimaging evidence. Participants involved in a mathematical task (Ulrich et al., 2016a) showed an inverted U pattern in the electrodermal activity (EDA), with the highest values observed in the flow condition, suggesting an up-modulation of sympathetic arousal. In the same vein, compared to performances in which they perceived low flow, professional pianists who perceived high flow during a music performance (de Manzano et al., 2010) showed higher heart rate and blood pressure (indicating arousal and increase in sympathetic ASN activity) as well as higher respiratory depth and smiling muscle activity (suggesting relaxation and increase in parasympathetic activity). Similar inverted U-shaped findings were observed during a computer game administered in three different conditions (Tian et al., 2017): Compared with the easy condition, the skill/demand balance condition was associated with higher respiratory and heart rate, deeper breath, lower HRV, and higher skin conductance; significant and opposite differences in all these indicators were observed between the balance condition and the high difficulty one. These findings support the view of flow as a state of moderate mental effort associated with increased parasympathetic modulation of sympathetic activity. Such a simultaneous activity increase in both branches of the ANS is physiologically linked to improved control and fine-tuning of behavioral responses (Berntson et al., 1997); at the experiential level, it can be related to the feeling of effortless attention characterizing flow (Ullén et al., 2010).

Regarding variations in cortisol levels observed in the flow condition, compared to boredom and overload, findings were partially consistent across studies. An inverted U-shaped relation was detected between flow and cortisol levels in two studies, inducing the increase of participants' physiological arousal through a stress test (Peifer et al., 2014) or the oral administration of exogenous cortisol (Peifer et al., 2015) before engagement in a complex computer task. In both studies, individuals with moderate cortisol response reported the highest flow levels compared to participants showing high or low cortisol response. Instead, expert chess players (Tozman et al., 2017) showed lower cortisol levels in both the balance and low-difficulty conditions compared to the overload one, while Keller et al. (2011) found no differences in the cortisol levels associated with conditions of skill/demand balance and high difficulty, both being higher that those detected in the easy one.

More controversial findings were obtained through the assessment of HRV in relation to different conditions of balance or imbalance between task demands and personal skills. Significant decreases in HRV, indicating sympathetic activation, were detected in conditions of flow and overload, compared to the low difficulty condition, using different computer tasks (Keller et al., 2011; Tozman et al., 2015). In the balanced skill-demand task, however, Tozman et al. found that flow was associated with a decreased LF-HRV activity compared to overload. An inverted U-shape pattern was instead observed in another study (Peifer et al., 2014) for LF-HRV (indicating a trend toward sympathetic predominance), with moderate levels being associated with higher flow ratings compared to the other two conditions; in the same study, higher flow values corresponded to higher HF-HRV levels, supporting a positive relationship between parasympathetic activation and flow. A significant increase in respiratory depth, matched with low levels of LF-HRV (both indicating parasympathetic activation), was detected in the flow condition during Tetris game performance (Harmat et al., 2015). During a math task (Knierim et al., 2019), no significant change in HF-HRV was instead observed from boredom to overload conditions, despite a decreased trend, with intermediate levels related to flow. Interestingly, the same study included an additional experimental task, consisting of writing a research project report (participants were students who were asked to develop a project from their own thesis), during which data were collected at three different timepoints. This task, closer to real-life than the math one, was associated with significantly lower HF-HRV levels, indicating stronger parasympathetic withdrawal than in the three math conditions. Finally, Colzato et al. (2018) examined the impact of the active transdermal stimulation of the vagus nerve (which is crucially involved in HRV) on perceived flow during an attention task: tVNS caused a decrease in self-reported flow levels compared to sham sessions. This finding was explained through the network reset theory (Bouret & Sara, 2005): tVNS produces a temporary increase in noradrenergic pathways involving the locus caeruleus, fostering attention divergence toward potential environmental changes (Steenbergen et al., 2015) and the simultaneous interruption of attention focus on a previously selected target.

Finally, data recorded through an eye tracker during netball and basketball shooting tasks (Harris et al., 2017) did not show significant variations in duration of quiet eye periods (indicating an optimal control of visual attention) across demand/skill conditions. Nevertheless, higher quiet eye duration was associated with self-reported flow, and mediation analyses revealed its indirect effect on performance through flow experience. This finding is consistent with a specific feature of flow, namely, prolonged concentration and attention focus (Jackson & Csikszentmihalyi 1999).

Several biological markers were also related to flow proneness, measured through SFPQ: the availability of dopamine D2-receptors in the dorsal striatum, which is functionally related to selective attention (De Manzano et al., 2013; O'Doherty et al., 2004); a significant increase in gray matter volume in the same region (Niksirat et al., 2019) and a D2 receptor coding gene (Gyurkovics et al., 2016). These studies suggest that higher levels of dopamine may be related to flow through reduced impulsivity and effective response inhibition.

Flow Experience

Overall, across studies, a strong consistency was detected between objective task difficulty and perceived challenge. Generally, inverted-U patterns were observed in the total score of flow scales, with the highest values corresponding to demands/skill balance, compared with boredom and overload conditions. Together with other measures, these findings are consistent with the view of flow as a moderate arousal condition of high and effortless concentration on the task at hand. For example, Keller et al. (2011) showed that involvement was highest in flow compared with the other two conditions, while mood did not vary across conditions. In the study by Harmat et al. (2015), flow and affect valence were significantly higher and attentional effort was significantly lower in the balance condition compared with boredom and overload. At the same time, arousal increased significantly with difficulty level, and concentration levels did not differ in the balance and overload conditions.

The study based on research report writing and math task (Knierim et al., 2019) included repeated samplings of KFS as well as the assessment of task demands, stress, and arousal/valence affect. Significant differences in flow scores emerged between the balance and the overload conditions during the math task. Overall, the flow levels reported across writing samplings did not differ from those reported during math tasks in the balance condition. At the same time, stress and arousal levels were significantly lower during writing sessions than in the balance and overload conditions during math tasks.

Specific patterns of variation emerged within flow measures including multiple dimensions. This was particularly evident for the widely-used FKS, which consists of two subscales: absorption and fluency. In most studies including FKS, only the absorption scale scores were consistent with expectations and aligned with the physiological findings; on the contrary, the fluency dimension did not show remarkable variations across demand conditions, and it could not be considered a reliable indicator of flow (Peifer et al., 2014, 2015). Moreover, the flow scores detected in some studies (e.g., Harris et al., 2017, who administered FKS), were only in a mid-range, indicating a relatively low engagement of participants in the task at hand.

Choosing a Flow Measure in Basic and Applied Research: Some Suggestions

Basic Research

Despite a long history, our understanding of flow as a construct requires additional research. Only in the context of computer games have its basic components been systematically studied through the joint use of psychological, biological, and neurophysiological measures. This is the greatest limitation of basic flow research: Laboratory tasks cannot be equated to real-life experiences. Moreover, the laboratory studies rely on models of flow in which objective task difficulties, rather than subjectively perceived challenges, are used as indicators of flow, boredom, or anxiety. This poses a substantial caveat: Demands appraised as challenging can lead to flow experience; but, because of low motivation, they may be perceived as difficult, albeit meaningless. Although most studies in this domain also include the participants' evaluation of the associated experience, this is measured through short scales, such as the Flow Kurz Skala, which are, of course, short and time-sparing but too rough compared to the sophistication of the physiological data. Except for the FKS, which allows for distinguishing the two dimensions of absorption and fluency and for comparing perceived challenges and demands, these scales usually provide a single global flow score (measured as intensity or frequency, depending on the measure). This makes it impossible to understand which facets of flow are predominant or whether challenge perception is consistent with task demand level. Finally, computer games may not be sufficiently varied and unpredictable to allow for differentially characterizing the experience across difficult conditions. For this reason, findings often point to similarities between flow and anxiety, compared to boredom, in terms of arousal (measured in the FKS as absorption), while no variation across conditions is often detected for the dimension of fluency.

In addition, information on flow through neuroimaging substantially derives from experiments relying on computer games or mental mathematical operations. Unsurprisingly, these tasks specifically activate prefrontal areas associated with the recruitment of attentional resources and cognitive networks, to the detriment of DMN areas. Regarding reward networks, the controversial findings point to the lack of meaningful motivations to perform the task. For these reasons, this line of research must be substantially implemented, and related findings must be carefully contextualized within the task features.

Physiological biomarkers can be used more flexibly in flow research, as their assessment is compatible with a variety of tasks. While some findings are substantially consistent across studies (e.g., cortisol level fluctuations), others – such as the assessment of HRV – need further investigation and a more diversified range of conditions.

At the psychological level, flow antecedents, core features, and outcomes could be better contextualized. We still know very little about the phenomenology of flow across daily domains. As Moneta (2012) highlighted, flow experience is highly dependent on the performed activity, which represents a potential source of bias. Systematic studies are few, and to appropriately delve into this topic, comparative research across cultures, age stages, and activity domains is still needed. For example, how is flow experienced in different work or leisure activities, based on the differential involvement of body and mind functions, presence or absence of competitiveness, other people's involvement in the task, and activity relevance for the person's life theme and psychological selection? Short scales are not the best solutions to delve into these issues, while long ones, such as the Flow State Scale-2, allow the comparative identification of the specific contribution of different experiential variables.

ESM studies relying on the classical sampling form – or including FSS-2 in repeated assessment – may contribute to clarifying these issues at the within-person level as well as across samples. Although the collection of neural and physiological biomarkers is quite challenging in real life, the development of NIRS techniques may be more fruitfully used than MRI, which imposes substantial constraints to task selection.

Overall, we think that, to better understand flow in its basic features, within real-life and across activity conditions, the use of short scales is insufficient. As a gold standard, we suggest the use of repeated samplings such as ESM as well as long scales. In association with neural and biological markers, in the context of experimental tasks, we recommend FKS in its full version, including the three additional items, though additional information should be collected among participants concerning their motivation in performing the task. In real-life settings, information concerning perceived intrinsic and extrinsic rewards in the ongoing task can be directly collected through ESM open-ended questions; in other cases, researchers could use already available instruments such as the Flow Questionnaire and the Life Theme Questionnaire (possibly by selecting specific sections). Finally, personality facets could contribute to the understanding of findings. While the contents of measures such as DFS-2 or SFPQ overlap with flow scales, the newly published measure to assess autotelic personality (APQ) may be fruitfully employed to elucidate the relationship between this trait and flow features and frequency.

Flow Across Cultures, Life Domains, and Bio-Psycho-Social Conditions

Only a few studies have investigated flow in real time during daily life among participants from non-Western cultures (Csikszentmihalyi & Asakawa, 2016; Moneta, 2004), children (Mesurado & Richaud de Minzi, 2013), elderly participants (Bassi et al., 2018; Collins et al., 2008), and people experiencing adversity related to suboptimal health or social conditions (Cortinovis et al., 2011; Delle Fave & Bassi, 2009; Delle Fave & Massimini, 2005b; Sartori et al., 2014). ESM represents the gold standard, when applicable, as it also provides information on daily life activities and experience fluctuations. In addition, its structure can be adapted and simplified according to participants' clinical conditions (Bassi et al., 2012; Sartori et al., 2019). Less time-consuming instruments can be used in less favorable contexts. Qualitative tools such as the Flow Questionnaire can be usefully employed with participants unacquainted with filling out scales (a recurrent situation among people with lower education levels living in rural areas). Moreover, culture-specific aspects, such as those briefly outlined in the previous sections and usually overlooked, may emerge. Regarding quantitative evaluations, for studies involving populations not previously investigated, we strongly suggest the use of long scales such as the FSS-2.

To date, the only two domains for which specific flow measures were developed are work and sport. The WoLF is widely used for studying flow at work, together with ESM that provided interesting information on the dynamics of flow onset (Ceja & Navarro, 2011). Modified ESM forms can be also designed to investigate specific dimensions of work experience (Peifer & Zipp, 2019). The recent attention to teamwork led researchers to study flow through ad-hoc items, combined with measures of collective efficacy beliefs (Salanova et al., 2014). A more specific tool to investigate team flow is TFM. While promising, this instrument assesses team features rather than individual flow. We, therefore, recommend its use in combination with ESM, the WoLF, or the FKS, depending on the constraints and research goals.

Regarding sports, the FSS-2 and the DFS-2 were purposefully developed to investigate flow in this domain, even though they later proved to be useful in a variety of other settings. Recently, researchers have started to focus on other dimensions of sports experience, investigating them through qualitative interviews, which is shedding interesting light on other aspects of sports performance that can be variously related to or distinguished from flow (Jackman et al., 2016; Swann et al., 2017).

Conclusions

After many decades of flow studies, this fascinating optimal experience has become even more intriguing and worth studying. While it apparently represents a unitary construct, studies contextualizing it in activity domains, social, and cultural contexts have shed light on its multifaceted nature. These aspects deserve careful attention in the future.

The recent explosion of interest in studying flow through neuroimaging techniques has produced interesting evidence, and its potential is relevant. However, absorption or immersion differ under experimental and everyday conditions. Moreover, the mental operations associated with experimental tasks are limited, compared to those associated with daily behaviors in a highly varying environment. This represents a crucial issue for future investigations, both at the psychological and neurophysiological levels.

To conclude, at this stage of flow research we think that psychologists should more seriously consider the unexplored sides of flow, made even more invisible today through the pervasive use of short scales. These are very fruitful for studies including flow as a side variable, but not as a core target. The appropriate characterization of flow across life domains, typologies of activities within a single domain, developmental stages, cultures, and health conditions will benefit from a renewed interest in a more systematic evaluation of this phenomenon through more detailed instruments, including qualitative interviews where necessary. In addition, the dialogue between psychologists and neuroscientists could lead to the development of new paradigms in the different domains of the application of flow. A still long and exciting way to go.

References

Asakawa, K. (2010). Flow experience, culture, and well-being: How do autotelic Japanese college students feel, behave, and think in their daily lives? *Journal of Happiness Studies, 11,* 205–223. https://doi.org/10.1007/s10902-008-9132-3

Bakker, A. B. (2005). Flow among music teachers and their students: The cross-over of peak experiences. *Journal of Vocational Behavior, 66,* 26–44. https://doi.org/10.1016/j.jvb.2003.11.001

Bakker, A. B. (2008). The work-related flow inventory: Construction and initial validation of the WOLF. *Journal of Vocational Behavior, 72,* 400–414. https://doi.org/10.1016/j.jvb.2007.11.007

Bassi, M., Coppa, R., & Delle Fave, A. (2008). Studiare medicina per condividere benessere: una ricerca transculturale in Ciad e in Italia [Studying medicine to share well-being: A cross-cultural research in Chad and Italy]. *Psicologia della Salute, 1,* 93–107.

Bassi, M., & Delle Fave, A. (2012). Optimal experience and self-determination at school: Joining perspectives. *Motivation and Emotion, 36,* 425–438. https://doi.org/10.1007/s11031-011-9268-z

Bassi, M., Ferrario, N., Ba, G., Delle Fave, A., & Viganò, C. (2012). Quality of experience during psychosocial rehabilitation: A real-time investigation with experience sampling method. *Psychiatric Rehabilitation Journal, 35,* 447–453. https://doi.org/10.1037/h0094578

Bassi, M., Rassiga, C., Fumagalli, N., & Senes, G. (2018). Quality of experience during horticultural activities: An experience sampling pilot study among older adults living in a nursing home. *Geriatric Nursing, 39*(4), 457–464. https://doi.org/10.1016/j.gerinurse.2018.01.002

Bassi, M., Steca, P., Monzani, D., Greco, A., & Delle Fave, A. (2014). Personality and optimal experience in adolescence: Implications for well-being and development. *Journal of Happiness Studies, 15,* 829–843. https://doi.org/10.1007/s10902-013-9451-x

Baumann, N., & Scheffer, D. (2011). Seeking flow in the achievement domain: The achievement flow motive behind flow experience. *Motivation and Emotion, 35,* 267–284. https://doi.org/10.1007/s11031-010-9195-4

Berntson, G. G., Bigger, J. T. Jr., Eckberg, D. L., Grossman, P., Kaufmann, P. G., Malik, M.,Nagaraja, H. N., Porges, S. W., Saul, J. P., Stone, P. H., & vand er Molen, M. W. (1997). Heart rate variability: Origins, methods, and interpretive caveats. *Psychophysiology, 34*(6), 623–648. https://doi.org/10.1111/j.1469-8986.1997.tb02140.x

Bouret, S., & Sara, S. J. (2005). Network reset: a simplified overarching theory of locus coeruleus noradrenaline function. *Trends in Neuroscience, 28,* 574–582. https://doi.org/10.1016/j.tins.2005.09.002

Calvo, C. T., Catuera, R. J., Ruano, F. J., Vaillo, R. R., & Gimeno, E. C. (2008). Psychometric properties of the Spanish versions of the flow state scale. *The Spanish Journal of Psychology, 11,* 660–669. https://doi.org/10.1017/S1138741600004662

Ceja, L., & Navarro, J. (2009). Dynamics of flow: A nonlinear perspective. *Journal of Happiness Studies, 10,* 665–684. https://doi.org/10.1007/s10902-008-9113-6

Ceja, L., & Navarro, J. (2011). Dynamic patterns of flow in the workplace: Characterizing within-individual variability using a complexity science approach. *Journal of Organizational Behavior, 32,* 627–651. https://doi.org/10.1002/job.747

Chen, Y., Yu, X., & Huang, B. (2016). The Chinese version of Work-reLated Flow Inventory (WOLF): An examination of reliability and validity. In Y. C. Chang, M. K. Ng., & D. S. Ma (Eds.), *Proceedings of the 2016 International Conference on Humanities and Social Science* (pp. 554–558). Atlantis Press. https://doi.org/10.2991/hss-26.2016.94

Clarke, S. G., & Haworth, J. (1994). "Flow" experience in the daily lives of sixth-form college students. *British Journal of Psychology, 85,* 511–523. https://doi.org/10.1111/j.2044-8295.1994.tb02538.x

Collins, A. M., Sarkisian, N., & Winner, E. (2008). Flow and happiness in later life: An investigation into the role of daily and weekly flow experiences. *Journal of Happiness Studies, 10*, 703–719. https://doi.org/10.1007/s10902-008-9116-3

Colzato, L., Wolters, G., & Peifer, C. (2018). Transcutaneous vagus nerve stimulation (tVNS) modulates flow experience. *Experimental Brain Research, 236*, 253–257. https://doi.org/10.1007/s00221-017-5123-0

Conner, T. S., Tennen, H., Fleeson, W., & Feldman Barrett, L. (2009). Experience sampling methods: A modern idiographic approach to personality research. *Social and Personality Psychology Compass, 3*, 1–22. https://doi.org/10.1111/j.1751-9004.2009.00170.x

Cortinovis, I., Intini, E., Luraschi, S., Sessa, M., & Delle Fave, A. (2011). The daily experience of people with achondroplasia. *Applied Psychology: Health and Well-being, 3*, 217–227. https://doi.org/10.1111/j.1758-0854.2010.01046.x

Critchley, H. D. (2002). Electrodermal responses: What happens in the brain. *Neuroscientist, 8*, 132–142. https://doi.org/10.1177/107385840200800209

Csikszentmihalyi, M. (1975). *Beyond boredom and anxiety*. Jossey Bass.

Csikszentmihalyi, M. (1996). *Creativity: Flow and the psychology of discovery and invention*. HarperPerennial.

Csikszentmihalyi, M. (1997). *Finding flow. The psychology of engagement with everyday life*. Basic Books.

Csikszentmihalyi, M., & Asakawa, K. (2016). Universal and cultural dimensions of optimal experiences. *Japanese Psychological Research, 58*, 4–13. https://doi.org/10.1111/jpr.12104

Csikszentmihalyi, M., & Beattie, O. (1979). Life themes: A theoretical and empirical exploration of their origins and effects. *Journal of Humanistic Psychology, 19*, 45–63. https://doi.org/10.1177/002216787901900105

Csikszentmihalyi, M., & Csikszentmihalyi, I. (Eds.). (1988). *Optimal experience: Psychological studies of flow in consciousness*. Cambridge University Press. https://doi.org/10.1017/CBO9780511621956

Csikszentmihalyi, M., & Larson, R. W. (1987). Validity and reliability of the experience sampling method. *Journal of Nervous and Mental Disease, 175*, 526–536. https://doi.org/10.1097/00005053-198709000-00004

Csikszentmihalyi, M., Larson, R. W., & Prescott, S. (1977). The ecology of adolescent activity and experience. *Journal of Youth and Adolescence, 6*, 281–294. https://doi.org/10.1007/BF02138940

Csikszentmihalyi, M., & LeFevre, J. (1989). Optimal experience in work and leisure. *Journal of Personality and Social Psychology, 56*, 815–822. https://doi.org/10.1037/0022-3514.56.5.815

Csikszentmihalyi, M., & Massimini, F. (1985). On the psychological selection of bio-cultural information. *New Ideas in Psychology, 3*, 115–138. https://doi.org/10.1016/0732-118X(85)90002-9

Csikszentmihalyi, M., & Schneider, B. (2000). *Becoming adult: How teenagers prepare for the world of work*. Basic Books.

Davey, C. G., & Harrison, B. J. (2018). The brain's center of gravity: How the default mode network helps us to understand the self. *World Psychiatry, 17*, 278–279. https://doi.org/10.1002/wps.20553

Delle Fave, A., & Bassi, M. (2000). The quality of experience in adolescents' daily lives: developmental perspectives. *Genetic, Social and General Psychology Monographs, 126*, 347–367.

Delle Fave, A., & Bassi, M. (2009). Sharing optimal experiences and promoting good community life in a multicultural society. *Journal of Positive Psychology, 4*, 280–289. https://doi.org/10.1080/17439760902933716

Delle Fave, A., Bassi, M., & Massimini, F. (2003a). Coping with boundaries: The quality of daily experience of Rom Nomads in Europe. *Psychology and Developing Societies, 15*, 87–102. https://doi.org/10.1177/097133360301500106

Delle Fave, A., Bassi, M., & Massimini, F. (2003b). Quality of experience and risk perception in high-altitude rock climbing. *Journal of Applied Sport Psychology, 15*, 82–99. https://doi.org/10.1080/10413200305402

Delle Fave, A., & Massimini, F. (1988). Modernization and the changing contexts of flow in work and leisure. In M. Csikszentmihalyi & I. Csikszentmihalyi (Eds.), *Optimal experience: Psychological studies of flow in consciousness* (pp. 193–213). Cambridge University Press.

Delle Fave, A., & Massimini, F. (1991). Modernization and the quality of daily experience in a Southern Italy village. In N. Bleichrodt & P. J. D. Drenth (Eds.), *Contemporary issues in cross cultural psychology* (pp. 110–119). Swets & Zeitlinger.

Delle Fave, A., & Massimini, F. (1992). Experience sampling method and the measuring of clinical change: A case of anxiety syndrome. In M. W. deVries (Ed.), *The experience of psychopathology: Investigating mental disorders in their natural settings* (pp. 280–298). Cambridge University Press. https://doi.org/10.1017/CBO9780511663246.025

Delle Fave, A., & Massimini, F. (2000). Living at home or in institution: Adolescents' optimal experience and life theme. Paideia. *Cadernos de Psicologia e Educaçao, 19*, 55–66.

Delle Fave, A., & Massimini, F. (2003). Optimal experience in work and leisure among teachers and physicians: Individual and bio-cultural implications. *Leisure Studies, 22*, 323–342. https://doi.org/10.1080/02614360310001594122

Delle Fave, A., & Massimini, F. (2004a). Bringing subjectivity into focus: Optimal experiences, life themes and person-centred rehabilitation. In P. A. Linley & S. Joseph (Eds.), *Positive psychology in practice* (pp. 581–597). Wiley. https://doi.org/10.1002/9780470939338.ch35

Delle Fave, A., & Massimini, F. (2004b). The cross-cultural investigation of optimal experience. *Ricerche di Psicologia, 27*, 79–102.

Delle Fave, A., & Massimini, F. (2004c). Parenthood and the quality of experience in daily life: a longitudinal study. *Social Indicators Research, 67*, 75–106. https://doi.org/10.1023/B:SOCI.0000007335.26602.59

Delle Fave, A., & Massimini, F. (2005a). The relevance of subjective well-being to social policies: Optimal experience and tailored intervention. In F. Huppert, N. Baylis, & B. Keverne (Eds.), *The science of well-being* (pp. 379–404). Oxford University Press. https://doi.org/10.1093/acprof:oso/9780198567523.003.0015

Delle Fave, A., & Massimini, F. (2005b). The investigation of optimal experience and apathy: Developmental and psychosocial implications. *European Psychologist, 10*, 264–274. https://doi.org/10.1027/1016-9040.10.4.264

Delle Fave, A., Massimini, F., & Bassi, M. (2011). *Psychological selection and optimal experience across cultures*. Springer Science.

De Manzano, Ö., Cervenka, S., Jucaite, A., Hellenäs, O., Farde, L., & Ullén, F. (2013). Individual differences in the proneness to have flow experiences are linked to dopamine D2 receptor availability in the dorsal striatum. *Neuroimage, 67*, 1–6. https://doi.org/10.1016/j.neuroimage.2012.10.072

De Manzano, Ö., Theorell, T., Harmat, L., & Ullén, F. (2010). The psychophysiology of flow during piano playing. *Emotion, 10*, 301–311. https://doi.org/10.1037/a0018432

Demerouti, E. (2006). Job characteristics, flow, and performance: The moderating role of conscientiousness. *Journal of Occupational Health Psychology, 11*, 266–280. https://doi.org/10.1037/1076-8998.11.3.266

Demerouti, E., Bakker, A. B., Sonnentag, S., & Fullagar, C. J. (2012). Work-related flow and energy at work and at home: A study on the role of daily recovery. *Journal of Organizational Behavior, 33*(2), 276–295. https://doi.org/10.1002/job.760

deVries, M. W. (Ed.). (1992). *The experience of psychopathology: Investigating mental disorders in their natural settings*. Cambridge University Press.

Duncan, J. (2010). The multiple-demand (MD) system of the primate brain: Mental programs for intelligent behaviour. *Trends in Cognitive Sciences, 14*, 172–179. https://doi.org/10.1016/j.tics.2010.01.004

Engeser, S. (Ed.). (2012). *Advances in flow research*. Springer. https://doi.org/10.1007/978-1-4614-2359-1

Engeser, S., & Baumann, N. (2015). Fluctuation of flow and affect in everyday life: A second look at the paradox of work. *Journal of Happiness Studies, 17*(1), 105–124. https://doi.org/10.1007/s10902-014-9586-4

Engeser, S., & Rheinberg, F. (2008). Flow, performance and moderators of challenge-skill balance. *Motivation and Emotion, 32*, 158–172. https://doi.org/10.1007/s11031-008-9102-4

Essig, M., Shiroishi, M. S., Nguyen, T. B., Saake, M. Provenzale, J. M., Enterline, D. Anzalone, N., Dörfler, A., Rovira, A., Wintermark, M., & Law, M. (2013). Perfusion MRI: The five most frequently asked technical questions. *American Journal of Roentgenology, 200,* 24–34. https://doi.org/10.2214/AJR.12.9543

Fournier, J., Gaudreau, P., Demontrond-Behr, P., Visioli, J., Forest, J., & Jackson, S. (2007). French translation of the Flow State Scale-2: Factor structure, crosscultural invariance, and associations with goal attainment. *Psychology of Sport and Exercise, 8,* 897–916. https://doi.org/10.1016/j.psychsport.2006.07.007

Freire, T. (2006). Experiências óptimas e lazer: Sobre a qualidade da experiência subjectiva na vida diária [Optimal experiences and leisure: About the quality of subjective experience in daily life]. *Psicologia: Teoria, Investigação e Prática, 11,* 243–258.

Fullagar, C., & Delle Fave, A. (2017). *Flow at work: Measurement and implications.* Taylor & Francis. https://doi.org/10.4324/9781315871585

Fullagar, C. J., & Kelloway, E. K. (2009). "Flow" at work: An experience sampling approach. *Journal of Occupational Health Psychology, 82,* 595–615. https://doi.org/10.1348/096317908X357903

González-Cutre, D., Sicilia, A., Moreno, J. A., & Fernández-Balboa, J. M. (2009). Dispositional flow in physical education: Relationships with motivational climate, social goals, and perceived competence. *Journal of Teaching in Physical Education, 28,* 422–440. https://doi.org/10.1123/jtpe.28.4.422

Gouveia, M. J., Pais-Ribeiro, J. L., Marques, M., & Carvalho, C. (2012). Measuring dispositional flow in exercise. Validity and reliability of a Portuguese version of the Dispositional Flow Scale-2 (DFS-2). *Revista de Psicologìa del Deporte, 21,* 81–88.

Gu, S., Satterthwaite, T. D., Medaglia, J. D., Yang, M., Gur, R. E., Gur, R. C., & Bassett, D. S. (2015). Emergence of system roles in normative neurodevelopment. *PNAS, 112,* 13681–13686. https://doi.org/10.1073/pnas.1502829112

Guo, Y. M., & Poole, M. S. (2009). Antecedents of flow in online shopping: A test of alternative models. *Information Systems Journal, 19,* 369–390. https://doi.org/10.1111/j.1365-2575.2007.00292.x

Gyurkovics, M., Kotyuk, E., Katonai, E. R., Horvath, E. Z., Vereczkei, A., & Szekely, A. (2016). Individual differences in flow proneness are linked to a dopamine D2 receptor gene variant. *Consciousness and Cognition, 42,* 1–8. https://doi.org/10.1016/j.concog.2016.02.014

Harari, Y. N. (2008). Combat flow: Military, political, and ethical dimensions of subjective well-being in war. *Review of General Psychology, 12*(3), 253–264. https://doi.org/10.1037/1089-2680.12.3.253

Harmat, L., de Manzano, Ö., Theorell, T., Högman, L., Fischer, H., & Ullén, F. (2015). Physiological correlates of the flow experience during computer game playing. *International Journal of Psychophysiology, 97,* 1–7. https://doi.org/10.1016/j.ijpsycho.2015.05.001

Harmat, L., Ørsted Andersen, F., Ullén, F., Wright, J., & Sadlo, G. (Eds.). (2016). *Flow experience: Empirical research and applications.* Springer. https://doi.org/10.1007/978-3-319-28634-1

Harris, D. J., Vine, S. J., & Wilson, M. R. (2017). Flow and quiet eye: The role of attentional control in flow experience. *Cognitive Processes, 18,* 343–347. https://doi.org/10.1007/s10339-017-0794-9

Haworth, J., & Evans, S. T. (1995). Challenge, skill and positive subjective states in the daily life of a sample of YTS students. *Journal of Occupational and Organizational Psychology, 68*(2), 109–121. https://doi.org/10.1111/j.2044-8325.1995.tb00576.x

Hektner, J. (2001). Family, school, and community predictors of adolescent growth-conducive experiences: Global and specific approaches. *Applied Developmental Science, 5,* 172–183. https://doi.org/10.1207/S1532480XADS0503_5

Hektner, J. M., Schmidt, J., & Csikszentmihalyi, M. (2007). *Experience sampling method: Measuring the quality of everyday life.* Sage.

Hox, J. J. (2002). *Multilevel Analysis: Techniques and applications* (2nd ed.). Routledge, Taylor & Francis.

Huskey, R., Craighead, B., Miller, M. B., & Weber, R. (2018). Does intrinsic reward motivate cognitive control? A naturalistic-fMRI study based on the synchronization theory of flow. *Cognitive, Affective, & Behavioral Neuroscience, 18*(5), 902–924. https://doi.org/10.3758/s13415-018-0612-6

Inkinen, M., Lonka, K., Hakkarainen, K., Muukkonen, H., Litmanen, T., & Salmela-Aro, K. (2014). The interface between core affects and the challenge-skill relationship. *Journal of Happiness Studies, 15,* 891–913. https://doi.org/10.1007/s10902-013-9455-6

Jackman, P.C., Crust, L., & Swann, C. (2016). Systematically comparing methods used to study flow in sport: A longitudinal multiple-case study. *Psychology of Sport and Exercise, 32*, 113–123. https://doi.org/10.1016/j.psychsport.2017.06.009

Jackson, S.A. (1996). Toward a conceptual understanding of the flow experience in élite athletes. *Research Quarterly for Exercise and Sport, 67*, 76–90. https://doi.org/10.1080/02701367.1996.10607928

Jackson, S.A., & Csikszentmihalyi, M. (1999). *Flow in sports: The keys to optimal experience and performances*. Human Kinetics.

Jackson, S.A., & Eklund, R.C. (2002). Assessing flow in physical activity: The flow State Scale-2 and Dispositional Flow Scale-2. *Journal of Sport & Exercise Psychology, 24*, 133–150. https://doi.org/10.1123/jsep.24.2.133

Jackson, S.A., Eklund, R.C., & Martin, A. (2010). *The Flow Scales Manual*. Mind Garden Inc.

Jackson, S.A., Ford, S.K., Kimiecik, J.C., & Marsh, H.W. (1998). Psychological correlates of flow in sport. *Journal of Sport and Exercise Psychology, 20*, 358–378. https://doi.org/10.1123/jsep.20.4.358.

Jackson, S.A., & Marsh, H.W. (1996). Development and validation of a scale to measure optimal experience: The flow state scale. *Journal of Sport & Exercise Psychology, 18*, 17–35. https://doi.org/10.1123/jsep.18.1.17

Jackson, S.A., Martin, A.J., & Eklund, R.C. (2008). Long and short measures of flow: The construct validity of the FSS-2, DFS-2, and new brief counterparts. *Journal of Sport & Exercise Psychology, 30*, 561–587. https://doi.org/10.1123/jsep.30.5.561

Jones, B., & Cooper, C.E. (2018). Near infrared spectroscopy (NIRS) observation of vastus lateralis (muscle) and prefrontal cortex (brain) tissue oxygenation during synchronised swimming routines in élite athletes. In O. Thews, J. LaManna & D. Harrison (Eds.), *Oxygen transport to tissue XL* (Advances in Experimental Medicine and Biology, Vol. 1072, pp. 111–117). Springer. https://doi.org/10.1007/978-3-319-91287-5_18

Jueptner, M., Stephan, K.M., Frith, C.D., Brooks, D.J., Frackowiak, R.S., & Passingham, R.E. (1997). Anatomy of motor learning: I. Frontal cortex and attention to action. *Journal of Neurophysiology, 77*, 1313–1324. https://doi.org/10.1152/jn.1997.77.3.1313

Katahira, K., Yamazaki, Y., Yamaoka, C., Ozaki, H., Nakagawa, S., & Nagata, N. (2018). EEG correlates of the flow state: A combination of increased frontal theta and moderate frontocentral alpha rhythm in the mental arithmetic task. *Frontiers in Psychology, 9*, Article 300. https://doi.org/10.3389/fpsyg.2018.00300

Kawabata, M., Mallett, C.J., & Jackson, S.A. (2008). The Flow State Scale-2 and Dispositional Flow State Scale-2: Examination of factorial validity and reliability for Japanese adults. *Psychology of Sport and Exercise, 9*, 465–485. https://doi.org/10.1016/j.psychsport.2007.05.005

Kawabata, M., & Mallett, C.J. (2011). Flow experience in physical activity: Examination of the internal structure of flow from a process-related perspective. *Motivation and Emotion, 35*, 393–402. https://doi.org/10.1007/s11031-011-9221-1

Keller, J., & Bless, H. (2008). Flow and regulatory compatibility: An experimental approach to the flow model of intrinsic motivation. *Personality and Social Psychology Bulletin, 34*, 196–209. https://doi.org/10.1177/0146167207310026

Keller, J., Bless, H., Blomann, F., & Kleinböhl, D. (2011). Physiological aspects of flow experiences: Skills-demand compatibility effects on heart rate variability and salivary cortisol. *Journal of Experimental Social Psychology, 47*, 849–852. https://doi.org/10.1016/j.jesp.2011.02.004

Keller, J., & Blomann, F. (2008). Locus of control and the flow experience: An experimental analysis. *European Journal of Personality, 22*, 1–19. https://doi.org/10.1002/per.692

Klasen, M., Weber, R., Kircher, T.T.J., Mathiak, K.A., & Mathiak, K. (2012). Neural contributions to flow experience during video game playing. *Social Cognitive and Affective Neuroscience, 7*, 485–495.

Knierim, M.T., Rissler, R., Hariharan, A., Nadj, M., Weinhardt, C. (2019). Exploring flow psychophysiology in knowledge work. In F. Davis, R. Riedl, J. vom Brocke, P.M. Léger, & A. Randolph (Eds.), *Information systems and neuroscience. Lecture notes in information systems and organisation* (Vol. 29, pp. 239–249). Springer. https://doi.org/10.1007/978-3-030-01087-4_29

Kyriazos, T.A., Stalikas, A., Prassa, K., Galanakis, M., Flora, K., & Chatzilia, V. (2018). The Flow Short Scale (FSS) dimensionality and what MIMIC shows on heterogeneity and invariance. *Psychology, 9,* 1357–1382. https://doi.org/10.4236/psych.2018.96083

Larson, R.W., & Delespaul, P.A.E.G. (1992). Analyzing experience sampling data: A guidebook for the perplexed. In M. deVries (Ed.), *The experience of psychopathology: Investigating mental disorders in their natural settings* (pp. 58–78). Cambridge University Press. https://doi.org/10.1017/CBO9780511663246.007

Leff, D.R., Orihuela-Espina, F., Elwell, C.E., Athanasiou, T., Delpy, D.T., Darzi, A.W., & Yang, G.Z. (2011). Assessment of the cerebral cortex during motor task behaviours in adults: A systematic review of functional near infrared spectroscopy (fNIRS) studies. *Neuroimage, 54,* 2922–2936. https://doi.org/10.1016/j.neuroimage.2010.10.058

Mann, D.T., Williams, A.M., Ward, P., & Janelle, C.M. (2007). Perceptual cognitive expertise in sport: A meta-analysis. *Journal of Sport and Exercise Psychology, 29,* 457–478. https://doi.org/10.1123/jsep.29.4.457

Marsh, H.W., & Jackson, S.A. (1999). Flow experiences in sport: Construct validation of multidimensional hierarchical state and trait responses. *Structural Equation Modelling, 6,* 343–371. https://doi.org/10.1080/10705519909540140

Martin, A.G., & Jackson, S.A. (2008). Brief approaches to assessing task absorption and enhanced subjective experience: Examining "short" and "core" flow in diverse performance domains. *Motivation and Emotion, 32,* 141–157. https://doi.org/10.1007/s11031-008-9094-0

Massimini, F., Csikszentmihalyi, M., & Carli, M. (1987). Optimal experience: A tool for psychiatric rehabilitation. *Journal of Nervous and Mental Disease, 175,* 545–549. https://doi.org/10.1097/00005053-198709000-00006

Massimini, F., Csikszentmihalyi, M., & Delle Fave, A. (1988). Flow and biocultural evolution. In M. Csikszentmihalyi & I. Csikszentmihalyi (Eds.), *Optimal experience: Psychological studies of flow in consciousness* (pp. 60–81). Cambridge University Press.

Massimini, F., & Delle Fave, A. (2000). Individual development in a bio-cultural perspective. *American Psychologist, 55,* 24–33. https://doi.org/10.1037/0003-066X.55.1.24

Massimini, F., & Inghilleri, P. (Eds.). (1986). *L'esperienza quotidiana: teoria e metodo d'analisi* [Everyday experience: Theory and analysis method]. FrancoAngeli.

Mathiak, K., & Weber, R. (2006). Toward brain correlates of natural behavior: fMRI during violent video games. *Human Brain Mapping, 27,* 948–956. https://doi.org/10.1002/hbm.20234

Mesurado, B. (2008). Factorial validity and reliability of Optimal Experience (Flow) Survey in children and teenagers. *Revista Iberoamericana de Diagnóstico y Evaluación Psicológica, 25,* 159–178.

Mesurado, B., & Richaud de Minzi, M.C. (2013). Child's personality and perception of parental relationship as correlates of optimal experience. *Journal of Happiness Studies, 14,* 199–214. https://doi.org/10.1007/s10902-012-9324-8

Mill, A., Kööts-Ausmees, L., Allik, J., & Realo, A. (2018). The role of co-occurring emotions and personality traits in anger expression. *Frontiers in Psychology, 9,* Article 123. https://doi.org/10.3389/fpsyg.2018.00123

Moneta, G.B. (2004). The flow model of intrinsic motivation in Chinese: Cultural and personal moderators. *Journal of Happiness Studies, 5,* 181–217. https://doi.org/10.1023/B:JOHS.0000035916.27782.e4

Moneta, G.B. (2010). Flow in work as a function of trait intrinsic motivation, opportunity for creativity in the job, and work engagement. In S. Albrecht (Ed.), *The handbook of employee engagement: Perspectives, issues, research and practice* (pp. 262–269). Edward Elgar.

Moneta, G.B. (2012). On the measurement and conceptualization of flow. In S. Engeser (Ed.), *Advances in flow research* (pp. 23–50). Springer. https://doi.org/10.1007/978-1-4614-2359-1_2

Moneta, G.B., & Csikszentmihalyi, M. (1996). The effect of perceived challenges and skills on the quality of subjective experience. *Journal of Personality, 64,* 275–310. https://doi.org/10.1111/j.1467-6494.1996.tb00512.x

Mosing, M.A., Magnusson, P.K.E., Pedersen, N.L., Nakamura, J., Madison, G., & Ullén, F. (2012). Heritability of proneness for psychological flow experiences. *Personality and Individual Differences, 53,* 699–704. https://doi.org/10.1016/j.paid.2012.05.035

Nakamura, J., & Csikszentmihalyi, M. (2009). Flow theory and research. In S. Lopez & C.R. Snyder (Eds.), *Oxford handbook of positive psychology* (2nd ed., pp. 195–206). Oxford University Press.

Napa Scollon, C., Kim-Prieto, C., & Diener, E. (2003). Experience sampling: Promises and pitfalls, strengths and weaknesses. *Journal of Happiness Studies, 4*, 5–34. https://doi.org/10.1023/A:1023605205115

Niendam, T.A., Laird, A.R., Ray, K.L., Dean, Y.M., Glahn, D.C., & Carter, C.S. (2012). Meta-analytic evidence for a superordinate cognitive control network subserving diverse executive functions. *Cognitive Affective and Behavioural Neuroscience, 12*, 241–268. https://doi.org/10.3758/s13415-011-0083-5

Niksirat, K.S., Park, K., Silpasuwanchai, C., Wang, Z., & Ren, X. (2019). The relationship between flow proneness in everyday life and variations in the volume of gray matter in the dopaminergic system: A cross-sectional study. *Personality and Individual Differences, 141*, 25–30. https://doi.org/10.1016/j.paid.2018.12.013

O'Doherty, J., Dayan, P., Schultz, J., Deichmann, R., Friston, K., Dolan, R.J. (2004). Dissociable roles of ventral and dorsal striatum in instrumental conditioning. *Science, 304*, 452–454. https://doi.org/10.1126/science.1094285

Páez, D., Rimé, B., Basabe, N., Wlodarczyk, A., & Zumeta, L. (2015). Psychosocial effects of perceived emotional synchrony in collective gatherings. *Journal of Personality and Social Psychology, 708*, 711–729. https://doi.org/10.1037/pspi0000014

Pearce, J.M., Ainley, M., & Howard, S. (2005). The ebb and flow of online learning. *Computers in Human Behavior, 21*, 745–771. https://doi.org/10.1016/S0747-5632(04)00036-6

Peifer, C., Schächinger, H., Engeser, S., & Antoni, C.H. (2015). Cortisol effects on flow-experience. *Psychopharmacology, 232*, 1165–1173. https://doi.org/10.1007/s00213-014-3753-5

Peifer, C., Schulz, A., Schächinger, H., Baumann, N., & Antoni, C.H. (2014). The relation of flow experience and physiological arousal under stress: Can u shape it? *Journal of Experimental Social Psychology, 53*, 62–69. https://doi.org/10.1016/j.jesp.2014.01.009

Peifer, C., & Zipp, G. (2019). All at once? The effects of multitasking behavior on flow and subjective performance. *European Journal of Work and Organizational Psychology, 28*(5), 682–690. https://doi.org/10.1080/1359432X.2019.1647168

Rathunde, K. (2001). Family context and the development of undivided interest: A longitudinal study of family support and challenge and adolescents' quality of experience. *Applied Developmental Science, 5*, 158–171. https://doi.org/10.1207/S1532480XADS0503_4

Raudenbush, S.W., & Bryk, A.S. (2002). *Hierarchical linear models: Applications and data analysis methods* (2nd ed.). Sage.

Rheinberg, F., Manig, Y., Kliegl, R., Engeser, S., & Vollmeyer, R. (2007). Flow bei der Arbeit, doch Glück in der Freizeit [Flow during work but happiness during leisure time]. *Zeitschrift für Arbeits- und Organisationspsychologie, 51*, 105–115. https://doi.org/10.1026/0932-4089.51.3.105

Rheinberg, F., Vollmeyer, R., & Engeser, S. (2003). Measuring flow experiences. In J. Stiensmeier-Pelster & F. Rheinberg (Eds.), *Diagnostik von Motivation und Selbstkonzept. Tests und Trends* (pp. 261–279). Hogrefe.

Riva, E.F.M., Riva, G., Talò, C., Boffi, M., Rainisio, N., Pola, L., Diana, B., Villani, D., Argenton, L., & Inghilleri, P. (2017). Measuring dispositional flow: Validity and reliability of the Dispositional Flow State Scale 2, Italian version. *PLoS ONE, 12*, e0182201. https://doi.org/10.1371/journal.pone.0182201

Rodríguez-Sánchez, A.M., Schaufeli, W., Salanova, M., Cifre, E., & Sonnenschein, M. (2011). Enjoyment and absorption: An electronic diary study on daily flow patterns. *Work & Stress, 25*(1), 75–92. https://doi.org/10.1080/02678373.2011.565619

Sakatani, K., Yamashita, D., Yamanaka, T., Oda, M., Yamashita, Y., Hoshino, T., Fujiwara, N., Murata, Y., & Katayama, Y. (2006). Changes of cerebral blood oxygenation and optical pathlength during activation and deactivation in the prefrontal cortex measured by time-resolved near infrared spectroscopy. *Life Sciences, 78*, 2734–2741. https://doi.org/10.1016/j.lfs.2005.10.045

Salanova, M., Bakker, A., & Llorens, S. (2006). Flow at work: Evidence for an upward spiral of personal and organizational resources. *Journal of Happiness Studies, 7*, 1–22. https://doi.org/10.1007/s10902-005-8854-8

Salanova, M., Rodríguez-Sánchez, A. M., Schaufeli, W. B., & Cifre, E. (2014). Flowing together: A longitudinal study of collective efficacy and collective flow among workgroups. *The Journal of Psychology, 148*, 435–455. https://doi.org/10.1080/00223980.2013.806290

Sartori, R. D. G., & Delle Fave, A. (2014). First aid activities and well-being: The experience of professional and volunteer rescuers. *Journal of Social Service Research, 40*, 242–254. https://doi.org/10.1080/01488376.2013.876954

Sartori, R. D. G., Marelli, M., D'Angelo, M. G., & Delle Fave, A. (2019). Autonomy level and quality of everyday experience of people with hereditary spastic paraplegia. *Health and Social Care in the Community, 27*(5), 850–860. https://doi.org/10.1111/hsc.12812

Sartori, R. D. G., Marelli, M., Garavaglia, P., Castelli, L., Busin, S., & Delle Fave, A. (2014). The assessment of patients' quality of experience: Autonomy level and perceived challenges. *Rehabilitation Psychology, 59*, 266–277. https://doi.org/10.1037/a0036519

Schiepe-Tiska, A., & Engeser, S. (2017). Measuring flow at work. In C. Fullagar & A. Delle Fave (Eds.), *Flow at work: Measurement and implications* (pp. 28–49). Taylor & Francis.

Schimmack, U. (2003). Affect measurement in experience sampling research. *Journal of Happiness Studies, 4*, 79–106. https://doi.org/10.1023/A:1023661322862

Schüler, J., Brandstätter, V., & Sheldon, K. M. (2013). Do implicit motives and basic psychological needs interact to predict well-being and flow? Testing a universal hypothesis and a matching hypothesis. *Motivation and Emotion, 37*, 480–495. https://doi.org/10.1037/t03592-000

Shaffer, F., & Combatalade, D. C. (2013). Don't add or miss a beat: A guide to cleaner heart rate variability recordings. *Biofeedback, 41*, 121–130. https://doi.org/10.5298/1081-5937-41.3.04

Shaffer, F., & Ginsberg, J. P. (2017). An overview of heart rate variability metrics and norms. *Frontiers in Public Health, 5*, Article 258. https://doi.org/10.3389/fpubh.2017.00258

Shernoff, D., & Csikszentmihalyi, M. (2009). Flow in schools: Cultivating engaged learners and optimal learning environments. In R. Gilman, E. Huebner, & M. Furlong (Eds.), *Handbook of positive psychology in schools* (pp. 131–145). Taylor & Francis.

Shulman, G. L., Fiez, J. A., Corbetta, M., Buckner, R. L., Miezin, F. M., Raichle, M. E., & Petersen, S. E. (1997). Common blood flow changes across visual tasks: II. Decreases in cerebral cortex. *Journal of Cognitive Neurosciences, 9*, 648–663. https://doi.org/10.1162/jocn.1997.9.5.648.

Steenbergen, L., Sellaro, R., Stock, A. K., Verkuil, B., Beste, C., & Colzato, L. S. (2015). Transcutaneous vagus nerve stimulation (tVNS) enhances response selection during action cascading processes. *European Neuropsychopharmacology, 25*, 773–778. https://doi.org/10.1016/j.euroneuro.2015.03.015

Swann, C., Crust, L., & Vella, S. A. (2017). New directions in the psychology of optimal performance in sport: Flow and clutch states. *Current Opinion in Psychology, 16*, 48–53. https://doi.org/10.1016/j.copsyc.2017.03.032

Sznitman, S., Baruc, Y. B., Green, T., & Gelkopf, N. (2018). The association between physical pain and cannabis use in daily life: An experience sampling method. *Drug and Alcohol Dependence, 191*, 294–299. https://doi.org/10.1016/j.drugalcdep.2018.07.014

Tenenbaum, G., Fogarty, G., & Jackson, S. (1999). The flow experience: A Rasch analysis of Jackson's Flow State Scale. *Journal of Outcome Measurement, 3*, 278–294.

Tian, Y., Bian, Y., Han, P., Wang, P., Gao, F., & Chen, Y. (2017). Physiological signal analysis for evaluating flow during playing of computer games of varying difficulty. *Frontiers in Psychology, 8*, Article 1121. https://doi.org/10.3389/fpsyg.2017.01121

Tozman, T., Magdas, E. S., MacDougall, H. G., & Vollmeyer, R. (2015). Understanding the psychophysiology of flow: A driving simulator experiment to investigate the relationship between flow and heart rate variability. *Computers in Human Behavior, 52*, 408–418. https://doi.org/10.1016/j.chb.2015.06.023

Tozman, T., Zhang, Y. Y., & Vollmeyer, R. (2017). Inverted U-shaped function between flow and cortisol release during chess play. *Journal of Happiness Studies, 18*, 247–268. https://doi.org/10.1007/s10902-016-9726-0

Trull, T. J., & Ebner-Priemer, U. W. (2009). Using experience sampling methods/ecological momentary assessment (ESM/EMA) in clinical assessment and clinical research: Introduction to the special section. *Psychological Assessment, 21*(4), 457–462. https://doi.org/10.1037/a0017653

Tse, D.C.K., Lau, V.W., Perlman, R., & McLaughlin, M. (2020). The development and validation of the Autotelic Personality Questionnaire. *Journal of Personality Assessment, 102*(1), 88–101. https://doi.org/10.1080/00223891.2018.1491855

Ullén, F., de Manzano, Ö., Almeida, R., Magnusson, P.K.E., Pedersen, N.L., Nakamura, J., Csikszentmihalyi, M., & Madison, G. (2012). Proneness for psychological flow in everyday life: Associations with personality and intelligence. *Personality and Individual Differences, 52*, 167–172. http://doi.org/10.1016/j.paid.2011.10.003 https://doi.org/10.1016/j.paid.2011.10.003

Ullén, F., de Manzano, Ö., Theorell, T., & Harmat, L. (2010). The physiology of effortless attention: Correlates of state flow and flow proneness. In B. Bruya (Ed.), *Effortless attention: A new perspective in the cognitive science of attention and action* (pp. 205–218). MIT Press. https://doi.org/10.7551/mitpress/9780262013840.003.0011

Ulrich, M., Keller, J., & Grön, G. (2016a). Neural signatures of experimentally induced flow experiences identified in a typical fMRI block design with BOLD imaging. *Social Cognitive and Affective Neuroscience, 11*, 496–507. https://doi.org/10.1093/scan/nsv133

Ulrich, M., Keller, J., Hoenig, K., Waller, C., & Grön, G. (2014). Neural correlates of experimentally induced flow experiences. *NeuroImage, 86*, 194–202. https://doi.org/10.1016/j.neuroimage.2013.08.019

Ulrich, M., Keller, J., & Grön, G. (2016b). Dorsal raphe nucleus downregulates medial prefrontal cortex during experience of flow. *Frontiers in Behavioral Neuroscience, 10*, Article 169. https://doi.org/10.3389/fnbeh.2016.00169

Van den Heuvel, M.P., & Sporns, O. (2011). Rich-club organization of the human connectome. *Journal of Neuroscience, 31*, 15775–15786. https://doi.org/10.1523/JNEUROSCI.3539-11.2011

Van den Hout, J.J.J., Davis, O.C., & Weggeman, M.D.C.P. (2018). The conceptualization of team flow. *The Journal of Psychology, 152*, 388–423. https://doi.org/10.1080/00223980.2018.1449729

Van den Hout, J.J.J., Gevers, J.M.P., Davis, O.C., & Weggeman, M.D.C.P. (2019). Developing and testing the Team Flow Monitor (TFM). *Cogent Psychology, 6*, 1643962. https://doi.org/10.1080/23311908.2019.1643962

Van Der Poel, E.G., & Delespaul, P.A.E.G. (1992). The applicability of ESM in personalized rehabilitation. In M.W. deVries (Ed.), *The experience of psychopathology: Investigating mental disorders in their natural settings* (pp. 290–303). Cambridge University Press. https://doi.org/10.1017/CBO9780511663246.026

Ventureyra, E.C. (2000). Transcutaneous vagus nerve stimulation for partial onset seizure therapy. *Child's Nervous System, 16*,101–102. https://doi.org/10.1007/s003810050021

Vickers, J.N. (1996). Control of visual attention during the basketball free throw. *American Journal of Sports Medicine, 24*, S93–S97. https://doi.org/10.1177/036354659602406S25

Vlachopoulos, S.P., Karageorghis, C.I., & Terry, P.C. (2000). Hierarchical confirmatory factor analysis of the Flow State Scale in exercise. *Journal of Sports Sciences, 18*, 815–823. https://doi.org/10.1080/026404100419874

Volkow, N.D., Wang, G.J., Telang, F., Fowler, J.S., Logan, J., Childress, A.R., Jayne, M., Ma, Y.M., & Wong, C. (2006). Cocaine cues and dopamine in dorsal striatum: Mechanism of craving in cocaine addiction. *Journal of Neuroscience, 26*, 6583–6588. https://doi.org/10.1523/JNEUROSCI.1544-06.2006

Walker, C.J. (2010). Experiencing flow: Is doing it together better than doing it alone? *The Journal of Positive Psychology, 5*(1), 3–11. https://doi.org/10.1080/17439760903271116

Wang, C.K.J., Liu, W.C., & Khoo, A. (2009). The psychometric properties of disposition flow scale in internet gaming. *Current Psychology, 28*, 194–201. https://doi.org/10.1007/s12144-009-9058-x

Waterink, W., & van Boxtel, A. (1994). Facial and jaw-elevator EMG activity in relation to changes in performance level during a sustained information processing task. *Biological Psychology, 37*, 183–198. https://doi.org/10.1016/0301-0511(94)90001-9

Weiskopf, N., Klose, U., Birbaumer, N., & Mathiak, K. (2005). Single-shot compensation of image distortions and BOLD contrast optimization using multi-echo EPI for real-time fMRI. *NeuroImage, 22*, 1068–1079. https://doi.org/10.1016/j.neuroimage.2004.10.012

Wilson, E. E., & Moneta, G. B. (2012). Flow as a way of coping: A qualitative study of the metacognitions of flow. In B. Molinelli, & V. Grimaldo (Eds.), *Handbook of the psychology of coping: New research* (pp. 133–150). Nova Science Publishers.

Wilson, E. E., & Moneta, G. B. (2016). The flow metacognitions questionnaire (FMQ): A two factor model of flow metacognitions. *Personality and Individual Differences, 90,* 225–230. https://doi.org/10.1016/j.paid.2015.11.004

Woolgar, A., Duncan, J., Manes, F., & Fedorenko, E. (2018). Fluid intelligence is supported by the multiple-demand system not the language system. *Nature Human Behaviour, 2,* 200–204. https://doi.org/10.1038/s41562-017-0282-3

Yoshida, K., Asakawa, K., Yamauchi, T., Sakuraba, S., Sawamura, D., Murakami, Y., & Sakai, S. (2013). The Flow State Scale for Occupational Tasks: Development, reliability, and validity. *Hong Kong Journal of Occupational Therapy, 23,* 54e61. https://doi.org/10.1016/j.hkjot.2013.09.002

Yoshida, K., Sawamura, D., Inagaki, Y., Ogawa, K., Ikoma, K., & Sakai, S. (2014). Brain activity during the flow experience: A functional near-infrared spectroscopy study. *Neuroscience Letters, 573,* 30–34. https://doi.org/10.1016/j.neulet.2014.05.011

Zito, M., Bakker, A. B., Colombo, L., & Cortese, C. G. (2015). A two-steps study for the Italian adaptation of the WorkreLated Flow (WOLF) inventory: The I-WOLF. *TPM–Testing, Psychometrics, Methodology in Applied Psychology, 22,* 553–570. https://doi.org/10.4473/TPM22.4.8

Zito, M., Cortese, C. G., & Colombo, L. (2018). The Italian adaptation of the WOrk-reLated Flow Inventory (WOLF) to sport: The I-WOLFS scale. *Bollettino di Psicologia Applicata, 64,* 38–45.

Zumeta, L., Basabe, N., Wlodarczyk, A., Bobowik, M., & Páez, D. (2016). Shared flow and positive collective gatherings. *Anales de Psicología, 32,* 717–727. https://doi.org/10.6018/analesps.32.3.261651

Chapter 11

Self-Efficacy

Ralf Schwarzer[1] and Aleksandra Luszczynska[2]

[1]Department of Education and Psychology, FU Berlin, Germany
[2]Wroclaw Faculty of Psychology, SWPS University of Social Sciences and Humanities, Wroclaw, Poland

Self-efficacy is concerned with individuals' beliefs in their capability to exercise control over challenging demands and their own functioning. In his landmark book *Social Foundations of Thought and Action: A Social Cognitive Theory*, Bandura (1986) developed the social cognitive theory (SCT) of human functioning based on his earlier social learning theory and his pioneering article on self-efficacy (Bandura, 1977). This work was crowned by the 1997 volume *Self-Efficacy: The Exercise of Control* (Bandura, 1997). The construct of self-efficacy reflects an optimistic self-belief, that is, the belief that one can perform a novel or difficult task or cope with adversity in various domains of human functioning. Self-efficacy facilitates goal-setting, effort investment, persistence in face of barriers, and recovery from setbacks. It can be regarded as a resilience factor. Self-efficacy is an operative construct, that is, it is related to subsequent behavior and, therefore, is relevant for professional or academic practice and behavior change. Thus, self-efficacy can guide behavioral changes and support optimal functioning.

Self-efficacy indicates a subjective estimate of the amount of personal control an individual expects to have in any given situation. If we hold a strong belief that we can master an upcoming task (i.e., have high self-efficacy), then we are likely to work toward it; if we feel confident that we can overcome an upcoming threat or challenge (e.g., an exam), then we are more likely to approach than to avoid this situation. In contrast, if we have self-doubts (i.e., low self-efficacy), we might hesitate to act instrumentally. Self-efficacy, therefore, affects how much effort individuals expend to change a particular behavior to obtain a particular goal and the extent to which they persist in striving to attain that goal in the face of barriers and setbacks that may undermine their motivation. Thus, self-efficacy provides guidance to behavioral engagement and is critical to attaining the goal-directed behaviors that individuals experience daily.

Numerous sources give rise to self-efficacy (Bandura, 1997). First, self-efficacy can be enhanced through personal accomplishment or mastery, insofar as success is attributed internally and perceived to be repeatable. A second source is a vicarious experience: When a role model, similar in ability to the individual, is viewed as successfully mastering a behavior or task in a difficult situation, upward social comparison processes are likely to enhance self-efficacy. Third, self-efficacy may be enhanced through verbal persuasion by others (e.g., a coach reassures an athlete that they can adopt a new training routine because of their competence). The fourth source of influence is emotional arousal, that is, when individuals experience no apprehension in a threatening environment, they may feel capable of mastering the situation. These four informational sources vary in strength and importance in the order presented here, with personal mastery being the strongest source of self-efficacy (Warner et al., 2014). Clearly, self-efficacy can be more strongly prompted by offering persons the chance to try new behaviors themselves (mastery experience) than by observing others (vicarious experience), listening to persuasive messages (verbal persuasion), or by trying to interpret their own nervousness (affective states), in that order. Self-efficacy is not the same as unrealistic optimism, as it is mainly based on experience and does not lead to unreasonable risk-taking. Instead, it leads to venturesome behavior that lies within the reach of one's capabilities. The main difference between optimism and self-efficacy lies in the focus on agency: Self-efficacy implies an internal attribution, believing that oneself is competent and can handle the challenges; in contrast, optimism does not require a sense of agency: Help by others or favorable circumstances alone can lead to an optimistic outlook. Moreover, compared to other similar constructs such as self-esteem, self-concept, or sense of control, the essential distinction between these constructs and self-efficacy lies in three aspects: (a) Self-efficacy implies an internal attribution (oneself is the cause of the action), (b) it is prospective, referring to future behaviors, and (c) it is an operative construct, which means that this cognition is proximal to the critical behavior (for an overview on how self-efficacy differs from similar constructs, see Warner & Schwarzer, 2017). Mastery experience as the best source of self-efficacy is at the same time the best source of self-concept of ability, which often makes it hard to distinguish between these two constructs. The main difference lies in the operative nature of self-efficacy, about future behavior (see Figure 11.1).

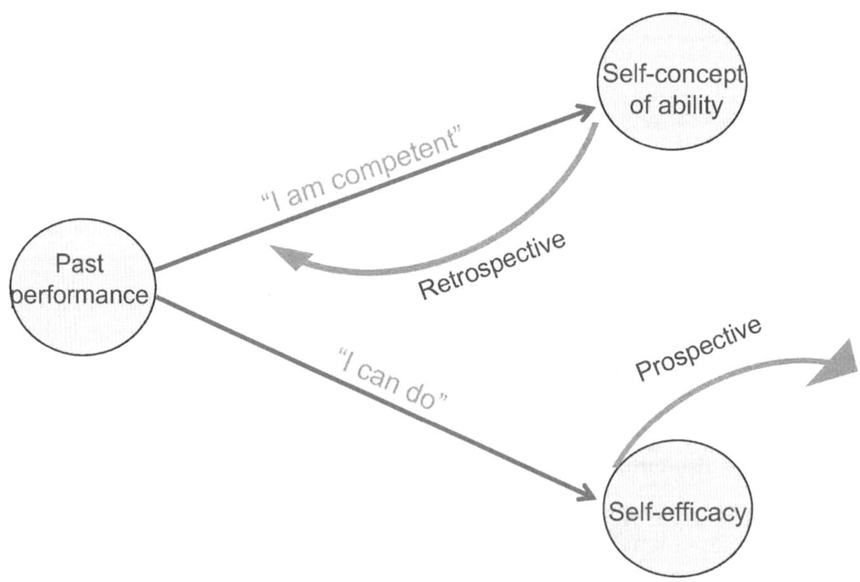

Figure 11.1. The distinction between self-efficacy as a prospective competence construct and self-concept of ability as a retrospective competence construct.

Diagnostic Relevance

Self-efficacy beliefs affect behaviors indirectly through their impact on goals. Self-efficacy, among other factors, influences which challenges people decide to meet and how high they set their goals. Persons with high self-efficacy in a specific domain select more challenging and ambitious goals. Optimistic self-beliefs about one's capability to exert control over one's actions influence how people respond to discrepancies between their personal goals and their performance (Jerusalem, & Schwarzer, 1992). Compared to those with low optimistic self-beliefs, self-efficacious individuals invest more effort when the discrepancies are larger (DeVellis & DeVellis, 2000). High self-efficacy not only improves goal setting but leads to more persistence in pursuing the goal. Self-efficacy also promotes the effective use of cognitive resources, diagnosing, and searching for solutions when obstacles arise (Maddux & Lewis, 1995).

Self-efficacy is considered to operate in various ways. It contributes to the forming of good intentions to change behaviors, and it is associated with efforts to maintain a novel behavior and to counteract temptations to relapse into an undesired behavior (such as smoking). Because most research is not limited to a bivariate design, the question arises of how self-efficacy operates in multivariate designs. Here, it can be specified either as a mediator or as a moderator, depending on the context of variables and the theoretical backdrop. As a mediator, it may translate some part of an initial independent variable, such as social support, to a chosen outcome, such as well-being or proactive behavior; as a moderator, it may reflect the association between other variables at one level, but the lack of associations at the other level.

Self-efficacy is related to various kinds of mental and physical performances. In nine meta-analyses published from 1990 to 2002, self-efficacy was positively associated with individuals' performance outcomes with effect sizes r from 0.27 to 0.40 (Bandura & Locke, 2003). A great deal of research has been done in the area of health behavior change (Schwarzer & Luszczynska, 2015, 2016), but self-efficacy interventions have also been found effective in numerous other contexts such as behaviors in organizational settings like career exploration and decision-making (Lent et al., 2016, 2017), productivity and attendance in occupational settings (Cherian & Jacob, 2013), behaviors in educational contexts like persistence with studying and attention in class (Schunk, & Zimmerman. 2007; Unrau et al., 2018), reading performance (Aro et al., 2018; Unrau et al., 2018), academic attainment (Honicke, & Broadbent, 2016; Huang, 2016; Talsma et al., 2018), goal attainment in sports (Te Velde et al., 2018), parenting (Liyana-Amin et al., 2018), and breastfeeding (Galipeau et al., 2018).

Application Example: Prediction of Health Behaviors and Health Behavior Change

Changing one's behavior may often be desirable but difficult to do. For example, quitting smoking, eating healthily, and sticking to a physical exercise regimen all require motivation, effort, and persistence. While many psychological factors play a role in behavior change, self-efficacy is one of the most important (Schwarzer & Luszczynska, 2015, 2016). High self-efficacy predicts engagement with many health behaviors, including cigarette smoking cessation, weight control, contraception, alcohol abuse, fruit and vegetable intake, dental flossing, and physical exercise. Additionally, intervention studies indicate that increasing self-efficacy leads to improvements in behavior (e.g., dietary behaviors and physical activity). Taken together, these findings indicate that individuals need a certain amount of self-efficacy to practice recommended health behaviors and achieve desired outcomes (e.g., weight loss).

Application Example: Teacher Self-Efficacy

One domain where research on professional self-efficacy has been conducted is teaching in schools. Why do some teachers succeed in continuously enhancing students' achievements, in setting high goals for themselves, and pursuing these goals persistently, while others cannot meet expectations imposed on them and tend to collapse under the burden of daily stress? There are many reasons, one of which pertains to a teacher's self-efficacy as a job-specific disposition (Schwarzer & Hallum, 2008; Schwarzer et al., 1999; Skaalvik & Skaalvik, 2016; Tschannen-Moran & Woolfolk Hoy, 2001).

Application Example: General Self-Efficacy

Self-efficacy is commonly understood as being task-specific or domain-specific. That is, one can hold more or less firm self-beliefs in different domains or particular situations of functioning. But there is also a general sense of self-efficacy, which refers to global confidence in one's coping ability across a wide range of demanding or novel situations. General self-efficacy aims at a broad and stable sense of personal competence to deal effectively with a variety of stressful situations (Shelton, 1990; Sherer et al., 1982). If self-efficacy is employed as a predictor of broad outcomes, such as quality of life, well-being, or overall adaptation and health, it is justified to use a correspondingly broad measure of general self-efficacy. For example, a meta-analysis of associations between types of self-efficacy and quality of life among people with cardiovascular diseases showed that general self-efficacy formed significantly stronger associations with quality of life than self-efficacy related to cardiovascular disease management (Banik et al., 2018). This general construct may be assessed with an inventory such as the General Self-Efficacy (GSE) scale (Schwarzer & Jerusalem, 1995).

Assessment of Self-Efficacy

Self-efficacy is a unipolar construct. As self-efficacy is important when guiding people to behavior change, the question remains how can we tell whether someone has high or low self-efficacy. The most common way is to ask individuals to endorse certain statements. A suggested rule for the behavior-specific assessment of self-efficacy is: "I am confident that I can do ... (perform an action), even if ... (a barrier)." An example of a self-efficacy statement is: "I am confident that I can skip desserts even if my family continues to eat them." This semantic rule need not be applied rigidly but might serve as a useful heuristic. A comprehensive book chapter with detailed guidelines on the construction of various kinds of self-efficacy measures was provided by Bandura (2006), who also introduced a variety of possible response formats. Some examples include scales from 0 to

100, though there is no general recommendation for the choice of response formats. Most research uses Likert-type formats (either 1 to 4, 1 to 5, or 1 to 6).

When assessing self-efficacy, it is important to note that low self-efficacy for one behavior does not imply low self-efficacy for different behavior. Depending on the particular application, it is a good idea that self-efficacy be assessed concerning a specific behavior. In health psychology, for example, self-efficacy scales have been developed for the measurement of all kinds of health behaviors. There are scales to assess self-efficacy for diet, exercise, sunscreen use, dental flossing, hand hygiene, and alcohol intake.

Health-Behavioral Self-Efficacy

When it comes to addictive behaviors, there are two basic methods to designing a risk-behavior self-efficacy scale: One is to confront the individual with a list or hierarchy of tempting situations and to assess situation-specific self-efficacy in line with these demands; the second approach aims at the restricted use of substances, asking participants whether they generally feel competent to control the behavior in question (irrespective of specific risk situations). In the domain of smoking, for example, the first method was chosen by Colletti et al. (1985) and Velicer et al. (1990). Dijkstra and DeVries (2000) elaborated a smoking self-efficacy scale to reflect different barriers that might arise during adoption, maintenance, and recovery after lapses. For example, barriers about emotional states (e.g., being stressed), social situations (e.g., seeing someone enjoying a smoke), or lack of skills (e.g., telling smokers to quit smoking during a party) might occur during the maintenance period. Godding and Glasgow (1985), Shiffman et al. (2000), and Gwaltney et al. (2002) chose the second approach to assess smoking cessation self-efficacy.

Thus, when it comes to changing a particular behavior, one should assess self-efficacy with a narrow scope, targeting specific situations. In the behavior-change context, people should not be categorized into high or low self-efficacious personalities; rather, they should be seen as having a profile of high scores in some behaviors and low scores in other behaviors. For example, people may harbor optimistic self-beliefs for swimming regularly and at the same time pessimistic self-beliefs for eating more vegetables. Some health behavior self-efficacy instruments can be downloaded from http://www.psyc.de/hapascales.pdf

Teacher Self-Efficacy

Among the instruments often used in school settings to assess teachers' optimistic beliefs about their professional actions, three inventories are quite popular. The Teachers' Sense of Efficacy Scale (TSES; Tschannen-Moran, & Woolfolk Hoy, 2001) is designed to identify what creates the most difficulties for teachers in daily school activities. It is a 24-item scale that includes three moderately correlated factors indicating teachers' efficacy in student engagement, instructional practices, and classroom management.

The multidimensional 24-item Norwegian Teacher Self-Efficacy Scale (NTSES) has six dimensions, namely, self-efficacy for instruction, adapting education to individual students' needs, motivating students, keeping discipline, cooperating with colleagues and parents, and coping with changes and challenges. Responses are on a 7-point scale. A reliability of $\alpha=.92$ and good validity were reported (Skaalvik & Skaalvik, 2016).

The Teacher Self-Efficacy Scale (TSE, Schwarzer et al., 1999) is a 10-item inventory that addresses a broad range of professional activities. An example item is: "Even if I get disrupted while teaching, I am confident that I can maintain my composure and continue to teach well." The scale reflects an optimistic coping resource and has been used, among others, as a predictor of job stress and job burnout (Schwarzer & Hallum, 2008). It is noncommercial and can be downloaded from the public domain (http://userpage.fu-berlin.de/~health/teacher_se.htm). Reliability was found to be between $\alpha=.76$, and $\alpha=.82$, test-retest reliability resulted in $r_{tt}=.67$ ($N=158$) and $r_{tt}=.76$ ($N=193$), respectively, for the period of 1 year.

General Self-Efficacy

Situation-specific self-efficacy is typically not measured with standardized inventories but rather with brief sets of items matched to the particular research context. However, self-efficacy can also be assessed at a general level, for which several instruments have become popular. The GSE scale (Schwarzer & Jerusalem, 1995) was originally developed in Germany in the 1970s and was later adapted to 33 languages. All versions are available in the public domain and can be downloaded from

Of its 10 items, a typical one is: "Thanks to my resourcefulness, I can handle unforeseen situations." Possible responses are *not at all true* (1), *hardly true* (2), *moderately true* (3), and *exactly true* (4), yielding a total score between 10 and 40. Bilingual speakers have adapted the self-efficacy items to foreign languages based on the German and English versions of the GSE scale (Scholz et al., 2002). The adaptations followed the group consensus model, including backtranslations and group discussions (Brislin, 1970). High internal consistency, temporal stability, and construct validity of the GSE scale were confirmed in many studies (Leganger et al., 2000). The scale was found to be configurally equivalent across 28 nations, and it forms usually a single global dimension (Scholz et al., 2002) although in some data sets one could have also extracted two factors.

Psychometric Research

There are hundreds of inventories of behavior-specific self-efficacy which have been generated for a particular research context, from single-item scales to full-size multidimensional scales. It is a characteristic of narrow, behavior-specific scales that they are not designed to serve a general purpose but to be affiliated to a unique research question. Therefore, we do not present such scales here; instead, we present a very brief overview of studies using the General Self-Efficacy (GSE) questionnaire.

The GSE has been used internationally with success for four decades, including population-representative norming (e.g., Hinz et al., 2006). It is suitable for a broad range of applications. It can be taken to predict adaptation after life changes, but it is also suitable as an indicator of well-being or quality of life at any point in time. In samples from 23 nations, Cronbach's alphas ranged from .76 to .90, with the majority in the high .80s (Scholz et al., 2002). Test-retest reliabilities were around $r_{tt}=.70$, depending on timespan and context. Criterion-related validity is documented in numerous correlation studies where positive coefficients were found with favorable emotions, dispositional optimism, and work satisfaction. Negative coefficients were found with depression, anxiety, stress, burnout, and health complaints. For example, Luszczynska et al. (2005) conducted multicultural validation studies with the GSE and found meaningful relationships between general self-efficacy and social cognitive variables, self-regulation, behavior-specific self-efficacy, health behaviors, well-being, and coping strategies among 1,933 respondents in three countries: Germany (n=633), Poland (n=359), and South Korea (n=941). Participants were between 16 and 86 years old, and some were dealing with stressful situations such as recovery from myocardial events or tumor surgery. The correlation with self-regulation was .42, with quality of life .32, with active coping .27, and with fighting spirit .39. Among cases of gastrointestinal disease, GSE was related to less frequent use of passive coping and more frequent use of active coping with pain. Among patients with cancer, GSE was related to the more frequent use of active coping, planning, positive reframing, humor, and fighting spirit, and to a more frequent seeking of information. Patients with cancer who had lower GSE more frequently used coping strategies such as self-blame or behavioral disengagement.

Negative correlations between GSE and negative affect were also documented. Two indicators of depressive symptoms correlated at –.36 and –.39. High general self-efficacy beliefs were related to lower levels of depression in patients with cardiovascular diseases and to lower levels of anxiety in individuals with gastrointestinal diseases. The latter also reported lower levels of pain intensity. In patients with cancer, efficacious individuals were less depressed and less tired. They reported better health and better quality of life in the areas of emotional, social, and cognitive functioning.

A study based on a representative German sample (N=2,019, age: 16–95 years) found a high correlation of the GSE with the Resilience Scale (r=.68) (Hinz et al., 2006), which underscores the positive resource nature of the general self-efficacy construct.

Necessary Decisions to Assess Self-Efficacy

When choosing an instrument, one must make some decisions. The first one pertains to the generality, domain-specificity, or behavior-specificity addressed in a particular research context. If the researcher or practitioner is interested in the prediction of a broad outcome such as quality of life, well-being, depression, or resilience in the context of life changes, one might want to use the general self-efficacy construct, which can be understood as a personality trait. General self-efficacy relates to a broad range of psychological constructs and outcomes pertaining to various domains of human functioning.

However, this was not Bandura's original idea (1977) when introducing the construct. Instead, self-efficacy was defined as being different from most other constructs because of its operative nature, which suggests an application in a situation-specific or behavior-specific manner (Bandura, 1997). This has consequences for its assessment. Situation-specific self-efficacy is typically not measured with standardized inventories, but rather with brief sets of items that are matched to the particular research context where self-regulatory processes are at stake. It is sufficient to apply principles for the construction of items to attain a content-valid scale (Bandura, 2006). Sticking to item construction rules (see above) leads to content-valid tests if there is a correspondence between item content and the situation targeted in the research or practice.

The discrepancy between self-efficacy as a personality trait and self-efficacy as a narrow behavior-specific operative construct need not pose a major problem, because one can combine measures of both kinds, and one can also address intermediate levels of generality. Teacher self-efficacy is a good example of an intermediate-level domain-specific construct. An item such as "When I try really hard, I am able to reach even the most difficult students" pertains to the daily professional demands. Starting such an item either with the word "Today" or "In the next school year" defines a temporal perspective that makes the content narrower or broader.

Thus, when deciding how to measure self-efficacy, one needs to clearly anticipate which domain is to be targeted and whether a personality trait should be assessed or only specific behaviors in specific contexts. One then can select scales or items from a boilerplate or design one's own instrument. The latter is often preferred to attain content-valid items that work in a given environment and fit the characteristics of the target population (e.g., age, health status; cf. Banik et al., 2018; Luszczynska, Hagger et al., 2016; Luszczynska, Horodyska et al., 2016). Sometimes, a single item appears to be sufficient to make a valid self-efficacy assessment. Although single-item measures should be used with caution because their internal consistency cannot be identified, several studies have found that single-item measures have comparable validity to multiitem measures for a variety of different constructs (e.g., Bergkvist & Rossiter, 2007; Hamilton et al., 2012; Milton et al., 2010; Wanous et al., 1997; West et al., 2012).

Future Directions

One future direction for self-efficacy diagnostics pertains to ecological momentary assessment (EMA). Advanced technology allows for more fine-grained process characteristics and for immediate feedback loops that keep users engaged, monitor progress, and provide resource information that is individually tailored. Identifying the current status of self-efficacy for interventions can improve behavior in various areas of human functioning. Frequent diagnostics allow the reclassification of individuals into concurrent stages of change, tailored for individual needs. For example, in eHealth applications, participants are guided to set goals, monitor their behavior, receive tailored feedback, make action plans, and increase their self-efficacy by vicarious experience via testimonials and by problem-solving tasks. In such EMA situations, one cannot administer extended standardized assessment tools. Rather, one would include single items to assess self-efficacy states at many points in time. Narrow behavior-specific operationalizations are appropriate to guide and tailor treatments to the current needs of the user.

References

Aro, T., Viholainen, H., Koponen, T., Peura, P., Räikkönen, E., Salmi, P., Sorvo, R., & Aro, M. (2018). Can reading fluency and self-efficacy of reading fluency be enhanced with an intervention targeting the sources of self-efficacy? *Learning and Individual Differences, 67*, 53–66. https://doi.org/10.1016/j.lindif.2018.06.009

Bandura, A. (1977). Self-efficacy: Toward a unifying theory of behavioral change. *Psychological Review, 84*, 191–215. https://doi.org/10.1037/0033-295X.84.2.191

Bandura, A. (1986). *Social foundations of thought and action*. Prentice-Hall.

Bandura, A. (1997). *Self-efficacy: The exercise of control*. Freeman.

Bandura, A. (2006). Guide for constructing self-efficacy scales. In F. Pajares & T. Urdan (Eds.), *Self-efficacy beliefs of adolescents* (Vol. 5, pp. 307–337). Information Age Publishing.

Bandura, A., & Locke, E. A. (2003). Negative self-efficacy and goal effects revisited. *Journal of Applied Psychology, 88*(1), 87–99. https://doi.org/10.1037/0021-9010.88.1.87

Banik, A., Schwarzer, R., Knoll, N., Czekierda, K., & Luszczynska, A. (2018). Self-efficacy and quality of life among people with cardiovascular diseases: A meta-analysis. *Rehabilitation Psychology, 63*, 295–312. https://doi.org/10.1037/rep0000199

Bergkvist, L., & Rossiter, J. R. (2007). The predictive validity of multiple-itemversus single item measures of the same constructs. *Journal of Marketing Research, 44*, 175–184. https://doi.org/10.1509/jmkr.44.2.175

Brislin, R. W. (1970). Back-translation for cross-cultural research. *Journal of Cross-Cultural Psychology, 1*, 185–216. https://doi.org/10.1177/135910457000100301

Cherian, J., & Jacob, J. (2013). Impact of self-efficacy on motivation and performance of employees. *International Journal of Business and Management, 8*(14), 80–88.. https://doi.org/10.5539/ijbm.v8n14p80

Colletti, G., Supnick, J. A., & Payne, T. J. (1985). The Smoking Self-Efficacy Questionnaire (SSEQ): Preliminary scale development and validation. *Behavioral Assessment, 7*, 249–620. https://doi.org/10.1037/t04891-000

DeVellis, B. M., & DeVellis, R. F. (2000). Self-efficacy and health. In A. Baum, T. A. Revenson, & J. E. Singer (Eds.), *Handbook of health psychology* (pp. 235–247). Erlbaum.

Dijkstra, A., & DeVries, H. (2000). *Self-efficacy expectations regarding different tasks in smoking cessations, Psychology and Health, 15*, 501–511. https://doi.org/10.1080/08870440008402009

Galipeau, R., Baillot, A., Trottier, A., & Lemire, L. (2018). Effectiveness of interventions on breastfeeding self-efficacy and perceived insufficient milk supply: A systematic review and meta-analysis. *Maternal & Child Nutrition, 14*(3), e12607–e12607. https://doi.org/10.1111/mcn.12607

Godding, P. R., & Glasgow, R. E. (1985). Self-efficacy and outcome expectations as predictors of controlled smoking status. *Cognitive Therapy and Research, 9*, 583–590. https://doi.org/10.1007/BF01173011

Gwaltney, C. J., Shiffman, S., Paty, J. A., Liu, K. S., Kassel, J. D., Gnys, M., & Hickcox, M. (2002). Using self-efficacy judgements to predict characteristics of lapses to smoking. *Journal of Consulting and Clinical Psychology, 70*, 1140–1149. https://doi.org/10.1037//0022-006X.70.5.1140

Hamilton, K., White, K. M., & Cuddihy, T. (2012). Using a single-item physical activity measure to describe and validate parents' physical activity pattern. *Research Quarterly in Exercise and Sport, 83*, 340–345. https://doi.org/10.1080/02701367.2012.10599865

Hinz, A., Schumacher, J., Albani, G., Schmid, G., & Brähler, E. (2006). Bevölkerungsrepräsentative Normierung der Skala zur Allgemeinen Selbstwirksamkeitserwartung [Population representative norming of the General Self-Efficacy Scale]. *Diagnostica, 52*, 26–32. https://doi.org/10.1026/0012-1924.52.1.26

Honicke, T., & Broadbent, J. (2016). The influence of academic self-efficacy on academic performance: A systematic review. *Educational Research Review, 17*, 63–84. https://doi.org/10.1016/j.edurev.2015.11.002

Huang, C. (2016). Achievement goals and self-efficacy: A meta-analysis. *Educational Research Review, 19*, 119–137. https://doi.org/10.1016/j.edurev.2016.07.002

Jerusalem, M., & Schwarzer, R. (1992). Self-efficacy as a resource factor in stress appraisal processes. In R. Schwarzer (Ed.), *Self-efficacy: Thought control of action* (pp. 195–213). Hemisphere.

Leganger, A., Kraft, P., & Røysamb, E. (2000). Perceived self-efficacy in health behavior research: Conceptualisation, measurement and correlates. *Psychology and Health, 15*, 51–69. https://doi.org/10.1080/08870440008400288

Lent, R.W., Ezeofor, I., Morrison, M.A., Penn, L.T., & Ireland, G.W. (2016). Applying the social cognitive model of career self-management to career exploration and decision-making. *Journal of Vocational Behavior, 93*, 47–57. https://doi.org/10.1016/j.jvb.2015.12.007.

Lent, R.W., Ireland, G.W., Penn, L.T., Morris, T.R., & Sappington, R. (2017). Sources of self-efficacy and outcome expectations for career exploration and decision-making: A test of the social cognitive model of career self-management. *Journal of Vocational Behavior, 99*, 107–117. https://doi.org/10.1016/j.jvb.2017.01.002

Liyana Amin, N.A., Tam, W.W.S., & Shorey, S. (2018). Enhancing first-time parents' self-efficacy: A systematic review and meta-analysis of universal parent education interventions' efficacy. *International Journal of Nursing Studies, 82*, 149–162. https://doi.org/10.1016/j.ijnurstu.2018.03.021

Luszczynska, A., Hagger, M.S., Banik, A., Horodyska, K., Knoll, N., & Scholz, U. (2016). Self-efficacy, planning, or a combination of both? A longitudinal experimental study comparing effects of three interventions on adolescents' body fat. *PloS ONE, 11*(7), e0159125. https://doi.org/10.1371/journal.pone.0159125

Luszczynska, A., Horodyska, K., Zarychta, K., Liszewska, N., Knoll, N., & Scholz, U. (2016). Planning and self-efficacy interventions encouraging replacing energy-dense foods intake with fruit and vegetable: A longitudinal experimental study. *Psychology & Health, 31*, 40–64. https://doi.org/10.1080/08870446.2015.1070156

Luszczynska, A., Scholz, U., & Schwarzer, R. (2005). The general self-efficacy scale: Multicultural validation studies. *The Journal of Psychology, 139*(5), 439–457. https://doi.org/10.3200/JRLP.139.5.439-457

Maddux, J.E., & Lewis, J. (1995). Self-efficacy an adjustment: Basic principles and issues. In J.E. Maddux (Ed.), *Self-efficacy, adaptation, and adjustment: Theory, research, and application* (pp. 37–68). Plenum. https://doi.org/10.1007/978-1-4419-6868-5_2

Milton, K., Bull, F.C., & Bauman, A. (2010). Reliability and validity testing of a single-item physical activity measure. *British Journal of Sports Medicine, 45*, 203–208. https://doi.org/10.1136/bjsm.2009.068395

Scholz, U., Gutiérrez-Doña, B., Sud, S., & Schwarzer, R. (2002). Is general self-efficacy a universal construct? Psychometric findings from 25 countries. *European Journal of Psychological Assessment, 18*(3), 242–251. https://doi.org/10.1027//1015-5759.18.3.242

Schunk, D.H., & Zimmerman, B.J. (2007). Influencing children's self-efficacy and self-regulation of reading and writing through modeling. *Reading & Writing Quarterly, 23*, 7–25. https://doi.org/10.1080/10573560600837578

Schwarzer, R., & Hallum, S. (2008). Perceived teacher self-efficacy as a predictor of job stress and burnout: Mediation analyses. *Applied Psychology, 57*, 152–171. https://doi.org/10.1111/j.1464-0597.2008.00359.x

Schwarzer, R., & Jerusalem, M. (1995). Generalized Self-Efficacy Scale. In J. Weinman, S. Wright, & M. Johnston (Eds.), *Measures in health psychology: A user's portfolio. Causal and control beliefs* (pp. 35–37). NFER-NELSON.

Schwarzer, R., & Luszczynska, A. (2015). The role of self-beliefs and self-regulation in health behavior change. In F. Guay, D. McInerney, R. Craven, & H. Marsh (Eds.), *Self-concept, motivation, and identity: Underpinning success with research and practice* (pp. 201–223). Information Age Publishing.

Schwarzer, R., & Luszczynska, A. (2016). Self-efficacy and outcome expectancies. In Y. Benyamini, M. Johnston, & E.C. Karademas (Eds.), *Assessment in health psychology* (pp. 31–44). Hogrefe.

Schwarzer, R., Schmitz, G., & Daytner, G.T. (1999). *Teacher self-efficacy*. http://userpage.fu-berlin.de/~health/teacher_se.htm

Shelton, S.H. (1990). Developing the construct of general self-efficacy. *Psychological Reports, 66*, 987–994. https://doi.org/10.1177/003329419006600301

Sherer, M., Maddux, J.E., Mercandante, B., Prentice-Dunn, S., Jacobs, B., & Rogers, R.W. (1982). The Self-Efficacy Scale: Construction and validation. *Psychological Reports, 51*(2), 663–671. https://doi.org/10.2466/pr0.1982.51.2.663

Shiffman, S., Balabanis, M.H., Paty, J.A., Engberg, J., Gwaltney, C.J., Liu, K.S., Gnys, M., Hickcox, M., & Paton, S.M. (2000). *Dynamic effects of self-efficacy on smoking lapse and relapse, Health Psychology, 19,* 315–323. https://doi.org/10.1037//0278-6133.19.4.315

Skaalvik, E., & Skaalvik, S. (2016). Teacher stress and teacher self-efficacy as predictors of engagement, emotional exhaustion, and motivation to leave the teaching profession. *Creative Education, 7,* 1785–1799. https://doi.org/10.4236/ce.2016.713182

Talsma, K., Schüz, B., Schwarzer, R., & Norris, K. (2018). I believe, therefore I achieve (and vice versa): A meta-analytic cross-lagged panel analysis of self-efficacy and academic performance. *Learning and Individual Differences, 61,* 136–150. https://doi.org/10.1016/j.lindif.2017.11.015

Te Velde, S.J., Lankhorst, K., Zwinkels, M., Verschuren, O., Takken, T., de Groot, J., & the HAYS Study Group. (2018). Associations of sport participation with self-perception, exercise self-efficacy and quality of life among children and adolescents with a physical disability or chronic disease-a cross-sectional study. *Sports Medicine - Open, 4,* Article 38. https://doi.org/10.1186/s40798-018-0152-1

Tschannen-Moran, M., & Woolfolk Hoy, A. (2001). Teacher efficacy: Capturing an elusive construct. *Teaching and Teacher Education, 17,* 783–805. http://doi.org/10.1016/S0742-051X(01)00036-1 https://doi.org/10.1016/S0742-051X(01)00036-1

Unrau, N.J., Rueda, R., Son, E., Polanin, J.R., Lundeen, R.J., & Muraszewski, A.K. (2018). Can reading self-efficacy be modified? A meta-analysis of the impact of interventions on reading self-efficacy. *Review of Educational Research, 88*(2), 167–204. https://doi.org/10.3102/0034654317743199

Velicer, W.F., DiClemente, C.C., Rossi, J.S., & Prochaska, J.O. (1990). Relapse situations and self-efficacy: An integrative model. *Addictive Behaviors, 15,* 271–283. https://doi.org/10.1016/0306-4603(90)90070-E

Wanous, J.P., Reichers, A.E., & Hudy, M.J. (1997). Overall job satisfaction: How good are single-item measures? *The Journal of Applied Psychology, 82,* 247–252. https://doi.org/10.1037//0021-9010.82.2.247

Warner, L.M., Schüz, B., Wolff, J.K., Parschau, L., Wurm, S., & Schwarzer, R. (2014). Sources of self-efficacy for physical activity. *Health Psychology, 33,* 1298–1308. https://doi.org/10.1037/hea0000085

Warner, L.M., & Schwarzer, R. (2017). Self-efficacy. In A. Wenzel (Ed.), *The Sage encyclopedia of abnormal and clinical psychology* (Vol. 1, pp. 3036–3038). Sage.

West, C.P., Dyrbye, L.N., Satele, D.V., Sloan, J., & Shanafelt, T.D. (2012). Concurrent validity of single-item measures of emotional exhaustion and depersonalization in burnout assessment. *Journal of General Internal Medicine, 27,* 1445–1452. https://doi.org/10.1007/s11606-012-2015-7

Chapter 12

Assessing the Trait of Appreciation of Beauty

Rhett Diessner

Department of Psychology, Lewis-Clark State College, Lewiston, ID, USA

We know beauty is important – but how important? The existential psychologist-philosopher Rollo May, interpreting Plato, wrote: "When Plato considered the great trilogy of Beauty, Truth, and Goodness, he placed Beauty at the top because Beauty is harmony, and whether Truth or Goodness are harmonious is the test of their integrity" (1985, p. 27).

Beauty makes life worth living. The visual, auditory, and olfactory beauty of nature makes life worthwhile; the visual, musical, gustatory works of beautiful art make life a pleasure; the moral beauty demonstrated in acts of human virtue encourages a flourishing and the eudaimonic life.

What Is Appreciation of Beauty?

Positive psychology, following Peterson and Seligman (2004), has typically focused on an appreciation of beauty *and* excellence, which lumps appreciation of beauty with the appreciation of excellence in skills into a single construct of appreciation. Admiration/appreciation of skills overlaps with the appreciation of beauty but is different (Algoe & Haidt, 2009). In this chapter, we focus only on the appreciation of beauty.

Haidt and Keltner (2004) defined appreciation as "the ability to find, recognize, and take pleasure in the existence of goodness in the physical and social worlds" (p. 537). They wrote: "[T]he trait of being emotionally *responsive* to all forms of excellence, including beauty, [i]s appreciation" (p. 538; italics added), and also:

> We think of appreciation as a specific *emotional* responsiveness, the tendency to experience a least subtle self-transcendent emotions such as awe, admiration, and elevation, triggered by the frequent perception of beauty and excellence in one's surroundings. (p. 539)

Güsewell and Ruch (2012), based on their empirical findings, showed that Haidt and Keltner's (2004) emphasis on emotional *responsiveness* is well warranted. Güsewell and Ruch also showed that responsiveness generates multiple channels (physical natural beauty, physical artistic beauty, social moral beauty) of engagement with various forms of beauty. Adler and Fagley (2005) emphasized that appreciation always involves recognizing the value and meaning of the object of appreciation.

Taking these various perspectives into account indicates that appreciation (of beauty) has at least these relevant aspects: (a) It is a *response* to subjectively, and perhaps objectively, beautiful stimuli, (b) appreciation has a cognitive component (recognize, acknowledge, esthetic judgment, a pattern of cognitive processing); (c) there is an emotional component, an emotional responsiveness to beauty, which may be the central component of a beauty experience (Armstrong & Detweiler-Bedell, 2008); (d) appreciation always involves *valuing* the object of the beauty experience.

Positive psychologists have studied three kinds of appreciation of beauty: natural beauty, artistic beauty, and moral beauty (Diessner, Pohling et al., 2018; Güsewell & Ruch, 2012; Haidt & Keltner, 2004). These three domains of appreciation of beauty have significant correlations with each other. For instance, subscales measuring appreciation of natural and artistic beauty, $r=.61$; artistic and moral beauty, $r=.48$; and natural and moral beauty, $r=.65$ (Diessner et al., 2008). The CFA of the Engagement with Beauty Scale (EBS; Diessner et al., 2008) found its three subscales of engagement with natural beauty, artistic beauty, and moral beauty to be distinct factors, while a single second-order factor (EBS total score) explained the correlations among the three factors. Thus, there may be a general trait of appreciation of beauty across domains, but also semidistinct separate traits of appreciating natural, appreciating artistic, and appreciating moral beauty.

Supporting this notion of both a general trait of appreciation of beauty (AoB) and subtraits of AoB is a review of the neuroscience of esthetic appreciation, wherein evidence is presented for both domain generality for when the brain processes esthetics, and also considerable domain specificity (Jacobsen & Beudt, 2017). Regarding domain generality, Ishizu and Zeki's (2011) showed that the medial orbital frontal cortex (mOFC) is a major staging area in the brain for beauty, including the beauty of paintings and music. Other brain-based studies found moral beauty and human facial beauty processed in the mOFC as well (reviewed in Diessner, Pohling et al., 2018).

Another possible domain of AoB is appreciating beautiful ideas (Pohling et al., 2019a). One fMRI study examined beautiful mathematical ideas and found that mathematicians processed them primarily in the mOFC (Zeki et al., 2014). The Noble Prize winner in physics, Frank Wilczek (2015), described how beautiful ideas helped lead him to discover the equations that explain the strong force.

Relevance

> "[Beauty is] central to human life ... I came to view that in writing about beauty as a philosopher, I was addressing the deepest kind of issue there is ... beauty is the only one of the esthetic qualities that is also a virtue, like truth and goodness. It is not simply among the values we live by, but one of the values that defines what a fully human life means." (Danto, 2003, pp. 14–15)

AoB is highly relevant to all three forms of the good life emphasized by positive psychology: a life of hedonic pleasure, the engaged life, and the meaningful life. The pleasures of the senses include the auditory beauty of music, the visual beauty of nature and the arts, the beautiful touch of your lover, not to mention gustatory and olfactory beauty (Diessner et al., 2019). Beauty can completely engage us (Diessner et al., 2008; Diessner, Pohling et al., 2018). And as the philosopher of esthetics Arthur Danto noted (2003), it is deeply meaningful. It is an essential aspect of eudemonia.

Empirically, AoB is intimately connected to transcendence, love, and inquiry (Diessner, Pohling et al., 2018). Martínez-Martí et al. (2016) report evidence that people with high scores on an appreciation of beauty and excellence scale tend to be self-transcendent, get easily absorbed, lose awareness of self and time and self (the engaged life), feel that all creatures are aspects of oneness and are vitalized by spiritual experiences. Other studies showed that AoB is significantly associated with most of the positive psychology character strengths of transcendence, such as spiritual transcendence and gratitude (Diessner et al., 2008) and hope (Diessner et al., 2006).

Regarding love, AoB is significantly correlated with Haidt's moral foundation of care, with the trait of agreeableness, with a love of all humanity, and with empathic concern (Diessner et al., 2013). As to inquisitiveness, McGrath's (2015) factor analysis of over 1 million VIA tests showed that appreciation of beauty and excellence (ABE) loaded most heavily on inquisitiveness and is associated with love of learning and curiosity; although ABE also loaded nearly as strongly on McGrath's caring factor (the love factor) as it did on the inquiry factor. The Openness trait of the Big Five is highly correlated with the AoB (Diessner et al., 2016), and Openness includes the search for truth and the pleasures of the intellect (i.e., inquiry).

The Relevance of Appreciation of Natural Beauty

The Engagement with Natural Beauty (EnB) subscale of the Engagement with Beauty Scale (Diessner et al., 2008) predicts proenvironmental behavior (Diessner, Genthôs et al., 2018), prosocial behavior (Zhang et al., 2014), a variety of forms of well-being (Capaldi et al., 2017; Zhang et al., 2014), connectedness to nature (Capaldi et al., 2017; Diessner et al., 2013; Zhang, Howell et al., 2014), positive emotions and elevating emotions (Passmore & Holder, 2016), mindfulness (Cattron, 2009), and awe (Güsewell & Ruch, 2014). EnB has also been shown to predict connectedness to the sacred and daily spiritual experiences (Feuille, 2013). The national campaign in the UK, *30 Days Wild*, has been shown to increase EnB, validating measurement of the construct as a measure of intervention success (Richardson, & McEwan, 2018).

The Relevance of Appreciation of Artistic Beauty

The Engagement with Artistic Beauty (EaB) subscale of the EBS (Diessner et al., 2008) has been shown to predict openness (Diessner et al., 2013; Zabihian & Diessner, 2016) and self-actualization (Howell et al., 2020). The EaB can also predict being in an artistic profession (e.g., musician, painter, or architect; Güsewell & Ruch, 2012) as well as differentiate professional musicians from nonmusicians (Güsewell & Ruch, 2015).

The Relevance of Appreciation of Moral Beauty

The Engagement with Moral Beauty (EmB) subscale of the EBS (Diessner et al., 2008) has been shown to predict susceptibility to experience the moral emotion of elevation; levels of moral identity; Schwartz values of universalism, benevolence, and spirituality; forgiving others (Diessner et al., 2013); moral identity development (Pohling et al., 2018); engaging with the moral beauty of senior citizens (Diessner et al., 2017); generosity and trust in economic games (Pohling et al., 2019b); preference for experiences over possessions (Howell et al., 2012); and a wide range of transcendent traits and emotions (see review in Diessner, Pohling et al., 2018). EmB also shows negative correlations with saving face (i.e., one's public image; Popov et al., 2016) and with materialism (Diessner et al., 2008).

Assessment Instruments

The assessment of AoB can take a variety forms (for an overview see Table 12.1). The most common is self-report. Peer-report results are available for the ABE of the VIA-IS in German (Ruch et al., 2010) and correlate relatively highly with self-report (r=.55). Peer-report is also available for the NEO-PI Aesthetics facet (McCrae et al., 2011), also with r>.50 with self-report. Self-report of esthetically oriented behavior is also an option and has been related to the ABE (Ruch et al., 2010) and The Desire for Aesthetics Scale (Lundy ct al., 2010; scc below). The actual behavioral observation of esthetic behavior might be the gold standard for empiricists, but little of this has been reported regarding trait AoB. Yet, a known-group study did show that students who electively take art classes score higher on trait engagement with artistic beauty than students not electively taking such classes (Diessner et al., 2008), and active artists also score higher than nonartists on that trait (Zabihian & Diessner, 2016). Another gold standard for assessment of AoB would be a stimulus-based test, one of which exists (Güsewell & Ruch, 2012; see Table 12.1). However, there appear to be no studies utilizing an experiencing sampling methodology (ESM) to relate esthetic behavior or esthetic feelings to trait AoB.

The Esthetics Facet of the Openness Factor of the Big Five or Five-Factor Model

The first popular, reliable, and perhaps valid measure of the personality trait of AoB is the esthetics facet of the Openness scale of the NEO-PI-R (Costa & McCrae, 1992). The NEO-PI-R makes use of a 5-point Likert scale, from 1 (*strongly disagree*) to 5 (*strongly agree*) (Table 12.1). The esthetic facet of the trait of Openness has the highest correlation to the general factor of Openness of any of the Openness facets, indicating that appreciation of esthetics may be the most prototypical trait of Openness (Costa & McCrae, 1992). There are many Big Five or Five-Factor scales besides the NEO-PI-R which have esthetic interest/sensitivity facets, such as the revised the Big Five Inventory (BFI-2; Soto & John, 2017) and Lee and Ashton's (2008) six-factor HEXACO.

The esthetic facet has been shown to predict a wide variety of variables. Low scores on the facet predict cognitive decline and dementia (Williams et al., 2013). Esthetic facet

Table 12.1. Measures of trait appreciation of beauty

Instrument	Author(s)	Number of items	Reliability	Validity	Instrument details
Aesthetics facet of the trait of Openness NEO-PI-R	Costa & McCrae (1992)	8	α: .77 *Test-retest:* .91 for 1 week; .86 for 6 years (McCrae et al., 2011).	Content validity for appreciation of art, a wide variety of nonesthetic predictive validity	7½ items refer to art [music, dance, poetry, art], and ½ question refers to patterns in nature
ABE subscale of the VIA-IS (240 item)	Peterson & Seligman (2004)	10	α: > .70 to .86 *Test-retest:* > .70 for 4 weeks; German version .72 for > 3.5 years (Gander et al., 2020; Ruch et al., 2010).	Strong content validity, concurrent validity, and a variety of predictive validity	3 items general beauty, 1 moral beauty, 1 beauty in a movie, 1 natural beauty, 2 artistic beauty, 1 awe with simple things, and 1 created something of beauty
ABE subscale of the VIA-IS (120 item)	VIA Institute on Character (2018)	5	α: .85 Test-retest information not available	Positive correlation with positive emotions (.31) and no correlation with negative emotions (–.02) (Littman-Ovadia & McGrath, (2015)	1 item natural beauty, 1 beauty in a movie, 2 items beauty in general, and 1 awe with simple things
EBS and EBS-R	Diessner et al. (2008); Pohling et al. (2019a)	EBS – 14 EBS-R – 18	α: .90 (total core);.80–.87 (subscales) *Test-retest:* .85 (total score); .67 to .79 (subscales, 1 week)	Content validity, concurrent validity, and a wide range of predictive validity	4 items on natural beauty, 4 on artistic beauty, 6 on moral beauty, 4 on beautiful ideas
DFAS	Lundy et al. (2010)	36	α: .82 *Test-retest:* .74 (3 months)	Wide content validity, concurrent validity, and a range of predictive validity	18 areas of esthetics: General beauty, architecture, visual art, music/sound quality, literature, films, creating art, traveling/nature, cars, physical attractiveness/dating, food, pets, clothing, stationery, interior décor, college campuses, houses/neighborhoods, and general surroundings.

Table 12.1. continued

Instrument	Author(s)	Number of items	Reliability	Validity	Instrument details
ABET	Güsewell & Ruch (2012)	30	α: the three subscales ranged from .69 (ABET Talent) to .88 (ABET Moral) Test-retest results not available	Strong content validity, and variety of criterion, concurrent, and predictive validity	3 subscales (Art, Talent, and Moral) assessment involves viewing paintings and listening to music excerpts (6 items each) and short poems read by professionals (6 items); reading short stories about people displaying moral goodness or moral beauty (6 items); and watching three short video clips of persons displaying great artistic, sportive or acrobatic skills, or reading short texts describing brilliant persons with particular intellectual or professional talents (6 items).
ABES	Martínez-Martí et al. (2016)	9	α: .89 (total score);.75–.87 (subscales) *Test-retest:* .67 to .79 (subscales, 1 month)	A variety of criterion, concurrent, and predictive validity	3 items tapping AoB in general, 3 on moral beauty, and 3 about nonmoral excellence or skills

Note. ABE = Appreciation of Beauty and Excellence; ABET = Appreciation of Beauty and Excellence Test; ABES = Appreciation of Beauty and Excellence Scale; DFAS = Desire for Aesthetics Scale; EBS = Engagement with Beauty Scale; EBS-R = Engagement with Beauty Scale – Revised; VIA-IS = Values in Action Inventory of Strengths. α = Cronbach's α scores predict a variety of workplace behaviors (Woo et al., 2014) as well as compulsive buying behavior (Otero-López & Pol, 2013). A 24-year longitudinal study found that the esthetic factor was unrelated to one's love life but did predict being motivated to go into nontraditional careers (Schwaba et al., 2019). A study with counselor trainees (Thompson et al., 2002) showed a measure of universal-diverse orientation (UDO; scores reflect an endorsement of acceptance and awareness of the differences and similarities within humanity) strongly correlated with the esthetics facet. As to predicting esthetic preferences, Rawlings et al. (2000) found U.K. college students' esthetics facet scores significantly correlated with liking classical, jazz, and world music, but that college students scores from Barcelona did not significantly correlate with any music genre. On the other hand, Japanese college students' esthetic facet scores also correlated with liking fine art music such as jazz, classical, opera, gospel, and *enka* (Brown, 2012).

Strengths and Weaknesses

The eight questions on the NEO-PI-R Aesthetic facet are 94% about art and 6% about nature. Thus. its face validity focuses on a trait of appreciation of the esthetics of *art*, much more than on appreciation of beauty in general. This could be a strength if trait engagement with artistic beauty is the focus of a study but a disadvantage if the study focuses on trait appreciation of beauty in general. Another strength is the massive amount of research published using Big Five and FFM measures, thus allowing researchers to connect and explain their findings in the context of a wide range of prior studies. A weakness is the paucity of studies predicting esthetic thoughts, feelings, or behavior from the Aesthetic facet.

Appreciation of Beauty and Excellence (ABE) of the VIA-IS

Integrated within the 240-item Values in Action Inventory of Strengths (VIA-IS; Peterson & Seligman, 2004) is the 10-item Appreciation of Beauty and Excellence (ABE) subscale; the ABE uses a 5-point Likert-type scale ranging from 1 (*very much unlike me*) to 5 (*very much like me*) on questions such as "I experience deep emotions when I see beautiful things" and "I see beauty that other people pass by without noticing." Scores can vary from 10 to 50 on the 10-item ABE, with higher scores indicating higher levels of trait AoB (Table 12.1). The ABE taps all of the concepts mentioned in Haidt and Keltner's (2004) theoretical description of ABE:

> We propose that there are three principal types of goodness for which it is beneficial to be responsive: (a) physical beauty (primarily the beauty of the visual environment but also auditory beauty such as music); (b) skill or talent (displays of virtuosity or superhuman ability by other people); and (c) virtue or moral goodness (displays of kindness, compassion, forgiveness, or many of the other virtues in this book). Each of these three kinds of goodness can produce awe-related emotions in observers. (p. 538)

In terms of predictive validity, a large web-based study found that ABE may lessen the negative effects of psychological disorders, such as depression and anxiety. It was found that, when people had suffered from a disorder, only two of the 24 character strengths served as mediators between experiencing the disorder and later moving on to increased life satisfaction: love of learning and ABE (Peterson et al., 2006). Similarly, Huta and Hawley (2010) found only three pretreatment strengths predicted posttreatment recovery from depression: hope, spirituality, and ABE. Pang et al. (2019) found the language used in Twitter tweets (after analyzing almost 4 million tweets from over 4,000 people) could predict ABE fairly well, with the ABE score of $r = .36$ with words relevant to ABE.

Immoderate use/overuse of appreciating beauty predicts obsessive-compulsive behavior (Littman-Ovadia & Freidlin, 2019); however, ABE can also predict a variety of positive emotions, especially awe (Güsewell & Ruch, 2012). ABE is also intimately connected with mindfulness: The more mindful one is, the more one appreciates beauty. And mindfulness training can lead to a substantial increase in AoB (Pang & Ruch, 2019).

Strengths and Weaknesses

The ABE has the strengths of being short, easy to administer, reliable, and has predictive validity. It measures both AoB and appreciation of excellence (skills), which is an advantage if a researcher is interested in those two traits together, but a disadvantage if one wants to focus on simple beauty.

The Engagement with Beauty Scale (EBS and EBS-R)

The 14-item Engagement with Beauty Scale (EBS; Diessner et al., 2008) was the first personality measure entirely dedicated to AoB and the first to contain multiple questions concerning each of the three major domains of beauty (natural, artistic, and moral). A revised version of the EBS was constructed by including a subscale on engagement with beautiful ideas and is currently undergoing validity testing (Pohling et al., 2019a).

The Engagement with Beauty Scale-Revised (EBS-R; Pohling et al., 2019a) is an 18-item self-report scale indicating various levels of cognitive and emotional engagement concerning natural beauty, artistic beauty, moral beauty, and beautiful ideas. It uses a 7-point Likert-type scale ranging from 1 (*very unlike me*) to 7 (*very much like me*) on questions such as "When perceiving beauty in nature I feel changes in my body, such as a lump in my throat, an expansion in my chest, faster heartbeat, or other bodily responses," "When perceiving beauty in a work of art I feel something like a spiritual experience, perhaps a sense of oneness or being united with the universe or a love of the entire world," and "When perceiving an act of moral beauty I find that I desire to become a better person." The Engagement with Moral Beauty subscale scores can range from 6–42, and the other three subscales can range from 4–28; the EBS-R total score ranges from 18–126. Higher scores indicate higher levels of engagement with beauty (Table 12.1).

A range of international studies with translations of the EBS show strong internal consistency and similar factor structure (three first-order factors and a second-order factor) across a variety of cultures, including Russia (Sabadosh, 2016, 2017, 2018), Cyprus, Germany, Iran, Croatia, Samoa, the United States (Richel et al., 2008), and India (Pohling et al., 2019a), although a Chinese sample from Hong Kong showed a single-factor structure (Hui & Diessner, 2015). A variety of studies showed the predictive validity for the original three subscales (reviewed in Diessner, Pohling et al., 2018; also, see the studies cited above in the Relevance section). EBS total score strongly predicts cognitive developmental stages of understanding beauty (Diessner et al., 2016), mildly predicts Kohlbergian moral reasoning stage, and moderately predicts levels of the character strength of fairness (Diessner et al., 2009).

Strengths and Weaknesses

The EBS-R is the only instrument dedicated to the appreciation of beauty; all other measures include items aimed to tap traits other than AoB, such as nonmoral excellence (skills) or other aspects of esthetics. The strengths of the EBS-R lie in the quantity and breadth of studies indicating its predictive validity as well as its availability in several languages. Its main weakness is the same as its strength: It *only* assesses trait AoB and no other esthetic traits, states, or emotions.

The Desire for Aesthetics Scale (DFAS)

Lundy et al. (2010) developed The Desire for Aesthetics Scale to measure esthetic motivation, aiming to reveal levels of how important beauty and/or esthetics are to those who complete it. The finalized scale included 36 items tapping 18 areas of esthetics: general beauty, architecture, visual art, music/sound quality, literature, films, creating art, traveling/nature, cars, physical attractiveness/dating, food, pets, clothing, stationery, interior décor, college campuses, houses/neighborhoods, and general surroundings. Using a 7-point Likert scale, response choices range from *strongly agree* (6) to *strongly disagree* (0), with 3 representing a neutral response (Table 12.1). The authors state that a maximum score of 216 indicates a strong interest in esthetics, 144 shows mild interest, and 108 is neutral. Items include, “Some of my best experiences in life have occurred because of listening to amazing songs” and “I prefer to see films that are immediately entertaining rather than deeply artistic” (reversed). The DFAS has demonstrated predictive validity in a variety of studies, including predicting a

> willingness to travel a long distance to visit a particular museum (.31), self-rating of ability to judge the quality of artistic works (.41), saying one has a large music collection (.24), saying one owns a lot of movies (.21), willingness to wait in line to see a truly artistic film (.28), and interest in wine and/or beer tasting (.22). (Lundy et al., 2010, pp. 84–85)

The DFAS is also effective at predicting esthetic bias (Lundy et al., 2018) and familiarity with music and musicians (Lundy et al., 2018). It has also revealed that esthetic similarity between partners is positively related to relationship satisfaction (Lundy et al., 2013) and other esthetic-related topics (Lundy & Smith, 2017).

Strengths and Weaknesses

A major strength is the wide diversity of esthetic stimuli mentioned in its items, giving strong face validity that the measure into is tapping a general trait of esthetic motivation. It is not the ideal scale for measuring trait AoB, as many of its items do not directly mention beauty (although two-thirds of the items mention beauty or a related term, such as gorgeous, attractive, or ugly [reverse scored]). But because beauty is only one element of esthetics (albeit perhaps the most important), this scale is still excellent for examining the importance of esthetics among research participants. It is relatively quick and easy to administer and score.

The Appreciation of Beauty and Excellence Test (ABET)

The 30-item Appreciation of Beauty and Excellence Test (ABET) was developed (Güsewell & Ruch, 2012) based on the structure of appreciation of beauty and excellence, as described by Haidt and Keltner (2004). It has three subscales: ABET Art (comprising music, paintings, and lyrics), ABET Talent, and ABET Moral (see Table 12.1 for the types of items). It is the first and only reliable and valid stimulus-based test assessing the sensitivity to beautiful paintings and music, excellence in skills and talents, and virtue or moral goodness. It comes in an online format and has strong content validity as well as predictive validity (Güsewell & Ruch, 2012).

The extent to which each of the items (i.e., pictures, musical excerpts, texts, and video clips) elicits the experience of beauty or excellence is rated on a 5-point Likert scale (ranging from 1 = *not at all* to 5 = *absolutely*). The ABET Art subscale has been shown to predict differences between nonartists and musicians and other artists, artistic profession, frequency of concert attendance (Güsewell & Ruch, 2012, 2015), degree of involvement in musical practice, and the ability to differentiate soloists from other musicians (Güsewell & Ruch, 2014).

Strengths and Weaknesses

The ABET has the strongest ecological and construct validity of any beauty measure and is the only stimulus-based and objective measure of AoB. It has solid reliability as well as predictive and concurrent validity. Its main drawbacks are that it is somewhat time-consuming to complete, does not include natural beauty, and is difficult to access the scale. The ABET is in German, which is a nice strength for German speakers (but not so good for non-German speakers).

The Appreciation of Beauty and Excellence Scale (ABES)

Martínez-Martí et al. (2016) developed the Appreciation of Beauty and Excellence Scale (ABES), which is based on Haidt and Keltner's (2004) description of appreciation of beauty and excellence and measures the tendency to appreciate beauty (B), moral excellence (ME), and nonmoral excellence (NME). A sample item to measure AB is "I am a person who is very sensitive to beauty." The scale has shown good validity (construct, factorial, incremental) and reliability (internal and temporal). Responses range from 1 (*completely disagree*) to 7 (*completely agree*) .

Studies of the criterion and concurrent validity of the ABES demonstrated it predicts self-transcendence, Openness, Agreeableness, empathy, tender mindedness, trust, and altruism as well as such well-being states/traits as satisfaction with life, positive emotions, vitality, personal growth, purpose in life, and hope (Martínez-Martí et al., 2016). It has demonstrated predictive validity regarding the effects of an appreciation of beauty intervention (Martínez-Martí et al., 2018).

Strengths and Weaknesses

The ABES is a refined version of the VIA-IS's ABE subscale (Peterson & Seligman, 2004) and has shown incremental validity beyond the ABE (Martínez-Martí et al., 2016). It is short and easy to use and has solid reliability and validity. Any study in which one needs short scales for appreciation of beauty in general, appreciation of moral beauty, and appreciation of skill would find the ABES a useful and valid measure to use. A possible weakness is that the ABES has no items directly tapping natural beauty or artistic beauty, but rather focuses on the main general trait of AoB in its 3-item B subscale.

Future Directions

The predictive validity of most trait AoB measures focuses on nonesthetic behavior and constructs, such as satisfaction with life, or as a buffer to depression or dementia. Such studies are worthwhile, but the field needs more studies that also validate the ability of trait measures to predict esthetic behavior (behavioral observation), such as actually enjoying the beauty of nature, going to museums and appreciating the art, or noticing the moral beauty in others' behavior. A step in that direction is the stimulus-based measure by Güsewell and Ruch (2012), which is currently available only on a web-based platform not available to other researchers.

A possibly neglected thread in AoB is assessing the trait of appreciation of beautiful ideas. A measure has been developed to do so, but validation studies concerning it have not been published (Pohling et al., 2019a). Another neglected area is examining whether traits of appreciating gustatory and olfactory beauty exist. Most researchers have focused on beauty experienced through visual and auditory channels, but there is some evidence that people may experience tastes and scents as "beautiful" (Diessner et al., 2019).

Experience-sampling methodology (ESM) has not been used in the AoB field. Although it relies on self-report, it does have ecological validity, and its use in the study of AoB is warranted.

Schindler et al. (2017) developed a comprehensive measure of esthetic emotions (the AESTHEMOS), with 42 items tapping 21 emotions, ranging from prototypical esthetic emotions to pleasing, epistemic, and negative esthetic emotions. One study (Diessner et al., 2019) briefly examined the relationship between trait AoB and the AETHEMOS, but more such studies are called for.

Perhaps the most important application of AoB currently regards natural beauty. If we loved the beauty of our natural world, would we be more motivated to stop polluting it and take immediate and drastic steps to slow climate change and global warming? There is some evidence that indeed we might (Diessner, Genthôs et al., 2018). Studies that could find ways to increase people's AoB of natural beauty and connectedness to nature, and then orient that increase toward proenvironmental behavior, are crucially needed at this time.

"Beauty will save the world!" (Dostoevsky, 2004, p. 351)

Acknowledgments

I thank Duane Lundy, Maria Louisa Martínez-Martí, and Angelika Güsewell for reading sections of this chapter and giving me feedback. I also thank Kianna Arthur for proofing the whole chapter (twice!). Nevertheless, all infelicities are mine. I also thank two anonymous reviewers who helped improve the content and structure of the chapter.

References

Adler, M.G., & Fagley, N.S. (2005). Appreciation: Individual differences in finding value and meaning as a unique predictor of subjective well-being. *Journal of Personality, 73,* 79–114. https://doi.org/10.1111/j.1467-6494.2004.00305.x

Algoe, S., & Haidt, J. (2009). Witnessing excellence in action: The other-praising emotions of elevation, admiration, and gratitude. *Journal of Positive Psychology, 4,* 105–127. https://doi.org/10.1080/17439760802650519

Armstrong, T., & Detweiler-Bedell, B. (2008). Beauty as an emotion: The exhilarating prospect of mastering a challenging world. *Review of General Psychology, 12,* 305–329. https://doi.org/10.1037/a0012558

Brown, R.A. (2012). Music preferences and personality among Japanese university students. *International Journal of Psychology, 47*(4), 259–268. https://doi.org/10.1080/00207594.2011.631544

Capaldi, C.A., Passmore, H.-A., Ishii, R., Chistopolskaya, K.A., Vowinckel, J., Nikolaev, E.I., & Semikin, G.I. (2017). Engaging with natural beauty may be related to well-being because it connects people to nature: Evidence from three cultures. *Ecopsychology, 9,* 199–211. https://doi.org/10.1089/eco.2017.0008

Cattron, R. (2009). Beauty and mindfulness. *Lewis-Clark State College Undergraduate Student Research Excellence Journal, 2,* 1–15.

Costa, P.T., & McCrae, R.R. (1992). *The Revised NEO Personality Inventory (NEO-PI-R) and NEO Five Factor Inventory (NEO-FFI) professional manual.* Psychological Assessment Resources.

Danto, A.C. (2003). *The abuse of beauty: Esthetics and the concept of art.* Open Court.

Diessner, R., Davis, L., & Toney, B. (2009). Empirical relationships between beauty and justice: Testing Scarry and elaborating Danto. *Psychology of Aesthetics, Creativity and the Arts, 3,* 249–258. https://doi.org/10.1037/a0014683

Diessner, R., Genthôs, R., Arthur, K., Adkins, B., & Pohling, C. (2019). Olfactory and gustatory beauty: Aesthetic emotions and trait appreciation of beauty. *Psychology of Aesthetics, Creativity and the Arts, 15*(1), 38–50. https://doi.org/10.1037/aca0000262

Diessner, R., Genthôs, R., Praest, K., & Pohling, R. (2018). Identifying with nature mediates the influence of valuing nature's beauty on proenvironmental behaviors. *Ecopsychology, 10,* 97–105. https://doi.org/10.1089/eco.2017.0040

Diessner, R., Iyer, R., Smith, M., & Haidt, J. (2013). Who engages with moral beauty? *Journal of Moral Education, 42,* 139–163. https://doi.org/10.1080/03057240.2013.785941

Diessner, R., Kirk, C., Guenthner, C., Pohling, R., & Mobasher, S. (2017). Teaching the psychology of engagement with beauty: State and trait. *Teaching of Psychology, 44,* 63–67. https://doi.org/10.1177/0098628316679969

Diessner, R., Parsons, L., Solom, R., Frost, N., & Davidson, J. (2008). Engagement with beauty: Appreciating natural, artistic and moral beauty. *The Journal of Psychology: Interdisciplinary and Applied, 142,* 303–329. https://doi.org/10.3200/JRLP.142.3.303-332

Diessner, R., Pohling, R., Stacy, S., & Güsewell, A. (2018). Appreciation of beauty: A story of love, transcendence, and inquiry. *Review of General Psychology, 22*(4), 377–397. https://doi.org/10.1037/gpr0000166

Diessner, R., Rust, T., Solom, R., Frost, N., & Parsons, L. (2006). Beauty and hope: A moral beauty intervention. *Journal of Moral Education, 35*(3), 301–317. https://doi.org/10.1080/03057240600874430

Diessner, R., Schuerman, L., Smith, A., Marker, K., Wilson, A., & Wilson, K. (2016). Cognitive-developmental education based on stages of understanding experiences of beauty. *Journal of Aesthetic Education, 50*, 27–52. https://doi.org/10.5406/jaesteduc.50.3.0027

Dostoevsky, F. (2004). *The idiot* (C. Garnett, Trans.). Barnes & Noble Classics. (Original work published ca. 1868–1869).

Feuille, M.H. (2013). *Migraines and mindfulness meditation: Does engaging spirituality make a difference?* Master's thesis, Bowling Green State University. Retrieved from https://etd.ohiolink.edu/!etd.send_file?accession=bgsu1365431728&disposition=inline

Gander, F., Hofmann, J., Proyer, R.T., & Ruch, W. (2020). Character strengths: Stability, change, and relationships with well-being changes. *Applied Research in Quality of Life, 15*(2), 349–367. https://doi.org/10.1007/s11482-018-9690-4

Güsewell, A., & Ruch, W. (2012). Are there multiple channels through which we connect with beauty and excellence? *The Journal of Positive Psychology, 7,* 516–529. https://doi.org/10.1080/17439760.2012.726636

Güsewell, A., & Ruch, W. (2014). Are musicians particularly sensitive to beauty and goodness? *Psychology of Aesthetics, Creativity, and the Arts, 8,* 96–103. https://doi.org/10.1037/a0035217

Güsewell, A., & Ruch, W. (2015). Character strength profiles of musicians and nonmusicians. *Journal of Arts and Humanities, 4*, 1–17. Retrieved from https://www.theartsjournal.org/index.php/site

Haidt, J., & Keltner, D. (2004). Appreciation of beauty and excellence [Awe, wonder, elevation]. In C. Peterson & M.E.P. Seligman (Eds.), *Character strengths and virtues: A handbook of classification* (pp. 537–552). Oxford University Press & American Psychological Association.

Howell, B.M., Diessner, R., & Robinson, R.M. (2020). Self-actualization and the tragedy of beauty. *Journal of Humanistic Psychology, 60*(2), 227–243. https://doi.org/10.1177/0022167817696836

Howell, R.T., Pchelin, R., & Iyer, R. (2012). The preference for experiences over possessions: Measurement and construct validation of the Experiential Buying Tendency Scale. *Journal of Positive Psychology, 7*, 57–71. https://doi.org/10.1080/17439760.2011.626791

Hui, R., & Diessner, R. (2015). Engagement with beauty in Hong Kong. *Indian Journal of Positive Psychology, 6,* 356–360.

Huta, V., & Hawley, L. (2010). Psychological strengths and cognitive vulnerabilities: Are they two ends of the same continuum or do they have independent relationships with well-being and ill-being? *Journal of Happiness Studies, 11*, 71–93. https://doi.org/10.1007/s10902-008-9123-4

Ishizu, T., & Zeki, S. (2011). Toward a brain-based theory of beauty. *PLoS ONE, 6,* e21852. https://doi.org/10.1371/journal.pone.0021852

Jacobsen, T., & Beudt, S. (2017). Domain generality and domain specificity in aesthetic appreciation. *New Ideas in Psychology, 47*, 97–102. https://doi.org/10.1016/j.newideapsych.2017.03.008

Lee, K., & Ashton, M.C. (2008). The HEXACO personality factors in the indigenous personality lexicons of English and 11 other languages. *Journal of Personality, 76*, 1001–1053. https://doi.org/10.1111/j.1467-6494.2008.00512.x

Littman-Ovadia, H., & Freidlin, P. (2019). Positive psychopathology and positive functioning: OCD, flourishing and satisfaction with life through the lens of character strength underuse, overuse and optimal use. *Applied Research in Quality of Life, 15*(2), 529–549. https://doi.org/10.1007/s11482-018-9701-5

Littman-Ovadia, H., & McGrath, R. (2015). Short form of the VIA Inventory of Strengths: Construction and initial tests of reliability and validity. *International Journal of Humanities Social Sciences and Education, 2*(4), 229–237. Retrieved from https://www.arcjournals.org/international-journal-of-humanities-social-sciences-and-education

Lundy, D. E., Allred, G. E., & Peebles, B. L. (2018, June 21). How good is this song? Expertversus nonexpert aesthetic appraisal. *Psychology of Aesthetics, Creativity, and the Arts, 13*(3), 293–304. https://doi.org/10.1037/aca0000181

Lundy, D. E., Barker, B. C., & Glenn, A. J. (2013). The role of aesthetic preferences similarity in attraction. *Empirical Studies of the Arts, 31*(2), 195–221. https://doi.org/10.2190/EM.31.2.e

Lundy, D. E., Schenkel, M. B., Akrie, T. N., & Walker, A. M. (2010). How important is beauty to you? The development of the Desire for Aesthetics Scale. *Empirical Studies of the Arts, 28*, 73–92. https://doi.org/10.2190/EM.28.1.e

Lundy, D. E., & Smith, J. L. (2017). It's tough to be a critic: Professional versus nonprofessional music judgment. *Empirical Studies of the Arts, 35*(2), 139–168. https://doi.org/10.1177/0276237416661989

Lundy, D. E., Stephens, L. A., Hinners, C. T., & Whitton, J. R. (2018). What it means to be (un)professional: The presence of nonaesthetic bias within differing levels of music and film expertise. *Psychology of Aesthetics, Creativity, and the Arts, 12*(2), 205–215. https://doi.org/10.1037/aca0000111

Martínez-Martí, M. L., Avia, M. D., & Hernández-Lloreda, M. J. (2018). Effects of an appreciation of beauty randomized-controlled trial web-based intervention on appreciation of beauty and well-being. *Psychology of Aesthetics, Creativity, and the Arts, 12*(3), 272–283. https://doi.org/10.1037/aca0000164

Martínez-Martí, M. L., Hernández-Lloreda, M. J., & Avia, M. D. (2016). Appreciation of beauty and excellence: Relationship with personality, prosociality and well-being. *Journal of Happiness Studies, 16*, 1–22. https://doi.org/10.1007/s10902-015-9709-6

May, R. (1985). *My quest for beauty.* Saybrook Publishing Company.

McCrae, R. R., Kurtz, J. E., Yamagata, S., & Terracciano, A. (2011). Internal consistency, retest reliability, and their implications for personality scale validity. *Personality and Social Psychology Review, 15*(1), 28–50. https://doi.org/10.1177/1088868310366253

McGrath, R. (2015). Integrating psychological and cultural perspectives on virtue: The hierarchical structure of character strengths. *The Journal of Positive Psychology, 10*, 407–424. https://doi.org/10.1080/17439760.2014.994222

Otero-López, J. M., & Pol, E. V. (2013). Compulsive buying and the five factor model of personality: A facet analysis. *Personality and Individual Differences, 55*(5), 585–590. https://doi.org/10.1016/j.paid.2013.05.005

Pang, D., Eichstaedt, J. C., Buffone, A., Slaff, B., Ruch, W., & Ungar, L. H. (2019). The language of character strengths: Predicting morally valued traits on social media. *Journal of Personality, 88*(2), 287–306. https://doi.org/10.1111/jopy.12491

Pang, D., & Ruch, W. (2019). The mutual support model of mindfulness and character strengths. *Mindfulness, 10*(8), 1545–1559. https://doi.org/10.1007/s12671-019-01103-z

Passmore, H.-A., & Holder, M. D. (2016). Noticing nature: Individual and social benefits of a two-week intervention. *The Journal of Positive Psychology, 11*, 1–10. https://doi.org/10.1080/17439760.2016.1221126

Peterson, C., Park, N., & Seligman, M. E. P. (2006). Greater strengths of character and recovery from illness. *The Journal of Positive Psychology, 1*, 17–26. https://doi.org/10.1080/17439760500372739

Peterson, C., & Seligman, M. E. P. (Eds.). (2004). *Character strengths and virtues. A handbook of classification*. American Psychological Association.

Pohling, R., Diessner, R., Iyer, R., Stacy, S., Woodward, D., & Ströbel, A. (2019a). *Reliability, validity, and measurement invariance of the revised Engagement with Beauty Scale (EBS-R).* Manuscript in preparation.

Pohling, R., Diessner, R., Stacy, S., Woodward, D., & Strobel, A. (2019b). Moral elevation and economic games: The moderating role of personality. *Frontiers in Psychology, section Personality and Social Psychology, 10*, Article 1381. https://doi.org/10.3389/fpsyg.2019.01381

Pohling, R., Diessner, R., & Strobel, A. (2018). The role of gratitude and moral elevation in moral identity development. *International Journal of Behavioral Development, 42*, 405–415. https://doi.org/10.1177/0165025417727874

Popov, V. O., Khona, N. N., & Harnisch, D. L. (2016). Art appreciation: Ability, development and components relating. In Z. Bekirogullari, M. Y. Minas, & R. X. Thambusamy (Eds.), *ICEEPSY 2016: Education and Educational Psychology, vol 16. European Proceedings of Social and Behavioural Sciences* (pp. 810–816). Future Academy. https://doi.org/10.15405/epsbs.2016.11.83

Rawlings, D., Barrantes i Vidal, N., & Furnham, A. (2000). Personality and aesthetic preference in Spain and England: Two studies relating sensation seeking and openness to experience to liking for paintings and music. *European Journal of Personality, 14,* 553–576. https://doi.org/10.1002/1099-0984(200011/12)14:6_553::AID-PER384_3.0.CO;2-H

Richardson, M., & McEwan, K. (2018). 30 days wild and the relationships between engagement with nature's beauty, nature connectedness and well-being. *Frontiers in Psychology, 9,* Article 1500. https://doi.org/10.3389/fpsyg.2018.01500

Richel, T., Diessner, R., Merchi, J., Dachs, I., Addison, D., Wilson, K., & Nasrullah, S. (2008, March). *International reliability studies of the Engagement with Beauty Scale (EBS).* Poster session presented at the International Counseling Psychology Conference, Chicago, IL.

Ruch, W., Proyer, R. T., Harzer, C., Park, N., Peterson, C., & Seligman, M. E. P. (2010). Values in action inventory of strengths (VIA-IS): Adaptation and validation of the German version and the development of a peer-rating form. *Journal of Individual Differences, 31,* 138–149. https://doi.org/10.1027/1614-0001/a000022.

Sabadosh, P. A. (2016). Engagement with beauty: Natural, artistic, moral, ideal ... How long is the list in Russian? *International Journal of Psychology, 51*(S1), 62. https://doi.org/10.1002/ijop.12296

Sabadosh, P. A. (2017). A Russian version of the Engagement with Beauty Scale: The multitrait-multimethod model. *Psychology: Journal of the Higher School of Economics, 14,* 7–21. https://doi.org/10.17323/1813-8918.2017.1.7.21

Sabadosh, P. A. (2018). Aesthetic responsiveness in Russian and Azerbaijani youths [Elektronnyi resurs] [article in Russian, abstract in English]. *Sovremennaia zarubezhnaia psikhologiia, 7*(2), 90–99. https://doi.org/10.17759/jmfp.2018070209

Schindler, I., Hosoya, G., Menninghaus, W., Beermann, U., Wagner, V., Eid, M., & Scherer, K. R. (2017). Measuring aesthetic emotions: A review of the literature and a new assessment tool. *PLoS ONE, 12*(6), e0178899. https://doi.org/10.1371/journal.pone.0178899

Schwaba, T., Robins, R. W., Grijalva, E., & Bleidorn, W. (2019). Does Openness to Experience matter in love and work? Domain, facet, and developmental evidence from a 24-year longitudinal study. *Journal of Personality, 87*(5), 1074–1092. https://doi.org/10.1111/jopy.12458

Soto, C. J., & John, O. P. (2017). The next Big Five Inventory (BFI-2): Developing and assessing a hierarchical model with 15 facets to enhance bandwidth, fidelity, and predictive power. *Journal of Personality and Social Psychology, 113*(1), 117–143. https://doi.org/10.1037/pspp0000096

Thompson, R. L., Brossart, D. F., Carlozzi, A. F., & Miville, M. L. (2002). Five-factor model (Big Five) personality traits and universal-diverse orientation in counselor trainees. *Journal of Psychology, 136*(5), 561–572. https://doi.org/10.1080/00223980209605551

VIA Institute on Character. (2018). *VIA assessments psychometrics.* Author. Retrieved from https://www.viacharacter.org/www/VIA-Assessments-Psychometrics

Wilczek, F. (2015). *A beautiful question: Finding nature's deep design.* Penguin.

Williams, P. G., Suchy, Y., & Kraybill, M. L. (2013). Preliminary evidence for low openness to experience as a pre-clinical marker of incipient cognitive decline in older adults. *Journal of Research in Personality, 47,* 945–951. https://doi.org/10.1016/j.jrp.2013.09.006

Woo, S. E., Chernyshenko, O. S., Stark, S. E., & Conz, G. (2014). Validity of six openness facets in predicting work behaviors: A meta-analysis. *Journal of Personality Assessment, 96*(1), 76–86. https://doi.org/10.1080/00223891.2013.806329

Zabihian, S., & Diessner, R. (2016). Engagement with beauty and levels of happiness among artists in the U. K. *Global Journal of Human-Social Science: Arts & Humanities, 16,* 1–9. Retrieved from http://globaljournals.us/index.php?option_com_content&view_article&id_89&Itemid_73

Zeki, S., Romaya, J.P., Benincasa, D.M., & Atiyah, M.F. (2014). The experience of mathematical beauty and its neural correlates. *Frontiers of Human Neuroscience, 8*, Artcile 68. https://doi.org/10.3389/fnhum.2014.00068

Zhang, J.W., Howell, R.T., & Iyer, R. (2014). Engagement with natural beauty moderates the positive relation between connectedness with nature and psychological well-being. *Journal of Environmental Psychology, 38*, 55–63. https://doi.org/10.1016/j.jenvp.2013.12.013

Zhang, J.W., Piff, P.K., Iyer, R., Koleva, S., & Keltner, D. (2014). An occasion for unselfing: Beautiful nature leads to prosociality. *Journal of Environmental Psychology, 37*, 61–72. https://doi.org/10.1016/j.jenvp.2013.11.008

Chapter 13

Assessing Posttraumatic Growth

Sara Etz Mendonca, A. Demaske, Emma Sims, and Eranda Jayawickreme

Department of Psychology, Wake Forest University, Winston-Salem, NC, USA

Research in positive psychology has grown exponentially in the past two decades. Notably, researchers, and clinical psychologists in particular, have been interested in understanding the impact of positive change after adversity. Logically, this would be a fruitful area of inquiry given that experiencing hardship and trauma is an ubiquitous feature of life (Jayawickreme & Blackie, 2014). Moreover, most people recover from their adversity within an acceptable amount of time, and some individuals may even benefit from the difficulty they experienced (Boals & Schuler, 2018). Despite myriad studies and the creation of multiple measures, posttraumatic growth is still a relatively new construct in psychology, with interest in the idea starting to take hold in the late 1980s (e.g., Frazier & Burnett, 1994; Tedeschi & Calhoun, 1996).

Tedeschi and Calhoun's (2004) conceptualization of posttraumatic growth (PTG) is perhaps the most prominent in the field, and their Post-Traumatic Growth Inventory (PTGI) is the most widely cited in recent research (Infurna & Jayawickreme, 2019; Jayawickreme & Blackie, 2016). They define PTG as positive psychological change posttrauma and measure it by examining five distinct life domains: personal relationships, personal strength, spirituality/religiosity, life appreciation, and new life possibilities (Tedeschi & Calhoun, 1996). Of note, some variation in this five-domain PTG structure has been observed across cultures, in part because of differences in spiritual, religious, and existential concerns (Tedeschi et al., 2017). Conceptualized in this way, PTG is different from resilience or optimism or other traits that allow people to cope with adversity healthily because people are posited to experience positive changes, or growth, beyond their baseline personality pretrauma. Additionally, it may be possible for PTG to occur while the individual is experiencing negative reactions to trauma, including symptoms of posttraumatic stress. Tedeschi and Calhoun (2004) justify the co-occurrence of positive and negative changes in multiple domains by arguing that PTG occurs by restructuring the core schemas that individuals use for understanding, meaning, and decision-making. Experiencing trauma can challenge people's sense of identity, future, safety, predictability, and controllability of their world.

This chapter provides a broad view of the main assessments used in PTG research and then briefly presents some key results found using the measures. We also examine the controversy surrounding what may be measured using certain assessments of PTG vs. what is thought to be measured (e.g., Infurna & Jayawickreme, 2019). The debate centers around whether the positive *retrospective* changes individuals report following adversity in these assessments are associated with actual positive changes in personality. The beliefs about growth captured in these measures may *not* be related to meaningful changes in behavior; therefore, we present assessment tools that may push science further by more accurately measuring actual change (Jayawickreme & Blackie, 2016).

Current Measures

Beyond Tedeschi and Calhoun's conceptualization and measurement of PTG, researchers have used other terms to describe the positive psychological changes resulting from coping with a variety of life challenges, such as thriving, benefit-finding, or stress-related growth (Abraído-Lanza et al., 1998; Park et al., 1996). Moreover, the way researchers have chosen to examine the phenomenon and create scales differs in areas as basic as deeming important the creation of a way to measure both positive and negative change to creating scales specifically adapted to assess the effect of one disease or traumatic event (Frazier et al., 2001; Mohr et al., 1999). By only assessing positive transformation after a struggle, only part of the potential change in each individual is considered and may misrepresent the overall adjustment after coping with the event. As noted, some research has focused narrowly on populations dealing with chronic illnesses such as arthritis or multiple sclerosis. These scales are valuable, but, clearly, caution must be taken when applying them to individuals dealing with other issues, regardless of whether they involve chronic health issues. The differing viewpoints of researchers on how to assess positive transitions after adversity also led to variation in domains and which domains are most important to examine.

When examining the various scales created to measure PTG, it must be kept in mind that crossover exists in many domains identified using both exploratory and confirmatory factor analyses, such as growth in personal relationships. Nevertheless, differences can also be found. For example, while focusing on psychological well-being more specifically, Joseph et al. (2012) discovered six domains when creating the Psychological Well-Being/ Post-Traumatic Changes Questionnaire (PWB-PTC): self-acceptance, life purpose, personal growth, environmental mastery, autonomy, and relationships – as opposed to the five domains of the PTGI. This perspective views humans as active and developing beings who both want to integrate their schemas and experiences into one sense of self and also innately pursue well-being and fulfillment. This circumstance is found through the pursuit of PWB in the wake of trauma. The new self-concept that is created through this pursuit of PWB is subsequently perceived as more authentic to the self (Joseph & Linley, 2005). Given the different conceptualizations, domains, and forms of measurement used by researchers, it is interesting to note that many scales were created using previously established measures as a base, such as with the PWB-PTC.An overview of measures for the assessment of posttraumatic growth is presented in Table 13.1.

Table 13.1. Overview of measures on posttraumatic growth

Measure	Authors	Number of items	Growth domains	Internal reliability	Convergent validity	Discriminant validity	Incremental validity
Benefit-Finding Scale (for patients with multiple sclerosis)	Mohr et al. (1999)	48	• Demoralization • Deterioration in relationships • Benefit-finding	$\alpha = .87$	Yes	No	No
Benefit-Finding in Breast Cancer Scale	Tomich & Helgeson (2004)	20	• Personal priorities • Daily activities (interest) • Family (sensitivity) • World views • Relationships	$\alpha = .95$	Yes	No	No
Changes in Outlook Questionnaire (CiOP)	Joseph et al. (2005)	26 (11 pos., 15 neg.)	• Positive changes • Negative changes	$\alpha = .86–.88$ $\alpha = .83(+)$ $\alpha = .90\ (–)$	Yes	Yes	No
Posttraumatic Life Change Measure	Frazier, Conlon, & Glaser (2001)	17	• Self • Relationships • Beliefs • Spirituality	$\alpha = .91$	Yes	Yes	No
Posttraumatic Growth Inventory (PTGI)	Tedeschi & Calhoun (1996)	21	• Relating to others • New possibilities • Personal strength • Spiritual change • Appreciation of life	$\alpha = .90$	Yes	Yes	No

Table 13.1. continued

Measure	Authors	Number of items	Growth domains	Internal reliability	Convergent validity	Discriminant validity	Incremental validity
Psychological Well-Being – Post-Traumatic Changes Questionnaire (PWB-PTCQ)	Joseph et al. (2012)	18	• Self-acceptance • Autonomy • Purpose in life • Relationships • Personal growth • Sense of mastery	α = .87–.95	Yes	Yes	Yes
Stress-Related Growth Scale (SRGS)	Park et al. (1996)	50	• Personal resources • Social relationships • Coping skills	α = .94	Yes	No	No
Thriving Scale	Abraido-Lanza et al. (1998)	20	• Appreciation: family • Appreciation: life • Appreciation: friends • Positive attitude • Personal strength • Enhance spirituality • Empathy • Patience	α = .92	Yes	No	No

Note. α = Cronbach's α

Assessments of Posttraumatic Growth

The Benefit-Finding Scale (Mohr et al., 1999)

This scale was developed using qualitative responses to open-ended questions provided by patients with multiple sclerosis focusing on how they changed as a person and how their relationships changed over time as a result of the disease. Psychosocial effects were broken down into two negative sections and one positive section: demoralization (distress, helplessness, subjective incompetence, decreased self-esteem, alienation), deterioration in relationships (personal inadequacy, victimization by partner), and benefit-finding (deepening of relationships, enhanced appreciation of life, spiritual focus). Importantly, the patients reported benefit-finding twice as often as demoralization and three times as often deterioration. Benefit-finding was positively related to adaptive coping strategies, but unexpectedly it was also positively related to higher levels of anxiety, anger, and unemployment, yet unrelated to depression.

The Benefit-Finding in Breast Cancer Scale (Tomich & Helgeson, 2004)

This scale was created using growth items from Behr's Positive Contribution Scale (Behr et al., 1992. Benefit-finding was conceptualized as being focused on positive changes experienced because of trauma caused specifically by cancer diagnosis. Growth domains represented in the scale are personal priorities, interest in daily activities, sensitivity to family issues, concern about humankind, and relationships. Upon examining patients at three timepoints postdiagnosis, the authors found correlations between the scale and demographic variables, such that SES and race were associated with benefit-finding at baseline. Women with a lower SES perceived more benefits, and African American and Hispanic women perceived more benefits, but worse physical functioning, than Caucasian women after diagnosis. Women diagnosed with more severe disease identified more benefits than those with less severe disease, but for those with more severe disease, greater benefit-finding was related to greater negative affect and worse mental functioning over time. In addition, benefit-finding was associated with more negative affect at baseline. This study showed how the more severe the disease, the more benefits found from it (Tomich & Helgeson, 2004).

The Changes in Outlook Post-Trauma Questionnaire (CiOQ; Joseph et al., 2005)

Joseph et al. (2005) developed the items for this measure by asking survivors of disaster how their lives had changed and designed it specifically to assess both positive and negative changes, intending to measure schematic change. Importantly, no statistically significant relationship was found between the positive and negative changes scales, suggesting that they were independent dimensions. Results from studies conducted to specifically examine internal reliability and convergent and discriminant validity suggest sound psychometric properties. The two scales were posited to be related to measures of psychopathology. They found evidence indicating that the negative change scale was positively related to measures of distress, intrusion, avoidance, and arousal, with positive changes related only to intrusion (Joseph et al., 2005).

The Posttraumatic Life Change Measure (Frazier et al., 2001)

This measure was developed using both open-ended responses from female sexual assault survivors and extant literature examining changes following traumatic events (Frazier et al., 1994). The measure was designed to look at both negative and positive changes over time, and in this study, it was used at four time points posttrauma to determine the importance of timing in PTG. Items were grouped into five domains: self, relationship, spirituality, empathy, and beliefs. Distress was assessed by measuring PTSD and depression. Notably, even just 2 weeks posttrauma some positive changes were reported (increased empathy, better relationships, greater life appreciation). Over time, positive changes increased and negative changes decreased, whereas significant variability was found between individuals in domains and change patterns. The greatest change was seen between 2 weeks and 2 months. Both positive and negative changes were related to distress, with the relationship stronger for negative changes (positive changes mean less distress, negative changes mean more distress). Negative changes were seen as far as 1-year posttrauma, including negative beliefs about the goodness of others and safety/fairness of the world. Those who indicated higher levels of positive change at 2 weeks and 12 months postassault reported the least distress at 12 months. Interestingly, the distress of those who failed to maintain positive changes from 6 to 12 months intensified over time, but in those who never experienced positive changes, it did not demonstrate an increase over time.

The Posttraumatic Growth Inventory (PTGI; Tedeschi and Calhoun, 1996)

The PTGI is likely the most widely used scale to assess PTG. Tedeschi and Calhoun (1996) were inspired by their clinical work with patients who had experienced traumatic events and reviewed extant literature to create their measure related to areas of positive perceived change in the domains (see Table 13.1). No relationship was observed between the PTGI and age of participant nor time since the tragic event. Women's scores were significantly higher than men's scores on all domains except for new possibilities. The PTGI was not related to social desirability nor neuroticism, but it was positively associated with optimism, religiosity, and all major dimensions of personality except for neuroticism. There were several relationships between scoring high on PTGI dimensions and personality traits as assessed by the NEO-PI. Specifically, all domains were positively associated with optimism and extraversion. In addition, openness to experience was positively associated with new possibilities and personal strength, relating to others was positively related to agreeableness, and personal strength was associated with conscientiousness. Finally, spiritual change was positively associated with religiosity. It is worth noting a 10-item short-form of this measure was developed in 2010 (Cann et al., 2010).

The Psychological Well-Being – Post-Traumatic Changes Questionnaire (PWB-PTCQ; Joseph et al., 2012)

The PWB-PTCQ was designed to assess not only the absence of negative functioning, but the presence of positive psychological functioning based on Ryff's conceptualization of PWB considering six domains: self-acceptance, autonomy, purpose in life, relationships, sense of mastery, and personal growth. The advantages of this scale include an established concept framework, a PTG definition that incorporates PWB and positive psychology, evidence of incremental validity, and positive and negative respondent ratings. To establish convergent validity, the researchers found that higher scores on the PWB-PTCQ were positively associated with scores on the PTGI and the CiOP but lower scores on the CiON. Higher scores on the PWB-PTCQ were also positively associated with self-esteem, optimism, reappraisal, and, in contrast, lower scores on neuroticism. Higher scores were also positively associated with gratitude and authenticity. The was no connection between responses to this scale and social desirability. Incremental validity was demonstrated over and above existing growth measures when predicting SWB. There was a moderate correlation between this scale and actual change determined by changes in Ryff's PWB scale, indicating that actual change and perceived change are not interchangeable (Joseph et al., 2012).

Stress-Related Growth Scale (SRGS; Park et al., 1996)

Park et al. (1996) posited that three main positive outcomes can result from stress: enhanced social resources, personal resources, and new/improved coping skills. Half of the items in the scale reflect positive changes in personal resources, and the rest of the items are divided equally between positive changes in social relationships and coping skills. This conceptual model of growth includes a person's characteristics, environmental characteristics, trauma characteristics, coping behavior, and acceptance. Notably, as with other measures, women reported higher scores than men. The SRGS was positively correlated with participants' ratings of the targeted negative events' initial stressfulness. Importantly, this is the only scale that used informants to establish validity and found that participant-informant SRGS scores reached significant intrapair agreement on many items. One study conducted to establish the scale collected data at two time points 6 months apart. At time 1 and time 2, SRGS was positively correlated with event-related growth, intrinsic religiousness, positive affectivity, and social support satisfaction. At time 2, SRGS was positively associated with optimism, the number of social support sources, the impact of event scale, number of positive life events, coping strategies, acceptance, positive reinterpretation, and religious coping. Predictors that were significantly related to SRGS include intrinsic religiousness, social support satisfaction, initial stress, positive reinterpretation, acceptance coping, and recent positive life events. Time 2 SRGS scores predicted time 2 positive change in optimism, positive affectivity, satisfaction with social support, and the number of social support scores in demonstrating the validity of the SRGS (Park et al.,1996).

The Thriving Scale (Abraido-Lanza et al., 1998)

When creating this scale, the authors operationalized thriving as a value-added model, where people grow beyond baseline and find strength, insight, and life-meaning despite dealing with multiple adversities, in this case, chronic poverty and arthritis. Researchers used open-ended questions to determine how participants may have thrived and then examined possible crossover in domains established with the PTGI and SRGS. Four factors were established with eight domains: appreciation for family, life, and friends; gained positive attitude; personal growth and strength; enhanced spirituality; more empathy; and more patience. The sample narrowly focused on Latinas to determine what social/cultural and personal resources promote thriving. Thriving did not demonstrate a relationship with age, illness characteristics, or sociocultural resources (emotional support, disability acceptance, acculturation) but did have a positive relationship with personal competence resources (self-esteem/self-efficacy), and psychological well-being. Greater self-esteem predicted thriving. In contrast, negative affect contributed to a decrease in both self-esteem and self-efficacy but did not affect thriving. In addition, positive affect had a direct effect on thriving but did not contribute to any of the competence measures. Psychological well-being (as opposed to ill-being) also encouraged thriving. Illness characteristics were not related to thriving, neither were sociocultural resources.

Challenges of Current Assessment Strategies

There are multiple issues with measures commonly used in PTG research which must be addressed if PTG research is going to move forward and accurately measure this important phenomenon. Despite promising psychometric properties, such as strong internal consistency and test-retest reliability, retrospective self-reports may suggest that individuals have experienced growth when, in fact, they have not (Boals & Schuler, 2018; Jayawickreme & Blackie, 2014). This is a real concern considering that the most commonly used measures, the PTGI (Tedeschi & Calhoun, 1996) and the SRGS (Park, Cohen, and Murch, 1996), are both retrospective self-report surveys. Beyond illusory growth, the lack of longitudinal data with baselines established before the trauma occurred presents challenges to researchers and participants alike (Ford et al., 2008). Lastly, the wording of questions or statements on measures may be such that participants are primed to respond in a positive manner creating a misrepresentation of true growth.

Retrospective Self-Reported Change

As with all events, individuals experience traumatic events through their own lens and based on their own perspective and personal biases, and this is no different for PTG. In addition to subjective viewpoints that may distort reality, living through a stressful situation is taxing and already presents study participants with potential emotional challenges when asked to recollect how they felt in the moment, not to mention the cognitive demands. Tennen and Affleck (2009) outlined five steps respondents must take to complete a retrospective PTG questionnaire: (1) assess their current state, (2) accurately recall their previous, pretrauma state, (3) compare the two, (4) assess the degree of difference, (5) judge to what degree the change occurred because of trauma. Confusion or inaccuracies in any one of these could lead to error. Thus, researchers use this type of scale expecting that participants can recall previous trait levels accurately (Infurna & Jayawickreme, 2019). However, studies have demonstrated that self-reported perceptions of change are often only weakly associated with actual change (Jayawickreme & Blackie, 2014).

Frazier et al. (2009) examined this issue more closely in a significant study highlighting the need for improved measures. They evaluated the construct validity of PTG by examining the difference from pretrauma to posttrauma between perceived growth and actual growth using five measures thought to assess the distinct concepts that encompass PTG (Boals & Schuler, 2018). Surprisingly, they found that PTGI scores tended not to be associated with actual growth in PTG-related domains. Importantly, when growth was perceived, it was related to increased distress pretrauma to posttrauma. In contrast, actual growth was associated with decreased distress. This critical difference suggests that different processes are responsible for perceived growth vs. actual growth. Moreover, the people who *reported* growth were not always the same people who *showed* growth. Other studies provide evidence of the same issue (Blackie et al., 2015).

Data were collected from patients who had suffered spinal-cord injuries, using the short-form PTGI along with measures assessing self-efficacy and purpose in life, constructs related to PTG, at three time points (Kunz et al., 2019). In line with Frazier et al. (2009), the researchers found only a small correlation between PTG and changes in self-efficacy and purpose in life. The discrepancies between perceived and measured PTG question the reliability of retrospective reports as a whole. Additional studies demonstrate the dissociation between experienced change and the perception of it (Henry et al., 1994; Herbst et al., 2000; Robins et al., 2005). For example, in a study focused on the stability of adult personality, although participants fell into three different profiles of self-reported perceived change – stayed the same, changed a little, changed a lot – stability coefficients were virtually the same between groups (Herbst et al., 2000). Thus, it is unclear why claims are made about positive psychological changes when they have been measured with retrospective measures of PTG, because such measures are often found to be only weakly associated with actual change (Jayawickreme & Blackie, 2014).

Demand Characteristics

When considering problematic perceptions of growth that may or may not have happened, it is important to examine various sources of this mismeasurement and misinformation. The inherent social desirability of experiencing and demonstrating growth after trauma may lead to participant response that is biased in favor of change (McLean & Syed, 2015). Western society, particularly the United States, is dominated by a cultural script in favor of strength being gained as a result of adversity (Jayawickreme & Blackie, 2014). Even retrospective self-perceived measures may reflect a certain amount of change, though they are also plagued by selective appraisals, adaptive and maladaptive coping strategies, distorted reality, individual personality characteristics, individual implicit theories of change, and tendencies to disparage past selves to report positive growth (Tennen & Affleck, 2009). Furthermore, participating in a research study may bias response because reflecting on growth may be an artifact of the study itself prompted by measure items (Infurna & Jayawickreme, 2019). It is difficult to accept that difficulty and strife had no meaning, yet these experiences are equally valid. If we are to truly study PTG, our measures must be sensitive and give a platform to nongrowth experiences. Unfortunately, most scales do not allow for such responses promoting the likelihood of skewed data.

Scales that only include positively-worded items create *demand characteristics* priming respondents to answer more positively than they otherwise would (Jayawickreme & Blackie, 2014). These demand characteristics positively skew scales and inflate reports of PTG, leading to flawed measures and biased results. Therefore, the PTGI and SRGS both implicitly and explicitly promote reports of PTG which are likely only illusory (Boals & Schuler, 2018). With a lack of neutral wording on measures, the positively worded items only allow for reports of positive change.

Lack of Longitudinal Studies

With few exceptions (e.g., Frazier et al., 2001), there is a dearth of longitudinal studies focused on the timing at which growth begins. PTG literature expounds on the benefits of growth after adversity but has yet to explicate the path this growth takes (Infurna & Jayawickreme, 2019). Most studies that considered longitudinal data assessed growth from 2 months to 1 year posttrauma; however, pretrauma data are missing which would give a full picture of growth. A 2006 meta-analysis focused only on cross-sectional studies because of the paucity of longitudinal studies found (Helgeson et al., 2006). This lack of longitudinal studies is concerning beyond the complications of accurate measurement. Fundamentally, posttraumatic growth is growth – change – over time. More longitudinal studies have been published since 2006, but they remain underrepresented and mostly lack crucial pretrauma data that would allow researchers to examine growth more accurately using posttrauma growth-relevant domains (Jayawickreme & Blackie, 2014). For a more valid assessment, studies should incorporate longitudinal measures, ideally multiple points before and after events.

Control Groups

Control groups should be used to provide a baseline, particularly when cross-sectional data are used, yet this is rarely done in PTG research (Jayawickreme & Blackie, 2014). This is problematic because most of the evidence provided for PTG has been drawn from data from participants who completed retrospective measures but were not compared with a group that did not. Cordova et al. (2001) used an age- and education-level matched control group when examining women who had gone through breast cancer treatment. They also measured concurrent self-reported social support, depression, well-being in personal growth, purpose in life, and self-acceptance. They found no difference between the two groups in depression or well-being, but the breast cancer patients had higher reports of PTG, which suggests that PTG is caused by different mechanisms than depression or well-being. Such findings could not have been found with only one group.

Improved Scales

Some scales address some of the limitations of the PTGI and other similar scales through the use of bipolar items and more neutral wording, limiting priming redemptive narratives, and giving researchers more flexible, state-based measures.

The Stress-Related Growth Scale – Revised (SRGS-R) (Boals & Schuler, 2018)

This measure has neutral wording in the items to avoid implying positive change and to limit demand characteristics. Moreover, a bipolar scale includes both positive and negative effects. The SRGS-R is a better indicator than the PTGI as it seems to capture adaptive perceived growth as opposed to illusory perceived growth. In contrast to the PTGI, which was positively related to PTSD symptoms but not related to depression, anxiety, global distress, or quality of life, the SRGS-R was significantly related to less depression, anxiety, global distress, and greater quality of life. Furthermore, the SRGS-R was negatively related to symptoms of PTSD. Convergent validity scores are acceptable and like those of the PTGI and SRGS.

The PTGI-42 – State Measure (Blackie et al., 2017)

An experience-sampling methodology was used to create a state measure of PTG to capture high-resolution, momentary standings on PTG dimensions by asking participants what they are thinking and feeling in the moment, using the same five PTG domains as the original PTGI. The purpose was to capture the degree to which PTG was demonstrated in individuals' everyday lives after as a result of a recent stressful or traumatic incident by asking participants whether, in the last 30 min, they had experienced a stressful event, along with follow-up questions. The newly developed state measure of PTG had a comparable factor structure to trait PTG, and there was significant variability in individuals' PTG moment-to-moment. However, individuals' trait PTG was unrelated to their state PTG. The state level uses the same information and rating scales used at the trait level (PTGI-42) (Blackie et al., 2017).

Conclusion

Although still too focused on using retrospective self-report measures, research on posttraumatic growth is evolving and learning to understand the need to move on from complete reliance on exploratory observations and positively-focused scales. The PTGI is still the most widely used scale, but other scales are available that take both positive and negative changes into account or examine particular phenomena such as specific chronic illnesses. Researchers have expanded the scope of life events into more neutral and even positive life events. This expansion has and should continue to be aided through the analysis of large-scale samples.

Researchers should seek a better understanding of what self-perceived PTG is both theoretically and empirically. Researchers should also continue to refine methods and measures to distinguish between adaptively and maladaptively perceived growth. This can be done by integrating multiple methods into data collection, including informant reports and experience-sampling. Finally, researchers should look to integrate methods of other disciplines into PTG research, seeking to create a wholistic theory of personal growth.

Future Directions

Improvements can be made to study design with some simple modifications. For example, incorporating control groups drawn from the larger initial sample would allow researchers to determine whether the growth found stems from trauma. Moreover, informant reports should be incorporated whenever possible, taking into consideration the danger of informants being influenced by the targets and the relationship between the informant and target. In addition, collecting data more often allows researchers to discover whether PTG occurs within hours, years, or continuously after the initial event through the use of path modeling (Roisman & Fraley, 2013).

There has been an increased focus on longitudinal research, and this area of study should continue to grow. Although a meta-analysis of posttraumatic change focused on cross-sectional studies because of the dearth of longitudinal ones (Helgeson et al., 2006), a subsequent meta-analysis examined 122 longitudinal studies (Mangelsdorf et al., 2019). One option for improving longitudinal studies is to use an existing dataset. Samples from existing longitudinal datasets are often large, representative, diverse, and include three or more waves of data. These measures provide researchers the opportunity to map the psychological trajectories of life events, including trajectories of PTG. While often without specialized PTG measures, proxies such as well-being or depression can be used (Seery et al., 2010).

Researchers should broaden their methodology beyond trait measures of PTG and work to capture PTG day-to-day. Experience-sampling and day-reconstruction are two methods to this end. Experience-sampling enables researchers to gain a real-time view of possible growth, and with technology such as computers and smartphones, this method has become more viable. Similar to experience-sampling, the day-reconstruction method combines the activity-based data of experience-sampling with techniques of time-budget measurement (Kahneman et al., 2004). Participants systematically recall their activities of the previous day, using procedures to minimize recall bias. While it has had limited use in PTG research, its use in capturing participants' daily life has been proposed (Jayawickreme & Blackie, 2014).

Lastly, researchers should broaden the events studied to encompass both nontraumatic stressors and positive events. While highly traumatic events are being reported, previous research indicates that moderate stressors may be illuminating as well. Moreover, studies indicate that the relationship between growth and stress may be a U-shaped curve (Seery et al., 2010), so moderate adversity may provide important examples of growth going forward.

References

Abraído-Lanza, A. F., Guier, C., & Colón, R. M. (1998). Psychological thriving among Latinas with chronic illness. *Journal of Social Issues, 54*(2), 405–424. https://doi.org/10.1111/0022-4537.741998074

Behr, S. K., Murphy, D. L., & Summers, J. A. (1992). *User's manual: Kansas Inventory of Parental Perceptions (KIPP)*. Resource document. Lawrence, K.S.: Beach Center on Families and Disability. https://beachcenter.lsi.ku.edu/sites/default/files/KIPP%20manual.pdf

Blackie, L. E. R., Jayawickreme, E., Helzer, E. G., Forgeard, M. J. C., & Roepke, A. M. (2015). Investigating the veracity of self-perceived posttraumatic growth: A profile analysis approach to corroboration. *Social Psychological and Personality Science, 6*(7), 788–796. https://doi.org/10.1177/1948550615587986

Blackie, L. E. R., Jayawickreme, E., Tsukayama, E., Forgeard, M. J., Roepke, A. M., Fleeson, W. (2017). Posttraumatic growth as positive personality change: Developing a measure to assess within-person variability. *Journal of Research in Personality, 69*, 22–32. https://doi.org/10.1016/j.jrp.2016.04.001

Boals, A., & Schuler, K. L. (2018). Reducing reports of illusory posstraumatic growth: A revised version of the Stress-Related Growth Scale (SRGS-R). *Psychological Trauma: Theory, Research, Practice, and Policy, 10*(2), 190–198. https://doi.org/10.1037/tra0000267

Cann, A., Calhoun, L. G., Tedeschi, R. G., Taku, K., Vishnevsky, T., Triplett, K. N., & Danhauer, S. C. (2010). A short form of the Posttraumatic Growth Inventory. *Anxiety, Stress & Coping, 23*(2), 127–137. https://doi.org/10.1080/10615800903094273

Cordova, M. J., Cunningham, L. L. C., Carlson, C. R., & Andrykowski, M. A. (2001). Posttraumatic growth following breast cancer: A controlled comparison study. *Health Psychology, 20*(3), 176–185. https://doi.org/10.1037/0278-6133.20.3.176

Ford, J. D., Tennen, H., & Albert, D. (2008). A contrarian view of growth following adversity. In S. Joseph & P. A. Linley (Eds.), *Trauma, recovery, and growth: Positive psychological perspectives on posttraumatic stress*. (pp. 297–324). Wiley.

Frazier, P. A., & Burnett, J. W. (1994). Immediate coping strategies among rape victims. *Journal of Counseling & Development, 72*(6), 633–639. https://doi.org/10.1002/j.1556-6676.1994.tb01694

Frazier, P., Conlon, A., & Glaser, T. (2001). Positive and negative life changes following sexual assault. *Journal of Consulting and Clinical Psychology, 69*(6), 1048–1055. https://doi.org/10.1037/0022-006X.69.6.1048

Frazier, P., Tennen, H., Gavian, M., Park, C., Tomich, P., & Tashiro, T. (2009). Does self-reported posttraumatic growth reflect genuine positive change? *Psychological Science, 20*(7), 912–919. https://doi.org/10.1111/j.1467-9280.2009.02381.x

Helgeson, V. S., Reynolds, K. A., & Tomich, P. L. (2006). A meta-analytic review of benefit finding and growth. *Journal of Consulting and Clinical Psychology, 74*(5), 797–816. https://doi.org/10.1037/0022-006X.74.5.797

Henry, B., Moffit, T. E., Caspi, A., Langley, J., & Silva, P. A. (1994). On the "remembrance of things past": A longitudinal evaluation of the retrospective method. *Psychological Assessment, 6*(2), 92–101. https://doi.org/10.1037/1040-3590.6.2.92

Herbst, J. H., McCrae, R. R., Costa, P. T., Jr., Feaganes, J. R., & Siegler, I. C. (2000). Self-perceptions of stability and change in personality at midlife: The UNC Alumni Heart Study. *Assessment, 7*(4), 379–388. https://doi.org/10.1177/107319110000700406

Infurna, F. J., & Jayawickreme, E. (2019). Fixing the growth illusion: New directions for research, resilience and posttraumatic growth. *Current Directions in Psychological Science, 28*(2), 152–158. https://doi.org/10.1177/0963721419827017

Jayawickreme, E., & Blackie, L. E. R. (2014). Post-traumatic growth as positive personality change: Evidence, controversies and future directions: post-traumatic growth. *European Journal of Personality, 28*(4), 312–331. https://doi.org/10.1002/per.1963

Jayawickreme, E., & Blackie, L. E. R. (2016). *Exploring the psychological assessment of posttraumatic growth*. Springer. https://doi.org/10.1007/978-3-319-47989-7

Joseph, S., & Linley, P.A. (2005). Positive adjustment to threatening events: An organismic valuing theory of growth through adversity. *Review of General Psychology, 9*(3), 262–280. https://doi.org/10.1037/1089-2680.9.3.262

Joseph, S., Linley, P.A., Andrews, L., Harris, G., Howle, B., Woodward, C., & Shevlin, M. (2005). Assessing positive and negative changes in the aftermath of adversity: Psychometric evaluation of the Changes in Outlook Questionnaire. *Psychological Assessment, 17*(1), 70–80. https://doi.org/10.1037/1040-3590.17.1.70

Joseph, S., Maltby, J., Wood, A.M., Stockton, H., Hunt, N., & Regel, S. (2012). The Psychological Well-Being – Post-Traumatic Changes Questionnaire (PWB-PTCQ): Reliability and validity. *Psychological Trauma: Theory, Research, Practice, and Policy, 4*(4), 420–428. https://doi.org/10.1037/a0024740

Kahneman, D., Krueger, A.B., Schkade, D.A., Schwarz, N., & Stone, A.A. (2004). A survey method for characterizing daily life experience: The day reconstruction method. *Science (New York, N.Y.), 306*(5702), 1776–1780. https://doi.org/10.1126/science.1103572

Kunz, S., Joseph, S., Geyh, S., Peter, C. (2019). Perceived posttraumatic growth and depreciation after spinal cord injury: Actual or Illusory? *Health Psychology, 38*(1), 53–62. https://doi.org/10.1037/hea0000676

Mangelsdorf, J., Eid, M., Luhmann, M. (2019). Does growth require suffering? A systematic review and meta-analysis on genuine posttraumatic and postecstatic growth. *Psychological Bulletin, 145*(3), 302–338. https://doi.org/10.1037/bul0000173

McLean, K.C., & Syed, M. (2015). Personal, master, and alternative narratives: An integrative framework for understanding development in context. *Human Development, 58*(6), 318–349. https://doi.org/10.1159/000445817

Mohr, D.C., Dick, L.P., Russo, D., Pinn, J., Boudewyn, A.C., Likosky, W., & Goodkin, D.E. (1999). The psychosocial impact of multiple sclerosis: Exploring the patient's perspective. *Health Psychology, 18*(4), 376–382. https://doi.org/10.1037/0278-6133.18.4.376

Park, C.L., Cohen, L.H., & Murch, R.L. (1996). Assessment and prediction of stress-related growth. *Journal of Personality, 64*(1), 71–105. https://doi.org/10.1111/j.1467-6494.1996.tb00815.x

Robins, R.W., Noftle, E.E., Trzesniewski, K.H., & Roberts, B.W. (2005). Do people know how their personality has changed? Correlates of perceived and actual personality change in young adulthood. *Journal of Personality, 73*(2), 489–522. https://doi.org/10.1111/j.1467-6494.2005.00317.x

Roisman, G.I., & Fraley, R.C. (2013). Developmental mechanisms underlying the legacy of childhood experiences. *Child Development Perspectives, 7*(3), 149–154. https://doi.org/10.1111/cdep.12030

Seery, M.D., Holman, E.A., & Silver, R.C. (2010). Whatever does not kill us: Cumulative lifetime adversity, vulnerability, and resilience. *Journal of Personality and Social Psychology, 99*(6), 1025–1041. https://doi.org/10.1037/a0021344

Tedeschi, R.G., & Calhoun, L.G. (1996). The Posttraumatic Growth Inventory: Measuring the positive legacy of trauma. *Journal of Traumatic Stress, 9*(3), 455–471. https://doi.org/10.1002/jts.2490090305

Tedeschi, R.G., & Calhoun, L.G. (2004). Posttraumatic growth: Conceptual foundations and empirical evidence. *Psychological Inquiry, 15*(1), 1–18. https://doi.org/10.1207/s15327965pli1501_01

Tedeschi, R.G., Cann, A., Taku, K., Senol-Durak, E., & Calhoun, L.G. (2017). The posttraumatic growth inventory: A revision integrating existential and spiritual change. *Journal of Traumatic Stress, 30*(1), 11–18. https://doi.org/10.1002/jts.22155

Tennen, H., & Affleck, G. (2009). Assessing positive life change: In search of meticulous methods. In C.L. Park, S.C. Lechner, M.H. Antoni, & A.L. Stanton (Eds.), *Medical illness and positive life change: Can crisis lead to personal transformation?* (pp. 31–49). American Psychological Association. https://doi.org/10.1037/11854-000

Tomich, P.L., & Helgeson, V.S. (2004). Is finding something good in the bad always good? Benefit finding among women with breast cancer. *Health Psychology, 23*(1), 16–23. https://doi.org/10.1037/0278-6133.23.1.16

Chapter 14

On the Passion Scale

Theory, Research, and Psychometric Properties

Robert J. Vallerand and Sonia Rahimi

Laboratoire de Recherche sur le Comportement Social,
Université du Québec à Montréal, QC, Canada

Over the past 20 years or so, research in positive psychology has experienced tremendous growth worldwide. One area in positive psychology that has generated a lot of attention is the field of passion – and for good reason, as passion is thought to promote positive outcomes. For instance, the famous rock singer John Bon Jovi stated that "Nothing is as important as passion. No matter what you do with your life, be passionate." However, contrary to the opinions of popular figures like Bon Jovi, our work has found that not all passions are equal, and that the type of passion one has for a given activity can lead to either optimal or suboptimal outcomes (Vallerand, 2010, 2015; Vallerand & Houlfort, 2019).

One major instrument that has been used in passion research for over 15 years is the Passion Scale (Marsh et al., 2013; Vallerand et al., 2003). This scale was developed to allow us to conduct the first series of studies testing the role of passion in optimal and suboptimal outcomes based on the dualistic model of passion (DMP; Vallerand et al., 2003) and was later used in well over 200 studies conducted worldwide by several scientists. This chapter reviews the evidence on the psychometric properties of the Passion Scale, including its factorial validity, invariance, reliability, and construct validity. We begin our discussion of the Passion Scale with an overview of the passion construct, including the DMP that serves as the basis for this scale.

On the Psychology of Passion

Dualistic Model of Passion

Vallerand et al. first postulated the DMP in 2003. It posits that, throughout life, people engage in various activities in hopes of experiencing self-growth and, in line with self-determination theory (Ryan & Deci, 2017), the basic psychological needs of autonomy (to feel a sense of personal initiative), competence (to interact effectively with the environment), and relatedness (to feel connected to significant others). With time and experience, most people eventually display preferences for a select few activities, especially when these activities are enjoyable, allow for the satisfaction of the aforementioned basic psychological needs, and have become part of one's identity. After a regular engagement in these activities, people become passionate about them. In line with the above, passion is thus defined as a strong inclination toward a self-defining activity that one loves, finds important, and in which one invests time and energy (Vallerand et al., 2003).

The DMP further posits the existence of two types of passion, harmonious and obsessive passion, which differ based on how they are internalized into one's identity. In line with self-determination theory, the DMP suggests that the activities people love and engage in regularly eventually become internalized into their identities, especially when they are highly valued and meaningful. Such internalization takes place through either a controlled or an autonomous process (see Deci et al., 1994; Vallerand, 1997, 2001, 2007; Vallerand et al., 1997). Harmonious passion (HP) results from an autonomous internalization of the beloved activity into the person's identity and self, which occurs when individuals have freely accepted the activity as important for themselves without any contingencies attached to it. This type of internalization emanates from the intrinsic and integrative tendencies of the self (Ryan & Deci, 2003); it produces a motivational force to willingly engage in the activity that one loves and engenders a sense of volition and personal endorsement about pursuing that activity. When HP is at play, the activity occupies a significant but not overpowering space in the person's identity and harmonizes with other aspects of the person's life, thereby allowing them to fully partake in the passionate activity in a mindful (St-Louis et al., 2018), nondefensive, and open way (Hodgins & Knee, 2002) that is conducive to flexible persistence (Vallerand, Chichekian, et al., 2022) and positive experiences.

For instance, if a university professor has an HP for playing basketball, they should be able to resist playing basketball with their friends to complete an unfinished research grant due tomorrow. Thus, they could readily tell their friends that they'll take a raincheck on the basketball game and proceeds to be fully immersed in the grant without thinking about the missed opportunity to play basketball. People with HP can choose not to play on a given day if needed or even to eventually terminate the relationship with the activity if they decide that it has become a permanent negative factor in their life.

Conversely, obsessive passion (OP) results from a controlled internalization of the activity one loves into one's identity. A controlled internalization originates from intra- and/or interpersonal pressure typically because certain contingencies are attached to the beloved activity such as feelings of social acceptance or self-esteem (Mageau et al., 2011), or because the sense of excitement derived from activity engagement is uncontrollable. Consequently, they risk experiencing conflict and other negative affective, cognitive, and behavioral consequences during and after activity engagement (Vallerand, 2015). For instance, if the university professor in the preceding example has an OP for playing basketball, they might not be able to resist an invitation to play with their friends. During the basketball scrimmage, they might feel upset with themselves for playing ball instead of working on the grant, have difficulties focusing on the task at hand (playing basketball), may not experience much positive affect and flow while playing, and may even experience guilt and anxiety as they should be doing something else instead (i.e., working on her research grant). It is thus proposed that individuals with OP display a rigid persistence toward the activity that they love (Vallerand, Chichekian, et al., 2022), as oftentimes they can't help but engage in it and may become dependent on the activity. Thus, people with OP should experience conflict between the passionate activity and other life activities, negative affect while doing the activity, and less adaptive outcomes than with HP.

The Passion Scale – Beginnings and Improvements

To assess the two types of passion, Vallerand et al. (2003, Study 1) developed the Passion Scale, which includes items assessing HP, OP as well as some criterion items used to examine whether or not people are passionate about a given activity. In this, the first contemporary study on passion, Vallerand et al. recruited 539 college students to complete a questionnaire including scales that measured passion. The students were first asked to think of an activity "that was very dear to their heart." After listing such an activity, participants were asked to complete 34 items about that activity on a 7-point Likert-type scale ranging from 1 (*do not agree at all*) to 7 (*completely agree*). The authors created these items to reflect the descriptions of the two types of passion. For instance, items assessing HP involved feeling control over the activity a person loves and the activity remaining in harmony with other activities in the person's life, whereas OP items involved "feelings of obsession" for the activity that the person loves (see Box 14.1 for scale items).

Box 14.1. The Passion Scale

Please name an activity that you love, highly value, and regularly spend time on, and respond to the various items while referring yourself to this activity.

Harmonious and Obsessive Passion

1. This activity is in harmony with the other activities in my life.
2. I have difficulties controlling my urge to do my activity.
3. The new things that I discover with this activity allow me to appreciate it even more.
4. I have almost an obsessive feeling for this activity.
5. This activity reflects the qualities I like about myself.
6. This activity allows me to live a variety of experiences.
7. This activity is the only thing that really turns me on.
8. My activity is well integrated in my life.
9. If I could, I would only do my activity.
10. My activity is in harmony with other things that are part of me.
11. This activity is so exciting that I sometimes lose control over it.
12. I have the impression that my activity controls me.

Passion Criteria

13. I spend a lot of time doing this activity.
14. I love this activity.
15. This activity is important for me.
16. This activity is a passion for me.
17. This activity is part of who I am.

Note. Key: harmonious passion: # 1, 3, 5, 6, 8, 10; obsessive passion: # 2, 4, 7, 9, 11, 12; passion criteria: # 13, 14, 15, 16, 17.

Factorial Validity

To evaluate the factorial validity of the Passion Scale, Vallerand et al. (2003, Study 1) randomly separated the participants into two groups. Using the first set of participants (N=284), they conducted an exploratory factor analysis with the 34 items to create a parsimonious preliminary version of the scale assessing HP and OP. Results of the analysis revealed the presence of two factors with 14 items (7 items for each type of passion) that loaded as expected. Using those 14 items, they conducted a second exploratory factor analysis, the results showing these items adequately reflect the two factors of HP and OP. Using the second group of randomly selected participants (N=235), Vallerand et al. conducted a confirmatory factor analysis that provided statistical support for the two-factor model, as indicated by acceptable fit indices. In addition, acceptable levels of reliability were also obtained (i.e., internal consistency, Cronbach's alphas of .79 for HP and α=.89 for OP).

Vallerand et al.'s findings (2003, Study 1) provided support for the Passion Scale. Nevertheless, subsequent minor changes were made to the scale to allow for generalizability (i.e., to use the scale for a variety of activities), resulting in 6 items for each subscale (instead of the 7 that were initially found). The refined version of the Passion Scale is very similar to the original (correlation between the original and refined versions above .80; see Vallerand, 2015). This condensed 12-item version is the most often used scale assessing HP and OP (although subscales with fewer items have been used in some studies).

Since the initial study on passion, well over 20 other studies have conducted exploratory/confirmatory factor analysis and/or exploratory structural equation modeling to validate the Passion Scale. These studies took place in a variety of different settings, such as work, education (for both teachers and students), marketing, music, driving, religion, the environment, romantic relationships, sports (from the perspective of athletes, coaches, referees, and fans; see Vallerand & Verner-Filion, 2020, for a review), gambling, outdoor activities, and plenty of other activities (for an overview, see Table 14.1.).

In addition to the HP and OP subscales, the Passion Scale also includes 5 passion criterion items based on the definition of passion which address the different elements of this construct. They are used to assess whether people are truly passionate about a given activity or not (e.g., "This activity is a passion for me"; see items 13–17 in Box 14.1). Because most studies were conducted in life domains about which most people were indeed passionate, this subscale has not been used regularly. However, when studying samples of participants who may not be passionate, researchers should use these items to first identify whether a person is passionate and, then, if they are, proceed to examine the relationships between HP and/or OP and outcomes (see Carbonneau et al., 2008, on this issue with passion for teaching). Furthermore, the passion criteria items can be used to determine whether passion has developed over time (see Mageau et al., 2009, Study 3).

Invariance of the Factor Structure

To further examine the psychometric properties of the Passion Scale, several authors have assessed the degree to which the structure of the measurement model is equivalent (invariant) between different groups of participants on some dimensions (e.g., between females and males). In a first such study, Marsh et al. (2013) used a sample of 3,570 in-

Table 14.1. Overview of studies validating the Passion Scale

Authors	Scale used	Language	Population	Number of items	Statistical technique	Reliability	Main findings
Anagnostopoulos et al. (2016)	The Passion Scale – adapted to The Passion for Your Job Scale	English	236 employees from the UK football industry	12 1 CP	CFA *t*-test ANOVA	HP $\alpha = .73$ OP $\alpha = .75$	CFA supported the two-factor model of passion. Better fit was found for 8-item, two-factor model. Employees who worked for football foundations (charitable organizations) had more HP and OP than those who worked for football clubs.
Bonneville-Roussy & Vallerand (2018)	The Passion Scale – adapted to The Passion for Music Scale	English	225 professional/student musicians from the UK	12 5 CP	ESEM Structural Equation Modeling	HP $\alpha = .83$ OP $\alpha = .77$ CP $\alpha = .89$	ESEM supported the two-factor model of passion. HP positively related to well-being ($\beta = .50$), and negatively to musical anxiety ($\beta = -.28$), whereas OP negatively related to well-being ($\beta = -.18$). Musical anxiety negatively related to well-being ($\beta = -.40$).
Burke et al. (2012)	The Passion Scale	French and English	177 breast cancer survivors from Montreal	12 5 CP	CFA Path Analysis	HP $\alpha = .87$ OP $\alpha = .85$	CFA supported the two-factor model of passion. HP positively related to positive affect ($\beta = .24$), and negatively to cancer worry ($\beta = -.19$), whereas OP positively related to negative affect ($\beta = .23$), posttraumatic growth ($\beta = .24$), and cancer worry ($\beta = .21$).
Carbonneau et al. (2008) Longitudinal Study	The Passion for Work Scale – adapted to The Passion for Teaching Scale	French	494 teachers from the Quebec City area	12 4 CP	CFA Cross-lagged Structural Equal Modeling	T1/T2 HP $\alpha = .87/.87$ OP $\alpha = .76/.80$ CP $\alpha = .79/.78$	CFA supported the two-factor model of passion. HP (T1) positively related to positive student behaviors (T2, $\beta = .14$), work satisfaction (T2, $\beta = .22$), and negatively to burnout (T2, $\beta = -.14$), whereas OP (T1) positively related to positive student behaviors (T2, $\beta = .11$).

Table 14.1. continued

Authors	Scale used	Language	Population	Number of items	Statistical technique	Reliability	Main findings
Castelda et al. (2007)	The Passion for Gambling Scale Scale translated from French to English	English	147 students from Binghamton University, NY	10	CFA Correlations Partial correlations	HP $\alpha = .89$ OP $\alpha = .90$	CFA supported two-factor model of passion (with some error variances correlated). HP ($r = .39$) and OP ($r = .37$) were positively correlated with pathological gambling (partial correlations: $r = .16, .22$). Partial correlations were not statistically different from one another.
Gousse-Lessard et al. (2013) Study 1	The Passion Scale – adapted to The Passion Toward an Environmental Cause Scale	French	110 volunteers from Quebec engaged in a cause	12 5 CP	CFA Path analysis	HP $\alpha = .81$ OP $\alpha = .85$ CP $\alpha = .74$	CFA supported the two-factor model of passion. HP positively related to the endorsement of mainstream behaviors ($\beta = .35$), whereas OP positively related to the endorsement of both mainstream ($\beta = .25$) and radical behaviors ($\beta = .32$).
Junot et al. (2017)	The Passion Scale – adapted to The Passion for an Outdoor Activity Scale	French	212 residents of and visitors to Reunion Island engaged in outdoor activities	12 5 CP	CFA Path analysis	HP $\alpha = .88$ OP $\alpha = .88$ CP $\alpha = .79$	CFA supported the two-factor model of passion. HP positively related to positive emotions ($\beta = .74$), whereas OP positively related to negative emotions ($\beta = .47$). Positive emotions were subsequently negatively related with an affiliation with nature and environmental behaviors, whereas negative emotions were negatively related. Lastly, an affiliation with nature is positively related to environmental behaviors.

Table 14.1. continued

Authors	Scale used	Language	Population	Number of items	Statistical technique	Reliability	Main findings
Lafrenière et al. (2011)	The Passion for Work Scale – adapted to The Passion for Coaching Scale	No mention	103 athlete–coach dyads	12	CFA Path analysis	HP α = .78 OP α = .87	CFA supported the two-factor model of passion. HP for coaching predicted coaches' autonomy support (β = .54), which positively predicted quality relationships between athletes and coaches that led to athletes' happiness. OP for coaching predicted controlling behaviors (β = .32).
Lafrenière et al. (2008) Study 2	The Passion Scale – adapted to The Passion for Coaching Scale	French	106 French-Canadian coaches	12	CFA Path analysis	HP α = .83 OP α = .85	CFA supported the two-factor model of passion. HP, not OP predicted the quality of coach-athlete relationship (β = .58), mediated by positive emotions. The quality of the coach-athlete relationship subsequently positively predicted subjective well-being.
Lajom et al. (2018)	The Passion for Work Scale – adapted to reflect passion for computer science in sample 4	English	767 participants from the Philippines (four samples)	12	CFA EFA Correlation	Across samples: HP α = .75–.95 OP α = .82–.92	CFA and EFA results showed support for the two-factor model. HP related to more adaptive constructs (learning goals and work engagement), whereas OP related to less adaptive constructs (performance-avoidance goals and workaholism). Also, participants with HP were more likely to feel confident when making career-related decisions and persist in their careers.

Table 14.1. continued

Authors	Scale used	Language	Population	Number of items	Statistical technique	Reliability	Main findings
Philippe et al. (2009) Study 1	The Passion Scale – adapted to The Passion for Driving Scale	French	113 undergraduate/graduate students from a French-Canadian University	12 4 CP	CFA Correlation Partial correlation	HP $\alpha = .85$ OP $\alpha = .80$	CFA results supported the two-factor model of passion. CP correlated with HP and OP (*r*s range .49–.76; convergent validity). OP for driving was positively associated with three types of aggression (*r*s range .21–.33) and HP was not (discriminant validity).
Ratelle et al. (2004)	The Passion for Gambling Scale	French	412 gamblers recruited from the Montreal Casino	10	EFA Partial correlation	HP $\alpha = .79$ OP $\alpha = .91$	EFA results supported the two-factor model of passion. HP negatively correlated with concentration ($r = -.17$), whereas OP positively related to negative consequences associated with gambling dependence and negatively related to positive consequences not associated with gambling dependence.
Ratelle et al. (2013) Study 1	The Passion Scale – adapted to The Passion for Romantic Relationships Scale	French	176 undergraduate students	14	EFA (from Ratelle, 2002) Regression	HP $\alpha = .86$ OP $\alpha = .89$	EFA results supported the two-factor model of passion. HP positively predicted all components of relationship quality, whereas OP positively predicted commitment and love, and negatively predicted trust.
Rip et al. (2012) Study 1	The Passion Scale – adapted to The Passion for Quebec Sovereignty Scale	French	114 Quebec sovereignty activists recruited from Quebec	12 4 CP	CFA Regression	HP $\alpha = .86$ OP $\alpha = .85$ CP $\alpha = .87$	CFA results supported the two-factor model of passion. Individuals with HP were peaceful/democratic about advancing their cause, whereas individuals with OP were radical and aggressive.

Table 14.1. continued

Authors	Scale used	Language	Population	Number of items	Statistical technique	Reliability	Main findings
Rip et al. (2012) Study 2	The Passion Scale – adapted to The Passion for Islam Scale	French	111 Muslims from Montreal	12 4 CP	CFA Path Analysis	HP α = .74 OP α = .67 CP α = .82	CFA results supported the two-factor model of passion. In identity-threatening situations, individuals with HP engage in peaceful religious activism, whereas individuals with OP engage in religious extremism.
Rousseau et al. (2002) Study 1	The Passion for Gambling Scale	French	312 participants from the Montreal Casino	10	EFA/CFA Partial Correlations	HP α = .76 OP α = .90	EFA and CFA results supported the two-factor structure of the scale. Partial correlations showed men to report more HP than women (*r* = .17). OP was more strongly associated with negative behaviors related to gambling than HP.
Rousseau et al. (2002) Study 2	The Passion for Gambling Scale	French	28 participants from the Montreal Casino	10	Test-retest correlations	HP α = .83, .84 OP α = .96, .89 Test-retest = HP r = .82 OP r = .83	The test-retest correlations were significant and high, supporting the temporal stability of the GPS.
Salama-Younes (2018) Study 1 *Two samples	The Passion Scale – adapted to The Passion for Running Scale	French	Sample 1: 567 adult runners from Rennes Sample 2: 163/154 participants	12	CFA Test-retest correlations	HP α = .78, .77 OP α = .75, .73 Test-retest = .29 < r > .76, *p* < .001)	CFA results supported the two-factor model of passion.

Table 14.1. continued

Authors	Scale used	Language	Population	Number of items	Statistical technique	Reliability	Main findings
Schellenberg et al. (2014)	The Passion Scale	English	$N = 1,256$ from 3 studies: recreational athletes, competitive athletes, sports fans	12	ICM-CFA/ ESEM Invariance		Invariance was found across the three samples.
Skitch and Hodgins (2005)	The Passion for Gambling Scale	English	162 students from the University of Calgary	10	Correlations Test-retest correlations	HP $\alpha = .90$ OP $\alpha = .76$ 4-week test-retest ($r = .82$)	OP was consistently more related to problematic gambling than HP ($r = .55$ vs. .29).
Swimberghe et al. (2014) Study 2	The Passion Scales – adapted to The Passion for the Consumer Brand Scale	English	121 US university students	10	CFA	HP $\alpha = .87$ OP $\alpha = .89$	CFA results supported the two-factor model of passion.
Vallerand et al. (2006) Study 1	The Passion Scale – adapted to The Passion Toward Sports Scale	English	206 participants (collegiate recreational sports)	14	CFA Structural Equation Modeling	HP $\alpha = .80$ OP $\alpha = .89$	CFA results supported the two-factor model of passion. Autonomous personality was positively related with HP ($\beta = .43$), whereas controlled personality was positively related with OP ($\beta = .22$).
Vallerand et al. (2008) Study 1	The Passion Scale – adapted to The Passion Toward Your Favorite Team Scale	English	165 UK adults	12	CFA Correlations Regressions	HP $\alpha = .83$ OP $\alpha = .82$	CFA results supported the two-factor model of passion. HP was positively associated with adaptive behaviors (e.g., celebrating), whereas OP was positively associated with negative behaviors (e.g., risking job to go to a game).

dividuals to assess the invariance of the Passion Scale concerning the language of the scale (English vs. French), sex (female vs. male), and types of activities that participants indicated being passionate about. Note that different types of invariance can be conducted. While Marsh et al. (2013) examined some of these different types of invariance, not all of their results are presented in the present paper. For more information on this issue, refer to Marsh et al. (2013). Similarly, we don't discuss the different types of invariance tested by other authors (e.g., Schellenberg et al., 2014).

The original Passion Scale was created in French but was later translated to English using the double translation/backtranslation technique (Vallerand, 1989). Results showed that the English and French versions of the scales were equivalent and provided strong support for the factor structure of the Passion Scale. Other tests conducted by Marsh et al. supported the invariance of the Passion Scale for sex as well as five types of activities: leisure, sports, social activities, work, and education.

The invariance of the Passion Scale has also been tested in sport/exercise settings (Schellenberg et al., 2014). Using many participants involved with exercise or sports, Schellenberg et al. replicated the factor structure of the Passion Scale and investigated whether there was equivalence across three different samples (recreational athletes/exercisers, competitive athletes, and sports fans). The results showed that there was indeed invariance among these groups. Finally, additional support was also found for invariance on several dimensions of the Passion Scale as translated into a dozen different languages such as Arabic (Salama-Younes & Hashim, 2018), Brazilian Portuguese (Peixoto et al., 2019), Chinese (Zhao et al., 2015), Hungarian (Tóth-Király et al., 2017) , Portuguese (Cid et al., 2019), Spanish (Chamarro et al., 2015), and many others. Thus, overall, there is impressive support for the invariance of the Passion scale regarding several dimensions including sex, languages, age, levels of competition (in sports), and types of activities (see Table 14.1 for more information on this issue).

Reliability and Temporal Stability

In Study 1 by Vallerand et al. (2003), each of the two passion subscales demonstrated a relatively high reliability (HP, α=.79; OP, α=.89). In addition, to the best of our knowledge, *all* published studies using the Passion Scale (well over 200 studies) have shown the scale to be reliable (α above .60). For example, the reliability indices for the papers cited in Table 14.1 are the following: HP range between α=.70–.95 and OP range between α=.66–.99. Finally, it should be underscored that high reliability has been found in both field and laboratory studies (e.g., Bélanger et al., 2013a, 2013b, α=.70–.89), demonstrating that, regardless of the research method, the reliability of the Passion Scale is satisfactory.

We should also note that some studies have examined the temporal stability of the Passion Scale. The DMP would hypothesize some stability to exist without expecting unity because if there is a passion for a given activity, there should be some stability over time, as the passion should remain relatively constant. However, at the same time, the DMP posits that passion can also be influenced by contextual factors. Overall, support was found for the temporal stability of the scale. For instance, Carbonneau et al. (2008) found that passion for teaching was relatively stable over 3 months (e.g., βs ranging from .67–.88); Rousseau et al. (2002, Study 2) found that passion for gambling to be comparatively stable for participants who gambled twice over 1 month (test-retest correlation: HP, r=.82, OP, r=.83); and Ratelle (2002, reported in Vallerand, 2015) found support for temporal stability in participants who reported passion for their romantic relationships (HP=.63; OP=.77). Thus, overall, there is good support for the reliability and temporal stability of the Passion Scale as expected.

Construct Validity of the Passion Scale

Given that the Passion Scale was constructed to empirically test various hypotheses derived from the DMP, to the extent that results support these hypotheses, there is evidence for the construct validity of the scale. In this regard, two types of construct validity have been studied. The first concerns convergent validity, which is established if both HP and OP positively correlate with a variable with which they should be similarly correlated. Most studies have tested this hypothesis using the passion criterion items (e.g., loving the activity, etc.), and given that both HP and OP reflect passion, they should be positively correlated with the passion criteria. The second issue deals with divergent/discriminant validity. The DMP posits that each type of passion is qualitatively different, so that, whereas HP is expected to lead to more adaptive outcomes (e.g., flow), OP is hypothesized to lead to less adaptive consequences and at times even to maladaptive outcomes (e.g., burnout).

Convergent Validity

Two prominent studies assessing the convergent validity of the Passion Scale are those of Marsh et al. (2013) and Vallerand et al. (2003, Study 1). The latter study investigated how the HP and OP subscales correlated with the passion criterion subscale and, using over 500 participants, found convergent validity as both the HP and OP subscales positively correlated with elements of the passion criterion subscale described previously (except for love for the activity, which was not assessed). The other major study (Marsh et al., 2013) looked at correlations between the HP and OP subscales and the criterion items (except for identity inclusion which was not measured). Results with close to 3,000 participants yielded the same findings as the Vallerand et al. (2003, Study 1) study: Both subscales positively correlated with all passion criterion items. In addition, tests of invariance revealed that these correlations were the same as a function of sex, age, language, and types of activities (while some minor distinctions took place in some activities relative to others).

Divergent Validity

As mentioned previously, in line with the DMP, it is hypothesized that HP should lead to more adaptive outcomes than OP. Overwhelming support has been obtained for this major hypothesis from the DMP. For instance, in the initial study (Vallerand et al., 2003, Study 1), HP was more positively correlated with the adaptive outcomes than OP (e.g., positive emotions, concentration), whereas OP was more positively correlated with less adaptive outcomes (conflict, negative emotions, ruminations, etc.) than HP. These findings were also replicated in the Marsh et al. (2013) study regarding conflict and ruminations. In addition, Marsh et al. also showed HP to be positively – and OP negatively – correlated with life satisfaction.

In addition to the two major studies mentioned above, several studies have focused on the divergent validity of HP and OP using the Passion Scale. A complete review of such literature is beyond the scope of this chapter as it includes more than 200 studies (for major reviews, see Curran et al., 2015; Vallerand, 2010, 2015; Vallerand & Houlfort, 2019). However, Table 14.1 provides some examples of such research about a variety of outcomes, such as psychological well-being, physical health, burnout, chronic injuries in dancers and runners, satisfaction in personal and romantic relationships, and contributing to one's community and society at large. Finally, although both HP and OP for a given activity lead to high levels of performance in the passionate activity, the process through which such performance is attained is much more adaptive and involves having a richer and fuller life with HP than with OP (see Vallerand et al., 2007, 2008).

The Cross-Cultural Use of the Passion Scale

As seen above, the psychometric properties of the Passion Scale have been extensively assessed through investigations in several languages. The Passion Scale was found to be invariant for language (French vs. English; Marsh et al., 2013), and since then, it has been translated and validated into at least the following languages: Arabic, Chinese, Greek, Hungarian, Italian, Norwegian, Portuguese, Brazilian Portuguese, Russian, and Spanish.

Considering the number of studies conducted in these various cultures, we can draw some conclusions on the crosscultural validity of the Passion Scale. A first conclusion is an overwhelming support for the two-factor structure of the Passion Scale in the various languages. The 21 studies presented in Table 14.2 used either an EFA or CFA, and all found support for the two-factor structure of the Passion Scale in a variety of languages. Of note, sometimes the Passion Scale was found to be appropriate concerning the same language as used in different countries such as Arabic with Saudi women and Arabic with older adults in Egypt, French in Canada (Quebec) and in France, and Portuguese in Brazil and Portugal.

Second, several researchers have also investigated the invariance of the Passion Scale in different languages and cultures, such as Chamarro et al. (2015), who found the Spanish version of the scale to be invariant across sex, type of activities, and age; Cid et al. (2019), who found the Portuguese version of the scale to be invariant across sex and sports; and Peixoto et al. (2019), who found the Brazilian Portuguese version of the Passion Scale to be invariant across sex and competition levels among athletes. Salama-Younes and Hashim (2018) also found invariance across sex and physical activity types in older adults in Egypt, and Tóth-Király et al. (2017) found invariance across sex and age in adults in Hungary.

Third, *all* versions, irrespective of language, have shown acceptable levels of internal consistency. Specifically, the internal consistency of the HP subscale of studies in Table 14.2 showed a range of α=.70–.94, whereas OP yielded a range of α=.79–.99. In addition, one study conducted in Arabic looked at the temporal stability of the Passion

Table 14.2. Overview of studies validating the Passion Scale in different languages or populations

Authors	Scale used	Language	Population	Number of items	Statistical technique	Reliability	Main findings
Abdelati & Salama-Younes (2016) Study 1	The Passion Scale Scale translated to Arabic	Arabic	474 female Saudi undergraduate students from Riyadh	12	CFA	HP α = .74 OP α = .66 OP after deleting item 10: α = .72	CFA demonstrated good fit indices for the 11-item version of the Passion Scale in Arabic (item 10 was deleted).
Abdelati & Salama-Younes (2016) Study 2	The Passion Scale Scale translated to Arabic	Arabic	Female Saudi undergraduate students from Riyadh	11	Correlation	HP α = .75 OP α = .73 Test-retest subscales/total (r = 0.59–.68)	HP and OP positively related to emotional (r = 63, r = .32), and psychosocial well-being (r = .48, r = .34), as well as overall mental health (r = .66, r = .34). Temporal stability for 4–5 weeks apart.
Balon et al. (2013)	The Passion Scale	French	241 Belgian and French participants	12 4 CP	EFA Correlation	HP α = .74 OP α = .83 CP α = .70	EFA supported the two-factor model of passion. HP positively related to conscientiousness (r = .30), extraversion (r = .18), agreeableness (r = .23), and openness (r = .20), whereas OP negatively related to agreeableness (r = −.19).
Birkeland & Buch (2015) Study 1	The Passion for Work Scale Scale translated to Norwegian	Norwegian	385 participants from Norway	12	CFA/ESEM Correlations	HP α = .86 OP α = .75	CFA/ESEM were done with HP, OP, work engagement (physical, emotional, and cognitive engagement), and workaholism. Model showed good fit. Results showed support for convergent and divergent validity HP and OP, concerning work engagement and workaholism.

Table 14.2. continued

Authors	Scale used	Language	Population	Number of items	Statistical technique	Reliability	Main findings
Birkeland & Buch (2015) Study 2 Longitudinal Study	The Passion for Work Scale	Norwegian	223 employees from Norway	12	CFA Correlations Hierarchical Multilevel Modeling	HP $\alpha = .83$ OP $\alpha = .82$	Controlling for work engagement and workaholism, HP was positively related to life satisfaction ($\beta = .19$)/negatively related to burnout ($\beta = -.18$). OP was negatively related to life satisfaction ($\beta = -.27$)/positively related to burnout ($\beta = .29$).
Burke et al. (2015)	The Passion for Work Scale	Russian and Chinese	233 participants from Russia and 193 participants from China	14	CFA Regression	Russia: HP $\alpha = .94$ OP $\alpha = .94$ China HP $\alpha = .88$ OP $\alpha = .89$	CFA showed the eight latent factor model to have a better fit over the seven latent factor model where HP and OP were combined. Russia: HP positively predicted all adaptive job outcomes (e.g., job satisfaction, $\beta = .45$), whereas OP only positively predicted job satisfaction ($\beta = .16$) and occupational commitment ($\beta = .21$). China: HP positively predicted all adaptive job outcomes (e.g., job satisfaction, $\beta = .40$), where OP did not predict anything.
Chamarro et al. (2015)	The Passion Scale Scale translated from English to Spanish	Spanish	1007 participants engaged in a variety of activities	12 4 CP	ESEM Invariance	HP $\alpha = .81$ OP $\alpha = .87$	ESEM results supported the two-factor model of passion. Invariance was supported for sex, type of activity, and age. Overall, pattern of results supported both convergent and divergent validity of the passion scale.

Table 14.2. continued

Authors	Scale used	Language	Population	Number of items	Statistical technique	Reliability	Main findings
Chen (2014)	The Passion Scale for Sport and Exercise Scale translated from English to Chinese	Chinese	172 boys, 140 girls, and 312 mothers/fathers from southern Taiwan	14	CFA ANOVA MANOVA	HP α = .91 OP α = .93	CFA results supported the two-factor model of passion. Children with passionate parents in sports and exercise (HP and OP) scored higher on intrinsic interest value, ability/expectancy, task difficulty, and required effort than those with parents who had lower levels of passion.
Cid et al. (2019)	The Passion Scale	Portuguese	1316 Portuguese athletes	14	CFA Invariance	14 item: HP α = .79 OP α = .90 8 item (two samples): HP α = .80/81 OP α = .90/91	CFA showed initial model did not fit the data, however, support was obtained for short subscales of 4 items each. 8 item version of the scale was found to be invariant across sexes and sports types.
Gonçalves et al. (2014)	The Passion Scale Scale translated from English to Portuguese	Portuguese	551 Portuguese workers	14	EFA (two Samples) Correlations	HP α = .92 OP α = .93	EFA's supported the two-factor model of passion. HP (r = .50) and OP (r = .32) positively correlated with job satisfaction. When controlling for OP, HP positively related to js (r = .48).
Orgambídez-Ramos et al. (2014)	Passion for Work Scale Scale translated from English to Spanish	Spanish	423 Spanish workers	14	EFA Correlations	HP α = .92 OP α = .94	EFA results supported the two-factor model of passion. HP and OP positively correlated with intrinsic job satisfaction (r = .68, 46), and extrinsic job satisfaction (r = .57, 38).

Table 14.2. continued

Authors	Scale used	Language	Population	Number of items	Statistical technique	Reliability	Main findings
Parastatidou et al. (2012)	The Passion Scale Scale translated from English to Greek	Greek	516 participants who exercise	14	CFA Correlations	HP $\alpha = .88$ OP $\alpha = .91$	CFA results supported the two-factor model of passion. HP was more related to several exercise variables than OP (e.g., intrinsic motivation), whereas OP was more strongly related with introjected regulation, exercise inclusion in self and total months of exercise than HP.
Peixoto et al. (2019)	The Passion Scale Scale translated from English to Brazilian Portuguese	Brazilian Portuguese	789 Brazilian athletes	12 5 CP	ESEM Invariance Correlations	HP $\alpha = .79$ OP $\alpha = .89$	ESEM supported the two-factor model of passion. Invariance was obtained for sex and competition level. HP and OP were positively related to CP ($r = .67, .55$), time of practice ($r = .19, 16$) and weekly hours dedicated to activity ($r = .27, 22$).
Ruiz-Alfonso & León (2017)	The Passion Scale – Harmonious passion in the educational context Scale translated to Spanish	Spanish	1157 high-school students from Spain	6 HP	CFA Multilevel Structural Equation Model	McDonald Omega = .95	CFA supported the proposed single factor of HP. Students reported viewing HP and motivation as different constructs. HP positively predicted math achievement, mediated by the motivation to learn. Teachers' emphasis on the usefulness of class content also predicted HP.

Table 14.2. continued

Authors	Scale used	Language	Population	Number of items	Statistical technique	Reliability	Main findings
Ruiz-Alfonso & León (2019)	The Passion Scale – Harmonious passion in the educational context Scale translated to Spanish	Spanish	1121 high-school students from Spain	6 HP	CFA Multilevel Structural Equation Model	McDonald Omega = .89	CFA supported the proposed single factor of HP. Teaching quality predicted HP, HP predicted deep strategy to learn and epistemic curiosity.
Salama-Younes & Hashim (2018) Study 1	The Passion Scale Scale translated to Arabic	Arabic	354 physically active older adults from Egypt	12	CFA Invariance	HP $\alpha = .76$ OP $\alpha = .72$	CFA results supported the two-factor model of passion. Invariance was supported for sex and physical activity.
Serrano-Fernández Boada-Grau et al. (2017)	The Passion Toward Work Scale Scale translated to Spanish	Spanish	513 workers from Spain	14	ESEM Correlations	HP $\alpha = .70$ OP $\alpha = .85$	ESEM showed support for the two-factor model, however, only 9 items were retained (4 for HP, $\alpha = .77$; and 5 for OP, $\alpha = .89$). Validity also confirmed given the pattern of correlations between various variables and HP (e.g., positive relationship with personal efficacy), and HP (e.g., positive relationship with burnout).
Tóth-Király et al. (2017) *Two samples	The Passion Scale Scale translated to Hungarian	Hungarian	7466 adults from Hungary 504 adults who use the computer 1 x/week from Hungary	12	CFA/ESEM Invariance	HP $\alpha = .80$ OP $\alpha = .88$	CFA and ESEM showed support for the two-factor model, however, some error variances were correlated to obtain a better model fit. After combining both samples, invariance was found for sex, and partial invariance was found for age.

Table 14.2. continued

Authors	Scale used	Language	Population	Number of items	Statistical technique	Reliability	Main findings
Tóth-Király et al. (2019) Study 1	The Passion Scale – adapted to The Passion for Sex Scale	Hungarian	679 adults from Hungary	12	ESEM Latent Profile Analysis	HP α = .87 OP α = .87	ESEM showed support for the two-factor model. Four distinct sexual motivation profiles were found (highly self-determined, moderately self-determined, moderately non-self-determined, and highly non-self-determined).
Zhao et al. (2015)	The Passion Scale – adapted to The Passion for One's Studies Scale	Chinese	286 university students from China	12 5 CP	CFA Invariance Correlations	HP α = .74 OP α = .84 CP α = .84	CFA results supported the two-factor model of passion. Invariance was fully supported between the Chinese version of the scale and the French-Canadian version of the scale. Both HP and OP had positive correlations with CP items (convergent validity). HP correlated more strongly to positive outcomes than OP (flow, $r = .39$ vs. .12, positive emotions, $r = .63$ vs .38), and OP correlated positively with negative emotions ($r = .28$), whereas HP was negatively related to them ($r = -.14$; discriminant validity)
Zito & Colombo (2017) *Two samples	The Passion Scale – adapted to The Passion for Work Scale Scale translated into Italian	Italian	101 participants 243 participants belonging to a professional association of managers	14	EFA CFA Correlations	HP α = .92 OP α = .87	The results of the EFA led to deleting item 7 (HP item). CFA confirmed the 13-item version as representing the two-factor model of passion (with some error terms correlated). Correlations showed HP to be related to more adaptive outcomes (e.g., life satisfaction and flow), where OP was more strongly related to negative outcomes (e.g., negative emotions at work), but also positively with flow.

Note. HP = harmonious mpassion; OP = obsessive passion. α = Cronbach's α.

Scale, finding relatively moderately strong correlations (r=0.59–.068; Abdelati & Salama-Younes, 2016, Study 2).

Finally, regarding the scale construct validity, overall the conclusions obtained in Western cultures have been replicated in other cultures. For instance, Zhao et al. (2015) found that HP in Chinese university students was more strongly related to flow and positive emotions than OP, which was more strongly related to negative emotions. Similarly, in a Norwegian sample, Birkeland and Buch (2015, Study 2) found HP to be more related to work engagement than OP, whereas OP was more related to workaholism than HP. Finally, using the Italian version of the Passion Scale, Zito and Colombo (2017) found HP to positively predict adaptive outcomes (life satisfaction and flow), whereas OP only predicted negative emotions. Other similar findings appear in Table 14.2.

Note that some cultural variations have been reported. For instance, using the Spanish version of the Passion Scale, Gonçalves et al. (2014) found that HP and OP for work were *both* positively correlated with job satisfaction. However, as hypothesized by the DMP, the correlation involving HP (r=.52) was stronger than that with OP (r=.32). Similarly, also using the Spanish Passion Scale, Orgambídez-Ramos et al. (2014) found HP and OP for work to be both positively correlated with intrinsic job satisfaction but more so for HP, whereas both types of passion were positively related to extrinsic job satisfaction. Although, overall, most findings support the distinction between HP and OP about outcomes, future research is nevertheless necessary to shed light on some of the differences as to the role of OP in adaptive outcomes obtained in these cultures vs. the North American culture.

Discussion

Taken together, the findings regarding the psychometric properties of the Passion Scale are impressive and lead to several conclusions. First, the Passion Scale demonstrates high levels of factorial validity – indeed, over 20 studies have validated the factor structure of the two-factor model of passion, and extensive support has been found for the invariance of the scale across a variety of modalities (e.g., sex, age, types of activities, etc.). Second, there is substantial evidence for the construct validity of the scale, including both convergent and divergent validity. Convergent validity was established as both HP and OP positively correlated with the passion criterion items, and divergent validity was obtained as HP was more strongly related to adaptive outcomes than OP, whereas the latter was related to negative outcomes but not HP. Of interest is the fact that the range of outcomes assessed is truly notable and includes cognitions, emotions, and behaviors, to mention a few (for a comprehensive review, see Vallerand, 2015; Vallerand & Houlfort, 2019).

Third, the Passion Scale is reliable, as demonstrated by the high levels of internal consistency (average α of both subscales were typically in the mid-70s), reflecting how the subscales assess the two types of passion with high levels of homogeneity without redundancy. Furthermore, support was also obtained for the temporal stability of both subscales, underscoring the fact that passion is not a fleeting interest, and once established, it may remain relatively stable. However, the fact that test-retest correlations were not in the .90s supports the hypothesis from the DMP that passion may also fluctuate because of situational variables (e.g., autonomy support). Fourth, the Passion Scale is valid and reliable in at least 13 languages and numerous countries such as France, Spain, Canada, the United States, Australia, as well as in Hungary, Portugal, China, and Russia. Studies conducted across the globe have consistently provided support for the factorial and construct validity of the scale, and high levels of internal consistency and temporal reliability have also been found.

In closing, we would like to make two major recommendations concerning future research with the scale. First, there is a huge interest in translating the Passion Scale into languages other than the 13 for which the scale already exists. To this end, we would like to underscore that scientists interested in this endeavor should use the double-backtranslation procedures recommended by Vallerand (1989). Such procedures imply that one individual translates the scale from English to Spanish, for instance, and that another takes the Spanish translation and translates the scale back into English (of course, without having access to the original English version). This process is done twice, and then all parties involved in the translation meet in a committee and go over the whole process and determine which items from the two translated scales best reflect the original items. Using such a translation process may explain in part the excellent psychometric properties of the translated versions so far. A second recommendation is that future research should start looking into the differential role of passion in objective outcomes such as physiological indicators of health (see Vallerand, Paquette et al., 2022). So far, most studies have focused on affective and well-being variables. A fresh look at other types of variables would go a long way in testing the ramifications of the DMP and the use of the Passion Scale.

The Passion Scale has been used in well over 200 studies and found to be highly valid and reliable. Although strong empirical support for the scale and the DMP exists, we hasten to underscore that research is still in its infancy, and that additional research is necessary to allow us to move forward toward a more comprehensive understanding of the passion construct. We submit that such research should be fertile for the field of positive psychology, and that the Passion Scale will lie at the heart of such research.

References

Abdelati, S. B., & Salama-Younes, M. (2016). Passion types and subjective well-being for Saudi women: Exploratory study. *Indian Journal of Positive Psychology, 7*(3), 325–334.

Anagnostopoulos, C., Winand, M., & Papadimitriou, D. (2016). Passion in the workplace: empirical insights from team sport organisations. *European Sport Management Quarterly, 16*(4), 385–412. https://doi.org/10.1080/16184742.2016.1178794

Balon, S., Lecoq, J., & Rimé, B. (2013). Passion and personality: Is passionate behaviour a function of personality? *Revue Européenne de Psychologie Appliquée/European Review of Applied Psychology, 63*(1), 59–65. https://doi.org/10.1016/j.erap.2012.06.001

Bélanger, J. J., Lafreniere, M. A. K., Vallerand, R. J., & Kruglanski, A. W. (2013a). Driven by fear: The effect of success and failure information on passionate individuals' performance. *Journal of Personality and Social Psychology, 104*(1), 180–195. https://doi.org/10.1037/a0029585

Bélanger, J., Lafrenière, M.-A., Vallerand, R. J., Kruglanski, A. W. (2013b). When passion makes the heart grow colder: The role of passion in alternative goal suppression. *Journal of Personality and Social Psychology, 104,* 126–147. https://doi.org/10.1037/a0029679

Birkeland, I. K., & Buch, R. (2015). The dualistic model of passion for work: Discriminate and predictive validity with work engagement and workaholism. *Motivation and Emotion, 39*(3), 392–408. https://doi.org/10.1007/s11031-014-9462-x

Bonneville-Roussy, A., & Vallerand, R. J. (2018). Passion at the heart of musicians' well-being. *Psychology of Music, 48*(2), 266–282. https://doi.org/10.1177/0305735618797180
Burke, R. J., Astakhova, M. N., & Hang, H. (2015). Work passion through the lens of culture: Harmonious work passion, obsessive work passion, and work outcomes in Russia and China. *Journal of Business and Psychology, 30*(3), 457–471. https://doi.org/10.1007/s10869-014-9375-4
Burke, S. M., Sabiston, C. M., & Vallerand, R. J. (2012). Passion in breast cancer survivors: Examining links to emotional well-being. *Journal of Health Psychology, 17*(8), 1161–1175. https://doi.org/10.1177/1359105311429202
Carbonneau, N., Vallerand, R. J., Fernet, C., & Guay, F. (2008). The role of passion for teaching in intrapersonal and interpersonal outcomes. *Journal of Educational Psychology, 100*(4), 977–987. https://doi.org/10.1037/a0012545
Castelda, B. A., Mattson, R. E., Mackillop, J., Anderson, E. J., & Donovick, P. J. (2007). Psychometric validation of the Gambling Passion Scale (GPS) in an English-speaking university sample. *International Gambling Studies, 7*(2), 173–182. https://doi.org/10.1080/14459790701387485
Chamarro, A., Penelo, E., Fornieles, A., Oberst, U., Vallerand, R. J., & Fernández-Castro, J. (2015). Psychometric properties of the Spanish version of the Passion Scale. *Psicothema, 27*(4), 402–409.
Chen, C. Y. (2014). An exploratory study on the relationship between parents' passion for sport/exercise and children's self-and task-perceptions in sport/exercise. *Perceptual and Motor Skills, 118*(3), 909–925. https://doi.org/10.2466/10.08.PMS.118k26w3
Cid, L., Vitorino, A., Bento, T., Teixeira, D. S., Rodrigues, F., & Monteiro, D. (2019). The Passion Scale – Portuguese version: Reliability, validity, and invariance of gender and sport. *Perceptual and Motor Skills, 129*(4), 694–712. https://doi.org/10.1177/0031512519849744
Curran, T., Hill, A. P., Appleton, P. R., Vallerand, R. J., & Standage, M. (2015). The psychology of passion: A meta-analytical review of a decade of research on intrapersonal outcomes. *Motivation and Emotion, 39*(5), 631–655. https://doi.org/10.1007/s11031-015-9503-0
Deci, E. L., Eghrari, H., Patrick, B. C., & Leone, D. R. (1994). Facilitating internalization: The self-determination theory perspective. *Journal of Personality, 62*(1), 119–142. https://doi.org/10.1111/j.1467-6494.1994.tb00797.x
Gonçalves, G., Orgambídez-Ramos, A., Ferrão, M. C., & Parreira, T. (2014). Adaptation and initial validation of the Passion Scale in a Portuguese sample. *Escritos de Psicología – Psychological Writings, 7*(2), 19–27. https://doi.org/10.24310/espsiescpsi.v7i2.13255
Gousse-Lessard, A. S., Vallerand, R. J., Carbonneau, N., & Lafrenière, M. A. K. (2013). The role of passion in mainstream and radical behaviors: A look at environmental activism. *Journal of Environmental Psychology, 35*, 18–29. https://doi.org/10.1016/j.jenvp.2013.03.003
Hodgins, H. S., & Knee, R. (2002). The integrating self and conscious experience. In E. L. Deci & R. M. Ryan (Eds.), *Handbook on self-determination research: Theoretical and applied issues* (pp. 87–100). University of Rochester Press.
Junot, A., Paquet, Y., & Martin-Krumm, C. (2017). Passion for outdoor activities and environmental behaviors: A look at emotions related to passionate activities. *Journal of Environmental Psychology, 53*, 177–184. https://doi.org/10.1016/j.jenvp.2017.07.011
Lafrenière, M. A. K., Jowett, S., Vallerand, R. J., & Carbonneau, N. (2011). Passion for coaching and the quality of the coach-athlete relationship: The mediating role of coaching behaviors. *Psychology of Sport and Exercise, 12*(2), 144–152. https://doi.org/10.1016/j.psychsport.2010.08.002
Lafrenière, M. A. K., Jowett, S., Vallerand, R. J., Donahue, E. G., & Lorimer, R. (2008). Passion in sport: On the quality of the coach-athlete relationship. *Journal of Sport and Exercise Psychology, 30*(5), 541–560. https://doi.org/10.1123/jsep.30.5.541
Lajom, J. A. L., Amarnani, R. K., Restubog, S. L. D., Bordia, P., & Tang, R. L. (2018). Dualistic passion for work and its impact on career outcomes: Scale validation and nomological network. *Journal of Career Assessment, 26*(4), 631–648. https://doi.org/10.1177/1069072717723096
Mageau, G. A., Carpentier, J., & Vallerand, R. J. (2011). The role of self-esteem contingencies in the distinction between obsessive and harmonious passion. *European Journal of Social Psychology, 41*(6), 720–729. https://doi.org/10.1002/ejsp.798

Mageau, G.A., Vallerand, R.J., Charest, J., Salvy, S.J., Lacaille, N., Bouffard, T., & Koestner, R. (2009). On the development of harmonious and obsessive passion: The role of autonomy support, activity specialization, and identification with the activity. *Journal of Personality, 77*(3), 601–646. https://doi.org/10.1111/j.1467-6494.2009.00559.x

Marsh, H.W., Vallerand, R.J., Lafrenière, M.-A.K., Parker, P., Morin, A.J.S., Carbonneau, N., Jowett, S., Bureau, J.S., Fenet, C., Guay, F., Salah Abduljabbar, A., & Paquet, Y. (2013). Passion: Does one scale fit all? Construct validity of two-factor Passion Scale and psychometric invariance over different activities and languages. *Psychological Assessment, 25*(3), 796–809.

Orgambídez-Ramos, A., Borrego-Alés, Y., & Gonçalves, G. (2014). Passionate workers: A Spanish adaptation of the Passion Scale. *Revista de Psicología del Trabajo y de las Organizaciones, 30*(2), 43–48. https://doi.org/10.1016/j.rpto.2014.06.005

Parastatidou, I.S., Doganis, G., Theodorakis, Y., & Vlachopoulos, S.P. (2012). Exercising with passion: Initial validation of the Passion Scale in exercise. *Measurement in Physical Education and Exercise Science, 16*(2), 119–134. https://doi.org/10.1080/1091367X.2012.657561

Peixoto, E.M., Nakano, T.D.C., Castillo, R.A., Oliveira, L.P., & Balbinotti, M.A.A. (2019). Passion Scale: Psychometric properties and factorial invariance via exploratory structural equation modeling (ESEM). *Paidéia (Ribeirão Preto), 29*, 1–9. https://doi.org/10.1590/1982-4327e2911

Philippe, F.L., Vallerand, R.J., Richer, I., Vallieres, É., & Bergeron, J. (2009). Passion for driving and aggressive driving behavior: A look at their relationship. *Journal of Applied Social Psychology, 39*(12), 3020–3043. https://doi.org/10.1111/j.1559-1816.2009.00559.x

Ratelle, C.F. (2002). *Une nouvelle conceptualisation de la passion amoureuse* [A new conceptualization of romantic passion] [Unpublished doctoral dissertation]. University of Quebec in Montreal, Montreal, QC, Canada.

Ratelle, C.F., Carbonneau, N., Vallerand, R.J., & Mageau, G. (2013). Passion in the romantic sphere: A look at relational outcomes. *Motivation and Emotion, 37*(1), 106–120. https://doi.org/10.1007/s11031-012-9286-5

Ratelle, C.F., Vallerand, R.J., Mageau, G.A., Rousseau, F.L., & Provencher, P. (2004). When passion leads to problematic outcomes: A look at gambling. *Journal of Gambling Studies, 20*(2), 105–119. https://doi.org/10.1023/B:JOGS.0000022304.96042.e6

Rip, B., Vallerand, R.J., & Lafrenière, M.A.K. (2012). Passion for a cause, passion for a creed: On ideological passion, identity threat, and extremism. *Journal of Personality, 80*(3), 573–602. https://doi.org/10.1111/j.1467-6494.2011.00743.x

Rousseau, F.L., Vallerand, R.J., Ratelle, C.F., Mageau, G.A., & Provencher, P.J. (2002). Passion and gambling: On the validation of the Gambling Passion Scale (GPS). *Journal of Gambling Studies, 18*(1), 45–66. https://doi.org/10.1023/A:1014532229487

Ruiz-Alfonso, Z., & León, J. (2017). Passion for math: Relationships between teachers' emphasis on class contents usefulness, motivation and grades. *Contemporary Educational Psychology, 51*, 284–292. https://doi.org/10.1016/j.cedpsych.2017.08.010

Ruiz-Alfonso, Z., & León, J. (2019). Teaching quality: relationships between passion, deep strategy to learn, and epistemic curiosity. *School Effectiveness and School Improvement, 30*(2), 212–230. https://doi.org/10.1080/09243453.2018.1562944

Ryan, R.M., & Deci, E.L. (2003). On assimilating identities to the self: A self-determination theory perspective on internalization and integrity within cultures. In M.R. Leary & J.P. Tangney (Eds.), *Handbook of self and identity* (pp. 253–272). Guilford.

Ryan, R.M., & Deci, E.L. (2017). *Self-determination theory: Basic psychological needs in motivation, development and wellness.* Guilford. https://doi.org/10.1521/978.14625/28806

Salama-Younes, M. (2018). Passion types and subjective well-being for French older adult runners. *Journal of Leisure Research, 49*(3–5), 177–195. https://doi.org/10.1080/00222216.2018.1505160

Salama-Younes, M., & Hashim, M. (2018). Passion, vitality and life satisfaction for physically active old adults. *The Journal of Positive Psychology, 13*(3), 309–319. https://doi.org/10.1080/17439760.2017.1291848

Schellenberg, B. J., Gunnell, K. E., Mosewich, A. D., & Bailis, D. S. (2014). Measurement invariance of the Passion Scale across three samples: An ESEM approach. *Measurement in Physical Education and Exercise Science, 18*(4), 242–258. https://doi.org/10.1080/1091367X.2014.942453

Serrano-Fernández, M. J., Boada-Grau, J., Gil-Ripoll, C., & Vigil-Colet, A. (2017). Spanish adaptation of the passion toward work scale (PTWS). *Anales de Psicología/Annals of Psychology, 33*(2), 403–410. https://doi.org/10.6018/analesps.33.2.240521

Skitch, S. A., & Hodgins, D. C. (2005). A passion for the game: Problem gambling and passion among university students. *Canadian Journal of Behavioural Science/Revue canadienne des sciences du comportement, 37*(3), 193–197. https://doi.org/10.1037/h0087256

St-Louis, A. C., Verner-Filion, J., Bergeron, C. M., & Vallerand, R. J. (2018). Passion and mindfulness: Accessing adaptive self-processes. *The Journal of Positive Psychology, 13*(2), 155–164. https://doi.org/10.1080/17439760.2016.1245771

Swimberghe, K. R., Astakhova, M., & Wooldridge, B. R. (2014). A new dualistic approach to brand passion: Harmonious and obsessive. *Journal of Business Research, 67*(12), 2657–2665. https://doi.org/10.1016/j.jbusres.2014.04.003

Tóth-Király, I., Bőthe, B., Rigó, A., & Orosz, G. (2017). An illustration of the exploratory structural equation modeling (ESEM) framework on the passion scale. *Frontiers in Psychology, 8*, Article 1968. https://doi.org/10.3389/fpsyg.2017.01968

Tóth-Király, I., Vallerand, R. J., Bőthe, B., Rigó, A., & Orosz, G. (2019). Examining sexual motivation profiles and their correlates using latent profile analysis. *Personality and Individual Differences, 146*, 76–86. https://doi.org/10.1016/j.paid.2019.04.002

Vallerand, R. J. (1989). Vers une méthodologie de validation transculturelle de questionnaires psychologiques: Implications pour la recherche en langue française [Toward a methodology to crossculturally validate psychological questionnaires: Implications for research in the French language]. *Psychologie Canadienne, 30*, 662–678. https://doi.org/10.1037/h0079856

Vallerand, R. J. (1997). Toward a hierarchical model of intrinsic and extrinsic motivation. *Advances in Experimental and Social Psychology, 29*, 271–360. https://doi.org/10.1016/S0065-2601(08)60019-2

Vallerand, R. J. (2001). A hierarchical model of intrinsic and extrinsic motivation in sport and exercise. In G. Roberts (Ed.), *Advances in motivation in sport and exercise* (pp. 263–319). Human Kinetics.

Vallerand, R. J. (2007). Intrinsic and extrinsic motivation in sport and physical activity: A review and a look at the future. In G. Tenenbaum & E. Eklund (Eds.), *Handbook of sport psychology* (3rd ed., pp. 59–83). Wiley. https://doi.org/10.1002/9781118270011.ch3

Vallerand, R. J. (2010). On passion for life activities: The dualistic model of passion. *Advances in Experimental Social Psychology, 42*, 97–193. Academic Press. https://doi.org/10.1016/S0065-2601(10)42003-1

Vallerand, R. J. (2015). *The psychology of passion: A dualistic model.* Oxford University Press. https://doi.org/10.1093/acprof:oso/9780199777600.001.0001

Vallerand, R. J., Blanchard, C. M., Mageau, G. A., Koestner, R., Ratelle, C., Léonard, M., Gagné, M., & Marsolais, J. (2003). Les passions de l'âme: On obsessive and harmonious passion [Passions of the soul: On obsessive and harmonious passion]. *Journal of Personality and Social Psychology, 85*, 756–767. https://doi.org/10.1037/0022-3514.85.4.756

Vallerand, R. J., Chichekian, T., Verner-Filion, J., & Rapaport, M. (2022). *A Look at the persistence of passionate individuals: On the role of rigid and flexible persistence in activity and life outcomes* [Manuscript submitted for publication].

Vallerand, R. J., Fortier, M. S., & Guay, F. (1997). Self-determination and persistence in a real-life setting: Toward a motivational model of high school dropout. *Journal of Personality and Social Psychology, 72*, 1161–1176. https://doi.org/10.1037/0022-3514.72.5.1161

Vallerand, R. J., & Houlfort, N. (Eds.). (2019). *Passion for work: Theory, research, and applications*. Oxford University Press.

Vallerand, R. J., Ntoumanis, N., Philippe, F. L., Lavigne, G. L., Carbonneau, N., Bonneville, A., Lagacé-Labonté, C., & Maliha, G. (2008). On passion and sports fans: A look at football. *Journal of Sports Sciences, 26*(12), 1279–1293. https://doi.org/10.1080/02640410802123185

Vallerand, R. J., Paquette, V., & Richard, C. (2022). The role of passion in psychological and cardiovascular responses: Extending the field of passion and positive psychology in new directions. *Frontiers in Psychology, 12*, 744629. https://doi.org/10.3389/fpsyg.2021.744629

Vallerand, R. J., Rousseau, F. L., Grouzet, F. M., Dumais, A., Grenier, S., & Blanchard, C. M. (2006). Passion in sport: A look at determinants and affective experiences. *Journal of Sport and Exercise Psychology, 28*(4), 454–478. https://doi.org/10.1123/jsep.28.4.454

Vallerand, R. J., Salvy, S. J., Mageau, G. A., Elliot, A. J., Denis, P., Grouzet, F. M. E., & Blanchard, C. B. (2007). On the role of passion in performance. *Journal of Personality, 75*, 505–534. https://doi.org/10.1111/j.1467-6494.2007.00447.x

Vallerand, R. J., & Verner-Filion, J. (2020). Theory and research in passion for sport and exercise. In G. Tenenbaum & R. Eklund (Eds.), *Handbook of sport psychology* (4th ed.). Wiley. https://doi.org/10.1002/9781119568124.ch11

Zhao, Y., St-Louis, A., & Vallerand, R. J. (2015). On the validation of the passion scale in Chinese. *Psychology of Well-Being, 5*(1), Article 3. https://doi.org/10.1186/s13612-015-0031-1

Zito, M., & Colombo, L. (2017). The Italian version of the Passion for Work Scale: First psychometric evaluations. *Revista de Psicología del Trabajo y de las Organizaciones, 33*(1), 47–53. https://doi.org/10.1016/j.rpto.2017.01.003

Chapter 15

Work Engagement

A Critical Assessment of the Concept and Its Measurement

Wilmar B. Schaufeli[1,2] and Arnold B. Bakker[3]

[1]Social, Health & Organizational Psychology, Utrecht University, The Netherlands
[2]Work & Organizational Psychology and Professional Learning, KU Leuven, Belgium
[3]Center of Excellence for Positive Organizational Psychology, Erasmus University Rotterdam, The Netherlands

Today, engaging employees is a critical agenda for organizations worldwide. Although the origin of the term is not entirely clear, most likely the Gallup Organization coined "employee engagement" in the 1990s (Buckingham & Coffman, 1999). Precisely in that period, an organization's human capital became increasingly important because of the increase in knowledge work. Moreover, more work had to be done with fewer people, among other things. Therefore, it became increasingly important for organizations to employ workers who were able and willing to invest in their jobs psychologically. In other words, they needed employees who, instead of merely bringing their bodies to work, bring their entire selves to work. Perhaps not so coincidentally, around the same time, the first scholarly article about engagement appeared as a new approach to employee motivation (Kahn, 1990). Yet, it took about a decade before the topic was picked up in academia.

This chapter clarifies the concept of work engagement as well as how it is assessed using self-report questionnaires. Although "work engagement" and "employee engagement" are typically used interchangeably, we prefer the former because it is more specific and refers to the individuals' relationship with work. In contrast, "employee engagement" – commonly used in business and human resource management – also includes the relationship with the organization, which blurs the distinction with established concepts such as organizational commitment and extra-role behavior.

Assessing their employees' levels of work engagement is important for organizations because this is ultimately related to their future financial business performance (Schneider et al., 2018). Moreover, levels of work engagement can be fostered by organizational measures, such as job and personal resources building (Knight et al., 2017). Not surprisingly, consultants have successfully marketed the concept together with their own proprietary employee engagement surveys. As a result, particularly larger organizations regularly monitor engagement levels of their employees and use this information as input for their HR and managerial policies to promote work engagement and ultimately business success (Attridge, 2009).

This chapter addresses five issues: (1) the nature of work engagement, (2) a model for understanding work engagement, (3) the Utrecht Work Engagement Scale, (4) questionnaires of limited applicability, and (5) practical use of work engagement questionnaires.

The Nature of Work Engagement

Everyday colloquial connotations of engagement refer to involvement, commitment, passion, enthusiasm, absorption, focused effort, zeal, immersion, dedication, and energy. In a similar vein, the Merriam-Webster dictionary describes the state of being engaged as "emotional involvement or commitment" and as "being in gear." However, neither practitioners nor scholars agree on the conceptualization of engagement to work. Consequently, different perspectives on work engagement exist both in business and in academia.

Work Engagement in Business

Virtually every major HR consultancy firm offers tools to assess and improve levels of what is commonly called employee engagement. Almost without exception, these firms claim to have conclusive and compelling evidence that employee engagement – as measured by their own tools – increases profitability through higher productivity, sales, customer satisfaction, effectiveness, employee retention, and so on. However, except for the Gallup Organization (Harter et al., 2002), this claim has not been evidenced by publications in peer-reviewed journals. Although the descriptions of work engagement of leading HR consultancy firms such as Towers Perrin, Mercer, Hewitt, and BlessingWhite may differ at first glance, a closer look reveals that, in essence, they define employee engagement as a blend of three existing concepts (Schaufeli, 2014): (1) job satisfaction, (2) extra-role behavior (i.e., discretionary behavior that promotes the organization's effective functioning), and (3) commitment to the organization and its goals, more particularly, emotional attachment to the organization (affective commitment) and the desire to stay with the organization (continuance commitment). Hence, how business conceptualizes employee engagement comes close to putting old wine in a new bottle.

Work Engagement in Academia

Based on over 200 eligible publications, Shuck (2011) reviewed academic definitions of work engagement and distinguished four approaches:

- *The needs-satisfying approach.* Kahn (1990) defined personal engagement as the "harnessing of organization members' selves to their work roles: in engagement, people employ and express themselves physically, cognitively, emotionally, and mentally during role performances" (p. 694). He conceptualized personal engagement as the employment and expression of one's preferred self in task behaviors. Although important for theoretical thinking, this approach has only occasionally been used in empirical research. According to a recent systematic review of 172 high-quality papers on work engagement, Kahn's conception was used in only 6% (k=11) of the cases (Bailey et al., 2017). The operationalization of Kahn's concept of personal engagement is discussed in the section about questionnaires with limited application.

- *The burnout-antithesis approach.* Rooted in occupational health psychology, this approach views work engagement as the positive antithesis of burnout. According to Maslach and Leiter (1997), work engagement and burnout are endpoints of a single continuum. The second, alternative view considers work engagement as a distinct concept that is negatively related to burnout. Work engagement, in this view, is defined as "a positive, fulfilling, work-related state of mind that is characterized by vigor, dedication, and absorption" (Schaufeli, Salanova et al., 2002, p. 74). Vigor refers to high levels of energy and mental resilience while working, the willingness to invest effort in one's work, and persistence even in the face of difficulties. Dedication refers to being strongly involved in one's work and experiencing a sense of significance, enthusiasm, inspiration, pride, and challenge. Finally, absorption refers to being fully concentrated and happily engrossed in one's work, whereby time passes quickly, and one has difficulties detaching oneself from work. According to Bailey et al. (2017), an overwhelming 86% of all academic research on work engagement used the Utrecht Work Engagement Scale (UWES), a questionnaire based on the definition of work engagement as a combination of vigor, dedication, and absorption. Because of its predominance, in this chapter, we focus mainly on the UWES.
- *The satisfaction-engagement approach.* According to the Gallup Organization, "The term employee engagement refers to an individual's involvement and satisfaction with as well as enthusiasm for work" (Harter et al., 2002, p. 269). Thus, like the definitions of other consultancy firms, Gallup's work engagement concept seems to overlap with well-known constructs such as job involvement and job satisfaction. This is illustrated by the fact that, after controlling for measurement error, Gallup's Q^{12} correlates almost perfectly (r=.91) with a single item that taps job satisfaction (Harter et al., 2002), meaning that both are virtually identical. Furthermore, rather than the *experience* of work engagement, the Q^{12} measures its *antecedents* in terms of perceived job resources. This is also acknowledged by Harter et al. (2002, p. 269), who stated that the items of the Q^{12} gauge "employee perceptions of the quality of people-related management practices in business units" (e.g., "My supervisor, or someone at work, seems to care about me as a person"). For these obvious reasons, we do not further consider this approach in this chapter.
- *The multidimensional approach.* Saks (2006) defined employee engagement as "a distinct and unique construct consisting of cognitive, emotional, and behavioral components that are associated with individual role performance" (p. 602). This definition is quite like that of Kahn (1990), because it also focuses on role performance at work. The innovative aspect is that Saks (2006) distinguishes between "job engagement" (performing one's work role) and "organizational engagement" (performing one's role as a member of the organization). Although both are moderately related (r=.62), they seem to have different antecedents and consequences. Despite its intuitive appeal, the research community has hardly taken up the multidimensional approach, which is used in only 3% of the empirical papers (Bailey et al., 2017). The measure based on

Saks' (2006) concept of employee engagement is discussed below in the section about questionnaires with limited application.

Taken together, the approaches noted above each focus on a different aspect of work engagement: (1) its relationship with role performance, (2) its positive, energetic nature as opposed to burnout, (3) its representation in resourceful jobs, and (4) its relationship with both the job as well as with the organization.

A Model for Understanding Work Engagement

To assess the content validity of measures that tap work engagement, we need a conceptual framework that includes its antecedents and consequences. Bakker and Demerouti (2007, 2008) developed a model of work engagement that may serve the purpose of a nomological network for work engagement. Figure 15.1 displays the motivational process of the job demands-resources (JD-R) model.

Accordingly, job resources have a motivational potential and lead to positive organizational outcomes, via work engagement (Schaufeli & Bakker, 2004a). The JD-R model is, with 38 %, the most frequently used model in publications on work engagement, against only 4 % for the needs-satisfying approach (Bailey et al., 2017). By the way, most studies do not use any conceptual model at all.

According to the JD-R model, job resources, such as job control, social support, and career opportunities, may either play an intrinsic motivational role because they foster employees' growth, learning and development, or an extrinsic motivational role because they are instrumental in achieving work goals. In addition, the JD-R model postulates that job resources become more salient and gain their motivational potential when em-

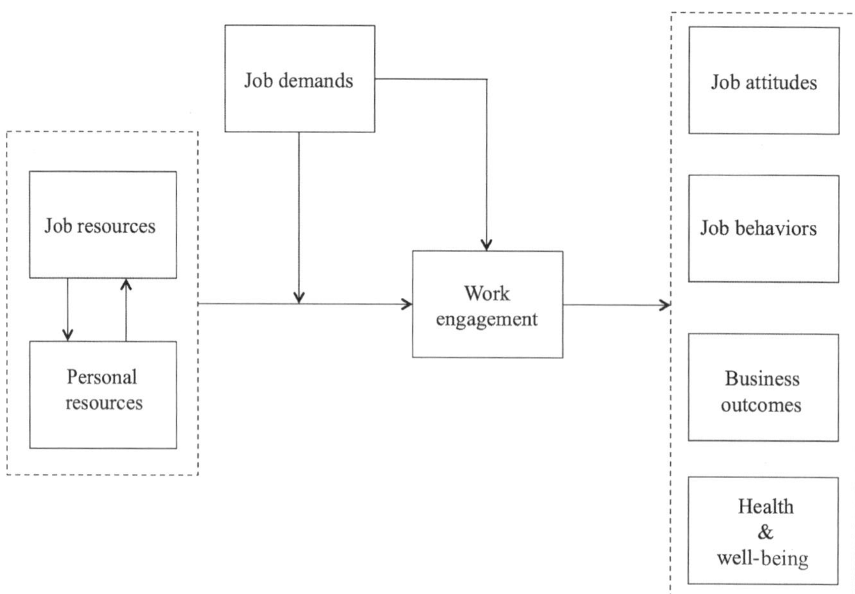

Figure 15.1. A model of work engagement

ployees are confronted with high job demands, such as work overload, role conflicts, and emotional demands (e.g., Bakker et al., 2007). Furthermore, Xanthopoulou et al. (2009a, 2009b) showed that job and personal resources (i.e., positive self-evaluations that refer to an individual's sense of their ability to control and impact upon the environment) are mutually related, and that personal resources are independent predictors of work engagement. Based on Fredrickson's (2001)broaden-and-build theory of positive emotions, Bakker and Demerouti (2008) argued that work engagement boosts performance because it can broaden the employee's momentary thought and action repertoires and to mobilize job and personal resources. Moreover, as we will see below, work engagement has a positive impact on health and well-being and can be distinguished from various organizational outcomes (see Figure 15.1). The latter is at odds with the view of most consultancy firms who define work engagement in terms of these very outcomes. In contrast, this chapter considers work engagement as a psychological state that *drives* employees' behavioral investment of personal energy. That means that work engagement should be theoretically distinguished from task performance, concomitant attitudes, and business outcomes.

The Utrecht Work Engagement Scale (UWES)

The UWES was developed using 30 in-depth interviews with employees (Schaufeli et al., 2001). Based on these interviews, the authors initially formulated 24 items, which were subsequently reduced as a result of preliminary psychometric studies in two independent samples (Schaufeli & Bakker, 2004b). As noted above, the UWES contains three subscales that assess vigor, dedication, and absorption. In addition to the original UWES, which contains 17 items (Schaufeli, Salanova et al., 2002), a shortened version of nine items is also available (Schaufeli, Bakker et al., 2006) as well as an ultrashort version of only three items, including a single item for each dimension of work engagement (Schaufeli et al., 2017). In a separate section, we briefly discuss alternative versions of the UWES: the team-level version, the daily version, and the student version. Over 30 foreign-language versions of the UWES are now available (see www.wilmarschaufeli.nl) and its psychometric features have been reported in peer-reviewed international journals for 22 different countries. (A complete list of publications is available upon request from the first author.) Because of the abundance of studies that use the UWES – Google Scholar produced almost 14,000 hits in April 2020 – in what follows, we focus particularly on literature reviews and meta-analyses.

Factorial Validity

A debate exists about the factorial validity of the UWES. Recently, Kulikowski (2017) carried out a systemic review and evaluated 21 studies on the UWES that used confirmative factor analysis to test its factorial validity. The originally proposed three-factor structure was superior in six studies, whereas this was the case for the one-factor structure in another further six studies. Eight studies concluded that the one- and three-factor structures could be considered equivalent. Only one study failed to confirm either the one- or the three-factor structure of the UWES. From a practical perspective, though, the dimensionality of the UWES is not so relevant because the correlations between the three factors are usually rather high, exceeding .80 (e.g., Schaufeli, Bakker et al., 2006, using 10 national samples).

Factorial Invariance

Confirmatory factor analyses using the so-called multiple group method, in which samples of two or more countries are simultaneously included, showed that the three-factor structure of the UWES is invariant across nations such as Australia, Belgium, Canada, Finland, France, Germany, The Netherlands, Norway, South Africa, and Spain (Schaufeli, Bakker et al., 2006). In contrast, Klassen et al. (2012) found that the one-factor structure was preferable over the three-factor structure across five national teacher samples. Moreover, the UWES was invariant *within* Western (Canada, Australia) and non-Western countries (Indonesia, China, Oman), but not *across* Western and non-Western countries. Storm and Rothmann (2003) concluded that the equivalence of the UWES is acceptable for white, black, colored, and Indian members of the South African Police Service, and that no evidence was found for item bias in these racial groups. Factorial invariance was generally demonstrated for various occupational groups, such as Dutch (Schaufeli & Bakker, 2004a) and Japanese (Shimazu et al., 2008) white-collar employees and healthcare professionals, Spanish workers and students (Schaufeli, Salanova et al., 2002), and Finnish healthcare workers, educators, and both white- and blue-collar workers (Seppälä et al., 2009). Also, Seppälä et al. demonstrated that the correlated three-factor structure of the UWES was invariant across a time interval of 3 years.

Internal Consistency

A meta-analysis of the original and the short versions of the UWES indicated good internal consistencies for vigor, dedication, and absorption. (Details of this unpublished meta-analysis may be obtained from the first author.) More particularly, analyses across 33 samples (total N=19,940) from nine different countries (Australia, Belgium, Finland, Greece, The Netherlands, Norway, Spain, South Africa, and Sweden) revealed that sample-weighted values for Cronbach's α of all three scales of the original and short versions of the UWES exceeded .80. Moreover, Cronbach's α for the composite score exceeded .90.

Stability

An analysis across five samples from three countries (Australia, The Netherlands, and Norway; total N=1,057) revealed that the mean stability coefficient of the original and short versions of the UWES across a one-year time interval is .65 (ranging from .56 to .75). (Details of this unpublished analysis may be obtained from the first author.) A longitudinal study among Finnish dentists spanning 7 years found similar stabilities for the subscales of the UWES ranging from .61 to .65 (Hakanen & Peeters, 2015). Furthermore, Seppälä et al. (2009) found high rank-order stability coefficients, ranging from .82 to .86, for the three scales of the UWES across a 3-year time interval, indicating that the relative ordering of individuals within the sample was largely maintained over time.

Discriminant Validity

Work engagement – as tapped with the UWES – is conceived as a distinct concept that is negatively related to burnout (González-Roma et al., 2006). Yet, meta-analytic findings of Cole et al. (2012) suggest that the UWES assesses the same as the reversed scored Maslach Burnout Inventory (MBI; Maslach et al., 2016). According to Cole et al., this would imply that work engagement is *not* a unique construct. However, Byrne et al. (2016) challenged this implication by applying a more rigorous and appropriate procedure that uses multiple constructs and measures at different time points. They concluded: "[W]e determined empirically that the construct of work engagement is *not* the same as the opposite of the burnout construct" (p. 1219). This conclusion is further supported by a study by Goering et al. (2017) testing a meta-analytic structural equation model (MASEM) that used input data from 10 other meta-analyses on the relationship between burnout and work engagement, including the one of Cole et al. This study not only found a *weak* negative correlation between the UWES and the MBI (r=–.29), but also that both were differentially related to challenge and hindrance demands as well as job resources. In other words, low scores on burnout do not imply high work engagement (and vice versa), and the root causes of burnout and work engagement are different.

Work engagement and workaholism are two forms of heavy work investment. Although, like workaholics, engaged workers work very hard, it seems their underlying motivation differs: Engaged employees are intrinsically motivated, whereas workaholics are characterized by an extrinsic – introjected or identified – motivation (Van Beek et al., 2012). Furthermore, confirmatory factor analyses showed that work engagement and workaholism – assessed as working excessively and working compulsively – are two distinct constructs (Schaufeli, Taris et al., 2006, 2008). However, the absorption scale of the UWES also loads on the latent workaholism factor, suggesting that absorption could also entail a compulsive tendency to work. In a similar vein, Andreassen et al. (2007) found that work engagement was predicted by enjoyment but *not* by drive, whereas the reverse was true for workaholism. Finally, a study by Mazetti et al. (2018), which included employees' self-reports as well as ratings from their colleagues, showed a considerable agreement between raters for work engagement (r=.59) and workaholism (r=.66). The authors concluded that "the present research corroborates the evidence that work engagement and workaholism represent two conceptually and empirically distinct forms of heavy work investment" (p. 38).

A meta-analysis of 13 studies found, on the one hand, correlations (corrected for unreliability) between work engagement – as measured with the UWES – and job satisfaction, job involvement as well as, on the other hand, affective organizational commitment of .55, .51, and .59, respectively (Christian et al., 2011). The authors conclude that "work engagement is unique although it shares conceptual space with job attitudes" (p. 120). This is confirmed by another meta-analysis that found a correlation of .77 between work engagement and a *composite,* latent measure of satisfaction, involvement, and commitment, dubbed the "A-factor" (Newman et al., 2010).

Conclusion

As expected, it appears that the UWES consists of three subscales (i.e., vigor, dedication, and absorption), and that this three-factor structure is generally – but not always – invariant across nations, race as well as across occupational groups and time. However, the three subscales are highly correlated, so it is recommended to use one composite score, particularly for practical purposes. Moreover, the three scales of the UWES as well as the composite questionnaire are sufficiently internally consistent and the scores are relatively stable across periods up to 7 years, which agrees with the definition of work engagement as a persistent psychological state. Finally, it seems that – despite some overlap – the UWES can be discriminated from measures tapping burnout, workaholism, and job attitudes such as job satisfaction, job involvement, and affective organizational commitment. In short: it seems that the UWES is a psychometrically sound instrument with sufficient factorial validity, factorial invariance, internal consistency, stability, and discriminant validity.

Content Validity of the Utrecht Work Engagement Scale (UWES)

Only very few studies have compared the UWES with other work engagement instruments. Byrne et al. (2016) carried out the most comprehensive convergent validity study so far by comparing the UWES with the Job Engagement Scale (JES; Rich et al., 2010 – see below). Using five independent samples, they concluded that the UWES and the JES are moderately positively related to each other, but that they measure different aspects of work engagement, whereby the UWES assesses a broader domain than the JES (see below).

Job Demands and Job Resources

Halbesleben (2010) carried out a meta-analysis that included 74 unique samples and 45,683 participants to assess the associations between work engagement, and job demands and resources. As expected, job resources (i.e., social support, job control, feedback, and climate) were positively related to work engagement ($\rho = .35$), whereas job demands (i.e., work overload and work-family conflict) were weakly negatively associated ($\rho = -.09$). Recently, Lesener et al. (2019) carried out a meta-analysis including 77 *longitudinal* samples and showed that job demands were not related to work engagement over time, whereas job resources are *reciprocally* related with work engagement. The latter is compatible with the notion of gain cycles; because of their motivational potential, job resources increase work engagement, which, in turn, leads to the accumulation of more resources, and so on (Salanova et al., 2010). A previous meta-analysis using 64 samples (Crawford et al., 2010), made an important distinction between hindering and challenging job demands, whereby the former thwart personal growth, learning, and goal attainment (e.g., role conflict, red tape), while the latter have the potential to promote mastery, personal growth, and future gains (i.e., time pressure, responsibility). Using MASEM, their study showed that hindrance demands were *negatively* ($r = -.19$) and challenge demands ($r = .21$) like resources ($r = .34$), were *positively* related to work engagement. Similar to the analysis of Halbesleben (2010), undifferentiated demands were virtually unrelated to work engagement (r=–.06). Finally, a recent meta-analysis (k=69, N=32,924) showed that work engagement was positively correlated with various leadership styles, including transformational (ρ=.45), servant (ρ=.40), and authentic (ρ=.35) leadership (DeCuypere & Schaufeli, in press).

Personal Resources

A meta-analysis involving 114 samples and focusing on the link with personality factors showed that, overall, the eight reviewed traits explained 48 % of the variance in work engagement (Young et al., 2018). Moreover, relative weights analysis revealed that positive affectivity was by far the strongest predictor of work engagement (ρ=.62), followed by proactive personality (ρ=.49), conscientiousness (ρ=.39), and extraversion (ρ=.40), respectively, whereas the remaining Big Five traits were less important. Focusing on more malleable personal resources, Halbesleben (2010) found similarly strong meta-analytic associations between work engagement and self-efficacy (ρ=.59) and optimism (ρ=.44). In their systematic review, Bailey et al. (2017) identified 11 studies that found a positive link between work engagement and other multifaceted personal resources, such as psychological capital (i.e., self-efficacy, hope, optimism, and resilience), core-self-evaluation (i.e., self-efficacy, self-esteem, internal locus of control, and emotional stability), hardiness (i.e., commitment, control and challenge), emotional intelligence, personal initiative, and achievement striving.

Outcomes

Four kinds of outcomes that have been associated with work engagement can be distinguished:

- *Attitude-based outcomes.* Not only can organizational commitment be discriminated from work engagement (see above), but work engagement also *predicts* commitment 2 years later, after controlling for commitment levels at baseline (Hakanen et al., 2008). A study using three independent samples showed that work engagement was negatively related to turnover intention, when controlling for burnout (Schaufeli & Bakker, 2004a). Finally, work engagement is positively related to workability, after controlling for prior workability 10 years ago (Airila et al., 2012). In addition, and consistent with this finding, the same study showed that work engagement was negatively related to lifestyle factors, such as BMI and smoking frequency.
- *Behavior-based outcomes.* In their meta-analysis, Christian et al. (2011) confirmed the incremental validity of work engagement by showing that it significantly contributed to task performance and contextual performance, after controlling for job satisfaction, job involvement, and organizational commitment. In addition, they also confirmed that work engagement mediated the relationship between job and personal resources, on the one hand, and performance, on the other hand. Moreover, work engagement has been *negatively* associated with counterproductive work behavior (Balducci et al., 2011), self-reported medical errors (Prins et al., 2010), and safety behaviors (meta-analysis; Nahrgang et al., 2011), and *positively* with active learning (Bakker et al., 2012),

supervisor-rated and coworker-rated performance (Halbesleben & Wheeler, 2008), creativity (Bakker et al., 2020), and personal initiative (Salanova & Schaufeli, 2008). Also, work engagement *predicts* registered future sickness absence (Schaufeli et al., 2009). Finally, the UWES can be used as a screening device to identify employees who are at risk for future long-term mental sickness absence (Roelen et al., 2015).

- *Business outcomes.* Work engagement is positively associated with customer satisfaction in the hospitality industry (Salanova et al., 2005), university departments' research productivity (Christensen et al., 2019) as well as business growth and business success in entrepreneurs (Gorgievski et al., 2014). Recently, Friesenbichler and Selenko (2017) found that managers' level of work engagement was positively related to firm performance (labor productivity), after controlling for various firm-based variables, such as type of industry and ownership. Although most outcomes that were included in the previous studies are objective, all studies used a cross-sectional design. However, work engagement also predicts work-unit innovativeness (Hakanen, Perhomeini et al., 2018) and clinical productivity (Hakanen & Koivumäki, 2014) of Finnish dentists, as well as petroleum company's work-unit service performance (Chen et al., 2018), restaurant's daily revenues (Xanthopoulou et al., 2009b), and future financial and personal success of entrepreneurs (Dijkhuizen et al., 2018).
- *Health and well-being outcomes.* Work engagement not only predicts future self-reported outcomes, such as low levels of depressive symptoms and life satisfaction (Hakanen & Schaufeli, 2012), low levels of psychological distress and physical symptoms (Shimazu et al., 2015), and low levels of burnout and job satisfaction (Hakanen, Peeters et al., 2018), but work engagement is also an important predictor of the nonoccurrence of major depression diagnosis (Imamura et al., 2016). Moreover, prospective cohort studies showed that engaged employees had low levels of C-reactive protein, which is an established risk factor for cardiovascular disease (Eguchi et al., 2015). Finally, work engagement is associated with healthy, cardiac autonomic activity (Seppälä et al., 2012). These last two studies seem to suggest that work engagement fosters cardiovascular health.

The associations described above refer to direct relationships between work engagement and various types of outcomes. Yet, it is important to note that several studies also confirmed that work engagement *mediates* the relationship between resources, on the one hand, and outcomes, on the other hand, as Figure 15.1 shows (e.g., Bakker et al., 2020; Chen et al., 2018; Nahrgang et al., 2011; Schaufeli & Bakker, 2004a; Schaufeli et al., 2009).

Job Crafting

Although research has provided considerable evidence for the contention that job characteristics influence employee work engagement, it is important to recognize that employees can also actively modify their own job demands and resources. This process is known as "job crafting," defined as "the physical and cognitive changes individuals make in their task or relational boundaries at work" (Wrzesniewski & Dutton, 2001, p. 179). Thus, employees may proactively change the content of their work, seek or avoid others with whom they interact (colleagues, suppliers, clients), or give a different meaning to their work activities. Tims, Bakker, and Derks (2013) developed the JD-R approach of job crafting and argued that individuals can proactively change the characteristics of their work to achieve a better person-job fit. Accordingly, job crafting can take the form of increasing social job resources (e.g., asking for feedback, seeking social support), increasing structural job resources (e.g., negotiating autonomy, developing competence through training), increasing challenge job demands (e.g., starting new projects), or decreasing hindrance job demands (e.g., decreasing emotionally demanding interactions with others at work). Meta-analytic findings indicate that job crafting is an important predictor of work engagement (Rudolph et al., 2017), particularly expansion-oriented job crafting behaviors through which employees increase their job challenges and resources. Several interventional studies showed that employees can learn to craft their jobs through training, and that the enactment of job crafting behaviors was related to work engagement and other positive outcomes including job performance (e.g., Van Wingerden et al., 2017; Gordon et al., 2018).

Conclusion

The content validity of the UWES is demonstrated by numerous studies that confirmed the relationships displayed in Figure 15.1. More specifically, cross-sectional evidence suggests that hindrance demands are negatively related to work engagement. In contrast, challenge demands, job resources, personal resources, and various leadership styles (e.g., transformational leadership) are positively related to work engagement. Moreover, longitudinal evidence indicates that job resources and work engagement are reciprocally related, which suggests the existence of so-called gain cycles. Work engagement predicts various attitudinal and behavioral outcomes, such as organizational commitment, workability, and sickness absence, as well as business outcomes such as creativity, productivity, service performance, and financial success. Work engagement also predicts various health and well-being outcomes such as cardiovascular health, life satisfaction, the non-occurrence of major depression, and low levels of psychological and physical health. Finally, employees may actively modify their own job demands and resources (i.e., job crafting), which has a positive impact on work engagement. Studies that evaluate the effects of job crafting training interventions have shown that the UWES is sensitive for detecting positive changes in levels of work engagement.

Special Applications of the UWES

Collective, Team Version

Costa et al. (2014) have proposed that teamwork engagement is functionally equivalent to individual work engagement. Therefore, they define teamwork engagement as a shared, fulfilling, and motivational state of work-related well-being, characterized by team vigor, team dedication, and team absorption. Work engagement may emerge at the team level through various social processes, including emotional contagion, role modeling, and adherence to social norms. Thus, energetic and enthusiastic team members influence each other so that levels of vigor, dedication, and absorption converge. Empirical evidence is still limited, but the first studies suggest that teamwork engagement results particularly from team job resources and team job crafting behaviors (e.g., Tims, Bakker, Derks et al., 2013). Also, teamwork engagement has been related to team job performance (e.g., Costa et al., 2015; Torrente et al., 2012; Rahmadani et al., 2020).

Daily Approach

Daily work engagement refers to transient states of vigor, dedication, and absorption that exist in a given moment and that fluctuate within the same individual over short periods of time (e.g., day to day or hour to hour; Sonnentag et al., 2010). Daily work engagement can be assessed with the 3- or 9-item version of the UWES, whereby the items are adjusted and refer to the specific "week," "day," or "hour." Breevaart et al. (2012) performed a multilevel factor-analytic study on the daily version of the 9-item UWES. Comparisons of competing models revealed that the multilevel model that captured the interdependency between the two levels of analysis (i.e., between-person and within-person level) was the model that best fitted the data. The three-factor structure of the work engagement construct was confirmed on a day-to-day basis, and it showed a better fit than the one-factor solution. In his review, Bakker (2014) showed that daily fluctuations in job resources explained daily fluctuations in work engagement, partly through their influence on daily personal resources like daily self-efficacy and daily optimism. In addition, daily work engagement was an important predictor of daily task performance.

Student Version

Although students do not "work" in the sense of being employed, they nevertheless carry out structured, goal-directed activities that are compulsory. They follow classes, carry out assignments, and prepare for obligatory exams and tests. Hence, from a psychological perspective, their activities can be considered as "work." And since they may pursue their activities with great energy and determination, the concept of academic work engagement emerged, which can be measured with the student version of the UWES in which "work" has been substituted by "study." The three-factor structure was confirmed for the 17-item (Cadime et al., 2016) as well as the 9-item version of the UWES (Schaufeli, Martínez et al., 2002; Carmona-Halty et al., 2019). As with the original version of the UWES, correlations between the subscales were very high, so a single composite academic work engagement score can be used just as well for practical purposes.

Several studies confirmed the positive relationship between students' engagement and their academic performance, as assessed by their grade point average (GPA; e.g., Schaufeli, Martínez et al., 2002; Ketonen et al., 2016). More specifically, it was found that – after controlling for exhaustion and cynicism – only vigor was associated with GPA (Cadime, Pinto et al., 2016). Moreover, student engagement mediated the relationship between academic resources and GPA (Salanova et al., 2009). Bakker et al. (2015) conducted a weekly diary study among first-year students who filled in a questionnaire twice per week over 3 weeks – during the days they had tutorial group meetings. The tutors evaluated each student's active learning behaviors during these meetings. Results showed that study engagement fully mediated the relationship between personal resources and observed learning activities; study resources (e.g., support, feedback, autonomy) were indirectly positively related to learning activities through study engagement. In addition, observed learning activities were positively related to the course grade. Finally, a longitudinal study (Ouweneel et al., 2011) suggested that student engagement is reciprocally related to personal resources (i.e., optimism, hope, and self-efficacy). So, taken together, these results with the student version of the UWES map into the model displayed in Figure 15.1 and therefore support its content validity.

Criticisms of the UWES

Although, overall, it seems that the UWES is a sound instrument to assess work engagement, not all that glitters is gold. The UWES has been criticized on three grounds: First, as noted above, it was claimed that work engagement – as assessed with the UWES – overlaps with burnout – as assessed with the MBI. In fact, Cole et al. (2012) argue that engagement is a redundant construct. In a similar vein, others showed that scores on the UWES correlate substantially with job attitudes, such as job satisfaction, job involvement, and affective organizational commitment (Christian et al., 2011). According to Newman et al. (2010), this is not surprising because the content of the items of the UWES resembles the content of other attitude measures. Finally, Meyer (2017) argues at the conceptual level that the definition of engagement that underlies the UWES raises questions about how it differs from satisfaction and commitment. In sum: the discriminant validity of the UWES is not beyond question, both empirically as well as conceptually.

Second, the UWES has been criticized because it lacks a firm theoretical basis (Viljevac et al., 2012), in contrast to the Job Engagement Scale (JES; see the next section), which is based on the seminal work of Kahn (1990) on personal engagement. Indeed, the UWES was developed inductively, based on in-depth interviews with employees and on the notion of work engagement being the positive antipode of burnout. Third, the meta-analysis by Kulikowski (2017) discussed above showed that the factorial validity of the UWES is not completely free from controversy; that is, not all studies confirm its three-factor structure unambiguously. In a somewhat similar vein, this also applies to the factorial invariance of the UWES across nations, races, and occupational groups, which has not been convincingly demonstrated in all cases (see above).

Questionnaires With Limited Application

Kahn's (1990) conceptualization of personal engagement inspired several researchers to develop self-report scales to assess employee engagement. For instance, May et al. (2004) and Rich et al. (2010) developed the Job Engagement Scale (JES), which includes cognitive, emotional, and physical engagement. The wording of the items shows a striking resemblance with those included in the absorption, dedication, and vigor subscales of the UWES, respectively (Schaufeli, 2014, p. 21).

Basing themselves somewhat more loosely on the seminal work of Kahn, Rothbard (2001) distinguished between attention and absorption, whereby the former refers to the cognitive availability and the amount of time one spends thinking about the work role, and the latter refers to being engrossed in the work role. The same applies to Saks (2006), who distinguished between job engagement and organizational engagement that were described as the employee's psychological presence in their job and their organization, respectively. Finally, the ISA Engagement scale of Soane, Truss et al. (2012) is also inspired by Kahn's conceptualization and includes *i*ntellectual, *s*ocial, and *a*ffective engagement. These three dimensions refer to (1) being intellectually absorbed in work; (2) being socially connected with the working environment and sharing common values with colleagues; and (3) feeling positive about one's work role, respectively. The first and the third dimension of the ISA resemble the absorption and vigor of the UWES, whereas the second dimension has not been considered before.

More recently, and based on a synthetic review of conceptualizations of work engagement, Shuck et al. (2017) proposed the Employee Engagement Scale (EES), which includes cognitive, emotional, and behavioral engagement. These three dimensions refer to an employee's intensity and willingness to invest mentally, emotionally, and behaviorally in positive organizational outcomes. A closer look at the items of these three dimensions reveals that they are reminiscent of absorption, affective organizational commitment, and extra-role behavior, respectively. Like most proprietary engagement measures, the EES can be criticized – at least partly – for putting old wine in a new bottle (Schaufeli, 2014).

It seems that all four operationalizations agree that engagement is a multidimensional construct, and that it includes absorption as its common denominator. Except for the JES, these questionnaires are only sporadically used in academic research (Bailey et al., 2017).

Two studies were carried out that compared the UWES with the JES. The first study used the preliminary, 13-item version of the JES (May et al., 2004) and showed that there is considerable overlap between both instruments. However, both measures could be discriminated from organizational commitment, and the UWES could also be discriminated from job involvement and intention to stay, whereas the JES could not. Moreover, compared to the JES, the UWES showed better predictive validity regarding perceptions of person-job fit and person-organization fit. The authors conclude that, overall, the UWES demonstrated a better validity than the JES.

The second comparative study is more elaborate and includes five samples to study the factor structure of both measures, their patterns of relationships with a host of antecedents and consequences, and the construct-level relationships between engagement and related variables (Byrne et al., 2016). First, the factor structures of the UWES and the more recent 18-item version of the JES (Rich et al., 2010) were each independently confirmed as three-factor structures. Second, both questionnaires were positively related with average correlations between the corresponding subscales ranging between .45 and .64 across the five samples. Third, the UWES and the JES were *not* interchangeable because they displayed different patterns of relationships with six variables, similar relationships with eight variables, and disparate relationships with five of the variables in the nomological network. However, overall, the relationships of the UWES with most variables in the network (e.g., job stress, job performance, strains, organizational commitment, job commitment, and burnout) were stronger than for the JES; this led the authors to conclude that the UWES assesses a broader domain than the JES.

In sum: only the JES is truly based on the needs-satisfying approach of Kahn (1990), whereas three other questionnaires of limited application are more loosely based on this approach, and one questionnaire emerged from a synthesis of the literature. According to the papers in which they were introduced, the psychometric quality of these questionnaires looks promising at first glance, but – except for the JES – this needs to be corroborated in future independent studies.

The Practical Use of Work Engagement Questionnaires

In this final section, we elaborate on which engagement questionnaire to choose in which context, and how to use the UWES for practical purposes.

Which Questionnaire to Use?

Recently, Mackay et al. (2017) tested a meta-analytic path model to examine the incremental validity of work engagement and a higher-order job attitude construct, consisting of job satisfaction, job involvement, and organizational commitment vis-à-vis employee effectiveness (i.e., in- and extra-role performance, turnover intention, and absenteeism). Indeed, they found evidence for moderate incremental validity of work engagement over-and-above the higher-order job attitude constructs as well as the three individual job attitudes. The authors concluded that work engagement " ... represents a quick and efficient way of assessing a key predictor of employee effectiveness and arguably makes the addition of other job attitude measures unnecessary" (p. 116). Also, the authors investigated whether the type of work engagement questionnaire (UWES vs. other instruments) moderated the effects, but that was not the case. Therefore, they recommend the use of the UWES for practitioners because " ... it represents a quick and efficient way of assessing a key predictor of employee effectiveness" (p. 116).

This agrees with the recommendation of Byrne et al. (2016), who – as noted in the previous section – found that the UWES taps a broader domain than the JES. Therefore, they recommend using the UWES in applied settings "where the intention is to assess with a wide net to capture global perceptions across several employee issues" (p. 1218). More specifically, they wrote that: "Practitioners' goals are typically to get a quick reading on how employees feel [...]. Their strategy is not to focus on one construct only, but to gather information on multiple constructs using the most efficient method. When a measure shares substantial content with existing measures and consequently demonstrates high correlations, its strength lies in providing summative information" (p.1218). In contrast, they recommend using the JES in research settings where the aim is to distinguish between concepts. The reason is that the JES has less overlap with associated attitudes than the UWES, rendering it potentially more useful in identifying the edges of the work-engagement construct domain. It should be noted here that Mackay et al.'s (2017) meta-analysis did *not* show a systematic difference between the UWES and other instruments including the JES, which might call this recommendation of Byrne et al. (2016) into question.

How to Use the UWES?

Work engagement as assessed with the UWES is regarded as a multifaceted experience; a set of experiences that occur together and refer to the same underlying entity. Hence, the recommendations of Schaufeli, Bakker et al. (2006) and Kulikowski (2017) to use a single, comprehensive score to assess work engagement make perfect sense. Unless, of course, one is interested in vigor, dedication, and absorption as separate components. However, it should be noted that no a priori theoretical reasons exist why these components would be related differently to other variables. At least, this is not how the UWES was conceived.

Originally, the UWES included 17 items that were later reduced to 9 items, which essentially provide the same information (Schaufeli, Taris et al., 2006). Some authors (Kulikowski, 2017; Seppälä et al., 2009) explicitly recommend using the more efficient short version, mainly because of better factorial validity and invariance across samples and time. Encouraging results were obtained with the 3-item ultrashort UWES across five countries (Schaufeli et al., 2017), which opens the possibility of measuring work engagement in national and international epidemiological surveys. For instance, the European Working Conditions Survey revealed that work engagement at the national level is curvilinearly related to a country's gross domestic product and linearly related to various indicators of good governance, such as public integrity, quality of democracy, and gender equality (Schaufeli, 2018).

The UWES can also be integrated into a more comprehensive, online tool based on the job demands-resources model (Bakker et al., 2014; Schaufeli, 2017). Hence, it assesses not only an employee's levels of work engagement but also the drivers and consequences (see Figure 15.1). Participants receive an individualized personal report, and by aggregating the individual information specific researchers can make suggestions about how to enhance levels of work engagement of teams, departments, or the organization as a whole (Knight et al., 2017).

Despite its cross-national validity, caution is warranted when comparing levels of work engagement between countries using the UWES, particularly when Asian countries are involved. For instance, it has been observed that Japanese employees scored consistently *lower* on work engagement than employees from Western countries, most likely because of the prevailing tendency in Japan to suppress the expression of positive affect (Shimazu et al., 2010). This underscores the necessity for establishing country-specific cutoff points that can be used for classifying employees as low, average, or high on work engagement compared with the working population (Schaufeli, 2017).

Conclusion and Outlook

Clearly, the field is dominated by the UWES, which is used in almost 9 out of 10 academic studies (Bailey et al., 2017). Although the validity of the UWES has occasionally been questioned, the current chapter shows that a vast body of psychometric studies exists demonstrating its internal consistency, stability, factorial validity, and invariance as well as its convergent and discriminant validity. Furthermore, this chapter shows that the UWES fits well into the nomological network that is based on the JD-R model (Figure 15.1). Taken together, the UWES seems to be the most promising tool to assess work engagement since, to date, no other viable alternative measure exists, perhaps except for the JES. Hence, future research with the JES – and other, alternative measures such as the ISA and EES – needs to be encouraged. In addition to psychometric work (e.g., about the incremental validity of different engagement measures; Mackay et al., 2017), three lines of research seem crucially important; (1) intervention studies on how to improve work engagement (Knight et al., 2017), (2) studies on the underlying mechanisms that explain why engagement leads to better individual, team, and business performance (Kim et al., 2012), and (3) studies on the still-underresearched dark side of work engagement (Albrecht, 2010). In other words, can we have too much engagement? For the time being, the UWES might not be the perfect measure of work engagement, but it is certainly backed up by the most elaborate and convincing body of empirical evidence demonstrating its psychometric and conceptual soundness.

References

Airila, A., Hakanen, J., Punakallio, A., Lusa, S., & Luukkonen, R. (2012). Is work engagement related to work ability beyond working conditions and lifestyle factors? *International Archives of Occupational and Environmental Health, 85*, 915–925. https://doi.org/10.1007/s00420-012-0732-1

Albrecht, S.L. (2010). Employee engagement: 10 key questions for research and practice. In S.L. Albrecht (Ed.), *The handbook of employee engagement: Perspectives, issues, research and practice* (p. 3–19). Edward-Elgar. https://doi.org/10.4337/9781849806374

Andreassen, C.S., Ursin, H., & Eriksen, H.R. (2007). The relationship between strong motivation to work, "workaholism," and health. *Psychology and Health, 22*, 615–629. https://doi.org/10.1080/14768320600941814

Attridge, M. (2009). Measuring and managing employee work engagement: A review of the research and business literature. *Journal of Workplace Behavioral Health, 24*, 383–398. https://doi.org/10.1080/15555240903188398

Bailey, C., Madden, A., Alfes, K., & Fletcher, L. (2017). The meaning, antecedents and outcomes of employee engagement: A narrative synthesis. *International Journal of Management Reviews, 19*, 31–53. https://doi.org/10.1111/ijmr.12077

Bakker, A.B. (2014). Daily fluctuations in work engagement: An overview and current directions. *European Psychologist, 19*, 227–236. https://doi.org/10.1027/1016-9040/a000160

Bakker, A.B., & Demerouti, E. (2007). The job demands-resources model: State of the art. *Journal of Managerial Psychology, 22*, 309–328. https://doi.org/10.1108/02683940710733115

Bakker, A.B., & Demerouti, E. (2008). Toward a model of work engagement. *Career Development International, 13*, 209–223. https://doi.org/10.1108/13620430810870476

Bakker, A.B., Demerouti, E., & Sanz-Vergel, A.I. (2014). Burnout and work engagement: The JD-R approach. *Annual Review of Organizational Psychology and Organizational Behavior, 1*, 389–411. https://doi.org/10.1146/annurev-orgpsych-031413-091235

Bakker, A.B., Demerouti, E., & ten Brummelhuis, L.L. (2012). Work engagement, performance, and active learning: The role of conscientiousness. *Journal of Vocational Behavior, 80*, 555–564. https://doi.org/10.1016/j.jvb.2011.08.008

Bakker, A.B., Hakanen, J.J., Demerouti, E., & Xanthopoulou, D. (2007). Job resources boost work engagement, particularly when job demands are high. *Journal of Educational Psychology, 99*, 274–284. https://doi.org/10.1037/0022-0663.99.2.274

Bakker, A.B., Petrou, P., Op den Kamp, E.M., & Tims, M. (2020). Proactive vitality management, work engagement, and creativity: The role of goal orientation. *Applied Psychology, 69*, 351–378. https://doi.org/10.1111/apps.12173

Bakker, A.B., Sanz-Vergel, A.I., & Kuntze, J. (2015). Student engagement and performance: A diary study on the role of openness. *Motivation and Emotion, 39*, 49–62. https://doi.org/10.1007/s11031-014-9422-5

Balducci, C., Fraccaroli, F., & Schaufeli, W.B. (2011). The job demands-resources model and counterproductive work behavior: The role of job-related affect. *European Journal of Work & Organizational Psychology, 20*, 467–496. https://doi.org/10.1080/13594321003669061

Breevaart, K., Bakker, A.B., Demerouti, E., & Hetland, J. (2012). The measurement of state work engagement: A multilevel factor analytic study. *European Journal of Psychological Assessment, 28*, 305–312. https://doi.org/10.1027/1015-5759/a000111

Buckingham, M., & Coffman, C. (1999). *First, break all the rules: What the world's greatest managers do differently*. Simon & Schuster.

Byrne, Z.S., Peters, J.M., & Weston, J.W. (2016). The struggle with employee engagement: Measures and construct clarification using five samples. *Journal of Applied Psychology, 101*, 1–27. https://doi.org/10.1037/apl0000124

Cadime, I., Lima, S., Marques Pinto, A., & Ribeiro, I. (2016). Measurement invariance of the Utrecht Work Engagement Scale for Students: A study across secondary school pupils and university students. *European Journal of Developmental Psychology, 13,* 254–263. https://doi.org/10.1080/17405629.2016.1148595

Cadime, I., Pinto, A.M., Lima, S., Rego, S., Pereira, J., & Ribeiro, I. (2016b). Well-being and academic achievement in secondary school pupils: The unique effects of burnout and engagement. *Journal of Adolescence, 53,* 169–179. https://doi.org/10.1016/j.adolescence.2016.10.003

Carmona-Halty, M., Schaufeli, W.B., & Salanova, M. (2019). The Utrecht Work Engagement Scale for Students (UWES-9S): Factorial validity, reliability, and measurement invariance in a Chilean sample of undergraduate university students. *Frontiers in Psychology, 10*, Article 1017. https://doi.org/10.3389/fpsyg.2019.01017

Chen, S.-L., Shih, C.-T., & Chi, N.-W. (2018). A multilevel job demands–resources model of work engagement: Antecedents, consequences, and boundary conditions. *Human Performance, 31*, 1–23. https://doi.org/10.1080/08959285.2018.1531867

Christensen, M., Dyrstad, J.M., & Innstrand, S.T. (2019). Academic work engagement, resources and productivity: Empirical evidence with policy implications. *Studies in Higher Education, 45*(1), 86–99. https://doi.org/10.1080/03075079.2018.1517304

Christian, M.S., Garza, A.S., & Slaughter, J.E. (2011). Work engagement: A quantitative review and test of its relations with task and contextual performance. *Personnel Psychology, 64*, 89–136. https://doi.org/10.1111/j.1744-6570.2010.01203.x

Cole, M.S., Walter, F., Bedeian, A.G., & O'Boyle, E.H. (2012). Job burnout and employee engagement: A meta-analytic examination of construct proliferation. *Journal of Management, 38*, 1550–1581. https://doi.org/10.1177/0149206311415252

Costa, P., Passos, A., & Bakker, A.B. (2015). Direct and contextual influence of team conflict on team resources, team work engagement and team performance. *Negotiation and Conflict Management Research, 8,* 211–227. https://doi.org/10.1111/ncmr.12061

Costa, P.L., Passos, A.M., & Bakker, A.B. (2014). Team work engagement: A model of emergence. *Journal of Organizational and Occupational Psychology, 87,* 414–436. https://doi.org/10.1111/joop.12057

Crawford, E.R., Lepine, J.A., & Rich, B.L. (2010). Linking job demands and resources to employee engagement and burnout: A theoretical extension and meta-analytic test. *Journal of Applied Psychology, 95*, 834–848. https://doi.org/10.1037/a0019364

DeCuypere, A., & Schaufeli, W.B. (in press). Positive leadership styles and engagement: A meta-analytic review. In S.K. Dhiman (Ed.), *Routledge companion to leadership and change*. Routledge.

Dijkhuizen, J., Gorgievski, M., van Veldhoven, M., & Schalk, R. (2018). Well-being, personal success and business performance among entrepreneurs: A two-wave study. *Journal of Happiness Studies, 19*, 2187–2204. https://doi.org/10.1007/s10902-017-9914-6

Eguchi, H., Shimazu, A., Kawakami, N., Inoue, A., Nakata, A., & Tsutsumi, A. (2015). Work engagement and high-sensitivity C-reactive protein levels among Japanese workers: A 1-year prospective cohort study. *International Archives of Occupational and Environmental Health, 88*, 651–658. https://doi.org/10.1007/s00420-014-0995-9

Frederickson, B.L. (2001). The role of positive psychology: The broaden-and-build theory of positive emotions. *American Psychologist*, *56*(3), 218–226. https://doi.org/10.1037/0003-066X.56.3.218

Friesenbichler, K., & Selenko, E. (2017). Firm performance in challenging business climates: Does managerial work engagement make a difference? *Asian Business and Management, 16,* 25–49. https://doi.org/10.1057/s41291-017-0016-4

Goering, D.D., Shimazu, A., Zhou, F., Wada, T., & Sakai, R. (2017). Not if, but how they differ: A meta-analytic test of the nomological networks of burnout and engagement. *Burnout Research, 5*, 21–34. https://doi.org/10.1016/j.burn.2017.05.003

González-Roma, V., Schaufeli, W.B., Bakker, A.B., & Lloret, S. (2006). Burnout and engagement: Independent factors or opposite poles? *Journal of Vocational Behavior, 68*, 165–174. https://doi.org/10.1016/j.jvb.2005.01.003

Gordon, H.J., Demerouti, E., LeBlanc, P.M., Bakker, A.B., Bipp, T., & Verhagen, M.A. (2018). Individual job redesign: Job crafting interventions in health care. *Journal of Vocational Behavior, 104*, 98–114. https://doi.org/10.1016/j.jvb.2017.07.002

Gorgievski, M., Moriano, A.J., & Bakker, A.B. (2014). Relating work engagement and workaholism to entrepreneurial performance. *Journal of Managerial Psychology, 29*, 106–121. https://doi.org/10.1108/JMP-06-2012-0169

Hakanen, J.J., & Koivumäki, J. (2014). Engaged or exhausted: How does it affect dentists' clinical productivity? *Burnout Research, 1*, 12–18. https://doi.org/10.1016/j.burn.2014.02.002

Hakanen, J.J., & Peeters, M.C.W. (2015). How do work engagement, workaholism, and the work-to-family interface affect each other? A 7-year follow-up study. *Journal of Occupational and Environmental Medicine, 57*, 601–609. https://doi.org/10.1097/JOM.0000000000000457

Hakanen, J.J., Peeters, M.C.W., & Schaufeli, W.B. (2018). Different types of employee wellbeing across time and their relationships with job crafting. *Journal of Occupational Health Psychology, 23*, 289–301. https://doi.org/10.1037/ocp0000081

Hakanen, J.J., Perhomeini, L., & Toppinen-Tanner, S. (2018). Positive gain spirals at work: From job resources to work engagement, personal initiative and work-unit innovativeness. *Journal of Vocational Behavior, 73*, 78–91. https://doi.org/10.1016/j.jvb.2008.01.003

Hakanen, J.J., & Schaufeli, W.B. (2012). Do burnout and work engagement predict depressive symptoms and life satisfaction? A three-wave seven-year prospective study. *Journal of Affective Disorders, 141*, 415–424. https://doi.org/10.1016/j.jad.2012.02.043

Hakanen, J.J., Schaufeli, W.B., & Ahola, K. (2008). The job demands-resources model: A three-year cross-lagged study of burnout, depression, commitment, and work engagement. *Work & Stress, 22*, 224–241. https://doi.org/10.1080/02678370802379432

Halbesleben, J.R.B. (2010). A meta-analysis of work engagement: Relationships with burnout, demands, resources, and consequences. In A.B. Bakker & M.P. Leiter (Eds.), *Work engagement: A handbook of essential theory and research* (pp. 102–117). Psychology Press.

Halbesleben, J.R.B., & Wheeler, A.R. (2008). The relative roles of engagement and embeddedness in predicting job performance and intention to leave. *Work & Stress, 22*, 242–256. https://doi.org/10.1080/02678370802383962

Harter, J.K., Schmidt, F.L., & Hayes, T.L. (2002). Business-unit-level relationships between employee satisfaction, employee engagement, and business outcomes: A meta-analysis. *Journal of Applied Psychology, 87*, 268–279. https://doi.org/10.1037/0021-9010.87.2.268

Imamura, K., Kawakami, N., Inoue, A., Shimazu, A., Tsutsumi, A., Takahashi, M., & Totsuzaki, T. (2016). Work engagement as a predictor of onset of major depressive episode (MDE) among workers, independent of psychological distress: A 3-year prospective cohort study. *PLoS ONE, 11*, 1–14. https://doi.org/10.1371/journal.pone.0167862

Kahn, W.A. (1990). Psychological conditions of personal engagement and disengagement at work. *Academy of Management Journal, 33*, 692–724.

Ketonen, E.E., Haarala-Muhonen, A., Hirsto, L., Hänninen, J., Wähälä, K., & Lonkaa, K. (2016). Am I in the right place? Academic engagement and study success during the first years at university. *Learning and Individual Differences, 51*, 141–148. https://doi.org/10.1016/j.lindif.2016.08.017

Kim, W., Kolb, J.A., & Kim, T. (2012). The relationship between work engagement and performance: A review of empirical literature and a proposed research agenda. *Human Resource Development Review, 12*, 248–276. https://doi.org/10.1177/1534484312461635

Klassen, R.M., Aldhafri, S., Mansfield, C.F., Purwanto, E., Siu, A.F.Y., Wong, M.W., & Woods-McConney, A. (2012). Teachers' engagement at work: An international validation study. *The Journal of Experimental Education, 80*, 317–337. https://doi.org/10.1080/00220973.2012.678409

Knight, C., Patterson, M., & Dawson, J. (2017). Building work engagement: A systematic review and meta-analysis investigating the effectiveness of work engagement interventions. *Journal of Organizational Behavior, 38*, 792–812. https://doi.org/10.1002/job.2167

Kulikowski, K. (2017). Do we all agree on how to measure work engagement? Factorial validity of Utrecht Work Engagement Scale as a standard measurement too: A literature review. *International Journal of Occupational Medicine and Environmental Health, 30*, 161–175. https://doi.org/10.13075/ijomeh.1896.00947

Lesener, T., Gusy, B., & Wolter, C. (2019). The job demands-resources model: A meta-analytic review of longitudinal studies. *Work & Stress, 33*, 76–103. https://doi.org/10.1080/02678373.2018.1529065

Mackay, M.M., Allen, J.A., & Landis, R.S. (2017). Investigating the incremental validity of employee engagement in the prediction of employee effectiveness: A meta-analytic path analysis. *Human Resource Management Review, 27*, 108–120. https://doi.org/10.1016/j.hrmr.2016.03.002

Maslach, C., Jackson, S.E., & Leiter, M.P. (2016). *The Maslach Burnout Inventory* (4th ed.). Mind Garden, Inc.

Maslach, C., & Leiter, M.P. (1997). *The truth about burnout*. Jossey-Bass.

May, D.R., Gilson, R.L., & Harter, L.M. (2004). The psychological conditions of meaningfulness, safety and availability and the engagement of the human spirit at work. *Journal of Occupational and Organizational Psychology, 77*, 11–37. https://doi.org/10.1348/096317904322915892

Mazetti, G., Schaufeli, W.B., & Guglielmi, D. (2018). Are workaholism and work engagement in the eye of the beholder? A multirater perspective on different forms of working hard. *European Journal of Psychological Assessment, 34*, 30–40. https://doi.org/10.1027/1015-5759/a000318

Meyer, J.P. (2017). Has engagement had its day: What's next and does it matter? *Organizational Dynamics, 46*, 87–95. https://doi.org/10.1016/j.orgdyn.2017.04.004

Nahrgang, J.D., Morgeson, F.P., & Hofmann, D. (2011). Safety at work: A meta-analytic investigation of the link between job demands, job resources, burnout, engagement, and safety outcomes. *Journal of Applied Psychology, 96*, 71–94. https://doi.org/10.1037/a0021484

Newman, D.A., Joseph, D.L., & Hulin, C.J. (2010). Job attitudes and employee engagement: Considering the attitude "A-factor." In S. Albrecht (Ed.), *The handbook of employee engagement: Perspectives, issues, research, and practices* (pp. 43–62). Edward Elgar.

Ouweneel, E., Le Blanc, P., & Schaufeli, W. (2011). Flourishing students: A longitudinal study on positive emotions, personal resources, and study engagement. *Journal of Positive Psychology, 6*, 142–153. https://doi.org/10.1080/17439760.2011.558847

Prins, J.T., Van der Heijden, F.M., Hoekstra-Weebers, J.E., Bakker, A.B., Jacobs, B., & Gazendam-Donofrio, S.M. (2010). Burnout, engagement and resident physicians' self-reported errors. *Psychology, Health & Medicine, 6*, 654–667.

Rahmadani, V., Schaufeli, W.B., Stouten, J., Zhang, Z., & Zulkarmain, Z. (2020). Engaging leadership and its implication for work engagement and job outcomes at individual and team level: A multilevel longitudinal study. *International Journal of Environmental Research and Public Health, 17*, 776. https://doi.org/10.3390/ijerph17030776

Rich, B.L., Lepine, J.A., & Crawford, E.R. (2010). Job engagement: Antecedents and effects on job performance. *The Academy of Management Journal, 53*, 617–635. https://doi.org/10.5465/amj.2010.51468988

Roelen, C.A.M., Van Hoffen, M.F.A., Groothoff, J.W., De Bruin, J., Schaufeli, W.B., & Van Rhenen, W. (2015). Can the Maslach Burnout Questionnaire and the Utrecht Work Engagement Scale be used to screen for risk of long-term sickness absence? *International Achieves for Occupational and Environmental Health, 88*, 467–475. https://doi.org/10.1007/s00420-014-0981-2

Rothbard, N.P. (2001). "Enriching or depleting?" The dynamics of engagement in work and family roles. *Administrative Science Quarterly, 46*, 655–684. https://doi.org/10.2307/3094827

Rudolph, C.W., Katz, I.M., Lavigne, K.N., & Zacher, H. (2017). Job crafting: A meta-analysis of relationships with individual differences, job characteristics, and work outcomes. *Journal of Vocational Behavior, 102*, 112–138. https://doi.org/10.1016/j.jvb.2017.05.008

Saks, A. M. (2006). Antecedents and consequences of employee engagement. *Journal of Managerial Psychology, 21*, 600–619. https://doi.org/10.1108/02683940610690169

Salanova, M., Agut, S., & Peiró, J. M. (2005). Linking organizational resources and work engagement to employee performance and customer loyalty: The mediation of service climate. *Journal of Applied Psychology, 90*, 1217–1227. https://doi.org/10.1037/0021-9010.90.6.1217

Salanova, M., & Schaufeli, W. B. (2008). A cross-national study of work engagement as a mediator between job resources and proactive behavior: A cross-national study. *International Journal of Human Resources Management, 19*, 226–231.

Salanova, M., Schaufeli, W. B., Martinez, I., & Bresó, E. (2009). How obstacles and facilitators predict academic performance: The mediating role of study burnout and engagement. *Anxiety, Stress, & Coping, 26*, 1–18.

Salanova, M., Schaufeli, W. B., Xanthopoulou, D., & Bakker, A. B. (2010). Gain spirals of resources and work engagement. In A. B. Bakker & M. P. Leiter (Eds.), *Work engagement: A handbook of essential theory and research* (pp. 118–131). Psychology Press.

Schaufeli, W. B. (2014). What is engagement? In C. Truss, R. Delbridge, K. Alfes, A. Shantz, & E. Soane (Eds.), *Employee engagement in theory and practice* (pp. 15–35). Routledge.

Schaufeli, W. B. (2017). The job demands-resources model: A "how to" guide to increase work engagement and prevent burnout. *Organizational Dynamics, 46*, 120–132. https://doi.org/10.1016/j.orgdyn.2017.04.008

Schaufeli, W. B. (2018). Work engagement in Europe: Relations with national economy, governance and culture. *Organizational Dynamics, 47*, 99–106. https://doi.org/10.1016/j.orgdyn.2018.01.003

Schaufeli, W. B., & Bakker, A. B. (2004a). Job demands, job resources and their relationship with burnout and engagement: A multi-sample study. *Journal of Organizational Behavior, 25*, 293–315. https://doi.org/10.1002/job.248

Schaufeli, W. B., & Bakker, A. B. (2004b). Bevlogenheid: Een begrip gemeten [Work engagement: The measurement of a concept]. *Gedrag & Organisatie, 17*, 89–112. https://doi.org/10.5117/2004.017.002.002

Schaufeli, W. B., Bakker, A. B., & Salanova, M. (2006). The measurement of work engagement with a short questionnaire: A cross-national study. *Educational and Psychological Measurement, 66*, 701–716. https://doi.org/10.1177/0013164405282471

Schaufeli, W. B., Bakker, A. B., & Van Rhenen, W. (2009). How changes in job demands and resources predict burnout, work engagement, and sickness absenteeism. *Journal of Organizational Behavior, 30*, 893–917. https://doi.org/10.1002/job.595

Schaufeli, W. B., Martínez, I., Marques Pinto, A., Salanova, M., & Bakker, A. B. (2002). Burnout and engagement in university students: A cross-national study. *Journal of Cross- Cultural Psychology, 33*, 464–481. https://doi.org/10.1177/0022022102033005003

Schaufeli, W. B., Salanova, M., Gonzélez-Romá, V., & Bakker, A. B. (2002). The measurement of engagement and burnout: A confirmative analytic approach. *Journal of Happiness Studies, 3*, 71–92. https://doi.org/10.1023/A:1015630930326

Schaufeli, W. B., Shimazu, A., Hakanen, J., Salanova, M., & De Witte, H. (2017). An ultra-short measure for work engagement: The UWES-3 validation across five countries. *European Journal of Psychological Assessment, 35*(4), 577–591. https://doi.org/10.1027/1015-5759/a000430

Schaufeli, W. B., Taris, T. W., & Bakker, A. B. (2006). Dr. Jekyll and Mr. Hyde: On the differences between work engagement and workaholism. In R. Burke (Ed.), *Work hours and work addiction* (pp. 193–252). Edward Elgar.

Schaufeli, W., Taris, T., Le Blanc, P., Peeters, M., Bakker, A., & De Jonge, J. (2001). Maakt arbeid gezond? Op zoek naar de bevlogen werknemer. [Does work make healthy? The quest for the engaged worker]. *De Psycholoog, 36*, 422–428.

Schaufeli, W. B., Taris, T. W., & Van Rhenen, W. (2008). Workaholism, burnout and engagement: Three of a kind or three different kinds of employee well-being? *Applied Psychology, 57*, 173–203. https://doi.org/10.1111/j.1464-0597.2007.00285.x

Seppälä, P., Mauno, S., Feldt, T., Hakanen, J., Kinnunen, U., Tolvanen, A., & Schaufeli, W.B. (2009). The construct validity of the Utrecht Work Engagement Scale: Multisample and longitudinal evidence. *Journal of Happiness Studies, 10*, 459–481. https://doi.org/10.1007/s10902-008-9100-y

Seppälä, P., Mauno, S., Kinnunen, M.L., Feldt, T., Juuti, T., Tolvanen, A., & Rusku, H. (2012). Is work engagement related to healthy cardiac autonomic activity? Evidence from a field study among Finnish women workers. *Journal of Positive Psychology, 7*, 95–106. https://doi.org/10.1080/17439760.2011.637342

Shimazu, A., Miyanaka, D., & Schaufeli, W.B. (2010). Work engagement from a cultural perspective. In S. Albrecht (Ed.), *The handbook of employee engagement: Perspectives, issues, research and practice* (pp. 364–372). Edward-Elgar.

Shimazu, A., Schaufeli, W.B., Kamiyama, L., & Kawakami, N. (2015). Workaholism vs. work engagement: The two different predictors of future well-being and performance. *International Journal of Behavioral Medicine, 22*, 18–23.

Shimazu, A., Schaufeli, W.B., Kosugi, S., Suzuki, A., Nashiwa, H., Kato, A., Sakamoto, M., Irimajiri, H., Amano, S., Hirohata, K., Goto, R., & Kitaoka-Higashiguchi, K. (2008). Work engagement in Japan: Development and validation of the Japanese version of the Utrecht Work Engagement Scale. *Applied Psychology, 57*, 510–523.

Schneider, B., Yost, A.B., Kropp, A., Kind, C., & Lam, H. (2018). Workforce engagement: What it is, what drives it, and why it matters for organizational performance. *Journal of Organizational Behavior, 39*, 462–480. https://doi.org/10.1002/job.2244

Shuck, B. (2011). Integrative literature review: Four emerging perspectives of employee engagement: an Integrative literature review. *Human Resource Development Review, 10*, 304–328. https://doi.org/10.1177/1534484311410840

Shuck, B., Adelson, J., & Reio, T.G. (2017). The employee engagement scale. *Human Resource Management, 56*, 95–977. https://doi.org/10.1002/hrm.21811

Soane, E., Truss, C., Alfes, K., Shantz, A., Gatenby, M., & Rees, C. (2012). Development and application of a new measure of employee engagement: The ISA Engagement Scale. *Human Resource Development International, 15*, 37–41. https://doi.org/10.1080/13678868.2012.726542

Sonnentag, S., Dormann, C., & Demerouti, E. (2010). Not all days are created equal: The concept of state work engagement. In A.B. Bakker & M.P. Leiter (Eds.), *Work engagement: A handbook of essential theory and research* (pp. 25–38). Psychology Press.

Storm, K., & Rothmann, I. (2003). A psychometric analysis of the Utrecht Work Engagement Scale in the South African police service. *South African Journal of Industrial Psychology, 29*, 62–70. https://doi.org/10.4102/sajip.v29i4.129

Tims, M., Bakker, A.B., & Derks, D. (2013). The impact of job crafting on job demands, job resources, and well-being. *Journal of Occupational Health Psychology, 18*, 230–240. https://doi.org/10.1037/a0032141

Tims, M., Bakker, A.B., Derks, D., & Van Rhenen, W. (2013). Job crafting at the team and individual level: Implications for work engagement and performance. *Group and Organization Management, 38*, 427–454. https://doi.org/10.1177/1059601113492421

Torrente, P., Salanova, M., Llorens, S., & Schaufeli, W.B. (2012). Teams make it work: How team work engagement mediates between social resources and performance in teams. *Psicothema, 24*, 106–112.

Van Beek, I., Hu, Q., Schaufeli, W.B., Taris, T., & Schreurs, B.H. (2012). For fun, love or money. What drives workaholic, engaged and burned-out employees at work? *Applied Psychology, 61*, 30–55.

Van Wingerden, J., Derks, D., & Bakker, A.B. (2017). The impact of personal resources and job crafting interventions on work engagement and performance. *Human Resources Management, 56*, 51–67. https://doi.org/10.1002/hrm.21758

Viljevac, A., Cooper-Thomas, H.D., & Saks, A.M. (2012). An investigation into the validity of two measures of work engagement. *The International Journal of Human Resource Management, 23*, 3692–3709. https://doi.org/10.1080/09585192.2011.639542

Wrzesniewski, A., & Dutton, J.E. (2001). Crafting a job: Revisioning employees as active crafters of their work. *Academy of Management Review, 26*, 179–201. https://doi.org/10.2307/259118

Xanthopoulou, D., Bakker, A. B., Demerouti, E., & Schaufeli, W. B. (2009a). Reciprocal relationships between job resources, personal resources and work engagement. *Journal of Vocational Behavior, 74,* 235–244. https://doi.org/10.1016/j.jvb.2008.11.003

Xanthopoulou, D., Bakker, A. B., Demerouti, E., & Schaufeli, W. B. (2009b). Work engagement and financial returns: A diary study on the role of job and personal resources. *Journal of Occupational and Organizational Psychology, 82,* 183–200. https://doi.org/10.1348/096317908X285633

Young, H. R., Glerum, D. R., Wang, W., & Joseph, D. L. (2018). Who are the most engaged at work? A meta-analysis of personality and employee engagement. *Journal of Organizational Behavior, 39,* 1330–1346. https://doi.org/10.1002/job.2303

Part IV

Applied Settings

Chapter 16

School-Based Approaches for the Universal Assessment of Adolescent Psychosocial Strengths

Jennica Paz[1], Eui Kyung Kim[2], Erin Dowdy[3], Michael J. Furlong[3], Tameisha Hinton[3], José A. Piqueras[4], Tíscar Rodríguez-Jiménez[5], Juan C. Marzo[4], and Susan Coats[6]

[1]College of Education, San Diego State University, CA, USA
[2]Graduate School of Education, University of California Riverside, CA, USA
[3]International Center for School-Based Youth Development, University of California Santa Barbara, CA, USA
[4]Department of Health Psychology, University Miguel Hernandez de Elche, Spain
[5]Department of Health Psychology, Catholic University of Murcia, Spain
[6]California Association of School Psychologists

Several terms are used to describe youth strengths such as psychological assets, attributes, functioning, and orientation. This chapter uses the term *psychosocial strengths* to refer to the combination of positive psychological domains that are conceptualized in the Covitality framework. The assessment of psychosocial strengths in adolescents has focused on the measurement of single traits and constructs, such as grit (Christopoulou et al., 2018), optimism (Oberle et al., 2018), hope (Pedrotti, 2018), and gratitude (Gottlieb & Froh, 2019). Although there is substantial value in assessing and evaluating the beneficial correlates of individual constructs, we suggest that a whole-child paradigm (Alford & White, 2015) provides the opportunity to examine the contributions of comprehensive measures of psychosocial strengths to better understand adolescents' quality of life. Note that several terms are used to describe positive life functioning such as quality of life, psychological well-being, mental well-being, and life satisfaction. Throughout, this chapter uses the term *quality of life*.

Strength-based measures have a clinical purpose when used by school psychologists as part of an individual child psychoeducational assessment. In addition, such measures have broader benefits when used to monitor the psychosocial strengths of *all* students within the context of local education agencies. This chapter focuses on two strength-based measures developed for schoolwide universal monitoring among adolescents that emerged from the positive education movement (Seligman et al., 2009; Waters & Loton, 2019).

Comprehensive Strengths Assessment Frameworks for School Contexts

This chapter reviews two comprehensive, strength-focused assessments that monitor components of psychosocial strengths of all youth specifically designed to support positive education research and practice. We advocate for a holistic approach that examines strengths in combination rather than in isolation; that is, the assessment of the integrative effects of the core components of positive psychosocial development (Lenzi et al., 2015). The assessments included in this chapter were selected based on (a) being grounded in a conceptual framework of positive education psychosocial strengths, (b) feasibility and utility as school-based universal screening measures (reasonable length and availability of self-report), and (c) evidence of compelling psychometric properties, including replicated validity and generalizability with diverse, crossnational samples of adolescents across three or more separate studies. We note that there are other assessments of youth personal character strengths that we did not review because their primary applications are not in school settings, or because they are discussed elsewhere in this volume. One example is the Values in Action (VIA) Youth Survey, which measures 24 strength constructs among youth aged 10 to 17 years. However, it is not used for schoolwide universal screening, and its many items (i.e., 96–198 items) limit practical use in schools. Another example is Lerner et al.'s (2005; Geldhof et al., 2014) Five Cs Framework of Positive Development (Competence, Confidence, Connection, Character, Caring), which has been used primarily in the United States to evaluate community youth-development initiatives. There are certainly other assessments such as those measuring specific strength constructs (e.g., school connectedness) and teacher ratings which we did not include because of this chapter's focus on comprehensive strength-based measures using adolescent self-reports, which is a practical method for schoolwide universal screening/monitoring that also recognizes the value of incorporating student voice (Halliday et al., 2019).

Two frameworks and their measures meet the above criteria and were thus selected for review: (a) Kern et al.'s (2016) Engagement, Perseverance, Optimism, Connectedness, and Happiness (EPOCH) framework and (b) Renshaw et al.'s (2014) Covitality Integrated Framework (Belief-in-Self, Belief-in-Others, Emotional Competence, and Engaged Living). For each measure, we provide an overview of the conceptual framework, a summary of the key psychometric studies, and illustrations of how the measures are being used in school-based research and practice. We include examples of how comprehensive positive psychology measures are employed by researchers and local education agencies in Spain and the United States. Additionally, we provide readers with descriptions of, and access to, online sources of information about school-based strength assessments.

Engagement, Perseverance, Optimism, Connectedness, and Happiness (EPOCH) Framework

The EPOCH measure is grounded in Seligman's (2011) PERMA (*P*ositive emotions, *E*ngagement, *R*elationships, *M*eaning and purpose, and *A*ccomplishment) psychosocial strengths-based framework. As the PERMA framework is currently applied and utilized in various countries to inform positive psychosocial education for youth in schools (Branson et al., 2019; Gregory & Brinkman, 2015; Kırca, & Ekşi, 2018; Lai et al., 2018), the EPOCH measure is highly relevant within the field of positive education. The EPOCH measure is a downward extension of Butler and Kern's (2016) PERMA-Profiler developed for use with adults. The EPOCH framework defines *Engagement* as the capacity to become absorbed in and focused on what one is doing, in addition to being involved and interested in life activities and tasks (e.g., "When I do an activity, I enjoy it so much that I lose track of time"). *Perseverance* is the ability to pursue one's goals to completion despite challenges (e.g., "Once I make a plan to get something done, I stick to it"). *Optimism* refers to one's hopefulness and confidence about the future marked by a tendency to have a positive outlook on life (e.g., "In uncertain times, I expect the best"). *Connectedness* is the sense that one has satisfying relationships with others, believes that one loves, values, and provides friendship or support to others (e.g., "When something good happens to me, I have people who I like to share the good news with"). *Happiness* is one's steady feeling of content with life, which is associated with a positive mood (e.g., "I feel happy"). Kern et al. (2016) posited that fostering these psychosocial strengths during adolescence promotes, and possibly predicts, adult psychosocial strengths based on PERMA's framework.

EPOCH Psychometric Properties

Kern et al. (2016) developed the EPOCH scale by selecting 60 items from comparable measures related to the aforementioned EPOCH characteristics. To develop a parsimonious measure, they compiled 10 sample groups of middle- to upper-income youths ages 10–18 from the U.S. and Australia. Based on measurement functioning across different sample groups and across time, the final EPOCH scale retained 20 items, with 4 items per subscale. Kern et al. (2019) further examined the EPOCH's structural validity employing samples of U.S., Australian, and Chinese students. Confirmatory factor analyses (CFA) indicated that there were adequate fit indices, favoring a five-factor model over a single-factor model and a higher-order model (additional psychometric information is available at https://journals.sagepub.com/doi/suppl/10.1177/0734282918789561). Overall, the authors reported good internal consistency estimates (Cronbach's alpha) for the full scale across sample groups (Kern et al., 2016). Table 16.1 provides a summary of key psychometric studies documenting the reliability and validity of the EPOCH scale (the scale is available online at http://www.peggykern.org/uploads/5/6/6/7/56678211/epoch_measure_of_adolescent_well-being_102014.pdf).

Regarding concurrent validity evidence, Kern et al. (2016) reported that the EPOCH subscales were negatively correlated with measures of depression, anxiety, and aggression. Despite the varying degrees of positive correlations with other constructs, the EPOCH subscales were positively associated with higher self-reported physical vitality, self-rated academic performance, and life satisfaction. As such, researchers suggested that the characteristics measured by the EPOCH scale could be used to assess the psychosocial strengths of youth and to predict the quality of life in adulthood via PERMA theory based on previous longitudinal studies.

EPOCH Research in Schools

Given the significance of quality of life as it relates to youth life satisfaction and success, researchers have incorporated the EPOCH framework for improving psychosocial strengths in schools. In Australia, the foundation for a multidimensional whole school framework based on PERMA theory was applied at an all-boys school to determine how well-being impacted the learning community, physical health, and job outcomes (Kern et al., 2015). To assess overall school climate factors, students anonymously completed the measure, and the results indicated that higher EPOCH scores were positively related to students' physical health. Similarly, researchers in the United Kingdom used the EPOCH to survey youth from the Americas, Asia Pacific, Europe, and the Middle East, to understand how school curricula might be modified to foster students' quality of life (Cooker et al., 2016).

A Slovakian version of the EPOCH was used to explore relations among high-school students' academic perceptions, social perceptions, and quality of life through school belonging (Šeboková et al., 2018). The results showed that school belongingness mediated self-competence and students' well-being. Specifically, higher self-competence was related to higher levels of connectedness, optimism, and happiness among youth. These studies highlight the relevance of EPOCH as an outcome measure and applied in education settings to establish supportive environments, facilitate learning, and improve youth outcomes.

EPOCH Considerations and Limitations

Rose et al. (2017) asserted that the promotion of psychosocial strengths and quality of life among adolescents is of "great public health and social significance" (p. 2360). For this reason, these researchers identified several scales aimed to measure psychosocial strengths and found the EPOCH to be one of four scales with empirical evidence for use with adolescents. Though the psychometric properties of the EPOCH continue to be assessed for norm values, order effects, use among special populations, and language translations, there is great interest in achieving a measure of the quality of life that is internationally useful (Kern et al., 2016; Zeng & Kern, 2019). Nevertheless, significant advances are being made using the PERMA framework and the EPOCH assessment to engage students in designing and implementing positive education programs in schools (Halliday et al., 2019).

Table 16.1. Summary of key Engagement, Perseverance, Optimism, Connectedness, and Happiness (EPOCH) measure psychometric studies

Study	Sample size (*N*)	Grade	Sex	Sample	Reliability[b]		Validity[c]
Kern et al. (2015)	514	8–11	100 % M	Australia	Engagement Perseverance Optimism Connectedness Happiness	.68 .83 .77 .78 .86	*Structural:* Acceptable fit five-factor model *Convergent:* EPOCH-E with School Engagement (.56), EPOCH-P with Grit (.78), EPOCH-O with Hope (.75), EPOCH-H with PANAS-P (.71)
Kern et al. (2016) 10 samples combined	3,826	7–12	Range[a]	USA, Australia	Engagement Perseverance Optimism Connectedness Happiness Overall	.74–.77 .79–.80 .76–.81 .77–.81 .83–.86 .90–.92	*Structural:* Acceptable fit five-factor model *Convergent:* Depression (–.13 – –.53) Anxiety (–.02 – –.36), Aggression (–.04 – –.44), Physical Vitality (.34–.58), Academic Performance (.29–.53), Life Satisfaction (.36–.83)
Loton & Waters (2017)	11,138	10–18 years	59 % M 41 % F	Australia	Engagement Perseverance Optimism Connectedness Happiness	– – – – .89	N/A
Šeboková et al. (2018)	248	9	38 % M 62 % F	Slovakia	Engagement Perseverance Optimism Connectedness Happiness	.76/.78[d] .73/.69 .77/.77 .80/.83 .86/.87	*Structural:* Acceptable fit five-factor model
Kern et al. (2019)	3,620 (China) 3,098 (Western)	9–19 years	55 % M 45 % F	China Western	Engagement Perseverance Optimism Connectedness Happiness	.77/.77[e] .79/.80 .77/.81 .77/.80 .90/.87	*Structural:* Acceptable fit five-factor model; invariance sex, age, and country

Note. M = male; F = female. EPOCH-E = Engagement; EPOCH-P = Perseverance; EPOCH-O = Optimism; EPOCH-H = Happiness. [a]The researchers used 10 sample groups; percentages are reported separately for each sample in Kern et al. (2016, p. 23). [b] All reliabilities are Cronbach's α coefficients unless otherwise indicated. [c] All validity coefficients are Pearson correlation coefficients. [d] Reliability coefficients reported based on 6-month test-retest. [e] Chinese/Western Omega coefficients

Covitality Framework

Furlong, You et al. (2014) hypothesized that youth psychosocial strengths are linked to a higher-order trait, called "covitality" and defined it as the "synergistic effect of positive mental health resulting from the interplay among multiple positive psychological building blocks" (p. 3). The term covitality takes a counterapproach to comorbidity, understood as the co-occurrence of multiple disorders, which often implies interactions associated with worse symptoms. Covitality proposes that the combination of psychosocial strengths and their synergistic effects matter more than any single individual strength for quality of life among youth.

The Social Emotional Health Surveys (SEHS; Furlong, You et al., 2014) were developed to measure covitality among youth. There are three self-report versions of the SEHS: Primary (SEHS-P; Furlong et al., 2013) for students ages 9–12, Secondary (SEHS-S; Furlong, You et al., 2014) for students ages 13–18, and Higher Education (SEHS-HE; Furlong et al., 2017) for college students (see https://www.covitalityucsb.info/sehs-measures/index.html). The SEHS framework views covitality through a transactional development lens: The development of core psychosocial strengths (e.g., gratitude, empathy, and persistence) promotes positive interpersonal transactions within a child's socioecological systems, which, in turn, contribute to better developmental outcomes. Youth thrive and flourish in life when they develop psychosocial strengths that promote positive, supportive day-to-day interactions with family, teachers, and peers.

Because of this chapter's focus on adolescence, we review the SEHS secondary version (SEHS-S; Furlong, You et al., 2014, 2021). The SEHS-S is a 36-item measure that assesses 12 psychosocial strengths derived from the social-emotional learning (SEL) and positive youth development (PYD) literature (e.g., Bandura et al., 1996; Furlong, Gilman et al., 2014; Masten et al., 2009; Zins et al., 2007). These 12 psychosocial strengths are associated with four second-order positive social-emotional constructs: (a) *belief-in-self* (self-awareness, self-efficacy, persistence); (b) *belief-in-others* (family coherence, peer support, school support); (c) *emotional competence* (emotion regulation, self-control, empathy); and (d) *engaged living* (optimism, zest, gratitude). The four domains load onto a higher-order latent trait, covitality.

SEHS-S Covitality Psychometric Properties

Table 16.2 provides a summary of key studies examining the psychometric properties of the SEHS-S. An increasing number of studies provide evidence for the psychometric properties of the SEHS-S, including evidence of the reliability and validity of the higher-order model, internal consistency, construct and predictive validity, and invariance across sociocultural and sex groups, including Japanese (Ito et al., 2015), South Korean (Lee et al., 2016), Turkish (Telef & Furlong, 2017), and U.S. samples (You et al., 2015). Additionally, the SEHS-S total covitality index has evidence of convergent validity with measures of youth global psychosocial strengths. For example, the covitality score had a significant positive relationship with the prosocial behavior subscale of the Strengths and Difficulties Questionnaire (SDQ; Goodman, 1997), and a negative relationship with the SDQ total difficulties scale among Turkish youths (Telef & Furlong, 2017). Furthermore, it was significantly correlated with other quality-of-life outcomes such as subjective well-

Table 16.2. Summary of key Social Emotional Health Survey-Secondary (SEHS-S) psychometric studies

Study	Sample size (*N*)	Grade	Sex	Sample		Reliability[a]		Validity[b]
Furlong, You et al. (2014)	4,189	8, 10, 12	50 % F 50 % M	USA Latin American	 72 %	Belief in Self Belief in Others Emo. Comp. Engaged Living Covitality	n/a n/a n/a n/a .92	*Structural:* Acceptable fit second-order model, invariance sex *Convergent*[c]: SWB (.89), Academic (.08), School safety (.12)
You et al. (2014)	2,240	9–12	47 % F 53 % M	USA Latin American	 72 %	Belief in Self Belief in Others Emo. Comp. Engaged Living Covitality	.76 .81 .78 .87 .91	*Structural:* Acceptable fit second-order model, invariance sex and age *Convergent:* BESS (–.63)
Kim et al. (2014)	118	10	56 % F 44 % M	USA Other European American Latin American	 50 % 24 % 12 %	Belief in Self Belief in Others Emo. Comp. Engaged Living Covitality	n/a n/a n/a n/a .90	*Structural:* n/a *Convergent:* SWB (.57)
You et al. (2015)	14,171	9–12	51 % F 49 % M	USA Latin American White American African American Asian American	 51 % 17 % 7 % 8 %	Belief in Self Belief in Others Emo. Comp. Engaged Living Covitality	n/a n/a n/a n/a .95	*Structural:* Acceptable fit second-order model, invariance sex and race/ethnicity
Ito et al. (2015)	975	7–9	52 % F 48 % M	Japan	100 %	Belief in Self Belief in Others Emo. Comp. Engaged Living Covitality	.78 .87 .82 .88 .93	*Structural:* Acceptable fit second-order model, invariance sex

Table 16.2. continued

Study	Sample size (*N*)	Grade	Sex	Sample		Reliability[a]		Validity[b]
Lee et al. (2016)	686	7–12	56 % F 44 % M	Korea	100 %	Belief in Self Belief in Others Emo. Comp. Engaged Living Covitality	.84 .85 .82 .88 .94	*Structural:* Acceptable fit second-order model, invariance sex *Convergent:* SWB (.56)
Telef & Furlong (2017)	2,242	9–12	55 % F 45 % M	Turkey USA	50 % 50 %	Belief in Self Belief in Others Emo. Comp. Engaged Living Covitality	.76 .77 .74 .80 .89	*Structural:* Latent mean differences on belief-in-self domain (ES = .16) *Convergent:* SWB (.66)
Xie et al. (2017)	3,750	7–12	52 % F 48 % M	China	100 %	Belief in Self Belief in Others Emo. Com. Engaged Living Covitality 3-week test-retest	.77 .81 .80 .88 .92 .89	*Structural:* Acceptable fit second-order model, invariance sex, and grade *Convergent:* LS (.46), PANAS-P (.46), DASS-D (–.36), DASS-A (–.25), DASS-S (–.22)

Note. M = male; F = female. BESS = Behavioral and Emotional Screening Scale; DASS-D = Depression Anxiety and Stress 21-Depression; DASS-A = Depression Anxiety and Stress 21-Anxiety; DASS-S = Depression Anxiety and Stress 21-Stress; Emo. Comp. = emotional competence domain; PSSM-A = Psychological Sense of School Membership-Acceptance; PANAS-P = Positive and Negative Affect Scale-Positive; PANAS-N = Positive and Negative Affect Scale-Negative; PSSM-R = Psychological Sense of School Membership-Rejection; SEHS = Social Emotional Health Survey Covitality = SEHS-S and SEHS-P total score; SWB = subjective well-being. [a]All reliabilities are Cronbach's α coefficients unless otherwise indicated. [b]All validity coefficients are Pearson correlation coefficients or structural equation model path coefficients. [c]Covitality scores are the sum of all SEHS-S and SEHS-P items.

being among Korean youth (Kim et al., 2019; Lee et al., 2016) and depression, anxiety, and stress in Chinese youth (Xie et al., 2017). These studies highlight some of the growing empirical support for using the SEHS-S to identify students' quality of life outcomes in various sociocultural contexts.

SEHS-S Covitality Framework

Research in Schools

Recognizing the importance of internal strengths for youth quality of life, international school-psychology scholars have adapted the SEHS-S to identify students' psychosocial strengths and their relationships with various school outcomes. The SEHS-S has been administered in middle and high schools within the U.S. (Carnazzo et al., 2019; Dougherty & Sharkey, 2017), Australia (Boman et al., 2017), South Korea (Kim et al., 2019; Lee et al., 2016), Japan (Ito et al., 2015), and Turkey (Telef & Furlong, 2017). It was utilized to identify positive psychological factors that improve academic achievement (Dougherty & Sharkey, 2017) and school connectedness (Kim et al., 2019), and to reduce behavioral concerns such as truancy (Wroblewski et al., 2019). Furthermore, Dowdy et al. (2015) discussed the utility of the SEHS-S in assisting schools in developing strengths-based prevention plans for students.

SHES-S Covitality Framework Considerations and Limitations

Overall, the crossnational SEHS-S Covitality validation and application studies provide empirical evidence on its utility in diverse educational settings. Ongoing international efforts in research and practice (e.g., Proyecto Covitalidad in Spain; https://www.facebook.com/pages/category/Mental-Health-Service/Proyecto-CoVitalidad-1733667443390967/) using the SEHS-S will further build evidence of its psychometric properties and utility in school settings globally. Additionally, further validations of the associations between the SEHS-S results and youth positive functioning in schools will support educators and school psychologists in identifying and promoting psychosocial strengths among youth to improve their quality of life. A final development is that Project Covitality, funded by the US Department of Education Institute of Education Sciences, received a four-year grant to enhance and standardize the SEHS-S, which will further examine its validity (for updated information and resources, see https://www.covitalityucsb.info/). In particular, the large cross-sectional database will be used to create updated norming information on the measure, and the longitudinal database will provide updated information on its stability across time and the ability to predict a wide range of educational and psychosocial outcomes.

From Research to Practice: Application Within Diverse School Contexts

Thus far, this chapter has focused on describing and reviewing comprehensive strength-based assessments that can be used to monitor youth psychosocial strengths. In addition to understanding the theoretical underpinnings and psychometric support for each of the reviewed measures, it is also critical for practitioners and researchers to understand how these comprehensive strength-based assessments may be used in school-based practice. In general, information obtained from these assessments may be used to monitor the well-being of individual students and that of an entire population, taking a public health approach to assessment (Dowdy et al., 2010), and can be used to help school-based practitioners direct resources appropriately for both students and school systems. For example, individual-level results on the SEHS-S may suggest that a particular student may benefit from additional asset-building preventions or early interventions. Additionally, population-level results may highlight that the ninth-grade cohort of males does not feel particularly bonded to the school, suggesting a targeted intervention to increase school belongingness among ninth-grade male students.

For both individual and population-level assessment goals, schools need a comprehensive means of measuring psychosocial strengths. The measures discussed thus far have been useful for research (Moore, Mayworm et al., 2019; Moore, Dowdy et al., 2019a, 2019b), but are also valuable for providing schools with readily-available measures with which to assess and monitor the psychosocial strengths of students. As an illustration, we provide two brief overviews of the use of the SEHS-S across two unique school-based contexts, one in the United States and the other in Spain. These examples may be more intensive than what all schools may choose to do, but these selected case examples demonstrate how comprehensive strength-based assessments may be integrated within school service delivery models to improve data-based decision-making and effectively plan for and deliver interventions.

Illustrative School-Based Applications

Illustration 1: California Local Education Agency Context

The Flores School District, located in an urban Southern California community, enrolls more than 13,000 students across 20 schools. The SEHS-S is administered as a universal monitoring measure to the students in Grades 7, 9, and 10. During the 2018–2019 academic year, 2,912 students completed the SEHS via an online format during the first semester. Screening and responding to students' needs was coordinated and provided by school-employed mental-health professionals and professionals provided by collaborating community mental-health agencies. These professionals included 14 school counselors, six school psychologists, and five community mental-health professionals.

Education Agency's Wellness Assessment Goals

In 2017, the education agency began discussing and developing their student mental-health framework and multitiered systems of support (MTSS) to address student behavioral and mental-health concerns and improve psychosocial strengths. The district's mental-health framework focuses on three tiers:

- Tier 1 supports a positive school climate and promotes well-being and psychosocial resilience for all youth;
- Tier 2 focuses on selected and brief evidence-based strategies to support some students (approximately 15 %) at risk of, or already with, mild mental health challenges;
- Tier 3 offers intensive, ongoing strategies to support those few students (approximately 5 %) with significant coping, functioning, and recovery needs, including referrals to school-employed mental health professionals and school-based mental-health providers.

Student Wellness Screening and Follow-Up

At the Tier 1 level, after obtaining parental consent, all students were asked to complete the social-emotional screening assessment, which included the SEHS-S, the Student Emotional Distress Scale (SEDS; Dowdy et al., 2018), and brief measures of life satisfaction and school belonging. The SEHS-S and the SEDS were employed to evaluate students' psychosocial wellness using a dual-factor (Suldo & Shaffer, 2008) complete mental health model that includes a balance of both distress and strength indicators. Students who reported experiencing elevated personal distress on the SEDS in the past month (among the top 15 % of peers) and who reported low levels of SEHS-S psychosocial strengths (among the lowest 15 % of peers) were identified for Tier 2 school support services – across eight secondary schools 3 % to 10 % of students screened positive.

The high-need students were individually interviewed by site administrators, school counselors, school psychologists, and school-based mental health agency personnel within a few days after taking the survey to clarify needs and link them to available services. Interviewers were asked to thank the student for their participation, commend the student on being a positive social-change agent by participating in the survey, and provide information to the student on their SEHS-S profile strengths. For the highest-need students, a structured interview form documenting the youth's comments was later used to identify areas of concern, available site resources, and the mental-health service gaps within the school and community.

Screening Effects on Education Agency Programs and Services

Principals and school team interviewers were invited to a debriefing meeting after all surveys had been completed and students with elevated risk profiles had been interviewed. The meeting began with a discussion of the successes and challenges in the process, student and school climate results, and any follow-up comments regarding those students with elevated risk profiles. Challenges to the survey process were noted to improve the process for the next school year. Toward the end of the debriefing meeting, a school wellness action plan was developed and given out to school site teams. The teams discussed screening results concerning their school's climate and the concerns of students with elevated risk profiles. The next steps included a district office mental-health administration meeting with each school site team to go over their wellness action plans by defining their strengths and concerns, analyzing their student group results and timelines in achieving their tiered student mental-health support goals. Additionally, school site wellness action plans were shared with the district leadership team for the future professional development of site administration, school-employed mental-health staff, and parents. School-based mental-health agencies work collaboratively with school sites to develop parent workshops and Tier 2 student support groups. Overall, this district exemplifies how the comprehensive assessment of youth psychosocial strengths (and distress) can be used to inform multitiered systems of support for all students within a school district.

Illustration 2: Strengths-Based Assessment in Diverse Spanish School Ecosystems

Until a few years ago, school-based preventive interventions for mental health in Spain had focused on detection, identification, and early intervention, exclusively targeting the presence of psychological problems. Recently, assessment approaches have focused not only on identifying the presence of distress and risk factors, but also on psychosocial strengths or resources. Since 2016, the Covitality-Spain team has been implementing psychological assessment practices including strengths and difficulties in children, adolescents, and university students. The survey instruments were administered online schoolwide within a universal prevention framework and were designed to assist youth while also collecting additional validity information for use of the SEHS-S with a population of Spanish youth.

Among adolescents, the first study involved 1,042 high-school students and included distress and strength variables. Findings indicated that Covitality was negatively associated with internalizing and externalizing symptoms as well as with peer and parent relationship problems. Large, positive associations were found with measures of positive covariates (well-being, health-related quality of life, and prosocial behaviors). A subsequent longitudinal study collected data from a sample of 5,172 secondary and high-school students. Distress, well-being, health-related quality of life, psychopathology, and relationships with parents, among other variables, were examined. Results indicated that social-emotional competencies predicted psychosocial adjustment and mediated the influence of stressful events on psychosocial adjustment. Additionally, SEHS-S results were used to create group and individual reports to identify adolescents who present a risk for suicide and/or low mental health. Overall, the comprehensive assessment of strengths among Spain has helped inform the use of strength-based measures while also providing data to inform prevention and intervention services for individuals and groups.

Conclusion

Psychosocial strengths-based assessment has its benefits and scientific rationale when grounded in a sound conceptual framework that offers an understanding of the process and factors associated with quality-of-life outcomes among adolescents. This chapter examined two recently developed comprehensive measures with sound conceptual frameworks that can be used schoolwide to monitor multiple psychosocial strengths of all students. Other scholars have identified over 140 additional measures with acceptable psychometric properties that may be incorporated into strengths-based assessment practices to assess a variety of positive attributes among diverse populations (Simmons

& Lehmann, 2013). Having stated this, we recognize that each potential measure of psychosocial strengths has unique strengths and weaknesses. The decision which measure to use may vary depending on the purpose of assessment, and local education agencies may wish to consider whether the measure has established validity regarding the intended culturally and linguistically diverse population. This chapter highlighted the EPOCH and SEHS-S as comprehensive strength-focused measures for use in monitoring student well-being in schools. In addition to the review of the EPOCH and SEHS-S measures provided in this chapter, Box 16.1 provides key resources that educators can openly access to carefully consider which psychosocial strength and asset measures would be optimal for use in each school context. As researchers and practitioners continue to emphasize further understanding the psychosocial strengths of students, there will likely be continued developments toward a standard of practice for the universal assessment of adolescent psychosocial strengths. As with any contemporary approach to assessment, we look forward to the continued progress in the comprehensive assessment of youths' psychosocial strengths, particularly as it helps students and school systems across the globe.

Box 16.1. Key positive psychology assessment resources for use in school contexts

Center for Social-Emotional Learning (CASEL) Assessment Guide

CASEL established an assessment workgroup to identify validated measures of social-emotional learning (SEL) skills and orientations to include in an SEL assessment guide. This guide includes a catalog of measures and resources for researchers and practitioners to select and use appropriately.

https://measuringsel.casel.org/access-assessment-guide/

Children's Worlds: International Study of Children's Well-Being

In 2009, UNICEF hosted a meeting involving researchers from the International Society for Child Indicators (ISCI) to develop a child well-being measure that supported international research. Subsequently, a measure was developed and has been employed in several studies. The latest study includes students (ages 8, 10, and 12) from 40 countries. The measures used in this study are available online.

https://www.isciweb.org/

Office of Economic Development Study on Social-Emotional Skills

This is an ambitious multiyear project (2016–2020) that set out to carefully define a set of social-emotional learning constructs and to craft a measure that can be used internationally. The main study will gather information on students' social and emotional skills; family, school, and community learning contexts; and the background characteristics of students, teachers, and parents. The student SEL measurement is grounded in the Big 5 personality model and assesses the following constructs: *Task Performance* (achievement motivation, responsibility, persistence, self-control); *Emotional Regulation* (stress resistance, optimism, emotional control); *Collaboration* (empathy, trust, cooperation); *Openmindedness* (tolerance, curiosity, creativity); *Engaging with Others* (sociability, assertiveness, energy); and *Compound Skills* (critical thinking, metacognition, self-efficacy).

https://www.oecd.org/education/ceri/social-emotional-skills-study

Project overview document: Office of Economic Development. (n.d.). https://bit.ly/2zWFtW9

Project Covitality

This multiyear (2016–2020) project was funded by the U.S. Office of Education, Institute of Education Sciences. It focused on the further validation of the Social-Emotional Health Survey-Secondary. A cross-sectional sample of 120,000 students and a three-year longitudinal sample of 1,000 high-school students were used in validation studies. These measures support the use of universal school complete social-emotional wellness screening and monitoring.

https://www.covitalityucsb.info/index.html

RAND Education Assessment Finder: Measuring Social, Emotional, and Academic Competencies

The RAND research group has created an online searchable resource that education agencies can use to identify measures of social and emotional constructs, including a range of positive psychological constructs. This resource includes a user guide on how to access and search the measure repository and a practitioner guide that education agencies can use to consider which measures best match interests and needs.

https://www.rand.org/education-and-labor/projects/assessments.html

User Guide: Hamilton, L.S., Stecher, B.M., Schweig, J., & Baker, G. (2018). RAND education assessment finder: User instructions. Available from https://www.rand.org/content/dam/rand/pubs/tools/TL300/TL308/RAND_TL308z1.pdf

Practitioner Guide: Taylor, J.J., Buckley, K., Hamilton, L.S., Stecher, B.M., Read, L., & Scgweig, J. (2018). *Choosing and using SEL competency assessments: What schools and districts need to know*. Available from https://measuringsel.casel.org/pdf/Choosing-and-Using-SEL-Competency-Assessments_What-Schools-and-Districts-Need-to-Know.pdf

Acknowledgments

Preparation of this chapter was supported by a research grant from the US Department of Education, Institute of Education Sciences (#R305A160157) awarded to Michael Furlong, Erin Dowdy, and Karen Nylund-Gibson, and by a research grant from the Spanish Ministry of Economy and Competitiveness – RETOS 2017 (PSI2017-88280-R) awarded to Jose A. Piqueras, Juan C. Marzo, Tíscar Rodríguez-Jiménez, and Michael Furlong.

References

Alford, Z., & White, M. (2015). Positive school psychology. In M. White & A. Murray (Eds.), *Evidence-based approaches in positive education* (pp. 93–109). Springer. https://doi.org/10.1007/978-94-017-9667-5_5

Bandura, A., Barbaranelli, C., Caprara, G.V., & Pastorelli, C. (1996). Multifaceted impact of self-efficacy beliefs on academic functioning. *Child Development, 67,* 1206–1222. https://doi.org/10.2307/1131888

Boman, P., Mergler, A., & Pennell, D. (2017). The effects of covitality on well-being and depression in Australian high school adolescents. *Clinical Psychiatry, 3*(2), Article 15. https://doi.org/10.21767/2471-9854.100045

Branson, V., Palmer, E., Dry, M.J., & Turnbull, D. (2019). A holistic understanding of the effect of stress on adolescent well-being: A conditional process analysis. *Stress and Health, 35*(5), 626–641. https://doi.org/10.1002/smi.2896

Butler, J., & Kern, M.L. (2016). The PERMA-Profiler: A brief multidimensional measure of flourishing. *International Journal of Wellbeing, 6,* 1–48. https://doi.org/10.5502/ijw.v6i3.526

Carnazzo, K., Dowdy, E., Furlong, M.J., & Quirk, M.P. (2019). An evaluation of the Social Emotional Health Survey–Secondary for use with students with learning disabilities. *Psychology in the Schools, 56,* 433–446. https://doi.org/10.1002/pits.22199

Christopoulou, M., Lakioti, A., Pezirkianidis, C., Karakasidou, E., & Stalikas, A. (2018). The role of grit in education: A systematic review. *Psychology, 9,* 2951–2971. https://doi.org/10.4236/psych.2018.915171

Cooker, L., Bailey, L., Stevenson, H., & Joseph, S. (2016). *Social and emotional well-being in IB world schools (age 3–19): Final report.* University of Nottingham, School of Education.

Dougherty, D., & Sharkey, J.D. (2017). Reconnecting youth: Promoting emotional competence and social support to improve academic achievement. *Children and Youth Services Review, 74,* 28–34. https://doi.org/10.1016/j.childyouth.2017.01.021

Dowdy, E., Furlong, M.J., Nylund-Gibson, K., Moore, S., & Moffa, K. (2018). Initial validation of the Social Emotional Distress Scale to support complete mental health screening. *Assessment for Effective Intervention, 43,* 241–248. https://doi.org/10.1177/1534508417749871

Dowdy, E., Furlong, M.J., Raines, T.C., Bovery, B., Kauffman, B., Kamphaus, R., Dever, B.V.,Price, M., & Murdock, J. (2015). Enhancing school-based mental health services with a preventive and promotive approach to universal screening for complete mental health. *Journal of Educational and Psychological Consultation, 25,* 178–197. https://doi.org/10.1080/10474412.2014.929951

Dowdy, E., Ritchey, K., & Kamphaus, R.W. (2010). School-based screening: A population-based approach to inform and monitor children's mental health needs. *School Mental Health, 2,* 166–176. https://doi.org/10.1007/s12310-010-9036-3

Furlong, M.J., Dowdy, E., Nylund-Gibson, K., Wagle, R., Carter, D., & Hinton, T. (2021). Enhancement and standardization of a universal social-emotional health measure for students' psychological strengths. *Journal of Well-Being Assessment, 4,* 245–267. https://doi.org/10.1007/s41543-020-00032-2

Furlong, M.J., Gilman, R., & Huebner, E.S. (Eds.). (2014). *Handbook of positive psychology in schools* (2nd ed.). Routledge/Taylor & Francis.

Furlong, M.J., You, S., Renshaw, T.L., O'Malley, M.D., & Rebelez, J. (2013). Preliminary development of the Positive Experiences at School Scale for elementary school children. *Child Indicators Research, 6,* 753–775. https://doi.org/10.1007/s12187-013-9193-7

Furlong, M.J., You, S., Renshaw, T.L., Smith, D.C., & O'Malley, M.D. (2014). Preliminary development and validation of the Social and Emotional Health Survey for Secondary Students. *Social Indicators Research, 117,* 1011–1032. https://doi.org/10.1007/s11205-013-0373-0

Furlong, M.J., You, S., Shishim, M., & Dowdy, E. (2017). Development and validation of the Social Emotional Health Survey–Higher Education version. *Applied Research in Quality of Life, 12,* 343–367. https://doi.org/10.1007/s11482-016-9464-9

Geldhof, G.J., Bowers, E.P., Boyd, M.J., Mueller, M.K., Napolitano, C.M., Schmid, K.L., Lerner, J.V., & Lerner, R.M. (2014). Creation of short and very short measures of the Five Cs of positive youth development. *Journal of Research on Adolescence, 24,* 163–176. https://doi.org/10.1111/jora.12039

Goodman, R. (1997). The Strengths and Difficulties Questionnaire: A research note. *Journal of Child Psychology and Psychiatry, 38*, 581–586. https://doi.org/10.1111/j.1469-7610.1997.tb01545.x

Gottlieb, R., & Froh, J. (2019). Gratitude and happiness in adolescents: A qualitative analysis. In N.R. Silton (Ed.), *Scientific concepts behind happiness, kindness, and empathy in contemporary society* (pp. 1–19). IGI Global. https://doi.org/10.4018/978-1-5225-5918-4.ch001

Gregory, T., & Brinkman, S. (2015). *Development of the Australian Student Wellbeing Survey: Measuring the key aspects of social and emotional well-being during middle childhood.* Frasier Mustard Centre, Department of Education and Child Development and the Telethon Kids Institute, Adelaide.

Halliday, A.J., Kern, M.L., Garrett, D.K., & Turnbull, D.A. (2019). The student voice in well-being: A case study of participatory action research in positive education. *Educational Action Research, 27*, 173–196. https://doi.org/10.1080/09650792.2018.1436079

Ito, A., Smith, D.C., You, S., Shimoda, Y., & Furlong, M.J. (2015). Validation of the Social Emotional Health Survey–Secondary for Japanese students. *Contemporary School Psychology, 19*, 243–252. https://doi.org/10.1007/s40688-015-0068-4

Kern, M.L., Benson, L., Steinberg, E.A., & Steinberg, L. (2016). The EPOCH measure of adolescent well-being. *Psychological Assessment, 28*, 586–597. https://doi.org/10.1037/pas0000201

Kern, M.L., Waters, L.E., Adler, A., & White, M.A. (2015). A multidimensional approach to measuring well-being in students: Application of the PERMA framework. *The Journal of Positive Psychology, 10*, 262–271. https://doi.org/10.1080/17439760.2014.936962

Kern, M.L., Zeng, G., Hou, H., & Peng, K. (2019). The Chinese version of the EPOCH measure of adolescent well-being: Testing cross-cultural measurement invariance. *Journal of Psychoeducational Assessment, 37*, 757–769. https://doi.org/10.1177/0734282918789561

Kim, E., Dowdy, E., & Furlong, M.J. (2014). An exploration of using a dual-factor model in school-based mental health screening. *Canadian Journal of School Psychology, 29*, 127–140. https://doi.org/10.1177/0829573514529567

Kim, E., Dowdy, E., Furlong, M.J., & You, S. (2019). Complete mental health screening: Psychological strengths and life satisfaction in Korean students. *Child Indicator Research, 12*, 901–915. https://doi.org/10.1007/s12187-018-9561-4

Kırca, B., & Ekşi, H. (2018). Turkish adaptation of the comprehensive inventory of mindfulness experiences-adolescents: A reliability and validity study. *SHS Web of Conferences, Vol. 48*, Article 1038. EDP Sciences. https://doi.org/10.1051/SHSCONF/20184801038

Lai, M.K., Leung, C., Kwok, S.Y., Hui, A.N., Lo, H.H., Leung, J.T., & Tam, C.H. (2018). A multidimensional PERMA-H positive education model, general satisfaction of school life, and character strengths use in Hong Kong senior primary school students: Confirmatory factor analysis and path analysis using the APASO-II. *Frontiers in Psychology, 9*, 1–11. https://doi.org/10.3389/fpsyg.2018.01090

Lee, S., You, S., & Furlong, M.J. (2016). Validation of the Social Emotional Health Survey for Korean school students. *Child Indicators Research, 9*, 73–92. https://doi.org/10.1007/s12187-0149294-y

Lerner, R.M., Lerner, J.V., Almerigi, J.B., Theokas, C., Phelps, E., Gestsdottir, S., Naudeau, S., Jelici, H., Alberts, A., Ma, L., Smith, L.M., Bobek, D.L., Richman-Raphael, D., Simpson, I., DiDenti Christiansen, E., & von Eye, A. (2005). Positive youth development, participation in community youth development programs, and community contributions of fifth-grade adolescents: Findings from the first wave of the 4-H Study of Positive Youth Development. *Journal of Early Adolescence, 25*, 17–71. https://doi.org/10.1177/0272431604272461

Lenzi, M., Dougherty, D., Furlong, M.J., Dowdy, E., & Sharkey, J.D. (2015). The configuration protective model: Factors associated with adolescent behavioral and emotional problems. *Journal of Applied Developmental Psychology, 38*, 49–59. https://doi.org/10.1016/j.appdev.2015.03.003

Loton, D.J., & Waters, L.E. (2017). The mediating effect of self-efficacy in the connections between strength-based parenting, happiness and psychological distress in teens. *Frontiers in Psychology, 8*, 1707. https://doi.org/10.3389/fpsyg.2017.01707

Masten, A. S., Cutuli, J. J., Herbers, J. E., & Reed, M.-G. J. (2009). Resilience in development. In S. J. Lopez & C. R. Snyder (Eds.), *Oxford handbook of positive psychology* (2nd ed., pp. 117–131). Oxford University Press.

Moore, S., Dowdy, E., Nylund-Gibson, K., & Furlong, M. J. (2019a). An empirical approach to complete mental health classification in adolescents. *School Mental Health, 11*(3), 438–453. https://doi.org/10.1007/s12310-019-09311-7

Moore, S., Dowdy, E., Nylund-Gibson, K., & Furlong, M. J. (2019b). A latent transition analysis of the longitudinal stability of dual-factor mental health in adolescence. *Journal of School Psychology, 73,* 56–73. https://doi.org/10.1016/j.jsp.2019.03.003

Moore, S., Mayworm, A. M., Stein, R., Sharkey, J. D., & Dowdy, E. (2019). Languishing students: Linking complete mental health screening in schools to Tier II intervention. *Journal of Applied School Psychology, 35*(3), 257–289. https://doi.org/10.1080/15377903.2019.1577780

Oberle, E., Guhn, M., Gadermann, A. M., Thomson, K., & Schonert-Reichl, K. A. (2018). Positive mental health and supportive school environments: A population-level longitudinal study of dispositional optimism and school relationships in early adolescence. *Social Science & Medicine, 214*, 154–161. https://doi.org/10.1016/j.socscimed.2018.06.041

Office of Economic Development. (n.d.) *Social and emotional skills: Well-being, connectedness, and success.* https://bit.ly/2zWFtW9

Pedrotti, J. T. (2018). The will and the ways in school hope as a factor in academic success. In M. W. Gallagher & S. J. Lopez (Eds.), *The Oxford handbook of hope* (pp. 107–115). Oxford University Press.

Renshaw, T. L., Furlong, M. J., Dowdy, E., Rebelez, J., Smith, D. C., O'Malley, M. D., Lee, S., & Strom, I. F. (2014). Covitality: A synergistic conception of adolescents' mental health. In M. J. Furlong, R. Gilman, & E. S. Huebner (Eds.), *Handbook of positive psychology in schools* (2nd ed., pp. 12–32). Routledge/ Taylor & Francis.

Rose, T., Joe, S., Williams, A., Harris, R., Betz, G., & Stewart-Brown, S. (2017). Measuring mental wellbeing among adolescents: A systematic review of instruments. *Journal of Child and Family Studies, 26*, 2349–2362. https://doi.org/10.1007/s10826-017-0754-0

Šeboková, G., Uhláriková, J., & Halamová, M. (2018). Cognitive and social sources of adolescent wellbeing: Mediating role of school belonging. *Studia Psychologica, 60*, 16–29. https://doi.org/10.21909/sp.2018.01.749

Seligman, M. E. P. (2011). *Flourish: A visionary new understanding of happiness and well-being.* Simon and Schuster.

Seligman, M. E. P., Ernst, R. M., Gillham, J., Reivich, K., & Linkins, M. (2009). Positive education: Positive psychology and classroom interventions. *Oxford Review of Education, 35*, 293–311. https://doi.org/10.1080/03054980902934563

Simmons, C. A., & Lehmann, P. (2013). *Tools for strength-based assessment and evaluation.* Springer.

Suldo, S. M., & Shaffer, E. J. (2008). Looking beyond psychopathology: The dual-factor model of mental health in youth. *School Psychology Review, 37,* 52–68. https://doi.org/10.1080/02796015.2008.12087908

Telef, B. B., & Furlong, M. J. (2017). Adaptation and validation of the Social Emotional Health Survey-Secondary into Turkish culture. *International Journal of School & Educational Psychology, 5,* 255–265. https://doi.org/10.1080/21683603.2016.1234988

Waters, L., & Loton, D. (2019). SEARCH: A meta-framework and review of the field of positive education. *International Journal of Applied Positive Psychology*, *4*(1–2), 1–46. https://doi.org/10.1007/s41042-019-00017-4

Wroblewski, A. P., Dowdy, E., Sharkey, J. D., & Kim, E. K. (2019). Social-emotional screening to predict truancy severity: Recommendations for educators. *Journal of Positive Behavior Interventions, 21,* 19–29. https://doi.org/10.1177/1098300718768773

Xie, J., Liu, S., Yang, C., & Furlong, M. J. (2017). Chinese version of Social and Emotional Health Survey-Secondary. *Chinese Journal of Clinical Psychology, 25*(6), 1012–1016. https://doi.org/10.16128/j.cnki.1005-3611.2017.06.004

You, S., Dowdy, E., Furlong, M.J., Renshaw, T., Smith, D.C., & O'Malley, M.D. (2014). Further validation of the Social and Emotional Health Survey for high-school students. *Applied Quality of Life Research, 9,* 997–1015. https://doi.org/10.1007/s11482-013-9282-2

You, S., Furlong, M.J., Felix, E., & O'Malley, M.D. (2015). Validation of the Social and Emotional Health Survey for five sociocultural groups: Multigroup invariance and latent mean analyses. *Psychology in the Schools, 52,* 349–362. https://doi.org/10.1002/pits.21828

Zeng, G., & Kern, M. (2019). The Chinese EPOCH measure of adolescent well-being: Further testing of the psychometrics of the measure. *Frontiers in Psychology, 10,* 1–11. https://doi.org/10.3389/fpsyg.2019.01457

Zins, J.E., Bloodworth, M.R., Weissberg, R.P., & Walberg, H.J. (2007). The scientific base linking social and emotional learning to school success. *Journal of Educational & Psychological Consultation, 17*(2–3), 191–210. https://doi.org/10.1080/10474410701413145

Chapter 17

Dyadic Coping as a Concept of Positive Psychology

Mirjam Senn and Guy Bodenmann

Department of Psychology, University of Zurich, Switzerland

Positive Psychology and Relationship Functioning

In the last decades, research on relationship functioning has primarily focused on relationship distress and marital dissolution, in an attempt at finding and understanding the predictors and mechanisms of the deterioration of close and intimate relationships. This line of research documented various risk factors for distressed intimate relationships, such as dysfunctional communication patterns (e.g., Weiss & Heyman, 1997) and hence built an important basis for helping distressed couples using relationship education programs as well as couple or family therapy.

Recognizing the role of positivity concerning negative and dysfunctional patterns in couples' communication in Gottman's balance theory (Gottman, 1994; Gottman et al., 1998) was the first step in the direction of exploring partners' well-being and the positive dimensions of relationship functioning (e.g., relationship stability, positive communication). Research on couples' resources for relationship functioning, such as dyadic coping (Bodenmann, 1995, 1997a; Coyne & Smith, 1991) and social support in close relationships (Cutrona, 1990; Sullivan et al., 2010), further developed this track.

Furthermore, studies showed that factors such as love, attractiveness, status, intelligence, and sex appeal are not predictive of long-term happiness in relationships, as they erode over time and partners become habituated to these positive characteristics (Karney & Bradbury, 1995). The best predictors of relationship functioning and positive relationship outcomes are personal and relational skills in addition to commitment (Bodenmann, Charvoz et al., 2007). Thus, couples scoring high in functional communication, dyadic coping, and problem-solving who have a strong established commitment for their relationship are more likely to be in a satisfied and stable intimate relationship. Moreover, studies point out the important role of capitalization for intimate relationships (Gable et al., 2004; Pagani, Parise et al., 2019), embracing the concept of relationship flourishing (Fincham & Beach, 2010). Dyadic coping research is another resource-oriented approach that is grounded in positive psychology.

Nevertheless, positive psychology does not have a long tradition in basic research in couples, which long focused on understanding couples' deficient functioning and differences between satisfied and dissatisfied couples; it has a rich tradition in couples' interventions aiming to strengthen dyadic skills and resources (Jakubowski et al., 2004). An accurate assessment of the positive dimensions of relationship functioning (e.g., dyadic coping) forms an important basis for designing appropriate interventions. Thus, diagnostic tools grounded in positive psychology enable both researchers and practitioners to analyze and understand the strengths and resources that can be empowered in interventions. The following introduces the importance of relationship functioning and the concept of dyadic coping as a pivotal skill in relationships. Further, it presents and discusses the assessment of dyadic coping utilizing self-report and overt behavior observation.

Importance of Relationship Functioning

The significance of intimate relationships is reflected in the high number of people in Western industrial countries who are at least once in their lives married or in a stable relationship and as well as in the high remarriage rate of divorced people (e.g., Peuckert, 2019). Not only is living together in an intimate relationship a fundamental need of most human beings, it also proves to be highly beneficial for both physical and psychological well-being (Diener et al., 2000). On the one hand, some studies support the notion that relationship functioning and healthy relationships account for higher life satisfaction (Ruvolo, 1998), higher longevity of the relationship (Kiecolt-Glaser & Newton, 2001), and healthier children (Cummings & Davies, 2010); also, partners in relationships have a lower risk for mental disorders (Scott et al., 2010). On the other hand, distressed relationships simultaneously play an important role in the development of physical illnesses such as diabetes and epilepsy (Wearden et al., 2000); different mental diseases are associated with a higher likelihood of general health risks (Kiecolt-Glaser & Wilson, 2017) and relapse after successful recovery (Hooley, 2007). Relational tensions, arguments, and chronic conflicts lead to alienation, dissatisfaction, and a higher likelihood of divorce (Bodenmann, 1997b; Nussbeck et al., 2012). Although interventions for couples would provide a high benefit, only 10 % of all couples take advantage of marriage counseling or therapy when in a crisis, and not many more engage in relationship education (Halford, 2011). While for decades destructive communication patterns were assumed to be the best predictors of relationship dissatisfaction, dissolution, and divorce (Karney & Bradbury, 1995), a more recent study indicates that dyadic coping even outperforms communication variables (Nussbeck et al., 2012). Thus, a large body of research documents that relationship functioning matters most for one's physical, psychological, and social well-being, and that strengthening dyadic coping through positive psychology-oriented interventions seems to be a valuable and important aim.

The Background of Dyadic Coping

In the early 1990s, using experimental, cross-sectional, longitudinal, and retrospective designs, scholars started research on stress and coping in couples and its influence on the romantic relationship (Bodenmann, 2000; Bodenmann, Ledermann et al., 2007; Story & Bradbury, 2004). In the last decades, several concepts of coping in romantic relationships (dyadic coping) have been proposed. Dyadic coping in committed couples entails shared stress appraisal, shared goals, and joint coping efforts (Bodenmann, 1995, 1997a). With this shift from an individual toward a more interpersonal view of stress and coping in couples, various models were proposed (Falconier & Kuhn, 2019): the congruence coping model (CM; Revenson, 1994), the relationship-focused model (RFM; Coyne & Smith, 1991; DeLongis & O'Brien, 1990), the communal coping model (CCM; Lyons et al., 1998), the developmental-contextual model (DCCM; Berg & Upchurch, 2007), the relational-cultural model (RCCM; Kayser & Revenson, 2016), and the systemic-transactional model (STM; Bodenmann, 1995, 2005). All of these models share the notion of interdependence between partners regarding stress and coping. Among these different models, the STM is today the most widespread and internationally applied approach. For this reason, we describe this model below, whereas Table 17.1 presents further measurements based on different models.

The systemic-transactional model (STM; Bodenmann, 1995, 2005) considers stress and coping in close relationships to be dyadic processes. This model is based on the transactional stress theory by Lazarus and Folkman (1984) and integrates process-related and systemic perspectives. Dyadic coping is a process in which three factors of stress communication and coping operate and interact: the stress signals of one partner, the perception of these signals by the other partner, and the reaction of this partner to the stress signals (Bodenmann, 2000, 2005). The reaction can either be one of not reacting (ignoring the partner's stress), of getting equally affected (stress contagion), or of engaging in support provision, e.g., supportive positive or negative dyadic coping. Dyadic coping serves two main functions: a stress-related and a relationship-related function. The former relies on the reduction of stress primarily affecting one partner and spilling over to the other partner, or it affects both partners at the same time ("we-stress"). It targets the maintenance or restoration of the general well-being of both partners and becomes relevant if individual coping was unsuccessful in reducing negative emotions or solving the problem. The second, but maybe more important function of dyadic coping is that dyadic coping fosters the feeling of "we-ness" among partners, their mutual trust and intimacy, and strengthens partners' mutual attachment and commitment (Cutrona, 1996).

The Dimensions of Dyadic Coping

The STM is a comprehensive model that entails various dimensions of positive, negative, and conjoint coping behaviors (Bodenmann et al., 2016). Dyadic coping includes partner-oriented behaviors (supportive dyadic coping, delegated dyadic coping, negative dyadic coping) or couple-oriented behaviors (joint/common dyadic coping).

Supportive dyadic coping typically refers to the partner's or couple's emotion regulation or problem-solving. Emotion-focused supportive dyadic coping includes empathic understanding, encouraging the partner, helping them to reframe the situation, solidarizing with them and telling the partner that one also knows those negative feelings, helping the partner to calm down and obtain an emotional distance to the problem. Problem-focused supportive dyadic coping includes behaviors such as giving practical advice, helping to seek further information, and sharing information with the partner that might be helpful for an adequate solution. Delegated dyadic coping, another category of dyadic coping, includes assuming tasks that the partner usually does to reduce their stress.

Table 17.1. An overview of dyadic coping measurement: Self-report and overt behavior

Instrument	Author(s)	Number of Items	Response options	Reliability	Validity	Description and notes
Self-report measures of dyadic coping						
Collaborative Coping Questionnaire (CCQ)	Berg et al. (2003); Hemphill (2013)	5 items	5-point Likert scale: 0 (*not at all*) to 4 (*every day*)	$\alpha_{patient} = .89$ $\alpha_{spouse} = .87$		Degree of collaboration between the partners in collaborating to manage a stressful (medical) condition (e.g., "The two of you shared feelings and concerns about managing ...")
Dyadic Coping Inventory (DCI)	Bodenmann (2008a)	37 items (10 subscales)	5-point Likert scale: 1 (*very rarely*) to 5 (*very often*)	$\alpha_{men} = .92$ $\alpha_{women} = .93$ (total scale)	PCA/CFA, structures for men and women Convergent validity with PFB, RAS, DAS, CPQ, MCQ, MCI, CTS; divergent validity with COPE; correlations with FACES, EFB, GHQ-28, DASS, NEO-FFI	Degree of stress communication and dyadic coping (e.g., "My partner shows empathy and understanding to me") Further validation in different languages: Ledermann et al. (2010), Levesque et al. (2014), Randall et al. (2016), Vedes et al. (2013), Wendołowska et al. (2020)
Empathic Responding Scale (ERS)	O'Brien & DeLongis (1996)	10 items (2 subscales)	3-point Likert scale: 0 (*not at all*) to 2 (*a lot*)	$\alpha = .93$ (total scale)	Correlations with personality (NEO-FFI), stressful situation	Cognitive-affective empathic responding (e.g., "I imagined myself in the other person's shoes") and behavioral empathic responding (e.g., "I tried to help the other person(s) involved by listening to them") Short version (6 items): O'Brien et al. (2009)

Table 17.1. continued

Instrument	Author(s)	Number of Items	Response options	Reliability	Validity	Description and notes
Relationship-Focused Coping Scale (RFCS)	Coyne & Smith (1991)	28 items (2 subscales)	5-point Likert scale: 1 (*never*) to 5 (*very often*)	Active engagement: $\alpha_{patient} = .90$ $\alpha_{wife} = .89$ Protective buffering: $\alpha_{patient} = .92$ $\alpha_{wife} = .91$	CFA and correlations with wives' distress	Active engagement (12 items, e.g., "My partner tries to talk about it when something bothers me," "I try to talk about it with my partner when something bothers him or her") and protective buffering (16 items, e.g., "My partner thinks that I don't know what's right for me," "I think my partner doesn't know what's right for him or her") subscales with one version for self-perception and another one for partner perception Short version: Suls et al. (1997)
Ways of Providing Support Scale (WPS)	Buunk et al. (1996) Hagedoorn et al. (2011)	19 items (2 subscales)	5-point Likert scale: 1 (*never*) to 5 (*very often*)	Active engagement: $\alpha_{patient} = .83$ $\alpha_{partners} = .85$ Protective buffering: $\alpha_{patient} = .68$ $\alpha_{partners} = .79$	CFA and correlations with past spousal support and relationship satisfaction	Adapted Version of the RFCS in Dutch Active engagement (8 items) and protective buffering (6 items) subscales with one version for self-perception and another one for partner perception Further validation: Hinnen et al. (2008)

Table 17.1. continued

Instrument	Author(s)	Number of Items	Response options	Reliability	Validity	Description and notes
Assessment of overt behavior of dyadic coping						
Protective Buffering Observation Coding System (PBOCS)	Langer et al. (2007)		Degree of protective buffering: ratio of negative emotion words used when a partner was absent to when a partner was present	Interrater reliabilities $r > .80$	Negative correlation of verbal protective buffering with marital satisfaction	Based on the RFCS, the PBOCS uses observations to assess protective buffering as a dimension of dyadic coping Partners were instructed to describe their deepest thoughts and feelings of their relationship alone and in front of their partner for 10 min each. Observations were recorded and transcribed to count negative and positive emotional words (see also Langer et al., 2000; Pennebaker et al., 2001).
Coding System to Assess Dyadic Coping (SADC)	Bodenmann (2000, 2008b)		Verbal and nonverbal stress communication and dyadic coping	Interrater agreement Cohen's kappa > .90		Partners talk about their own stress issues to each other for 8 min each. Interaction is videotaped and coded.

Note. CFA = confirmatory factor analysis, PCA = principal component analysis. PFB = Partnership Questionnaire (Hahlweg 1996); RAS = Relationship Assessment Scale (Hendrick, 1988); DAS = Dyadic Adjustment Scale (Spanier, 1976); CPQ = Communication Patterns Questionnaire (Christensen & Sullaway, 1984); MCQ = Marital Communication Questionnaire (Bodenmann, 2000); MCI = Marital Communication Inventory (Bienvenu, 1971); CTS = Conflict Tactics Scales (Straus, 1979); COPE = COPE Inventory (Carver et al., 1989); FACES = Family Adaptability and Cohesion Evaluation Scale (Olson et al., 1985); EFB = Erziehungsfragebogen (Naumann et al., 2010); GHQ-28 = General Health Questionnaire-28 (Goldberg & Williams, 1988); DASS = Depression Anxiety Stress Scales (Lovibond & Lovibond, 1995); NEO-FFI = NEO Five-Factor Inventory (Costa & McCrae, 1992).

Negative dyadic coping distinguishes between hostile dyadic coping, ambivalent dyadic coping, and superficial dyadic coping. Negative dyadic coping likely occurs when the supporting partner is stressed or when they are not motivated or unable to support the stressed partner. This is typically the case when the relationship commitment is low or the potential support provider makes negative attributions about the partner (e.g., that they caused the stress and are guilty of the bad outcome). Often, negative dyadic coping is observed in situations where support is provided by necessity or coercion rather than voluntarily. Poor personal emotional resources, negative mood, or difficult personality traits (e.g., lack of empathy, egoism, dominance, intolerance) are further reasons for hostile, ambivalent, or superficial dyadic coping.

In addition to supportive, delegated, and negative dyadic coping, the STM also includes joint/common dyadic coping, which denotes the symmetric or complementary involvement of both partners in a shared coping process, typically based on shared appraisals. This can be expressed through reframing the stress together, searching jointly for more information, establishing mutual efforts to calm down, praying together, or sharing emotional or physical intimacy. The model predicts joint/common dyadic coping occurs when the stressor affects both partners, typically at the same time, and when both partners perceive that their own resources may contribute to the coping process (Bodenmann, 1995, 1997a).

The Significance of Dyadic Coping

Research on romantic relationships has yielded strong empirical evidence that stress (and mainly stress outside the close relationship) is negatively associated with various facets of relationship functioning (e.g., less relationship satisfaction, negative partner interaction, higher likelihood of divorce) (Bodenmann & Cina, 2006; Neff & Karney, 2007; Randall & Bodenmann, 2009; Story & Bradbury, 2004). Further, manifold studies support the importance of dyadic coping for relationship satisfaction (Falconier, Jackson et al., 2015), general well-being (Bodenmann et al., 2011; Falconier, Nussbeck et al., 2015), severe illness (Badr et al., 2010; Revenson & Lepore, 2012; Rottmann et al., 2015), or mental disorders (Bodenmann & Randall, 2013; Leuchtmann & Bodenmann, 2017). Dyadic coping proves to be a consistent and robust predictor of relationship satisfaction in different cultures (Hilpert, Randall et al., 2016) and a stronger predictor than individual coping strategies, but it is positively linked to individual emotion regulation strategies (Papp & Witt, 2010). Rusu et al. (2019) found that adaptive cognitive emotion regulation strategies such as putting into perspective, positive refocusing, positive reappraisal, and planning refocusing, were related to positive dyadic coping (supportive, common, and delegated coping) in couples, which in turn increased both partners' relationship satisfaction.

Research on overt observation is particularly fruitful as it yields insights into the dynamics and the process of couples' shared stress management. Recent studies based on behavioral data on dyadic coping illustrated that couples with high dyadic coping skills show a tight pattern of stress-related self-disclosure followed by active, interested, and empathic listening by the other partner as well as the provision of support matching the needs of the stressed partner. In unsatisfied couples, characterized by low dyadic coping resources, there is a lot of talking about stress, poor listening, and poor dyadic coping provision, indicating a poor match between disclosure, listening, and support provision (Kuhn et al., 2018).

The Assessment of Dyadic Coping

Self-Report Instruments for Assessing Dyadic Coping

Most studies assess dyadic coping using self-report scales (for an overview, see Falconier, Jackson et al., 2015). Several questionnaires were developed for this purpose (see Table 17.1): The Collaborative Coping Questionnaire (CCQ; Berg et al., 2003), the Dyadic Coping Inventory (DCI; Bodenmann, 2008a), the Empathic Responding Scale (ERS; O'Brien & DeLongis, 1996), the Relationship-Focused Coping Scale (RFCS; Coyne & Smith, 1991), and the Ways of Providing Support Scale (WPS; Buunk et al., 1996). All of these questionnaires are self-report instruments in which respondents rate how often each member of the couple (self and partner) engages in dyadic coping. Based on the DCI, a few studies even applied a daily diary format using certain subscales over 7 or 14 days (Lüscher et al., 2019; Pagani, Donato et al., 2019). Because the DCI by Bodenmann (2008a) is the most widely used self-report scale for assessing dyadic coping and the only questionnaire in which psychometrics were examined in a large validation study, we refer to this scale in the following.

The Dyadic Coping Inventory (DCI)

The DCI (Bodenmann, 2008a) is a 37-item questionnaire for the assessment of stress communication and dyadic coping in romantic relationships. It is used internationally and has to date been translated into 24 languages (Brazilian, Chinese, Danish, Dutch, English, French, German, Greek, Hebrew, Hindi, Hungarian, Indonesian, Italian, Japanese, Korean, Norwegian, Persian, Polish, Portuguese, Russian, Tamil, Thai, Turkish, and Urdu). The questionnaire has been validated in 11 languages (Chinese, English, French, German, Italian, Japanese, Polish, Portuguese, Rumanian, Spanish, and Urdu) (Falconier & Kuhn, 2019).

The Structure of the DCI

The scales assess stress communication (stress-related self-disclosure) and dyadic coping on the following dimensions, from one's own view ("What do I do?") and from the perceived partner's view ("What does my partner do?") in both partners scoring on their own and the perceived dyadic coping of the partner. That yields four scales of dyadic coping (see Figure 17.1; one's perception of one's own dyadic coping and one's perceived partner's dyadic coping by partner A and B separately). Based on this conceptualization, one can compute a sum score and scores of subscales or aggregated scales as well as different perception indices such as the index of reciprocity (partner A's self-perceived dyadic coping in relation to partner B's self-perceived dyadic coping), the index of congruence (partner A's perception of partner B's dyadic coping and partner B's self-perceived dyadic coping) and the equity index (partner A's or B's perception of their own dyadic coping compared to their perception of their partner's dyadic coping).

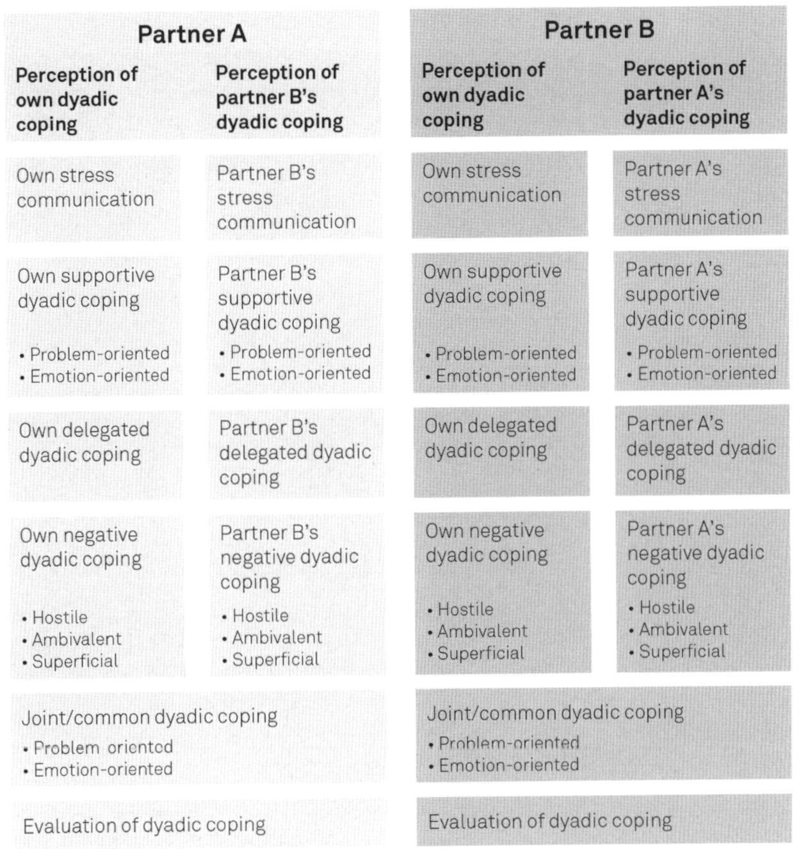

Figure 17.1. The structure of the Dyadic Coping Inventory.

The Scales of the DCI

The DCI assesses dyadic coping with nine subscales: stress communication, supportive dyadic coping, delegated dyadic coping, negative dyadic coping (each for partner A and B), joint/common dyadic coping. In addition, the satisfaction with the dyadic coping and the effectiveness of the dyadic coping are evaluated with one item each (evaluation of dyadic coping). Answers are given on a 5-point Likert-scale (1=*never/very rarely*, 2=*rarely*, 3=*sometimes*; 4=*often*; 5=*very often*). Administration time is about 10 min. The total DCI score is a sum of items 1 through 35 with a range from 35 to 175 points after reverse coding the eight negatively keyed items. Items 36 and 37 are evaluation items and are not included in the total score. The DCI has established cutoff scores to include the following: DCI total scores <111 represent dyadic coping below average, DCI scores between 111–145 represent dyadic coping in the normal range, and DCI total scores >145 represent dyadic coping above average. The German manual also provides age and sex norm values and specific cutoff scores (*N*=2,399) (Bodenmann, 2008a). For an overview of the different scales and item examples, see Table 17.2.

Table 17.2. Description of the subscales of the Dyadic Coping Inventory (Bodenmann, 2008a)

Scale	Number of items	Item example
Own stress communication *(How do you communicate your stress to your partner?)*	4	I let my partner know that I would appreciate his/her practical support, advice, or help.
Partner's stress communication *(How does your partner communicate when he/she is feeling stressed?)*	4	My partner shows me through his/her behavior that he/she is not doing well or when he/she has problems.
Own supportive dyadic coping *(What do you do when your partner makes known his/her stress?)*	5	I express to my partner that I am on his/her side.
Partner's supportive dyadic coping *(What does your partner do when you are stressed?)*	5	My partner shows empathy and understanding to me.
Own delegated dyadic coping *(What do you do when your partner makes known his/her stress?)*	2	I take on things that my partner would normally do to help him/her out.
Partner's delegated dyadic coping *(What does your partner do when you are stressed?)*	2	My partner asks me to do things for him/her when he has too much to do.
Own negative dyadic coping *(What do you do when your partner makes known his/her stress?)*	4	When my partner is stressed, I tend to withdraw.
Partner's negative dyadic coping *(What does your partner do when you are stressed?)*	4	My partner does not take my stress seriously.
Joint/common dyadic coping *(What do we do when we are both feeling stressed?)*	5	We help one another to put the problem in perspective and see it in a new light.
Evaluation of dyadic coping *(How do you evaluate your coping as a couple?)*	2	I am satisfied with the support I receive from my partner and the way we deal with stress together.
Total	37	

The Psychometrics of the DCI

The DCI was first validated with a sample of 2,399 subjects in German (Bodenmann, 2008a) and later with a total of 1,647 subjects in English (Levesque et al., 2014; Randall et al., 2016). The reliability and validity of the scale and measurement invariance across different cultures are well established (Falconier et al., 2016). Internal consistencies range from .71 to .92 for subscales and for the total score from .92 (men) to .93 (women). Test-retest reliabilities lay between r_{tt} = .52 and .80 with higher scores for women. High convergent (e.g., relationship quality) and discriminant validity (e.g., individual coping) is observed (Bodenmann, 2008a).

The factor structure of the original inventory was replicated and further validated by Ledermann et al. (2010) in three language groups (German, French, Italian). It showed mixed reliabilities for the subscales (German = .61 to .86, Italian = .62 to .89, French = .50 to .89). Negative dyadic coping was rarely reported in these samples, so it is more likely to observe high means of negative dyadic coping in couples with low relationship quality and in more diverse samples. High construct validity was detected for correlations with marital quality (PFB; Hahlweg, 1996) and marital communication patterns (CPQ; Christensen & Sullaway, 1984). The psychometric properties for the DCI in English (Levesque et al., 2014; Randall et al., 2016) showed significant correlations with relationship satisfaction (RAS; Hendrick, 1988) and, as expected, lower correlations for individual coping (BriefCOPE; Carver, 1997). Reliabilities in English range from .69 to .85 (Levesque et al., 2014) and .54 to .95 (Randall et al., 2016).

The factor structure of the DCI has been further replicated. In most studies, a five-factor structure (stress communication, emotion-focused supportive dyadic coping, problem-focused supportive dyadic coping, delegated dyadic coping, and negative dyadic coping) for women and men and a two-factor structure (emotion-focused and problem-focused common/joint dyadic coping) are reported (e.g., Wendołowska et al., 2020). Depending on language and nation, several items of the DCI must be occasionally excluded to permit a good model fit.

Within convergent validity, the DCI shows moderate associations with questionnaires assessing relationship satisfaction, communication, and self-disclosure. Within criterion validity, the DCI is significantly associated with health and life satisfaction. Within divergent validity, the DCI is weakly correlated with individual coping, reflecting two independent constructs.

Overall, the DCI correlates substantially and significantly with measures of relationship quality and satisfaction but additionally represents an independent construct. It suggests that couples who use positive dyadic coping strategies and avoid negative dyadic coping strategies report being more satisfied in their romantic relationship.

Analyzing Dyadic Data Assessed by the DCI

Like other relationship measurements, the DCI has the advantage of providing non-independent dyadic data either for distinguishable (e.g., different-sex) or indistinguishable (e.g., same-sex) couples. Data analysis should consider the widely used actor–partner interdependence models (APIM; Kenny et al., 2006; Ledermann et al., 2011) or dyadic growth curve models (GCM, Raudenbush et al., 1995) because of the interdependent nature of dyadic data. Ledermann and Kenny (2017) provide an overview of the particular advantages and applications of these methods.

Assessment of Overt Dyadic Coping Behavior

Several studies are based on overt dyadic coping in real couple interactions. Currently, two coding systems are used in dyadic coping research (see Table 17.1): the Protective Buffering Observation Coding System (PBOCS; Langer et al., 2007) and the Coding System to Assess Dyadic Coping (SADC; Bodenmann, 2008b).

Table 17.3. Categories of overt behavioral dyadic coping

Categories	Subcategories	Examples
Verbal stress communication (stress-related self-disclosure)	• Problem-focused stress communication with appeal for problem-focused dyadic coping • Neutral and latent emotional stress communication • Verbal implicit emotion-focused stress communication • Verbal explicit emotion-focused stress communication	• Asking the partner for advice or specific assistance • Neutral or factual descriptions • Superficial feelings such as "stressed" or "frustrated" • "I have never been that embarrassed" or "I was really hurt by that person's behavior"
Nonverbal stress communication	• Nonverbal stress	• Sigh, groan, discard hands, shake head
Verbal dyadic coping	• Verbal problem-focused dyadic coping • Verbal problem-focused joint/common dyadic coping • Inquiring • Verbal emotion-focused dyadic coping • Verbal emotion-focused joint/common dyadic coping • Verbal negative dyadic coping	• Giving advice • E.g., empathic understanding, showing solidarity with the partner, encouraging the partner: "I understand that this must have been very stressful" • E.g., hostile, insensitive, superficial support behavior
Nonverbal dyadic coping	• Attentive/interested listening • Nonverbal emotion-focused dyadic coping • Nonverbal negative dyadic coping	• E.g., listening • E.g., holding, hugging, kissing • E.g., ignoring partner's stress communication, eye-rolling

The PBOCS is based on word counts of observations to assess dyadic coping (protective buffering) of couples with cancer. Partners were instructed to describe their deepest thoughts and feelings about their relationship alone and in front of their partner for 10 min each. A ratio of negative emotion words used when the partner is absent to negative emotion words used when the partner is present is computed and declared the degree of protective buffering dyadic coping (Falconier, Jackson et al., 2015). In contrast, the SADC allows the microanalytic coding of dyadic coping of both partners in the interaction itself and contains the categories of stress communication and dyadic coping in a verbal and a nonverbal type (see Table 17.3). Thereby, dyadic coping is examined in the lab in a standardized setting. Couples are invited to talk about a bothersome stressful event (daily hassle) that occurred outside of the relationship (referred to as couple external stress; see Randall & Bodenmann, 2009). Then, the stressed partner talks for 8 min about the event and how they experienced it. Afterward, the other partner is invited to do the same on their own topic. This yields two situations, where one partner has the role of the speaker (self-disclosing about a stressful experience) and the other the role of the listener (and vice versa). These interactions are videotaped, split into 48 10-second sequences, and subsequently microanalytically coded by trained observers. Coders are trained for a minimum of 60 hours and until they reach a high level of interrater reliability (Cohen's $\kappa \geq .90$) (Kuhn et al., 2018; Zemp et al., 2016). Meuwly et al. (2012) report an interrater agreement of Cohen's $\kappa \geq .87$ in their study. Each videotape is rated by two coders simultaneously in three laps (review all sequences, rating nonverbal categories, rating verbal categories), whereby the strongest dimension is coded per category. The coding requires about 60 min per videotaped interaction (with a duration of 8 min), which sums up to 4 hours per couple for trained coders.

Recommendations for Instrument Selection

For assessing dyadic coping, there were specific conceptual and practical considerations. Among the Collaborative Coping Questionnaire (CCQ; Berg et al., 2003), the Empathic Responding Scale (ERS; O'Brien & DeLongis, 1996), Relationship-Focused Coping Scale (RFCS; Coyne & Smith, 1991), and the Ways of Providing Support Scale (WPS; Buunk et al., 1996), the Dyadic Coping Inventory (DCI; Bodenmann, 2008a) is the only scale that measures all facets of dyadic coping (positive/negative; self/partner; supportive/common), allowing the use of scales (different subscales or global score as well as perception indices). In contrast to instruments measuring generally social support (e.g., Winkeler & Klauer, 2003), the various dyadic coping questionnaires focus exclusively on the support provided by the partner and do not consider other support sources. With an administration time of 10 min, the DCI is easily applicable, and with the various translations in different languages the most frequently used instrument. Its psychometric properties are well established.

Studies involving behavior observation of dyadic coping are marginal compared to the total volume of published studies on dyadic coping. One major reason lies in the fact that behavioral observation is very time-consuming, expensive, and laborious. Nevertheless, more research should be conducted with this approach as many aspects of dyadic coping (timing, matching of stress expression and support behaviors, sequences of behaviors, relative duration and relative frequency, development during a support interaction, etc.) can only be captured by this means. The available coding system allows reliable coding in German and English.

Conclusion and Future Directions

With dyadic coping, a new concept of positive relationship behavior and its assessment has been established in research and practice. Positive forms of relationship behavior, most notably dyadic coping in couples, proved to be beneficial for each partner's individual and relational well-being (Falconier & Kuhn, 2019; Hilpert, Bodenmann et al., 2016; Nussbeck et al., 2012).

By now, the scope of assessments for dyadic coping includes questionnaires, diaries, and systematic overt behavior observation with broad possibilities for application in research and practice. Research conducted with the assessment instruments discussed revealed associations of dyadic coping with relationship quality, dyadic communication, and the developmental course of close relationships (Falconier, Jackson et al., 2015), yet several domains require further research: What kind of couples benefit from dyadic coping and what kind do not (e.g., according to attachment style, stage in couple's development, personality traits)? What further benefits can positive dyadic coping of couples have for different contexts (e.g., workplace and organizations, subjective well-being)? How are the self-report and overt behavior assessments related? Furthermore, dyadic coping could play an important role outside of the intimate relationship context, even if in a somewhat different and less intimate form such as in athlete-trainer relationships, in the professional context or in the context of parent-child dyads. Dyadic coping should therefore be studied in workgroups in companies, families, and various socioeconomic groups.

Finally, the knowledge gained about the benefits of positive dyadic coping and the harms of negative dyadic coping has important clinical implications. To help couples cope with their stress, specific interventions have been established: the Couples Coping Enhancement Training (Bodenmann & Shantinath, 2004) to teach couples to cope with stress to prevent relationship distress, the Coping-Oriented Couple Therapy (Bodenmann et al., 2008) to deliver a clinical intervention focused on dyadic coping, or the TOGETHER program (Falconier, 2015) to help couples cope with financial stress. Improving couples functioning through these interventions could even help people experience more happiness (Hilpert, Bodenmann et al., 2016). With these findings in mind, researchers should further expand their knowledge about positive relationship functioning, and relationship education programs should focus on positive psychological interventions by strengthening couples' functional communication and their dyadic coping.

References

Badr, H., Carmack, C.L., Kashy, D.A., Cristofanilli, M., & Revenson, T.A. (2010). Dyadic coping in metastatic breast cancer. *Health Psychology, 29*(2), 169–180. https://doi.org/10.1037/a0018165

Berg, C.A., Johnson, M.M.S., Meegan, S.P., & Strough, J. (2003). Collaborative problem-solving interactions in young and old married couples. *Discourse Processes, 35*(1), 33–58. https://doi.org/10.1207/S15326950DP3501_2

Berg, C.A., & Upchurch, R. (2007). A developmental-contextual model of couples coping with chronic illness across the adult life span. *Psychological Bulletin, 133*(6), 920–954. https://doi.org/10.1037/0033-2909.133.6.920

Bienvenue, M.J. (1971). An Interpersonal Communication Inventory. *Journal of Communication, 21*(4), 381–388. https://doi.org/10.1111/j.1460-2466.1971.tb02937.x

Bodenmann, G. (1995). A systemic-transactional conceptualization of stress and coping in couples. *Swiss Journal of Psychology, 54*(1), 34–49.

Bodenmann, G. (1997a). Dyadic coping: A systemic-transactional view of stress and coping among couples: Theory and empirical findings. *European Review of Applied Psychology, 47*(2), 137–141.

Bodenmann, G. (1997b). Can divorce be prevented by enhancing the coping skills of couples? *Journal of Divorce & Remarriage, 27*(3–4), 177–194. https://doi.org/10.1300/J087v27n03_12

Bodenmann, G. (2000). *Stress und Coping bei Paaren* [Stress and coping in couples]. Hogrefe.

Bodenmann, G. (2005). Dyadic coping and its significance for marital functioning. In T.A. Revenson, K. Kayser, & G. Bodenmann (Eds.), *Couples coping with stress: Emerging perspectives on dyadic coping.* (pp. 33–49). American Psychological Association. https://doi.org/10.1037/11031-002

Bodenmann, G. (2008a). *Dyadisches Coping Inventar (DCI). Testmanual* [Dyadic Coping Inventory]. Huber.

Bodenmann, G. (2008b). *Kodiersystem zur Erfassung des dyadischen Copings (SEDC): Erweiterte und adaptierte Version*[Coding system to assess dyadic coping (SADC): Modified and adapted version] [Unpublished manual].

Bodenmann, G., Charvoz, L., Bradbury, T.N., Bertoni, A., Iafrate, R., Giuliani, C., Banse, R., & Behling, J. (2007). The role of stress in divorce: A three-nation retrospective study. *Journal of Social and Personal Relationships, 24*(5), 707–728. https://doi.org/10.1177/0265407507081456

Bodenmann, G., & Cina, A. (2006). Stress and coping among stable-satisfied, stable-distressed and separated/divorced Swiss couples: A 5-year prospective longitudinal study. *Journal of Divorce & Remarriage, 44*(1–2), 71–89. https://doi.org/10.1300/J087v44n01_04

Bodenmann, G., Ledermann, T., & Bradbury, T.N. (2007). Stress, sex, and satisfaction in marriage. *Personal Relationships, 14*(4), 551–569. https://doi.org/10.1111/j.1475-6811.2007.00171.x

Bodenmann, G., Meuwly, N., & Kayser, K. (2011). Two conceptualizations of dyadic coping and their potential for predicting relationship quality and individual well-being: A comparison. *European Psychologist, 16*(4), 255–266. https://doi.org/10.1027/1016-9040/a000068

Bodenmann, G., Plancherel, B., Beach, S.R.H., Widmer, K., Gabriel, B., Meuwly, N., Charvoz, L., Hautzinger, M., & Schramm, E. (2008). Effects of coping-oriented couples therapy on depression: A randomized clinical trial. *Journal of Consulting and Clinical Psychology, 76*(6), 944–954. https://doi.org/10.1037/a0013467

Bodenmann, G., & Randall, A.K. (2013). Close relationships in psychiatric disorders. *Current Opinion in Psychiatry, 26*(5), 464–467. https://doi.org/10.1097/YCO.0b013e3283642de7

Bodenmann, G., Randall, A.K., & Falconier, M.K. (2016). Coping in couples: The systemic transactional model (STM). In M.K. Falconier, A.K. Randall, & G. Bodenmann (Eds.), *Couples coping with stress: A cross-cultural perspective* (pp. 2–22). Routledge, Taylor & Francis Oxford University Press.

Bodenmann, G., & Shantinath, S.D. (2004). The Couples Coping Enhancement Training (CCET): A new approach to prevention of marital distress based upon stress and coping. *Family Relations, 53*(5), 477–484. https://doi.org/10.1111/j.0197-6664.2004.00056.x

Buunk, B.P., Berkhuysen, M.A., Sanderman, R., & Nieuwland, W. (1996). Actieve betrokkenheid, beschermend bufferen en overbescherming. Meetinstrumenten voor de rol van de partner bij hartrevalidatie [The role of the partner in heart disease: Active engagement, protective buffering, and overprotection]. *Gedrag & Gezondheid: Tijdschrift Voor Psychologie En Gezondheid, 24*(6), 304–313.

Carver, C.S. (1997). You want to measure coping but your protocol's too long: Consider the Brief COPE. *International Journal of Behavioral Medicine, 4*, 92–100. https://doi.org/10.1207/s15327558ijbm0401_6

Carver, C.S., Scheier, M.F., & Weintraub, J.K. (1989). Assessing coping strategies: A theoretically based approach. *Journal of Personality and Social Psychology, 56*, 267–283. https://doi.org/10.1037/0022-3514.56.2.267

Christensen, A., & Sullaway, M. (1984). *Communication Patterns Questionnaire* [Unpublished manuscript]. University of California Los Angeles.

Costa, P.T., & McCrae, R.R. (1992). *NEO PI-R professional manual: Revised NEO Personality Inventory (NEO PI-R) and NEO Five-Factor Inventory (NEO-FFI).* Psychological Assessment Resources.

Coyne, J.C., & Smith, D.A. (1991). Couples coping with a myocardial infarction: A contextual perspective on wives' distress. *Journal of Personality and Social Psychology, 61*(3), 404–412. https://doi.org/10.1037/0022-3514.61.3.404

Cummings, E.M., & Davies, P. (2010). *Marital conflict and children: An emotional security perspective.* Guilford.

Cutrona, C.E. (1990). Stress and social support: In search of optimal matching. *Journal of Social and Clinical Psychology, 9*(1), 3–14. https://doi.org/10.1521/jscp.1990.9.1.3

Cutrona, C.E. (1996). *Social support in couples: Marriage as a resource in times of stress.* Sage. https://doi.org/10.4135/9781483327563

DeLongis, A., & O'Brien, T. (1990). An interpersonal framework for stress and coping: An application to the families of Alzheimer's patients. In M.A.P. Stephens, J.H. Crowther, S.E. Hobfoll, & D.L. Tennenbaum (Eds.), *Stress and coping in later-life families.* (pp. 221–239). Hemisphere.

Diener, E., Gohm, C.L., Suh, E., & Oishi, S. (2000). Similarity of the relations between marital status and subjective well-being across cultures. *Journal of Cross-Cultural Psychology, 31*(4), 419–436. https://doi.org/10.1177/0022022100031004001

Falconier, M.K. (2015). Together – A couples' program to improve communication, coping, and financial management skills: Development and initial pilot-testing. *Journal of Marital and Family Therapy, 41*(2), 236–250. https://doi.org/10.1111/jmft.12052

Falconier, M.K., Jackson, J., Hilpert, P., & Bodenmann, G. (2015). Dyadic coping and relationship satisfaction: A meta-analysis. *Clinical Psychology Review, 42*, 28–46. https://doi.org/10.1016/j.cpr.2015.07.002

Falconier, M.K., & Kuhn, R. (2019). Dyadic coping in couples: A conceptual integration and a review of the empirical literature. *Frontiers in Psychology, 10*, Article 571. https://doi.org/10.3389/fpsyg.2019.00571

Falconier, M.K., Nussbeck, F., Bodenmann, G., Schneider, H., & Bradbury, T.N. (2015). Stress from daily hassles in couples: Its effects on intradyadic stress, relationship satisfaction, and physical and psychological well-being. *Journal of Marital and Family Therapy, 41*(2), 221–235. https://doi.org/10.1111/jmft.12073

Falconier, M.K., Randall, A.K., & Bodenmann, G. (Eds.). (2016). *Couples coping with stress: A cross-cultural perspective.* Routledge, Taylor & Francis, Oxford University Press.

Fincham, F.D., & Beach, S.R.H. (2010). Of memes and marriage: Toward a positive relationship science. *Journal of Family Theory & Review, 2*(1), 4–24. https://doi.org/10.1111/j.1756-2589.2010.00033.x

Gable, S.L., Reis, H.T., Impett, E.A., & Asher, E.R. (2004). What do you do when things go right? The intrapersonal and interpersonal benefits of sharing positive events. *Journal of Personality and Social Psychology, 87*(2), 228–245. https://doi.org/10.1037/0022-3514.87.2.228

Goldberg, D.P., & Williams, P. (1988). *A user's guide to the General Health Questionnaire.* NFER-Nelson.

Gottman, J.M. (1994). *What predicts divorce? The relationship between marital processes and marital outcomes.* Erlbaum.

Gottman, J.M., Coan, J., Carrere, S., & Swanson, C. (1998). Predicting marital happiness and stability from newlywed interactions. *Journal of Marriage and the Family, 60*(1), 5–22. https://doi.org/10.2307/353438

Hagedoorn, M., Dagan, M., Puterman, E., Hoff, C., Meijerink, W.J.H.J., DeLongis, A., & Sanderman, R. (2011). Relationship satisfaction in couples confronted with colorectal cancer: The interplay of past and current spousal support. *Journal of Behavioral Medicine, 34*(4), 288–297. https://doi.org/10.1007/s10865-010-9311-7

Hahlweg, K. (1996). *Fragebogen zur Partnerschaftsdiagnostik (FPD)* [Partnership Questionnaire (PFB)]. Hogrefe.

Halford, W.K. (2011). *Marriage and relationship education: What works and how to provide it.* Guilford.

Hemphill, R.C. (2013). *Disease-related collaboration and adjustment among couples coping with type 2 diabetes.* Dissertation Abstracts International: The Sciences and Engineering, B 75/08 (E).

Hendrick, S.S. (1988). A generic measure of relationship satisfaction. *Journal of Marriage and the Family, 50*(1), 93–98. https://doi.org/10.2307/352430

Hilpert, P., Bodenmann, G., Nussbeck, F.W., & Bradbury, T.N. (2016). Improving personal happiness through couple intervention: A randomized controlled trial of a self-directed couple enhancement program. *Journal of Happiness Studies, 17*(1), 213–237. https://doi.org/10.1007/s10902-014-9591-7

Hilpert, P., Randall, A.K., Sorokowski, P., Atkins, D.C., Sorokowska, A., Ahmadi, K., Aghraibeh, A.M., Aryeetey, R., Bertoni, A., Bettache, K., Błażejewska, M., Bodenmann, G., Borders, J., Bortolini, T.S., Butovskaya, M., Castro, F.N., Cetinkaya, H., Cunha, D., David, O.A. ... Yoo, G. (2016). The associations of dyadic coping and relationship satisfaction vary between and within nations: A 35-nation study. *Frontiers in Psychology, 7*, Article 1106. https://doi.org/10.3389/fpsyg.2016.01106

Hinnen, C., Hagedoorn, M., Ranchor, A. V., & Sanderman, R. (2008). Relationship satisfaction in women: A longitudinal case-control study about the role of breast cancer, personal assertiveness, and partners' relationship-focused coping. *British Journal of Health Psychology, 13*(4), 737–754. https://doi.org/10.1348/135910707X252431

Hooley, J. M. (2007). Expressed emotion and relapse of psychopathology. *Annual Review of Clinical Psychology, 3*(1), 329–352. https://doi.org/10.1146/annurev.clinpsy.2.022305.095236

Jakubowski, S. F., Milne, E. P., Brunner, H., & Miller, R. B. (2004). A review of empirically supported marital enrichment programs. *Family Relations, 53*(5), 528–536. https://doi.org/10.1111/j.0197-6664.2004.00062.x

Karney, B. R., & Bradbury, T. N. (1995). The longitudinal course of marital quality and stability: A review of theory, methods, and research. *Psychological Bulletin, 118*(1), 3–34. https://doi.org/10.1037/0033-2909.118.1.3

Kayser, K., & Revenson, T. A. (2016). Including the cultural context in dyadic coping: Directions for future research and practice. In M. K. Falconier, A. K. Randall, & G. Bodenmann (Eds.), *Couples coping with stress: A cross-cultural perspective* (pp. 285–299). Routledge, Taylor & Francis, Oxford University Press.

Kenny, D. A., Kashy, D. A., & Cook, W. L. (2006). *Dyadic data analysis*. Guilford.

Kiecolt-Glaser, J. K., & Newton, T. L. (2001). Marriage and health: His and hers. *Psychological Bulletin, 127*(4), 472–503. https://doi.org/10.1037/0033-2909.127.4.472

Kiecolt-Glaser, J. K., & Wilson, S. J. (2017). Lovesick: How couples' relationships influence health. *Annual Review of Clinical Psychology, 13*(1), 421–443. https://doi.org/10.1146/annurev-clinpsy-032816-045111

Kuhn, R., Bradbury, T. N., Nussbeck, F. W., & Bodenmann, G. (2018). The power of listening: Lending an ear to the partner during dyadic coping conversations. *Journal of Family Psychology, 32*(6), 762–772. https://doi.org/10.1037/fam0000421

Langer, S. L., Rudd, M. E., & Syrjala, K. L. (2007). Protective buffering and emotional desynchrony among spousal caregivers of cancer patients. *Health Psychology, 26*(5), 635–643. https://doi.org/10.1037/0278-6133.26.5.635

Langer, S. L., Wilson, J. F., Pettigrew, L. C., & Blonder, L. X. (2000). Channel-consistency following unilateral stroke: An examination of patient communications across verbal and nonverbal domains. *Neuropsychologia, 38*(4), 337–344. https://doi.org/10.1016/S0028-3932(99)00100-1

Lazarus, R. S., & Folkman, S. (1984). *Stress, appraisal, and coping*. Springer.

Ledermann, T., Bodenmann, G., Gagliardi, S., Charvoz, L., Verardi, S., Rossier, J., Bertoni, A., & Iafrate, R. (2010). Psychometrics of the dyadic coping inventory in three language groups. *Swiss Journal of Psychology, 69*(4), 201–212. https://doi.org/10.1024/1421-0185/a000024

Ledermann, T., & Kenny, D. A. (2017). Analyzing dyadic data with multilevel modeling vs. structural equation modeling: A tale of two methods. *Journal of Family Psychology, 31*(4), 442–452. https://doi.org/10.1037/fam0000290

Ledermann, T., Macho, S., & Kenny, D. A. (2011). Assessing mediation in dyadic data using the actor-partner interdependence model. *Structural Equation Modeling: A Multidisciplinary Journal, 18*(4), 595–612. https://doi.org/10.1080/10705511.2011.607099

Leuchtmann, L., & Bodenmann, G. (2017). Interpersonal view on physical illnesses and mental disorders. *Swiss Archives of Neurology, Psychiatry and Psychotherapy, 168*, 170–174.

Levesque, C., Lafontaine, M.-F., Caron, A., & Fitzpatrick, J. (2014). Validation of the English version of the dyadic coping inventory. *Measurement and Evaluation in Counseling and Development, 47*(3), 215–225. https://doi.org/10.1177/0748175614522272

Lovibond, S. H., & Lovibond, P. F. (1995). The structure of negative emotional states: Comparison of the Depression Anxiety Stress Scales (DASS) with the Beck Depression and Anxiety Inventories. *Behaviour Research and Therapy, 33*(3), 335–343. https://doi.org/10.1016/0005-7967(94)00075-U

Lüscher, J., Kowatsch, T., Boateng, G., Santhanam, P., Bodenmann, G., & Scholz, U. (2019). Social support and common dyadic coping in couples' dyadic management of type II diabetes: Protocol for an ambulatory assessment application. *JMIR Research Protocols, 8*(10), e13685. https://doi.org/10.2196/13685

Lyons, R.F., Mickelson, K.D., Sullivan, M.J. L., & Coyne, J.C. (1998). Coping as a communal process. *Journal of Social and Personal Relationships, 15*(5), 579–605. https://doi.org/10.1177/0265407598155001

Meuwly, N., Bodenmann, G., Germann, J., Bradbury, T.N., Ditzen, B., & Heinrichs, M. (2012). Dyadic coping, insecure attachment, and cortisol stress recovery following experimentally induced stress. *Journal of Family Psychology, 26*(6), 937–947. https://doi.org/10.1037/a0030356

Naumann, S., Bertram, H., Kuschel, A., Heinrichs, N., Hahlweg, K., & Döpfner, M. (2010). Der Erziehungsfragebogen (EFB): Ein Fragebogen zur Erfassung elterlicher Verhaltenstendenzen in schwierigen Erziehungssituationen [The parenting questionnaire (EFB): A questionnaire for the assessment of parental behavior tendencies in difficult parenting situations]. *Diagnostica, 56*(3), 144–157. https://doi.org/10.1026/0012-1924/a000018

Neff, L.A., & Karney, B.R. (2007). Stress crossover in newlywed marriage: A longitudinal and dyadic perspective. *Journal of Marriage and Family, 69*(3), 594–607. https://doi.org/10.1111/j.1741-3737.2007.00394.x

Nussbeck, F., Hilpert, P., & Bodenmann, G. (2012). Der Zusammenhang von positivem und negativem Interaktionsverhalten in der Partnerschaft mit Partnerschaftszufriedenheit und Trennungsabsichten [The connection between positive and negative interactional behavior in partnerships with partnership satisfaction and separation intention]. *Zeitschrift für Familienforschung, 24*(1), 85–103. https://doi.org/10.20377/jfr-193

O'Brien, T.B., & DeLongis, A. (1996). The interactional context of problem-, emotion-, and relationship-focused coping: The role of the big five personality factors. *Journal of Personality, 64*(4), 775–813. https://doi.org/10.1111/j.1467-6494.1996.tb00944.x

O'Brien, T.B., DeLongis, A., Pomaki, G., Puterman, E., & Zwicker, A. (2009). Couples coping with stress: The role of empathic responding. *European Psychologist, 14*(1), 18–28. https://doi.org/10.1027/1016-9040.14.1.18

Olson, D.H., Portner, J., & Lavee, Y. (1985). *FACES-III – Family Adaptability and Cohesion Evaluation Scales* [Unpublished test]. University of Minnesota Saint Paul.

Pagani, A.F., Donato, S., Parise, M., Bertoni, A., Iafrate, R., & Schoebi, D. (2019). Explicit stress communication facilitates perceived responsiveness in dyadic coping. *Frontiers in Psychology, 10*, Article 401. https://doi.org/10.3389/fpsyg.2019.00401

Pagani, A.F., Parise, M., Donato, S., Gable, S.L., & Schoebi, D. (2019). If you shared my happiness, you are part of me: Capitalization and the experience of couple identity. *Personality and Social Psychology Bulletin, 46*(2), 258–269. https://doi.org/10.1177/0146167219854449

Papp, L.M., & Witt, N.L. (2010). Romantic partners' individual coping strategies and dyadic coping: Implications for relationship functioning. *Journal of Family Psychology, 24*(5), 551–559. https://doi.org/10.1037/a0020836

Pennebaker, J.W., Francis, M.E., & Booth, R.J. (2001). *Linguistic inquiry and word count: LIWC 2001.* Erlbaum.

Peuckert, R. (2019). *Familienformen im sozialen Wandel* [Family types in changing social contexts]. Springer Fachmedien Wiesbaden. https://doi.org/10.1007/978-3-658-25077-5

Randall, A.K., & Bodenmann, G. (2009). The role of stress on close relationships and marital satisfaction. *Clinical Psychology Review, 29*(2), 105–115. https://doi.org/10.1016/j.cpr.2008.10.004

Randall, A.K., Hilpert, P., Jimenez-Arista, L.E., Walsh, K.J., & Bodenmann, G. (2016). Dyadic coping in the U.S.: Psychometric properties and validity for use of the English version of the dyadic coping inventory. *Current Psychology, 35*(4), 570–582. https://doi.org/10.1007/s12144-015-9323-0

Raudenbush, S.W., Brennan, R.T., & Barnett, R.C. (1995). A multivariate hierarchical model for studying psychological change within married couples. *Journal of Family Psychology, 9*(2), 161–174. https://doi.org/10.1037/0893-3200.9.2.161

Revenson, T.A. (1994). Social support and marital coping with chronic illness. *Annals of Behavioral Medicine, 16*(2), 122–130. https://doi.org/10.1093/abm/16.2.122

Revenson, T.A., & Lepore, S.J. (2012). Coping in social context. In A. Baum, T.A. Revenson, & J.E. Singer (Eds.), *Handbook of health psychology* (pp. 193–217). Psychology Press.

Rottmann, N., Hansen, D.G., Larsen, P.V., Nicolaisen, A., Flyger, H., Johansen, C., & Hagedoorn, M. (2015). Dyadic coping within couples dealing with breast cancer: A longitudinal, population-based study. *Health Psychology, 34*(5), 486–495. https://doi.org/10.1037/hea0000218

Rusu, P.P., Bodenmann, G., & Kayser, K. (2019). Cognitive emotion regulation and positive dyadic outcomes in married couples. *Journal of Social and Personal Relationships, 36*(1), 359–376. https://doi.org/10.1177/0265407517751664

Ruvolo, A.P. (1998). Marital well-being and general happiness of newlywed couples: Relationships across time. *Journal of Social and Personal Relationships, 15*(4), 470–489. https://doi.org/10.1177/0265407598154002

Scott, K.M., Wells, J.E., Angermeyer, M., Brugha, T.S., Bromet, E., Demyttenaere, K., de Girolamo, G., Gureje, O., Haro, J.M., Jin, R., Karam, A.N., Kovess, V., Lara, C., Levinson, D., Ormel, J., Posada-Villa, J., Sampson, N., Takeshima, T., Zhang, M., & Kessler, R.C. (2010). Gender and the relationship between marital status and first onset of mood, anxiety and substance use disorders. *Psychological Medicine, 40*(9), 1495–1505. https://doi.org/10.1017/S0033291709991942

Spanier, G.B. (1976). Measuring dyadic adjustment: New scales for assessing the quality of marriage and similar dyads. *Journal of Marriage and Family, 38*(1), 15–28. https://doi.org/10.2307/350547

Story, L.B., & Bradbury, T.N. (2004). Understanding marriage and stress: Essential questions and challenges. *Clinical Psychology Review, 23*(8), 1139–1162. https://doi.org/10.1016/j.cpr.2003.10.002

Straus, M.A. (1979). Measuring intrafamily conflict and violence: The Conflict Tactics Scales. *Journal of Marriage and the Family, 41*, 75–88. https://doi.org/10.2307/351733

Sullivan, K.T., Pasch, L.A., Johnson, M.D., & Bradbury, T.N. (2010). Social support, problem solving, and the longitudinal course of newlywed marriage. *Journal of Personality and Social Psychology, 98*(4), 631–644. https://doi.org/10.1037/a0017578

Suls, J., Green, P., Rose, G., Lounsbury, P., & Gordon, E. (1997). Hiding worries from one's spouse: Associations between coping via protective buffering and distress in male post-myocardial infarction patients and their wives. *Journal of Behavioral Medicine, 20*(4), 333–349. https://doi.org/10.1023/A:1025513029605

Vedes, A., Nussbeck, F.W., Bodenmann, G., Lind, W., & Ferreira, A. (2013). Psychometric properties and validity of the dyadic coping inventory in Portuguese. *Swiss Journal of Psychology, 72*(3), 149–157. https://doi.org/10.1024/1421-0185/a000108

Wearden, A.J., Tarrier, N., Barrowclough, C., Zastowny, T.R., & Rahill, A.A. (2000). A review of expressed emotion research in health care. *Clinical Psychology Review, 20*(5), 633–666. https://doi.org/10.1016/S0272-7358(99)00008-2

Weiss, R.L., & Heyman, R.E. (1997). A clinical-research overview of couples interactions. In W.K. Halford & H.J. Markman (Eds.), *Clinical handbook of marriage and couples interventions* (pp. 13–41). Wiley.

Wendołowska, A.M., Czyżowska, D., & Bodenmann, G. (2020). Psychometric properties and measurement invariance of the Polish version of the dyadic coping inventory. *Current Psychology, 41*(3), 1159–1173. https://doi.org/10.1007/s12144-020-00623-5

Winkeler, M., & Klauer, T. (2003). Inventar zur sozialen Unterstützung in Dyaden (ISU-DYA) [Inventory of Social Support in Dyads (ISU-DYA)]. *Diagnostica, 49*(1), 14–23. https://doi.org/10.1026//0012-1924.49.1.14

Zemp, M., Bodenmann, G., Backes, S., Sutter-Stickel, D., & Revenson, T.A. (2016). The importance of parents' dyadic coping for children: The importance of parents' dyadic coping. *Family Relations, 65*(2), 275–286. https://doi.org/10.1111/fare.12189

Chapter 18

Health and Clinical Settings

Carmelo Vazquez[1], Gonzalo Hervas[1], Cristian Ochoa[2,3], Covadonga Chaves[1], and Pablo Roca[1]

[1]Department of Personality, Assessment and Clinical Psychology, School of Psychology, Complutense University, Madrid, Spain
[2]Clinical Psychology and Psychobiology Department, Faculty of Psychology, University of Barcelona, Spain
[3]Institut d'Investigació Biomèdica de Bellvitge, L'Hospitalet de Llobregat, Barcelona, Spain

Why a Positive Perspective on Clinical Problems? Old vs. New Approaches

One of the ultimate challenges to incorporating a positive perspective into the assessment of psychological functioning is the clinical field. Apparently, there is nothing more distant from positive functioning than having mental difficulties or psychological disorders. Yet, issues such as quality of life, well-being, full recovery, or adaptive functioning – to name but a few – have occupied the clinical field for decades (Bech, 1990). The emergence of the positive psychology movement (Seligman & Csikszentmihalyi, 2000) helped to provide both an impetus and a more robust theoretical background to the growing need of including those relatively neglected issues in conceptualizing psychological problems (Vázquez & Chaves, 2016).

The positive psychology movement is aligned with the emergence of new "positive" metrics to assess the cost of interventions and the impact of public and private investments in terms of quality of life and well-being. Given the limitations of psychiatric diagnostic labels as indicators of functioning, two decades ago, the World Bank and the World Health Organization jointly coined the concept of "burden" as a way of quantifying the cost of diseases in terms of the disability associated with the disease (Murray, 1994). Linked to this idea, several indexes like the Quality Adjusted Life Years (QALYs; Weinstein et al., 2009), which measure the severity of the disease and disabilities in terms of the number of years of life in perfect health, have been developed. Positive psychology fits well with this new interest from the fields of epidemiology and health economy to find sound indicators of having fulfilling lives. Another index was recently proposed, the Well-Being Adjusted Life Years (WALYs; Johnson et al., 2016), which measures the number of years with well-being. Although at the societal level it is possible to propose indicators and measures of national or collective well-being (Joshanloo, 2018; Summers et al., 2017), this chapter focuses on measures at the individual level. This approach is relevant for the fields of mental health and public policy as the reduction of well-being is significantly greater in persons with mental health difficulties than in persons with physical illnesses (Vázquez et al., 2015).

Yet, the inertia of focusing on symptoms, difficulties, and life problems may lead experts in clinical and health psychology to become inattentive to the positive aspects of functioning, thereby biasing their view about the complexity of human problems (Maddux, 2016). The prevailing implicit model of human functioning in psychology considers "bad is stronger than good" (Baumeister et al., 2001). However, as we argue below, positive emotions, cognitions, and traits *coexist* with symptoms and problems. Thus, a model of human functioning, that *simultaneously* considers the possible existence of positive and negative aspects offers a more realistic and less biased perspective of human nature (Keyes, 2007; Ruini, 2017).

The Science Behind a Positive Perspective in the Clinical Field

There are comprehensive collections of instruments available to assess almost any imaginable symptom, sign, or syndrome (e.g., Rush et al., 2008), much as there are widely used instruments to assess difficulties in functioning (e.g., WHO Disability Assessment Schedule -WHODAS 2.0; WHO, 2012). Yet, there can be no doubt that a complementary approach that focuses on positive aspects of functioning is still needed to understand the true nature of psychological problems and disorders (Vázquez, 2017). Large-scale studies conducted in the general population found that feelings of happiness (Bergsma et al., 2011) and judgments of life satisfaction (Vázquez et al., 2015) are significantly diminished in persons with mental health problems compared to healthy individuals. Yet, well-being is not equally affected across all diagnostic categories: Individuals with depression and some anxiety problems (in particular, obsessive-compulsive disorders) report the lowest levels of happiness, whereas, for instance, individuals with alcohol use or abuse report similar levels to healthy individuals (Bergsma & Veenhoven, 2011). Other research has also found that levels of life satisfaction are particularly low when comorbidity of anxiety and depression is present (Spinhoven et al., 2015). Thus, there can be no doubt that common mental disorders must also be analyzed from the well-being perspective as they are the best predictors of low life satisfaction, above and beyond factors like unemployment or physical illnesses (Layard et al., 2013). More research is needed to clarify when and how well-being deficits are part of the contributing factors, the maintaining factors (e.g., efforts to increase well-being finally fuel psychological symptoms), or just appear concomitantly.

Research on positive emotions and positive cognitions has provided a solid ground to understand key aspects of some clinical disorders (e.g., Gruber et al., 2019). From our point of view, some of the milestones of this accumulated knowledge in clinical science are the following:

The Negative and the Positive Are Relatively Independent

Research on the architecture of emotions has consistently found that positive and negative emotions can be considered as two dimensions that are relatively independent of each other (Watson, 2016). This basic distinction has profound theoretical and practical implications as it provides legitimacy to separate assessments of both aspects. Although most of the extant research on emotions in mental health problems has focused on the study of negative emotions (fear, anxiety, sadness, etc.), there is growing evidence that positive emotions play a distinctive role in different disorders (e.g., depression, social phobia, schizophrenia, and stress-related disorders), both in adults (Kashdan & Breen, 2008; Kashdan et al., 2011; Watson & Naragon-Gainey, 2010) and children and adolescents (Gilbert, 2012).

The Negative and the Positive Can Coexist

Perhaps one of the best compasses clinicians may have to go on is that the presence of psychological pain or stress does not exclude the existence of strengths, abilities, growth, and virtues (see Box 18.1). Moreover, it seems that, in adverse situations like suffering from severe medical diseases, the perception of uncertainty and threat to one's own life may be the source for both negative and positive emotional responses (Cordova et al., 2001). As a close recent example, the SARS-COVID-19 pandemic has helped us to make it clear that topics of resilience, posttraumatic growth, or positive beliefs about the world and others are crucial to understanding the complex process of adaptation to adversities (Vazquez et al., 2021). Clinical and therapeutic assessment focused on the facilitation of a constructive balance of this positive/negative coexistence needs to foster active and flexible coping including positive reappraisal, acceptance, and behavioral changes sustained over time (Pat-Horenczy et al., 2015).

Box 18.1. Coexistence of positive and negative emotions: The case of cancer

In cancer, the coexistence of stress and posttraumatic growth suggests that it is likely that both "responses" of chaos (stress/trauma) or positive life changes (growth) reflect similar homeostatic mechanisms. This coexistence spawns different clinical interpretations during the disease process, aiming to achieve a new constructive life meaning and balance to incorporate mortality as an existential concern that cannot be postponed (Ochoa et al., 2017). For example, many patients in full emotional shock and uncertainty about their cancer diagnosis consider, or refer to, being willing to "positively" change their lives completely. Many times, directly or indirectly, they relate this previous life with the origin of their cancer. In those cases, this actual "growth" is usually focused more on avoiding the cancer threat than on a real positive vital change to accommodate disturbing/traumatic information. Therefore, the coexistence of stress and growth in the initial stages of cancer (diagnosis and treatment) has been linked to its illusory nature, seen as cognitive avoidance and a short-term palliative coping strategy with a buffering effect that is lost over time (Sumalla et al., 2009). On the other hand, the coexistence of stress-growth processes at the end of primary cancer treatments could reflect a preliminary assimilation of an initial cancer-related stress threat and the beginning of incipient constructive growth. It is precisely in this stage that positive psychological interventions have demonstrated better results than other stress-management therapies (Ochoa-Arnedo et al., 2021).

The Role of Positive Elements in Clinical Disorders

Contrary to the neglect of the DSM to consider any aspect of well-being as a relevant vector of psychopathology (Bech, 2015), the Research Domain Criteria (RDoC) offer new means of promoting research on positive aspects of functioning. Interestingly, one of the five large domains or "constructs" acknowledged in the RDoC as the robust pillars of the psychological and neurobiological human systems is the positive valence system (PVS). Within the PVS, aspects like the regulation and maintenance of approach behaviors, hedonic and reward responses, satisfaction, novelty, and reward learning might help pave the road for sound scientific advancements in theory-guided research on mental health problems. For example, meta-analytic evidence showed deficits in several reward-processing behaviors in depression (Halahakoon et al., 2020), though, in general, a reward dysfunction has also been found in other disorders like mania or schizophrenia (Whitton et al., 2015). Research from the clinical and experimental field has provided support for the existence of deficits in positive mood regulation (e.g., expressing or maintaining positive mood states; Vanderlind et al., 2020). It also used the term "positive emotion disturbances" to describe difficulties in anticipating, reacting, regulating, or understanding positive emotions (Gruber et al., 2020). There is accumulated evidence on the presence of these positive disturbances in disorders like depression, social anxiety, schizophrenia, anorexia nervosa, bipolar disorders, and alcohol use (see a review of the evidence, see Gruber et al., 2020). As we point out below, in the clinical context, an assessment may benefit from gathering information on the intensity, frequency, diversity, and maintenance of the processes (e.g., guilt, fear of happiness).

Contributions of Eudaimonic Perspectives on Well-Being

Well-being theories that emphasize the key role of optimal functioning are usually included within the category of "eudaimonic." Although each of the current frameworks includes a singular set of variables, most of them include relatedness/relationships, meaning/purpose, competence/achievement, or autonomy, among others (Ryan & Deci, 2001; Ryff, 1989; Seligman, 2011). Some authors have suggested that the *absence* of well-being creates conditions of vulnerability to possible future adversities (Ryff & Singer, 1996) or even feeds different kinds of symptoms (Ryan & Deci, 2000). Exploring the source of well-being deficits can shed light on the distant origin of the psychological problems that lead patients to ask for help. Although the connection between well-being deficits and mental disorders is not yet fully understood, some research supports its relevance. In a longitudinal study, Wood and Tarrier (2010) showed that people who had low scores on characteristics related to psychological well-being, such as self-acceptance, autonomy, purpose in life, positive relationships with others, environmental mastery, and personal growth, were up to seven times more likely to meet the cutoff for clinical depression at the 10-year follow-up. Similarly, depressive symptoms or even suicide ideation are commonly associated with a chronic deficit in the areas of relatedness (Erzen & Çikrikci, 2018) or life meaning (e.g., Kleiman & Beaver, 2013). Exploring the neural correlates of well-being, Urry et al. (2004) found that persons with lower levels of Ryff's psychological well-being (all scales except for autonomy) presented diminished left frontal activation which is a marker of depression vulnerability.

Additionally, assessing eudaimonic well-being can help us to better select the targets of the intervention and align the therapeutic objectives with respect to the patient's own perspective of their problems. Among other reasons, this assessment is useful because patients, when asked about their ultimate therapeutic goals, report that they want not to reduce their symptoms but to feel more confidence and more optimism, and to regain well-being in their life, etc. (e.g., Demyttenaere et al., 2015; Zimmerman et al., 2006). Moreover, some findings show the therapeutic effects of working on eudaimonic areas (i.e., relatedness, meaning, growth, etc.) in anxiety and mood disorders (e.g., Fava et al., 2017; Ruini & Fava, 2009).

A Schematic Proposal for a Positive Clinical Assessment

A close inspection of the assessment models in clinical psychology confirms that strengths and capabilities are only rarely formally assessed. One corollary of this absence of positive concepts (emotions, resilience, flexibility, skills, strengths, etc.) in the clinical framework of customary assessment is that what is not assessed cannot be viewed as a potential intervention target. For instance, well-being is not typically considered in disorders like schizophrenia as the vast majority of assessment protocols do not cover domains of positive functioning (Valiente et al., 2019).

Initial Assessment and Interview

The assessment and monitoring of positive functioning (including positive emotions, positive cognitions, and adaptive behavior), both using informal tools (e.g., interviews and dialogues with the patient) or instruments (e.g., self-records, questionnaires, objective measures), can be used throughout the therapeutic process. Clinicians should have a double agenda to assess, on the one hand, deficits and problems and resources and preserved interests, strengths, skills, and talents, on the other hand (Biswas-Diener, 2010; Rashid, 2015).

An assessment with an accent on positive functioning should start from the first encounter with the patient. Key areas to explore in the initial interview(s) are: What abilities does the patient still have? What strengths are still being put to work? What material resources does the patient have? What social connections do they have? Which symbolic connections (e.g., sense of belonging to the community or the workplace) work well? Is there any moment or situation when the problem does not appear?

The Life Graph (timeline) is often used in clinical assessment to explore distal factors that might be related to current problems. Patients are typically asked to chronologically enumerate previous negative events from infancy to the present. Also, including positive experiences in the graph as well is a useful addition that may allow the therapist to explore strengths and positive emotions or cognitions over time (see Suddaby & Landau, 1998).

Many techniques used by specialists in brief solution-focused therapy can be very valuable in these initial steps. For instance, one may use the so-called "formula task" to ask patients with any kind of psychological difficulty to make an elaborate list of the things that still work well for them. For instance, some helpful questions are: How will we know whether this therapy has worked? Who would be the first person to notice it? What would they see differently in you? Also, using language oriented to the future is recommended for patients who somehow feel anchored in their past, which is common in depression and trauma-related disorders (O'Hanlon, 2011).

Regarding positive emotions, in addition to anhedonia, it may be interesting to include an assessment of savoring and dampening to tap positive emotion regulation (e.g., Feldman et al., 2008). Excessive regulation of positive emotions has been found to be relevant not only in depression but also in social anxiety (Everaert et al., 2020) and posttraumatic stress disorder (Nawijn et al., 2015). If a deficit related to the experience of positive emotions is detected, one may include specific positive interventions during the treatment phase (Chaves et al., 2019). Another relevant aspect of the initial assessment, concerning positivity, is to screen for patients' attitudes toward happiness and well-being to assess cognitive obstacles to accepting or experiencing positive emotions and states of well-being in general. Some instruments related to "fear of happiness" are available (Gilbert, 2012; Joshanloo, 2018).

Daily Self-Records

A useful tool for assessment is to build specific daily records (Fava, 2016) that tap the patient's specific difficulties. These records may gather information on the recognition or ability to label positive emotions or cognitions, identification of the context where these emotions or cognitions appear, or the factors that affect their volatility. For instance, experimental studies on mood regulation have found that individuals who score high in depression react with a similar magnitude of positive emotions but have more difficulties than healthy individuals to sustain that positive mood over time (McMakin et al., 2009). In clinical contexts, short-lived positive emotions may occur because of the appearance of negative automatic thoughts (e.g., "I do not deserve to be happy") or the appearance of a person that systematically short-circuits positive moods. All this information can be detected by designing ad-hoc records that, for instance, might include the following information: Date/positive emotion/intensity (0–10 scale)/Where did you experience this emotion?/What interrupted the emotion? (e.g., Fava, 2016).

Criteria for Instrument Selection

As it is very well detailed in many chapters of this book, there are a myriad of available instruments that tap different aspects of positive functioning. A broad array of instruments is available for both researchers and professionals which have been summarized in previous comprehensive reviews of the literature (e.g., Lindert et al., 2015; Linton et al., 2016) including the clinical field (e.g., Cooke et al., 2016; Owens et al., 2015; Simmons & Lehmann, 2012).

In a systematic review of unique self-reported well-being instruments, Lindert et al. (2015) found that the most frequently assessed domains were affects (39 scales), social relations (17 scales), life satisfaction (13 scales), physical health (13 scales), meaning/achievement (9 scales), and spirituality (6 scales), with a broad range of length (between 1 and 100 items) and administration time (from 1 to 15 min).

Yet, the availability of many instruments may make it difficult to choose the best instrument(s) for one's own purposes. In selecting instruments and methodologies of assessment, assessors should pay attention to several key factors:

Psychometric Robustness

Many instruments measure positive aspects of human functioning but in many cases lack sound psychometric properties. With some exceptions (De Vries et al., 2016; Salsman et al., 2018; Stewart-Brown et al., 2009), well-being instruments have been developed using suboptimal construction strategies (e.g., not using high-standard psychometric tools, such as item response theory, to select items; no pilot testing; not using discussion groups to analyze the readability and interpretability of the items, etc.).

Quality assessments of the psychometric robustness of commonly used instruments in positive psychology have yielded rather disappointing conclusions on the reliability and validity of most of the instruments available to measure key concepts such as resilience (Windle et al., 2011), hope (Redlich-Amirav et al., 2018), or optimism (Malouff & Schutte, 2017), to name a few. As a result, a key issue before using an instrument is to ensure reliability, content validity, convergent and discriminant validity, incremental validity, cultural background, and the construction procedure.

Sensitivity to Change

One of the most important features of clinical instruments is that they are sensitive to changes over time or after interventions (Guidi et al., 2018). That may be a partial explanation for the still relatively modest effect size of positive interventions in the clinical field (Chakhssi et al., 2018; Weiss et al., 2016), namely, that we are using measures (e.g., broad overall judgments of satisfaction with life) that may not be sensitive enough to capture the efficacy of the interventions.

Adequacy and Pertinence

Also, it must be remembered, as part of a more general problem, that most of the current research published is embedded in Western frameworks of conceptualization and production, which is reflected in the very use and acceptance of assessment instruments. Many commonly used scales to assess emotions (e.g., PANAS, Bradburn's Affect Balance Scale, etc.) are saturated with high arousal emotions that, for instance, are not so common in Eastern cultures and are not associated with a core concept of what a "good life" in other cultures may be (Oishi & Schimmack, 2010). More broadly, these frequently used instruments are not a good choice when the assessor wishes to explore some kinds of positive emotions (e.g., calmness, peace of mind, etc.) that are not well represented in these instruments, which, furthermore, represent only a fraction of the positive and negative emotions that can be expressed in English (Cowen & Keltner, 2017).

Cognitive and emotional development are important aspects to consider when selecting instruments regarding child assessment. Studies show that children can reliably and validly report their symptoms and well-being from the age of 5. However, the measurement methods and instruments should be carefully selected. Some questionnaires are validated only for specific ages (e.g., the VIA-Youth can be used from 10 years of age), and other questionnaires have different age versions (e.g., Pediatric Quality of Life; Varni et al., 2002). Although a direct report by children or adolescents is irreplaceable (Achenbach, 1992), it is recommended to complement their evaluations with other informants (e.g., parents, teachers, health professionals). Multidimensional and multimethod assessments are also recommended. For instance, protocols may include interviews and/or the evaluation of different variables such as cognitive and emotional well-being, family and school relationships, or strengths. Besides self-report measures (e.g., Student Life Satisfaction Scale; Huebner, 1991), one can use more explicit indicators of skills for mental health (e.g., observing cooperative behaviors in a classroom or behavioral vignettes; Slemp et al., 2017; Waters, 2015). Finally, when children are very young or have cognitive problems, it is recommended to assess their ability to respond to questionnaires using Likert-scale response formats and, if possible, to teach them how to use these formats of response. A good example of this prior training can be reviewed on the Pediatric Quality of Life scale (Varni et al., 2002).

Time Framework

Depending on the nature of the problem, the appropriate time window (e.g., days, weeks, months, or lifetime) may vary. Many instruments assess feelings, values, strengths, or cognitions "in general," with no specific indication of time. While this is a valuable source of information, retrospective general judgments may be subjected to significant recall biases (Kahneman et al., 1990). In some instruments, the time window can be arbitrarily changed (e.g., "last week," "last month," "currently") depending on the evaluator's needs (Watson & Clark, 1994). Yet, in these cases, one must be cautious when interpreting the data or comparing them with published results.

Regarding the timeframe of the assessment, it is important to consider that one way of minimizing recall biases is to use experience-sampling methods (ESMs), which allow for capturing individuals' feelings and behaviors in a given moment (typically by using apps that randomly indicate participants to provide information on themselves several times a day over several days). Although ESMs have provided very innovative insights on the dynamics of emotions, cognition, and behavior (e.g., van Os et al., 2017), their utility may be limited in practice as such methods can often be experienced as intrusive or uncomfortable by the patients (Bos et al., 2019). Yet, despite their disadvantages, ESMs are some of the promising tools to make significant advancements in our comprehension of the nature of emotions, although their utility for clinicians is still limited (Trull & Ebner-Priemer, 2020).

Use of Standard Assessment Instruments

Finally, an interesting possibility is to use instruments that, despite being aimed at assessing symptoms, dysfunctions, and difficulties, include items of positive functioning. In some of these instruments, the standard psychometric procedure is to reach an overall score of psychopathologies (e.g., depression or lack of self-esteem) by adding scores of items directly assessing psychopathology (e.g., feelings of sadness) and inverted scores from items worded in a positive direction (e.g., feelings of happiness). For instance, the Center for Epidemiologic Studies Depression Scale (CES-D), a widely used instrument to assess the frequency of depressive symptoms in the last week (Radloff, 1977), includes 4 positive items (e.g., "I felt that I was just as good as other people," "I felt hopeful about the future," "I was happy," and "I enjoyed life") within the set of 20 items measuring depressive symptoms. Thus, clinicians might well provide separate scores of items related to well-being from those related to other depressive symptoms. This strategy would allow not only monitoring those two separate facets but also facilitating dialogues with patients about this dichotomy and ways to promote changes in both directions. Similar strategies have been conducted in separating positive and negative items of scales aimed at measuring general health status, like the Goldberg Health Questionnaire (QHQ-30; Huppert & Whittington, 2003) or the Rosenberg Self-Esteem Scale (RSES; Donnellan et al., 2016), both of which contain positive and negative items that are typically combined in a single composite score.

Concluding Comments

Paying attention to the assessment of positive functioning (either its presence or absence) is important because having positive mental health is a universal goal. In fact, in the case of persons with psychological difficulties, the issue of positivity may be even more important than for individuals with good mental health. One might think that a positive mental health framework is just a construction of well-intentioned clinicians. Yet, individuals with mental disorders seem to also share this positive perspective (Demyttenaere et al., 2015; Zimmerman et al., 2006). Thus, clinicians would do well to pay attention to issues related to the quality of life and well-being of their patients, as it seems that these factors are congruent with what patients rank as important goals in therapy.

All mental health professionals should take into consideration the advancements in the science of well-being (Diener et al., 2018). Since Maria Jahodas's urgent call in 1958 to pay attention to positive mental health, some clinicians have tried to formulate measures and protocols to include positive aspects of functioning (e.g., Bech, 2015; Tomba & Bech, 2012). Knowing more about basic concepts related to the field of positive functioning (e.g., the maps and structure of positive and negative emotions, emodiversity, hedonic adaptation, psychological strengths, full recovery, rehabilitation, posttraumatic growth, resilience, psychological flexibility, etc.) seems essential to building a more robust clinical science. Both positive and negative aspects of functioning belong to the science of psychology and should be naturally incorporated into the curriculum of mental health researchers and practitioners. In the case of the clinic field, knowing more about the basics of positive functioning may enrich the professional's perspectives while also humanizing their vision of their clients and patients in providing a more holistic view of their capabilities. Also, considering well-being as an outcome target (Valiente et al., 2019) may help the designing of more robust and comprehensive interventions to alleviate human suffering (Fava et al., 2017). Moreover, personalized treatments need to incorporate vast arrays of clinical and demographic information to predict who benefits most from which intervention (Cuijpers et al., 2020; López-Gómez et al., 2019). We can anticipate that including positive variables enhances personalized treatments.

A good example of the growing relevance of positive concepts in the clinical domain may be found in a document on the mental health research priorities in Europe, where one of the six declared priorities was the "focus on the development and causal mechanisms of mental health symptoms, syndromes, and *well-being* across the lifespan (including older populations)" (Wykes et al., 2015, p. 1040, *italics added*). Thus, the time to address these challenges – using the best scientific knowledge available – has arrived. Positive psychology has an undoubtedly important opportunity to fill that gap between institutional statements and promises, and the fulfillment of these rather abstract but desirable objectives that have been related to "positive mental health2 for many decades (Jahoda, 1958).

The assessment of positive aspects of functioning, with the support of the best available research in the fields of emotions, psychopathology, psychometrics, and neuroscience, may open new spaces to improve mental health. In sum, that assessment may help to (a) pay attention to issues (e.g., strengths) that can be easily ignored using clinical traditional mental frameworks, (b) identify and monitor new intervention targets, and (c) personalize treatments.

References

Achenbach, T.M. (1992). *Manual for Child Behavior Checklist/2-3 and 1992 Profile.* University of Vermont.

Baumeister, R.F., Bratslavsky, E., Finkenauer, C., & Vohs, K.D. (2001). Bad is stronger than good. *Review of General Psychology, 5*(4), 323–370. https://doi.org/10.1037//1089-2680.5.4.323

Bech, P. (1990). Measurement of psychological distress and well-being. *Psychotherapy and Psychosomatics, 54*, 77–89. https://doi.org/10.1159/000288382

Bech, P. (2015). Clinical assessments of positive mental health. In D.V. Jeste & B.W. Palmer (Eds.), *Positive psychiatry: A clinical handbook* (pp. 127–143). American Psychiatric Publishing. https://doi.org/10.1176/appi.books.9781615370818.dj07

Bergsma, A., ten Have, M., Veenhoven, R., & de Graaf, R. (2011). Most people with mental disorders are happy: A 3-year follow-up in the Dutch general population. *Journal of Positive Psychology, 6*(4), 253–259. https://doi.org/10.1080/17439760.2011.577086

Bergsma, A., & Veenhoven, R. (2011). The happiness of people with a mental disorder in modern society. *Psychology of Well-Being: Theory, Research, and Practice, 1*, Article 2. https://doi.org/10.1186/2211-1522-1-2

Biswas-Diener, R. (2010). *Practicing positive psychology coaching.* Wiley. https://doi.org/10.1002/9781118269633

Bos, F.M., Snippe, E., Bruggeman, R., Wichers, M., & van der Krieke, L. (2019). Insights of patients and clinicians on the promise of the experience sampling method for psychiatric care. *Psychiatric Services, 70*(11), 983–991. https://doi.org/10.1176/appi.ps.201900050

Chakhssi, F., Kraiss, J.T., Sommers-Spijkerman, M., & Bohlmeijer, E.T. (2018). The effect of positive psychology interventions on well-being and distress in clinical samples with psychiatric or somatic disorders: a systematic review and meta-analysis. *BMC Psychiatry, 18*, Article 211. https://doi.org/10.1186/s12888-018-1739-2

Chaves, C., Lopez-Gomez, I., Hervas, G., & Vazquez, C. (2019). The integrative positive psychological intervention for depression (IPPI-D). *Journal of Contemporary Psychotherapy, 49*(3), 177–185. https://doi.org/10.1007/s10879-018-9412-0

Cooke, P.J., Melchert, T.P., & Connor, K. (2016). Measuring well-being: A review of instruments. *The Counseling Psychologist, 44*(5), 730–757. https://doi.org/10.1177/0011000016633507

Cordova, M.J., Cunningham, L.L., Carlson, C.R., & Andrykowski, M.A. (2001). Posttraumatic growth following breast cancer: A controlled comparison study. *Health Psychology, 20*(3), 176–185. https://doi.org/10.1037/0278-6133.20.3.176

Cowen, A.S., & Keltner, D. (2017). Self-report captures 27 distinct categories of emotion bridged by continuous gradients. *Proceedings of the National Academy of Sciences, 114*(38), 201702247. https://doi.org/10.1073/pnas.1702247114

Cuijpers, P., Stringaris, A., & Wolpert, M. (2020). Treatment outcomes for depression: Challenges and opportunities. *The Lancet Psychiatry, 0366*(2019), 2019–2020. https://doi.org/10.1016/s2215-0366(20)30036-5

Demyttenaere, K., Donneau, A.-F., Albert, A., Ansseau, M., Constant, E., & Van Heeringen, C. (2015). What is important in being cured from depression? Discordance between physicians and patients. *Journal of Affective Disorders, 174,* 390–396. https://doi.org/10.1016/j.jad.2014.12.004

De Vries, M., Emons, W.H.M., Plantinga, A., Pietersma, S., Van Den Hout, W.B., Stiggelbout, A.M., & Elske Van Den Akker-Van Marle, M. (2016). Comprehensively measuring health-related subjective well-being: Dimensionality analysis for improved outcome assessment in health economics. *Value in Health, 19*(2), 167–175. https://doi.org/10.1016/j.jval.2015.11.010

Diener, E., Lucas, R.E., & Oishi, S. (2018). Advances and open questions in the science of subjective well-Being. *Collabra: Psychology, 4*(1), Article 15. https://doi.org/10.1525/collabra.115

Donnellan, M.B., Ackerman, R.A., & Brecheen, C. (2016). Extending structural analyses of the Rosenberg Self-Esteem Scale to consider criterion-related validity: Can composite self-esteem scores be good enough? *Journal of Personality Assessment, 98*(2), 169–177. https://doi.org/10.1080/00223891.2015.1058268

Erzen, E., & Çikrikci, Ö. (2018). The effect of loneliness on depression: A meta-analysis. *International Journal of Social Psychiatry, 64*(5), 427–435. https://doi.org/10.1177/0020764018776349

Everaert, J., Bronstein, M.V., Castro, A.A., Cannon, T.D., & Joormann, J. (2020). When negative interpretations persist, positive emotions don't! Inflexible negative interpretations encourage depression and social anxiety by dampening positive emotions. *Behaviour Research and Therapy, 124,* 103510. https://doi.org/10.1016/j.brat.2019.103510

Fava, G.A. (2016). *Well-being therapy*. Karger AG. https://doi.org/10.1159/isbn.978-3-318-05822-2

Fava, G.A., Cosci, F., Guidi, J., & Tomba, E. (2017). Well-being therapy in depression: New insights into the role of psychological well-being in the clinical process. *Depression and Anxiety, 34*(9), 801–808. https://doi.org/10.1002/da.22629

Feldman, G.C., Joormann, J., & Johnson, S.L. (2008). Responses to positive affect: A self-report measure of rumination and dampening. *Cognitive Therapy and Research, 32*(4), Article 507. https://doi.org/10.1007/s10608-006-9083-0

Gilbert, K.E. (2012). The neglected role of positive emotion in adolescent psychopathology. *Clinical Psychology Review, 32*(6), 467–481. https://doi.org/10.1016/j.cpr.2012.05.005

Gruber, J. (Ed.). (2019). *The Oxford handbook of positive emotion and psychopathology*. Oxford University Press. https://doi.org/10.1093/oxfordhb/9780190653200.001.0001

Gruber, J., Villanueva, C., Burr, E., Purcell, J.R., & Karoly, H. (2020). Understanding and taking stock of positive emotion disturbance. *Social and Personality Psychology Compass, 14*(1), 1–19. https://doi.org/10.1111/spc3.12515

Guidi, J., Brakemeier, E.-L., Bockting, C.L. H., Cosci, F., Cuijpers, P., Jarrett, R.B., Linden, M., Marks, I., Peretti, C.S., Rafanelli, C., Rief, W., Schneider, S., Schnyder, U., Sensky, T., Tomba, E., Vazquez, C., Vieta, E., Zipfel, S., Wright, J.H., & Fava, G.A. (2018). Methodological recommendations for trials of psychological interventions. *Psychotherapy and Psychosomatics, 87*(5), 276–284. https://doi.org/10.1159/000490574

Halahakoon, D.C., Kieslich, K., O'Driscoll, C., Nair, A., Lewis, G., & Roiser, J.P. (2020). Reward processing behavior in depressed participants relative to healthy volunteers: A systematic review and meta-analysis. *JAMA Psychiatry, 77*(12), 1286–1295. https://doi.org/10.1001/jamapsychiatry.2020.2139

Huebner, E.S. (1991). Initial development of the Student's Life Satisfaction Scale. *School Psychology International, 12*(3), 231–240. https://doi.org/10.1177/0143034391123010

Huppert, F.A., & Whittington, J.E. (2003). Evidence for the independence of positive and negative well-being: Implications for quality of life assessment. *British Journal of Health Psychology, 8*(1), 107–122. https://doi.org/10.1348/135910703762879246

Jahoda, M. (1958). *Current concepts of positive mental health.* Basic Books. https://doi.org/10.1037/11258-000

Johnson, R., Jenkinson, D., Stinton, C., Taylor-Phillips, S., Madan, J., Stewart-Brown, S., & Clarke, A. (2016). Where's WALY? A proof of concept study of the "well-being adjusted life year" using secondary analysis of cross-sectional survey data. *Health and Quality of Life Outcomes, 14*(1), Article 126. https://doi.org/10.1186/s12955-016-0532-5

Joshanloo, M. (2018). Optimal human functioning around the world: A new index of eudaimonic well-being in 166 nations. *British Journal of Psychology, 109*(4), 637–655. https://doi.org/10.1111/bjop.12316

Kahneman, D., Knetsch, J.L., & Thaler, R.H. (1990). Experimental tests of the endowment effect and the coase theorem. *Journal of Political Economy, 98,* 1325–1348. https://doi.org/10.1086/261737

Kashdan, T.B., & Breen, W.E. (2008). Social anxiety and positive emotions: A prospective examination of a self-regulatory model with tendencies to suppress or express emotions as a moderating variable. *Behavior Therapy, 39*(1), 1–12. https://doi.org/10.1016/j.beth.2007.02.003

Kashdan, T.B., Weeks, J.W., & Savostyanova, A. (2011). Whether, how, and when social anxiety shapes positive experiences and events: A self-regulatory framework and treatment implications. *Clinical Psychology Review, 31*(5), 786–799. https://doi.org/10.1016/j.cpr.2011.03.012

Keyes, C.L.M. (2007). Promoting and protecting mental health as flourishing: A complementary strategy for improving national mental health. *American Psychologist, 62*(2), 95–108. https://doi.org/10.1037/0003-066X.62.2.95

Kleiman, E.M., & Beaver, J.K. (2013). A meaningful life is worth living: Meaning in life as a suicide resiliency factor. *Psychiatry Research, 210*(3), 934–939. https://doi.org/10.1016/j.psychres.2013.08.002

Layard, R., Chisholm, D., Patel, V., & Saxena, S. (2013). Mental illness and unhappiness. In J. Helliwell, R. Layard, & J. Sachs (Eds.), *World happiness report 2013* (pp. 39–51). UN Sustainable Development Solutions Network. https://doi.org/10.2139/ssrn.2336397

Lindert, J., Bain, P.A., Kubzansky, L.D., & Stein, C. (2015). Well-being measurement and the WHO health policy Health 2010: Systematic review of measurement scales. *European Journal of Public Health, 25*(4), 731–740. https://doi.org/10.1093/eurpub/cku193

Linton, M.J., Dieppe, P., Medina-Lara, A., Watson, L., & Crathorne, L. (2016). Review of 99 self-report measures for assessing well-being in adults: exploring dimensions of well-being and developments over time. *BMJ Open, 6*(7), e010641. https://doi.org/10.1136/bmjopen-2015-010641

López-Gómez, I., Lorenzo-Luaces, L., Chaves, C., Hervas, G., DeRubeis, R.J., & Vazquez, C. (2019). Predicting optimal interventions for clinical depression: Moderators of outcomes in a positive psychological intervention vs. cognitive-behavioral therapy. *General Hospital Psychiatry, 61,* 104–110. https://doi.org/10.1016/j.genhosppsych.2019.07.004

Maddux, J.E. (2016). Toward a more positive clinical psychology. In A.M. Wood & J. Johnson, *The Wiley handbook of positive clinical psychology* (pp. 19–29). Wiley. https://doi.org/10.1002/9781118468197.ch2

Malouff, J.M., & Schutte, N.S. (2017). Can psychological interventions increase optimism? A meta-analysis. *Journal of Positive Psychology, 12*(6), 594–604. https://doi.org/10.1080/17439760.2016.1221122

McMakin, D.L., Santiago, C.D., & Shirk, S.R. (2009). The time course of positive and negative emotion in dysphoria. *The Journal of Positive Psychology, 4*(2), 182–192. https://doi.org/10.1080/17439760802650600

Murray, C. J. (1994). Quantifying the burden of disease: The technical basis for disability-adjusted life years. *Bulletin of the World Health Organization, 72*(3), 429–445.

Nawijn, L., van Zuiden, M., Frijling, J. L., Koch, S. B., Veltman, D. J., & Olff, M. (2015). Reward functioning in PTSD: A systematic review exploring the mechanisms underlying anhedonia. *Neuroscience & Biobehavioral Reviews, 51,* 189–204. https://doi.org/10.1016/j.neubiorev.2015.01.019

Ochoa, C., Casellas-Grau, A., Vives, J., Font, A., & Borràs, J.-M. (2017). Positive psychotherapy for distressed cancer survivors: Posttraumatic growth facilitation reduces posttraumatic stress. *International Journal of Clinical and Health Psychology, 17*(1), 28–37. https://doi.org/10.1016/j.ijchp.2016.09.002

Ochoa-Arnedo, C., Casellas-Grau, A., Lleras, M., Medina, J. C., & Vives, J. (2021). Stress management or post-traumatic growth facilitation to diminish distress in cancer survivors? A randomized controlled trial. *Journal of Positive Psychology, 16*(6), 715–725. https://doi.org/10.1080/17439760.2020.1765005

O'Hanlon, B. (2011). *Quick steps to resolving trauma.* Norton.

Oishi, S., & Schimmack, U. (2010). Culture and well-being: A new inquiry into the psychological wealth of nations. *Perspectives on Psychological Science, 5*(4), 463–471. https://doi.org/10.1177/1745691610375561

Owens, R. L., Magyar-Moe, J. L., & Lopez, S. J. (2015). Finding balance via positive psychological assessment and conceptualization: Recommendations for practice. *The Counseling Psychologist, 43*(5), 634–670. https://doi.org/10.1177/0011000015584956

Pat-Horenczyk, R., Perry, S., Hamama-Raz, Y., Ziv, Y., Schramm-Yavin, S., & Stemmer, S. M. (2015). Posttraumatic growth in breast cancer survivors: Constructive and illusory aspects. *Journal of Traumatic Stress, 28*(3), 214–222. https://doi.org/10.1002/jts.22014

Radloff, L. S. (1977). The CES-D Scale. *Applied Psychological Measurement, 1*(3), 385–401. https://doi.org/10.1177/014662167700100306

Rashid, T. (2015). Positive psychotherapy: A strength-based approach. *The Journal of Positive Psychology, 10*(1), 25–40. https://doi.org/10.1080/17439760.2014.920411

Redlich-Amirav, D., Ansell, L. J., Harrison, M., Norrena, K. L., & Armijo-Olivo, S. (2018). Psychometric properties of Hope Scales: A systematic review. *International Journal of Clinical Practice, 72*(7), 1–23. https://doi.org/10.1111/ijcp.13213

Ruini, C. (2017). *Positive psychology in the clinical domains.* Springer International Publishing. https://doi.org/10.1007/978-3-319-52112-1

Ruini, C., & Fava, G. A. (2009). Well-being therapy for generalized anxiety disorder. *Journal of Clinical Psychology, 65*(5), 510–519. https://doi.org/10.1002/jclp.20592

Rush, A. J., First, M. B., & Blaker, D. (2008). *Handbook of psychiatric measures* (2nd ed.). American Psychiatric Publishing.

Ryan, R. M., & Deci, E. L. (2000). The darker and brighter sides of human existence: Basic psychological needs as a unifying concept. *Psychological Inquiry, 11*(4), 319–338. https://doi.org/10.1207/S15327965PLI1104_03

Ryan, R. M., & Deci, E. L. (2001). On happiness and human potentials: A review of research on hedonic and eudaimonic well-being. *Annual Review of Psychology, 52,* 141–166. https://doi.org/10.1146/annurev.psych.52.1.141

Ryff, C. D. (1989). Happiness is everything, or is it? Explorations on the meaning of psychological well-being. *Journal of Personality and Social Psychology, 57,* 1069–1081. https://doi.org/10.1037/0022-3514.57.6.1069

Ryff, C. D., & Singer, B. (1996). Psychological well-being: Meaning, measurement, and implications for psychotherapy research. *Psychotherapy and Psychosomatics, 65*(1), 14–23. https://doi.org/10.1159/000289026

Salsman, J. M., Park, C. L., Hahn, E. A., Snyder, M. A., George, L. S., Steger, M. F., Merluzzi, T., & Cella, D. (2018). Refining and supplementing candidate measures of psychological well-being for the NIH PROMIS®: Qualitative results from a mixed cancer sample. *Quality of Life Research, 27*(9), 2471–2476. https://doi.org/10.1007/s11136-018-1896-2

Seligman, M. (2011). *Flourish.* Free Press.

Seligman, M. E. P., & Csikszentmihalyi, M. (2000). Positive psychology: An introduction. *American Psychologist, 55*(1), 5–14. https://doi.org/10.1037//0003-066X.55.1.5

Simmons, C., & Lehmann, P. (2012). *Tools for strengths-based assessment and evaluation.* Springer. Retrieved from https://www.springerpub.com/media/springer-downloads/Simmons_PTR_Ancillary.pdf

Slemp, G., Chin, T.-C., Kern, M. L., Siokou, C., Loton, D., Oades, L. G., Vella-Brodrick, D., & Waters, L. (2017). Positive education in Australia: Practice, measurement, and future directions. In E. Frydenberg, A. Martin & R. Collie (Eds.), *Social and emotional learning in Australia and the Asia- Pacific: Perspectives, programs and approaches* (pp. 101–122). Springer. https://doi.org/10.1007/978-981-10-3394-0_6

Spinhoven, P., Elzinga, B. M., Giltay, E., & Penninx, B. W. J. H. (2015). Anxious or depressed and still happy? *PLoS ONE, 10*(10), 1–17. https://doi.org/10.1371/journal.pone.0139912

Stewart-Brown, S., Tennant, A., Tennant, R., Platt, S., Parkinson, J., & Weich, S. (2009). Internal construct validity of the Warwick-Edinburgh Mental Well-being Scale (WEMWBS): A Rasch analysis using data from the Scottish Health Education Population Survey. *Health and Quality of Life Outcomes, 7*(1), Article 15. https://doi.org/10.1186/1477-7525-7-15

Suddaby, K., & Landau, J. (1998). Positive and negative timelines: A technique for restorying. *Family Process, 37*(3), 287–298. https://doi.org/10.1111/j.1545-5300.1998.00287.x

Sumalla, E. C., Ochoa, C., & Blanco, I. (2009). Posttraumatic growth in cancer: Reality or illusion? *Clinical Psychology Review, 29*, 24–33. https://doi.org/10.1016/j.cpr.2008.09.006

Summers, J. K., Smith, L. M., Harwell, L. C., & Buck, K. D. (2017). The development of a human well-being index for the United States. In A. A. Vilas Boas, *Quality of life and quality of working life.* InTech. https://doi.org/10.5772/intechopen.68596

Tomba, E., & Bech, P. (2012). Clinimetrics and clinical psychometrics: Macro- and micro-analysis. *Psychotherapy and Psychosomatics, 81*(6), 333–343. https://doi.org/10.1159/000341757

Trull, T. J., & Ebner-Priemer, U. W. (2020). Ambulatory assessment in psychopathology research: A review of recommended reporting guidelines and current practices. *Journal of Abnormal Psychology, 129*(1), 56–63. https://doi.org/10.1037/abn0000473

Urry, H. L., Nitschke, J. B., Dolski, I., Jackson, D. C., Dalton, K. M., Mueller, C. J., Rosenkranz, M. A., Ryff, C. D., Singer, B. H., & Davidson, R. J. (2004). Making a life worth living: Neural correlates of well-being. *Psychological Science, 15*(6), 367–372. https://doi.org/10.1111/j.0956-7976.2004.00686.x

Valiente, C., Espinosa, R., Trucharte, A., Nieto, J., & Martínez-Prado, L. (2019). The challenge of well-being and quality of life: A meta-analysis of psychological interventions in schizophrenia. *Schizophrenia Research, 208*, 16–24. https://doi.org/10.1016/j.schres.2019.01.040

Vanderlind, W. M., Millgram, Y., Baskin-Sommers, A. R., Clark, M. S., & Joormann, J. (2020). Understanding positive emotion deficits in depression: From emotion preferences to emotion regulation. *Clinical Psychology Review, 76*, 101826. https://doi.org/10.1016/j.cpr.2020.101826

van Os, J., Verhagen, S., Marsman, A., Peeters, F., Bak, M., Marcelis, M., Drukker, M., Reininghaus, U., Jacobs, N., Lataster, T., Simons, C., Lousberg, R., Gülöksüz, S., Leue, C., Groot, P. C., Viechtbauer, W., & Delespaul, P. (2017). The experience sampling method as an mHealth tool to support self-monitoring, self-insight, and personalized healthcare in clinical practice. *Depression and Anxiety, 34*(6), 481–493. https://doi.org/10.1002/da.22647

Varni, J. W., Burwinkle, T. M., Katz, E. R., Meeske, K., & Dickinson, P. (2002). The PedsQLTM in pediatric cancer: Reliability and validity of the Pediatric Quality of Life Inventory TM Generic Core Scales, multidimensional fatigue scale, and cancer module. *Cancer, 94*, 2090–2106. https://doi.org/10.1002/cncr.10428.

Vazquez, C. (2017). What does positivity add to psychopathology? An introduction to the special issue on "Positive emotions and cognitions in clinical psychology." *Cognitive Therapy and Research, 41*(3), 325–334. https://doi.org/10.1007/s10608-017-9847-8

Vazquez, C., & Chaves, C. (2016). Positive Psychology. In H. S. Friedman (Ed.), *Encyclopedia of mental health* (Vol. 3, 2nd ed., pp. 290–299). Academic Press. https://doi.org/10.1016/B978-0-12-397045-9.00049-5

Vazquez, C., Rahona, J.J., Gómez, D., Caballero, F.F., & Hervás, G. (2015). A national representative study of the relative impact of physical and psychological problems on life satisfaction. *Journal of Happiness Studies, 16*(1), 135–148. https://doi.org/10.1007/s10902-014-9501-z

Vazquez, C., Valiente, C., García, F.E., Contreras, A., Peinado, V., Trucharte, A., & Bentall, R.P. (2021). Post-traumatic growth and stress-related responses during the COVID-19 pandemic in a national representative sample: The role of positive core beliefs about the world and others. *Journal of Happiness Studies, 22,* 2915–2935. https://doi.org/10.1007/s10902-020-00352-3

Waters, L. (2015). The Relationship between strength-based parenting with children's stress levels and strength-based coping approaches. *Psychology, 6,* 689–699. https://doi.org/10.4236/psych.2015.66067

Watson, D. (2016). Positive mood dysfunction in psychopathology. In A.M. Wood & J. Johnson, *The Wiley handbook of positive clinical psychology* (pp. 57–71). Wiley. https://doi.org/10.1002/9781118468197.ch5

Watson, D., & Clark, L.A. (1994). *The PANAS-X: Manual for the Positive and Negative Affect Schedule-Expanded Form.* University of Iowa. https://doi.org/10.17077/48vt-m4t2

Watson, D., & Naragon-Gainey, K. (2010). On the specificity of positive emotional dysfunction in psychopathology: Evidence from the mood and anxiety disorders and schizophrenia/schizotypy. *Clinical Psychology Review, 30*(7), 839–848. https://doi.org/10.1016/j.cpr.2009.11.002

Weinstein, M.C., Torrance, G., & McGuire, A. (2009). QALYs: The basics. *Value in Health, 12,* S5–S9. https://doi.org/10.1111/j.1524-4733.2009.00515.x

Weiss, L.A., Westerhof, G.J., & Bohlmeijer, E.T. (2016). Can we increase psychological well-being? The effects of interventions on psychological well-being: A meta-analysis of randomized controlled trials. *PLoS ONE, 11*(6), 1–16. https://doi.org/10.1371/journal.pone.0158092

Whitton, A.E., Treadway, M.T., & Pizzagalli, D.A. (2015). Reward processing dysfunction in major depression, bipolar disorder and schizophrenia. *Current Opinion in Psychiatry, 28*(1), 7–12. https://doi.org/10.1097/YCO.0000000000000122

Windle, G., Bennett, K.M., & Noyes, J. (2011). A methodological review of resilience measurement scales. *Health and Quality of Life Outcomes, 9*(1), 8. https://doi.org/10.1186/1477-7525-9-8

Wood, A.M., & Tarrier, N. (2010). Positive clinical psychology: A new vision and strategy for integrated research and practice. *Clinical Psychology Review, 30,* 819–829. https://doi.org/10.1016/j.cpr.2010.06.003

World Health Organization. (2012). *Measuring health and disability: Manual for WHO Disability Assessment Schedule (WHODAS 2.0).* Author.

Wykes, T., Haro, J.M., Belli, S.R., Obradors-Tarragó, C., Arango, C., Ayuso-Mateos, J.L., Bitter, I., Brunn, M., Chevreul, K., Demotes-Mainard, J., Elfeddali, I., Evans-Lacko, S., Fiorillo, A., Forsman, A.K., Hazo, J.-B., Kuepper, R., Knappe, S., Leboyer, M., Lewis, S.W., ... Wittchen, H.U. (2015). Mental health research priorities for Europe. *The Lancet Psychiatry, 2*(11), 1036–1042. https://doi.org/10.1016/S2215-0366(15)00332-6

Zimmerman, M., McGlinchey, J.B., Posternak, M.A., Friedman, M., Attiullah, M., & Boerescu, D. (2006). How should remission from depression be defined? The depressed patient's perspective. *The American Journal of Psychiatry, 163,* 148–150. https://doi.org/10.1176/appi.ajp.163.1.148

Chapter 19

Measuring Leisure

Synopsis of Perspectives and Instruments

Lynn A. Barnett[1] and Joel A. Blanco[2]

[1]Department of Recreation, Sport & Tourism, University of Illinois, Champaign IL, USA
[2]Department of Exercise Science & Sport, Millikin University, Decatur IL, USA

Early writings reveal that even more than 2,000 years ago, philosophers of the time were expounding on what makes a good life and on how leisure is its essence. Work was defined as that which was "unleisurely," and leisure was to be sought only by those who could use it "wisely" (i.e., for mental inquiries, debate, poetry, or cultural pursuits). Greek philosophers characterized leisure in such lofty terms because they regarded it as contributing to an individual's life – more so than any other activity – distinguishing it as the "ultimate purpose of life" (Goodale & Godbey, 1988). In contemporary society, leisure is no longer regarded in such reverent terms, yet its influence on people's well-being and quality of life is still recognized. Research about leisure has a relatively short history, and researchers are still grappling with how to define and measure it. How leisure has been conceptualized and operationally defined is summarized below, and the remainder of the chapter scrutinizes the tools that have been employed to measure it.

Leisure as Activity

The measurement of leisure can generally be seen to follow a chronological path and reflects developments in how to define, conceptualize, and theorize about leisure. The earliest efforts viewed leisure as recreational pursuits – the activities people do to presumably enjoy and derive pleasure. Respondents were presented with an *a priori* generated (researcher-created) list of activities and requested to list the frequency of participation in each one. Response options ranged from specific quantities (once a month, twice a week or more, etc.), depending on the referent ("yesterday,“ "last week,“ "last month," "last year,“ "ever"), to more imprecise alternatives (e.g., "a lot,“ "a moderate amount,“ "a little," etc.), which left much to the subjective interpretation of the respondent. Equating leisure with recreational activity, and quantifying it in this way permitted comparisons between demographic subgroups and cultures. Critics of these activity profile inventories – regardless of how their lists were generated – have argued that the clustering of activities based on participation rates does nothing to inform scholars about the latent structure or meaning underlying leisure activities (cf., Tinsley & Tinsley, 1982). Leisure scholars were thus challenged to consider a different perspective.

Leisure as Free Time

A second approach was to consider leisure as time free from obligations, thus voluntary, and it was considered to be the life domain most under an individual's control. The scales that assessed how individuals spend their leisure ("free") time adopted the perspective that the passing of time was a central tenet. Measures of leisure focused on "discretionary time" and asked respondents to report their behaviors, contexts, companions, and feelings when asked to do so. These time-budget diaries segmented people's daily, weekly, or monthly time, and time sampling units were systematic or random (e.g., ESM "beeper" studies). More recently, technological advances have been employed to permit responses to be entered on preprogrammed devices (e.g., wristbands). In addition, much of this data is now available for use through resources such as the American Time Use Survey (National Research Council, 2012).

This approach presented researchers with possibilities for empirical questions that were different than those possible when leisure was viewed solely as an activity. The quantitative data that were output afforded opportunities for studies contrasting leisure time allocation across demographics and countries (Haller et al., 2013). However, as "progress" in technological devices has blurred the boundaries between the different domains of life and multitasking has become a typical occurrence, it is no longer easy to separate leisure from work or free from obligated time. For those who segment rather than integrate their work and leisure activities (cf. Kreiner, 2006), time-budget measures may be apposite.

Leisure as a Subjective Experience (State of Mind)

As leisure research progressed, sociological and psychological perspectives began to expand conceptualizations of leisure beyond mere categorization of time (Mommaas, 1997). Scholars deemed the activity- and time-based definitions of leisure to be lacking in ecological validity, and instead they came to regard leisure as a phenomenon or an experience. Leisure was now seen as any pursuit, at any time, with the qualities that it was intrinsically motivated, accompanied by positive affect, and in which the actor perceived there was the freedom to choose (Kleiber et al., 2011). Questions were posed about antecedents and outcomes, motivations, and how leisure choices might contribute to individuals' happiness and well-being.

While viewing leisure in this way spawned a cadre of new empirical questions, it also posed a quandary to researchers about how to measure it. For most academicians who had been trained in the scientific method, assessing leisure as blocks of time or frequency of activity participation presented few problems. However, the concepts that were now being used to define leisure were more abstract and intangible, and the challenge was to encapsulate them so they could be understood by both research participants and professional colleagues. This reflects the current state of affairs in designing tools and methods of measurement for the constructs and relationships thought to define and characterize leisure.

Relevance

How individuals forge a life for themselves that they find to be personally rewarding and meaningful suggests a natural linkage between research in the fields of positive psychology and leisure experience. Utilizing whatever their evaluative criteria are, people seek to live their lives in positive ways and thereby achieve a sense of well-being. One strategy for achieving this is to increase the frequency with which they experience positive affect (Seligman, 2011) by engaging in desired leisure activities, more so than in other areas/domains in their lives (Diener et al., 1999). The satisfaction that people have with the frequency and diversity of their leisure engagements has been shown to have a significant effect on their subjective well-being (SWB; Diener, 1984) in cross-sectional as well as longitudinal studies (Pinquart, & Schindler, 2009). Experimental interventions on leisure have been demonstrated to enhance SWB (Searle et al., 1995).

Research has provided insights into what the elements common to leisure experiences might be that contribute to people's SWB, and they most closely align with the subjective experience, or state-of-mind, perspective. The prevailing conceptualization proposes that leisure can be demarcated from other endeavors by the primacy of three qualities: intrinsic motivation, perceived freedom, and positive affect (Kleiber et al., 2011), each of which has also been shown to predict SWB (Kuykendall et al., 2015) and satisfaction with life (Iwasaki, 2007) in both research and theory (Fredrickson, 1998; Ryan & Deci, 2000).

In summary, the observed connections between leisure and positive psychology are strong and consistent. There is a growing number of empirical studies in both fields investigating the common theme of how individuals can live an enhanced and fulfilling life they themselves define and pursue. While several core concepts within the field of positive psychology can claim methodological maturity and rigor (Geerling & Diener, 2020), the measurement of leisure has not reached this status. This chapter represents an attempt to congregate the instruments that have been, and continue to be, utilized to assess leisure activities, time, and perceptions (see Table 19.1 for a summary).

The following section presents the characteristics and quality of each one under a critical lens, to enable the reader to advance how leisure can be operationalized, so that further scientific studies of relationships between leisure and aspects of positive psychology can be more aggressively pursued.

Assessment Instruments

Leisure as Activity

One of the first formalized instruments was the Leisure Activities Blank (LAB; McKechnie, 1974, 1975), which listed 121 activities presumed by the authors to be leisure, and respondents were asked to report the extent of their past participation and their intended future participation for each one. A multitude of studies followed suit, all assessing participation rates and utilizing factor analytic or scaling procedures to find ways to group them. Introducing variations in the response format, respondents were asked to assess the extent to which activities were similar or different (Russell & Hultsman, 1988), or to

Table 19.1. Summary of leisure instruments

Instrument	Authors	Leisure is	Items	Response scale	Reliability	Validity
Free Time Boredom (FTB) Scale	Ragheb & Merydith (2001)	Free time	33, 20 (short form)	1 (*strongly disagree*) to 5 (*strongly agree*)	Long form: α = .92 (global), .78–.91 (4 factors) Short form: α = .88 (global), .75–.83 (4 factors)	Convergent validity with boredom proneness (long form, short form) but low correlations
Intrinsic Leisure Motivation (ILM) Scale	Weissinger & Bandalos (1995)	State of mind	24	1 (*very strongly disagree*) to 7 (*very strongly agree*)	α = .87–.91 (global); .64–.83 (4 subscales); test-retest (8 weeks) .63 (global), .58–.70 (4 subscales)	CFA; convergent validity with leisure satisfaction, perceived freedom in leisure, activity participation, self-as-entertainment; discriminant validity with leisure boredom
Leisure Activities Blank (LAB)	McKechnie (1974, 1975)	Activity	242	Past participation: 1 (*never engaged*) to 4 (*engage regularly*) Future participation: 1 (*do not expect to do it*) to 3 (*do expect to do it sometime*)	α = .81–.89 (7 activity factors; past participation)	EFA
Leisure Activities Questionnaire (LAQ)	Tinsley et al. (1977)	State of mind	45	1 (*not true*) to 5 (*definitely true*)	α = .92(global), .29–.90 (needs); split-group *r* = .86 to .97	CFA; convergent & discriminant validity (MTMM 10 leisure activities x LAQ/PAL, factor structure)
Leisure Affect Scale	Kuykendall et al. (2017)	State of mind	20	1 (*never*) to 5 (*extremely often*)	α = .79–.85 (4 subscales); test-retest (1 month) .56 to .69	CFA; discriminant validity with subjective well-being, leisure needs
Leisure Attitude Scale (LAS)	Ragheb & Beard (1982)	State of mind	36	1 (*strongly disagree*) to 5 (*strongly agree*)	α = .94 (global); .89–.93 (3 subscales)	PCA; convergent & divergent validity (factor structure, intercorrelations)

Table 19.1. continued

Instrument	Authors	Leisure is	Items	Response scale	Reliability	Validity
Leisure Boredom Scale (LBS)	Iso-Ahola & Weissinger (1990)	Free time	16	1 (*strongly agree*) to 5 (*strongly disagree*)	α = .85–88 (global)	CFA; convergent validity with frequency, depth of boredom, substance use/abuse; divergent validity with leisure satisfaction, leisure participation, leisure ethic, intrinsic leisure motivation, self-as-entertainment, social competence, self-esteem, physical & mental health
Leisure Constraints Questionnaire (LCQ)	Alexandris & Carroll (1997)	Activity	29	1 (*not important*) to 4 (*very important*)	α = .85 (global), .59–.81 (7 dimensions)	PCA; discriminant validity by group comparisons (3 of 7 dimensions)
Leisure Diagnostic Battery (LDB) I. Perceived Freedom in Leisure (PFL)	Ellis & Witt (1982, 1984)	State of mind	95, 25 (short form)	1 (*completely disagree*) to 5 (*completely agree*)	α = .82–.90 (global); .86–.90 (5 subscales)	CFA; convergent validity with intrinsic leisure motivation, Big 5 personality traits, self-esteem, causal attributions, self-as-entertainment; discriminant validity with depression, shyness
Leisure Identity Salience Scale (LISS)	Shamir (1992)	State of mind		Rate 3 role identities, one is leisure, on bipolar scales then subtract 2 nonleisure roles from total	α = .87 (global), .89 (2 subscales)	Convergent validity with years in activity (but negative correlations with hours in activity, effort and skill in activity, intrinsic motivation
Leisure Meanings Inventory (LMI)	Schulz & Watkins (2007)	State of mind	23	1 (*strongly disagree*) to 5 (*strongly agree*)	α = .81 (global); .66- .81 (4 subscales)	PCA/CFA; concurrent validity with leisure needs, self-determination, REP scales (moderate to low correlations)
Leisure Motivation Scale (LMS)	Beard & Ragheb (1983)	State of mind	48	1 (*never true*) to 5 (*always true*)	α = .90–.92 (4 subscales)	PCA

Table 19.1. continued

Instrument	Authors	Leisure is	Items	Response scale	Reliability	Validity
Leisure Satisfaction Scale (LSS)	Beard & Ragheb (1980)	State of mind	51, 24(short form)	1 (*almost never true*) to 5 (*almost always true*)	Long form: α = .96 (global); .85–.92 (6 subscales); short form: α = .93 (global	PCA
Leisure Satisfaction Scale	Kuykendall et al., 2017	State of mind	5	1 (*strongly disagree*) to 7 (*strongly agree*)	α = .86 (global); test-retest *r* = .66 (4 weeks)	CFA; discriminant validity with subjective well-being, leisure need fulfillment
Paragraphs About Leisure (PAL)	Tinsley & Kass (1980b)	State of mind	27 paragraphs	1 (*not true*) to 5 (*definitely true*)	α = .93 (global); split-group *r* = .82–.97	CFA; convergent & discriminant validity (MTMM 10 leisure activities x LAQ/PAL, factor structure)
Recreation Experience Preference (REP) Scales	Bassett & Driver (1979); Driver (1983)	State of mind	328 (item bank) for 18 domains. Trip-specific or activity-specific instruction set.	0–7 scales within domains 4 response types Satisfaction: 1 (*strongly adds*) to 4 (*strongly detracts*) Importance: 1 (*not at all*) to 4 (*very*) Valence: 1 (*very unlikely outcome*) to 4 (*very likely outcome*) Experience 1 (*detracted from experience*) to 4 (*added to experience*) Domain or scale scoring	α = .17–.67 (domains); .37–.75 (scales within domains)	CFA (domains, scales within domains); concurrent validity (DFA double-cross validation); discriminant validity (interitem correlations); predictive validity (both scoring procedures) "hits" for leisure activities vs. chance
Victoria Longitudinal Study Leisure Activities Questionnaire (VSLAQ)	Jopp & Hertzog (2010)	Activity	69	0 (*never*) to 8 (*daily*)	α = .43–.79 (11 activity types); Test-retest (16 months) *r* = .41–.82	CFA; convergent validity with cognitive functioning, intelligence, Big 5 personality traits, health, education; divergent validity with depression

Note. CFA = confirmatory factor analysis, DFA = discriminant function analysis, EFA = exploratory factor analysis, MTMM = multitrait-multimethod, PCA = principal components analysis. α = Cronbach's α.

rank order all possible pairs of activities in terms of preference (Ritchie, 1975). What was regarded as an arduous list of activities in the LAB was shortened, although these rating directives did little to mitigate the demands placed on respondents.

One such effort was devised as part of a national study (Hultsch et al., 1993) to assess the leisure activities of adults of middle and older ages. Like their predecessors, the authors attempted to generate a comprehensive list of activities common to these age groups, and they requested information about participation rates and frequency. The scale has been revised several times, with the latest version being the Victoria Longitudinal Study Leisure Activities Questionnaire (VSLAQ; Jopp & Hertzog, 2010). Statistical testing on the VSLAQ has shown there is one general activities factor, and across several samples, it has been demonstrated to be both internally consistent and stable (with a 16-month interval). Subsequent research has demonstrated that the VSLAQ is equally effective at capturing the leisure activities of adults of any age, and that its factor structure and psychometrics could be reproduced. A similar activity-based scale was the Leisure Interest Questionnaire (Hansen, 1998), which assessed participant interest in 250 activities regardless of whether the activity was actually performed. Further study established the internal consistency and test-retest reliability of this measure (Hansen & Scullard, 2002).

Activity inventories have been generated with the advent of each new empirical effort, with the common intent that the instrument be comprehensive and inclusive. Toward that end, open-ended diaries have instead requested respondents generate their own list of leisure activities based upon their past and present participation. These instruments have predominantly utilized an event-sampling approach or have employed ESM pagers to beep at random or predetermined times throughout several days or weeks. The data are then converted to activity clusters, and participation data and frequencies again form the unit of analysis. Perhaps as a way of easing the burden on respondents, or following the recognition that it is a futile exercise to try to capture the leisure activities of adults of all ages, activity inventories became targeted toward specific subgroups (e.g., Adolescent Leisure Interest Profile, Henry 1998; Children's Leisure Assessment Scale, Rosenblum et al., 2010; Family Leisure Activity Profile, Zabriskie & McCormick, 2001).

Leisure scholars were challenged to consider a different perspective, resulting in a plethora of studies conducted on the concept of "leisure constraints" – an alternative approach that examines the factors that limit or prevent participation (Crawford et al., 1991). In the Leisure Constraints Questionnaire (LCQ; Alexandris & Carroll, 1997), respondents are first asked to indicate their frequency of participation in 28 activities and then to report the importance of several factors in deterring their participation the previous year. The LCQ currently enjoys widespread use, despite its original intent to be used for recreational sports, likely because it is one of the only such instruments currently available. It has been adapted for application to physically active leisure, outdoor recreation, and travel, and specific activities such as golf and skiing.

Leisure as Free Time

A new genre of measurement instruments focused on the absence of fulfilling leisure activities, or experience of boredom, during discretionary time. Several instruments have been developed that strive to assess "leisure boredom" – the most popular being the Leisure Boredom Scale (LBS; Iso-Ahola & Weissinger, 1990). The authors defined leisure boredom as the "mismatch between *desired* (authors' italics) arousal-producing characteristics of leisure experiences, and perceptual or actual *availability* (authors' italics) of such leisure experiences" (p. 5). It's not at all clear how operationalizing this definition led to the items in the LBS, and psychometric testing was conducted with data collected for other purposes. Nevertheless, its construct validity has been investigated in several studies, and all have shown satisfactory results (Weissinger, 1995; Weissinger & Bandalos, 1995; Weissinger et al., 1992).

Ragheb and Merydith (2001) criticized the LBS for having too narrow a focus by addressing only the leisure component of an individual's free time, which provided the rationale for their development of their Free Time Boredom Scale (FTBS). All items on the FTBS refer to "free time" rather than "leisure"; the incomplete stimulus statement "During my free time" is followed by several possibilities, and for each respondents are asked the extent to which they agree or disagree. Based on their findings, a definition of free time boredom was crafted as, "a subjective feeling, characterized as sensory deficit and dissatisfaction with passing time and in failing to reach an optimal level of flow or arousal, originating from underload because of the lack of meaning or purpose during a person's free time, and can be described as meaningless, with less mental and physical involvement and low speed of time" (Ragheb & Merydith, 2001, pp. 53–54). The FTBS is utilized by researchers interested in studies of free time use with samples of different ages and demographics.

Leisure as Subjective Experience

Frustration with employing leisure activities and free time data to elucidate the nature of leisure led to efforts to develop instruments that relied on different metrics. Researchers devised measures assessing the psychosocial benefits perceived to accrue to leisure participants. The Recreation Experience Preference scale (REP; Bassett & Driver, 1979) was initially developed for outdoor leisure enthusiasts but has been adapted to apply to a wide variety of leisure activities. The REP originators assembled a database of 328 possible motivations for recreation activities (Driver, 1983), and respondents can select the ones that closely approximate their activity interests. The REP provides a choice of four types of response options: a Satisfaction scale, an Importance scale, a Valence scale, and an Experience scale. Instruction sets can be one of two types – a "trip-specific" set or an "activity-specific set," and the data can be scored either by calculating domain scores (e.g., Escape Personal-Social Pressures) or by using scores from individual scales within the domains (e.g., Tension release). Validity has proved satisfactory, based on the collective findings of over 40 studies (Manfredo et al., 1996), although all were conducted on outdoor recreation pursuits. Hence, despite its current use, content validity testing should be conducted for different types of enthusiasts before it can be recommended for wide-ranging adoption.

Researchers then turned to the question of *why* individuals make the choices they do, that is, the underlying reasons they choose specific activities for their leisure and engage at a certain level of participation. Tinsley et al. (1977) thought the answer to this question lies in the individual's needs, and they developed two scales to measure the "need-satisfying properties" of leisure activities (the Leisure Activities Questionnaire, LAQ), which is organized into scales measuring need-satisfying dimensions (e.g., authority). Each item begins with the stem, "Participants in this activity ..." and sequentially appends statements assessing each leisure-activity-specific need (e.g., " ... have an opportunity to be in charge of others"). The Paragraphs about Leisure scale (PAL; Tinsley & Kass, 1980a) is an alternate means of measuring the same "leisure-activity-specific need-satisfier dimensions," although it consists of paragraphs for each need-satisfier and individuals respond to the paragraph with the same options as in the LAQ. Both scales have undergone extensive psychometric testing, and results have been satisfactory (Tinsley & Eldredge, 1995; Tinsley & Kass, 1978, 1979, 1980b).

Beard and Ragheb (1983) substituted the broader term "motivator" for "need satisfier" and developed the Leisure Motivation Scale (LMS). Individuals are asked to think of their "favorite leisure activities and make a short mental note" before responding to each of 48 possible motives for their participation in the activities. The LMS presents respondents with the stem, "One of my reasons for engaging in leisure activities is ...," followed by 48 possible motivations. Preliminary testing identified four dimensions to underlie the LMS (Intellectual, Social, Mastery, Escape); individuals were asked to think of their "favorite leisure activities and make a short mental note" before responding to each motive regarding the extent to which it was true of them. The LMS has been widely used for a variety of leisure settings and activities, although psychometric testing has been lacking.

It has been postulated that a motivation specific to leisure sets it apart from other behaviors as well as other motivators. Such a "leisure motivation disposition" (Iso-Ahola & Weissinger, 1990) was defined as the "tendency to seek intrinsic rewards in leisure behavior" (p. 379) and the authors conceptualized it to be stable within individuals and across situations. They conceived of intrinsic leisure motivation as being comprised of the four components of self-determination, competence, commitment, and challenge. A scale was designed to measure this disposition, the Intrinsic Leisure Motivation (ILM) scale (Weissinger & Bandalos, 1995), which assessed individual differences in ILM. The scale has shown good reliability and validity and has been extensively utilized, applying ILM to motivations for exercise, and tourism, for example.

Several instruments were developed that departed from a motivational approach to leisure, although they diverged in how they defined and operationalized subjective experience. In one approach, the question was posited as to what individuals derive from their leisure experiences – the outcomes – rather than why they entered into them. "Leisure satisfaction" was the label assigned to "the positive perceptions or feelings which an individual forms, elicits, or gains as a result of engaging in leisure activities and choices ... the degree to which one is presently content or pleased with their general leisure experiences and situations" (Beard & Ragheb, 1980, p. 22). Six themes were identified from the literature as underlying leisure outcomes (social, psychological, educational, physiological, relaxation, and esthetic), and the Leisure Satisfaction Scale (LSS; Beard & Ragheb, 1980) contained subscales to assess each one. A short form is also available (Ragheb & Beard, 1980) and is the one most extensively used. Validity testing continues to test its application with varying populations and topics. Further research by Kuykendall et al. (2017) developed and validated additional measures of leisure affect and leisure satisfaction while exploring the relationships between SAB and work-leisure conflict.

The LSS was criticized for not allowing participants to determine satisfaction based on what they consider to be most subjectively relevant, rather than providing them with a predetermined list (Kuykendall et al., 2015). To remedy this issue, a new Leisure Satisfaction Scale was devised consisting of five items (Kuykendall et al., 2017), where respondents are asked to think about leisure activities they had done in the past 4 weeks (free-time activities apart from work and household responsibilities). Psychometric testing determined that it was unidimensional, and internal consistency and 4-week test-retest reliability were acceptable. In research utilizing this new measure, the authors found that leisure experiences, compared to those for job and family, were a stronger influence on participants' subjective well-being, regardless of role salience (Kuykendall et al., 2017).

The study of attitudes has long been an interest of psychologists, and its application to leisure has been undertaken. These efforts date back more than 50 years (Burdge, 1961) and have undergone several iterations to improve on their scope, item development, and theoretical underpinning (Crandall & Slivken, 1980; Neulinger, 1974). After critically reviewing them for focusing only on one component of attitudes, Ragheb and Beard (1982) designed the Leisure Attitude Scale (LAS) to incorporate all three and to operationalize them from the perspective of leisure experience. The cognitive component of the LAS focused on general knowledge and beliefs about leisure, including its virtues, characteristics, and relationships to other concepts such as health, happiness, and work. Items comprising the affective component were seen as relating to the individual's immediate feelings toward their leisure activities and experiences, while the behavioral aspect concentrated on intentions and participation. The LAS is widely used today and has been translated into several other languages (e.g., Iranian, Korean, Malaysian, Chinese, Taiwanese).

Decrying all the approaches previously used to measure leisure as too cognitive, the remedy advanced shifted the focus to understanding the feelings participants have when engaging in leisure activities. The Leisure Affect Scale (Kuykendall et al., 2017) consisted of 20 items that represented the four valence-activity intersections: the positive activated (e.g., "My leisure activities make me feel excited"), positive deactivated (e.g., "My leisure activities make me feel at ease"), negative activated (e.g., "My leisure activities make me feel nervous"), and negative deactivated (e.g., "My leisure activities make me feel sluggish") leisure affects. Psychometric testing determined that, unlike the items in the other three subscales, the negative deactivated one did not show a good fit. Test-retest reliability over a 1-month interval was moderate to good for the subscales. The Leisure Affect Scale is now receiving more attention, and research studies utilizing it are awaiting publication.

Adopting a more phenomenological approach, Schulz and Watkins (2007) presented yet another alternative, the Leisure Meanings Inventory (LMI). The authors claimed that what was important to measure was how individuals derive meanings from leisure and how they experienced those meanings. Four ways in which this is typically done (achieving fulfillment, expressing choice, passing time, escaping pressure) were gleaned from the transcripts of open-ended interviews with university students (Watkins, 2000), and an item pool for each was crafted. The authors argued that what might be regarded as "poor" psychometric findings by traditional standards was to be expected, because of the unconventional phenomenographic approach they had adopted.

A different viewpoint was espoused by focusing on the individual's self-concept and the considerable role it plays in shaping motivation and behavior. Fashioned from identity theory (Stryker, 1980), Shamir (1988) argued that leisure is an additional role from which individuals may define themselves, and that their behaviors and attitudes may be influenced by a commitment to a particular leisure activity (cf. "serious leisure" Stebbins, 1992). He postulated that the stronger a person's "leisure identity" is, the more motivating it is and the more likely the individual actively seeks specific types of leisure opportunities. He devised the Leisure Identity Salience Scale (LISS; Shamir, 1992), which asked respondents to "think about your most important freely chosen activity, not including work, family, and student roles, write down what that activity is, and fill out the questionnaire with that activity in mind." Participants were then asked to utilize the same bipolar scales to rate three role identities (e.g., student, worker), one of which was leisure. The aggregate of the latter two roles is deducted from the one for leisure, indicating the importance that leisure plays in the individual's self-definition. The author concluded that knowing an individual's LIS increases our understanding of their leisure attitude and behavior.

One of the few attempts at grounding measurement in leisure theory (Neulinger, 1974) was the Leisure Diagnostic Battery (LDB; Ellis & Witt, 1982, 1984). The authors regarded "perceived freedom" to lie at the core of leisure functioning and added perceptions of intrinsic motivation, competence, and satisfaction to their conceptualization. They posited a single continuum as one part of the attribution process, ranging from freedom and independence ("self-serving") on the one end to dependence and learned helplessness ("self-degenerative") on the other. Those who fall toward the self-serving end are more intrinsically motivated to participate in leisure, which leads to a sense of competence and control and the inclination to have playful encounters with others. The LDB has two parts: The first purports to measure Perceived Freedom in Leisure (PFL), the second to examine factors that might inhibit PFL and it is intended to be used to design intervention strategies. The PFL scale has been predominantly used, and there is also a short form, with an adult and an adolescent version (Witt & Ellis, 1985, 1989). The PFL consists of subscales assessing the five constructs of Leisure Competence (the degree of competency a person feels they have in their leisure experiences and activities), Perceived Leisure Control Scale (the extent to which individuals believe they can control the outcomes that occur in their leisure, Depth of Involvement (how absorbed individuals can characteristically become while they are engaged in preferred leisure activities, the Leisure Needs Scale (whether individuals perceive their needs are met by participating in leisure activities), and the Playfulness Scale (how playful individuals feel they are when at leisure). Several versions of the PFL scale have been designed by the authors for different purposes. For example, a second version was constructed to be utilized with mentally challenged individuals, and a third form for those who might have difficulty using a writing implement, reading, or marshaling sufficient cognitive skills to complete the self-report format. The LDB has been utilized for investigating varying groups, ranging from Baptist Church recreation participants (Baack 1985) to stutterers (Black 1986), as well as the efficacy of therapeutic interventions for various recreation programs and populations (Peebles et al., 1999).

Key Findings

Leisure is universal, something that is done regardless of race, ethnicity, or culture, and yet its meaning varies among cultures (Huizinga, 1950). It has been difficult to define because it can mean something different to each person, and several prominent scholars have argued that it is so abstract as to defy definition (Kabanoff, 1980). Yet even though a precise definition of leisure has eluded scholars for centuries, it continues to be scientifically studied and measured.

Studies that have viewed leisure objectively have measured it as an activity that is done in free time. This approach presumes there are specific pursuits chosen by individuals because they are pleasurable (satisfying, enjoyable) to engage and allows for quantitative assessments (LAB, VLSAQ, LCQ) based on the frequency, duration, intensity, or commitment in their participation in each one. These types of instruments can be effective in addressing research questions about what people do and the conditions under which they do it. There are two considerations, however, investigators must be mindful of in designing, conducting, and interpreting the findings from these studies: One caveat lies in the supposition that each of the activities presented is construed by the respondent as a leisure activity – yet none ask the participant whether this is indeed the case before proceeding to participation queries. A second caution lies in the inadequacy of these instruments to provide any insights into the underlying structure, meaning, or significance of leisure by respondents. Hence, they are not useful for constructing models or theories about leisure, nor should they be employed when the purpose of the research is more conceptual than applied.

Leisure has also been defined as the time during which a person is at liberty to do as they choose, free from obligations, responsibilities, and commitments. This approach views leisure as residual time – left-over time – which is thus dependent on what "obligated" time is to determine leisure. Time-use data have been used in a plethora of studies, both cross-sectional and longitudinal, and with small to large-scale populations. For example, data about changes over 30 years in how Americans spend their leisure time (Robinson & Godbey, 1999) to relationships between work time and leisure time for lawyers (Wallace & Young, 2010) have emerged from this type of measurement. Scientists and professionals might be concerned with issues related to the allocation of time for leisure, such as how it might have a salutary effect on individuals' physical or mental health, so that leisure viewed as free time continues to be an important area for scholarship. While studies investigating the allocation and use of leisure time are plentiful, to date there is no standard measurement instrument. Current scales assessing boredom in leisure time (LBS, FTBS) represent a myopic view, making the development of instruments to address discretionary time with a broad range of applications sorely needed.

The state of mind that people have during, or just before or after, engaging in leisure is an important topic for study, yet extant measurement tools have been disunited. The instruments that are currently in use (REP, LAB, LAQ, PAL, LMS, ILM, LSS, LAS, LMI, LISS, LDB) range from describing motivations to satisfactions to attitudes, and the psychometric testing for each type warrants continued effort. As the field wrestles with defining leisure as a subjective experience and delineating its distinguishing characteristics, so too does the development of corresponding measures. While valid instruments to assess intrinsically motivated activity, positive affect, and perceived freedom currently exist, the synergies between these concepts, which are thought to uniquely define leisure, has escaped enumeration. There is an urgent need to better operationalize these constructs in the leisure realm of subjective experience.

Considerations and Recommendations for Instrument Selection

Ideally, the construction of instruments would be driven by an integrated theory and definition of leisure, yet the development of measures of leisure has been largely based on an absence of theoretical or conceptual foundations. Efforts to define leisure based on what people do in their pursuit of pleasure or enjoyment, or during times when they are free from obligations, have been criticized, although the instruments reflecting these approaches continue to be widely utilized in research. The consensus about defining leisure based on the "state of mind" of the individual appears to be firmly entrenched, however, when one attempts to identify any underlying framework there is divergence. Hence, the instruments available for generating knowledge about leisure are constructed without a clear blueprint or underlying conceptual framework. It is therefore imperative that, when considering the instrumentation for a research study, as a crucial first step in the process investigators should delve into how leisure has previously been approached, conceptualized, and delimited.

Accordingly, it becomes difficult to proffer recommendations to ignore measures with psychometric shortcomings or to attend only to those that are viable through ample testing. While it has been traditional to consider the construct validity of an instrument to be paramount, the lack of a theoretical underpinning doesn't suggest ways in which this can be examined with leisure. A nomological network has yet to be proposed that can provide direction about what constructs a leisure instrument should relate to and which it should oppose. In the same way, the content validity of leisure assessment is also an elusive metric to assess because all the facets of leisure are not at all clear. Thus, while methodologists almost unanimously espouse the importance of probing the psychometric evidence for an instrument under consideration, the above presents a dilemma for leisure researchers. Further, reliability estimates (predominantly internal consistency) are available for all instruments presented, yet efforts to assess their stability over time have been only sporadic. Researchers must search for studies that have examined the relationships between aspects of leisure perceptions and participation which are at least attentive to the scholarship available at the time. At this stage in the nascent leisure field, we must be at least tentatively satisfied with these approximations to more rigorous validity testing.

Conclusions, Challenges, and Future Directions

While it is quite clear to the academician and layman alike that leisure lies at the center of conversations about people's health, happiness, and well-being, what is less discernible is how to scientifically demonstrate this and contribute to knowledge about these interrelationships. If we've been too critical or harsh in our summary statements that studies of leisure are challenging to conduct because of the necessity of utilizing measures without theoretical underpinning, we see the reason for this state of affairs in the challenges in the study of the leisure construct itself, which currently struggles to adopt consistent terminology (Schlag et al., 2015) or definitional consensus. A bottom-up approach might be a route to take, by focusing on small clusters of research studies and ways of extending measurements of leisure. Investigators could identify behavioral metrics in addition to the self-report data currently in vogue, to learn more about the leisure construct and as a means to evaluate some of the leisure instruments. Measures that request data on leisure in real-time would increase the fidelity of time diaries to actual leisure experiences and minimize reliance on participants' recollections. Leisure should also be investigated with more divergent populations than undergraduate students and in a multitude of settings (e.g., organizational, educational, clinical). Many cultures (especially non-Westernized ones) do not have comparable terms for "leisure," and analogous descriptions are either absent or dissimilar (Iwasaki et al., 2007). A plethora of research has been conducted about the leisure of individuals across the lifespan, yet all of it has employed cross-sectional samples. Longitudinal studies should be undertaken to investigate the continuity and interruption of leisure from one life stage to the next, which would provide knowledge not only about the nature of the construct itself, but also about its contribution to the individual's optimal development and well-being. As a final suggestion, observations of the leisure of individuals with varying levels of leisure functioning and satisfaction could also be very informative, for example, conducting studies with populations of individuals who typically have many constraints to their leisure opportunities (e.g., those with low income, working several jobs) could provide insights into the implications for functioning in other areas that such disadvantages might implicate.

In conclusion, the positive and fulfilling aspects of our lives are no more evident than in the ways we pursue and experience our leisure. It is in the leisure arena, more so than in virtually every other domain in our life, that we are relatively unrestrained to choose what to do, with whom to do it, and how it will take place. The freedom to wander and have interludes in fantasy, imaginings, and creative expression are daily ventures of children and adults of all ages and circumstances. The individuality and nuanced expression of a person's desires and contemplations are precisely what present complex challenges to researchers trying to measure leisure. Those who have been less than successful would argue that leisure is ultimately something more to be experienced than explained. Yet science demands that we capture, define, systematize, and measure it. The development and refinement of measures of leisure signify the search for its underlying coherence and unity.

References

Alexandris, K., & Carroll, B. (1997). An analysis of leisure constraints based on different recreational sport participation levels: Results from a study in Greece. *Leisure Sciences, 19*(1), 1–15. https://doi.org/10.1080/01490409709512236

Baack, S. (1985). *Predictors of perceived freedom in leisure of Baptist Church members.* Unpublished doctoral dissertation, North Texas State University.

Bassett, J. R., & Driver, B. L. (1979). *Perceived immediate benefits of selected users of the Huron and Pine Rivers in Michigan.* Final report, USDA Contract No. 13-455. University of Michigan, School of Natural Resources.

Beard, J. G., & Ragheb, M. G. (1980). Measuring leisure satisfaction. *Journal of Leisure Research, 12*(1), 20–33. https://doi.org/10.1080/00222216.1980.11969416

Beard, J. G., & Ragheb, M. G. (1983). Measuring leisure motivation. *Journal of Leisure Research, 15*(3), 219–228. https://doi.org/10.1080/00222216.1983.11969557

Black, J. A. (1986). *A comparative study of the perception of freedom in leisure between stuttering and nonstuttering individuals.* Unpublished doctoral dissertation, Gonzaga University.

Burdge, R. (1961). *The development of a leisure orientation scale.* Ohio State University.

Crandall, R., & Slivken, K. (1980). Leisure attitudes and their measurement. In S. Iso-Ahola (Ed.), *Social psychological perspectives on leisure and recreation* (pp. 261–284). Charles C Thomas.
Crawford, D.W., Jackson, E.L., & Godbey, G. (1991). A hierarchical model of leisure constraints. *Leisure Sciences, 13*(4), 309–320. https://doi.org/10.1080/01490409109513147
Diener, E. (1984). Subjective well-being. *Psychological Bulletin, 95*(3), 542–575. https://doi.org/10.1037/0033-2909.95.3.542
Diener, E., Suh, E.M., Lucas, R.E., & Smith, H.L. (1999). Subjective well-being: Three decades of progress. *Psychological Bulletin, 125*(2), 276–302. https://doi.org/10.1037/0033-2909.125.2.276
Driver, B.L. (1983). *Master list of items for Recreation Experience Preference scales and domains.* USDA Forest Service, Rocky Mountain Forest and Range Experiment Station, Fort Colls, CO.
Ellis, G., & Witt, P.A. (1982). *The Leisure Diagnostic Battery: Theoretical and empirical structure.* North Texas State University.
Ellis, G., & Witt, P.A. (1984). The measurement of perceived freedom in leisure. *Journal of Leisure Research, 16*(1), 110–123. https://doi.org/10.1080/00222216.1984.11969579
Fredrickson, B.L. (1998). What good are positive emotions? *Review of General Psychology, 3*, 300–319. https://doi.org/10.1037/1089-2680.2.3.300
Geerling, D.M., & Diener, E. (2020). Effect size strengths in subjective well-being research. *Applied Research in Quality of Life, 15*(1), 167–185.https://doi.org/10.1007/s11482-018-9670-8
Goodale, T., & Godbey, G. (1988). *The evolution of leisure: Historical and philosophical perspectives.* Venture.
Haller, M., Hadler, M., & Kaup, G. (2013). Leisure time in modern societies: A new source of stress? *Social Indicators Research, 111*(2), 403–434. https://doi.org/10.1007/s11205-012-0023-y
Hansen, J.C. (1998). *Leisure Interest Questionnaire.* JCH Consulting.
Hansen, J.C., & Scullard, M.G. (2002). Psychometric evidence for the Leisure Interest Questionnaire and analyses of the structure of leisure interests. *Journal of Counseling Psychology, 49*(3), 331–341. https://doi.org/10.1037/0022-0167.49.3.331
Henry, A.D. (1998). Development of a measure of adolescent leisure interests. *American Journal of Occupational Therapy, 52*, 531–53. https://doi.org/10.5014/ajot.52.7.531
Huizinga, J. (1950). *Homo ludens: A study of play elements in culture.* Beacon Press.
Hultsch, D.F., Hammer, M., & Small, B.J. (1993). Age differences in cognitive performance in later life: Relationships to self-reported health and activity lifestyle. *Journal of Gerontology Series B: Psychological Sciences, 48*(1), 1–11. https://doi.org/10.1093/geronj/48.1.P1
Iso-Ahola, S.E., & Weissinger, E. (1990). Perceptions of boredom in leisure: Conceptualization, reliability and validity of the Leisure Boredom Scale. *Journal of Leisure Research, 22*(1), 1–17. https://doi.org/10.1080/00222216.1990.11969811
Iwasaki, Y. (2007). Leisure and quality of life in an international and multicultural context: What are major pathways linking leisure to quality of life? *Social Indicators Research, 82*(2), 233–264. https://doi.org/10.1007/s11205-006-9032-z
Iwasaki, Y., Nishino, H., Onda, T., & Bowling, C. (2007). Leisure research in a global world: Time to reverse the Western domination in leisure research? *Leisure Sciences, 29*(1), 113–117. https://doi.org/10.1080/01490400600983453
Jopp, D.S., & Hertzog, C. (2010). Assessing adult leisure activities: An extension of a self-report activity questionnaire. *Psychological Assessment, 22*(1), 108–120. https://doi.org/10.1037/a0017662
Kabanoff, B. (1980). Work and nonwork: A review of models, methods, and findings. *Psychological Bulletin, 88*, 60–77. https://doi.org/10.1037/0033-2909.88.1.60
Kleiber, D.A., Walker, G.J., & Mannell, R.C. (2011). *A social psychology of leisure* (2nd ed.). Venture.
Kreiner, G.E. (2006). Consequences of work-home segmentation or integration: A person-environment fit perspective. *Journal of Organizational Behavior, 27*(4), 485–507. https://doi.org/10.1002/job.386
Kuykendall, L., Lei, X., Cheung, K., Kolze, M.J., Lindsey, A., Silvers, M., & Engelsted, L. (2017). Subjective quality of leisure & worker well-being: Validating measures & testing theory. *Journal of Vocational Behavior, 103*, 14–40. https://doi.org/10.1016/j.jvb.2017.07.007

Kuykendall, L., Tay, L., & Ng, V. (2015). Leisure engagement and subjective well-being: A meta-analysis. *Psychological Bulletin, 141*(2), 364–403. https://doi.org/10.1037/a0038508
Manfredo, M.J., Driver, B.L., & Tarrant, M.A. (1996). Measuring leisure motivation: A meta-analysis of the Recreation Experience Preference Scales. *Journal of Leisure Research, 28*(3), 188–213. https://doi.org/10.1080/00222216.1996.11949770
McKechnie, G.E. (1974). The psychological structure of leisure: Past behavior. *Journal of Leisure Research, 6*, 27–45. https://doi.org/10.1080/00222216.1974.11970163
McKechnie, G.E. (1975). *Manual for the Leisure Activities Blank.* Consulting Psychology Press.
Mommaas, H. (1997). European leisure studies at the crossroads? A history of leisure research in Europe. *Leisure Sciences, 19*(4), 241–254. https://doi.org/10.1080/01490409709512253
National Research Council. (2012). *The Subjective Well-Being module of the American Time Use Survey: Assessment for its continuation.* The National Academies Press.
Neulinger, J. (1974). *The psychology of leisure.* Charles C. Thomas.
Peebles, J., McWilliams, L., Norris, L.H., & Park, K. (1999). Population-specific norms and reliability of the Leisure Diagnostic Battery in a sample of patients with chronic pain. *Therapeutic Recreation Journal, 33*, 135–141.
Pinquart, M., & Schindler, I. (2009). Change of leisure satisfaction in the transition to retirement: A latent-class approach. *Leisure Sciences, 31*(4), 311–329. https://doi.org/10.1080/01490400902988275
Ragheb, M.G., & Beard, J.G. (1980). Leisure satisfaction: Concept, theory and measurement. In S.E. Iso-Ahola (Ed.), *Social psychological perspectives on leisure and recreation.* Charles C Thomas.
Ragheb, M.G., & Beard, J.G. (1982). Measuring leisure attitude. *Journal of Leisure Research, 14*(2), 155–167. https://doi.org/10.1080/00222216.1982.11969512
Ragheb, M.G., & Merydith, S.P. (2001). Development and validation of a multidimensional scale measuring free time boredom. *Leisure Studies, 20*(1), 41–59. https://doi.org/10.1080/02614360122569
Ritchie, J.R.B. (1975). On the derivation of leisure activity types: A perceptual mapping approach. *Journal of Leisure Research, 7*, 128–140. https://doi.org/10.1080/00222216.1975.11970226
Robinson, J., & Godbey, G. (1999). *Time for life: The surprising ways Americans use their time* (2nd ed.). Pennsylvania State University Press.
Rosenblum, S., Sachs, D., & Schreuer, N. (2010). Reliability and validity of the Children's Leisure Assessment Scale. *American Journal of Occupational Therapy, 64*, 633–641. https://doi.org/10.5014/ajot.2010.08173
Russell, R.V., & Hultsman, J.T. (1988). An empirical basis for determining the multidimensional structure of leisure. *Leisure Sciences, 10*(1), 69–76. https://doi.org/10.1080/01490408809512177
Ryan, R.M., & Deci, E.L. (2000). Self-determination theory and the facilitation of intrinsic motivation, social development, and well-being. *American Psychologist, 55*(1), 68–78. https://doi.org/10.1037/0003-066X.55.1.68
Schlag, P.A., Yoder, D.G., & Sheng, Z. (2015). Words matter. *SCHOLE: Journal of Leisure Studies and Recreation Education, 30*(1), 25–38. https://doi.org/10.1080/1937156X.2015.11949724
Schulz, J., & Watkins, M. (2007). The development of the Leisure Meanings Inventory. *Journal of Leisure Research, 39*(3), 477–497. https://doi.org/10.1080/00222216.2007.11950118
Searle, M.S., Mahon, M.J., Iso-Ahola, S.E., Sdrolias, H.A., & Van Dyck, J. (1995). Enhancing a sense of independence and psychological well-being among the elderly: A field experiment. *Journal of Leisure Research, 27*(2), 107–124. https://doi.org/10.1080/00222216.1995.11949737
Seligman, M.E. (2011). *Flourish: A visionary new understanding of happiness and well-being.* Simon and Schuster.
Shamir, B. (1988). Commitment and leisure. *Sociological Perspectives, 31*(2), 238–258. https://doi.org/10.2307/1389084
Shamir, B. (1992). Some correlates of leisure identity salience: Three exploratory studies. *Journal of Leisure Research, 24*(4), 301–323. https://doi.org/10.1080/00222216.1992.11969898
Stebbins, R.A. (1992). *Amateurs, professionals, and serious leisure.* McGill-Queen's Press.
Stryker, S. (1980). *Symbolic interactionism: A social structural version.* Benjamin/Cummings.

Tinsley, H. E. A., Barrett, T. C., & Kass, R. A. (1977). Leisure activities and need satisfaction. *Journal of Leisure Research, 9*(2), 110–120. https://doi.org/10.1080/00222216.1977.11970317

Tinsley, H. E. A., & Eldredge, B. D. (1995). Psychological benefits of leisure participation: A taxonomy of leisure activities based on their need-gratifying properties. *Journal of Counseling Psychology, 42*(2), 123–132. https://doi.org/10.1037/0022-0167.42.2.123

Tinsley, H. E. A., & Kass, R. A. (1978). Leisure activities and need satisfaction: A replication and extension. *Journal of Leisure Research, 10*, 191–202. https://doi.org/10.1080/00222216.1978.11969353

Tinsley, H. E. A., & Kass, R. A. (1979). The latent structure of need satisfying properties of leisure activities. *Journal of Leisure Research, 11*(4), 278–291. https://doi.org/10.1080/00222216.1979.11969406

Tinsley, H. E. A., & Kass, R. A. (1980a). Discriminant validity of the Leisure Activity Questionnaire and the Paragraphs About Leisure. *Educational and Psychological Measurement, 40*(1), 227–233. https://doi.org/10.1177/001316448004000137

Tinsley, H. E. A., & Kass, R. A. (1980b). The construct validity of the Leisure Activities Questionnaire and of the Paragraphs About Leisure. *Educational and Psychological Measurement, 40*(1), 219–226. https://doi.org/10.1177/001316448004000136

Tinsley, H. E. A., & Tinsley, D. J. (1982). A holistic model of leisure counseling. *Journal of Leisure Research, 14*, 100–116. https://doi.org/10.1080/00222216.1982.11969508

Wallace, J. E., & Young, M. C. (2010). Work hard, play hard? A comparison of male and female lawyers' time in paid and unpaid work and participation in leisure activities. *Canadian Review of Sociology, 47*(1), 27–47. https://doi.org/10.1111/j.1755-618X.2010.01221.x

Watkins, M. (2000). Ways of learning about leisure meanings. *Leisure Sciences, 22*, 93–107. https://doi.org/10.1080/014904000272876

Weissinger, E. (1995). Effects of boredom on self-reported health. *Society and Leisure, 18*, 21–32. https://doi.org/10.1080/07053436.1995.10715488

Weissinger, E., & Bandalos, D. (1995). Development, reliability and validity of a scale to measure intrinsic motivation in leisure. *Journal of Leisure Research, 27*, 379–400. https://doi.org/10.1080/00222216.1995.11949756

Weissinger, E., Caldwell, L. L., & Bandalos, D. L. (1992). Relation between intrinsic motivation and boredom in leisure time. *Leisure Sciences, 14*, 317–325. https://doi.org/10.1080/01490409209513177

Witt, P. A., & Ellis, G. (1985). Development of a short form to assess perceived freedom in leisure. *Journal of Leisure Research, 17*(3), 225–233. https://doi.org/10.1080/00222216.1985.11969632

Witt, P. A., & Ellis, G. (1989). *The Leisure Diagnostic Battery, user's manual.* Venture.

Zabriskie, R. B., & McCormick, B. P. (2001). The influence of family leisure patterns on perceptions of family functioning. *Family Relations, 50*(3), 281–289. https://doi.org/10.1111/j.1741-3729.2001.00281.x

Chapter 20

Monitoring Well-Being Changes in Positive Psychology Interventions

Fabian Gander

Department of Psychology, University of Basel, Switzerland

Positive psychology interventions are "treatment methods or intentional activities aimed at cultivating positive feelings, positive behaviors, or positive cognitions" (Sin & Lyubomirsky, 2009, p. 468) or empirical-based interventions aimed at building "positive" variables (Parks & Biswas-Diener, 2013). Often, these interventions are designed for and evaluated with people from the general population who are not suffering from a psychological disease but would like to increase their well-being.

While the effectiveness of positive psychology interventions for increasing well-being (i.e., subjective and psychological well-being) has been confirmed in several meta-analyses (e.g., Bolier et al., 2013; Sin & Lyubomirsky, 2009; see also White et al., 2019), the focus of the present chapter lies on the assessment instruments for monitoring changes in such interventions. A review of the meta-analyses reveals that there is large variability regarding the assessment instruments used to evaluate an intervention's potential for increasing well-being. This may be partly because of the missing agreement in the field on how well-being should best be conceptualized (Huta & Waterman, 2014), but it may also be because of the large number of available instruments for the assessment of well-being (e.g., Cooke et al., 2016). Further, some instruments might not have been translated and validated in the required language or might not be suited for the assessment of well-being in a specific sample because of cultural differences.

The present chapter (1) discusses important properties of a well-being instrument for the evaluation of changes following positive psychology interventions in research and practice and (2) reviews the most commonly used well-being instruments in positive psychology interventions regarding the previously mentioned properties. The second part analyzes data of participants who completed several well-being instruments, which allows for a direct comparison of instruments.

Whereas most aspects discussed in this chapter also apply to intervention studies in other areas – or psychological assessment in general – the main focus here is on positive psychology intervention studies that aim at enhancing (aspects of) well-being.

Properties of Well-Being Instruments for Evaluating Positive Psychology Interventions

Objectivity

Objectivity within a study (i.e., that the procedure, scoring, and interpretation are independent of the researcher) should be a given if the basic standards for psychological testing are fulfilled. However, this is often questionable between studies. In many cases, the instructions for instruments are adapted to the necessities of a particular study, albeit not adequately reported in the publications (i.e., ideally verbatim). The scoring of the instruments is mostly defined by the developers of the instrument. However, several widely used research instruments offer both facet and total scores without clear instructions on how to compute the total score (i.e., the mean across all items vs. the mean across all facets) and how to weigh the facets, respectively. Finally, in many cases, the instruments are not interpreted as originally intended, without providing a convincing rationale for doing so (see below for examples).

Thus, it is sometimes uncertain whether the results of a positive psychology intervention study are independent of those who conducted the testing, scored the instruments, and interpreted the results. This hinders the comparability of findings, making more elaborate reporting standards of instructions and scoring procedures necessary. Researchers and practitioners should, whenever possible, adhere to the instructions, scoring key, and suggestions for the interpretation provided by the original author(s).

Reliability

Issues of reliability deserve special consideration in intervention studies. While most widely used instruments fulfill conventional reliability criteria, there are several concerns and potential tradeoffs to consider. First, if the length of an instrument is held constant, the internal consistency increases inversely to decreases in the breadth of the construct covered. Thus, if a very broad conceptualization of well-being is to be covered, more items are needed to achieve values of internal consistency considered satisfactory by conventional standards – very short instruments only allow for assessing rather narrow concepts such as life satisfaction (e.g., SWLS) or happiness (e.g., SHS), but they cannot assess very broad conceptualizations of well-being and simultaneously yield high internal consistencies. While instruments used in research should have at least an acceptable internal consistency, very high values come at the price of overly homogeneous instruments; in most cases, it is more important that the construct be well-represented by the items (i.e., content validity) than internal consistency maximized. The latter also comes with the disadvantage that longer instruments might be tiring for the participants to complete, especially if there are many measurement timepoints, which could lead to a higher dropout rate. Designs involving planned missingness might be a helpful alternative approach to avoid these problems (e.g., Graham et al., 2006). Also, it is worth noting that most studies rely on Cronbach's alpha, which has often been criticized; see Flora (2020) for an overview and recommendations for the use of different versions of McDonald's omega.

Second, there is a tradeoff between sample size and required reliability. In large studies, where only group comparisons are of interest, researchers might use instruments of lower precision. If only a few participants can be tested, or individual changes are of interest (e.g., whether a participant reported a reliable change in the outcomes; Christensen & Mendoza, 1986), using more reliable instruments is recommended.

Third, longer instruments allow for more fine-grained distinctions. A short instrument such as the SWLS, which uses 5 items on a 7-point scale, only allows for distinguishing among 30 different levels (i.e., participants can score between 5 and 35 points). Especially if only subtle changes in well-being are to be expected, instruments with more items (and with varying item difficulties) that allow for distinguishing among more levels could be helpful.

Fourth, positive psychology interventions are often used in general population samples that are, on average, generally rather satisfied with their life. Most instruments were developed to assess well-being in the midrange of the well-being continuum but might be less useful for separating happy from very happy people. Thus, when training well-being in samples of already very happy participants, there might be risks of ceiling effects or imprecise estimates at higher levels of well-being.

Fifth, several instruments can be adapted to different timespans, and there often is a tradeoff between stability and sensitivity for change. Take the example of the PANAS: "Indicate to what extent you feel this way right now, that is, at the present moment" (short timespan), vs. "Indicate how you have felt in the past year" (long timespan; Watson et al., 1988, p. 1070). Using instructions focusing on very short periods (e.g., "at the present moment" or "today") hardly qualifies for an intervention study but rather serves as a manipulation check (unless assessed on several consecutive moments or days). Using instruments with very long periods (e.g., "during the past year" or "in general") might make it difficult to trace potential changes because of the intervention. Thus, the instrument should be sensitive enough to allow detecting (positive) changes but still show a considerable degree of stability. Additionally, every intervention study should include, in addition to pretests and (immediate) posttests, at least one follow-up at a later point in time: If an intervention that lasts several weeks only affects well-being (or rather mood, in this case) immediately following the intervention and not at the follow-up timepoints, the efforts of engaging in such an intervention might not be worth it.

Validity

With instruments used to evaluate interventions, it should be ensured in advance that the items represent the underlying construct (content validity), that the test has a clear (factorial) structure, positively relates to other instruments of the same or similar constructs, and does not show undesired relationships to other instruments (construct validity). Criterion validity, however, seems of lesser importance, as long as the aim of an intervention is to foster well-being – in this case, well-being is the most relevant criterion at hand.

Often, it is recommendable to use a well-being instrument based on a theoretical framework, since this facilitates interpreting the outcomes. Several widely used instruments were explicitly derived from a specific model or definition of well-being (e.g., Satisfaction with Life Scale (SWLS), Diener et al., 1985; Subjective Happiness Scale (SHS), Lyubomirsky & Lepper, 1999; Positive and Negative Affect Schedule (PANAS), Watson et al., 1988; Mental Health Continuum – Short Form (MHC-SF), Keyes, 2002; Psychological Well-

Being Scales, Ryff, 1989), while this is less the case for other widely used instruments that represent collections of items covering several concepts relevant for well-being, as long as the weighting of these concepts (e.g., whether 5 items in a scale of 10 items address meaning and only a single item addresses positive relations) and the reasons for their weightings remains unclear. This seems especially relevant when working with manifest (as opposed to latent) scores, which is rather common in intervention studies.

In case the instrument has no clear theoretical foundation, especially content and construct validity seem more difficult to examine and evaluate; without a clearly formulated construct, it is difficult to establish whether the items are representative of this construct, what appropriate instruments for estimating convergent and discriminant validity should be, and how findings can be interpreted. While these aspects seem obvious, they are sometimes disregarded. This is highly problematic since one cannot evaluate something when one does not know whether it works (i.e., an intervention) with something (i.e., an instrument) of which one also does not know what it assesses. Nonetheless, the most widely used instruments in positive psychology intervention studies are well-validated (see below). However, this does not necessarily apply to translated versions of the instruments in non-English languages. After adapting an instrument to a different language/cultural setting, one should always examine the psychometric properties of the adapted version, which cannot be inferred from the original version (van de Vijver, 2016). Yet, in many cases, only limited information about the quality of adapted instruments is available.

In summary, instruments used in positive psychology interventions should (1) be applied, scored, and interpreted as initially intended; (2) be based on a theoretical framework, and their items should reflect the underlying construct in appropriate breadth; (3) have a clear factor structure; (4) show expected relationships to similar constructs; (5) show satisfactory reliabilities also at higher well-being levels; and (6) have a sensible degree of stability and be able to detect relevant changes in well-being.

Further, the instrument and its underlying concept should fit the aims of the intervention. Thus, researchers and practitioners should consider whether the intervention to be evaluated primarily addresses hedonic or eudemonic well-being and select the instruments accordingly. For example, interventions that primarily aim at increasing positive functioning or personal growth (e.g., such as in interventions based on increasing the use of signature strengths; Schutte & Malouff, 2019) should use an instrument that can monitor changes in eudemonic well-being, while interventions that aim at fostering positive emotions (e.g., such as in the "three good things" intervention; Seligman et al., 2005) should include a measure of hedonic well-being. Additionally, measures of hedonic well-being should fit the expected kind of positive emotions or mood elicited by the interventions. For example, one of the most widely used instruments for the assessment of positive affect, the PANAS (Watson et al., 1988), does not explicitly cover positively valenced emotional states with low arousal or activation, such as being content or serene, but has a strong focus on positively valenced high arousal states (e.g., excited, enthusiastic, active). However, most positive psychology interventions presumably elicit emotional states that are positive but less active (e.g., Gander et al., 2020; Lyubomirsky et al., 2011). In consequence, people who feel more content following an intervention (though not necessarily more active or aroused) might not show strong increases in the PANAS, so the effects of the intervention are more difficult to monitor.

Therefore, often studies have used alternative, newly developed instruments with selected emotional states to assess changes in emotional well-being (e.g., Lyubomirsky et al., 2011). This procedure has the downside of limiting the comparability of outcomes among studies since different studies often use different subsets of positive emotions. Researchers have tried to ameliorate this problem by considering valence in addition to positive and negative activation (i.e., by adding inactivated but positively and negatively valenced items; Schallberger, 2005). Recently, Diener et al. (2010) suggested an alternative instrument, the Scale of Positive and Negative Experience (SPANE), which has the advantage of covering positive states regardless of their level of arousal (with items such as positive, or pleasant) and avoiding asking people about a large number of discrete emotional states by assessing emotions on a much more abstract level (e.g., feeling good or feeling pleasant). On the other hand, it comes with the downside that more abstract emotional states might be more difficult for participants to remember and adequately judge. However, resulting consequences have yet to be examined empirically.

If the intervention has no clear focus in terms of the presumably affected outcomes but rather aims at increasing general well-being, researchers might want to consider instruments that use a broad underlying conceptualization of well-being encompassing both aspects of hedonic and eudemonic well-being.

Overall, it is recommended that properties of considered instruments should be considered and the selection of instruments should be well-tailored to the intervention at hand. Regarding reliability, for example, for low-intensity interventions (e.g., self-administered online interventions during 1 week) where more subtle changes in well-being are to be expected, instruments with more items that assess well-being in the past weeks or months and one or two follow-ups after a couple of weeks might be a sensible choice, while for high-intensity interventions (e.g., face-to-face delivered group interventions during multiple weeks), shorter, more stable instruments and longer follow-up periods might be considered. For the assessment of individuals, further criteria might be relevant, such as the existence of normative data (i.e., scores from a population-representative sample) that allow for determining whether a score can be considered average or above average.

The following section identifies the most common instruments currently used in positive psychology interventions, analyzes data from participants who completed these instruments, and discusses the instruments regarding their characteristics mentioned above.

Review of the Most Common Well-Being Instruments in Positive Psychology Interventions

Identification of the Most-Common Well-Being Instruments

To identify the most relevant assessment instruments in positive interventions, I reviewed the intervention studies covered in four meta-analyses (Bolier et al., 2013; Dickens, 2017; Hendriks et al., 2019; Sin & Lyubomirsky, 2009) with regard to how frequently each instrument was applied (see Table 20.1).

Table 20.1 shows that by far the most commonly employed instruments used with the largest number of participants are the Satisfaction with Life Scale (SWLS; Diener et al., 1985), followed by the Positive and Negative Affect Schedule (PANAS; Watson et al., 1988), the Authentic Happiness Inventory (AHI, also called Steen Happiness Index in older versions; Seligman et al., 2005), and the Subjective Happiness Scale (SHS; Lyubomirsky & Lepper, 1999), while many studies also used varying subsets of specific affect terms (e.g., "happy," "content," or "grateful"). Further, commonly used instruments include single items for the assessment of global happiness (*N*=1,281; 9 studies) and Ryff's (1989) Psychological Well-Being Scales (*N*=1,139; 13 studies). The following examines the SHS, SWLS, AHI, and PANAS Positive Affect Scale. While the absence of negative affect is also a constituting element of subjective well-being and positive-negative is often assessed in positive psychology intervention studies, we decided not to consider the Negative Affect Scale but rather to focus on scales assessing the positive aspects of well-being.

Table 20.1. Most frequently used well-being instruments in positive psychology intervention studies

Instrument	Authors	*N*	Number of studies
Satisfaction with Life Scale (SWLS)	Diener et al. (1985)	4,114	39
Positive and Negative Affect Schedule – Positive Affect Scale (PANAS-PA)	Watson et al. (1988)	2,806	32
Discrete affect terms	Various authors	2,420	23
Authentic Happiness Inventory (AHI)	Seligman et al. (2005)	2,335	8
Subjective Happiness Scale (SHS)	Lyubomirsky & Lepper (1999)	2,206	16

Note. Discrete affect terms = varying subsets of specific affect terms

Comparison of Well-Being Instruments

While extensive psychometric information is available in the construction articles for these scales, a direct comparison of the psychometric properties across the instruments is limited by the use of different samples and methods. Thus, for this chapter, I present data from participants who completed all these instruments.

Method

The sample consisted of *N*=251 participants (65.7% women) aged 18 to 77 years (*M*=44.05, *SD*=13.40). They completed German versions of the SHS, SWLS, AHI, and PANAS scales at two different timepoints within 6 months as a part of a large positive psychology intervention program or a waiting-list group.

For the SHS, SWLS, and PANAS, participants were instructed to describe their experiences *in general*, while the AHI was focusing on the experiences during the *last week*. Descriptive characteristics of all scales at pretest are given in Table 20.2. The table shows that all scales show a slight negative skew but can be considered more or less normally distributed based on the skewness and kurtosis.

Table 20.2. Descriptive statistics at pretest

Scale	Items	*N*	*M*	*SD*	Min	Max	Skewness (*SE*)	Kurtosis (*SE*)
SWLS	5 (7-point scale)	247	4.61	1.07	1.20	6.80	−0.54 (0.16)	0.07 (0.31)
PANAS-PA	10 (5-point scale)	245	3.37	0.55	1.70	4.90	−0.31 (0.16)	0.16 (0.31)
AHI	24 (5 sets of statements per item)	248	3.18	0.49	1.76	4.36	−0.35 (0.16)	0.24 (0.31)
SHS	4 (7-point scale)	251	4.72	1.19	1.25	7.00	−0.51 (0.15)	−0.16 (0.31)

Note. The original English versions of the instruments are available online: SWLS = Satisfaction with Life Scale (http://labs.psychology.illinois.edu/~ediener/SWLS.html); PANAS-PA = Positive and Negative Affect Schedule – Positive Affect Scale (https://doi.org/10.1037/0022-3514.54.6.1063); AHI = Authentic Happiness Inventory (https://www.authentichappiness.sas.upenn.edu/testcenter; versions with 20 and 33 items have also been developed, the present sample uses the 24-item version); SHS = Subjective Happiness Scale (http://sonjalyubomirsky.com/subjective-happiness-scale-shs/)

Objectivity

The SHS, SWLS, and PANAS all provide clear instructions for participants to complete the instrument, for the researcher to score it, and there is information available on how to interpret the obtained scores. For the AHI, while its instructions and scoring are available, its interpretation seems not to be straightforward. This has led to several different understandings of its interpretation in the literature. For example, results of the AHI have been interpreted as a measure of authentic happiness (Seligman et al., 2005), psychological well-being (e.g., Bolier et al., 2013), happiness (e.g., Abbott et al., 2009), or subjective well-being (e.g., Hendriks et al., 2019) – four rather different conceptualizations of well-being.

Validity

An inspection of the items reveals that, whereas the SHS, SWLS, and PANAS Positive Affect Scale have a rather narrow scope precisely addressed by the items, the AHI covers a much broader understanding of well-being. Content validity only seems potentially problematic in the AHI, because of its rather loose relationship to its theoretical framework. Seligman et al. (2005) state: "The items [...] reflect the three kinds of happy lives (the pleasant life, the engaged life, and the meaningful life): experiencing and savoring pleasures, losing the self in engaging activities, and participating in meaningful activities" (p. 414), whereas, usually, only a general score is computed. However, an inspection of the items suggests that its scope is much broader and also encompasses other aspects such as accomplishment, relationships, optimism, or work satisfaction; the process and criteria for item selection are unknown.

To examine construct validity, I examined the factor structures and intercorrelations of the instruments, first testing the fit of the data to one-dimensional models using confirmatory factor analyses (using a robust weighted least squares estimator; WLSMV) for all scales separately (see Table 20.3).

Table 20.3. Results of confirmatory factor analyses at pretest

	χ^2	*df*	CFI	RMSEA	SRMR
SWLS	10.02	5	.98	.06 [.00–.12]	.03
PANAS-PA	98.04	35	.87	.09 [.07–.11]	.07
AHI	253.91	152	.90	.05 [.04–.06]	.07
SHS	4.51	2	.99	.07 [.00–.16]	.02

Note. SWLS = Satisfaction with Life Scale; PANAS-PA = Positive and Negative Affect Schedule – Positive Affect Scale; AHI = Authentic Happiness Inventory; SHS = Subjective Happiness Scale. CFI = comparative fit index; RMSEA = root mean square error of approximation [in brackets: 90% confidence interval]; SRMR = standard root mean square residual. All models examined a one-dimensional model using a robust weighted least squares estimator.

Table 20.3 shows that, while the SHS and SWLS met widely used cutoff criteria for CFI, RMSEA, and SRMR (e.g., Hu & Bentler, 1999), the CFI was slightly below acceptable cutoffs for the AHI and the PANAS and thus showed a suboptimal fit of the data to the intended models. Next, I computed manifest and latent (i.e., based on the models estimated in the CFA) scale intercorrelations (see Table 20.4).

Table 20.4. Manifest (above diagonal) and latent (below diagonal) intercorrelations among the scales

	Scale intercorrelations			
	SWLS	PANAS-PA	AHI	SHS
SWLS	–	.44	.67	.83
PANAS-PA	.53	–	.73	.69
AHI	.78	.63	–	.87
SHS	.71	.60	.75	–

Note. N = 239–251. SWLS = Satisfaction with Life Scale; PANAS-PA = Positive and Negative Affect Schedule – Positive Affect Scale; AHI = Authentic Happiness Inventory; SHS = Subjective Happiness Scale.

Table 20.4 shows that SHS, SWLS, and AHI showed strong correlations (all latent rs ≥ .79) among each other, and they showed smaller but still robust relationships to (trait) positive affect. Thus, the SHS, SWLS, and AHI assess very similar, albeit nonredundant constructs. As expected, the PANAS positive affect scale showed smaller relationships with the other measures, since it has a different focus (i.e., assessment of positive affect vs. different concepts of well-being). Nonetheless, these results confirm good convergent validity for all instruments.

Reliability

For comparing the reliabilities of the instruments, I computed McDonald's omega (for categorical data, see Flora, 2020), Cronbach's α, and the test-retest reliabilities of the scales (see Table 20.5).

Table 20.5. Internal consistency and manifest and latent test-retest reliability (6 months)

	Internal consistency		Test-retest reliability	
	McDonald's ω	Cronbach's α	Manifest	Latent
SWLS	.84	.84	.79	.87
PANAS-PA	.88	.85	.62	.68
AHI	.95	.93	.79	.80
SHS	.86	.87	.82	.89

Note. N = 243–251 (internal consistency), N = 172–177 (test-retest reliability). SWLS = Satisfaction with Life Scale; PANAS-PA = Positive and Negative Affect Schedule – Positive Affect Scale; AHI = Authentic Happiness Inventory; SHS = Subjective Happiness Scale.

Table 20.5 shows that internal consistencies were high for all instruments. The scores on the SHS, SWLS, and AHI were very stable across 6 months, while the PANAS showed lower but still considerable test-retest reliability. This finding is somewhat surprising for the AHI, since it only asks about the well-being in the past week, while the other instruments ask about their experiences in general.

Next, I computed the propensity of the scales for floor- and ceiling effects. For this purpose, I computed the standardized difference of the group mean to the scale minima and maxima (i.e., the difference between the means and the theoretical minima and maxima of the scales, divided by the standard deviations; see Table 20.6).

Table 20.6 shows that all scale means are almost two standard deviations apart from reaching the scale maximum. However, there were considerable differences among the scales; among the well-being instruments, the AHI seemed to be the least and the SHS the most susceptible to ceiling effects. Assuming a normal distribution, this means that on the SHS approximately 2.7% of participants reach this ceiling, while only 0.01% of the participants do so on the AHI. All scale means were at least three standard deviations above the theoretical minima – thus, the scales were widely immune to floor effects.

Furthermore, I examined the reliabilities of the scales depending on different levels of the constructs. For this purpose, I conducted exploratory analyses based on item response theory, without concerning the underlying assumptions of item response theory (previous in-depth analyses of the SWLS suggested that these assumptions do not necessarily hold for all items; Schutte et al., 2019; Vittersø et al., 2005). I estimated the two-parameter item response models for all scales using the psych-package in R (Revelle, 2018). Reliability estimates for different levels of the underlying latent traits are given in Figure 20.1.

Figure 20.1 shows that the findings were widely parallel to earlier studies regarding floor and ceiling effects: While all scales yielded accurate (i.e., reliable) estimates at lower to middle expressions of the traits, the precision of the SHS, SWLS, and PANAS strongly decreased at the higher end of the spectrum, while the AHI still showed high reliability even in people with very high expressions of the underlying construct.

Finally, I examined the instruments' susceptibility for monitoring critical life events. For this purpose, I selected those events from the Social Readjustment Rating Scale (Holmes & Rahe, 1967) which can be – more or less clearly – considered of positive or

Table 20.6. Distances of group means to scale minima and maxima

Scale	Distance bottom (z-scores)	Distance top (z-scores)
SWLS	3.37	2.24
PANAS-PA	4.34	2.99
AHI	4.44	3.70
SHS	3.13	1.92

Note. Example: The group mean for the SHS (M = 4.72) is 3.13 standard deviations (SD = 1.19) above the theoretical minimum of the scales. SWLS = Satisfaction with Life Scale; PANAS-PA = Positive and Negative Affect Schedule – Positive Affect Scale; AHI = Authentic Happiness Inventory; SHS = Subjective Happiness Scale.

Table 20.7. Partial correlations of well-being scores at posttest with the experience of negative and positive life events, controlled for baseline scores

	Negative life events	Positive life events
SWLS	.07	.21**
PANAS-PA	.04	.17*
AHI	.00	.23**
SHS	−.03	.09

Note. N = 169–174. SWLS = Satisfaction with Life Scale; PANAS-PA = Positive and Negative Affect Schedule – Positive Affect Scale; AHI = Authentic Happiness Inventory; SHS = Subjective Happiness Scale. Positive and negative life events: whether a negative or positive life event was experienced during the last 6 months (= 1) or not (= 0). Positive life events include marriage, outstanding personal achievements, beginning or completion of education; negative life events include major personal injury or illness, being fired from work, sexual difficulties, death of a close friend, troubles with in-laws, troubles with the boss. *p < .05, **p < .01.

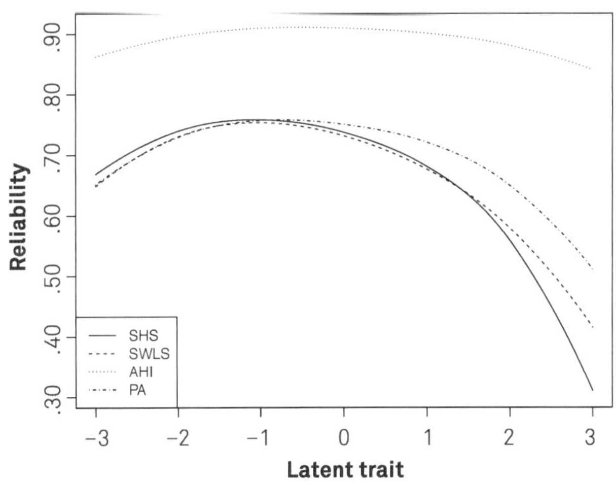

Figure 20.1. Reliability estimates of the SHS, SWLS, AHI, and PANAS Positive Affect Scale at different levels of the latent trait (z-scores).

negative valence and which do not occur too rarely in a period of 6 months (such as "death of a spouse," which was accordingly not considered). Positive life events included marriage, outstanding personal achievements, and beginning or completion of education. Negative life events major personal injury or illness, being laid off from a job, sexual difficulties, death of a close friend, troubles with in-laws, and troubles with the boss. The total scores were coded as 1 if participants experienced one of the positive or negative life events and as 0 if they did not experience any event. The total scores were correlated with the well-being scales at posttest (i.e., 6 months after pretest), while controlling for the scores at pretest (i.e., baseline), see Table 20.7.

Table 20.7 shows that the SWLS, AHI, and the Positive Affect Scale of the PANAS showed higher scores when a positive life event was experienced, while the SHS was widely unaffected by these events. The experience of negative life events was unrelated to all instruments.

Discussion

The results of the analyses suggested that the most widely used instruments in positive psychology interventions, the SHS, SWLS, AHI, and PANAS, fulfill most of the previously mentioned criteria regarding psychometric properties and are useful to assess changes in well-being following positive psychology interventions. However, there are also important differences among the instruments regarding most of the criteria. First, the lack of a clear theoretical framework in the AHI seems a potential issue for the interpretation of findings. The instrument has a very broad scope, which is also reflected in a less clear fit of the data to a one-dimensional model than in the other instruments; this has also been discussed before (see Kaczmarek et al., 2011; Proyer et al., 2017). One might argue that the instrument is more of an "index," that is, a collection of relevant items that do not necessarily share a common factor (as maybe suggested in its original name "Steen Happiness Index"), than a scale in which all items are representative of the same underlying latent concept. While indexes are helpful when different, not necessarily related dimensions should be summarized in one score; however, an index might have the downside that it is related to (unknown) other constructs, which may bias obtained results. A good rationale is required for what items should be included. Given the large intercorrelations among well-being measures reported in the literature, there is ample evidence that there is a general underlying "trait" of well-being (e.g., Goodman et al., 2018; Keyes et al., 2002), which makes the use of indexes somewhat questionable. Instead, models with a general factor, be it one-dimensional models, hierarchical, or bifactor models, seem to be more plausible representations of the data in this field. Regarding the AHI, Proyer et al. (2017) describe the instrument as "a valuable indicator of general well-being, encompassing a broad array of hedonic and eudemonic concepts" (p. 78). They conclude that the AHI is well-suited for use in intervention studies, but they also recommend it being further refined to address its shortcomings and to account for advancements in well-being theories.

Second, while all reviewed instruments show good internal consistency and test-retest reliability, there were differences regarding the proneness to ceiling effects and the sensitivity in higher levels of well-being. In my analyses, I found the AHI to be least affected by ceiling effects and showed high sensitivity also in very happy people, while the other measures failed to discriminate reliably among those in the upper end of the continuum and were more prone to ceiling effects (results for the SWLS were widely parallel to earlier findings; Schutte et al. 2019). This is mostly due to item difficulty; for assessing well-being across the full range of the spectrum, we need items reflecting very low and very high levels of the construct. Consequently, this is also related to the length of the instrument: Very short instruments can hardly accommodate items representing the low, middle, and high range of the continuum.

Third, while the SHS was unable to detect the experience of positive life events, the SWLS, AHI, and the PANAS all monitored these experiences to comparable degrees. One can assume that this finding can be translated into the detection of positive effects following a positive psychology intervention, though this proposal would need to be tested empirically.

In conclusion, this review of the most common well-being instruments in intervention research suggests recommending the AHI, SWLS, and the PANAS Positive Affect Scale for the evaluation of such interventions. An earlier study (Proyer et al., 2017) that directly compared the AHI with the SWLS further reported a stronger susceptibility to change in the AHI than in the SWLS following well-validated positive psychology interventions, suggesting that the AHI might be even better suited than the other instruments. However, as previously mentioned, instrument selection should be well-tailored to the intervention at hand as well as take the content of the intervention and the instruments into account. In many cases, it is more informative to look at more specific aspects of well-being presumably elicited by an intervention than at very general notions of well-being.

For working with people at the upper end of the well-being continuum, I can only recommend the AHI among the reviewed instruments. Finally, while the SHS cannot be recommended when one is interested in measuring change or discriminating among highly satisfied people, it might be better suited than the other instruments for other purposes, when one is interested in a measure of well-being widely unaffected by momentary influences or life experiences.

Of course, in this empirical review, I was only able to compare the few most-relevant well-being instruments currently in use. Given the larger number of existing well-being instruments, future studies might consider directly comparing further (and newer) instruments regarding the mentioned criteria here using similar procedures for furthering the knowledge on well-being instruments in positive psychology interventions.

References

Abbott, J.-A., Klein, B., Hamilton, C., & Rosenthal, A. J. (2009). The impact of online resilience training for sales managers on wellbeing and performance. *E-Journal of Applied Psychology*, 5(1), 89–95. https://doi.org/10.7790/ejap.v5i1.145

Bolier, L., Haverman, M., Westerhof, G., Riper, H., Smit, F., & Bohlmeijer, E. (2013). Positive psychology interventions: A meta-analysis of randomized controlled studies. *BMC Public Health, 13*, Article 119. https://doi.org/10.1186/1471-2458-13-119

Christensen, L., & Mendoza, J. L. (1986). A method of assessing change in a single subject: An alteration of the RC index. *Behavior Therapy, 17*, 305–308. https://doi.org/10.1016/S0005-7894(86)80060-0

Cooke, P. J., Melchert, T. P., & Connor, K. (2016). Measuring well-being: A review of instruments. *The Counseling Psychologist, 44*, 730–757. https://doi.org/10.1177/0011000016633507

Dickens, L. R. (2017). Using gratitude to promote positive change: A series of meta-analyses investigating the effectiveness of gratitude interventions. *Basic and Applied Social Psychology, 39*, 193–208. https://doi.org/10.1080/01973533.2017.1323638

Diener, E., Emmons, R. A., Larsen, R. J., & Griffin, S. (1985). The satisfaction with life scale. *Journal of Personality Assessment, 49*, 71–75. https://doi.org/10.1207/s15327752jpa4901_13

Diener, E., Wirtz, D., Tov, W., Kim-Prieto, C., Choi, D., Oishi, S., & Biswas-Diener, R. (2010). New well-being measures: Short scales to assess flourishing and positive and negative feelings. *Social Indicators Research, 97*, 143–156. https://doi.org/10.1007/s11205-009-9493-y

Flora, D.B. (2020). Your coefficient alpha is probably wrong, but which coefficient omega is right? A tutorial on using R to obtain better reliability estimates. *Advances in Methods and Practices in Psychological Science, 3*(4), 484–501. https://doi.org/10.1177/2515245920951747

Gander, F., Proyer, R.T., Hentz, E., & Ruch, W. (2020). Working mechanisms in positive interventions: A study using daily assessment of positive emotions. *The Journal of Positive Psychology, 15*, 633–638. https://doi.org/10.1080/17439760.2020.1789698

Goodman, F.R., Disabato, D.J., Kashdan, T.B., & Kauffman, S.B. (2018). Measuring well-being: A comparison of subjective well-being and PERMA. *The Journal of Positive Psychology, 13*(4), 321–332. https://doi.org/10.1080/17439760.2017.1388434

Graham, J.W., Taylor, B.J., Olchowski, A.E., & Cumsille, P.E. (2006). Planned missing data designs in psychological research. *Psychological Methods, 11*(4), 323–343. https://doi.org/10.1037/1082-989X.11.4.323

Hendriks, T., Schotanus-Dijkstra, M., Hassankhan, A., de Jong, J., & Bohlmeijer, E. (2019). The efficacy of multi-component positive psychology interventions: A systematic review and meta-analysis of randomized controlled trials. *Journal of Happiness Studies, 21*(1), 357–390. https://doi.org/10.1007/s10902-019-00082-1

Holmes, T.H., & Rahe, R.H. (1967). The social readjustment rating scale. *Journal of Psychosomatic Research, 11*, 213–218. https://doi.org/10.1016/0022-3999(67)90010-4

Hu, L., & Bentler, P.M. (1999). Cutoff criteria for fit indexes in covariance structure analysis: Conventional criteria vs. new alternatives. *Structural Equation Modeling, 6*, 1–55. https://doi.org/10.1080/10705519909540118

Huta, V., & Waterman, A.S. (2014). Eudaimonia and its distinction from hedonia: Developing a classification and terminology for understanding conceptual and operational definitions. *Journal of Happiness Studies, 15*, 1425–1456. https://doi.org/10.1007/s10902-013-9485-0

Kaczmarek, L., Stanko-Kaczmarek, M., & Dombrowski, S. (2011). Adaptation and validation of the Steen Happiness Index into Polish. *Polish Psychological Bulletin, 41*(3), 98–104. https://doi.org/10.2478/v10059-010-0013-3

Keyes, C.L. M. (2002). The mental health continuum: From languishing to flourishing in life. *Journal of Health & Social Behavior, 43*, 207–222. https://doi.org/10.2307/3090197

Keyes, C.L.M., Shmotkin, D., & Ryff, C.D. (2002). Optimizing well-being: The empirical encounter of two traditions. *Journal of Personality and Social Psychology, 82*, 1007–1022. https://doi.org/10.1037/0022-3514.82.6.1007

Lyubomirsky, S., Dickerhoof, R., Boehm, J.K., & Sheldon, K.M. (2011). Becoming happier takes both a will and a proper way: An experimental longitudinal intervention to boost well-being. *Emotion, 11*, 391–402. https://doi.org/10.1037/a0022575

Lyubomirsky, S., & Lepper, H.S. (1999). A measure of subjective happiness: Preliminary reliability and construct validation. *Social Indicators Research, 46*, 137–155. https://doi.org/10.1023/A:1006824100041

Parks, A.C., & Biswas-Diener, R. (2013). Positive interventions: Past, present, and future. In T.B. Kashdan & J. Ciarrochi (Eds.), *Mindfulness, acceptance, and positive psychology: The seven foundations of well-being* (pp. 140–165). Context Press/New Harbinger Publications.

Proyer, R.T., Gander, F., Wellenzohn, S., & Ruch, W. (2017). The Authentic Happiness Inventory revisited: Addressing its psychometric properties, validity, and role in intervention studies. *Journal of Well-Being Assessment, 1*, 77–96. https://doi.org/10.1007/s41543-018-0006-0

Revelle, W. (2018). *psych: Procedures for psychological, psychometric, and personality research.* Retrieved from https://CRAN.R-project.org/package=psych

Ryff, C.D. (1989). Happiness is everything, or is it? Explorations on the meaning of psychological well-being. *Journal of Personality and Social Psychology, 57*, 1069–1081. https://doi.org/10.1037/0022-3514.57.6.1069

Schallberger, U. (2005). *Kurzskalen zur Erfassung der Positiven Aktivierung, Negativen Aktivierung und Valenz in Experience Sampling Studien (PANAVA-KS). Theoretische und methodische Grundlagen, Konstruk-*

tvalidität und psychometrische Eigenschaften bei der Beschreibung intra- und interindividueller Unterschiede [Short scales for the assessment of positive activation, negative activation, and valence in experience sampling studies (PANAVA-KS). Theoretical and methodological foundations, construct validity, and psychometric properties for describing intra- and interpersonal differences]. Forschungsberichte aus dem Projekt: "Qualität des Erlebens in Arbeit und Freizeit," No. 6. Fachrichtung Angewandte Psychologie des Psychologischen Instituts der Universität Zürich.

Schutte, N.S., & Malouff, J.M. (2019). The impact of signature character strengths interventions: A meta-analysis. *Journal of Happiness Studies, 20*, 1179–1196. https://doi.org/10.1007/s10902-018-9990-2

Schutte, L., Negri, L., Delle Fave, A., & Wissing, M.P. (2019). Rasch analysis of the Satisfaction with Life Scale across countries: Findings from South Africa and Italy. *Current Psychology, 40*(10), 4908–4917. https://doi.org/10.1007/s12144-019-00424-5

Seligman, M.E.P., Steen, T.A., Park, N., & Peterson, C. (2005). Positive psychology progress: Empirical validation of interventions. *American Psychologist, 60*, 410–421. https://doi.org/10.1037/0003-066X.60.5.410

Sin, N.L., & Lyubomirsky, S. (2009). Enhancing well-being and alleviating depressive symptoms with positive psychology interventions: A practice-friendly meta-analysis. *Journal of Clinical Psychology, 65*, 467–487. https://doi.org/10.1002/jclp.20593

van de Vijver, P.J.R. (2016). Test adaptations. In F.T.L. Leong, D. Bartram, F.M. Cheung, K.F. Geisinger, & D. Iliescu (Eds.), *The ITC international handbook of testing and assessment* (pp. 364–376). Oxford University Press. https://doi.org/10.1093/med:psych/9780199356942.003.0025

Vittersø, J., Biswas-Diener, R., & Diener, E. (2005). The divergent meanings of life satisfaction: Item response modeling of the Satisfaction with Life Scale in Greenland and Norway. *Social Indicators Research, 74*, 327–348. https://doi.org/10.1007/s11205-004-4644-7

Watson, D., Clark, L.A., & Tellegen, A. (1988). Development and validation of brief measures of positive and negative affect: The PANAS scales. *Journal of Personality and Social Psychology, 54*, 1063–1070. https://doi.org/10.1037/0022-3514.54.6.1063

White, C.A., Uttl, B., & Holder, M.D. (2019). Meta-analyses of positive psychology interventions: The effects are much smaller than previously reported. *PLOS ONE, 14*(5), e0216588. https://doi.org/10.1371/journal.pone.0216588

Part V

New Directions

Chapter 21

Measuring Primal World Beliefs

Jeremy D.W. Clifton

Department of Psychology, University of Pennsylvania, Philadelphia, PA, USA

Background and Relevance

Human behavior is influenced by global judgments of situations. For example, in snake-infested jungles (i.e., any situation perceived as having a high base rate for threat), humans are more jumpy, irritable, and unhappy. Likewise, in places perceived as full of opportunity and resources (i.e., any situation assigned a high base rate for worthwhile engagement), humans respond by being more curious and experiencing more positive emotions. Yet, researchers have only recently begun to seriously consider the possibility that the behaviors and outcomes individuals experience seemingly wherever they go (i.e., personality and well-being) are explained by different global judgments of the one place humans never leave: the world.

Historically, personality variables have been attributed to individual differences in disposition (i.e., traits), which are often seen as biologically rooted (e.g., Eysenck, 1963; McCrae, 2004). Yet genetic markers of personality continue to elude researchers (Deary, 2009). Dweck (2008, 2017) recently suggested that beliefs might be major drivers of patterns of behavior associated with major personality traits. Yet, she also notes, such beliefs have yet to be identified. Given that behavior is highly responsive to global judgments of situations, is it possible that most variance in most major personality, clinical, and well-being outcomes is determined in part by normative reactions to global judgments of the world's basic character as if *the world* was one big heterogeneous yet still meaningfully characterizable place? For example, the pattern of thinking and acting that personality researchers call "optimism" could be largely a reaction to a perception that the world is a good place. Likewise, neuroticism could be partly a reaction to the belief the world is dangerous, depression partly a reaction to the belief the world is ugly and barren, and so forth. If such hypotheses were just partly true, that would have sweeping implications for the social sciences and improving human life.

My colleagues and I (Clifton et al., 2019; Clifton & Kim, 2019; Clifton, 2020a) recently suggested that humans hold many of these beliefs, which we call *primal world beliefs* or primals for short, and that primals may be central to personality and well-being, which can be referred to as the strong primals hypothesis. Primals are defined as simple, adjectival, goal-relevant beliefs about the general character of the world as a whole, such as "the world is an abundant place" or "the world is dangerous." They do not necessarily concern specific phenomena within the world, such as the self, intelligence, friends, and so forth, but the world as a whole. Primals are adjectival in the sense that they do not describe *why* or *how* the world came to be what it is, but merely *what* it is like now.

In the first systematic effort to empirically derive all major primals, we (Clifton et al., 2019) found that subjects varied along 26 empirically and conceptually distinct continua anchored by mutually exclusive conceptual opposites. As Figure 21.1 shows, most primals form a three-tiered hierarchy. Seven tertiary primals group together into the overall belief that the world is Safe (vs. dangerous); seven group into the belief that the world is Enticing (vs. dull); three group into the belief that the world is Alive (vs. mechanistic); and five are largely orthogonal to the rest. Safe, Enticing, and Alive – which we called secondary primals or informally the Big Three – in turn cluster into a single overarching primary primal, which concerns whether or not the world is a generally Good place that deserves to exist.

If the strong primals hypothesis is partially true and researchers can identify interventions that reliably alter primals like Enticing, researchers could theoretically alter personality and well-being with essentially endless applications. For example, couples may benefit from understanding alternative perceptions of the world that may underlie conflicts; citizens may find that primals underlie many political and policy differences. Clifton (2020a) identified 10 positive psychology variables that primals may influence, including gratitude, curiosity, hope/optimism, trust, self-efficacy, positive emotions, engagement, meaning, life satisfaction, and overall well-being. Clifton and Kim (2019) hypothesized that primals influence major health outcomes, including the risk of developing chronic diseases, such as cardiovascular disease, Alzheimer's disease, stroke, respiratory disease, infection, and cancer. Other promising dependent variables we (Clifton et al., 2019) mention includes clinical variables (depression, anxiety, stress, posttraumatic stress), personality variables (extraversion, agreeableness, neuroticism, and grit), and other well-being variables (such as zest, professional success, and having more friends).

Assessment Instruments

Although primals pose special measurement challenges, they are still just beliefs, a phenomenon psychologists frequently measure. Because all beliefs are based on meaningful exclusion, I suggest that measuring any belief requires the identification of adequately-performing reverse-scored items to achieve what Tay and Jebb (2018) call *continuum specification*. For example, if respondents are capable of indicating strong agreement with the item "I am a tall person" as well as "I am a short person," the validity of scores is suspect. Thus, we (Clifton et al., 2019) required that all subscales include reverse-scored items.

Beliefs are generally of two types, explicit or implicit. Primals are primarily implicit. Akin to beliefs often studied concerning depression such as "I am worthless" or "My spouse hates me," primals too are more felt than thought. Thus, items with affect-laden language may at times better pinpoint the latent variable than items stated as facts, which may engage overly cognitive System 2 processes.

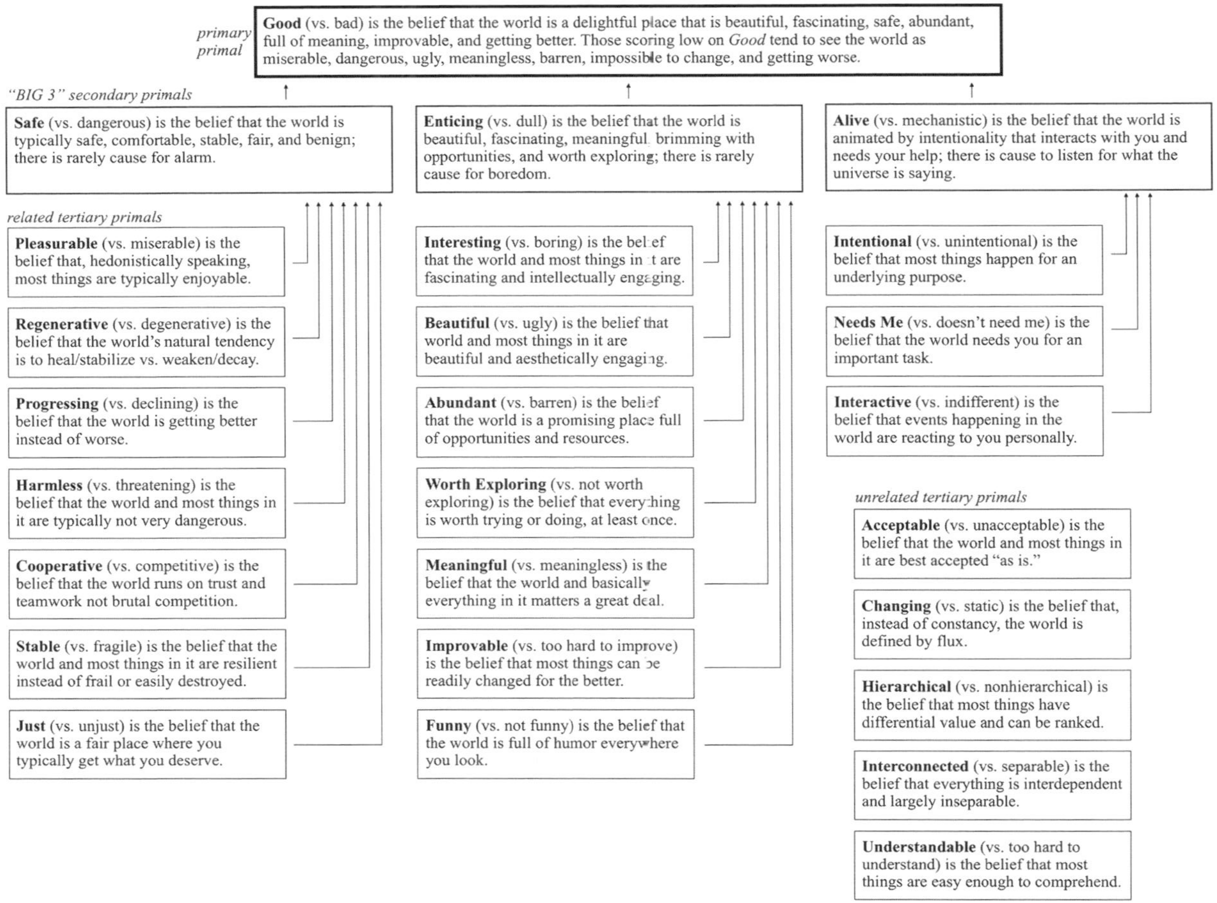

Figure 21.1. The structure of primal world beliefs with definitions (reprinted with permission from Clifton & Kim, 2019, p. 2).

Beliefs are not mere propositions, but meaningful psychological phenomena. Our biggest initial challenge in measuring primals was to establish that humans hold primals in the first place. Unlike other beliefs, where meaningful individual differences are obvious (e.g., belief about god), it is not obvious that humans profoundly disagree in numerous ways about the most basic character of an unusually large circumstance that we all inhabit, never leave, rarely discuss explicitly, do not have a proper term for in English, and usually do not consider a "circumstance." Most dictionaries assign over a dozen definitions to "the world," and various scholars say they study beliefs about "the world," even though these constructs rarely concern the world but various phenomena within it. Throughout our research, we (Clifton et al., 2019) found that many scholars were skeptical of the existence of primals: Some denied they held primals personally; some thought scale scores would reflect affect-driven hyperbole, temporary opinions respondents would make up to navigate vague items, or would be redundant with previously studied personality traits; some thought the world was too heterogeneous and large to be meaningfully characterizable - which is itself a primal and one that we tried to measure. This skepticism, and the need to establish the ontology of the category, drove our unusually extensive efforts to establish the validity, publish in the top measurement journal, and employ established measurement techniques for measuring similar beliefs.

A Brief History of Primals Assessment

Among the previously-measured constructs that can be considered a primal, the belief in a just world (BJW) has received by far the most research attention. This belief holds that the world is a place where one gets what one deserves and deserves what one gets. Lerner (e.g., 1980) thought this belief was part of "a fundamental delusion" that caused one to blame marginalized individuals for their misfortune (Montada & Lerner, 1998). After all, if a just world punishes you, you probably deserve it.

The first BJW scale was Rubin and Peplau's (1973) Just World Scale (JWS), followed by the slightly revised JWSR two years later (Rubin & Peplau, 1975). In creating items, they faced two options (the extent to which they weighed these options is only implicit in their writing). First, they could write direct items specific to the global character of the world as a whole, such as "Basically, the world is a just place." Second, they could write indirect items about a series of fairness subdomains such as grades, traffic tickets, court verdicts, sports, and so forth, and assume the mean response reflects an implicit belief about the world as a whole (i.e., a primal). An example indirect item is "Students almost always deserve the grades they receive in school."

In the early 1970s, the first option was fraught. Rubin and Peplau did not know if "the world as a whole" was a psychologically meaningful place or if individuals could accurately answer direct items about it. They also did not know if "just" is a meaningful modifier for this particular subject (are rocks or stars just?). However, they did know that a common mistake in survey design is employing vague terms - like "the world" - that have multiple meanings and interpretations (e.g., DeVellis, 2003). Doing so typically lowers internal reliability, test-retest reliability, and validity. Perhaps for this reason, Rubin and Peplau (1973, 1975) opted for the indirect approach. The 20-item BJWSR includes 19 indirect items about subdomains and one direct item, the aforementioned "Basically, the world is a just place."

Table 21.1. Some noteworthy instruments relevant to the measurement of primal world beliefs

Instrument	Author(s)	Total items	Reverse scored	Subscale information: Sub-scales	Label	Items	Reverse Scored	$\alpha^{\dagger}$	Example item	Belief(s) identified *a priori* to explain specific dependent variable	Primary dimension identification method
Just World Scale-Revised (JWSR)	Rubin & Peplau (1975)	20	9	1	Belief in a just world	20	9	.68	*Careful drivers are just as likely to get hurt in traffic accidents as careless ones.*	Yes, blame and racism	Conceptual
Global Belief in a Just World Scale (GBJWS)	Lipkus (1991)	7	0	1	Belief in a just world	7	0	.81	*I feel that people get what they deserve.*	Yes, blame and racism	Conceptual
Social World-View Scale – Revised (SWS-R)	Perry et al. (2013)	20	0	2	Dangerous worldview	10	0	.85	*There is really no such thing as "right" and "wrong." It all boils down to what you can get away with.* (Competitive)	Yes, political ideology	Conceptual
					Competitive worldview	10	0	.79			
World Assumptions Scale (WAS)	Janoff-Bulman (1989)	32	5	8	Benevolence of world	4	0	.84	*Human nature is basically good.* (Benevolence of people) *In general, life is mostly a gamble.* (Randomness)	Yes, trauma recovery	Conceptual
					Benevolence of people	4	2	.81			
					Justice	4	0	.83			
					Controllability	4	0	.81			
					Randomness	4	0	.69			
					Worthiness of self	4	3	.85			
					Luck of self	4	0	.86			
					Controllability of self	4	0	.72			

Table 21.1. continued

Instrument	Author(s)	Total items	Re-verse scored	Subscale information					Example item	Belief(s) identified *a priori* to explain specific dependent variable	Primary dimension identification method
				Sub-scales	Label	Items	Reverse Scored	α[†]			
Primals Inventory (PI-99)	Clifton et al. (2019)	99	39	26	Good	71	30	.97	*There's humor in everything.* (Funny) *In life, there's way more beauty than ugliness.* (Beautiful) *The world is an abundant place.* (Abundant) *What happens in the world is meant to happen.* (Intentional) *Most things and situations are responsive, workable, and totally possible to improve.* (Improvable) *On the whole, the world is a safe place.* (Safe)	No	Empirical
					Safe	29	15	.96			
					Pleasurable	5	2	.89			
					Regenerative	4	2	.85			
					Progressing	4	2	.91			
					Harmless	5	2	.90			
					Cooperative	4	3	.84			
					Stable	4	3	.81			
					Just	5	1	.81			
					Enticing	28	9	.95			
					Interesting	4	3	.86			
					Beautiful	4	1	.82			
					Abundant	4	1	.84			
					Worth Exploring	4	1	.77			
					Meaningful	4	3	.86			
					Improvable	5	1	.81			
					Funny	4	1	.88			
					Alive	14	4	.89			
					Intentional	5	2	.86			
					Needs Me	4	1	.91			
					Interactive	5	1	.84			
					Other tertiary primals						
					Acceptable	4	3	.81			
					Changing	5	1	.79			
					Hierarchical	5	1	.78			
					Interconnected	4	1	.85			
					Understandable	4	2	.80			

Note. [†]Representative Cronbach's α computed from 22 studies for JWS, 47 studies for JWS-R, and 20 studies for GBJWS (Hellman et al., 2008). Selected Cronbach's α for WAS (one study, $N = 122$) and PI-99 (six studies, $N = 2{,}454$) from Clifton et al. (2019).

Of course, the downside of Rubin and Peplau's (1975) approach is length and heterogeneity, for which they were criticized (e.g., Furnham & Procter, 1989). Furthermore, despite having 20 items, α often fell below .70. So, more scales were developed (for a review, see Furnham, 2003), most of which use subsets of Rubin and Peplau's (1975) items (e.g., Steensma et al., 1994), measure dimensions within BJW (e.g., Furnham & Procter, 1989), use a 6-point Likert scale, and use indirect items.

However, in creating the Global Belief in Just World Scale (GBJWS), Lipkus (1991; O'Connor et al., 1996) tried a more direct approach, relying on items such as "I feel that a person earns the rewards and punishments they get" and "I basically feel that the world is a fair place." Also, whereas Rubin and Peplau's (1975) items are written as facts, GBJWS items employ an "I feel that ..." format. Yet the empirical evidence suggests that the GBJWS and the JWSR measure the same latent variable (Lipkus, 1991; O'Connor et al., 1996) while being 14 items shorter and more reliable. This suggests that humans are capable of meaningfully answering more direct questions about the world as a whole, and that affect-related item wording can be useful. However, the GBJWS has no reverse-scored items and, like the JWSR, is somewhat specific to humanity rather than the world as a whole. Indeed, it is often unclear whether BJW researchers themselves see BJW as concerning the fairness of society or the cosmos generally.

As BJW measurement techniques improved, some other primals and primals-adjacent beliefs were identified in other fields to help explain other dependent variables – one-offs. For example, instead of racism in the case of BJW (Lerner, 1980), Altemeyer (1988) and Perry et al. (2013) were interested in political ideology, and their scales remain primarily used in that context. They intended to examine the social world rather than the world as a whole. Their subscale, often called "Belief in a Dangerous World," appears empirically and conceptually specific to a subdomain of danger (decline) and their "Belief in a Competitive World" subscale incorporates values that are not related to primals (Clifton et al., 2019; Clifton & Kerry, 2022).

In two instances, researchers used notable rigor to identify more than one primal at a time. Interested in the nature of control, Collins (1974) factor analyzed responses to items drawn from locus-of-control scales, finding a general good/bad factor as well as four subfactors he labeled, the *Difficult-easy world*, the *Just-unjust world*, the *Predictable-unpredictable world*, and the *Politically responsive-unresponsive world*. The other better-known effort comes from traumatologist Janoff-Bulman (1989). She theorized a priori that a few primals – the beliefs that the world is benevolent, just, controllable, and not random – along with some other beliefs about the self form what she called "the assumptive world," which gets shattered by trauma. Janoff-Bulman (1989) was arguably the first to (a) explicitly target beliefs about the world as a whole as one large place, (b) apply the schema concept to the world, (c) suggest that humans may hold several primals, and (d) may interact with each other to influence behavior. However, her process of identifying beliefs was top-down, constrained to a few beliefs she thought would be related to trauma recovery specifically, and her dimensions do not replicate (Kaler, 2009). Though Collins (1974) and Janoff-Bulman (1989) used factor analysis, both relied on a limited set of items concerning control.

The result of unsystematic research was the identification of a few beliefs that overlapped conceptually and nomologically. Works of literature rarely interacted, and many researchers were unaware they were coming at the same idea from different perspectives. Indeed, few were cognizant of the idea that humans held different beliefs about the world as a whole. For example, in his seminal review of the worldview literature, Koltko-Rivera (2004, p. 16) discusses BJW literature and muses that it could refer to some sort of "larger dimension, one that we might call *world nature*" and speculated that there might be other beliefs about this overall "world nature." Moreover, no theorists had noted that patterns of action an organism exhibits habitat-wide (i.e., personality and well-being) are theoretically explainable by individual differences in beliefs about typical habitat-wide conditions (i.e., primal world beliefs).

In sum, the relevant literature suggested that primals were measurable, multiple, and likely influence some behaviors. But this research was ad hoc. Primals remained underdefined, underexplored, and no theory like the strong primals hypothesis had been articulated.

Development of the Primals Inventory

After defining primals and articulating the strong primals hypothesis, we (Clifton et al., 2019) sought to identify all the major primals individuals hold, doing so with no particular dependent variable in mind. We drew inspiration from Kaler's (2009) multimethod approach to defining the assumptive world and the bottom-up lexical approach of personality psychologists that identified the BIG 5 in the 1970s (John et al., 1988). Recognizing that exploratory factor analysis cannot reveal latent phenomena no items tap and primals are implicit and easily overlooked, we pursued an unusually extensive empirically driven multimethod approach summarized in our 507-page supplement. For example, we analyzed over 80,000 tweets about the world as a whole gleaned from a database of over one billion; over 1,700 claims about the world as a whole gleaned from 358 of the most influential texts in world history; data from 12 focus groups eliciting descriptions of the world as a whole from adherents of all major world religions; and the 840 most-used adjectives in contemporary American English derived from 190,000 texts (450 million words) curated equally across five genres from 1990–2012. As we incorporated these and other inputs, we engaged dozens of scholars in several iterative stages of classification creation until we reached saturation. Despite months of searching, we could identify no new candidate primals; the 37 candidate primals already identified accounted for the overwhelming majority of the thousands of instances of world description we had gathered. Of these 37, we prioritized 25 for our first measurement effort based on frequency, exclusivity, and other criteria, and administered 234 items (8–12 per candidate primal) to 930 subjects for initial exploratory factor analysis – a sample approximately three times larger than Collins' (1974) and Janoff-Bulman's (1989) – which preceded two rounds of confirmatory analyses on subjects recruited from different online platforms (N=524, N=529). Our study administration and analysis strategy prioritized capturing the full breadth of the construct (i.e., content validity) and ensuring that dimensionality would emerge only if latent phenomena actually existed. For example, in follow-up studies, we removed various high-performing items to ensure that subscales relied more on signals from the underlying variable than variance defined by bloated specifics generated by item redundancy (i.e., artifacts).

As a result of these efforts, a basic structure of primal world beliefs emerged that we did not seek or expect (see Figure 21.1). Many primals were new to the literature, such as the belief that the world is Interesting (vs. boring), Funny (vs. not funny), and Abundant (vs. barren). Indeed, depending on how you count, only 1–5 of the 26 beliefs we identified had received previous research attention and all these relate to Safe, none to Enticing or Alive. Still, the dimensionality we unearthed finds parallels in earlier work, such as Collins' (1974) general good/bad factor.

The Primals Inventory and Its Psychometric Properties

Length and Dimensionality

Whereas most previous instruments were unidimensional, the PI-99 measures 26 subscales. This dimensionality is the result of the only effort to empirically derive a comprehensive set of primals. Fourteen tertiary subscales are measured with 4 items and eight subscales are measured with 5 items. The *Safe*, *Enticing*, *Alive*, and *Good* subscales include 29, 28, 14, and 71 items, respectively. Thus, most of the 99 items are used to compute scores at the primary, secondary, and tertiary levels.

Item Scoring and Content

Whereas most previous measures do not use reverse-scored items, nearly 40 % of PI-99 items are reverse-scored, and all subscales include at least one opposite scored item. As a result, each continuum is specified, which strengthens validity (Clifton, 2019). Primals researchers know, for example, that seeing the world as more Beautiful typically means seeing the world as less ugly, as opposed to less bland, disgusting, or meaningless. The PI-99 can measure many primals at once because we followed Lipkus' (1991) and Janoff-Bulman's (1989) strategy of using fewer more direct items rather than Rubin and Peplau's (1975) strategy of using numerous more indirect items.

Scale Instructions

Because of Lipkus' (1991) work, we also felt free to use affect language in some items, generally finding that such items performed equivalently to items phrased as facts. This may be partially because of the PI-99's unusually explicit instructions, which asks respondents to treat items as fact-like "statements about the world – not the world we wish we lived in, but the actual world as it is now."

Response Options

Like previous instruments, the PI-99 uses a 6-point Likert scale. Finding no rationale explaining why previous scale-builders did so, my own reasoning stemmed from the concern that a neutral point could be used as an "opt-out" option. Though study participants occasionally complain about the lack of a neutral point, item-level analysis (e.g., item characteristic curves) suggested that answering *slightly agree* vs. *slightly disagree* provides meaningful information (Clifton et al., 2019).

Reliability

The PI-99 is generally more reliable than other scales measuring similar constructs. We found that mean α across all subscales and studies was .84 (N=2,454) with none falling below .77. Test-retest reliability, assessed across 2 weeks, 9 months, and 19 months, ranging from .90 to .46, falling from an average of .74 across two weeks to .67 across 19 months. Such high reliability is remarkable given that (a) most subscales are only 4 items, including at least one opposite-scored item, (b) items are intermixed in a different random order for every participant each time the participant takes the survey, (c) items are intermixed across nearly 100 other items measuring 25 other variables, each of which includes reverse-scored items, and (d) test-retest subjects never learn the purpose of the survey, what constructs were being measured, or their own scores. All these practices are known to increase validity at the expense of reliability (Clifton, 2020b).

The GBJWS vs. the PI-99 Just Subscale

The *Just* subscale is the one PI-99 subscale that is empirically and conceptually fully redundant with pre-existing scales, specifically the Belief in a Just World, arguably the best measure of which is Lipkus' (1991) GBJWS, which correlates with *Just* at r(524)=.74. Though largely equivalent, the PI-99 *Just* subscale is marginally superior for four reasons. First, the *Just* subscale is more accurate because it was created by a comprehensive examination of primals in which items are selected to pinpoint the unique nomological space the latent variable occupies. Second, the GBJWS does not include any reverse-scored items. Third, the *Just* subscale is one item shorter than the GBJWS yet just as reliable (α for both hovers around .81). Fourth, whereas the GBJWS was created by administering items in a single unidimensional block and a fixed order, the *Just* subscale was created by randomly interspersing items across numerous other items measuring numerous other latent variables, which typically results in considerably less systematic error (Clifton, 2020b).

Validity

We (Clifton et al., 2019) employed unusually extensive efforts to establish convergent, divergent, concurrent, predictive, incremental, discriminant, and criterion validity. For example, we examined over 2,000 relationships between primals and other variables. Few of these relationships violated directional assumptions (+, –, or unrelated) and effect sizes mirrored expectations with few exceptions. Results from correlational and experimental research suggested that affect and social desirability play at most a minor role in scale scores. To determine whether it was necessary to retain all three levels of primal world beliefs (primary, secondary, and tertiary), we pitted the levels against each other in 63 three-way prediction contests when predicting outcomes such as depression and well-being. A similar methodology demonstrated that PI-99 subscales explain variance in several of these outcomes that BIG 5 scores did not. In fact, when it comes to interpersonal trust, gratitude, and life satisfaction, the predictive power of Big Three primals (Safe, Enticing, and Alive) exceeds that of BIG 5 scores by margins five times greater than established thresholds of *very strong evidence* of a superior model. Finally, pairwise relationships between PI-99 scores and nearly 100 personality and well-being variables showed moderate, to large, to very large effects. Given the obvious predictive value of PI-99 subscales, we concluded that "If nothing else, the PI-99 can help psychologists make predictions" (p. 96).

Future Measurement Possibilities

Psychometricians can improve upon the PI-99 in several ways. Some I am currently pursuing include validating shorter measures of Good, Safe, Enticing, and Alive (project completed prior to publication of this edited handbook; see Clifton & Yaden, 2021) and collecting large samples to power a confirmatory factor analysis of the PI-99's complex measurement model. Others are mentioned below.

Novel Approaches

Researchers should explore novel ways of measuring primals that move away from ~5-item scales with 6 Likert-style response options. For example, perhaps all 26 primals could be measured efficiently and accurately via just 22 items with 11 response options anchored by pairs of one-word opposites like beautiful/ugly with a common stem such as "I see the world as ..." Non-self-report methods, such as experience-sampling and postsurvey interviews, might also be used to triangulate the phenomenon.

Additional Primal-Specific Validation

Because the PI-99 includes an unusually large number of subscales, the validity of some remains underexamined, such as *Funny* and *Needs Me*.

Translation

The PI-99 and its short form versions (the PI-18 and PI-6) are currently being translated into over 20 languages, and more translation efforts are needed. Clifton et al. (in press) provide specific guidance for translators.

What Is the World?

More research is needed to unpack the object of primal world beliefs. For example, we do not know the relative importance of various subsets of phenomena (e.g., self vs. other, humans vs. nature, planet earth vs. outer space) in one's construal of everything.

Missing Tertiary Primals

Psychometricians might explore whether the PI-99 overlooks important primals. I currently see little value in another involved mixed-method approach to identifying candidate primals because ours was so recent and extensive. Instead, I recommend examining the following 15 candidate primals that we identified but dropped from initial measurement efforts: well-formed (vs. inelegant/clumsy/inefficient), orderly/organized (vs. chaotic/disorganized), vast/infinite (vs. small/finite), contradictory/inconsistent (vs. without contradiction/either-or), purely physical (vs. purely spiritual), young/fresh (vs. old/worn), affectionate/nurturing (vs. sinister/cold/cruel), unending/eternal (vs. ending/terminal), directional/narrative/linear (vs. directionless/erratic), magical/alive/mysterious/enigmatic (vs. straightforward/dead/direct/open), responsive to play (vs. responsive to being serious), responsive to high expectations (vs. responsive to low expectations), easy/manageable (vs. hard/difficult), responsive to attachment/caring (vs. detachment/stoicism), open to interpretation/subjective/hazy (vs. full of facts/objective/precise/clear). Items for each could be randomly interspersed within the PI-99 and subjected to factor analysis. See page 95 of our supplemental materials for more details. Please note that these proposed continuums have not been determined empirically but conceptually only.

Against Me

When, for empirical reasons, we dropped some candidate primals for being duplicative or not reflecting latent phenomena, one candidate primal was nonduplicative, seemed latent and important, but was dropped anyway: the belief that the world is For Me (vs. against me). Reverse-scored items cohered into a meaningful and reliable factor that was highly predictive of many outcomes, but no forward-scored items ever loaded on that factor. Also, unique among subscales, separate minimum average partial analysis of each candidate primal's items suggested multiple latent variables underscored this candidate primal (see page 127 of the supplemental). Future research should attempt to specify this continuum and restore it to the Primals Inventory.

Missing Secondary Primals

Other possible secondary primals warrant further study. In Study 1 (Clifton et al., 2019), "Bass-Ackwards" factor analysis found the beliefs that the world is against me, unjust, and barren cohered into an unusually stable factor across seven factor extractions (10–16). The exploratory factor analysis of Study 3 suggested a potential grouping concerning nonhierarchical, interconnected, and changing. A recent effort to translate the PI-99 into German duplicated Safe, Enticing, and Alive while finding three additional secondary primals: Fluid, Empowering, and Communal (Stahlmann et al., 2020). We speculate that perhaps Safe, Enticing, and Alive represent a universal trio across cultures but are not exhaustive within cultures.

Primal Self-Beliefs

Our process of identifying primal world beliefs has demonstrated the feasibility and value of empirically mapping all major beliefs about a topic. What about other topics, especially the self? A similar and complementary process which maps primal self-beliefs would likely have broad implications for clinical, well-being, and personality research.

Key Findings

So far researchers know that primals have four major empirical characteristics (Clifton et al., 2019). First, individuals seem to broadly disagree about the fundamental character of this world we presumably share; all 26 primals vary in quite normal nonleptokurtic unimodal distributions. Second, primals are orthogonal or weakly related to demographic variables such as income, age, and sex. Third, primals are among the most stable latent variables psychologists measure, roughly comparable to BIG 5 personality traits. Fourth, primals are highly predictive of numerous personality and well-being variables that primals theoretically influence, including BIG 5 traits. We (Clifton et al., 2019) list 42 example relationships described by highly significant ($p<.001$) and large effect sizes. For example, among 524 subjects, Safe correlates with life satisfaction at $r=.51$, Enticing correlates with curiosity at $r=.61$, and Good correlates with optimism at $r=.67$. Much previous research on Just/BJW can be summarized as follows: Those who see the world as Just tend to work harder, act nicer, and blame victims, presumably because of the expectation that effort and kindness will be rewarded (e.g., Furnham, 2003; Furnham & Procter, 1989; Montada & Lerner, 1998).

In sum, researchers know that humans behave *as if* much of their personality and enjoyment of life stems from their primals. In other words, the strong primals hypothesis may well be accurate. However, causation is not yet confirmed experimentally; nearly all research has been correlational. It is thus also possible that primals are overlooked, remarkably stable, unique cognitive symptoms of personality and well-being variables that are worth studying further because of their predictive value, though they play only a marginal causal role. I call this the *weak primals hypothesis*. More research is needed to determine whether the strong or weak primals hypothesis is more accurate.

Recommendations

For those interested in using the PI-99 (or short-form versions PI-18 and PI-6) in their research, I have several recommendations, some of which are based on speculation.

Study Design Recommendations

Consider Using Subscales

If length is a concern, I advise measuring Safe, Enticing, Alive, and Good, using either (a) the 18- or the 6-item short-form versions of the Primals Inventory (Clifton & Yaden, 2021) or (b) selecting individual PI-99 subscales for independent use. We created tertiary subscales with independent use in mind. Also, if the sole interest is a secondary primal like Safe, one might administer the seven subscales of the tertiary primals associated with it (*Cooperative*, *Harmless*, *Just*, *Pleasurable*, *Progressing*, *Regenerative*, and *Stable*) for 31 items total, which includes the 29 needed to compute Safe scores. However, we expect that administering the full PI-99 will often prove useful. When doing so, consider guarding against multiple comparisons by preregistering hypotheses.

Beware of Hypotheses Treating Primals as Dependent Variables

So far, hypotheses that treat primals as dependent variables have underperformed. For example, some researchers might hypothesize that believing the world is Abundant might stem largely from being wealthy when they are in fact orthogonal ($r(524) = .05$, Clifton et al., 2019). Such results suggest that researchers should be skeptical of simplistic intuitions conceiving primals as byproducts of easily defined categories of experiences (Clifton, 2020c). A bias may be at play, wherein individuals condescendingly imagine that other people cannot help but believe the things they do because of their backgrounds while our own beliefs stem from something more objective and clear-eyed.

Consider Hypotheses Consistent With the Normative Logic of Global Place Perceptions

The strong primals hypothesis is based on the idea that primals influence outcomes just like any place perception influences outcomes. We (Clifton et al., 2019, Table 2) standardized these normative assumptions with the phrase "In environments seen as X, Y is prudent and natural," where X is a quality of a place and Y is a given reaction to it. We then identified 30 normative statements, applied each statement to primals, and note that generally large effect sizes describe those relationships. For example, normative statement #15 states "In environments seen as positive, enjoyable, and predictable, well-being and positive emotions are prudent and natural." If so, we hypothesize, then "In worlds seen as Good and Understandable, overall PERMA scores (well-being) will be higher." We then provide the relevant correlation coefficients. In this case, even when controlling for age, sex, education, and income, the relationship between Good and overall PERMA scores was $\beta(524) = .64$, $p < .001$, and the relationship between Understandable and overall PERMA scores was $\beta(524) = .40$, $p < .001$.

Taking the PI-99 May Influence Affect

Experimentalists concerned with confounds should note that there is some evidence that taking the PI-99 causes affect to reflect the meaning of one's primals (Clifton et al., 2019).

Primal-Specific Recommendations

Consider Removing Subscales

Some primals are less relevant to positive psychology research. Interactive, Acceptable, Changing, Funny, Hierarchical, Interconnected, and Progressing did not correlate above .30 with life satisfaction or any PERMA elements. Dropping these subscales shortens the PI-99 by 31 items.

Alive Is Less Related to Well-Being

Safe and Enticing appear far more relevant to well-being research than Alive. See correlational relationships on page 312 of our supplement.

Avoid Underestimating Enticing or Overestimating Safe

The distinction between Safe and Enticing is the most important distinction between any two primals. Safe concerns threat, pain, and pleasure – lower-level animalistic concerns – while Enticing concerns higher-level motivations, such as beauty, cognitive engagement, meaning, and humor. Indeed, the hedonistic belief that the world is Pleasurable (vs. miserable) is more related to Safe than Enticing. Though the empirical evidence suggests that Enticing is just as important as Safe when it comes to well-being, individuals (including researchers) may be biased to overestimate the influence of Safe relative to Enticing. This sort of incongruity is consistent with some empirical literatures (e.g., actor-observer bias) and the fact that all previously studied primals relate to Safe and none to Enticing.

When Safe and Enticing Similarly Correlate to a Third Variable, the Relevant Primal Is Probably Good

Since primals exist at three levels of granularity, identifying the level most appropriate to each dependent variable is important. For example, narcissists tend to see the world as Alive, but only because narcissism is related to one of the tertiary subscales of Alive (Interactive; Clifton et al., 2019). Likewise, with substantial shared variance, Safe and Enticing are essentially the two main reasons for seeing the world as Good. If a DV correlates similarly with both, Good is likely most relevant. Indeed, Good is by far the most important primal. It explained ~35 % of the variance in all 99 items, single-handedly outperformed the three secondary primals and 22 tertiary primals in a third of our 63 three-way prediction contests, and explained more variance in gratitude, growth mindset, trust, and life satisfaction than BIG 5 traits combined (Clifton et al., 2019). Indeed, in many positive psychology studies, Good may be the only primal worth measuring.

Conclusion

Much psychological research and theory appears to be premised on the implicit assumption that humans agree with each other about the sort of world we are in and what sorts of actions this world calls for. However, the development and use of the PI-99 has shown that humans vary in their beliefs about the world along numerous previously unknown dimensions, and the PI-99 can be used to explore the implications of this variation. Regardless of whether this discovery represents an incremental step (the weak primals hypothesis) or a giant leap (the strong primals hypothesis), much further research is warranted. This chapter has sought to aid further research by introducing the PI-99 in the context of a brief but important history of primals measurement, to outline next steps for further scale development, and to provide some practical advice to positive psychologists seeking to examine primals in their research programs.

References

Altemeyer, B. (1988). *Enemies of freedom*. Jossey-Bass.

Clifton, A. B. W., Stahlmann, A. G., Hofmann, J., Chirico, A., Cadwallader, R., & Clifton, J. D. W. (in press). Improving scale equivalence by increasing access to scale-specific information. *Perspectives on Psychological Science*.

Clifton, J. D. W. (2020a). Happy in a crummy world: Implications of primal world beliefs for increasing wellbeing through positive psychology interventions. *Journal of Positive Psychology, 15*(5), 691–695. https://doi.org/10.1080/17439760.2020.1789703

Clifton, J. D. W. (2020b). Managing validity vs. reliability trade-offs in scale-building decisions. *Psychological Methods, 25*(3), 259–270. https://doi.org/10.1037/met0000236

Clifton, J. D. W. (2020c). Testing if primal world beliefs reflectexperiences – Or at least some experiencesidentified *ad hoc*. *Frontiers in Psychology, 11*, Article 1145. https://doi.org/10.3389/fpsyg.2020.01145

Clifton, J. D. W., Baker, J. D., Park, C. L., Yaden, D. B., Clifton, A. B. W., Terni, P., Miller, J. L., Zeng, G., Giorgi, S., Schwartz, H. A., & Seligman, M. E. P. (2019). Primal world beliefs. *Psychological Assessment, 31*(1), 82–99. https://doi.org/10.1037/pas0000639

Clifton, J. D. W., & Kerry, N. T. (2022). Belief in a dangerous world does not explain substantial variance in political attitudes, but other world beliefs do. *Social Psychological and Personality Science*. Advance online publication. https://doi.org/10.1177/19485506221119324

Clifton, J. D. W., & Kim, E. S. (2019). Healthy in a crummy world: Implications of primal world beliefs for health psychology. *Medical Hypotheses, 135*, Article 109463. https://doi.org/10.1016/j.mehy.2019.109463

Clifton, J. D. W., & Yaden, D. B. (2021). Brief measures of the four highest-order primal world beliefs. *Psychological Assessment, 33*(12), 1267–1273. https://doi.org/10.1037/pas0001055

Collins, B. E. (1974). Four components of the Rotter internal-external scale: Belief in a difficult world, a just world, a predictable world, and a politically responsive world. *Journal of Personality and Social Psychology, 29*, 381–391. https://doi.org/10.1037/h0036015

Deary, I. J. (2009). The trait approach to personality. In P. J. Corr & G. Matthews (Eds.), *The Cambridge handbook of personality psychology*. Cambridge University Press.

DeVellis, R. F. (2003). *Scale development: Theory and applications*. Sage.

Dweck, C. S. (2008). Can personality be changed? The role of beliefs in personality and change. *Current Directions in Psychological Science, 17*(6), 391–394. https://doi.org/10.1111/j.1467-8721.2008.00612.x

Dweck, C. S. (2017). From needs to goals and representations: Foundations for a unified theory of motivation, personality, and development. *Psychological Review, 124*(6), 689–719. https://doi.org/10.1037/rev0000082

Eysenck, H. J. (1963). Biological basis of personality. *Nature, 199*, 1031–1034. https://doi.org/10.1038/1991031a0

Furnham, A. (2003). Belief in a just world: Research progress over the past decade. *Personality and Individual Differences, 34*, 795–817. https://doi.org/10.1016/S0191-8869(02)00072-7

Furnham, A., & Procter, E. (1989). Belief in a just world: Review and critique of the individual difference literature. *British Journal of Social Psychology, 28*, 365–384. https://doi.org/10.1111/j.2044-8309.1989.tb00880.x

Hellman, C. M., Muilenburg-Trevino, E. M., & Worley, J. A. (2008). The belief in a just world: An examination of reliability estimates across three measures. *Journal of Personality Assessment, 90*(4), 399–401. https://doi.org/10.1080/00223890802108238

Janoff-Bulman, R. (1989). Assumptive worlds and the stress of traumatic events: Applications of the schema construct. *Social Cognition, 7*, 113–136. https://doi.org/10.1521/soco.1989.7.2.113

John, O. P., Angleitner, A., & Ostendorf, F. (1988). The lexical approach to personality: A historical review of trait taxonomic research. *European journal of Personality, 2*, 171–203. https://doi.org/10.1002/per.2410020302

Kaler, M. E. (2009). *The world assumptions questionnaire: Development of a measure of the assumptive world*. [Doctoral dissertation]. Retrieved from ProQuest (3371864).

Koltko-Rivera, M. E. (2004). The psychology of worldviews. *Review of General Psychology, 8*, 3–58. https://doi.org/10.1037/1089-2680.8.1.3

Lerner, M. J. (1980). *Belief in a just world: A fundamental delusion*. Plenum.

Lipkus, I. (1991). The construction and preliminary validation of a global belief in a just world scale and the exploratory analysis of the multidimensional belief in a just world scale. *Personality and Individual Differences, 12*, 1171–1178. https://doi.org/10.1016/0191-8869(91)90081-L

McCrae, R. R. (2004). Human nature and culture: A trait perspective. *Journal of Research in Personality, 38*(1), 3–14. https://doi.org/10.1016/j.jrp.2003.09.009

Montada, L., & Lerner, M. J. (Eds.). (1998). *Responses to victimizations and belief in a just world*. Springer. https://doi.org/10.1007/978-1-4757-6418-5

O'Connor, W. E., Morrison, T. G., & Morrison, M. A. (1996). The reliability and factor structure of the global belief in a just world scale. *Journal of Social Psychology, 136*(5), 667–668. https://doi.org/10.1080/00224545.1996.9714055

Perry, R., Sibley, C. G., & Duckitt, J. (2013). Dangerous and competitive worldviews: A meta-analysis of their associations with social dominance orientation and right-wing authoritarianism. *Journal of Research in Personality, 47*, 116–127. https://doi.org/10.1016/j.jrp.2012.10.004

Rubin, Z., & Peplau, A. (1973). Belief in a just world and reactions to another's lot: A study of participants in the national draft lottery. *Journal of Social Issues, 29*(4), 73–93. https://doi.org/10.1111/j.1540-4560.1973.tb00104.x

Rubin, Z., & Peplau, L. A. (1975). Who believes in a just world? *Journal of Social Issues, 31*, 65–89. https://doi.org/10.1111/j.1540-4560.1975.tb00997.x

Stahlmann, A. G., Hofmann, J., Ruch, W., Heinz, S., & Clifton, J. D. W. (2020). The higher-order structure of primal world beliefs in German-speaking countries: Adaptation and initial validation of the German Primals Inventory (GPI-66). *Personality and Individual Differences, 163*, 110054. https://doi.org/10.1016/j.paid.2020.110054

Steensma, H., den Hartigh, E., & Lucardie, E. (1994). Social categories, just world belief, locus of control, and causal attributions of occupational accidents. *Social Justice Research, 7*(3), 281–299. https://doi.org/10.1007/BF02334835

Tay, L., & Jebb, A. T. (2018). Establishing construct continua in construct validation: The process of continuum specification. *Advances in Methods and Practices in Psychological Science, 1*(3), 375–388. https://doi.org/10.1177/2515245918775707

Chapter 22
Imagination

Darya L. Zabelina

Department of Psychological Science, University of Arkansas, Fayetteville, AR, USA

Imagination has been defined as the formation of new ideas, images, or concepts in one's mind's eye. The late 19th century saw the first foray into the study of imagination and its related constructs, such as fantasy and daydreaming (Galton, 1880; James, 1890). James was the first to describe two different types of imagination: reproductive imagination, when imagined images closely represent previously experienced reality; and productive imagination, when the elements of such images are recombined in the service of a novel stimulus. Later work went on to examine imagination from the perspective of the ability for mental imagery (Kosslyn et al., 2001). Recent studies, however, have expanded the study of imagination to investigate its other features, including originality and transformative ability (Jankowska & Karwowski, 2015), satisfaction and implementation (Jung et al., 2016), kinesthetic imagery (Malouin et al., 2007), and frequency, emotional valence, and goal-directedness (vs. "free-floating") imagination (Zabelina & Condon, 2020). Finally, mental imagery has been proposed to include multiple sensory modalities, such as feelings and bodily sensations (Holmes & Mathews, 2010).

Relevance

A growing body of empirical evidence suggests that imagination is relevant in many aspects of our lives. Studies report that imagination is a unique and integral part of fictional story reading (Sadoski et al., 1990) and learning of mathematics (Arcavi, 2003), and may be involved in overall cognitive development (Thomas & Brown, 2011). The ability to imagine has been linked with increased creativity (LeBoutillier & Marks, 2003) and innovation (Samli, 2011). Affective forecasting, a concept closely related to imagination, has been reported to affect our ability to envision our "future selves," such as anticipating our future thoughts and feelings (Wilson & Gilbert, 2005) or the ability to save money for retirement (Hershfield et al., 2011). Additionally, episodic simulation, or imagining a specific situation, such as helping a person, increases the intensions to help others (Gaesser & Schacter, 2014), while having imaginary companions in childhood is linked with greater social understanding (Taylor et al., 2004).

The study of imagination has been discussed in clinical literature. Imagination is reported to be linked with clinical outcomes and at the same time is used to treat health outcomes. For example, mental imagery is the hallmark of symptomatology in people with posttraumatic stress disorder (PTSD; American Psychiatric Association, 2000) and also occurs in people with social phobia (Hackmann & Holmes, 2004) and substance abuse (Kavanagh et al., 2001). In terms of treatment, imagination is used in imaginal exposure (Foa et al., 1980) and systematic desensitization in psychotherapy (Wolpe, 1958). Other types of psychotherapeutic methods that involve imagination are autogenic training for biofeedback (Zitman et al., 1992) and virtual reality (Vincelli, 1999).

Wide variation in the reported vividness of mental imagery recently led to the discovery that some people are unable to voluntarily conjure up mental images in their mind's eye; this was termed *aphantasia* (Zeeman et al., 2015). People with aphantasia are reported to experience very low sensory and phenomenal imagery but have intact metacognition (Keogh & Pearson, 2018).

One of the challenges of studying imagination is the apparent subjectivity of mental imagery. However, studies from neuroscience show neurophysiological underpinnings are associated with some aspects of imagination. For example, subjectively reported vividness of mental imagery is correlated with activity in the early visual cortex (Cui et al., 2007), indicating some objective reliability of reported imagery.

Assessment Instruments

There are now numerous instruments available for measuring individual differences in imagination, some performance-based, others self-reported. Additionally, some instruments target typical imaginative practices and experiences (e.g., The Four-Factor Imagination Scale, Zabelina & Condon, 2020), while others focus more strongly on the intensity of imagination (e.g., Vividness of Visual Imagery Questionnaire, Marks, 1973.)

A summary of the instruments and their psychometric properties can be found in Table 22.1.

Imaginal Processing Inventory (IPI)

The IPI (Singer & Antrobus, 1963, 1966) consists of 344 items and comprises 28 scales measuring aspects of daydreaming. The scales of the IPI include (1) Daydreaming frequency, (2) Nightdreaming frequency, (3) Absorption in daydreaming, (4) Acceptance of daydreaming; (5) Positive reactions in daydreaming; (6) Frightened reactions to daydreaming, (7) Visual imagery in daydreams, (8) Auditory imagery in daydreams, (9) Problem-solving daydreams, (10) Present orientation in daydreams, (11) Future orientation in daydreams, (12) Past orientation in daydreams, (13) Bizarre-improbable daydreams, (14) Mind wandering, (15) Achievement-oriented daydreams, (16) Hallucinatory vividness of daydreams, (17) Fear of failure daydreams, (18) Hostile daydreams, (19) Sexual daydreams, (20) Heroic daydreams, (21) Guilt daydreams, (22) Interpersonal curiosity, (23) Impersonal mechanical curiosity, (24) Boredom susceptibility, (25) Mentation rate, (26) Distractibility, (27) Need for external stimulation, and (28) Selfrevelation.

The IPI is a comprehensive measure, although its length may preclude its use in some circumstances (completion of the entire instrument is estimated to be around 1 hour). Psychometric properties of the IPA are reported in Huba (1980). The internal consist-

Table 22.1. A summary of imagination instruments and their psychometric properties

Instrument • Subscales	**Author(s)**	**Number of items**	**Psychometric properties**
Imaginal Processing Inventory (IPI) • 28 subscales	Singer & Antrobus (1966, Revised 1970)	344	Internal consistency: $\alpha = .70–.90$
Short Imaginal Processing Inventory (SIPI) • Positive-constructive daydreaming • Guilt and fear of failure daydreaming • Poor attentional control	Huba et al. (1982)	45	Internal consistency: $\alpha = .80–.83$
Vividness of Visual Imagery Questionnaire (VVIQ)	Marks (1973)	16	Test-retest reliability: $r = .74$ Split-half consistency: $r = .85$
Tellegen Absorption Scale (TAS) • Absorption • Dissociative amnesia • Attentional dissociation	Tellegen & Atkinson (1974)	34	Internal consistency: $\alpha = .88$ Test-retest reliability: $r = .91$
Movement Imagery Questionnaire (MIQ) • Visual subscale • Kinesthetic subscale	Hall & Pongrac (1983)	18	Internal consistency: $\alpha = .87–.91$ Test-retest reliability: $r = .83$
Sport Imagery Questionnaire (SIQ) • Motivational-specific • Motivational-general-arousal • Cognitive-specific • Cognitive-general • Motivational-general-mastery	Hall et al. (1998)	46	Internal consistency: $\alpha = .70–.88$
Creative Experiences Questionnaire (CEQ)	Merckelbach et al. (2001)	25	Internal consistency: $\alpha = .72$ Test-retest reliability: $r = .95$ Criterion validity: $r = .47–.70$
The Kinesthetic and Visual Imagery Questionnaire (KVIQ) • Kinesthetic • Visual	Malouin et al. (2007)	20	Internal consistency: $\alpha = .87–.94$ Test-retest reliability: ICC = .72–.90

Table 22.1. continued

Instrument • Subscales	**Author(s)**	**Number of items**	**Psychometric properties**
Test of Creative Imagery Abilities (TCIA) • Vividness • Originality • Transformativeness	Jankowska & Karwowski (2015)	7	Internal consistency: α = .83–.87 Test-retest reliability: α = .43–.98 Criterion validity: r = .31–.42 Discriminant validity: r = .08–29
Hunter Imagination Questionnaire (HIQ)	Jung et al. (2016)	10	Internal consistency: α = .76–.79 Concurrent validity: r = .26–.31
Self-Descriptive Imagination Questionnaire (SIQ) • Expressive imagination • Openness to variations • Instrumental imagination • Past/future mindedness • Conventionality	Feng et al. (2017)	25	None available
The Fantasy Questionnaire (FQ) • Imaginative fantasy • Creative fantasy	Weibel et al. (2018)	27	Internal consistency: α = .88–.90 Test-retest reliability: r = .79–.82 Convergent validity: r = .42–.70 Discriminant validity: r = –.13–.18
The Four-Factor Imagination Scale (FFIS) • Frequency • Complexity • Emotional Valence • Directedness	Zabelina & Condon (2020)	26	Internal consistency: α = .76–.93 Convergent validity: r = .32–.48 Discriminant validity: r = .05–.12
Imaginative Behaviour Engagement Scale (IBES)	von Stumm & Scott (2019)	14	Internal consistency: α = .77–.82 Test-retest reliability: r = .88 Convergent validity: r = .26–.51

Note. α = Cronbach's α; ICC = intraclass correlation coefficient.

ency of the IPI's subscales ranges from α=.70–.90. Other scale and item information can be found in Giambra (1974, 1977, 1980). Items on the Visual Images in Daydreams may be the most closely related to the construct of imagination. Example items in this subscale include "The visual images in my daydreams are so vivid, I believe that they are actually happening" and "Visual scenes are an important part of my daydreams." Items are answered on a 5-point Likert-type scale from A=*definitely not true* to E=*very true.*

Short Imaginal Processing Inventory (SIPI)

The SIPI (Huba et al., 1982) consists of 45 items and is a shortened version of the IPI (Singer & Antrobus, 1963). It was designed to measure aspects of one's inner experience, including daydreaming style and content. The three subscales of the SIPI are (1) Positive-constructive daydreaming, (2) Guilt and fear of failure daydreaming, and (3) Poor attentional control. Positive-constructive daydreaming is the subscale that appears to most closely assess imaginative abilities, with sample items including "Pictures in my mind are as clear as photographs" and "I seldom think about the future." The internal consistency for the three subscales ranges between α=.80–.83. Items are answered on a Likert-type scale from 1=*definitely untrue or strongly uncharacteristic of me* to 5=*very true or strongly characteristic of me.*

Vividness of Visual Imagery Questionnaire (VVIQ)

The VVIQ (Marks, 1973) was developed to examine to what extent one can visualize familiar items or scenes. The instrument consists of 4 items, with 4 questions per item. The items are relative or a friend, rising sun, a familiar shop, and a country scene. Participants are asked to self-assess to what extent they can visualize these items on a 5-point Likert-type scale from 1=*perfectly clear and as vivid as normal vision* to 5=*No image at all, you only "know" that you are thinking of the object*. The test-retest reliability coefficient of the VVIQ is r=.74 (timespan not reported), and the split-half reliability coefficient is r=.85.

Tellegen Absorption Scale (TAS)

The TAS (Tellegen & Atkinson, 1974), although not tapping the imagination construct per se, examines the degree to which people find themselves absorbed in their perceptual or imaginative experiences. The TAS comprises 34 items and three subscales: Absorption, Dissociative amnesia, and Attentional dissociation. The Absorption subscale in particular taps into fantasy, or imagination, although its focus remains on how absorbed one tends to be in one's fantasies. For example, the TAS item "If I wish, I can imagine (or daydream) some things so vividly that they hold my attention in the way a good movie or story does" prioritizes the holding of attention, conflating vividness of imagination and absorption in it. Items are scored on a Likert-type scale ranging from 0=*never* to 4=*always*. Internal consistency of the TAS is α=.88, with the average interitem correlation r=.37 and 30-day test-retest reliability r=.91 (Kihlstrom et al., 1989; Tellegen, 1982), although see Carleton et al. (2010) for updated psychometric properties.

Movement Imagery Questionnaire (MIQ)

The MIQ (Hall & Pongrac, 1983) was developed to measure imagery of movement and consists of visual and kinesthetic subscales. Each of the 18 items on the MIQ asks a question about a specific movement involving arm, leg, and whole-body movements. On the MIQ, participants are initially asked to physically assume a given position and then produce a specified movement. Following this, participants are asked to reassume the starting position and imagine producing the same movement. They are then instructed to indicate to what extent they were able to image each movement on a 7-point Likert-type scale, where lower scores indicate that the movement was easy to imagine and higher scores indicate that it was difficult to imagine. The MIQ reports a good internal consistency of $\alpha=.87$ for the visual subscale and $\alpha=.91$ for the kinesthetic subscale. The one-week test-retest reliability is $r=.83$.

Sport Imagery Questionnaire (SIQ)

The SIQ (Hall et al., 1998) was designed to measure motivational and cognitive functions of imagery. The SIQ consists of 46 items and five separate factors: Motivational-specific (e.g., "I imagine the audience applauding my performance"), Motivational-general-arousal (e.g., "When I imagine a competition, I feel myself getting emotionally excited"), Cognitive-specific ("I can easily change an image of a skill"), Cognitive-general ("I imagine alternative strategies in case my event/game plan fails"), and Motivational-general-mastery ("I imagine myself being in control in difficult situations"). Responses are indicated on a 7-point Likert-type scale from 1=*rarely* to 7=*often*. Internal consistency of each scale is: $\alpha=.88$, $\alpha=.85$, $\alpha=.83$, $\alpha=.75$, and $\alpha=.70$, respectively. Predictive validity was supported in that higher imagery scores on the SIQ correlate with successful athletic performance.

Creative Experiences Questionnaire (CEQ)

The CEQ (Merckelbach et al., 2001) is a 25-item measure of proneness to fantasy. Example items are "As a child, I thought that the dolls, teddy bears, and stuffed animals that I played with were living creatures" and "Many of my fantasies are often just as lively as a good movie." Items are answered on a binary *yes/no* scale. The CEQ has good test-retest reliability over 6 weeks of $r=.95$ and internal consistency of $\alpha=.72$. The CEQ shows convergent validity with measures of absorption $r=.70$ and dissociation $r=.47$–$.63$.

Kinesthetic and Visual Imagery Questionnaire (KVIQ)

The KVIQ (Malouin et al., 2007) was designed to assess motor imagery in patients after stroke. Items consist of simple movements, such as foot tapping and shoulder flexion. The KVIQ uses a 5-point Likert-type scale to assess the clarity of the image (visual: V subscale) and the intensity of the sensation (kinesthetic: K subscale). The longer version of the KVIQ is comprised of 20 items, and the shorter version is comprised of 10 items. Internal consistency of the KVIQ-20 is $\alpha=.94$ (V) and $\alpha=.92$ (K), and internal consistency of the KVIQ-10 is α=.89 (V) and α=.87 (K). Test-retest reliabilities over 7–14 days are ICC=.72–.81 for healthy participants, and ICC=.81–.90 for people who had a stroke.

Test of Creative Imagery Abilities (TCIA)

The TCIA (Jankowska & Karwowski, 2015) is a performance-based measure of people's creative imagery abilities. Administering the TCIA involves three consecutive stages. In the first stage, participants are instructed to generate images from seven incomplete figures. Upon completion, they select the most original and draw a complete drawing accompanied by a description. Participants are encouraged to elaborate and transform their images even further. Finally, in an interview, they are questioned about their drawing. The test has two versions (A and B), is unlimited in time, and typically takes around 20 min to complete.

The TCIA was designed to bridge creativity and imagination constructs and is scored on three unrelated components: Vividness, which measures people's ability to visualize images that are complex and detailed; Originality, which measures the extent to which the visualized images are original or unique; and Transformativeness, which assesses the ability for controlling one's visualized images. The criterion validity for the TCIA with the VVIQ (Marks, 1973) measure is between r=.31–.42, discriminant validity against measures of IQ is r=.29 for Vividness, r=.10 for Originality, and r=.08 for Transformativeness. The interjudge consistency for the three components ranges between ICC=.89–.91. Finally, the 3-week test-retest reliabilities are between r=.43–.98, and internal consistency ranges between r=.83–.87.

Hunter Imagination Questionnaire (HIQ)

The HIQ (Jung et al., 2016) was designed to assess imagination over time and is completed over the time course of four different sessions (3–7 days apart). In Session 1, participants are asked to write down what they would like to "do, make, create, or achieve in the next few months." In Session 2, participants are asked to visualize a scene that invokes their senses. Session 3 asks participants to imagine what they would like to invent, discover, or change. Finally, Session 4 (like Session 1) asks participants what they would like to "do, make, create, or achieve in the next few months." Participants are given 8 min to make their responses in all four sessions, and the time between each session ranges between 3–7 days. Finally, participants are asked to select three of their best ideas and rate them on a series of 10 items on a scale from 1–10 (anchors depend on each question). Examples of items include "How passionate or engaged are you with the ideas you generated?" and "Are you satisfied with the number of ideas you generated?" The internal consistency of the HIQ ranges from α=.76–.79, and concurrent validity against the Creative Achievement Questionnaire (CAQ; Carson et al., 2005) is r=.31 for creative achievements in writing and r=.26 for creative achievements in the scientific domains.

Self-Descriptive Imagination Questionnaire (SIQ)

The SIQ (Feng et al., 2017) describes five features of imagination, namely, expressive imagination, openness to variations, instrumental imagination, past/future mindedness, and conventionality. It is a 25-item instrument that is answered on a 7-point Likert-type scale from 1=*not at all* to 7=*absolutely*. The central factor, expressive imagination, includes items such as "I like to take seemingly unrelated elements (characters, objects, ideas) and put them together in a story," and "I often have vivid and interesting dreams in color." Psychometric properties of the SIQ are reported.

Fantasy Questionnaire (FQ)

The FQ (Weibel et al., 2018) is a 27-item instrument that assesses individual differences in proneness to fantasy. Its two subscales are Imaginative Fantasy and Creative Fantasy. Imaginative Fantasy surveys people's tendency for vivid imagination and absorption. Sample items include "Many of my fantasies have a realistic intensity" and "When I read a book, the feelings of the character with whom I identify influence my own mood." Creative Fantasy surveys the tendency for using fantasy to create new ideas. Sample items include "Sometimes I think about new inventions" and "My ideas are usually considered as very creative." All items are answered on a Likert-type scale from 1=*strongly disagree* to 5=*strongly agree*.

The FQ has good psychometric properties. Its internal consistency is α=.88 for Imaginative Fantasy and α=.90 for Creative Fantasy. The 12-week test-retest reliability is r=.79 for the Imaginative Fantasy and r=.82 for the Creative Fantasy. Both subscales show good convergent validity with the personality trait of openness to experience (Costa & McCrae 1992): Imaginative Fantasy r=.53 and Creative Fantasy r=.62; the TAS (Tellegen & Atkinson, 1974): Imaginative Fantasy r=.70 and Creative Fantasy r=.58; and against the VVIQ (Marks, 1973): Imaginative Fantasy r=.42 and Creative Fantasy r=.32. The FQ also has good discriminant validity against the personality traits of extraversion (r=.18), and agreeableness (r=–.13). Normative data for different age groups for the two subscales are provided by the test developers (Weibel et al., 2018). For example, for respondents between 21–30 years, the mean score for the Imaginative Fantasy subscales is 3.24 (SD=.63), and the mean score for the Creative fantasy subscale is 3.31 (SD=.70; see Weibel et al., 2018 for the detailed normative data for the FQ).

Four-Factor Imagination Scale (FFIS)

The FFIS (Zabelina & Condon, 2020) is a 26-item scale that encompasses four features of the imaginative process, including (1) frequency – how much time an individual spends in an imaginative state; (2) complexity – how vivid or detailed someone's imagination tends to be; (3) emotional valence – the extent to which one's imaginings are largely positively or negatively valenced; and (4) directedness – the degree to which imaginings are oriented toward specific goals or outcomes, or are nondirected. Example items include: "I am lost in imagination most of the time" (Frequency), "My fantasies are less detailed than most peoples'" (Complexity – reverse-scored), "Imagining my future makes me feel blue" (Emotional Valence), "My daydreams have a clear goal" (Directedness).

The FFIS has good internal consistency of α=.87 (α=.76–.93 for the subscales). The Frequency subscale shows good convergent validity with the personality trait of openness to experience (r=.32). Complexity of imagination has good convergent validity with openness (r=.40) and with creativity (r=.37). Emotional valence has good convergent validity with neuroticism (r=.48). The FISS has good discriminant validity showing low associations with measures of intellectual abilities, where the highest correlations were with Complexity (r=.05–.12).

Imaginative Behaviour Engagement Scale (IBES)

The IBES (von Stumm & Scott, 2019) surveys typical imaginative behaviors, such as having an imaginary childhood friend ("Did you have one or more imaginary friend(s) as a child?) or becoming immersed in the story when watching a film ("When you watch a good movie, do you become immersed in the story as if you were part of it?"). Responses are made on a 5-item scale, with different anchors for each item.

The 3-week test-retest reliability for IBES is r=.88, and Cronbach's alphas range between α=.77–.82. The IBES shows good convergent validity with the personality trait of openness to experience (r=.26–.42), and with some creativity measures (e.g., with Runco Ideation Behavior Scale, r=.51), but not with others (divergent thinking, r=.01–.12).

Key Research Findings on the Described Measures

The Positive-Constructive Daydreaming subfactor of the SIPI (Huba et al., 1982) has been shown to relate to increased enjoyment of thinking, while Poor Attentional Control is associated with decreased enjoyment of thinking (Wilson et al., 2014). Further, Poor Attentional Control is elevated in people with a diagnosis of depersonalization disorder (DPD) – a dissociative disorder characterized by feelings of detachment and significant distress – compared to control participants (Levin et al., 2004). The Guilt and Fear of Failure Daydreaming subscale was reported to relate to increased instances of having nightmares (Levin & Fireman, 2001), while Positive-Constructive Daydreaming related to increased dream recall frequency and dream saliency (Levin & Young, 2002). Finally, engagement in videogame activities was positively correlated with Positive-Constructive Daydreaming (Dauphin & Heller, 2010).

When examining the ability to discriminate between memories derived from two sources of information while watching a film of a crime, people with higher (vs. lower) scores on the VVIQ (Marks, 1973) were found to make more source monitoring errors (Dobson & Markham, 1993), suggesting that vivid imagery may serve a role in eyewitness testimony. In another study investigating the link between imagination and physiological activity, people with higher scores on the VVIQ showed greater physiological activity during affective and action-oriented imagery, with the pattern of physiological activity varying depending on the imagery script (e.g., action, fear, anger; Miller et al., 1987).

The neuroimaging literature provides evidence for deactivation of the auditory cortex and increased activation of the visual cortex in participants with higher VVIQ scores during visual imagery (Amedi et al., 2005), suggesting that pure visual imagery, especially in people with a vivid imagination, relates to isolated activation of the visual cortical regions, while other "irrelevant" cortical areas go offline. Finally, ratings of vividness of imagery were linked with neural activity in the right lateral occipital complex during haptic imagery, whereas overall haptic imagery tended to activate bilateral parietal areas (Zhang et al., 2004).

Absorption as measured by the TAS (Tellegen & Atkinson, 1974) tends to correlate with several different constructs, including imagery, paranormal experiences, and synesthesia (Roche & McConkey, 1990) as well as with the childhood memories and imaginings (Lynn & Rhue, 1986). People scoring higher on the TAS reported being less bored in general and were more likely to keep themselves interested and entertained (Seib & Vodanovich, 1998).

In a study examining learning and retention of movements, participants scoring higher (vs. lower) on the MIQ (Hall & Pongrac, 1983) were quicker to learn new movements but were no more likely to remember the movements 2 days later (Goss et al., 1986).

Studies from the sports psychology literature show that people with higher scores on the SIQ (Hall et al., 1998) are more likely to experience benefits from sports imagery practice (Goss et al., 1986), although other studies present contradicting evidence (Corlett et al., 1989; Yágüez et al., 1998).

The CEQ (Merckelbach et al., 2001) was found to be correlated with the severity of delusions in a sample of patients with schizophrenia and Bipolar I disorder as well as in healthy controls (Tan et al., 2019). There was also a link between elevated scores on the CEQ and higher reported distress and preoccupation in patients only. Further, people with higher scores on the CEQ tended to have higher levels of emotional distress and maladaptive coping strategies, and they were more likely to ruminate and catastrophize to a greater degree (Bacon & Charlesford, 2018). In addition, higher CEQ scores correlated with several adaptive outcomes, including planning and positive reappraisal. In women who had suffered sexual abuse, higher CEQ scores were linked with higher instances of false recall and false recognition of both neutral and trauma-related critical lures on the Deese-Roediger-McDermott (DRM) paradigm (Geraerts et al., 2005).

The KVIQ (Malouin et al., 2007) was used to evaluate stroke patients and control participants (Malouin et al., 2008). Both groups showed higher visual than kinesthetic scores. In stroke patients, visual scores were higher when imagining upper limb movements on the unaffected side (vs. affected side), while kinesthetic scores were higher when imagining lower limb movements on the unaffected (vs. affected) side. Results suggest that overall motor imagery remains similar in poststroke patients compared to control participants, although in poststroke patients motor imagery is no longer symmetrical.

The TCIA (Jankowska & Karwowski, 2015) was used to examine the role of imagination in friendships. It was found that students with higher scores on the TCIA were more likely to be nominated as a friend by their peers (McKay et al., 2017), and students with similar scores on the TCIA were more likely to be friends.

The HIQ (Jung et al., 2016) and its subfactors were found to be linked with the anatomical brain regions that were previously implicated in imagination, namely, the bilateral hippocampi, lingual gyrus, and caudal/rostral middle frontal lobe, and with decreased volumes within the nucleus accumbens and regions within the default mode network (Jung et al., 2016).

Differences in imagination across three different countries were evaluated using the SIQ (Feng et al., 2017). Expressive imagination was found to be the highest in the Chinese sample, followed by the North American sample, and the sample from Germany (Feng et al., 2017). Openness to variations was highest in the North American sample and lowest in the Chinese sample. Instrumental imagination was highest in the German sample and lowest in the Chinese sample. Past/future mindedness was highest in the North American sample compared to the other two groups. Finally, Conventionality was highest in the Chinese sample compared to the other two groups.

To date, only one study has been published employing the FQ (Weibel et al., 2018), reporting no association between FQ scores and emotional distress (Bacon & Charlesford, 2018).

Several correlates of imagination were reported during the development of the FFIS (Zabelina & Condon, 2020). People who reported a higher frequency of imagination on the FFIS tended to be higher in introspection, anxiety, and impulsivity as well as in creativity and art appreciation, and lower in well-being and emotional stability. They also tended to be younger and have lower socioeconomic status. The complexity of imagination was related to introspection and conformity as well as to creativity and art appreciation. Negative emotional valence of imagination was related to lower levels of well-being, emotional stability, charisma, adaptability, sociability, honesty, and trust, and to higher levels of anxiety and irritability and higher art appreciation. Interestingly, the emotional valence of imagination was also linked with several health outcomes, most notably with worse overall health, lower exercise frequency, poorer sleep quality, and higher levels of stress. Finally, the directedness of imagination was related to higher levels of perfectionism, introspection, and creativity. There were no significant links between the FFIS subscales and biological sex.

The IBES (von Stumm & Scott, 2019) was found to be linked with the schizotypal personality trait, accounting for 22% of the variance, as well as a strong relationship with self-reported measures of creativity. The IBES showed weak associations with performance measures of creativity, such as divergent thinking.

Recommendations for Instrument Selection

The scientific interest in the study of imagination is relatively recent, spearheaded by the Imagination Institute (http://www.imagination-institute.org), although related constructs of fantasy, absorption, and daydreaming have been of interest to psychologists since the late 19th century (Galton, 1880; James, 1890). To date, several instruments have been developed for examining individual differences in various features of imagination. As Table 22.1 shows, some of the imagination instruments have good psychometric properties, although others are missing evaluations of construct validity, including factorial, content, convergent and/or discriminant validity, making it difficult to confirm whether or not they truly measure imagination. For the SIQ (Feng et al., 2017), the psychometric properties were not reported altogether by test developers.

For a comprehensive measure of imagination, the IPI (Singer & Angrobus, 1970) remains a useful tool, although both researchers and participants need to be prepared to spend around 1 hour to complete its 344 questions. Alternatively, for a quicker and more easily-accessible version of the IPI, one can employ the SIPI (Huba et al., 1982), in which the Positive-Constructive Daydreaming subfactor is the most relevant for the study of imagination. If the goal is to examine vividness of visual imagery of familiar scenes, rather than imagination of novel scenes, the VVIQ (Marks, 1973) is a useful and popular measure. If the goal is to examine absorption in one's daydreams, the TAS (Tellegen & Atkinson, 1974) is a suitable instrument.

There are several motor imagery instruments. For example, if interested in examining motor imagery in sports, researchers should use the MIQ (Hall & Pongrac, 1983) or the SIQ (Hall et al., 1998), while the KVIQ (Malouin et al., 2007) is well suited for the study of imagination in poststroke patients.

The HIQ (Jung et al., 2016) is a suitable instrument for studying imagination over time (4 separate sessions, 3–7 days apart), while the TCIA (Jankowska & Karwowski, 2015) is a performance-based measure of imagination that differentiates between vividness, originality, and transformativeness of one's imagination. It should be noted that the vividness factor of the TCIA reflects the ability for persistent and thorough work and has been shown to correlate with intelligence and the achievement test scores in math and reading.

For shorter, easy-to-administer self-report measures of imagination and related constructs, the following measures should be employed: The SIQ (Feng et al., 2017) – the Expressive Imagination subscale is especially relevant, although its use is contingent on the ability of future studies to support its reliability and validity; the FQ (Weibel et al., 2018) – both the imaginative and the creative fantasy subscales; the FFIS (Zabelina & Condon, 2020) – if the goal is to distinguish between frequency, complexity, emotional valence, and directedness of imagination; and the IBES (von Stumm & Scott, 2019) for typical imaginative behaviors.

Conclusion and Future Directions

Empirical investigations of imagination are on the rise, with several new instruments having been developed in recent years. The primary focus of many of these instruments remains on visual imagery or visual imagination. Imagination, however, is multifaceted and includes other senses, so developers of future instruments need to consider the other features of imagination as well as imagination that involves other senses, including auditory, olfactory, gustatory, and tactile imagination. Further, relationships between imagination and other constructs, such as cognitive abilities, should be examined in future investigations. Finally, the evaluation of construct validity of the existing measures is a worthwhile direction for future research.

References

Amedi, A., Malach, R., & Pascual-Leone, A. (2005). Negative BOLD differentiates visual imagery and perception. *Neuron, 48*(5), 859–872. https://doi.org/10.1016/j.neuron.2005.10.032

American Psychiatric Association. (2000). *Diagnostic and statistical manual of mental disorders* (4th ed., text rev.). Author.

Arcavi, A. (2003). The role of visual representations in the learning of mathematics. *Educational Studies in Mathematics, 52*(3), 215–241. https://doi.org/10.1023/A:1024312321077

Bacon, A. M., & Charlesford, J. J. (2018). Investigating the association between fantasy proneness and emotional distress: the mediating role of cognitive coping strategies. *Personality and Individual Differences, 135*, 157–165. https://doi.org/10.1016/j.paid.2018.07.003

Carleton, R. N., Abrams, M. P., & Asmundson, G. J. G. (2010). The Attentional Resource Allocation Scale (ARAS): Psychometric properties of a composite measure for dissociation and absorption. *Depression and Anxiety, 27*(8), 775–786. https://doi.org/10.1002/da.20656

Carson, S. H., Peterson, J. B., & Higgins, D. M. (2005). Reliability, validity, and factor structure of the creative achievement questionnaire. *Creativity Research Journal, 17,* 37–50. https://doi.org/10.1207/s15326934crj1701_4

Corlett, J. T., Anton, J., Kozub, S., & Tardif, M. (1989). Is locomotor distance estimation guided by visual imagery? *Perceptual and Motor Skills, 69*(3–2), 1267–1272. https://doi.org/10.1177/00315125890693-237

Costa, P., & McCrae, R. R. (1992). *NEO PI-R: Revised NEO Personality Inventory (NEO PI-R)*. Psychological Assessment Resources.

Cui, X., Jeter, C. B., Yang, D., Montague, P. R., & Eagleman, D. M. (2007). Vividness of mental imagery: Individual variability can be measured objectively. *Vision Research, 47*(4), 474–478. https://doi.org/10.1016/j.visres.2006.11.013

Dauphin, B., & Heller, G. (2010). Going to other worlds: The relationships between videogaming, psychological absorption, and daydreaming styles. *Cyberpsychology, Behavior, and Social Networking, 13*(2), 169–172. https://doi.org/10.1089/cyber.2009.0065

Dobson, M., & Markham, R. (1993). Imagery ability and source monitoring: Implications for eyewitness memory. *British Journal of Psychology, 32*, 111–118. https://doi.org/10.1111/j.2044-8295.1993.tb02466.x

Feng, Z., Logan, S., Cupchik, G., Ritterfeld, U., & Gaffin, D. (2017). A cross-cultural exploration of imagination as a process-based concept. *Imagination, Cognition and Personality, 37*(1), 69–94. https://doi.org/10.1177/0276236617712006

Foa, E. B., Steketee, G., Turner, R. M., & Fischer, S. C. (1980). Effects of imaginal exposure to feared disasters in obsessive-compulsive checkers. *Behaviour Research and Therapy, 18*, 449–455. https://doi.org/10.1016/0005-7967(80)90010-8

Gaesser, B., & Schacter, D. L. (2014). Episodic simulation and episodic memory can increase intentions to help others. *Proceedings of the National Academy of Sciences, 111*(12), 4415–4420. https://doi.org/10.1073/pnas.1402461111

Galton, F. (1880). Statistics of mental imagery. *Mind, 5*, 301–318. https://doi.org/10.1093/mind/os-V.19.301

Geraerts, E., Smeets, E., Jelicic, M., van Heerden, J., & Merckelbach, H. (2005). Fantasy proneness, but not self-reported trauma is related to DRM performance of women reporting recovered memories of childhood sexual abuse. *Consciousness and Cognition, 14*(3), 602–612. https://doi.org/10.1016/j.concog.2005.01.006

Giambra, L. M. (1974). Daydreaming across the life span: Late adolescent to senior citizen. *Journal of Aging and Human Development, 5*, 115–140. https://doi.org/10.2190/7AEJ-T3MA-QLGD-CCF5

Giambra, L. M. (1977). A factor analytic study of daydreaming, imaginal process, and temperament: A replication on an adult male life span sample. *Journal of Gerontology, 32,* 675–680. https://doi.org/10.1093/geronj/32.6.675

Giambra, L. M. (1980). A factor analysis of the items of the Imaginal Processes Inventory. *Journal of Clinical Psychology, 36*, 383–409. https://doi.org/10.1002/jclp.6120360203

Goss, S., Hall, C., Buckolz, E., & Fishburne, G. (1986). Imagery ability and the acquisition and retention of movements. *Memory & Cognition, 14*(6), 469–477. https://doi.org/10.3758/BF03202518

Hackmann, A., & Holmes, E. A. (2004). Reflecting on imagery: A clinical perspective and overview of the special edition on mental imagery and memory in psychopathology. *Memory, 12*(4), 389–402. https://doi.org/10.1080/09658210444000133

Hall, C. R., Mack, D. E., Paivio, A., & Hausenblas, H. A. (1998). Imagery use by athletes: Development of the Sport Imagery Questionnaire. *International Journal of Sport Psychology, 29,* 73–89.

Hall, C.R., & Pongrac, J. (1983). *Movement imagery Questionnaire*. Faculty of Physical Education, University of Western Ontario.

Hershfield, H.E., Goldstein, D.G., Sharpe, W.F., Fox, J., Yeykelis, L., Carstensen, L.L., & Bailenson, J.N. (2011). Increasing saving behavior through age-progressed renderings of the future self. *Journal of Marketing Research, 48*(SPL), S23–S37. https://doi.org/10.1509/jmkr.48.SPL.S23

Holmes, E.A., & Mathews, A. (2010). Mental imagery in emotion and emotional disorders. *Clinical Psychology Review, 30*(3), 349–362. https://doi.org/10.1016/j.cpr.2010.01.001

Huba, G.J. (1980). Daydreaming. In R.H. Woody (Ed.), *Encyclopedia of clinical assessment*. Jossey-Bass.

Huba, G.J., Singer, J.L., Aneshensel, C.S., & Antrobus, J.S. (1982). *The short imaginal processes inventory*. Research Psychologist Press.

James, W. (1890). *The principles of psychology*. Holt.

Jankowska, D.M., & Karwowski, M. (2015). Measuring creative imagery abilities. *Frontiers in Psychology, 6*, Article 1591. https://doi.org/10.3389/fpsyg.2015.01591

Jung, R.E., Flores, R.A., & Hunter, D. (2016). A new measure of imagination ability: Anatomical brain imaging correlates. *Frontiers in Psychology, 7*, Article 496. https://doi.org/10.3389/fpsyg.2016.00496

Kavanagh, D.J., Freese, S., Andrade, J., & May, J. (2001). Effects of visuospatial tasks on desensitization to emotive memories. *British Journal of Clinical Psychology, 40*(3), 267–280. https://doi.org/10.1348/014466501163689

Keogh, R., & Pearson, J. (2018). The blind mind: No sensory visual imagery in aphantasia. *Cortex, 105*, 53–60. https://doi.org/10.1016/j.cortex.2017.10.012

Kihlstrom, J.F., Register, P.A., Hoyt, I.P., Albright, J.S., Grigorian, E.M., Heindel, W.C., & Morrison, C.R. (1989). Dispositional correlates of hypnosis: A phenomenological approach. *International Journal of Clinical and Experimental Hypnosis, 37*(3), 249–263. https://doi.org/10.1080/00207148908414476

Kosslyn, S.M., Ganis, G., & Thompson, W.L. (2001). Neural foundations of imagery. *Nature Reviews: Neuroscience, 2*(9), 635–642. https://doi.org/10.1038/35090055

LeBoutillier, N., & Marks, D.F. (2003). Mental imagery and creativity: A meta-analytic review study. *British Journal of Psychology, 94*(1), 29–44. https://doi.org/10.1348/000712603762842084

Levin, R., & Fireman, G. (2001). The relation of fantasy proneness, psychological absorption, and imaginative involvement to nightmare prevalence and nightmare distress. *Imagination, Cognition and Personality, 21*(2), 111–129. https://doi.org/10.2190/C11Q-VQAW-G3YH-KCQD

Levin, R., Sirof, B., Simeon, D., & Guralnick, O. (2004). Role of fantasy proneness, imaginative involvement, and psychological absorption in depersonalization disorder. *The Journal of Nervous and Mental Disease, 192*(1), 69–71. https://doi.org/10.1097/01.nmd.0000106003.46153.54

Levin, R., & Young, H. (2002). The relation of waking fantasy to dreaming. *Imagination, Cognition and Personality, 21*(3), 201–219. https://doi.org/10.2190/EYPR-RYH7-2K47-PLJ9

Lynn, S.J., & Rhue, J.W. (1986). The fantasy-prone person: Hypnosis, imagination, and creativity. *Journal of Personality and Social Psychology, 51*, 404–408. https://doi.org/10.1037//0022-3514.51.2.404

Malouin, F., Richards, C.L., Durand, A., & Doyon, J. (2008). Clinical assessment of motor imagery after stroke. *Neurorehabilitation and Neural Repair, 22*(4), 330–340. https://doi.org/10.1177/1545968307313499

Malouin, F., Richards, C.L., Jackson, P.L., Lafleur, M.F., Durand, A., & Doyon, J. (2007). The Kinesthetic and Visual Imagery Questionnaire (KVIQ) for assessing motor imagery in persons with physical disabilities: a reliability and construct validity study. *Journal of Neurologic Physical Therapy, 31*(1), 20–29. https://doi.org/10.1097/01.NPT.0000260567.24122.64

Marks, D.F. (1973). Visual imagery differences in the recall of pictures. *British Journal of Psychology, 64*(1), 17–24. https://doi.org/10.1111/j.2044-8295.1973.tb01322.x

McKay, A.S., Grygiel, P., & Karwowski, M. (2017). Connected to create: A social network analysis of friendship ties and creativity. *Psychology of Aesthetics, Creativity, and the Arts, 11*(3), 284–294. https://doi.org/10.1037/aca0000117

Merckelbach, H., Horselenberg, R., & Muris, P. (2001). The Creative Experiences Questionnaire (CEQ): A brief self-report measure of fantasy proneness. *Personality and Individual Differences, 31*(6), 987–995. https://doi.org/10.1016/S0191-8869(00)00201-4

Miller, G.A., Levin, D.N., Kozak, M.J., Cook III, E.W., McLean Jr, A., & Lang, P.J. (1987). Individual differences in imagery and the psychophysiology of emotion. *Cognition and Emotion, 1*(4), 367–390. https://doi.org/10.1080/02699938708408058

Roche, S.M., & McConkey, K.M. (1990). Absorption: Nature, assessment, and correlates. *Journal of Personality and Social Psychology, 59*(1), 91–101. https://doi.org/10.1037/0022-3514.59.1.91

Sadoski, M., Goetz, E.T., Olivarez Jr, A., Lee, S., & Roberts, N.M. (1990). Imagination in story reading: The role of imagery, verbal recall, story analysis, and processing levels. *Journal of Reading Behavior, 22*(1), 55–70. https://doi.org/10.1080/10862969009547694

Samli, A.C. (2011). *From imagination to innovation: New product development for quality of life*. Springer Science & Business Media.

Seib, H.M., & Vodanovich, S.J. (1998). Cognitive correlates of boredom proneness: The role of private self-consciousness and absorption. *The Journal of Psychology, 132*(6), 642–652. https://doi.org/10.1080/00223989809599295

Singer, J.L., & Antrobus, J.S. (1963). A factor-analytic study of daydreaming and conceptually-related cognitive and personality variables. *Perceptual and Motor Skills, 17*(1), 187–209. https://doi.org/10.2466/pms.1963.17.1.187

Singer, J.L., & Antrobus, J.S. (1966, Revised 1970). *Imaginal Processes Inventory*. Center for Research in Cognition and Affect Graduate Center, City University of New York.

Tan, E.J., Fletcher, K., & Rossell, S.L. (2019). Exploring the relationship between fantasy proneness and delusional beliefs in psychosis and nonclinical individuals. *Psychiatry Research, 272*, 80–85. https://doi.org/10.1016/j.psychres.2018.12.081

Taylor, M., Carlson, S.M., Maring, B.L., Gerow, L., & Charley, C.M. (2004). The characteristics and correlates of fantasy in school-age children: Imaginary companions, impersonation, and social understanding. *Developmental Psychology, 40*(6), 1173–1187. https://doi.org/10.1037/0012-1649.40.6.1173

Tellegen, A. (1982). *Brief manual for the Multidimensional Personality Questionnaire*. Unpublished manuscript, Department of Psychology, University of Minnesota.

Tellegen, A., & Atkinson, G. (1974). Openness to absorbing and self-altering experiences ("absorption"), a trait related to hypnotic susceptibility. *Journal of Abnormal Psychology, 83*(3), 268–277. https://doi.org/10.1037/h0036681

Thomas, D., & Brown, J.S. (2011). *A new culture of learning: Cultivating the imagination for a world of constant change* (Vol. 219). CreateSpace.

Vincelli, F. (1999). From imagination to virtual reality: The future of clinical psychology. *CyberPsychology and Behavior, 2*(3), 241–248. https://doi.org/10.1089/109493199316366

von Stumm, S., & Scott, H. (2019). Imagination links with schizotypal beliefs, not with creativity or learning. *British Journal of Psychology, 110*(4), 707–726. https://doi.org/10.1111/bjop.12369

Weibel, D., Martarelli, C.S., Häberli, D., & Mast, F.W. (2018). The Fantasy Questionnaire: A measure to assess creative and imaginative fantasy. *Journal of Personality Assessment, 100*(4), 431–443. https://doi.org/10.1080/00223891.2017.1331913

Wilson, T.D., & Gilbert, D.T. (2005). Affective forecasting: Knowing what to want. *Current Directions in Psychological Science, 14*(3), 131–134. https://doi.org/10.1111/j.0963-7214.2005.00355.x

Wilson, T.D., Reinhard, D.A., Westgate, E.C., Gilbert, D.T., Ellerbeck, N., Hahn, C., Brown, C.L., & Shaked, A. (2014). Just think: The challenges of the disengaged mind. *Science, 345*(6192), 75–77. https://doi.org/10.1126/science.1250830

Wolpe, J. (1958). *Psychotherapy by reciprocal inhibition*. Stanford University Press.

Yágüez, L., Nagel, D., Hoffman, H., Canavan, A.G.M., Wist, E., & Hömberg, V. (1998). A mental route to motor learning: improving trajectorial kinematics through imagery training. *Behavioural Brain Research, 90*(1), 95–106. https://doi.org/10.1016/S0166-4328(97)00087-9

Zabelina, D.L., & Condon, D.M. (2020). The Four-Factor Imagination (FFIS) Scale: A measure for assessing frequency, complexity, emotional valence, and directedness of imagination. *Psychological Research, 84*, 2287–2299. https://doi.org/10.1007/s00426-019-01227-w

Zeeman, A., Dewar, M., & Della Sala, S. (2015). Lives without imagery: Congenital aphantasia. *Cortex, 73*, 378–380. https://doi.org/10.1016/j.cortex.2015.05.019

Zhang, M., Weisser, V.D., Stilla, R., Prather, S.C., & Sathian, K. (2004). Multisensory cortical processing of object shape and its relation to mental imagery. *Cognitive, Affective, and Behavioral Neuroscience, 4*(2), 251–259. https://doi.org/10.3758/CABN.4.2.251
Zitman, F.G., Van Dyck, R., Spinhoven, P., & Linssen, A.C.G. (1992). Hypnosis and autogenic training in the treatment of tension headaches: a two-phase constructive design study with follow-up. *Journal of Psychosomatic Research, 36*(3), 219–228. https://doi.org/10.1016/0022-3999(92)90086-H

Chapter 23

Assessing Self-Transcendent Experience

David Bryce Yaden[1] and Marianna Graziosi[2]

[1]Department of Psychiatry and Behavioral Sciences, Johns Hopkins University School of Medicine, Baltimore, MD, USA
[2]Department of Clinical Psychology, Hofstra University, Hempstead, NY, USA

In one of positive psychology's founding documents, Seligman and Csikszentmihalyi's *Positive Psychology: An Introduction* (2000), the authors outline three "pillars" of positive psychology: (1) positive institutions, (2) positive traits, and – most relevant for our purposes – (3) *positive states*. The study of positive mental states in the context of a well-being framework allows researchers to examine subjective qualities and outcomes that investigations in exclusively clinical contexts might miss. Research from a positive psychology perspective serves as an important corrective from a purely pathologizing approach and can thus help to illuminate psychological qualities and outcomes related to various positive mental states.

William James pioneered the psychological study of positive mental states by describing them in his classic book *The Varieties of Religious Experience* (1902). That volume includes many dozens of accounts of individuals describing the often (but not always) extremely positive experiences of conversion, personal transformation, and mystical experience. James provides a basis for studying these experiences by setting aside questions of their ultimate metaphysical or theological reality and rather focusing on their precipitating conditions, their subjective qualities, their physiological concomitants, and their outcomes in people's lives.

James (1902) characterized mystical experiences as involving four features: (1) passivity, (2) transiency, (3) a noetic quality, and (4) ineffability. Passivity refers to the feeling that such mental states are overwhelming and cannot generally be brought on in a straightforwardly volitional manner. Transiency refers to their relatively brief duration, generally in the range of seconds and minutes rather than hours or days. The noetic quality refers to a feeling of knowledge that is gained from the experience and/or the sense that the experience was somehow "real" and not merely a delusion. Lastly, ineffability refers to the difficulty of putting such experiences into words that adequately describe the experience. Furthermore, James also describes feelings of unity, self-surrender, and overwhelming positive emotions involved in these experiences. These qualities pose several unique challenges to assessing these states empirically.

Many of the personal accounts of mental states that James (1902) drew on came from earlier work by Edwin Starbuck, a former student of James's who had distributed one of the earliest self-report surveys on this topic. Starbuck published his findings from this self-report survey in *The Psychology of Religion* (1899). Of historical interest, in his earlier 1890 book, *The Principles of Psychology* (the field of psychology's major textbook for many decades), James declared his opposition to (or at least annoyance at) self-report survey methodologies, although James makes an about-face on the subject in the preface of Starbuck's book. James begins by describing his initial doubt about Starbuck's project of measuring the prevalence and subjective qualities of these experiences. This is then followed by James's confession of his own conversion (of sorts) regarding the value of psychometric self-report: "I must say that the results amply justify his own confidence in his methods, and that I feel somewhat ashamed at present of the littleness of my own faith." (Starbuck, 1899, viii)

This method described by James and Starbuck of employing psychometric self-report surveys to gather data on the prevalence, triggers, subjective qualities, and impact of positive mental states formed the most prominent theoretical approach and measurement paradigm in psychology around this topic. Although different particular mental states often have different theoretical and philosophical lineages, which are mentioned as they arise, the Jamesian approach remains central to psychology. James captures this entire area of study in a characteristically descriptive manner:

> "It is our normal waking consciousness, rational consciousness as we call it, is but one special type of consciousness, while all about it, parted from it by the filmiest of screens, there lie potential forms of consciousness entirely different. We may go through life without suspecting their existence; but apply the requisite stimulus, and at a touch they are there in all their completeness, definite types of mentality which probably somewhere have their field of application and adaptation. No account of the universe in its totality can be final which leaves these other forms of consciousness quite discarded. How to regard them is the question – for they are so discontinuous with ordinary consciousness." (James, 1902, p. 388)

The beginning of the contemporary collection of prevalence data on such experiences could be marked by the research of Alister Hardy, a Professor of Zoology at Oxford. Hardy founded The Religious Experience Research Centre at Oxford in 1969 to further the James-Starbuck approach, with an emphasis on large-scale psychometric self-report survey research. Its mission statement was explicit about this aim:

> An extension and development of those pioneer studies of Professor E. D. Starbuck (*The Psychology of Religion: An Empirical Study of the Growth of Religious Consciousness*, 1899) and by William James (*The Varieties of Religious Experience: A Study in Human Nature*, 1902). These classics have never been added to in the same spirit in which they were undertaken. (Hay, 1990, p. 27)

Since then, several single-item measures and multifactorial scales have been created to measure these experiences. These have come primarily from clinical (e.g., depersonalization disorders), religious/spiritual (e.g., religious, spiritual, mystical experiences; RSMEs), and emotion (e.g., awe) literatures in psychology. A primary concern in this area remains that of nomenclature. James himself wrote, "I am willing to accept almost any name" (1902, p. 39) for such experiences. The research literature accordingly ballooned with terms that are roughly equivalent to James's conception of mystical experience – to name only a few:

- religious experiences (James, 1902)
- spiritual experiences (Kass et al., 1991)
- hypoegoic states (Leary & Guadagno, 2011)
- transpersonal experiences (Grof, 1972; Tart, 2006)
- unitary experiences (Newberg & d'Aquili, 2000)
- quantum change (Miller & C'de Baca, 2001)
- sacred moments (Lomax et al., 2011)
- epiphanic experiences (Pawelski, 2012)
- ecstatic experiences (Laski, 1961)
- anomalous experiences (Cardeña et al., 2000)
- near-death experiences (Blackmore, 1996)
- numinous experiences (Jung, 2012)
- peak experiences (Maslow, 1964)
- mystical experiences (Hood et al., 2001; James, 1902; Newberg & d'Aquili, 2008; Wulff, 2000)
- religious, spiritual, and mystical experiences (RSME) (Beauregard, 2011)
- awe (Keltner & Haidt, 2003; Yaden et al., 2019)
- self-transcendent experiences (Yaden et al., 2017)

A review article, entitled "The varieties of self-transcendent experience" (Yaden et al., 2017) attempted to gain clarity on this multiplicity of labels by finding core underlying dimensions and placing these experiences on a common continuum. The authors identify several positive mental states that involve self-loss and/or connectedness. Self-loss refers to a temporary sense of self-diminishment or reduction in self-salience; and in the context of these experiences, connectedness refers to a sense of oneness with the universe as a whole (which may or may not include supernatural concepts). These qualities result from the brute self-report of the phenomenology of these experiences and have yet to be further specified through empirical investigation. The constructs included in this review of self-transcendent experience fulfill the following criteria: (1) they are transient mental states, (2) have been described by their authors as having an aspect of self-loss/connectedness, (3) have items related to self-loss and/or connectedness in scales used to measure them, (4) have generally positive outcomes, and (5) have been cited in the research literature at least several thousand times. Constructs that fit these criteria include mindfulness, flow, and awe as well as peak and mystical experiences.

Yaden et al. (2017) attempt to further the Jamesian framework regarding mystical-type experiences into the domain of contemporary psychological research, while placing rare and often transformative mystical experiences on a continuum with other more common mental states such as flow, mindfulness, and awe. Also, "self-transcendence" has relatively metaphysically neutral connotations, not cueing religious/spiritual beliefs nor negating them. Thus, we use the umbrella term "self-transcendent experience" most often in what follows (for an even more extended discussion, see Yaden & Newberg, 2022).

Relevance

The scientific study of self-transcendent experiences is important for several reasons: (1) their prevalence in the normal population, (2) the unusual manner in which they alter aspects of consciousness, and (3) their psychological impact on those who experience them.

In terms of prevalence, many people seem to have the impression that self-transcendent experiences are rather rare – but this is demonstrably not so. Almost everyone has experienced the mental states of flow, mindfulness, and awe. These are states that some people may experience almost daily. But even more surprising is the prevalence of intense and sometimes life-changing mystical-type experiences. For example, when the following question was posed in the General Social Survey (GSS): "Have you ever felt as though you were close to a powerful spiritual force that seemed to lift you out of yourself?" about 40% of the sample answered in the affirmative (Yamane & Polzer, 1994). When Gallup posed this question: "Would you say that you have had a 'religious or mystical experience' – that is, a moment of sudden religious awakening or insight?" 53% of a US sample reported that they had. The gestalt of the findings from these large-scale survey items supports a ~35% average commonly cited in reviews of the psychology of religious research (Hay, 1990, p. 69; Hood et al., 2009, p. 346). One reason for this somewhat surprisingly high number may be that there is a social taboo against speaking about religious, spiritual, or mystical experiences. Hay (1990) found that between 28% and 44% of those surveyed had never told anyone about their experience.

Self-transcendent experiences, particularly in their more intense manifestations, reveal alterations to several fundamental features of consciousness; in particular, people often report changes to the sense of time, space, and self. Time dilation – the subjective sense of time slowing – has been reported in mental states like awe (Rudd et al., 2012; Yaden et al., 2019). In flow, in contrast, the sense of time appears to speed up (Im & Varma, 2018). In some mystical experiences, time can seem to temporarily disappear completely, leaving the experiencer in a brief yet seemingly timeless moment (Hood et al., 2009). Neurologically, changes to the sense of self and space around an individual may relate to brain regions related to modeling self/other boundaries being temporarily inhibited (Newberg & d'Aquili 2000; Urgesi et al., 2010). That self-transcendent experiences both involve these changes to fundamental aspects of consciousness (time, space, self) and are related to well-being raise deeper questions about the nature of the relationships between certain basic categories of consciousness and well-being.

Perhaps the most important reason for measuring self-transcendent experiences is their psychological impact. Notably, there has been substantial disagreement as to whether the psychological impact of these experiences is positive or negative overall. Freud, for example, described "oceanic feelings of oneness" as neurotic and speculated that such experiences were caused by repressed memories surfacing into consciousness (Freud, 1930). James, on the other hand, provided a qualified endorsement of the positive effects of these experiences, though he did acknowledge that such experiences do sometimes need therapeutic support and can occur amid psychotic states. David Lukoff, a contemporary clinical psychologist, sensibly describes how some such experiences are purely positive, some purely pathological, and some have mixed features (Lukoff et al., 1992). The preponderance of empirical research demonstrates, however, that the incidence of positive experiences vastly outnumbers those associated with or resulting in psychopathology (for an extended discussion, see Yaden et al., 2017). Indeed, these experiences can sometimes consist of the *most* positive experiences in one's entire life (Griffiths et al., 2006, 2008; Miller & Bacag, 2001).

In terms of pathological outcomes, the DSM-5 includes several categories that share some subjective features with some self-transcendent experiences. This is particularly the case in the dissociative cluster of disorders, which can produce substantial suffering and dysfunction. This category is subdivided into depersonalization, involving feelings of being detached from one's mental processes or body; and derealization, in which one's surroundings seem unreal or dream-like and the sense of time changes (American Psychiatric Association, 2013). These symptoms can be exacerbated by stress, negative moods, overstimulating settings, and lack of sleep as well as psychedelic substances. Thus, there appears to be a close connection between dissociative disorders and some superficial qualities of self-transcendent experiences. The DSM-5 acknowledges such a connection, but in the context of cultural sensitivities related to religious or spiritual traditions; it states that "induced experiences of depersonalization/derealization can be a part of meditative practices that are prevalent in many religions and cultures and should not be diagnosed as a disorder." These statements are complicated by the fact that large percentages of the US and UK populations claim to have had spiritual/self-transcendent experiences. Can these kinds of experiences, therefore, be considered culturally normative? The DSM acknowledges that almost half of adults have had at least one episode of depersonalization/derealization, but that persisting episodes that result in suffering and dysfunction are much less common (ranging from .8 % to 2.8 % of the population; American Psychiatric Association, 2013, p. 303). Thus, rather than extrapolating from around 1 % of the population's pathological experiences to define experiences that more than 50 % of the population have had, it may make more sense to treat pathological outcomes as a special case of a more general psychological process.

The framework of positive psychology (Seligman & Csikszentmihalyi, 2000), with its interest in positive states, provides a useful basis for exploring more fine-grained beneficial outcomes. In terms of positive outcomes, most large-scale survey studies of self-transcendent experience report associations with aspects of well-being. Using the Hardy single-item question (described below), Hay (1982) found that most of his sample (61 %) who reported spiritual experiences endorsed feeling peace, happiness, or uplifted. However, this association only held for experiences of God, not for occult experiences (involving ghost experiences or telepathy). Byrd et al. (2000) found that mystical experience (measured by the M-Scale) was associated with subjective well-being in multivariate regression.

Causal evidence regarding positive outcomes from spiritual experience comes from experimental psychopharmacology research using psilocybin. An early study of this kind, the so-called "Good Friday Experiment," involved administering psilocybin to theology students during a church service at Marsh Chapel (Pahnke, 1963). Those in the experimental group reported positive changes to their attitudes about life, other people, and themselves, which persisted for at least 6 months. This preliminary study has now been replicated using a rigorous double-blind, crossover design. Psilocybin has been effectively administered to participants and the effects measured directly after the experiences as well as at 6 and 18 months follow-ups (Griffiths et al., 2006, 2008). As mentioned previously, about two-thirds of the participants reported a self-transcendent experience (as measured by the MEQ). Participants in the psilocybin condition showed significant positive mood changes, altruistic/positive social effects, positive behavior changes, all lasting 6 and 18 months. The positive behavior change was also confirmed by community observers (e.g., neighbors) blind to condition. Perhaps most importantly, about two-thirds of the participants reported that the experience was among the top five most meaningful and spiritually significant experiences of their entire lives.

The psilocybin research paradigm has had substantial success in clinical contexts. Subsequent studies demonstrated the efficacy of psilocybin as an effective treatment for depression, end-of-life anxiety, and addictions (Griffiths et al., 2016; Johnson et al., 2017). Treatment effects in these studies were predicted by the degree to which a participant reports having had a mystical experience, as operationalized by scores on the MEQ (Griffiths et al., 2018; Yaden & Griffiths, 2020), underscoring the importance of research on self-transcendent experiences in this clinical context.

Applications for self-transcendent experiences are advancing more quickly than the research on their efficacy and possible contraindications. Mindfulness, for example, has been shown to effectively help manage stress and pain (Carmody & Baer, 2008; Marchand, 2012). However, some emerging research has shown that serious practitioners may have experiences that are confusing or negative (Britton, 2019). The most potent emerging intervention for well-being as well as for treating several mood disorders (depression) and behavioral disorders (addiction) is the use of the psychoactive substance psilocybin in combination with a supportive therapeutic context. This intervention has been shown to increase mood, meaning, and prosocial behavior (Griffiths et al., 2006, 2008, 2011, 2016, 2018), and its efficacy is predicted by participant scores on a measure of mystical experience. This intervention is posed to make a serious impact on psychiatric practices and much more research is necessary to learn about its therapeutic mechanisms, contraindications, and relationship with well-being (Yaden et al., 2021, 2022).

Assessment Instruments

Empirical assessments of self-transcendent experiences have led to the development of a variety of single-item and multifactorial self-report measures. Tables 23.1 and 23.2 provide the reader with compilations of these self-report instruments.

Table 23.1. Single-item measures for the assessment of self-transcendent experiences

Item	Authors
"Would you say that you have had a 'religious or mystical experience' – that is, a moment of sudden religious awakening or insight?"	Back & Bourque (1970)
"Have you ever felt as though you were close to a powerful spiritual force that seemed to lift you out of yourself?"	Greeley (1974)
"Have you ever been aware of or influenced by a presence or power, whether you call it God or not, which is different from your everyday self?"	Hay & Morisy (1978)
"I have had a profound religious experience or awakening that changed the direction of my life."	Gallup (2003)

Table 23.2. Multifactorial scales for the assessment of self-transcendent experiences

Instrument	Author(s)	Number of items	Factors	Reliability	Validity
The Religious Experience Episodes Measure (REEM)	Hood (1970)	15	Religious experience	$\alpha = .90$	Responses correlate with the Intrinsic Motivation items on the Religious Orientation Scale (ROS) (Hood, 1970)
The Mysticism Scale (M-Scale)	Hood (1975)	32	Introvertive factor Extravertive factor Interpretation factor	$\alpha = .91$ in US ($N = 188$) $\alpha = .83$ in Iran ($N = 187$) (Hood et al., 2001)	Responses correlate with the Intrinsic Motivation items on the ROS, and with the REEM (Hood, 1975)
The Peak Scale	Mathes et al. (1982)	70	Peak experience	KR20 ≥ .92	Scale-times found to correlate with verbal descriptions of peak and mystical experience, as well as with the Absorption Scale, the Being-Values achievement measure, and five subscales of the Personal Orientation Inventory of Self-Actualization (Mathes et al., 1982)
Dissociative Experiences Scale (DES)	Bernstein & Putnam, (1986) Frischholz et al. (1990)	28	Nonpathological absorption Compartmentalization Detachment	Test-retest = 0.84 ($p < .0001$, $N = 26$) (Bernstein & Putnam, 1986)	Found to have construct validity and criterion-referenced validity (see Berenstein & Putnam, 1986)
Index of Core Spiritual Experience (INSPIRIT)	Kass et al. (1991)	7	Personal conviction of the existence of God Perception of an internalized relationship with God	$\alpha = .90$	Correlates with measures of health & positive treatment outcomes (Monod et al., 2011)
The Self-transcendence subscale of the Temperament and Character Inventory (TCI)	Cloninger et al. (1993)	51	Spiritual and religious beliefs Unifying interconnectedness Belief in the supernatural Dissolution of self in experience	$\alpha = .90$	Found to have criterion and convergent validity (see MacDonald & Holland, 2002)

Table 23.2. continued

Instrument	Author(s)	Number of items	Factors	Reliability	Validity
Flow State Scale (FSS)	Jackson & Marsh (1996)	36	Challenge-skill balance Action-awareness merging Clear goals Unambiguous feedback Concentration Sense of control Loss of self-consciousness Transformation of time Autotelic experience	α = .83	Found to have construct validity (Jackson & Marsh, 1996)
5 Dimension Altered States of Consciousness Profile (5D-ASC)	Dittrich et al. (2010)	94	Oceanic Boundlessness Anxious ego dissolution Visionary Restructuraliza-tion Auditory alterations Reduction of vigilance	Psychometrically, un-tested, however, found to be reliable across 43 studies; 591 sessions total (see Studerus et al., 2010)	Translated and widely used in dozens of studies testing the effects of psychoactive drugs on consciousness (Studerus et al., 2010)
The Daily Spiritual Expe-riences Scale (DSES)	Underwood & Teresi/2002)	16	Daily spiritual experience	α = .94	Found to have preliminary construct valid-ity (Underwood & Teresi, 2002)
Toronto Mindfulness Scale (TMS)	Lau et al. (2006)	35	Curiosity Decentering	α = .95	Found to have construct validity, discrimi-nant validity, criterion validity and incre-mental validity (Lau et al., 2006)
The Mystical Experience Questionnaire (MEQ)	Barrett et al. (2015)	30	Mystical Positive mood Transcendence of time & space Ineffability	α = .93	Found to have convergent validity and con-struct validity (MacLean et al., 2012; Barrett et al., 2015)

Table 23.2. continued

Instrument	Author(s)	Number of items	Factors	Reliability	Validity
Sacred Moment Qualities	Pargament et al. (2014)	20	Transcendence Ultimacy Boundlessness Interconnectedness Spiritual emotions	$\alpha = .88$	High predictive validity, correlates with client gains ($r = .63$, $p < .001$), provider gains ($r = .64$, $p < .001$)
The Nondual Awareness Dimensional Assessment (NADA)	Hanley et al. (2018)	13	Self-transcendence Bliss	$\alpha = .93$	Found to have consistent Construct Validity (see Hanley et al., 2018)
The Awe Experience Scale (AWE-S)	Yaden et al. (2019)	61	Vastness Need for accommodation Physiological changes Altered time perception Self-loss Connectedness	Each factor and total scale $\alpha \geq .80$	Found to have convergent and divergent validity (Yaden et al., 2019)

Note. α = Cronbach's α

Single-Item Measures

Hardy et al. (1970) collected written descriptions of religious experience from people living in the UK, along with responses to self-report survey items. The question circulated by these researchers to solicit responses read as follows: "All those who feel they have been conscious of, and perhaps influenced by, some Power, whether called God or not, which may either appear to be beyond their selves or partly, or even entirely, within their being, are asked to write a simple account of their feelings and their effects" (p. 20).

Four major survey questions form the bulk of early data on the prevalence of religious/spiritual forms of self-transcendent experience in the US and the UK (Hood et al., 2009). The first of these questions is a modification of Hardy's original question posed by Hay and Morisy (1978, p. 207), but is referred to as the "Hardy Question":

> "Have you ever been aware of or influenced by a presence or power, whether you call it God or not, which is different from your everyday self?"

About 36 % of a 1,865-person sample taken randomly in the UK agreed with this question (Hay & Morisy, 1978). When this question was posed to a sample of 985 participants in the UK about a decade later, a 48 % affirmative response rate was obtained (Hay & Heald, 1987). Three different samples of Gallup surveys showed similar rates in the US – a 3,232-person study in 1962, a 3,518-person study in 1966, and a 3,168-person study in 1969 yielded affirmative response rates of 21 %, 32 %, and 41 %, respectively (Back & Bourque, 1970). Participants who answered in the affirmative then described their experience in writing. Researchers sorted the answers into several categories: "presence of or help from God (28 %), assistance via prayer (9 %), intervention by a presence not identified as God (13.5 %), presence or help from deceased (9 %), premonitions (10 %), meaningful patterning of events (10 %), and miscellaneous (8 %)" (Hay & Morisy, 1985, p. 217). This analysis begins to hint at the variety of different experiences captured by this question.

The second major survey question was posed by Greeley (1974):

> "Have you ever felt as though you were close to a powerful spiritual force that seemed to lift you out of yourself?"

In a UK sample of 1,865 people, 36 % of the sample responded in the affirmative to this question (Hay & Morisy, 1978). In the US, the General Social Survey (GSS) included this question over several years. When four samples of the GSS collected in the 1980s were combined to create a sample of 5,420 individuals, the affirmative response rate was 40 % (Yamane & Polzer, 1994).

The GSS also included questions on other kinds of anomalous mental states that some consider being spiritual experiences. For example, other questions were about *extrasensory perception* ("Have you ever felt as though you were in touch with someone when they were far away from you?"; *clairvoyance* ("Have you ever seen events that were happening at a great distance as they were happening?"); and *contact with the dead* ("Have you ever felt as though you were in touch with someone who had died?"). In 1989, the prevalence of these experiences was extrasensory perception (58 %), clairvoyance (23 %), and contact with the dead (35 %; Fox, 1992, p. 422). These items tap experiences that many scholars have referred to as "paranormal" or "occult" experiences, but, notably, their prevalence is sometimes higher than more classically conceptualized spiritual experiences.

The third major survey question posed by Back & Bourque (1970, p. 489) reads:

> "Would you say that you have had a 'religious or mystical experience' – that is, a moment of sudden religious awakening or insight?"

A Gallup survey in the US of 1,500 people in 1976 reported an affirmative response rate of 31% (Gallup, 1978). When this question was administered by Gallup in the US to samples of 1,236 in 1990, a 53% affirmative response rate was reported (Yamane & Polzer, 1994).

The fourth major survey item was created by Gallup (2003):

> "I have had a profound religious experience or awakening that changed the direction of my life"

In a sample of 1,509 adults in the US (surveyed randomly by phone), participants were asked the degree to which the item applied to them on a Likert-style scale ranging from 0 (*does not apply at all*) to 5 (*applies completely*). In this sample, 41% responded that the item *applies completely* to them.

The gestalt of the findings from these large-scale survey items supports a ~35% average commonly cited in reviews of research on the topic in the psychology of religion (Hay, 1990, p. 69; Hood et al., 2009, p. 346). Although there is a substantial degree of variability around that figure. For many, the number of people affirming these experiences seems surprisingly high. One explanation for these relatively high numbers may reflect a readiness for individuals with religious or spiritual beliefs to report such experiences, when what they have in mind is something closer to a strongly felt religious/spiritual belief than a religious/spiritual experience in the Jamesian sense. In one study, Hay (1979) obtained a 65% affirmative response rate using the Hay and Morrisey question described above. Follow-up interviews were then conducted with participants, asking them to explain their responses. The researchers then found that the number of affirmative responses dropped to 29% that fit their stricter criteria. This may not be due entirely to issues of belief, however, as Vernon (1968) found that atheists and agnostics affirm having had spiritual experiences, even when the question is phrased using the word "God." This suggests that these questions may be successfully tapping into inner *experiences*, or positive mental states, and not merely religious/spiritual *beliefs*. However, the inclusion of religious/spiritual terminology poses several problems we will return to later in this chapter.

Multifactorial Scale Measures

Mindfulness

The Toronto Mindfulness Scale (TMS; Lau et al., 2006) was designed to capture changes in experience following mindfulness training in both experienced and inexperienced meditators. The scale has 35 Likert-type self-response items, where participants rate the extent to which they agree with statements from 0 (*Not at all*) to 4 (*Very much*). Statements were designed to reflect aspects related to existing definitions of mindfulness, such as: "I experienced myself as separate from my changing thoughts and feelings" (Lau et al., 2006). The scale assesses two factors: (1) Curiosity (toward the present moment) and (2) Decentering (the awareness of "distance or disidentification" with one's thoughts and experience; Lau et al., 2006, p. 1452). Lau et al. found the TMS to have high internal consistency overall ($\alpha = .95$), as well as for each of its two factors (curiosity, $\alpha = .93$; decentering, $\alpha = .91$). The scale has also been found to be valid, with the authors establishing construct validity, discriminant validity, criterion validity, and incremental validity (for a closer look at the validity of the TMS, see Lau et al., 2006).

Flow

The Flow State Scale (FSS; Jackson & Marsh, 1996) was developed to study the experience of flow in settings related to sports and physical activity. Researchers confirmed a 9-factor model of the 36-item FSS, which asks participants to rate the extent of their agreement with statements related to flow experience from 1 (*Strongly disagree*) to 5 (*Strongly agree*). The 9 factors of the FSS are (1) perceptions of Challenge-Skill Balance; (2) a sense of Action-Awareness Merging; (3) having Clear Goals; (4) sources of Unambiguous Feedback; (5) Concentration on Task at hand; (6) Sense of Control; (7) Loss of Self-Consciousness (which is analogous to the self-loss described throughout this chapter); (8) Transformation of Time, or the sense that it is speeding up or slowing down; and (9) Autotelic Experience, which refers to an activity done for its own sake, because it is inherently rewarding (Jackson & Marsh, 1996). Researchers found both the overall scale ($\alpha = .83$) and the nine subscales ($\alpha \geq .80$) to be reliable and provided evidence for the construct validity of the scale (Jackson & Marsh, 1996).

Peak Experience

The Peak Scale (Mathes et al., 1982) contains 70 true-false items related to peak experience as described by Abraham Maslow (1964), with half of the items presented in the affirmative and half of the items presented in the negative. An example of a true or false statement is "I have had an experience which made me extremely happy and, at least temporarily, helped me to appreciate wholeness, unity, and integration to a greater degree than I usually do" (Mathes et al., 1982, p. 97). Mathes et al. (1982) found the scale to have high internal consistency for both men (.94) and women (.92) by using Kuder-Richardson reliabilities because of the binary nature of the scale. In their 1982 paper, these researchers also found items on the Peak Scale to correlate with verbal descriptions of peak experience (Study 2), with the Absorption Scale, and the Being-Values achievement measure (Study 3), with verbal descriptions of peak experience (Study 4), and various subscales of the Personal Orientation Inventory of Self-Actualization (Study 5).

Religious/Spiritual Experience

The Religious Experience Episodes Measure (REEM; Hood, 1970) uses a "literary exemplar" approach. Specifically, the measure involves presenting 15 different accounts from *The Varieties* (James, 1902) and asking participants to indicate the extent to which they have had similar experiences. While this measure has the benefit of drawing from actual accounts of religious/spiritual experience, it does not provide a clear operationalization of a deeply theoretically rooted concept. Instead, it explicitly uses accounts included in *The Varieties* as the construct itself. Most of these experiences explicitly mention religious/spiritual terminology.

The Index of Core Spiritual Experience (INSPIRIT; Kass et al., 1991) was inspired by individuals reporting spiritual experiences in the context of psychotherapy and relaxation practices (Benson, 1975). The authors observed that "Many patients reported what we came to call 'core spiritual experiences'" (Kass et al., 1991, p. 204). The scale explicitly aims to measure experiences rather than beliefs. However, the authors describe the scale as measuring experiences that "convince a person that God exists and evoke feelings of closeness with God" (Kass et al., 1991, p. 205), belying a strong belief-based component. This scale, while covering a wide range of experiences (including items related to experiencing God, angels, communication with a deceased relative, feeling of unity) as well as religious beliefs, practices, and the degree to which the experience led to a belief in God. This scale is thus constructed more like a short survey than a psychometric scale with a diverse array of religious/spiritual experiences and practices (although the Cronbach's alpha of the items is high at .90). This underscores the importance of conceptual and empirically derived distinctions in such scales.

The Daily Spiritual Experiences Scale (DSES; Underwood & Teresi, 2002) was created from a process of interviews and focus groups of people of various belief systems (Christian, Jewish, Muslims, Buddhists, Hindus, agnostics, and atheists). The instructions for this measure are fairly typical: "The list that follows includes items which you may or may not experience, please consider how often you directly have this experience, and try to disregard whether you feel you should or should not have these experiences. Several items use the word God. If this word is not a comfortable one for you, please substitute another idea which calls to mind the divine or holy for you" (Underwood & Teresi, 2002, p. 25). The measure is treated as a single factor, though it includes a diverse array of experiences (God, unity, joy), beliefs (drawing strength from religion/spirituality), and practices (such as prayer). Despite the purported influence of individuals across various belief systems during the creation of the scale, it appears to use specifically monotheistic concepts. Additionally, it includes a couple of mentions of positive emotions in the scale, potentially including an outcome into the measure itself.

The Sacred Moment Qualities (SMQ; Pargament et al., 2014) was designed to capture self-transcendent experiences between therapists and clients. Pargament et al. (2014) describe sacred moments as having five qualities: (1) transcendence, (2) ultimacy (i.e., experiences of "deep truth" (p. 249), (3) boundlessness (or beyond the limitations of time and space), (4) interconnectedness (especially marked by mutuality and caring), and (5) spiritual emotions (which include awe, humility, gratitude, joy, etc.). The SMQ has been found to be highly reliable ($\alpha = .88$; Pargament et al., 2014) and to have high predictive validity, with scores correlating with client gains ($r = .63$, $p < .001$), provider gains ($r = .64$, $p < .001$), and provider well-being ($r = .40$, $p < .01$; Pargament et al., 2014). Research employing the SMQ has found that these transcendent experiences in therapy (i.e., sacred moments) are reported as commonly experienced by providers (Pargament et al., 2014).

Mystical Experience

The Mysticism Scale (M-Scale; Hood 1975) is derived from the chapter in *The Varieties* (James, 1902) on mystical experience as well as Stace's (1960) philosophical elaborations on James's work in his book, *Mysticism and Philosophy*. This scale consists of 32 positively and negatively worded items that describe several subjective qualities, including items related to a perception of unity, timelessness, spacelessness, ineffability, a noetic quality, and positive affect. Participants are asked whether "they have ever had" an experience with these various qualities, thus making the M-Scale a kind of trait measure that differentiates high and low mystical experiencers, as it were. These items clustered into two factors – one measuring feelings related to unity and another related to how the experience is interpreted, particularly regarding religious/spiritual interpretations (Caird, 1988; Reinert & Stifler, 1993), although later factor analyses recommended three factors (Hood et al., 1993; Hood & Williamson, 2000). This three-factor model was confirmed in samples of Christians (Chen et al., 2012), Iranian Muslims (Hood et al., 2001), and Israeli Jews (Lazar & Kravetz, 2005), although slight modifications to the factor structure were observed in crosscultural samples of Tibetan Buddhists (Chen et al., 2011) and Indian Hindus (Anthony et al., 2010). Similar scores were found across each of these cross-cultural samples (Hood, 2016).

The Mystical Experience Questionnaire (MEQ; Barrett et al., 2015; MacLean et al., 2012) was designed as a state scale to measure *recent* instances of mystical experiences elicited in laboratory settings using the psychoactive substance psilocybin. This measure takes its theory from the same sources as the M-Scale (e.g., James, 1902; Stace, 1960) as well as from early research on psychedelic substances at Harvard (Pahnke, 1963). The reverse-scored items used in the M-Scale had been shown to produce substantial method/error variance (Chen et al., 2011) and were therefore removed from this scale. The four factors derived through exploratory and confirmatory factor analysis in this scale include (1) Mystical (including the subjective elements of unity, noetic quality, sacredness), (2) Positive mood, (3) Transcendence of time/space, and (4) Ineffability. The scale initially had 43 items, but a factor analysis led to a 30-item version of the scale that was found to have high internal consistency overall ($\alpha = .83$), with each of the four subscales also having high reliability estimates ($\alpha \geq .80$; MacLean et al., 2012). Additionally, MacLean et al. found that the scale exhibited both convergent validity (correlating with the Hood Mysticism scale) and construct validity. The MEQ has since been used in several psilocybin studies (e.g., Griffiths et al., 2006, 2008, 2011, 2016, 2018). This scale includes religious/spiritual terminology in some items.

The 5-Dimension Altered States of Consciousness Profile (5D-ASC; Dittrich et al., 2010) seeks to measure the departure from ordinary consciousness by having participants rate changes in mood, perception, self-other awareness, and thought processes. The 5D-ASC contains 94 items in total and is divided into five subscales: (1) Oceanic Boundlessness, which assess self-loss alongside changes in affect; (2) Anxious Ego Dissolution, or the degree to which changes in self-control, thoughts, arousal, and anxiety correspond to a sense that the ego has dissolved; (3) Visionary Restructuralization, which refers to perceptual changes and processes (e.g., synesthesia); (4) Auditory Alterations, which measures whether an acoustic experience is altered; and (5) Reduction of Vigilance, which measures changes to alertness (e.g., drowsiness). The questionnaire is typically administered following a session of psychoactive drug administration, at which point participants are asked to rate the degree to which a statement applies to their experience from *No, not more than usually* to *Yes, much more than usually* on a line with no designated scales points beyond these descriptors of the endpoints. The 5D-ASC was originally developed in German but has been translated and widely used in more than dozens of studies testing the effects of various psychoactive drugs on consciousness. The measure has been found to be reliable when evaluated across 43 experimental studies (591 drug sessions total; Studerus et al., 2010).

The Self-Transcendence Subscale of the Temperament and Character Inventory (TCI; Cloninger et al., 1993) operationalizes self-transcendence as a trait-like tendency to both believe and feel that one is part of a larger whole, which is often presented in explicitly spiritual terms (Garcia-Romeu, 2010). In terms of experience, items include "Religious experiences have helped me understand the real purpose of my life," "The moral ideals within me fill my heart with awe and admiration," and "I have had moments of great joy in which I suddenly had a clear, deep feeling of oneness with all that exists." In addition to experiences, the scale also includes mention of practices like prayer, and the experiences often involve belief-based components (e.g., "divine," "spiritual"). This trait-based approach is supported by some other psychometric work arguing that spirituality could be considered a sixth dimension of personality because of its high degree of stability and low correlations with other personality traits (Piedmont, 1999). Recently, MacDonald and Holland (2002) evaluated the psychometric properties of the self-transcendence subscale of the TCI and revised the subscales to center around four factors: (1) Spiritual and Religious Beliefs (SRB), (2) Unifying Interconnectedness (UIC), (3) Belief in the Supernatural (BSN), and (4) Dissolution of Self in Experience (DSE). In a sample of 376 students, researchers found support for the reliability, criterion validity, and convergent validity of the scale, and all but the DSE factor were found to relate to similar constructs (MacDonald & Holland, 2002).

The Nondual Awareness Dimensional Assessment (Hanley et al., 2018) approaches self-transcendent experiences from both a trait and state perspective with the development of two scales: (1) The Nondual Awareness Dimensional Assessment-Trait (NADA-T) and (2) The Nondual Awareness Dimensional Assessment-State (NADA-S). Both scales follow the same factor structure, with the scale capturing two aspects of nondual awareness: (1) Self-transcendence, which involves a sense of oneness with all things both experientially, conceptually, or both; and (2) Bliss, an emotional state that involves extreme joy and boundless love (Hanley et al., 2018). Both the overall scale ($\alpha = .93$) and the two factors were found to be reliable (self-transcendence $\alpha = .94$; bliss $\alpha = .81$). Additionally, the two factors were positively correlated ($r = .62$, $p < .001$; Hanley et al., 2018).

Awe and Self-Transcendence

The Awe Experience Scale (AWE-S; Yaden et al., 2019) was introduced to provide a robust, state measure of awe. The AWE-S includes six factors: (1) Vastness, (2) Need for Accommodation, (3) Physiological Changes, (4) Altered Time Perception, (5) Self-Loss, and (6) Connectedness. Factors measuring Self-Loss and Connectedness were based on theoretical work linking the emotion of awe to mystical experiences because of these shared components (Yaden et al., 2017). The overall measure as well as each factor were found to have high internal consistency ($\alpha \geq .80$), and the AWE-S was found to have both convergent and divergent validity (Yaden et al., 2019). Additionally, the authors of the scale found that each factor of the AWE-S was significantly positively correlated with awe items of the Differential Emotions Scale (mDES) and with awe items of the Dispositional Positive Emotion Scale (D-PES).

In terms of well-being-related measurement, the Connectedness subscale of the Awe Experience Scale may be the most useful as it has been shown to correlate highly with well-being and with mystical experience measures. Notably, this subscale can be converted into a state measure of a recent experience, a measure of a recollected experience, or a trait measure. Items should be randomized when administered and rated on a 7-point scale ranging from strongly disagree to strongly agree.

Brief Presentation of Key Findings

The empirical investigation into the varieties of self-transcendent experiences has provided certain hallmarks that help to distinguish where a given STE could be on the continuum. Proceeding from the more mundane STEs to those that are more intense, we discuss the key findings of each. Taken as a whole, STEs are marked by varying degrees of self-loss, increased sensations of connectedness, are often rated as personally meaningful, and may have pathological manifestations (see Yaden et al., 2017, for a more detailed account of STEs).

The empirical literature approaches mindfulness as present-moment awareness, that is, open and nonjudgmental (Jha et al., 2007; Kabat-Zinn, 1994). A framework of mindfulness offered by Vago and Silbersweig (2012) parses the state into "self-awareness," "self-regulation," and "self-transcendence" (S-ART). Their work into the "self-transcendence" component of S-ART shows that the cultivation of mindfulness corresponds with a reduced sense of self-importance and increases in prosociality and empathy. Additionally, researchers found "decentering" to occur in states of mindfulness, which refers to feeling like the watcher or observer of one's own thoughts (Brown et al., 2007; Hölzel et al., 2011; Vago & Silbersweig, 2012). Mindfulness practitioners occasionally have more intense self-transcendent experiences (Vago & Zeidan, 2016). The state of mindfulness can be cultivated through meditation or mindfulness-based interventions such as mindfulness-based stress reduction (MBSR; Davidson et al., 2003), mindfulness-based cognitive therapy (MBCT; Segal et al., 2013), and mindfulness-based strengths practice (MBSP; Niemiec, 2014). Benefits associated with mindfulness practice include improved self-regulation skills and a greater sense of well-being (Baer, 2003; Davidson & McEwen, 2012; Goyal et al., 2014) as well as increases in prosociality (Condon et al., 2013; Leiberg et al., 2011; Weng et al., 2013).

Csikszentmihalyi (1990) first used the term flow to describe a mental state of complete absorption in a challenging but interesting task. The self-loss involved in a state of flow entails a sense of merging with the task one is engaged in. Common aspects of flow include absorption of attention, diminished sense of self, and feeling time pass faster than usual (Csikszentmihalyi, 1990). People often report positive emotions, such as feeling invigorated and refreshed after the experience (Csikszentmihalyi & LeFevre, 1989; Jackson, 2000; Rogatko, 2009). Research by Peterson, Park, & Seligman (2005) found that participants who scored high in engagement, along with high scores in meaning and pleasure (a combination they call the "full life") scored higher on life satisfaction. This suggests that flow states play a role in the optimal experience, and that this sort of experience is important for cultivating a satisfying life. On the other hand, Csikszentmihalyi (1990) himself describes a downside to flow states, "they can become addictive, at which point the self becomes captive of a certain kind of order" (p. 62). Therefore, while flow states can make human striving more effortless and enjoyable, they also run the risk of interfering with achievement because of their addictive nature, although more work is needed on distinguishing between healthy and potentially maladaptive forms of flow.

Contemporary accounts of awe place it as a self-transcendent positive emotion that is accompanied by perceptual and cognitive changes. Seminal work on awe describes it as having two essential features: (1) perception of vastness and (2) a need for accommodation (Keltner & Haidt, 2003). It is important to note that the "vastness" of awe can be elicited by both literally vast objects, such as expansive nature (Joye & Bolderdijk, 2015; Rudd et al., 2012; Silvia et al., 2015), or figuratively vast objects (e.g., grand theories; Preston & Shin, 2016; Yaden et al., 2016). Subsequent work on awe has isolated other qualities that are associated with awe experience, including the self-loss typical of STEs (Piff et al., 2015; Preston & Shin, 2016), alterations to the sense of time (Rudd et al., 2012; Joye & Dewitte, 2016), increased feelings of connectedness (Yaden et al., 2017), and physiological changes (Shiota et al., 2003, 2011). Awe experience has been found in past research to lead to prosociality (Piff et al., 2015; Prade & Saroglou, 2016), improved mood (Joye & Bolderdijk, 2015), and improved well-being (Anderson et al., 2018; Rudd et al., 2012).

The term *peak experience* has its origin in the work of Abraham Maslow (1964), who used it to describe the transformative or self-transcendent experiences of "self-actualized" persons. Peak experiences tend to involve both intense positive emotions (Panzarella, 1980; Kaufman, 2018) and self-transcendent unity (Davis et al., 1991; Wuthnow, 1978). The self-loss of peak experiences involves self-transcendence and feelings of merging with the universe, although these feelings need not involve references to God or higher powers, though many do (Bucke, 1901; Maslow, 1964). Peak experiences are rare throughout a lifetime, but when they do occur, they correlate with meaning in life (Magen, 1996), well-being (Margoshes & Litt, 1966), and empathy (Olson et al. 1998; Wilson & Spencer, 1990).

Perhaps the most intense type of STE are *mystical experiences*. The hallmark of this variety of STE involves complete self-loss and a unity with one's surroundings that arises out the collapsed boundaries between self and other (Hood, 2002; Newberg & d'Aquili 2000; Stace, 1960). William James (1902) outlines the following qualities of mystical experience in addition to self-loss: transiency, passivity, and a noetic quality. Recent work by Yaden et al. (2017) corroborated this noetic quality of mystical experience, showing that, to the participants who have had these experiences, they indeed feel "real." Substantial work has found that these experiences entail alterations in the perception of space and time (Hood, 1975; MacLean et al., 2012; Newberg & D'Aquili, 2008). Typically, mystical experiences are studied by analyzing the experience of participants who have had them (Hood et al., 2009; James, 1902; Yaden et al., 2015). More recently, however, researchers have attempted to induce mystical experience in the lab using pharmacology (Griffiths et al., 2006, 2008; Streib & Hood, 2016). Mystical experiences have been found to relate to improved perspectives on life and identity, increased meaning in life, improved mood, prosociality, and positive behavior change (Griffiths et al., 2006, 2008; Yaden et al., 2016; Yaden & Griffiths, 2020).

Recommendations for Instrument Selection

The language used in these instruments can result in slightly different findings. In particular, religious and spiritual language may play a substantial role in the measurement of these experiences. Additionally, one must consider whether the measurement of positive states in a given instance should focus on a particular mental state or a dispositional tendency to experience particular mental states, which is trait-like.

The first decision required is whether one wishes to expressly measure religious/spiritual experiences; if so, then the explicit mention of supernatural concepts is desirable. Most of the common items used in the GSS and by Gallup use explicitly religious/spiritual terminology. The REEM appears to measure largely religious experience, with the explicit mention of God. The INSPIRIT and DSES focus on experiences of God, explicitly using that term, though also have items related to "connection" and "unity." The INISPIRT additionally has items related to god, unity, angels, communicating with someone who has died, and experience of a historical spiritual teacher, all in a single factor. The self-transcendence subscale of the Temperament and Character Inventory includes mentions of divinity and a spiritual force.

Mystical experience measures largely, but not entirely, avoiding religious/spiritual language. While the M-Scale and the MEQ emphasize unity experiences, they do include concepts such as "sacredness" and "spiritual." These mystical experience scales are likely impacted by participants' beliefs, systematically lowering scores of nonreligious/spiritual individuals, the impact is likely to be relatively small in magnitude.

If religious/spiritual experiences are not the primary focus of measuring positive mental states, then other measures may be desirable. One option that may capture most, but not all, religious/spiritual experiences yet does not include explicit mention of supernatural concepts is the self-transcendence subscales of the Awe Experience Scale (AWE-S).

The second major decision is whether to focus on states or traits. Different measures are often needed if the focus is a single experience – a state – or a dispositional tendency to have certain kinds of experiences – a trait. Some scales are explicitly designed to measure positive mental states, such as the Mystical Experience Questionnaire (MEQ). Other scales measure traits, such as the Mysticism Scale (M-Scale), the Daily Spiritual Experience Scale (DSES), and the Self-Transcendence subscale of the TCI. Some scales, such as the Self-Transcendence subscale of the AWE-S, can be used as a state or trait scale with a modification to the instructions.

Most of the scales currently used in the literature have several problems. First, scales include multiple types of experiences that appear quite different; we recommend a data-driven differentiation of these various types of experiences as the field advances. Second, scales often include items that refer to triggers or outcomes; we recommend that future measures remove items referring to triggers and outcomes of experiences.

Conclusion

The study of positive states is a core component of positive psychology and has a long theoretical tradition that goes back to the very beginnings of the field of psychology. Many of the instruments used to measure these experiences employ explicitly religious/spiritual terminology, which may or may not be desirable, depending on the context. Additionally, several measures are intended to tap states or traits, and though scales may sometimes be altered to measure trait tendencies or to measure aspects of particular experiences, this should be done with care. Certain mental states are among the most important moments in many people's lives, and researchers must acknowledge the challenges of measuring these states while striving to investigate this source of ultimate significance in human life.

References

American Psychiatric Association. (2013). *Diagnostic and statistical manual of mental disorders* (5th ed.).

Anderson, C.L., Monroy, M., & Keltner, D. (2018). Awe in nature heals: Evidence from military veterans, at-risk youth, and college students. *Emotion, 18*(8), 1195–1202.

Anthony, F.V., Hermans, C.A., & Sterkens, C. (2010). A comparative study of mystical experience among Christian, Muslim, and Hindu students in Tamil Nadu, India. *Journal for the Scientific Study of Religion, 49*(2), 264–277.

Back, K.W., & Bourque, L.B. (1970). Can feelings be enumerated? *Behavioral Science, 15*(6), 487–496. https://doi.org/10.1002/bs.3830150603

Baer, R.A. (2003). Mindfulness training as a clinical intervention: A conceptual and empirical review. *Clinical Psychology: Science and Practice, 10*, 125–143. https://doi.org/10.1093/clipsy.bpg015

Barrett, F.S., Johnson, M.W., & Griffiths, R.R. (2015). Validation of the revised Mystical Experience Questionnaire in experimental sessions with psilocybin. *Journal of Psychopharmacology, 29*(11), 1182–1190. https://doi.org/10.1177/0269881115609019

Beauregard, M. (2011). Neuroscience and spirituality: Findings and consequences. In H. Walach & S. Schmidt (Eds.), *Neuroscience, consciousness and spirituality* (pp. 57–73). Springer. https://doi.org/10.1007/978-94-007-2079-4_4

Benson, H. (1975). *The relaxation response*. Morrow.

Bernstein, E.M., & Putnam, F.W. (1986). Development, reliability and validity of a dissociation scale. *The Journal of Nervous and Mental Disease, 174*(12), 727–735. https://doi.org/10.1097/00005053-198612000-00004

Blackmore, S.J. (1996). Near-death experiences. *Journal of the Royal Society of Medicine, 89*, 73–76. https://doi.org/10.1177/014107689608900204

Britton, W.B. (2019). Can mindfulness be too much of a good thing? The value of a middle way. *Current Opinion in Psychology, 28*, 159–165. https://doi.org/10.1016/j.copsyc.2018.12.011

Brown, K.W., Ryan, R.M., & Creswell, J.D. (2007). Mindfulness: Theoretical foundations and evidence for its salutary effects. *Psychological Inquiry, 18*, 211–237. https://doi.org/10.1080/10478400701598298

Bucke, R.M. (1901). *Cosmic consciousness: A study in the evolution o the human mind.* Merchant Books.

Byrd, K.R., Lear, D., & Schwenka, S. (2000). Mysticism as a predictor of subjective well-being. *The International Journal for the Psychology of Religion, 10*(4), 259–269. https://doi.org/10.1207/S15327582IJPR1004_04

Caird, D. (1988). The structure of Hood's mysticism scale: A factor-analytic study. *Journal for the Scientific Study of Religion, 27*(1), 122–127. https://doi.org/10.2307/1387407

Cardeña, E.E., Lynn, S.J.E., & Krippner, S.E. (2000). *Varieties of anomalous experience: Examining the scientific evidence.* American Psychological Association. https://doi.org/10.1037/10371-000

Carmody, J., & Baer, R.A. (2008). Relationship between mindfulness practice and levels of mindfulness, medical and psychological symptoms and well-being in a mindfulness-based stress reduction program. *Journal of Behavioral Medicine, 31*(1), 23–33. https://doi.org/10.1007/s10865-007-9130-7

Chen, Z., Hood Jr, R. W., Yang, L., & Watson, P. J. (2011). Mystical experience among Tibetan Buddhists: The common core thesis revisited. *Journal for the Scientific Study of Religion, 50*(2), 328–338. https://doi.org/10.1111/j.1468-5906.2011.01570.x

Chen, Z., Zhang, Y., Hood, R. W., & Watson, P. J. (2012). Mysticism in Chinese Christians and non-Christians: Measurement invariance of the mysticism scale and implications for the mean differences. *International Journal for the Psychology of Religion, 22*(2), 155–168. https://doi.org/10.1080/10508619.2011.638586

Cloninger, C. R., Svrakic, D. M., & Przybeck, T. R. (1993). A psychobiological model of temperament and character. *Archives of General Psychiatry, 50*(12), 975–990. https://doi.org/10.1001/archpsyc.1993.01820240059008

Condon, P., Desbordes, G., Miller, W. B., & DeSteno, D. (2013). Meditation increases compassionate responses to suffering. *Psychological Science, 24*, 2125–2127. https://doi.org/10.1177/0956797613485603

Csikszentmihalyi, M. (1990). *Flow: The psychology of optimal experience.* HarperCollins.

Csikszentmihalyi, M., & LeFevre, J. (1989). Optimal experience in work and leisure. *Journal of Personality and Social Psychology, 56,* 815–822. https://doi.org/10.1037/0022-3514.56.5.815

Davidson, R. J., Kabat-Zinn, J., Schumacher, J., Rosenkranz, M., Muller, D., Santorelli, S. F., Urbanowski, F., Harrington, A., Bonus, K., & Sheridan, J. F. (2003). Alterations in brain and immune function produced by mindfulness meditation. *Psychosomatic Medicine, 65*(4), 564–570. https://doi.org/10.1097/01.PSY.0000077505.67574.E3

Davidson, R. J., & McEwen, B. S. (2012). Social influences on neuroplasticity: Stress and interventions to promote well-being. *Nature Neuroscience, 15*, 689–695. https://doi.org/10.1038/nn.3093

Davis, J., Lockwood, L., & Wright, C. (1991). Reasons for not reporting peak experiences. *Journal of Humanistic Psychology, 31,* 86–94. https://doi.org/10.1177/0022167891311008

Dittrich, A., Lamparter, D., & Maurer, M. (2010). *5D-ASC: Questionnaire for the assessment of altered states of consciousness. A short introduction.* PSIN PLUS.

Fox, J. W. (1992). The structure, stability, and social antecedents of reported paranormal experiences. *Sociological Analysis, 53*(4), 417–431. https://doi.org/10.2307/3711436

Freud, S. (1930). *Civilization and its discontents.* WW Norton.

Frischholz, E. J., Braun, B. G., Sachs, R. G., Hopkins, L. (1990). The Dissociative Experiences Scale: Further replication and validation. *Dissociation: Progress in the Dissociative Disorders, 3*(3), 151–153.

Gallup, G., Jr. (1978). *The Gallup poll: Public opinion 1972–1977.* Scholarly Resources.

Gallup Organization. (2003). *Religious awakenings bolster Americans' faith.* Retrieved from https://news.gallup.com/poll/7582/religious-awakenings-bolster-americans-faith.aspx

Garcia-Romeu, A. (2010). Self-transcendence as a measurable transpersonal construct. *Journal of Transpersonal Psychology, 42*(1), 26–47.

Goyal, M., Singh, S., Sibinga, E. M., Gould, N. F., Rowland-Seymour, A., Sharma, R., Berger, Z., Sleicher, D., Maron, D. D., Shihab, H. M., Ranasinghe, P. D., Linn, S., Saha, S., Bass, E., & Haythornthwaite, J. A. (2014). Meditation programs for psychological stress and well-being: A systematic review and meta-analysis. *Journal of the American Medical Association Internal Medicine, 174*, 357–368.

Greeley, A. M. (1974). *Ecstasy: A way of knowing* (Vol. 324). Prentice Hall.

Griffiths, R. R., Johnson, M. W., Carducci, M. A., Umbricht, A., Richards, W. A., Richards, B. D., Cosimano, M. P., & Klinedinst, M. A. (2016). Psilocybin produces substantial and sustained decreases in depression and anxiety in patients with life-threatening cancer: A randomized double-blind trial. *Journal of Psychopharmacology, 30*(12), 1181–1197. https://doi.org/10.1177/0269881116675513

Griffiths, R. R., Johnson, M. W., Richards, W. A., Richards, B. D., Jesse, R., MacLean, K. A., Barrett, F. S., Cosimano, M. P., & Klinedinst, M. A. (2018). Psilocybin-occasioned mystical-type experience in combination with meditation and other spiritual practices produces enduring positive changes in psychological functioning and in trait measures of prosocial attitudes and behaviors. *Journal of Psychopharmacology, 32*(1), 49–69.

Griffiths, R. R., Johnson, M. W., Richards, W. A., Richards, B. D., McCann, U., & Jesse, R. (2011). Psilocybin occasioned mystical-type experiences: Immediate and persisting dose-related effects. *Psychopharmacology, 218*(4), 649–665. https://doi.org/10.1007/s00213-011-2358-5

Griffiths, R.R., Richards, W.A., Johnson, M.W., McCann, U.D., & Jesse, R. (2008). Mystical-type experiences occasioned by psilocybin mediate the attribution of personal meaning and spiritual significance 14 months later. *Journal of Psychopharmacology, 22*(6), 621–632. https://doi.org/10.1177/0269881108094300

Griffiths, R.R., Richards, W.A., McCann, U., & Jesse, R. (2006). Psilocybin can occasion mystical-type experiences having substantial and sustained personal meaning and spiritual significance. *Psychopharmacology, 187*(3), 268–283. https://doi.org/10.1007/s00213-006-0457-5

Grof, S. (1972). Varieties of transpersonal experiences: Observations from LSD psychotherapy. *Journal of Transpersonal Psychology, 4,* 45–80.

Hanley, A.W., Nakamura, Y., and Garland, E.L. (2018). The Nondual Awareness Dimensional Assessment (NADA): New tools to assess nondual traits and states of consciousness occurring within and beyond the context of meditation. *Psychological Assessment, 30*(12), 1625–1639. https://doi.org/10.1037/pas0000615

Hardy, A.C. (1970). A scientist looks at religion. *Proceedings of the Royal Institute of Great Britain, 43,* 201.

Hay, D. (1979). Religious experience amongst a group of post-graduate students: A qualitative study. *Journal for the Scientific Study of Religion, 18*(2), 164–182. https://doi.org/10.2307/1385938

Hay, D. (1982). *Exploring inner space: Scientists and religious experience.* Penguin Books.

Hay, D. (1990). *Religious experience today: Studying the facts.* Mowbray.

Hay, D., & Heald, G. (1987). Religion is good for you. *New Society, 80*(1268), 20–22.

Hay, D., & Morisy, A. (1978). Reports of esctatic, paranormal, or religious experience in GreatBritain and the United States: A comparison of trends. *Journal for the Scientific Study of Religion, 17*(3), 255–268. https://doi.org/10.2307/1386320

Hay, D., & Morisy, A. (1985). Secular society, religious meanings: A contemporary paradox. *Review of Religious Research, 26*(3), 213–227. https://doi.org/10.2307/3511273

Hölzel, B.K., Lazar, S.W., Gard, T., Schuman-Oliver, Z., Vago, D.R., & Ott, U. (2011). How does mindfulness meditation work? Proposing mechanisms of action from a conceptual and neural perspective. *Perspectives on Psychological Science, 6*(6), 537–559. https://doi.org/10.1177/1745691611419671

Hood, R.W., Jr. (1970). Religious orientation and the report of religious experience. *Journal for the Scientific Study of Religion, 9*(4), 285–291. https://doi.org/10.2307/1384573

Hood, R.W., Jr. (1975). The construction and preliminary validation of a measure of reported mystical experience. *Journal for the Scientific Study of Religion, 14*(1), 29–41. https://doi.org/10.2307/1384454

Hood, R.W., Jr. (2002). The mystical self: Lost and found. *The International Journal for the Psychology of Religion, 12,* 1–14. https://doi.org/10.1207/S15327582IJPR1201_01

Hood, R.W., Jr. (2016). Mysticism and hypo-egoicism. In K.W. Brown & M.R. Leary (Eds.), *Oxford handbook of hypo-egoicphenomena*(pp. 285–296). Oxford University Press. https://doi.org/10.1093/oxfordhb/9780199328079.013.19

Hood, R.W., Jr., Ghorbani, N., Watson, P.J., Ghramaleki, A.F., Bing, M.N., Davison, H.K., Morris, R.J., & Williamson, W.P. (2001). Dimensions of the mysticism scale: Confirming the three-factor structure in the United States and Iran. *Journal for the Scientific Study of Religion, 40,* 691–705. https://doi.org/10.1111/0021-8294.00085

Hood, R.W., Jr., Hill, P.C., & Spilka, B. (2009). *The psychology of religion: Am empirical approach.* Guilford.

Hood, R.W., Jr., Morris, R.J., & Watson, P.J. (1993). Further factor analysis of Hood's Mysticism Scale. *Psychological Reports, 73*(3), 1176–1178. https://doi.org/10.2466/pr0.1993.73.3f.1176

Hood, R.W., Jr., & Williamson, W.P. (2000). An empirical test of the unity thesis: The structure of mystical descriptors in various faith samples. *Journal of Psychology and Christianity, 19*(3), 232–244.

Im, S.H., & Varma, S. (2018). Distorted time perception during flow as revealed by an attention-demanding cognitive task. *Creativity Research Journal, 30*(3), 295–304. https://doi.org/10.1080/10400419.2018.1488346

Jackson, S.A. (2000). Joy, fun, and flow state in sport. In Y.C. Hanin (Ed.), *Emotions in sport* (pp. 136–156). Human Kinetics. https://doi.org/10.5040/9781492596233.ch-006

Jackson, S. A., & Marsh, H. W. (1996). Development and validation of a scale to measure optimal experience: The Flow State Scale. *Journal of Sport & Exercise Psychology, 18,* 17–35. https://doi.org/10.1123/jsep.18.1.17

James, W. (1890). *The principles of psychology.* H. Holt and Company.

James, W. (1902). *The varieties of religious experience.* Harvard University Press.

Jha, A. P., Krompinger, J., & Baime, M. J. (2007). Mindfulness training modifies subsystems of attention. *Cognitive, Affective & Behavioral Neuroscience, 7,* 109–119. https://doi.org/10.3758/CABN.7.2.109

Johnson, M. W., Garcia-Romeu, A., & Griffiths, R. R. (2017). Long-term follow-up of psilocybin-facilitated smoking cessation. *The American Journal of Drug and Alcohol Abuse, 43*(1), 55–60. https://doi.org/10.3109/00952990.2016.1170135

Joye, Y., & Bolderdijk, J. W. (2015). An exploratory study into the effects of extraordinary nature on emotions, mood, and prosociality. *Frontiers in Psychology, 5,* Article 1557. https://doi.org/10.3389/fpsyg.2014.01577

Joye, Y., & Dewitte, S. (2016). Up speeds you down. Awe-evoking monumental buildings trigger behavioral and perceived freezing. *Journal of Environmental Psychology, 47,* 112–125. https://doi.org/10.1016/j.jenvp.2016.05.001

Jung, C. G. (2012). *The red book: A reader's edition.* WW Norton.

Kabat-Zinn, J. (1994). *Wherever you go, there you are: Mindfulness meditation in everyday life.* Hyperion.

Kass, J. D., Friedman, R., Leserman, J., Zuttermeister, P. C., & Benson, H. (1991). Health outcomes and a new index of spiritual experience. *Journal for the Scientific Study of Religion, 30*(2), 203–211. https://doi.org/10.2307/1387214

Kaufman, S. B. (2018). Self-actualizing people in the 21st century: Integration with contemporary theory and research on personality and well-being. *Journal of Humanistic Psychology.* Advance online publication. https://doi.org/10.1177/0022167818809187

Keltner, D., & Haidt, J. (2003). Approaching awe: A moral, spiritual, and aesthetic emotion. *Cognition and Emotion, 17,* 297–314. https://doi.org/10.1080/02699930302297

Laski, M. (1961). *Ecstasy: A study of some secular and religious experiences.* Cresset Press.

Lau, M. A., Bishop, S. R., Segal, Z. V., Buis, T., Anderson, N. D., Carlson, L., Shapiro, S., Carmody, J., Abbey, S., & Devins, G. (2006). The Toronto mindfulness scale: Development and validation. *Journal of Clinical Psychology, 62*(12), 1445–1467. https://doi.org/10.1002/jclp.20326

Lazar, A., & Kravetz, S. (2005). Responses to the Mystical Scale by religious Jewish persons: A comparison of structural models of mystical experience. *The International Journal for the Psychology of Religion, 15*(1), 51–61. https://doi.org/10.1207/s15327582ijpr1501_4

Leary, M. R., & Guadagno, J. (2011). The role of hypo-egoic self-processes in optimal functioning and subjective well-being. In K. M. Sheldon, T. B. Kashdan & M. F. Steger (Eds.), *Designing positive psychology: Taking stock and moving forward* (pp.135–146). Oxford University Press.

Leiberg, S., Klimecki, O., & Singer, T. (2011). Short-term compassion training increases prosocial behavior in a newly developed prosocial game. *PLoS ONE, 6,* e17798. https://doi.org/10.1371/journal.pone.0017798

Lomax, J. W., Kripal, J. J., & Pargament, K. I. (2011). Perspectives on "sacred moments" in psychotherapy. *The American Journal of Psychiatry, 168,* 12–18. https://doi.org/10.1176/appi.ajp.2010.10050739

Lukoff, D., Lu, F., & Turner, R. (1992). Toward a more culturally sensitive DSM-IV. Psychoreligious and psychospiritual problems. *Journal of Nervous and Mental Disease, 180,* 673–682. https://doi.org/10.1097/00005053-199211000-00001

MacDonald, D. A., & Holland, D. (2002). Examination of the psychometric properties of the temperament and character inventory self-transcendence dimension. *Personality and Individual Differences, 32*(6), 1013–1027. https://doi.org/10.1016/S0191-8869(01)00107-6

MacLean, K. A., Leoutsakos, J. M. S., Johnson, M. W., & Griffiths, R. R. (2012). Factor analysis of the mystical experience questionnaire: a study of experiences occasioned by the hallucinogen psilocybin. *Journal for the Scientific Study of Religion, 51*(4), 721–737. https://doi.org/10.1111/j.1468-5906.2012.01685.x

Magen, Z. (1996). Commitment beyond self and adolescence: The issue of happiness. *Social Indicators Research, 37,* 235–267. https://doi.org/10.1007/BF00286233

Marchand, W.R. (2012). Mindfulness-based stress reduction, mindfulness-based cognitive therapy, and Zen meditation for depression, anxiety, pain and psychological distress. *Journal of Psychiatric Practice, 18*(4), 233–252. https://doi.org/10.1097/01.pra.0000416014.53215.86

Margoshes, A., & Litt, S. (1966). Vivid experiences: Peak and nadir. *Journal of Clinical Psychology, 22,* 175–195. https://doi.org/10.1002/1097-4679(196604)22:2<175::AID-JCLP2270220214>3.0.CO;2-U

Maslow, A.H. (1964). *Religions, values, and peak-experiences.* Ohio State University Press.

Mathes, E., Zevon, M., Rotter, P., & Joerger, S. (1982). Peak experience tendencies: Scale development and theory testing. *Journal of Humanistic Psychology, 22,* 92–108. https://doi.org/10.1177/0022167882223011

Miller, W.R., & C'de Baca, C.J. (2001). *Quantum change: When epiphanies and sudden insight transform ordinary lives.* Guilford.

Monod, S., Brennan, M., Rochat, E., Martin, E., Rochat, S., & Büla, C.J. (2011). Instruments measuring spirituality in clinical research: A systematic review. *Journal of General Internal Medicine, 26*(11), 1345–1357. https://doi.org/10.1007/s11606-011-1769-7

Newberg, A.B., & d'Aquili, E.G. (2000). The neuropsychology of religious and spiritual experience. *Journal of Consciousness Studies, 7,* 11–12.

Newberg, A.B., & d'Aquili, E.G. (2008). *Why God won't go away: Brain science and the biology of belief.* Ballantine Books.

Niemiec, R.M. (2014). *Mindfulness and character strengths: A practical guide to flourishing.* Hogrefe Publishing.

Olson, M.S., Hinds, P.S., Eull, K., Quargnenti, A., Milligan, M., Foppiano, P., & Powell, B. (1998). Peak and nadir experiences and their consequences described by pediatric oncology nurses. *Journal of Pediatric Oncology Nursing, 15,* 13–24. https://doi.org/10.1177/104345429801500103

Pahnke, W.N. (1963). *Drugs and mysticism: An analysis of the relationship between psychedelic drugs and the mystical consciousness: A thesis*[Doctoral dissertation]. Harvard University.

Panzarella, R. (1980). The phenomenology of aesthetic peak experiences. *Journal of Humanistic Psychology, 20,* 69–85. https://doi.org/10.1177/002216788002000105

Pargament, K.I., Lomax, J.W., McGee, J.S., & Fang, Q. (2014). Sacred moments in psychotherapy from the perspectives of mental health providers and clients: Prevalence, predictors, and consequences. *Spirituality in Clinical Practice, 1*(4), 248–262. https://doi.org/10.1037/scp0000043

Pawelski, J.O. (2012). *The dynamic individualism of William James.* SUNY Press.

Peterson, C., Park, N., & Seligman, M.E.P. (2005). Orientations to happiness and life satisfaction: The full life vs. the empty life. *Journal of Happiness Studies, 6,* 25–41. https://doi.org/10.1007/s10902-004-1278-z

Piedmont, R.L. (1999). Does spirituality represent the sixth factor of personality? Spiritual transcendence and the five-factor model. *Journal of Personality, 67*(6), 985–1013. https://doi.org/10.1111/1467-6494.00080

Piff, P.K., Dietze, P., Feinberg, M., Stancato, D.M., & Keltner, D. (2015). Awe, the small self, and prosocial behavior. *Journal of Personality and Social Psychology, 108*(6), 883–899. https://doi.org/10.1037/pspi0000018

Prade, C., & Saroglou, V. (2016). Awe's effects on generosity and helping. *The Journal of Positive Psychology, 11*(5), 522–530. https://doi.org/10.1080/17439760.2015.1127992

Preston, J.L., & Shin, F. (2016). Spiritual experiences evoke awe through the small self in both religious and non-religious individuals. *Journal of Experimental Social Psychology, 70,* 212–221. https://doi.org/10.1016/j.jesp.2016.11.006

Reinert, D.F., & Stifler, K.R. (1993). Hood's mysticism scale revisited: A factor-analytic replication. *Journal for the Scientific Study of Religion, 32*(4), 383–388. https://doi.org/10.2307/1387178

Rogatko, T.P. (2009). The influence of flow on positive affect in college students. *Journal of Happiness Studies, 10,* 133–148. https://doi.org/10.1007/s10902-007-9069-y

Rudd, M., Vohs, K. D., & Aaker, J. (2012). Awe expands people's perception of time, alters decision making & enhances well-being. *Psychological Science, 23*(10), 1130–1136. https://doi.org/10.1177/0956797612438731

Segal, Z., Williams, M., & Teasdale, J. (2013). *Mindfulness-based cognitive therapy for depression.* Guilford.

Seligman, M., & Csikszentmihalyi, M. (2000). Positive psychology: An introduction. *American Psychologist, 55*(1), 5–14. https://doi.org/10.1037/0003-066X.55.1.5

Shiota, M. N., Campos, B., & Keltner, D. (2003). The faces of positive emotion: Prototype displays of awe, amusement, and pride. *Annals of the New York Academy of Sciences, 1000,* 296–299. https://doi.org/10.1196/annals.1280.029

Shiota, M. N., Neufeld, S. L., Yeung, W. H., Moser, S. E., & Perea, E. F. (2011). Feeling good: Autonomic nervous system responding in five positive emotions. *Emotion, 11*(6), 1368–1378. https://doi.org/10.1037/a0024278

Silvia, P., Fayn, K., Nusbaum, E. C., Beaty, R. E. (2015). Openness to experience and awe in response to nature and music: Personality and profound aesthetic experiences. *Psychology of Aesthetics, Creativity, and the Arts, 9*(4), 376–384. https://doi.org/10.1037/aca0000028

Stace, W. T. (1960). *Mysticism and philosophy*. Lippincott.

Starbuck, E. D. (1899). *The psychology of religion: An empirical study of the growth of religious consciousness.* Walter Scott.

Streib, H., & Hood, R. W., Jr. (Eds.). (2016). *Semantics and psychology of "spirituality."* Springer International Publishing. https://doi.org/10.1007/978-3-319-21245-6

Studerus, E., Gamma, A., & Vollenweider, F. X. (2010). Psychometric evaluation of the altered states of consciousness rating scale (OAV). *PLoS One, 5*(8), e12412. https://doi.org/10.1371/journal.pone.0012412

Tart, C. (2006). Current status of transpersonal psychology. *Journal of Consciousness Studies, 13,* 83–87.

Underwood, L. G., & Teresi, J. A. (2002). The daily spiritual experience scale: Development, theoretical description, reliability, exploratory factor analysis, and preliminary construct validity using health-related data. *Annals of Behavioral Medicine, 24*(1), 22–33. https://doi.org/10.1207/S15324796ABM2401_04

Urgesi, C., Aglioti, S. M., Skrap, M., & Fabbro, F. (2010). The spiritual brain: Selective cortical lesions modulate human self-transcendence. *Neuron, 65*(3), 309–319. https://doi.org/10.1016/j.neuron.2010.01.026

Vago, D. R., & Silbersweig, D. A. (2012). Self-awareness, self-regulation, and self-transcendence (S-ART): A framework for understanding the neurobiological mechanisms of mindfulness. *Frontiers in Human Neuroscience, 6,* Article 296. https://doi.org/10.3389/fnhum.2012.00296

Vago, D. R., & Zeidan, F. (2016). The brain on silent: Mind wandering, mindful awareness, and states of mental tranquility. *Annals of the New York Academy of Sciences, 1373,* 96–113. https://doi.org/10.1111/nyas.13171

Vernon, G. M. (1968). The religious "nones": A neglected category. *Journal for the Scientific Study of Religion, 7*(2), 219–229. https://doi.org/10.2307/1384629

Weng, H. Y., Fox, A. S., Shackman, A. J., Stodola, D. E., Caldwell, J. Z. K., Olson, M. C., Rogers, G. M., & Davidson, R. J. (2013). Compassion training alters altruism and neural responses to suffering. *Psychological Science, 24,* 1171–1180. https://doi.org/10.1177/0956797612469537

Wilson, S. R., & Spencer, R. C. (1990). Intense personal experiences: Subjective effects, interpretations, and after-effects. *Journal of Clinical Psychology, 46,* 565–573. https://doi.org/10.1002/1097-4679(199009)46:5<565::AID-JCLP2270460504>3.0.CO;2-3

Wulff, D. M. (2000). Mystical experience. In E. Cardena, S. J. Lynn, & S. C. Krippner (Eds.), *Varieties of anomalous experience: Examining the scientific evidence* (pp. 397–440). American Psychological Association. https://doi.org/10.1037/10371-012

Wuthnow, R. (1978). Peak experiences: Some empirical texts. *Journal of Humanistic Psychology, 18,* 59–75. https://doi.org/10.1177/002216787801800307

Yaden, D. B., & Griffiths, R. R. (2020). The subjective effects of psychedelics are necessary for their enduring therapeutic effects. *ACS Pharmacology & Translational Science*, *4*(2), 568–572. https://doi.org/10.1021/acsptsci.0c00194

Yaden, D. B., Haidt, J., Hood, R. W., Jr., Vago, D. R., & Newberg, A. B. (2017). The varieties of self-transcendent experience. *Review of General Psychology, 21*(2), 143–160. https://doi.org/10.1037/gpr0000102

Yaden, D. B., Kaufman, S. B., Hyde, E., Chirico, A., Gaggioli, A., Zhang, J., & Keltner, D. (2019). The development of the awe experience scale (AWE-S): A multifactorial measure for a complex emotion. *The Journal of Positive Psychology, 14*(4), 474–488. https://doi.org/10.1080/17439760.2018.1484940

Yaden, D. B., Le Nguyen, K. D., Kern, M. L., Belser, A. B., Eichstaedt, J. C., Iwry, J., Smith, M. E., Wintering, N. A., Hood, R. W., Jr., & Newberg, A. B. (2016). Of roots and fruits: A comparison of psychedelic and nonpsychedelic mystical experiences. *Journal of Humanistic Psychology, 57*(4), 338–353. https://doi.org/10.1177/0022167816674625

Yaden, D. B., McCall, T. D., & Ellens, J. H. (2015). *Being called: Scientific, secular, and sacred perspectives.* Praeger.

Yaden, D. B., & Newberg, A. B. (2022). *The varieties of spiritual experience: 21st century research and perspectives.* Oxford University Press.

Yaden, D. B., Potash, J. B., & Griffiths, R. R. (2022). *Preparing for the Bursting of the Psychedelic Hype Bubble.* JAMA Psychiatry.

Yaden, D. B., Yaden, M. E., & Griffiths, R. R. (2021). Psychedelics in psychiatry -keeping the renaissance from going off the rails. *JAMA Psychiatry, 78*(5), 469–470. https://doi.org/10.1001/jamapsychiatry.2020.3672

Yamane, D., & Polzer, M. (1994). Ways of seeing ecstasy in modern society: Experiential-expressive and cultural-linguistic views. *Sociology of Religion, 55*(1), 1–25. https://doi.org/10.2307/3712173

Chapter 24

Measuring Nostalgia

Tim Wildschut and Constantine Sedikides

Center for Research on Self and Identity, School of Psychology,
University of Southampton, UK

The term *nostalgia* was coined in the 17th century by the Swiss medical student Johannes Hofer (1688/1934). It is a compound of the Greek words *nostos* (return) and *algos* (pain). Hofer conceptualized nostalgia as a medical or neurological disease. Based on his studies of Swiss mercenaries in foreign service who longed for their homeland, Hofer proposed that nostalgia was associated with despondency, bouts of weeping, fainting, indigestion, stomach pain, anorexia, high fever, cardiac palpitations, suicidal ideation, or even death. In his view, it was "a cerebral disease of essentially demonic cause" (p. 387). If Hofer were alive today, he would be dumbfounded to see nostalgia covered in the *Handbook of Positive Psychology Assessment*. What happened in the intervening centuries?

Historical Background

Hofer's (1688/1934) view of nostalgia as a medical or neurological disease remained influential throughout the 18th and 19th centuries. For some time, nostalgia was considered a condition confined to the Swiss, and acquired the label *mal du Suisse* (Swiss illness). This notion was abandoned, however, in light of documented cases of nostalgia in other groups, such as French soldiers fighting in the Revolutionary and Napoleonic armies (O'Sullivan, 2012) and American soldiers fighting in the Civil War (Matt, 2007). The first dissenting opinion was heard in the second half of the 19th century: None other than Darwin (1872/1896) offered a more positive outlook on nostalgia in *The Expression of the Emotions in Man and Animals*, discussing "the vivid recollection of our former home, or of long-past happy days" under the heading of tender emotions (Chapter VIII, p. 216). Regrettably, Darwin's voice was soon drowned out by the influential psychoanalytic movement. Scholars in this tradition labeled nostalgia an "immigrant psychosis" (Frost, 1938, p. 801) and pondered "the importance of the preoedipal mother in the emotional developments of nostalgics" (Kleiner, 1977, p. 17). As in Hofer's days, the construct came to be regarded as synonymous to homesickness and was presumed to be limited to very specific populations, such as soldiers, immigrants, and boarding school students (Jackson, 1986).

The publication of Davis's (1979) *Yearning for Yesteryear* toward the end of the 20th century was a turning point. He presented preliminary evidence that the term "homesickness" has more negative connotations than "nostalgia," steering the respective literatures onto separate paths. The homesickness literature focused on adjustment challenges (e.g., separation anxiety) that accompany young persons' transitions away from the home environment (Thurber & Walton, 2007), whereas the budding nostalgia literature began to uncover functional benefits of this emotion (Sedikides et al., 2008; Wildschut et al., 2006). In the four decades since Davis's groundbreaking work, nostalgia has attracted intense scholarly interest, within psychology and beyond. This literature has now established nostalgia as a predominantly (albeit not purely) positive emotion with far-reaching implications for motivation and behavior. Nostalgia can serve as an intrapersonal and interpersonal resource that fosters psychological equanimity. It is prevalent, universal, and experienced across the lifespan (for reviews, see Sedikides & Wildschut, 2016, 2019; Sedikides et al., 2015).

Nostalgia Measures

The sharp rise in nostalgia research has been mirrored by a remarkable proliferation of measures to assess this emotion, both as a relatively stable personality trait (i.e., nostalgia proneness) and as a short-lived, momentary state. This diversity is indicative of a vibrant research area, and it is inspiring to see "a hundred flowers bloom." Without claiming to be exhaustive, we present a selection of frequently used peer-reviewed measures in Table 24.1 (trait-level measures) and Table 24.2 (state-level measures). The information in these tables serves as a roadmap to primary sources and is intended to assist future researchers in identifying suitable measures for their specific research purposes. Space limitations do not permit a detailed discussion of scale development procedures, but this information is generally available from the primary sources. Rather than act as arbiters of quality, our main objective is to review common statistical and conceptual challenges we have encountered in almost two decades of nostalgia research – and to suggest possible solutions. Before so doing, however, we make one recommendation regarding the selection of trait-level measures which is based on results from studies in which researchers administered multiple measures of nostalgia proneness and reported their intercorrelations. We present the relevant data in Table 24.3.

Table 24.1. Examples of trait-level nostalgia measures

Instrument	Key source	Items	Reliability (α)	Comments
Southampton Nostalgia Scale for Children (SNS-C)	Juhl et al. (2020)	7	.87	This scale is an adaptation of the Southampton Nostalgia Scale. It uses cartoon drawings and accompanying vignettes to explain the meaning of the word "nostalgia" to children.
Personal Inventory of Nostalgic Experiences (PINE)	Newman et al. (2020)	4	.91	Newman et al. (2020) used this scale to measure trait-level nostalgia (Study 2) and daily nostalgia (Studies 3 and 5).
Nostalgia Scale	Baldwin et al. (2018)	16	Personal Experience: .76 Popular Culture: .87 Society: .78 Childhood: .90	This scale is an adaptation of Batcho's (1995) Nostalgia Inventory, with four subscales: Personal Experience, Popular Culture, Society, and Childhood.

Table 24.1. continued

Instrument	Key source	Items	Reliability (α)	Comments
Nostalgia Prototype Scale (NPS)	Cheung, Sedikides, & Wildschut (2017)	10	.86	Cheung, Sedikides, & Wildschut (2017, Study 1) instructed participants to rate both the frequency and importance of five behaviors related to prototypical features of nostalgia (e.g., "I bring to mind rose-tinted memories").
Southampton Nostalgia Scale (SNS, 7-item version)	Barrett et al. (2010)	7	.93	Barrett et al. (2010) added two items to the 5-item version of the scale developed by Routledge et al. (2008).
Southampton Nostalgia Scale (SNS, 5-item version)	Routledge et al. (2008)	5	.92	
Modified Holbrook (1993) Nostalgia Scale	Rousseau & Venter (2000)	38	Nostalgia: .77 Progressiveness: .74 Consumer Nostalgic Preference: .77 Vintage/ Antiques Propensity: .72	Rousseau and Venter (2000) used all 20 items generated by Holbrook (1993) and added 18 items, resulting in a 38-item scale with four subscales: Nostalgia, Progressiveness, Consumer Nostalgic Preference, and Vintage/Antiques Propensity.
Time Perspective Inventory (TPI): Past-Positive subscale (TPI:P-P)	Zimbardo & Boyd (1999)	9	.80	Routledge et al. (2008) used a subset of 8 items from the Time Perspective Inventory to assess nostalgia proneness (α = .71). For 4 items, higher ratings indicated greater nostalgia; for the other 4 items, higher ratings indicated lower nostalgia (reversed). 5 items were drawn from the Past-Positive subscale (one reversed), with the remaining 3 items being drawn from the Past-Negative subscale (all reversed). Cheung, Sedikides, & Wildschut (2017, Study 4) dropped one of the reverse-scored items from the Past-Positive scale (α = .65).
Nostalgia Inventory (NI)	Batcho (1995)	20	.84	Batcho (1995) instructed participants to rate how much they "miss" these 20 items from their past. Recently, researchers have instructed participants to rate how "nostalgic" they feel for the items from their past (e.g., Zou et al., 2019; α = .87).

Table 24.1. continued

Instrument	Key source	Items	Reliability (α)	Comments
Nostalgia Scale (NS, 8-item version)	Holbrook (1993)	8	.78	Holbrook (1993) generated a pool of 20 items, from which he selected 8. Other researchers have indexed nostalgia proneness with all 20 items generated by Holbrook (e.g., Schindler & Holbrook, 2003; α = .81).
Dispositions Toward the Past (DTP)	Taylor and Konrad (1980)	48	Conservation: .86 Interest: .87 Heritage: .84 Experience: .79	This scale comprises four sub-subscales: Conservation, Interest, Heritage, and Experience. Schindler and Holbrook (2003) used the Experience subscale as measure of nostalgia proneness (α = .71).
Environmental Response Inventory (ERI): Antiquarianism subscale (ERI:A)	McKechnie (1977)	20	.61	

Note. Reliability = Cronbach's α as reported in the key source. For NI (Batcho, 1995), α = 1-week test-retest reliability. For Antiquarianism subscale of Environmental Response Inventory (McKechnie, 1977), α as reported in Schindler and Holbrook (2003).

Table 24.2. Examples of state-level nostalgia measures

Key source	Items	Reliability (α)	Comments
Baldwin et al. (2018)	3	.93	Baldwin et al. (2018, Study 2) assessed state-level nostalgia with three items: "nostalgic," "sentimental," and "longing"
Zou et al. (2018)	10	.89	Zou et al. (2018) assessed nostalgia for a host culture. Repatriates rated their level of nostalgia for 10 objects they had encountered in their host culture (e.g., "the town where I lived").
Sedikides et al. (2016)	1	See comments	Five judges coded participant-generated autobiographical narratives for the intensity of expressed nostalgia ("How much nostalgia did the person who wrote this narrative experience?"). Interrater reliability was high (.98).
Baldwin et al. (2015)	4	.88	Studies 1 and 5 assessed state-level nostalgia with four items: "nostalgic," "wistful," "sentimental," and "a longing for my past."
Reid et al. (2015)	1	.80	Reid et al. (2015) assessed scent-evoked nostalgia. Participants evaluated 12 scents. For each scent, they rated the item: "How nostalgic does this scent make you feel?" Reid et al. indexed scent-evoked nostalgia by averaging these ratings across the 12 scents.

Table 24.2. continued

Key source	Items	Reliability (α)	Comments
Zhou et al. (2012)	1	–	Study 1 assessed daily nostalgia. Participants rated their daily level of nostalgia for 30 consecutive days.
Iyer & Jetten (2011)	4	.86	Study 2 used four items to assess first-year undergraduates' nostalgia about their lives and communities before university. Other researchers used all or some of these items to assess how nostalgic problem gamblers and/or problem drinkers felt for their life before addiction (e.g., Wohl et al., 2018, Experiment 1; α = .73).
Barrett et al. (2010)	1	–	Barrett et al. (2010) assessed music-evoked nostalgia. Participants listened to 30 musical excerpts. For each excerpt, they rated the item: "How nostalgic does this song make you feel?" Batcho (2007) used this single item ("nostalgic") to assess song-lyric evoked nostalgia.
Zhou et al. (2008)	5	.71	Study 2 adapted the Southampton Nostalgia Scale (Routledge et al., 2008) to create an index of state-level nostalgia (for a similar measure of daily nostalgia, see Van Tilburg et al., 2018, Study 2; α = .97).
Wildschut et al. (2006)	18	.88	Studies 3–4 created an 18-item state version of Batcho's (1995) Nostalgia Inventory. They did not include the items "church/religion" and "heroes/heroines." Other researchers have used all 20 items (e.g., Stephan et al., 2014, Study 2; α = .92).
Wildschut et al. (2006)	3	.95	This 3-item measure introduced by Wildschut, Sedikides et al. (2006, Study 3) has been frequently used as a manipulation check in studies with an experimental nostalgia induction. Van Tilburg, Sedikides et al. (2018, Study 1) adapted this measure to assess weather-evoked nostalgia (α = .96).

Note. Reliability = Cronbach's α as reported in the key source.

Although the correlation matrix is incomplete, certain patterns are discernible. First, the Southampton Nostalgia Scale (SNS) forms the core of a cluster that includes the Personal Inventory of Nostalgic Experiences (PINE; $.66 \leq r \leq .81$), the Nostalgia Prototype Scale (NPS; $r = .81$), the Nostalgia Inventory (NI; $.40 \leq r \leq .77$), and the Past-Positive subscale of the Time Perspective Inventory (TPI:P-P; $.36 \leq r \leq .61$). The substantial correlations support the construct validity of these five measures of personal nostalgia (Campbell & Fiske, 1959). Second, Holbrook's (1993) Nostalgia Scale, a measure frequently used in past research and still occasionally administered (Lammers & Baldwin, 2018), is relatively weakly correlated with the other scales ($-.01 \leq r \leq .32$). Holbrook generated an initial set of 20 items to index nostalgia proneness and then conducted a stepwise search to eliminate items until he obtained an acceptable chi-square fit for a single-factor model in an exploratory maximum-likelihood factor analysis. This process resulted in a final set of 8 items, which formed the Nostalgia Scale. A subsequent confirmatory maximum-likelihood factor analysis of these 8 items indicated good fit for a single-factor model. The Nostalgia Scale includes items such as "Things used to be better in the good old days,"

"Products are getting shoddier and shoddier," "Modern business constantly builds a better tomorrow" (reversed), and "Technological change will ensure a brighter future" (reversed). Batcho (1998) proposed that Holbrook's scale assesses sociohistorical nostalgia or "a respect or desire for the cultural values or political visions of an earlier historical period" (p. 413). Schindler and Holbrook (2003) conducted a principal components analysis on a set of 52 nostalgia-proneness items that comprised Holbrook's original 20 items, the 12 items of the Experience subscale from Taylor and Konrad's (1980) study of personal dispositions toward the past, and the 20 items of the Antiquarianism subscale from McKechnie's (1977) Environmental Response Inventory. This analysis yielded two dimensions. Items from the latter two instruments had high loadings on the first dimension, which Schindler and Holbrook labeled the Antiques dimension. These items mostly concerned liking for things or objects from the past (e.g., "I would be happy living in an old house full of antique furniture and mementos of the past," "I enjoy browsing in antique shops"). Holbrook's original 20 items loaded primarily on the second dimension, which Schindler and Holbrook labeled the Decline dimension. Echoing Batcho (1998), they proposed that these items tap "the belief that the passing of time is associated with a decline in conditions" (p. 289).

Table 24.3. Correlations among trait-level nostalgia measures

	PINE	NPS	SNS	TPI:P-P	NI	NS	DTP:E	ERI:A
PINE	–	5	5, 7	7	5			
NPS	.81	–	5		5			
SNS	.66 to .81	.81	–	6, 8	5, 8, 10, 11, 12, 13			
TPI:P-P	.40		.36 to .61		4	4		
NI	.74	.81	.40 to .77	.21	–	1, 2, 3, 4		
NS				.01	−.01 to .32	–	9	9
DTP:E						.14	–	9
ERI:A						.22	.56	–

Note. Zero-order correlations are presented below the diagonal. Sources are indicated above the diagonal. PINE = Personal Inventory of Nostalgic Experiences (Newman et al., 2020); NPS = Nostalgia Prototype Scale (Cheung, Sedikides, & Wildschut, 2017); SNS = Southampton Nostalgia Scale (Barrett et al., 2010; Routledge et al., 2008); TPI:P-P = Past-Positive subscale of the Time Perspective Inventory (Zimbardo & Boyd, 1999); NI = Nostalgia Inventory (Batcho, 1995); NS = Nostalgia Scale (Holbrook, 1993); DTP:E = Experience subscale of Dispositions Toward the Past Scales (Taylor & Konrad, 1980); ERI:A = Antiquarianism subscale of the Environmental Response Inventory (McKechnie, 1977).

Sources. [1]Batcho (1998); [2]Batcho (2007); [3]Batcho et al. (2008); [4]Batcho et al. (2011); [5]Kelley et al. (2022); [6]Luo et al. (2016); [7]Newman et al. (2020); [8]Routledge et al. (2008); [9]Schindler & Holbrook (2003); [10]Stephan et al. (2015); [11]Stephan et al. (2014); [12]Tullett et al. (2015); [13]Zhou et al. (2008).

In light of this evidence, we recommend that researchers who wish to assess trait-level nostalgia proneness select one or more measures from the intercorrelated set comprising (in chronological order) NI, TPI:P-P, SNS, NPS, and PINE. Under ideal circumstances, researchers could combine two or more measures from this set to meet Campbell and Fiske's (1959) desideratum of implementing multiple converging operations (for an example of this approach, see Stephan et al., 2015, Study 1). These measures have high internal consistency (Table 24.1), and their convergent validity is supported by sizeable positive correlations with multiple independent attempts to assess the same construct (Table 24.3). In addition, they have encouraging test-retest reliabilities. For the NI, Batcho (1995) reported a 1-week test-retest reliability of .84; for the TPI:P-P, Zimbardo and Boyd (1999) reported a 4-week test-retest reliability of .76; Newman et al. (2020) reported a 10-week test-retest correlation of .64 for the PINE, which equates to Spearman-Brown reliability of .78. We used our data from the Longitudinal Internet Studies for the Social Sciences panel (see below) to calculate 4-month (November 2012–March 2013) and 6½-year (November 2012–April 2019) test-retest reliabilities for the SNS, which equaled .82 and .73, respectively. (Test-retest reliability for NPS is currently unavailable.)

We recommend Holbrook's (1993) Nostalgia Scale, either in its 8- or 20-item version, to researchers with a specific interest in assessing sociohistorical nostalgia or the distinctly conservative belief that society, institutions, people, and products were better in days of yore. Researchers interested in the concept of antiquarianism could select (and, ideally, combine) Taylor and Konrad's (1980) Experience subscale and/or McKechnie's (1977) Antiquarianism subscale. Normative information from large, randomly selected representative samples of specific populations is scarce. However, we administered the SNS and NI to the Longitudinal Internet Studies for the Social Sciences panel, which comprises residents of The Netherlands who were selected based on a true probability sampling of households registered with Statistics Netherlands. Panel data can be accessed at www.surveydata.nl/liss-panel-data-archive.

Perils and Pitfalls

We now consider some perils and pitfalls we have encountered in past research and make several design recommendations to address them. These challenges are neither new nor unique to the study of nostalgia, as they relate to the perennial limitations of correlational research: the third-variable problem and the reverse-causation problem (Campbell & Stanley, 1966; Cook & Campbell, 1979).

Third-Variable Problem and the Perils of Partialling

A study by Cheung et al. (2018) illustrated the third-variable problem in the context of nostalgia research. They showed that nostalgia proneness, as assessed with the SNS (Barrett et al., 2010), shares variance with rumination and counterfactual thinking. How this overlap is treated can profoundly affect conclusions regarding the nature of nostalgia proneness. Rumination is defined as "thoughts and behaviors that focus an individual's attention on the negative mood, the causes and consequences of this mood, and self-evaluations related to the mood" (Rusting & Nolen-Hoeksema, 1998, p. 790). It was assessed with the Ruminative Responses Scale (Treynor et al., 2003). Counterfactual thinking is the cognitive process of imagining alternatives to the past and considering how certain events could have resulted in a different outcome. It was assessed with the Counterfactual Thinking for Negative Events Scale (Rye et al., 2008).

To characterize the similarities and differences among nostalgia, rumination, and counterfactual thinking, Cheung et al. (2018) examined their respective associations with the functions or uses of autobiographical memory, which they assessed with the 39-item Modified Reminiscence Functions Scale (Washington, 2009). These functions are Self-Regard (using memories to reaffirm positive self-attributes), Conversation (referring to shared past experiences to spice up conversations), Boredom Reduction (recalling past experiences to alleviate tedium and break monotony), Intimacy Maintenance (using memories to feel closer to important [deceased] others), Death Preparation (using memories to better accept one's own mortality), Teach/Inform (sharing memories to pass on important insights about life and/or oneself), and Bitterness Revival (using memories to rekindle resentment toward others).

Cheung et al. (2018) found that nostalgia proneness was positively correlated with rumination and counterfactual thinking (which were also positively correlated). We suggest that these correlations could point to a general or *g* factor reflecting global individual differences in past orientedness. More to the point, how one treats the overlap among these variables shapes one's conclusions regarding the nature of nostalgia proneness. For illustrative purposes, we focus on the association between nostalgia and Bitterness Revival scores. Evidence concerning the relation between memory functions and mental health indicates that using memories to rekindle resentment (as indexed by Bitterness Revival) is "negatively related to almost all aspects of mental health that have been studied" (Westerhof et al., 2010, p. 706). The significant, positive correlation between nostalgia proneness and Bitterness Revival ($r = .26$, $p < .001$) suggests, then, that nostalgia is maladaptive. However, rumination and counterfactual thinking were also positively correlated with Bitterness Revival and more strongly so than nostalgia. Controlling for these "third variables" in a multiple regression analysis significantly reduced the magnitude of the nostalgia – Bitterness Revival association and rendered it nonsignificant ($\beta = .06$). This result points to a different conclusion about nostalgia.

The process of controlling for, or partialling, "third variables" can be perilous, however. A key concern relates to the substantive interpretation of a predictor variable after the variance shared with other predictors is removed. This problem is most severe when the variables in the predictor set are highly correlated, have fuzzy boundaries, and are unreliable. The problem is ameliorated when correlations among predictors are modest, the constructs are homogeneous or clearly delineated, and the measures are reliable (Lynam et al., 2006). When these conditions can be met, controlling for "third variables," such as rumination, can provide a clearer picture of nostalgia's nomological net. Where there are discrepancies, prior theory and evidence should also play a role in deciding whether to place confidence in the zero-order or partial relations (Hoyle & Robinson, 2004). In our illustrative case, one could turn to findings by Van Tilburg, Wildschut et al. (2018), who instructed participants to rate the similarities/differences between nostalgia and 10 other emotions: embarrassment, gratitude, guilt, hurt feelings, inspiration, passion, pride, self-compassion, shame, and unrequited love. If nostalgia is associated with resentful recollection of perceived slights at the hands of others (Bitterness Revival), it should be perceived as relatively similar to hurt feelings and dissimilar to gratitude. Instead, the opposite was the case: Nostalgia was perceived as similar to gratitude and dissimilar to hurt feelings. This lends credence to the nonsignificant partial relation between nostalgia proneness and Bitterness Revival and casts doubt on the positive zero-order relation.

Reverse-Causation Problem and the Role of Experiments

The second issue that deserves scrutiny is the reverse-causation problem. This issue is, of course, endemic in correlational research, but it may have special relevance to nostalgia. To understand why this is the case, one must revisit Hofer (1688/1934) and his acolytes. They observed that nostalgia was associated with dysfunctional symptoms (e.g., anxiety, depression, bouts of weeping, loss of appetite, insomnia, anorexia, suicidal ideation) and rushed to the conclusion that nostalgia was the cause of such symptoms. Surprisingly, they never considered the reverse causal sequence; after all, the selectively studied populations (e.g., mercenaries, soldiers, immigrants) were facing considerable challenges under adverse, and sometimes life-threatening, circumstances in unfamiliar or dangerous environments. The possibility that nostalgia was triggered by (rather than being the cause of) psychological and physiological adversity was hiding in plain sight.

In more recent years, however, the idea that nostalgia acts as a coping mechanism in times of adversity has gained traction (Wildschut et al., 2011). The link between loneliness and nostalgia is an illustrative case. Initial evidence for a relation between loneliness and nostalgia emerged when we (Wildschut et al., 2006, Study 2) asked British undergraduates to write about the circumstances under which they become nostalgic. The most frequently mentioned trigger of nostalgia (38 % of responses) was negative affect (e.g., "Generally I think about nostalgic experiences when things are not going very well – lonely or depressed."). Within this broad category of negative affect, loneliness was by far the most common discrete affective state. One participant wrote, for example: "If I ever feel lonely or sad, I tend to think of my friends or family whom I haven't seen for a long time."

A series of studies by Zhou et al. (2008) threw the reverse-causation problem in stark relief. In their first study, they administered measures of loneliness (UCLA Loneliness Scale; Russell, 1996), nostalgia proneness (SNS), and perceived social support (Multidimensional Scale of Perceived Social Support; Zimet et al., 1988) to 758 Chinese children who had migrated with their parents from rural areas to a large city. (A pilot study established that Chinese elementary-school children understood the meaning of the Chinese word for nostalgia, *huaijiu*, and showed good comprehension of the SNS.) Zero-order correlations revealed that, not surprisingly, loneliness was negatively correlated with perceived social support ($r = -.17, p < .001$). Furthermore, nostalgia proneness was positively correlated with loneliness ($r = .14, p < .001$). At first glance, this finding would seem to support the bleak, Hoferian view of nostalgia. Yet, nostalgia proneness was also positively correlated with perceived social support ($r = .33, p < .001$). How to make sense of this perplexing pattern of correlations? Zhou et al. formulated a model that specified three causal paths: (1) Loneliness leads to reduced perceptions of perceived social support, (2) loneliness increases nostalgia, and (3) nostalgia fosters perceived social support (because it frequently pertains to close others; Wildschut et al., 2006). This model specifies that loneliness affects perceived social support in two distinct ways. Whereas the direct effect of loneliness is to reduce perceived social support, the indirect effect of loneliness is to increase perceived social support via nostalgia. In statistical terms, this pattern of relations gives rise to a situation of suppression or inconsistent mediation. When the intervening variable is controlled for, the direct effect of the initial predictor is strengthened (as opposed to weakened like in ordinary mediation models; Paulhus et al., 2004). Results supported these predictions: When the presumed palliative role of nostalgia proneness was controlled for, the negative association between loneliness and perceived social support became significantly more negative. In summary, lonely migrant children perceived little social support but were also the most nostalgic. This high level of nostalgia, in turn, predicted increased perceptions of social support.

To be sure, although Zhou et al. (2008, Study 1) showed that nostalgia need not cause loneliness, evidence for the postulated reverse effect of loneliness on nostalgia was suggestive at best; wishing for a causal relation does not make it so. Even when ignoring the third-variable problem, one must still contend with the fact that three variables can be ordered in six different sequences, with the number of possible sequences increasing exponentially with each added variable. One approach to this issue has been to use structural equation modeling to compare alternative sequences (e.g., Cheung, Sedikides, & Wildschut, 2017). The Akaike information criterion (AIC; Akaike, 1974) and the expected cross-validation index (ECVI; Browne & Cudeck, 1993) can be used to compare competing models. Another approach has been to implement longitudinal designs and crosslagged analyses (Newman et al., 2020). Whereas both approaches are informative, neither is conclusive. Experiments can furnish more decisive evidence.

Returning to our illustrative case, Zhou et al. (2008, Studies 2–3) implemented an experimental causal chain design (Spencer et al., 2005) to test their postulated model (loneliness ⇒ nostalgia ⇒ perceived social support). To examine the first link in the chain, they experimentally induced loneliness and then measured nostalgia. Participants completed the ostensibly valid and reliable Southampton Loneliness Scale, which consisted of 10 items drawn from the UCLA Loneliness Scale. In the high-loneliness condition, items were phrased to elicit agreement (e.g., "I sometimes feel alone"); in the low-loneliness condition, items were phrased to elicit disagreement (e.g., "I always feel alone"). As intended, participants in the high-loneliness condition agreed with more items than participants in the low-loneliness condition. Next, the researchers told those in the high-loneliness condition that they were "well above average on loneliness" compared to their peers. Those in the low-loneliness condition were informed that they were "very low on loneliness" compared to their peers. As a final step, participants were instructed to list the reasons for their loneliness score. Following the (successful) loneliness manipulation, momentary nostalgia was assessed with a state version of the SNS. In Table 24.2 we present additional information about this and other assessments of state-level nostalgia. As hypothesized, participants in the high-loneliness condition reported significantly higher levels of nostalgia than those in the low-loneliness condition. To test the second link in the chain, the researchers induced nostalgia and then measured perceived social support. Participants in the nostalgia condition were instructed to recall and reflect on a nostalgic event from their past. Participants in the control condition recalled and reflected on an ordinary event from their past. Next, participants completed two measures of perceived social support. One was a state version of the Multidimensional Scale of Perceived Social Support (Zimet et al., 1988), and the other involved estimating how many friends would volunteer their time to help one receive extra course credit. As hypothesized, compared to controls nostalgic participants reported higher overall levels of perceived social support.

Similar evidence has accumulated for the palliative or homeostatic role of nostalgia in reaction to other types of psychological and physiological threat: Nostalgia and adversity are linked, but the direction of causality is from adversity to increased nostalgia, rather than the reverse (for reviews, see Sedikides & Wildschut, 2016; Sedikides et al.,

2015, 2018). By drawing attention to this issue, we want to raise awareness that characterizing nostalgia as either adaptive or maladaptive solely based on correlational data is tenuous at best. This is not meant to say that experiments offer a methodological panacea or that correlations are uninformative, but correlations serve as an investigative starting point rather than a conclusion.

Varieties of Nostalgia

The sheer diversity of nostalgia research does not permit an exhaustive review, but, before closing, we touch briefly on notable contributions and developments. A well-established and generative tradition in consumer research concerns advertising- and brand-evoked nostalgia (Holbrook, 1993; Merchant et al., 2013). In a typical study, participants view several product advertisements and, for each, rate their level of evoked nostalgia, as well as product-related attitudes and purchase intentions. Findings consistently indicate that advertising-evoked nostalgia is positively associated with favorable product-related attitudes and purchase intentions (Pascal et al., 2002). We refer the interested reader to Jain et al. (2019), who provided a comprehensive overview of advertising- and brand-evoked nostalgia measures.

Another rich vein of research has explored nostalgia at the relational and collective levels of self-definition (Sedikides & Brewer, 2001). In a study by Hepper et al. (2016), dyads (friends and romantic couples) completed measures of attachment style, nostalgia-proneness within their relationship, and relationship satisfaction. Attachment anxiety was negatively associated with relationship satisfaction only for those low, not high, in relational nostalgia. At the collective level, organizational nostalgia (a sentimental longing or wistful affection for past events and aspects of one's organizational life, including buildings, colleagues, leaders, and technology) is positively associated with work meaning and reduces turnover intentions (Leunissen et al., 2018). Likewise, group-level nostalgia (Wildschut et al., 2014) and national nostalgia (Smeekes, 2015) have been linked with positive attitudes and behavior toward the ingroup. The link between these collective forms of nostalgia and outgroup attitudes is more nuanced and context-dependent, however, with some studies suggesting a negative association (Cheung, Sedikides, Wildschut et al., 2017) and others identifying potential benefits for intergroup harmony (Martinovic et al., 2017).

To conclude, the field of nostalgia is young, diverse, vibrant, and, admittedly, somewhat anarchic and in flux. Long may it stay that way.

References

Akaike, H. (1974). A new look at the statistical model identification. *IEEE Transactions on Automatic Control, 19,* 716–723. https://doi.org/10.1109/TAC.1974.1100705

Baldwin, M., Biernat, M., & Landau, M. J. (2015). Remembering the real me: Nostalgia offers a window to the intrinsic self. *Journal of Personality and Social Psychology, 108,* 128–147. https://doi.org/10.1037/a0038033

Baldwin, M., White, M. H., & Sullivan, D. (2018). Nostalgia for America's past can buffer collective guilt. *European Journal of Social Psychology, 48,* 433–446. https://doi.org/10.1002/ejsp.2348

Barrett, F.S., Grimm, K.J., Robins, R.W., Wildschut, T., Sedikides, C., & Janata, P. (2010). Music-evoked nostalgia: Affect, memory, and personality. *Emotion, 10*, 390–403. https://doi.org/10.1037/a0019006

Batcho, K.I. (1995). Nostalgia: A psychological perspective. *Perceptual and Motor Skills, 80,* 131–143. https://doi.org/10.2466/pms.1995.80.1.131

Batcho, K.I. (1998). Personal nostalgia, world view, memory, and emotionality. *Perceptual and Motor Skills, 87,* 411–432. https://doi.org/10.2466/pms.1998.87.2.411

Batcho, K.I. (2007). Nostalgia and the emotional tone and content of song lyrics. *American Journal of Psychology, 120,* 361–381. https://doi.org/10.2307/20445410

Batcho, K.I., DaRin, M.L., Nave, A.M., & Yaworsky, R.R. (2008). Nostalgia and identity in song lyrics. *Psychology of Aesthetics, Creativity, and the Arts, 2*(4), 236–244. https://doi.org/10.1037/1931-3896.2.4.236

Batcho, K.I., Nave, A.M., & DaRin, M.L. (2011). A retrospective survey of childhood experiences. *Journal of Happiness Studies, 12*, 531–545. https://doi.org/10.1007/s10902-010-9213-y

Browne, M.W., & Cudeck, R. (1993). Alternative ways of assessing model fit. In K.A. Bollen & J.S. Long (Eds.), *Testing structural equation models* (pp. 136–162). Sage.

Campbell, D.T., & Fiske, D.W. (1959). Convergent and discriminant validation by the multitrait-multimethod matrix. *Psychological Bulletin, 56,* 81–105. https://doi.org/10.1037/h0046016

Campbell, D.T., & Stanley, J.C. (1966). *Experimental and quasi-experimental designs for research.* Rand McNally.

Cheung, W.Y., Sedikides, C., & Wildschut, T. (2017). Nostalgia proneness and reduced prejudice. *Personality and Individual Differences, 15,* 89–97. https://doi.org/10.1016/j.paid.2016.12.045

Cheung, W.Y., Sedikides, C., Wildschut, T., Tausch, N., & Ayanian, A.H. (2017). Collective nostalgia is associated with stronger outgroup-directed anger and participation in ingroup-favoring collective action. *Journal of Social and Political Psychology, 5,* 301–319. https://doi.org/10.5964/jspp.v5i2.697

Cheung, W.Y., Wildschut, T., & Sedikides, C. (2018). Autobiographical memory functions of nostalgia in comparison to rumination and counterfactual thinking: Similarity and uniqueness. *Memory, 26,* 229–237. https://doi.org/10.1080/09658211.2017.1346129

Cook, T.D., & Campbell, D.T. (1979). *Quasi-experimentation: Design and analysis issues for field settings.* Houghton Mifflin.

Darwin, C. (1896). *The expression of the emotions in man and animals.* D. Appleton. (Original work published 1872)

Davis, F. (1979). *Yearning for yesterday: A sociology of nostalgia.* The Free Press.

Frost, I. (1938). Homesickness and immigrant psychoses. *Journal of Mental Science, 84*, 801–847. https://doi.org/10.1192/bjp.84.352.801

Hepper, E.G., Wildschut, T., & Sedikides, C. (2016, July). *Nostalgia buffers perceptions of relationship quality and partner behaviour for anxiously attached individuals.* Paper presented at International Association of Relationship Research Conference, Toronto, Canada.

Hofer, J. (1934). Medical dissertation on nostalgia. (C.K. Anspach, Trans.). *Bulletin of the History of Medicine, 2*, 376–391. (Original work published 1688)

Holbrook, M. (1993). Nostalgia and consumption preferences: Some emerging patterns of consumer tastes. *Journal of Consumer Research, 20,* 245–265. https://doi.org/10.1086/209346

Hoyle, R.H., & Robinson, J.I. (2004). A reasoned approach to measurement in social psychological research. In C. Sansone, C. Morf, & A.T. Panter (Eds.), *Handbook of methods in social psychology* (pp. 213–233). Sage.

Iyer, A., & Jetten, J. (2011). What's left behind: Identity continuity moderates the effect of nostalgia on well-being and life choices. *Journal of Personality and Social Psychology, 101*, 94–108. https://doi.org/10.1037/a0022496

Jackson, S.W. (1986). *Melancholia and depression: From Hippocratic times to modern times.* Yale University Press. https://doi.org/10.2307/j.ctt1xp3stn

Jain, V., Merchant, A., Roy, S., & Ford, J.B. (2019). Developing an emic scale to measure ad-evoked nostalgia in a collectivist emerging market, India. *Journal of Business Research, 99,* 140–156. https://doi.org/10.1016/j.jbusres.2019.02.039

Juhl, J., Wildschut, T., Sedikides, C., Diebel, T., Cheung, W. Y., & Vingerhoets, A. J. J. M. (2020). Nostalgia proneness and empathy: Generality, underlying mechanism, and implications for prosocial behavior. *Journal of Personality, 88*(3), 485–500. https://doi.org/10.1111/jopy.12505

Kelley, N. J., Davis, W. E., Dang, J., Liu, L., Wildschut, T., & Sedikides, C. (2022). Nostalgia confers psychological wellbeing by increasing authenticity. *Journal of Experimental Social Psychology*. Advance online publication. https://doi.org/10.1016/j.jesp.2022.104379

Kleiner, J. (1977). On nostalgia. In C. W. Socarides (Ed.), *The world of emotions* (pp. 471–498). International University Press.

Lammers, J., & Baldwin, M. (2018). Past-focused temporal communication overcomes conservatives' resistance to liberal political ideas. *Journal of Personality and Social Psychology, 114,* 599–619. https://doi.org/10.1037/pspi0000121

Leunissen, J., Sedikides, C., Wildschut, T., & Cohen, T. R. (2018). Organizational nostalgia increases work meaning: The moderating role of burnout. *Journal of Occupational Health Psychology, 23,* 44–57. https://doi.org/10.1037/ocp0000059

Luo, Y. L. L., Liu, Y., Cai, H., Wildschut, T., & Sedikides, C. (2016). Nostalgia and self-enhancement: Phenotypic and genetic approaches. *Social Psychological and Personality Science, 7,* 857–866. https://doi.org/10.1177/1948550616660158

Lynam, D. R., Hoyle, R. H., & Newman, J. P. (2006). The perils of partialling: Cautionary tales from aggression and psychopathy. *Assessment, 13,* 328–341. https://doi.org/10.1177/1073191106290562

Martinovic, B., Jetten, J., Smeekes, A., & Verkuyten, M. (2017). Collective memory of a dissolved country: Collective nostalgia and guilt as predictors of interethnic relations between diaspora groups from former Yugoslavia. *Journal of Social and Political Psychology, 5,* 588–607. https://doi.org/10.5964/jspp.v5i2.733

Matt, S. J. (2007). You can't go home again: Homesickness and nostalgia in U. S. history. *Journal of American History, 94,* 469–497. https://doi.org/10.2307/25094961

McKechnie, G. E. (1977). The Environmental Response Inventory in application. *Environment and Behavior, 9,* 255–276. https://doi.org/10.1177/001391657792006

Merchant, A., Latour, K., Ford, J. B., & Latour, M. S. (2013). How strong is the pull of the past? Measuring personal nostalgia evoked by advertising. *Journal of Advertising Research, 53,* 150–165. https://doi.org/10.2501/JAR-53-2-150-165

Newman, D. B., Sachs, M. E., Stone, A. A., & Schwarz, N. (2020). Nostalgia and well-being in daily life: An ecological validity perspective. *Journal of Personality and Social Psychology, 118*(2), 325–347. https://doi.org/10.1037/pspp0000236

O'Sullivan, L. (2012). The time and place of nostalgia: Re-situating a French disease. *Journal of the History of Medicine and Allied Sciences, 67,* 626–649. https://doi.org/10.1093/jhmas/jrr058

Pascal, V. J., Sprott, D. E., & Muehling, D. D. (2002). The influence of evoked nostalgia on consumers' responses to advertising: An exploratory study. *Journal of Current Issues and Research in Advertising, 24,* 39–49. https://doi.org/10.1080/10641734.2002.10505126

Paulhus, D., Robins, R., Trzesniewski, K., & Tracy, J. (2004). Two replicable suppressor situations in personality research. *Multivariate Behavioral Research, 39,* 301–326. https://doi.org/10.1207/s15327906mbr3902_7

Reid, C. A., Green, J. D., Wildschut, T., & Sedikides, C. (2015). Scent-evoked nostalgia. *Memory, 23,* 157–166. https://doi.org/10.1080/09658211.2013.876048

Rousseau, G. G., & Venter, D. J. L. (2000). The relationship between nostalgia and consumer preference: Replication and extension. *Journal of Industrial Psychology, 26,* 32–36. https://doi.org/10.4102/sajip.v26i2.705

Routledge, C., Arndt, J., Sedikides, C., & Wildschut, T. (2008). A blast from the past: The terror management function of nostalgia. *Journal of Experimental Social Psychology, 44,* 132–140. https://doi.org/10.1016/j.jesp.2006.11.001

Russell, D. (1996). The UCLA Loneliness Scale (Version 3): Reliability, validity, and factor structure. *Journal of Personality Assessment, 66,* 20–40. https://doi.org/10.1207/s15327752jpa6601_2

Rusting, C.L., & Nolen-Hoeksema, S. (1998). Regulating responses to anger: Effects of rumination and distraction on angry mood. *Journal of Personality and Social Psychology, 74,* 790–803. https://doi.org/10.1037/0022-3514.74.3.790

Rye, M.S., Cahoon, M.B., Ali, R.S., & Daftary, T. (2008). Development and validation of the Counterfactual Thinking for Negative Events Scale. *Journal of Personality Assessment, 90,* 261–269. https://doi.org/10.1080/00223890701884996

Schindler, R.M., & Holbrook, M.B. (2003). Nostalgia for early experience as a determinant of consumer preferences. *Psychology & Marketing, 20,* 275–302. https://doi.org/10.1002/mar.10074

Sedikides, C., & Brewer, M.B. (Eds.). (2001). *Individual self, relational self, collective self.* Psychology Press.

Sedikides, C., & Wildschut, T. (2016). Past forward: Nostalgia as a motivational force. *Trends in Cognitive Sciences, 20,* 319–321. https://doi.org/10.1016/j.tics.2016.01.008

Sedikides, C., & Wildschut, T. (2019). The sociality of personal and collective nostalgia. *European Review of Social Psychology, 30,* 123–173. https://doi.org/10.1080/10463283.2019.1630098

Sedikides, C., Wildschut, T., Arndt, J., & Routledge, C. (2008). Nostalgia: past, present, and future. *Current Directions in Psychological Science, 17,* 304–307. https://doi.org/10.1111/j.1467-8721.2008.00595.x

Sedikides, C., Wildschut, T., Cheung, W.-Y., Routledge, C., Hepper, E.G., Arndt, J., Vail, K., Zhou, X., Brackstone, K., & Vingerhoets, A.J.J.M. (2016). Nostalgia fosters self-continuity: Uncovering the mechanism (social connectedness) and the consequence (eudaimonic well-being). *Emotion, 16,* 524–539. https://doi.org/10.1037/emo0000136

Sedikides, C., Wildschut, T., Routledge, C., Arndt, J., Hepper, E.G., & Zhou, Z. (2015). To nostalgize: Mixing memory with affect and desire. *Advances in Experimental Social Psychology, 51,* 189–273. https://doi.org/10.1016/bs.aesp.2014.10.001

Sedikides, C., Wildschut, T., & Stephan, E. (2018). Nostalgia shapes and potentiates the future. In J.P. Forgas & R.F. Baumeister (Eds.), *The social psychology of living well* (pp. 181–199). Routledge. https://doi.org/10.4324/9781351189712-11

Smeekes, A. (2015). National nostalgia: a group-level emotion that benefits the in-group but hampers intergroup relations. *International Journal of Intercultural Relations, 49,* 54–67. https://doi.org/10.1016/j.ijintrel.2015.07.001

Spencer, S.J., Zanna, M., & Fong, G.T. (2005). Establishing a causal chain: Why experiments are often more effective than mediational analyses in examining psychological processes. *Journal of Personality and Social Psychology, 89,* 845–851. https://doi.org/10.1037/0022-3514.89.6.845

Stephan, E., Sedikides, C., Wildschut, T., Cheung, W.Y., Routledge, C., & Arndt, J. (2015). Nostalgia-evoked inspiration: Mediating mechanisms and motivational consequences. *Personality and Social Psychology Bulletin, 41,* 1395–1410. https://doi.org/10.1177/0146167215596985

Stephan, E., Wildschut, T., Sedikides, C., Zhou, X., He, W., Routledge, C., Cheung, W.Y., & Vingerhoets, A.J.J.M. (2014). The mnemonic mover: Nostalgia regulates avoidance and approach motivation. *Emotion, 14,* 545–561. https://doi.org/10.1037/a0035673

Taylor, S.M., & Konrad, V.A. (1980). Scaling dispositions toward the past. *Environment and Behavior, 12,* 283–307. https://doi.org/10.1177/0013916580123001

Thurber, C.A., & Walton, E.A. (2007). Preventing and treating homesickness. *Pediatrics, 119,* 843–858. https://doi.org/10.1542/peds.2006-2781

Treynor, W., Gonzalez, R., & Nolen-Hoeksema, S. (2003). Rumination reconsidered: A psychometric analysis. *Cognitive Therapy and Research, 27,* 247–259. https://doi.org/10.1023/A:1023910315561

Tullett, A., Wildschut, T., Inzlicht, M., & Sedikides, C. (2015). Right-frontal cortical asymmetry predicts increased proneness to nostalgia. *Psychophysiology, 52,* 990–996. https://doi.org/10.1111/psyp.12438

Van Tilburg, W.A.P., Sedikides, C., & Wildschut, T. (2018). Adverse weather evokes nostalgia. *Personality and Social Psychology Bulletin, 44,* 984–995. https://doi.org/10.1177/0146167218756030

Van Tilburg, W.A.P., Wildschut, T., & Sedikides, C. (2018). Nostalgia's place among self-relevant emotions. *Cognition and Emotion, 32,* 742–759. https://doi.org/10.1080/02699931.2017.1351331

Washington, G. (2009). Modification and psychometric testing of the Reminiscence Functions Scale. *Journal of Nursing Measurement, 17,* 134–147. https://doi.org/10.1891/1061-3749.17.2.134

Westerhof, G.J., Bohlmeijer, E., & Webster, J.D. (2010). Reminiscence and mental health: A review of recent progress in theory, research, and interventions. *Ageing & Society, 30,* 697–721. https://doi.org/10.1017/S0144686X09990328

Wildschut, T., Bruder, M., Robertson, S., Van Tilburg, W.A.P., & Sedikides, C. (2014). Collective nostalgia: A group-level emotion that confers unique benefits on the group. *Journal of Personality and Social Psychology, 107,* 844–863. https://doi.org/10.1037/a0037760

Wildschut, T., Sedikides, C., Arndt, J., & Routledge, C. (2006). Nostalgia: Content, triggers, functions. *Journal of Personality and Social Psychology, 91,* 975–993. https://doi.org/10.1037/0022-3514.91.5.975

Wildschut, T., Sedikides, C., & Cordaro, F. (2011). Self-regulatory interplay between positive and negative emotions: The case of loneliness and nostalgia. In I. Nyklicek, A.J.J.M. Vingerhoets, & M. Zeelenberg (Eds.), *Emotion regulation and well-being* (pp. 67–83). Springer. https://doi.org/10.1007/978-1-4419-6953-8_5

Wohl, M.J.A., Kim, H.S., Salmon, M., Santesso, D., Wildschut, T., & Sedikides, C. (2018). Discontinuity-induced nostalgia improves the odds of a self-reported quit attempt among people living with addiction. *Journal of Experimental Social Psychology, 75,* 83–94. https://doi.org/10.1016/j.jesp.2017.11.011

Zhou, X., Sedikides, C., Wildschut, C., & Gao, D.-G. (2008). Counteracting loneliness: On the restorative function of nostalgia. *Psychological Science, 19,* 1023–1029. https://doi.org/10.1111/j.1467-9280.2008.02194.x

Zhou, X., Wildschut, T., Sedikides, C., Chen, X., & Vingerhoets, A.J.J.M. (2012). Heartwarming memories: Nostalgia maintains physiological comfort. *Emotion, 12,* 678–684. https://doi.org/10.1037/a0028236

Zimbardo, P.G., & Boyd, J.N. (1999). Putting time in perspective: A valid, reliable individual-difference metric. *Journal of Personality and Social Psychology, 77,* 1271–1288. https://doi.org/10.1037/0022-3514.77.6.1271

Zimet, G.D., Dahlem, N.W., Zimet, S.G., & Farley, G.K. (1988). The Multidimensional Scale of Perceived Social Support. *Journal of Personality Assessment, 52,* 30–41. https://doi.org/10.1207/s15327752jpa5201_2

Zou, X., Lee, M., Wildschut, T., & Sedikides, C. (2019). Nostalgia increases financial risk taking. *Personality and Social Psychology Bulletin, 45,* 907–919. https://doi.org/10.1177/0146167218799717

Zou, X., Wildschut, T., Cable, D., & Sedikides, C. (2018). Nostalgia for host culture facilitates repatriation success: The role of self-continuity. *Self and Identity, 17,* 327–342. https://doi.org/10.1080/15298868.2017.1378123

Contributors

Arnold B. Bakker
Center of Excellence for Positive Organizational Psychology
Erasmus University Rotterdam
Woudestein Campus
Mandeville Building T13-47
PO Box 1738
3000 DR Rotterdam
The Netherlands
bakker@fsw.eur.nl

Lynn A. Barnett
Department of Recreation, Sport & Tourism
University of Illinois
1204 S. Fourth St.
Champaign, IL 61820
USA
lynnbm@illinois.edu

Marta Bassi
Department of Biomedical and Clinical Sciences
University of Milan
Via G.B. Grassi 74
20157 Milan
Italy
marta.bassi@unimi.it

Joel A. Blanco
Department of Exercise Science & Sport
Millikin University
1099 W. Wood St. D105
Decatur, IL 62522
USA
jblanco@millikin.edu

Guy Bodenmann
Department of Psychology
University of Zurich
Binzmuehlestrasse 14, Box 23
8050 Zurich
Switzerland
guy.bodenmann@psychologie.uzh.ch

Kay Brauer
Department of Psychology
Martin Luther University Halle-Wittenberg
Emil-Abderhalden-Straße 26-27
06108 Halle/Saale
Germany
kay.brauer@psych.uni-halle.de

Covadonga Chaves
Department of Personality, Assessment and Clinical Psychology
Complutense University of Madrid
Campus de Somosaguas
28223 Pozuelo de Alarcón
Madrid
Spain
cchavesv@ucm.es

Jeremy D. W. Clifton
Department of Psychology
University of Pennsylvania
Solomon Labs
3720 Walnut St., Office C2
Philadelphia, PA 19104
USA
cliftonj@sas.upenn.edu

Susan Coats
Azusa Pacifc University
21003 Evergreen Circle
Walnut, CA 91789
USA
coatslep@gmail.com

Antonella Delle Fave
Department of Pathophysiology and Transplantation
University of Milan
via Francesco Sforza 35
20122 Milan
Italy
antonella.dellefave@unimi.it

A. Demaske
Department of Psychology
Wake Forest University
PO Box 7778
Winston-Salem, NC 27109
USA
demaas18@wfu.edu

Rhett Diessner
Department of Psychology
Lewis-Clark State College
500 8th Avenue
Lewiston, ID 83501
USA
diessner@lcsc.edu

Erin Dowdy
International Center for School-Based Youth Development
University of California Santa Barbara
Building 275
Santa Barbara, CA 93106-9490
USA
edowdy@education.ucsb.edu

Barbara L. Fredrickson
Department of Psychology and Neuroscience
University of North Carolina at Chapel Hill
Davie Hall, Campus Box 3270
Chapel Hill, NC 27599-3270
USA
blf@unc.edu

Michael J. Furlong
International Center for School-Based Youth Development
University of California Santa Barbara
Building 275
Santa Barbara, CA 93106-9490
USA
mfurlong@ucsb.edu

Fabian Gander
Department of Psychology
University of Basel
Missionsstrasse 62
4055 Basel
Switzerland
mail@fabiangander.ch

Marianna Graziosi
Department of Clinical Psychology
Hofstra University
135 Hofstra University
Hempstead, NY 11549
USA
marigraz@sas.upenn.edu

Sonja Heintz
School of Psychology
Faculty of Health
University of Plymouth
Drake Circus
Plymouth, PL4 8AA
UK
sonja.heintz@plymouth.ac.uk

Gonzalo Hervas
Department of Personality, Assessment and Clinical Psychology
Complutense University of Madrid
Campus de Somosaguas
28223 Pozuelo de Alarcón
Madrid
Spain
ghvervas@psi.ucm.es

Tameisha Hinton
International Center for School-Based Youth Development
University of California Santa Barbara
Building 275
Santa Barbara, CA 93106-9490
USA
thinton@ucsb.edu

Stefan Höfer
Department of Medical Psychology
Medical University Innsbruck
Christoph-Probst-Platz 1
6020 Innsbruck
Austria
stefan.hoefer@i-med.ac.at

Jennifer Hofmann
Department of Psychology
University of Zurich
Hirschengraben 84
8001 Zurich
Switzerland
jennifer.hofmann@sae.uzh.ch

Indra Alam Syah Bin Aziz
School of Social Sciences
Singapore Management University
90 Stamford Road, Level 4
Singapore 178903
Republic of Singapore
indra.rc@gmail.com

Eranda Jayawickreme
Department of Psychology
Wake Forest University
PO Box 7778
Winston-Salem, NC 27109
USA
jayawide@wfu.edu

Jun Sheng Keh
School of Social Sciences
Singapore Management University
90 Stamford Road, Level 4
Singapore 178903
Republic of Singapore
jskeh.2017@phdps.smu.edu.sg

Eui Kyung Kim
Graduate School of Education
University of California Riverside
Sproul Hall
W. Campus Drive
Riverside, CA 92507
USA
euikyung.kim@ucr.edu

Aleksandra Luszczynska
Wroclaw Faculty of Psychology
SWPS University of Social Sciences and Humanities
30B Ostrowskiego St.
53-238 Wroclaw
Poland
aluszczy@uccs.edu

Frank Martela
Department of Industrial Engineering and Management
Aalto University
PO Box 15500
00076 Aalto
Finland
frank.martela@aalto.fi

Juan C. Marzo
Department of Health Psychology
University Miguel Hernandez de Elche
Avenida de la Universidad, s/n
03202 Elche, Alicante
Spain
jc.marzo@umh.es

Sara Etz Mendonca
Department of Psychology
Wake Forest University
PO Box 7778
Winston-Salem, NC 27109
USA
mendons@wfu.edu

Cristian Ochoa
Faculty of Psychology
Clinical Psychology and Psychobiology Department
University of Barcelona
Passeig de la Vall D'Hebron, 171
08035 Barcelona
Spain
cochoa@ub.edu

Jennica Paz
College of Education
San Diego State University
5500 Campanile Drive
San Diego, CA 92182-1154
USA
jennica.paz@sdsu.edu

José A. Piqueras
Department of Health Psychology
University Miguel Hernandez de Elche
Avenida de la Universidad, s/n
03202 Elche, Alicante
Spain
jpiqueras@umh.es

René T. Proyer
Department of Psychology
Martin Luther University Halle-Wittenberg
Emil-Abderhalden-Straße 26–27
06108 Halle/Saale
Germany
rene.proyer@psych.uni-halle.de

Sonia Rahimi
Department of Psychology
Université du Québec à Montréal
PO Box 8888, Station Centre-Ville
Montréal, QC H3C 3P8
Canada
sonia.rahimi@mail.mcgill.ca

Pablo Roca
Department of Personality, Assessment and Clinical Psychology
Complutense University of Madrid
Campus de Somosaguas
28223 Pozuelo de Alarcón
Madrid
Spain
pabloroc@ucm.es

Tíscar Rodríguez-Jiménez
Department of Psychology and Sociology
University of Zaragoza
C/ Atarazanas, 4
44003 Teruel
Spain
trodriguez@unizar.es

Willibald Ruch
Department of Psychology
University of Zurich
Binzmuehlestrasse 14, Box 1
8050 Zurich
Switzerland
w.ruch@psychologie.uzh.ch

Wilmar B. Schaufeli
Department of Psychology
KU Leuven
Dekenstraat 2, Box 3725
3000 Leuven
Belgium
wilmar.schaufeli@kuleuven.be

Ralf Schwarzer
Department of Education and Psychology
Freie Universität Berlin
Habelschwerdter Allee 45
14195 Berlin
Germany
ralf.schwarzer@fu-berlin.de

Constantine Sedikides
Center for Research on Self and Identity
School of Psychology
University of Southampton
University Road
Southampton SO17 1BJ
UK
C.Sedikides@soton.ac.uk

Mirjam Senn
Department of Psychology
University of Zurich
Binzmuehlestrasse 14, Box 23
8050 Zurich
Switzerland
mirjam.senn@psychologie.uzh.ch

Emma Sims
Department of Psychology
Wake Forest University
PO Box 7778
Winston-Salem, NC 27109
USA
emmasims1996@gmail.com

Michael F. Steger
Department of Psychology
Colorado State University
Mail Stop 1876
Fort Collins, CO 80523-1876
USA
Michael.F.Steger@colostate.edu

Qin Ying Tan
School of Social Sciences
Singapore Management University
90 Stamford Road, Level 4
Singapore 178903
Republic of Singapore
qinying.tan.2017@phdps.smu.edu.sg

Yan Qiang Tan
School of Social Sciences
Singapore Management University
90 Stamford Road, Level 4
Singapore 178903
Republic of Singapore
yqtan.2017@msps.smu.edu.sg

Louis Tay
Department of Psychological Sciences
Purdue University
703 Third Street
West Lafayette, IN 47907
USA
stay@purdue.edu

William Tov
School of Social Sciences
Singapore Management University
90 Stamford Road, Level 4
Singapore 178903
Republic of Singapore
williamtov@smu.edu.sg

Robert J. Vallerand
Department of Psychology
Université du Québec à Montréal
PO Box 8888, Station Centre-Ville
Montréal, QC H3C 3P8
Canada
vallerand.bob@gmail.com

Carmelo Vazquez
Department of Personality, Assessment and Clinical Psychology
Complutense University of Madrid
Campus de Somosaguas
28223 Pozuelo de Alarcón
Madrid
Spain
cvazquez@ucm.es

Lisa Wagner
Department of Psychology
Jacobs Center for Productive Youth Development
University of Zurich
Andreasstrasse 15
8050 Zurich
Switzerland
l.wagner@psychologie.uzh.ch

Tim Wildschut
Center for Research on Self and Identity
School of Psychology
University of Southampton
University Road
Southampton SO17 1BJ
UK
timw@soton.ac.uk

David Bryce Yaden
Department of Psychiatry and Behavioral Sciences
Johns Hopkins University School of Medicine
5510 Nathan Shock Drive, Room 3037
Baltimore, MD 21224
USA
dyaden1@jhmi.edu

Darya L. Zabelina
Department of Psychological Science
University of Arkansas
480 Campus Drive
Fayetteville, AR 72701
USA
dlzabeli@uark.edu

Fanyi Zhang
Department of Psychological Sciences
Purdue University
703 Third Street
West Lafayette, IN 47907
USA
zhan3822@purdue.edu

Jieni Zhou
Department of Psychology and Neuroscience
University of North Carolina at Chapel Hill
Davie Hall, Campus Box 3270
Chapel Hill, NC 27599-3270
USA
jieniz@live.unc.edu

Peer Commentaries

"The Handbook of Positive Psychology Assessment *is a tremendously rich resource for researchers, students, and practitioners interested in positive psychology and basic aspects of human flourishing, including happiness, meaningfulness, emotion, playfulness, humor, and plenty more. The chapters are written by highly regarded experts who explain the currently available methods and measures, summarize best practices, and offer useful advice."*

Roy F. Baumeister, PhD, Professor emeritus, University of Queensland, Brisbane, Australia; President-Elect (2023), International Positive Psychology Association

"Locating and evaluating scales that measure aspects of positive psychology was a difficult task before this highly readable volume was published. It is designed to help researchers, students, and practitioners find suitable assessment tools and will be invaluable for all serious researchers in positive psychology and its applications."

Colin Cooper, PhD, President, International Society for the Study of Individual Differences

"Psychology research and also evidence-based psychology practice both require reliable and valid assessment methods. This book brings together leading researchers in positive psychology who provide a comprehensive, scientifically sound, and highly readable overview of the state of the art of assessment methods in positive psychology. It covers a very broad range of constructs and is a veritable goldmine for researchers and applied psychologists. This book has the potential to become the standard reference for assessment methods in positive psychology."

Michael Eid, PhD, Professor of Methods and Evaluation, Freie Universität Berlin, Germany

"Positive psychology has now come of age and this handbook provides an invaluable, comprehensive, and critical overview of the field."

Adrian Furnham, DPhil (Oxon), DSc (London), Adjunct Professor, Department of Leadership and Organizational Behaviour, Norwegian Business School, Oslo, Norway

"This handbook is a welcome and invaluable addition to the positive psychology field. Each chapter uses a helpful outline that enables readers to easily learn about each construct and the best instruments for measuring it. Easy-to-use tables and straightforward reviews of strengths, weaknesses, and recommendations are strong features. This is a handbook that will not simply sit on your shelf – it will be perpetually open on your desk to be eagerly and actively read and reread!"

James C. Kaufman, PhD, Professor of Educational Psychology, University of Connecticut, Storrs, CT, USA

"This book brings insightful, practical perspectives to foundational concepts in positive psychology. Its careful attention to measurement and method strengthens the foundations of the field, encouraging research that addresses issues of critical theoretical and practical significance. The book does an excellent job of confirming the core constructs in positive psychology while pointing the way to innovative approaches and concepts that are necessary for a thriving field of endeavor."

Michael Leiter, PhD, Honorary Professor, School of Psychology, Deakin University, Melbourne, Australia

"Finally, the GO-TO book for measuring positive psychology."

Martin E. P. Seligman, PhD, Zellerbach Family Professor of Psychology and Director of the Positive Psychology Center, University of Pennsylvania, Philadelphia, PA, USA

"This book provides an excellent overview of key constructs in the field of positive psychology and the instruments that have been developed to measure them. The authors give a critical review of the reliability and validity of available instruments, thereby helping researchers and practitioners to choose an instrument that suits their purposes."

Prof. Dr. Marianne van Woerkom, Tilburg University/Erasmus University Rotterdam, The Netherlands

Volumes in the series

Psychological Assessment – Science and Practice

Vol. 1
Tuulia M. Ortner, Fons J. R. van de Vijver (Eds.)
Behavior-Based Assessment in Psychology
Going Beyond Self-Report in the Personality, Affective, Motivation, and Social Domains
2015 (July), vi + 232 pages
ISBN 978-0-88937-437-9

Vol. 2
Yael Benyamini, Marie Johnston, Evangelos C. Karademas (Eds.)
Assessment in Health Psychology
2016 (February), vi + 345 pages
ISBN 978-0-88937-452-2

Vol. 3
Karl Schweizer, Christine DiStefano (Eds.)
Principles and Methods of Test Construction
Standards and Recent Advances
2016 (April), vi + 336 pages
ISBN 978-0-88937-449-2

Vol. 4
Peter Karl Jonason (Ed.)
Shining Light on the Dark Side of Personality
Measurement Properties and Theoretical Advances
2022 (July), viii + 320 pages
ISBN 978-0-88937-615-1

Vol. 5
Willibald Ruch, Arnold B. Bakker, Louis Tay, Fabian Gander (Eds.)
Handbook of Positive Psychology Assessment
2022 (November), vi + 464 pages
ISBN 978-0-88937-619-9

Vol. 6
Adrian Meule (Ed.)
Assessment of Eating Behavior
2023 (April), ca. viii + 320 pages
ISBN 978-0-88937-616-8

For more information and further volumes, please see www.hogrefe.com

Gian Vittorio Caprara / Guido Alessandri / Patrizia Steca

Positivity Test

Available on the Hogrefe Testsystem.

The Positivity Test is a self-report questionnaire for the assessment of positive attitude. It explores how people view themselves, their futures, their lives and their general trust in others.

Positive thought, or positivity, can be described as a basic general tendency to approach everyday life with hope and trust. It has also been shown to be a successful predictor of professional success. Positivity corresponds to a pervasive tendency in how people look at reality, which can have a profound effect on the way in which they assign significance and value to their existence in the world.

The Positivity Test assesses positivity by presenting a series of statements reflecting three positive constructs:

- **Self-esteem** captures the individual's general opinion of their self-worth as a person.
- **Optimism** captures individual expectations regarding the future.
- **Satisfaction with life** reflects the individual's expression of a very general evaluation of their existence.

Each statement is rated on a scale ranging from strongly agree to strongly disagree, thus providing an insight into the individual's overall positivity. In definitive terms, self-esteem, optimism and life satisfaction are 'global evaluations' that have a pervasive influence on individual emotions, cognition and actions. All three constructs have also demonstrated correlations with a consistent number of indicators of good psychological adjustment or success in life and at work.

The Positivity Test is a useful tool for businesses, as evidence links positivity to job performance. It can also be used by clinical psychologists as a predictor for mood changes or disorders such as depression. Cross-cultural studies have shown that it is equally appropriate for people from different cultural backgrounds.

www.hogrefe.com

hogrefe

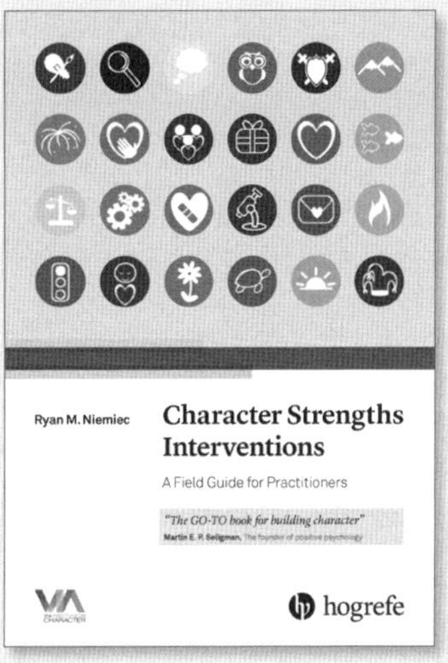

Ryan M. Niemiec

Character Strengths Interventions

A Field Guide for Practitioners

2018, xx + 300 pp.
US $59.00 / € 46.95
ISBN 978-0-88937-492-8
Also available as eBook

This book is the epitome of positive psychology – it takes character strengths, the "backbone" of positive psychology, and builds a bridge between science and practice. The experienced author does so in such a way that both new and experienced practitioners will benefit. Working with clients' character strengths boosts well-being, fosters resilience, improves relationships, and creates strong, supportive cultures in our practices, classrooms, and organizations – including in the context of clinical treatment. Hands-on tips throughout the book provide valuable hints on how to take a truly strengths-based approach in your practice.

The 24 summary sheets spotlighting each of the universal character strengths are an indispensable resource for client sessions, succinctly summarizing the core features of and research on each strength. 70 evidence-based activity handouts can be given to clients to help them develop character strengths awareness and use, increase resilience, develop positive relationships, and find meaning and engagement in their daily lives. No matter what kind of practitioner you are, this one-of-a-kind field guide is a goldmine in science-based applications.

Matthijs Steeneveld / Anouk van den Berg

Character Strengths Intervention Cards

To use with the book

2020, 50 cards + 16-page booklet
US $34.80 / € 27.95
ISBN 978-0-88937-566-6

These character strengths cards are the ideal resource to use with the *Character Strengths Interventions* book. With these cards, you can help clients learn about their character strengths.

The full-color 50-card set provides cards for each of the 24 VIA character strengths and 6 virtues as well as information cards to hand out in groups and individual sessions. 16 ready-to-use, intervention cards help clients discover and explore their strengths and practice applying them more often. The cards are a valuable addition to the toolboxes of coaches, trainers, and therapists from any background.

www.hogrefe.com

hogrefe